a world history of styles and techniques

Credits

I would like to thank John Trotter for playing drums and percussion on the CDs. His understanding and knowledge of the wide range of styles is exceptional. His skill and sensitivity is always a pleasure to hear, and his contribution to this book is invaluable. He is currently living in Australia, where he is performing regularly in concerts and recording sessions.

The recording was done at Greystone Studios, London (e-mail for studio bookings; gigsmcg@msn.com), and I would like to thank John McGinley for his expertise in organising the hundreds of recordings we made there. He also played guitar on several tracks. He made the CDs possible through his infinite patience and care.

All the staff at AMA have become personal friends since we began this project, and I would like to express my appreciation also for the professional way in which the whole company operates. An author could not be in better hands. Detlef Kessler, Axel Mütze, Julius Müller and Karin Stuhrmann have taken enormous care to do a great job in publishing this book. I understand and share their vision and enthusiasm in trying to achieve a standard of excellence.

Thanks to you all.

Paul

■ Imprint

revised edition 2005 by
AMA Verlag GmbH
Postfach 1168
D-50301 Brühl
Germany

www.ama-verlag.de
e-mail: mail@ama-verlag.de

Cover graphics: identität, Solingen
Desktop publishing: Steffen Weber-Freytag
Overall production: Detlef Kessler

Printed in Germany

Order code: 610164E
ISBN 978-3-927190-67-2
ISMN M-700136-96-3

Contents

■ BOOK TWO

■ BOOK THREE

Introduction

The main role of the bass guitar is to provide a musical foundation for the rhythm section, and together with the drums in particular, to play an interesting groove which drives the band along. In order to keep the audience involved, the bass line must often be fairly varied.

Consequently, whether you use a walking bass line, riffs, improvisation, or even a simple pattern, the fundamental purpose of the bass guitar is to play more or less repetitive phrases, solidly and with a good sense of time.

Learning an instrument can be like learning a language. The first step is usually to become familiar with short phrases aurally. You then learn to speak these as accurately as possible. As you learn more phrases, your vocabulary becomes increasingly varied and sophisticated. Reading usually comes later. Enthusiasm can be dulled by getting bogged down by too much theory too early. This book is designed like a dictionary of musical phrases, which can be opened at the point that interests you. Therefore, in putting this book together, I have worked on the premise that if you learn a whole series of musical phrases, riffs, rhythms and patterns, it provides the basic language to be able to perform within a group. I have avoided excessively repetitive exercises because they can be boring, and practising being bored is dangerous if you are learning to entertain people. There are more interesting and practical phrases which will keep your attention and be of use in providing a good, solid, fluent technique.

Once you have absorbed a whole series of phrases in a certain style, alternatives will then come to mind. This is where it becomes really fascinating. Only after experiencing many alternatives can you invent your own original ideas. Convincing improvisation follows on from learning sufficient, basic phrases. What I have tried to do with each section is to capture the essence of what the style is about. It is by no means complete or definitive. It is merely the beginning, or a springboard from which to start.

In many cases I have included the ideas which got me interested in the first place. They may be simple or complex, but they all work, and have each formed the basis of a whole new series of my own ideas.

The book can be used in various ways. If you are interested in slap bass playing, open the book at that point. You will find beginners' phrases and more advanced ones. You will also find that many slap ideas are based on old boogie lines, which are to be found in the chapter before. Studying walking bass lines will lead you to examine certain scales and arpeggios which are related. In this way you can explore your own interests and expand your own horizons.

Many bass players play by ear and do not read, so with them in mind, I have recorded the CDs which accompany this book. Even so, I suggest that non-readers do look at the appropriate phrase they are listening to, as eventually they will learn to recognise it. We read by pattern recognition. For instance, we do not read the individual letters of a word, but the group of letters as a whole.

Manuscript is a useful way of storing ideas. When you learn to read, you have access to a whole new world of music, information and experiences which the non-reader does not share. It is all about enthusiasm and effort.

Finally, I must explain that I did not set out to write a book at all. It evolved as a way of helping my pupils, whom I discovered were desperately short of ideas and ways of expressing themselves musically. Each pupil has his own set of problems. Only when I had amassed a pile of musical examples did I realise that I had actually developed a system which could help others too. My aim was therefore to provide each student with a sort of armoury of phrases; an arsenal of musical weapons.

In this fashion, you can be prepared for most eventualities. Your vocabulary will be expanded enough so that you are able to express yourself better in the language of music.

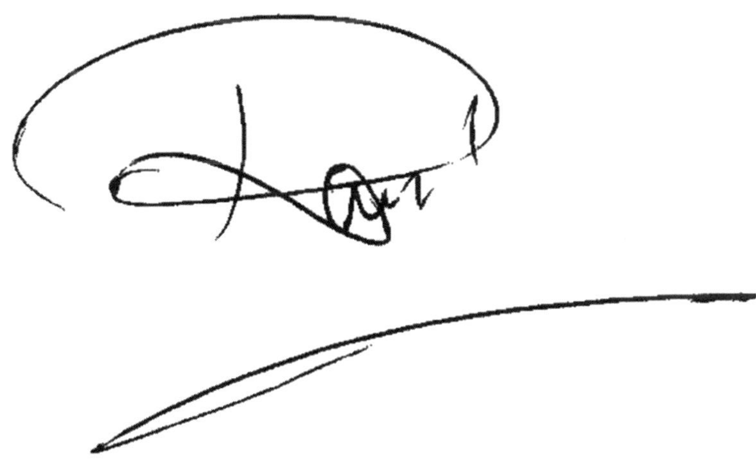

P.S. The publishers have at times used a new and modified version of music notation. I am reliably informed that it is widely used and makes reading easier in certain circumstances.

BOOK ONE

■ Techniques

Finger Style

The left hand should be able to grip the guitar neck firmly. Place each of the four fingers between consecutive frets, producing a stretch of four semitones. To produce the maximum grip, the thumb is best placed opposite the second finger, on the rounded side of the neck. There are exceptions, but this is a good starting position for getting into good habits early on. Bad habits start, for instance, when you play a scale of G with the thumb under the first finger. You will find it difficult to stretch the little finger (4th).

The right hand position is based on the pizzicato, double-bass style of plucking with the first and second fingers. For a straight 8th note pattern, it is often better to use just the first finger to produce a steady, strong, even-sounding feel. Using two fingers can sometimes sound uneven. It is an advantage to be able to play as evenly as possible with two fingers, because you do not want a great difference between the volume and tone produced by each finger.

The most natural way for the arms to be positioned is for the elbow to be bent at 90°. You will find that tighter angles make your muscles work harder and you become more easily tired. Greater angles can result in loss of control, as the guitar is further away from your body and not gripped to prevent it swinging out of control. The right hand thumb can rest on a pick-up, using it as a pivot. The thumb can also be placed on the fourth string (E), and even moved across to the third string (A) for greater control and precision.

Soft/Hard Playing

To provide a laid back feel, it is not always necessary to underplay. Nor is it always necessary to overplay for a hard driving feel. It is a question of where the note is placed in relation to the beat which determines the feel. If you play slightly late, it will be laid back and lazy. If you play on top of the beat (or even early), the feel will be driving. You can play with heavy or light dynamics, or somewhere between the two. A driving rhythm can be intense when played more quietly, and more aggressive when played louder. Laid-back feels can be firm or gentle. It all depends on the mood of the song, and the intensity of the music around you.

Tone

Part of the art of bass playing is to have the right tone. A bright tone can be useful for a more exposed, harder sound. It can be used for solo or lead lines, for greater clarity or for a driving effect.

A bassier tone can be effective in other ways. In the same way that a double bass often provides a subtle pulse, the bass guitar can have a similar role. The sound comes out "beneath" the band, where it is not in competition with harder, higher sounding instruments. The right tone can make a band swing; the wrong one can destroy the feel.

Spanish Style

The Spanish guitar is often played with the thumb and fingers. The bass guitar can be played in a similar way. By using the thumb, first and second fingers, it is possible to play in a whole new variety of ways. You have greater dynamic control, even with 16 semiquavers to the bar. You are more able to jump between strings, which is usually awkward when they are not adjacent (this is one advantage of the slap style). Other advantages are created for greater flexibility, arpeggio playing, chordal and harmonic uses, and a brighter, clearer tone. The palm of the hand can be used to dampen the strings, to provide a shorter note.

Plectrums & Picks

Pick-playing can be useful in certain situations. It provides a clearer start to the note, so you can produce a "click" sound at one extreme, and quite a solid "thump" at the other. Deeper tones can be used which would be unacceptable for normal finger-style playing. Repetitive phrases can be made very punchy, more like a synthesizer effect. Ad-libbed phrases can be made tighter and cleaner sounding. Alternatively, you can blend in with deeper sounding instruments and still maintain your clarity without being "buried".

It is important to keep pick-playing as even as possible, because any unevenness is far more apparent with a clearer sound.

Nail Playing

An alternative to pick playing is to use the finger nail. It produces a harder sound than skin and is more subtle than a plectrum. Some bass players use this method, and I have even used finger picks (which clip onto the fingers) to achieve this sound. With nails that are too long you are limited to one sound, but if they can be kept at just the right length, a slight change of angle can vary the sound from skin to nail playing.

Slap Bass

To maintain complete control, the guitar has to be held against the player's body to prevent the instrument moving about while the right hand moves freely. The slap method basically involves the right hand thumb striking or "popping" out the bass line, and the first finger providing extra percussive effects. The thumb is slapped down onto the string just where the fretboard starts, giving a metallic edge to the note. The obvious part of the thumb to use is the hardest part, where the bone is near the surface on the side of the joint.

The first finger is placed under either of the top two strings, where it pulls out the string, and releases it quickly to snap or slap against the frets.
The wrist must be kept quite loose, as this provides the rocking motion between thumb and finger, giving both power and subtlety.

The Squeeze

An alternative to the slap technique is to squeeze, pull and release the string. Place the thumb and first finger of your right hand either side of the string, squeeze it, and pull it away from the body of the guitar. When it is quickly released you get a similar sound to the slap. It is more controlled but less versatile. Some guitars do not sound good when slapped, but respond well with this method. It also means that the right hand does not have to change to the slap position to get the sound.

Right Hand Tapping

If the first two fingers of the right hand are held together and gently tap the string against the 19th fret, the left hand can play the usual fingering on the two bottom strings. It produces a picked, almost hollow sound. The pitch of the note is the same as if it was plucked normally, and because the tapping is not too heavy, the right hand fingers do not sound the pitch of the note.

Damping

Damping can be done in various ways. If you put foam rubber underneath the strings by the bridge, then the sounds produced are uniformly shorter. You must be careful not to reach the point where the guitar sounds out of tune because the foam is too tight, providing an extra, false bridge which alters the pitch.

Right hand damping can be done with the palm (the part next to the little finger). The string is plucked with the thumb. This technique allows the correct amount of damping and you vary it simply by adding or releasing pressure on the string.

Walking 4 and Damping

In the same way that a double bass player will often play a steady 4 feel with his first finger (right hand), the bass guitarist will achieve a more even sound if he plays in this fashion. The solidity of the bass line is the foundation that others rely on. Obviously, skips and musical variations will necessitate using other fingers also, but the basic 4 has to be even and solid. Palming the string can provide a shorter note, rather more like a double bass. It can solve a problem if the sound is otherwise too metallic or sustained. The thumb then provides a solid 4 feel, with a slightly duller, rounder sound.

Patting

If you hold a chord down with the left hand and then pat the strings with the straight fingers of the open right hand, you can get effects as varied as power chords and subtle running 8th note patterns. Obviously, a hard pat will produce a loud metallic chord, which can sustain for quite a while. Try also patting a gentle Bossa Nova rhythm, keeping the right hand patting 8 notes to the bar. By sustaining and deadening the notes with the left hand, you can get some interesting rhythm patterns.

Harmonics

Harmonics are achieved by placing a left-hand finger gently on certain points of the string (without pressing it down), plucking with the right hand, and then releasing the string quickly with the left hand. This allows maximum sustain, which is needed to bring out the harmonic. The harmonic is a note above the open string, and the slight damping effect stops the normal open string note from ringing. Harmonics do not exist at every part of the string, and you have to experiment to find out where the most useful ones are. The obvious ones are above the 4th, 5th, 7th, 9th and 12th frets.

False or artificial harmonics can be played by holding a note down with the left hand, whilst resting the first finger of the right hand on the note an octave above on the same string, and plucking it with the third finger of the right hand. Then remove the first finger to allow the sustain. False harmonics allow you to play any note on the instrument, whereas natural harmonics are limited to the notes of the harmonic series of the open strings. It is technically far easier, though, to play natural harmonics.

Pedals and Effects

It is very important to get the chain of pedals in the correct order. There are of course exceptions, but I will suggest a tried, tested and successful order. The guitar plugs into the compressor, then next comes the octave divider, high flanger, chorus, echo, volume pedal, DI box and amplifier.

A bowing effect can be created using the volume pedal to simulate the double bass. Play a note with the volume pedal set to minimum, then gradually increase it. Imagine a bow which starts from a stationary position, begins to move, and slowly increases the vibration of the string.

A synthesizer effect can be produced by using the compressor, octave divider, high flanger and a plectrum. A big sound can be produced by just using the octave divider with a touch of echo.

The chorus effect gives an illusion of two basses playing in unison, but very slightly differently. This is because the tuning sweep varies, and the delay makes one sound fractionally late.

Be careful with pedals, though, because they can sometimes distract you from the notes you really should be playing. It is important not to let effects rule your head. Pedals can also result in the loss of bottom end and clarity. Very often, subtlety is the best method. Used correctly, they can add the extra colour which is needed, but always try to avoid competing with the guitar and synthesizer effects. The more colour these instruments use, the less I tend to use effects.

■ 49 Steps to Basic Theory

1

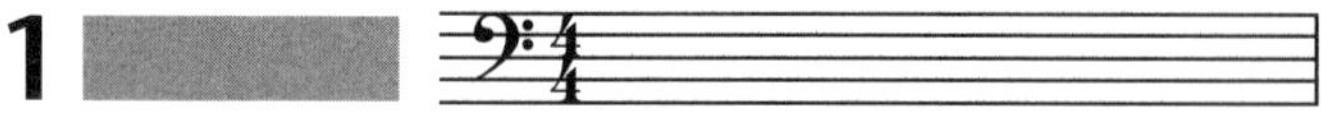

The bass clef sign means the music is written for instruments which play in the lower registers. The bass guitar is one.

2 The five lines on which the clef and the notes are written is called a stave.

Notes of a scale are given letter names A B C D E F G

3

4

The four-string bass guitar begins on low E.

E A D G

The four open strings are low E, A, D and high G.

5 = a semibreve or whole note. 1 note lasts 4 beats. There is 1 semibreve in a 4 beat bar.

6 = minims or 1/2 notes. 1 note lasts 2 beats. There are 2 minims in a 4 beat bar.

7 = crotchets or 1/4 notes. 1 note lasts 1 beat. There are 4 crotchets in a 4 beat bar.

8 = quavers or 8th notes. 1 note lasts 1/2 beat. There are 8 quavers in a 4 beat bar. 2 notes = 1 beat.

9 = semiquavers or 16th notes. 1 note lasts 1/4 beat. There are 16 semiquavers in a 4 beat bar. 4 notes = 1 beat.

A dot after a note means it becomes half as long again.

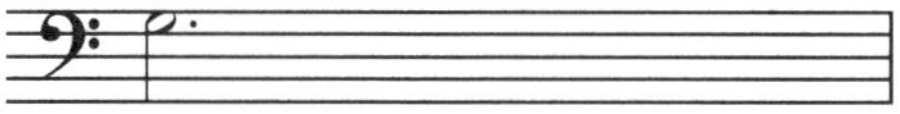

= 2 beats + 1 = 3 beats. 10

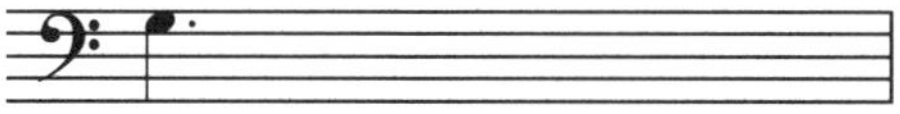

= 1 beat + 1/2 = 1 1/2 beats. 11

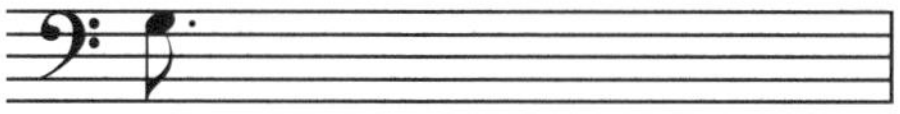

= 1/2 beat + 1/4 = 3/4 beat. 12

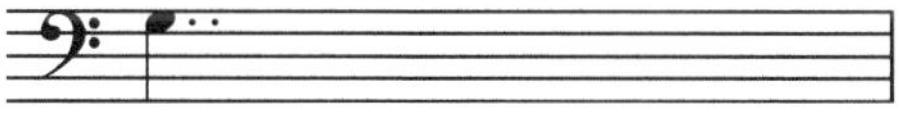

= 1 beat + 1/2 + 1/4 = 1 3/4 beats. 13

1 2 3 4

= semibreve or whole note rest. This lasts 4 beats. There is 1 semibreve rest in a 4 beat bar. 14

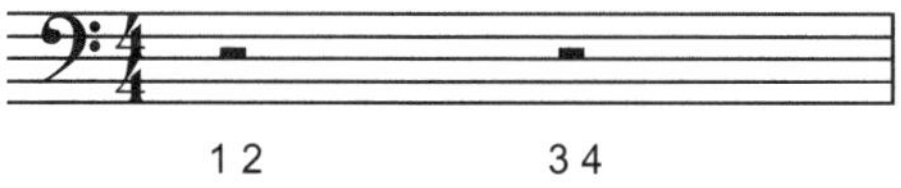

1 2 3 4

= minim or 1/2 note rests. Each one lasts 2 beats. 15

1 2 3 4

= crotchet or 1/4 notes rests. Each one lasts 1 beat. 16

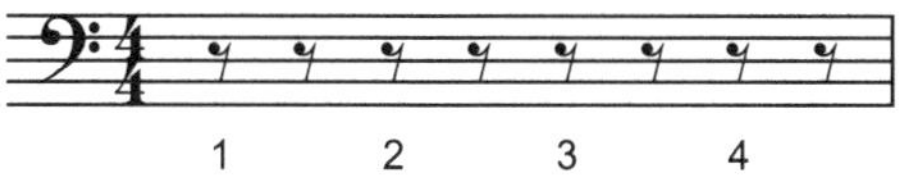

1 2 3 4

= quaver or 8th note rests. Each one lasts 1/2 beat. 17

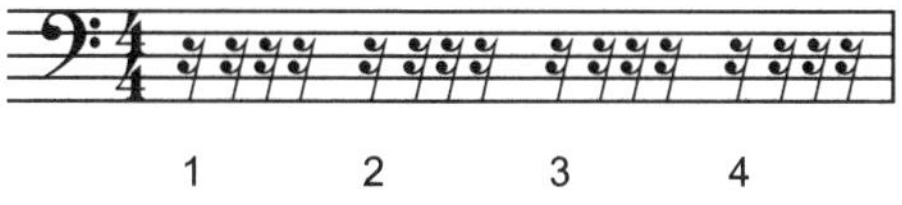

1 2 3 4

= semiquaver or 16th note rests. Each one lasts 1/4 beat. 18

A dot after a rest means it becomes half as long again.

19 = 2 beats rest + 1 = 3 beats.

20 = 1 beat rest + 1/2 = 1 1/2 beats.

21 = 1/2 beat rest + 1/4 = 3/4 beat.

22 = 4 beats in a bar.

23 = 3 beats in a bar.

24 = 12 half beats in a bar, or 4 groups of 3 quavers.

= a swing or shuffle feel

Compare this with example 24a.

24a = 4 beats in a bar with a shuffle or swing feeling.

count: 1 2 3 4

Compare this with example 24.

25 = a tie is between 2 or more notes. 1 note is played for the length of the tied notes together.

26 = 1 note lasts 4 beats.

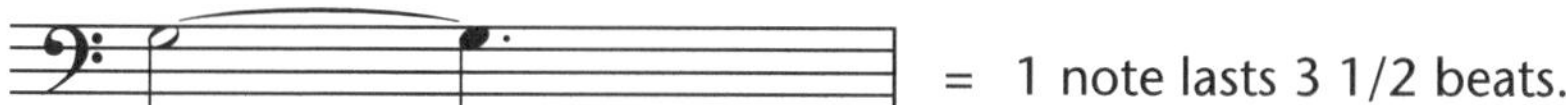

= 1 note lasts 3 1/2 beats. 27

= 1 note lasts 3 beats. 28

= 1 note lasts 2 1/2 beats. 29

= 1 note lasts 2 1/4 beats. 30

= 1 note lasts 2 beats. 31

= 1 note lasts 1 1/2 beats. 32

= 1 note lasts 1 1/4 beats. 33

= 1 note lasts 1 beat. 34

= 1 note lasts a 1/2 beat. 35

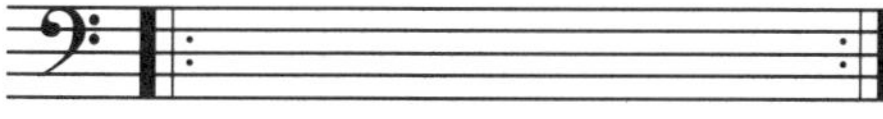

= Means all the bars within these signs are repeated.  36

37

a) Raising a note by one fret is called a semitone.

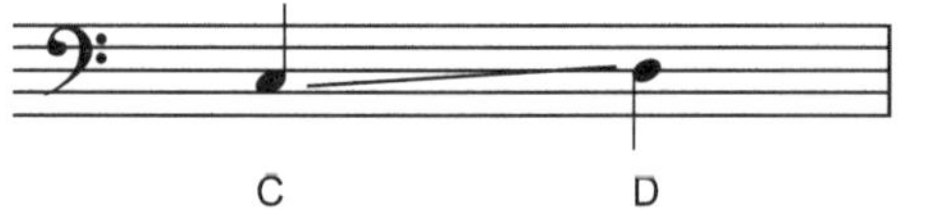

b) Raising a note by 2 frets is called a tone.

38 ♯ = sharp. The note is raised a semitone.

39 ♭ = flat. The note is lowered a semitone.

40 ♮ = natural. If the same note previously in the bar had a ♯ or ♭ before it, the ♮ sign cancels the accidental.

41 Means the key of the piece of music has no sharps or flats. It is the key signature for C or Am. The notes are C D E F G A B C oder A B C D E F G A.

42 one sharp = the key of G or Em. The notes are G A B C D E F♯ G or E F♯ G A B C D E.

43 2 sharps = the key of D or Bm. The notes are D E F♯ G A B C♯ D or B C♯ D E F♯ G A B.

44 3 sharps = the key of A or F♯m. The notes are A B C♯ D E F♯ G♯ A or F♯ G♯ A B C♯ D E F♯.

45 4 sharps = the key of E or C♯m. The notes are E F♯ G♯ A B C♯ D♯ E or C♯ D♯ E F♯ G♯ A B C♯.

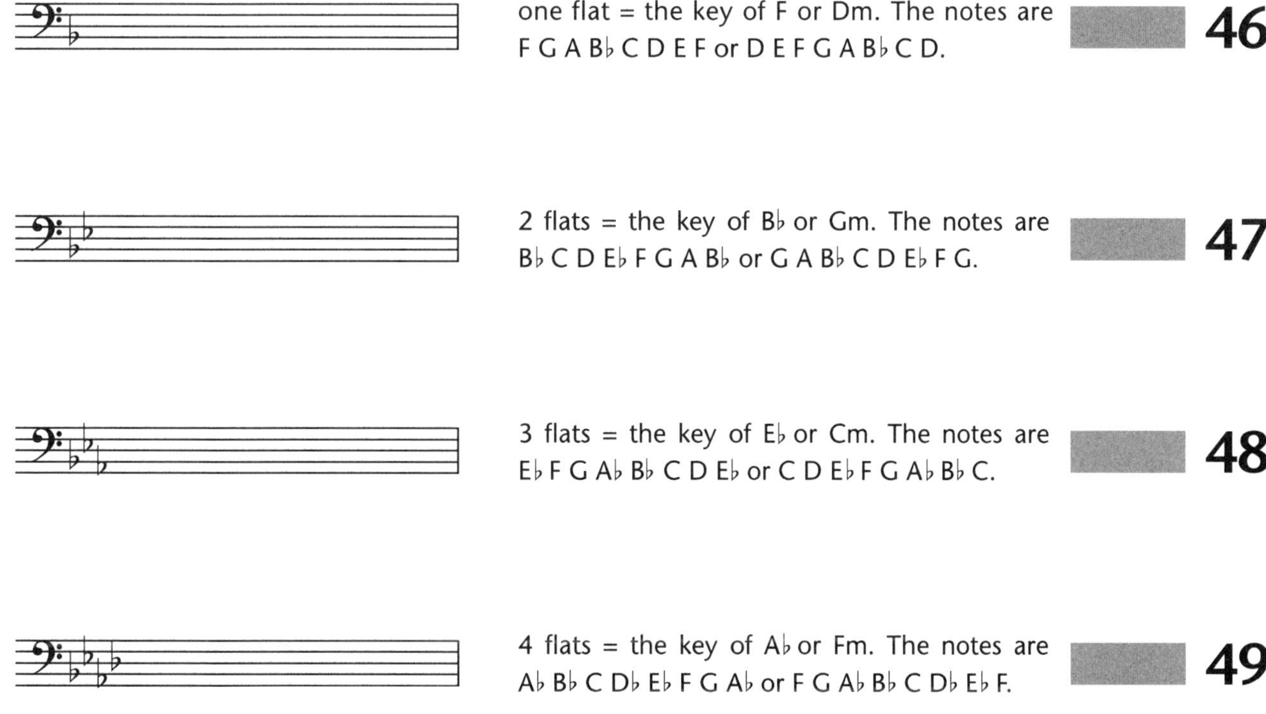

one flat = the key of F or Dm. The notes are F G A B♭ C D E F or D E F G A B♭ C D. 46

2 flats = the key of B♭ or Gm. The notes are B♭ C D E♭ F G A B♭ or G A B♭ C D E♭ F G. 47

3 flats = the key of E♭ or Cm. The notes are E♭ F G A♭ B♭ C D E♭ or C D E♭ F G A♭ B♭ C. 48

4 flats = the key of A♭ or Fm. The notes are A♭ B♭ C D♭ E♭ F G A♭ or F G A♭ B♭ C D♭ E♭ F. 49

Walking Bass Lines ■

The walking bass line is common to many kinds of music. Bach wrote many classical pieces of music with what are essentially walking bass lines; hence the interest shown by jazz musicians in his work. Later on, when more contemporary bands wanted to make people dance, one answer was a simple walking bass line. Jazz musicians discovered that it made their music swing, and when used in their particular way, it converted what had been a rather clumsy, military-style marching band into an exciting jazz group.

Country music adopted the walking bass line, as did Gospel music, the Blues, Boogie Woogie, Rock and Roll and even modern day Pop music.

Vocalists found a steady 4 notes to the bar easy to sing with, as it provided a simple rhythm to follow, without the beat necessarily being overstated by the drummer or rest of the band. The swing 4 determined the dynamic of the whole band. The lowest volume, for instance, in many Sinatra recordings is that set by the solo bass playing a walking 4.

The rest of the band consequently relies on being able to hear that rhythm, and the musicians' balance within the band is dictated by the role of the bass. Therefore, at times the bass has to be the solid backbone to the band, played firmly and clearly. If the bass is too loud, the music does not swing, because dynamically the band cannot decrease or increase its volume when it has to play too loudly to compete. A loud walking bass line is not a pleasant sound. It is clumsy, unsympathetic and obliterates whole sections of the band. Bass guitarists have to be particularly careful, because electric amplification gives them obvious advantages over acoustic instruments. Besides, the role of the bass guitar is fundamentally the same as a double bass; to provide a basic rhythm.

The walking bass line is also the life-giving pulse of the band. It can be used in many ways. It can be a straightforward means of establishing a kind of marching feel (as used by Glenn Miller), which swings but deliberately overstates the rhythm, or it can be subtly used (e.g. Oscar Peterson's recordings with Ray Brown).

The basic musical difference between the two is not just a question of how loud you play, but what you play. Glenn Miller used a lot of basic arpeggio swing lines, which outlined the simplicity of the chords, and made it easy for the audience to understand what was essentially commercial music. Ray Brown, however, used a subtle blend of arpeggios, scales, extensions to the chords (e.g. ma7th, 6th, 9th, flat 5th, etc.), passing notes and triplets to make the music more flowing, hip and far more sophisticated. Of course it does not please everyone. It is all a matter of taste and using the right feel at the right moment.

■ Scales, Arpeggios and Scale Exercises

Scales form the basis to most forms of music. The scales included in this book are what most bass players need.

Arpeggios are formed from the root, 3rd, 5th and chordal extension, e.g. major 7th. This is again an oversimplification, but for practical purposes you can see how the system works fairly easily. Any variations will be self-evident.

Scale exercises are useful because they get the fingers used to repetitive rising and falling patterns. You can develop the technical dexterity necessary to play in unison with other instruments. Exercises also form the basis of solo playing, by building up flowing movements and regular, melodic runs.

Exercises should never be ignored if you want to progress to the more advanced and interesting roles of the instrument. It is a good idea to master these exercises in all keys. It could be the difference between success and failure, as there is not always enough rehearsal time before a performance.

Major Scales

(C major)

* Note: △ = major

C△♯4 *scale*

(C augmented 4th)
(Lydian)
(Cmaj 7♯11 chord)

C△♭6 *scale*

(C flat 6th)
(C harmonic major)
(Cmaj 7♭13 chord)

C△♯4♯5 *scale*

(C aug 5th, aug 4th)
(Lydian aug)
(Cmaj7♯5♯11 chord)

C7 *scale*

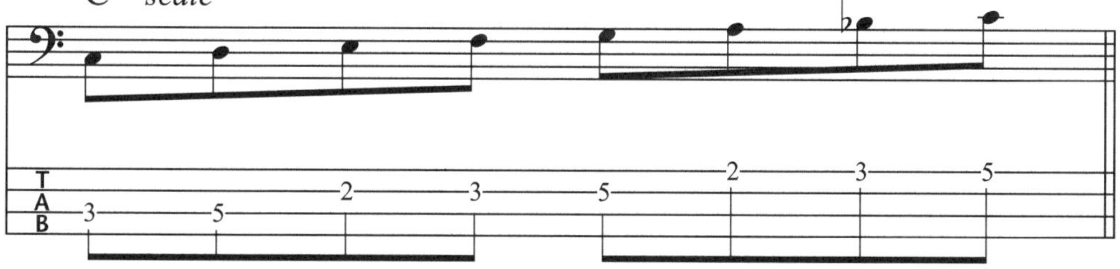

(C seventh)
(Mixolydian)
(dominant 7th)

C7♯4 *scale*

(C seventh, aug 4th)
(Lydian dominant)
(Lydian flat 7th)
(C 7♯11 chord)

C7♭6 *scale*

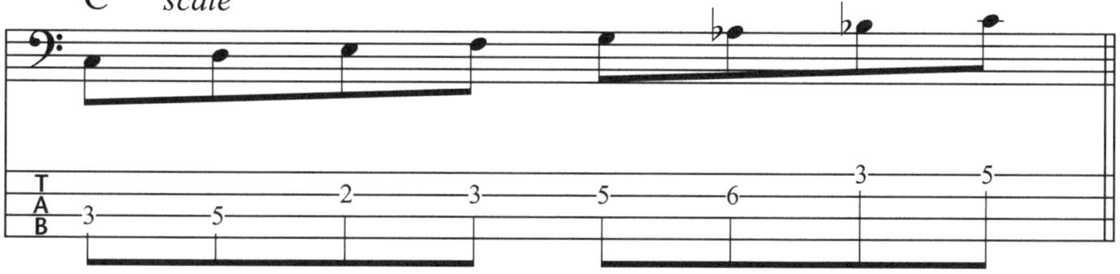

(C seventh, flat 6th)
(Hindu)
(C 7♭13 chord)

(C major Blues)
(C 7th Blues)
(C Blues)

C7 *(Blues)*

* Note: Often used as a passing note.

(C 7th suspended 4th)

C7sus4

(C 7th aug 9th)
(diminished whole tone)
(C♭9♯9♯4♯5 7th)
(super Locrian)

C7♯9 (also C7+/♯9, C+7♯9, C7♯9, C7/♯9, C7(alt))

(C augmented)
(alternative augmented scale)

C+ *(occasionally used)*

(C 7th aug)
(whole tone)
(more commonly used augmented scale)

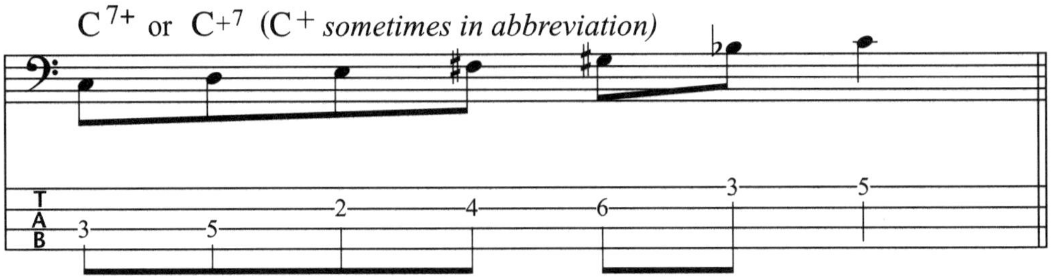

C7+ or C+7 (C+ *sometimes in abbreviation)*

(half tone whole tone scale)
(C 7th flat 9th)

C7♭9 *(sounds diminished)*

Minor Scales

Cm^7 *(Dorian)*

(C minor)
(C Dorian)
(Cm^7)

Cm *(pure minor or natural minor)*

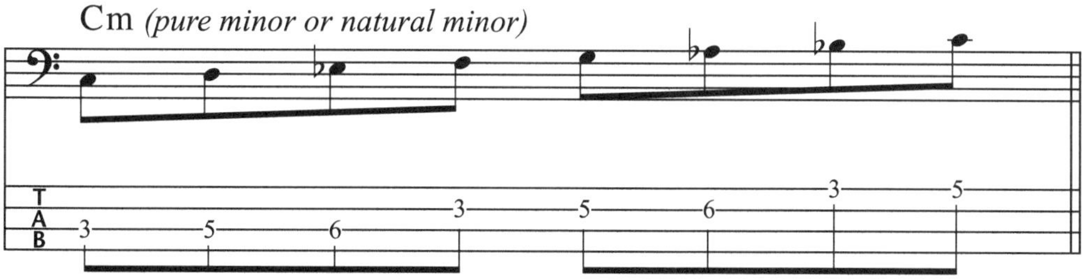

(C minor)

Cm *(Melodic) [classical music tradition]*

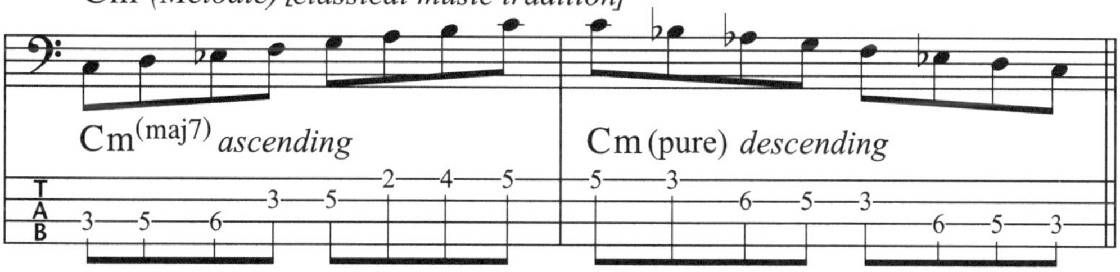

Cm$^{(maj7)}$ *ascending* — Cm (pure) *descending*

(C melodic minor)

Note: In Jazz Cm$^{(maj7)}$ melodic minor ascends and descends on the first scale only.

Cm *(Harmonic)*

(C harmonic minor)
(Cm$^{(maj7/\flat 6)}$ scale)
(Cm$^{(maj7/\flat 13)}$ chord)

Cm *(Phrygian)*

(C minor, Phrygian)
(C Phrygian)

Cm *(Blues)*

(C Blues)
(C minor Blues)

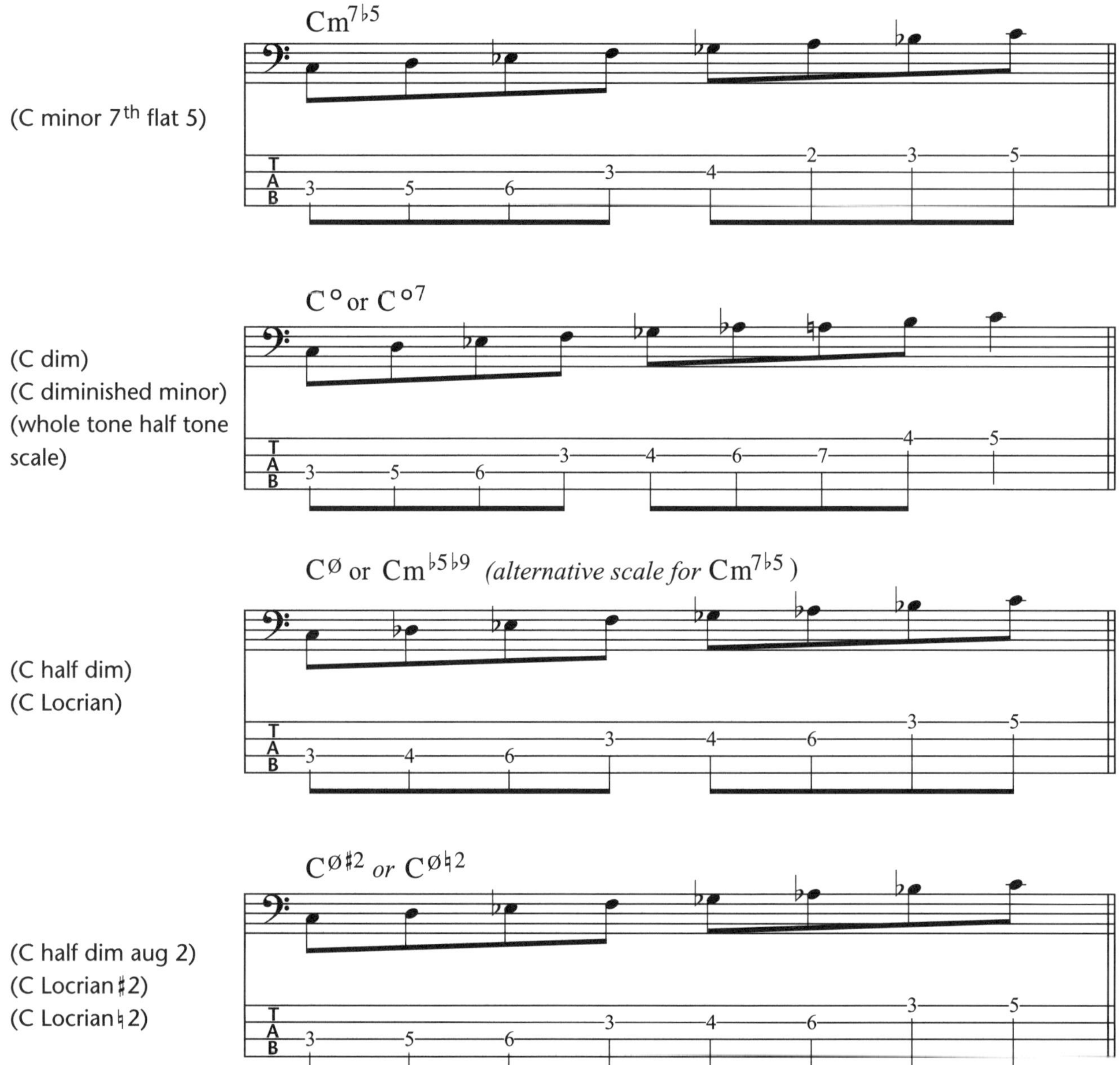
Cm7♭5
(C minor 7th flat 5)
C° or C°7
(C dim)
(C diminished minor)
(whole tone half tone scale)
Cø or Cm♭5♭9 (alternative scale for Cm7♭5)
(C half dim)
(C Locrian)
Cø♯2 or Cø♮2
(C half dim aug 2)
(C Locrian♯2)
(C Locrian♮2)

Diatonic Modes

Ionian

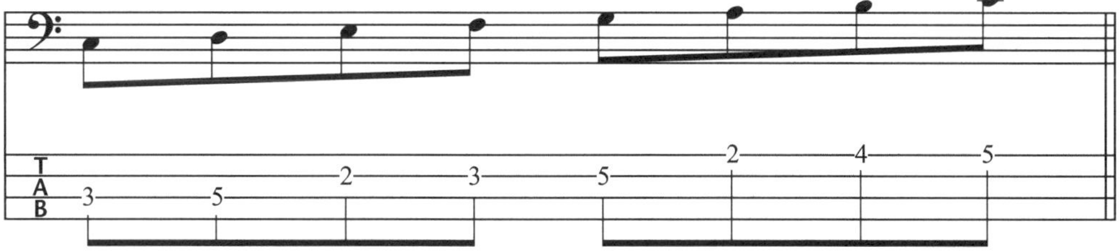

(C major scale)
(C^{maj7})

Dorian

($Cm^{\natural 6}$)
(Cm^{7})

Phrygian

($Cm^{\flat 9}$)
($D\flat^{\sharp 4}$ scale/C root)

Lydian

($C^{\sharp 4}$ scale)
($C^{maj7\sharp 11}$ chord)

Mixolydian

(C^{7})

Aeolian

(Cm)
(pure or natural minor)

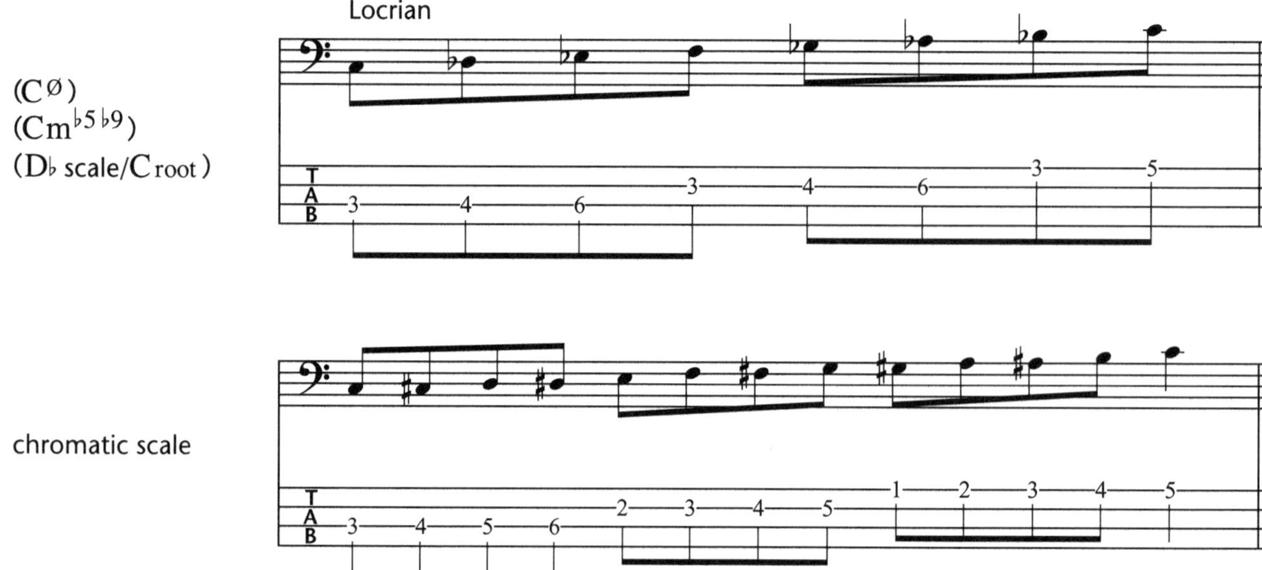

Arpeggios (Major)

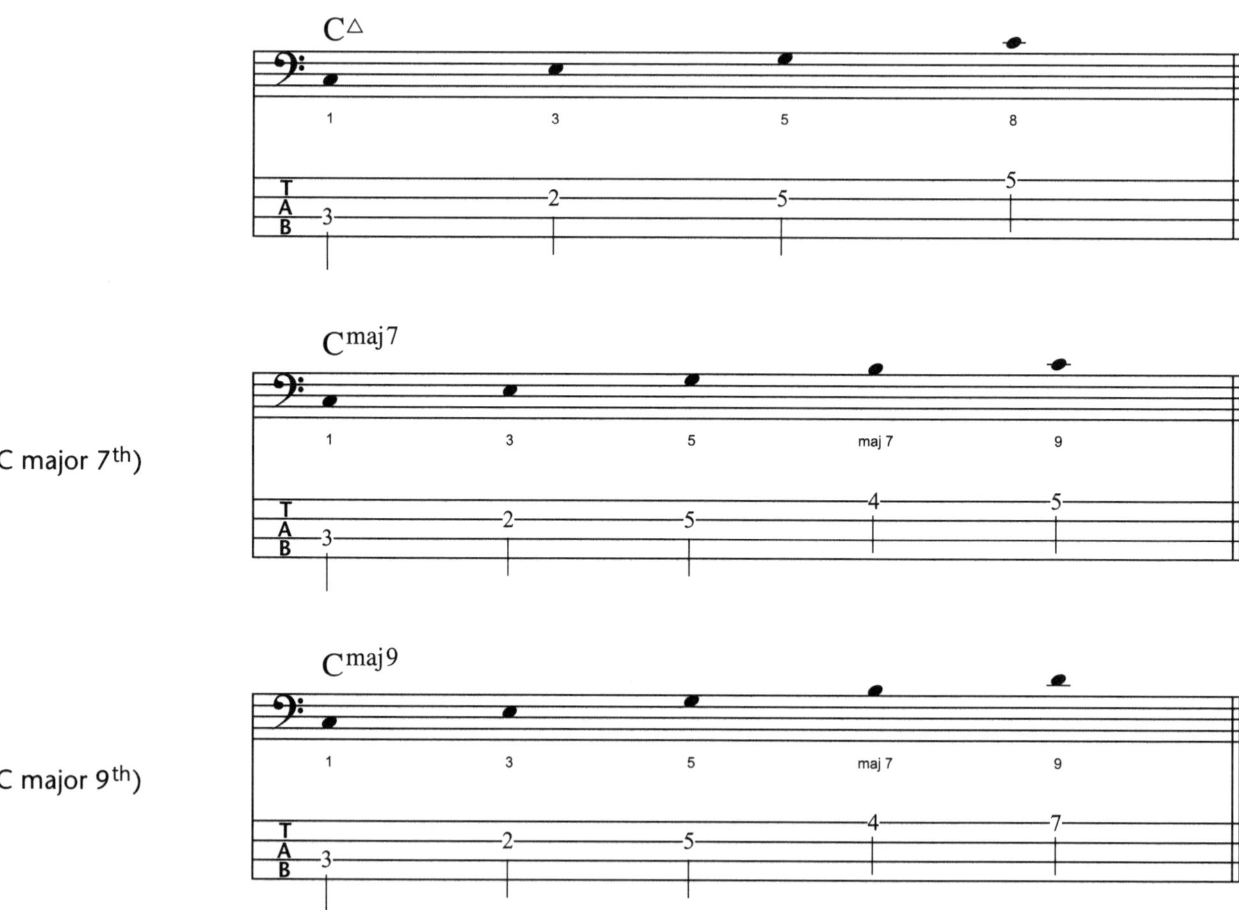

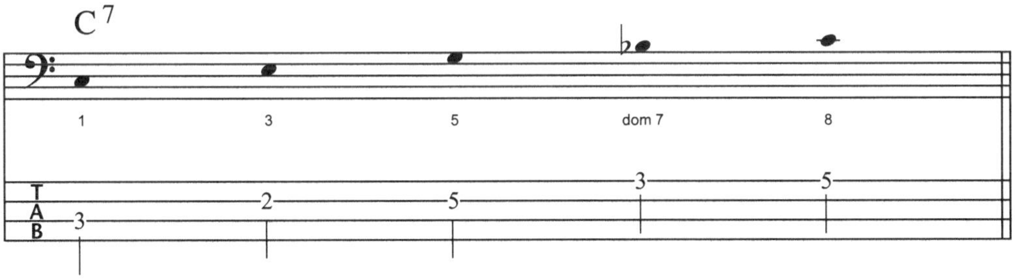

C7

1 3 5 dom 7 8

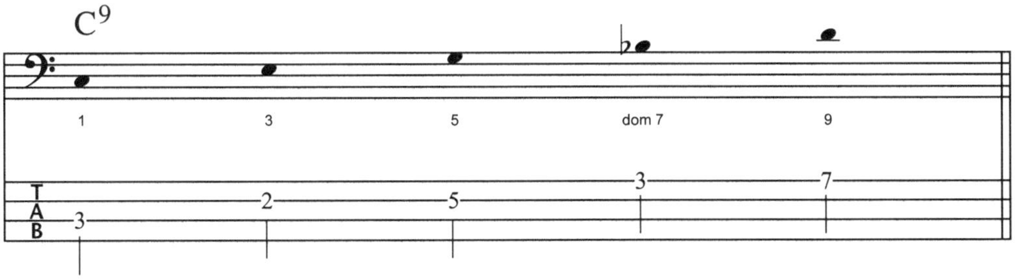

T A B: 3 2 5 3 5

C9

1 3 5 dom 7 9

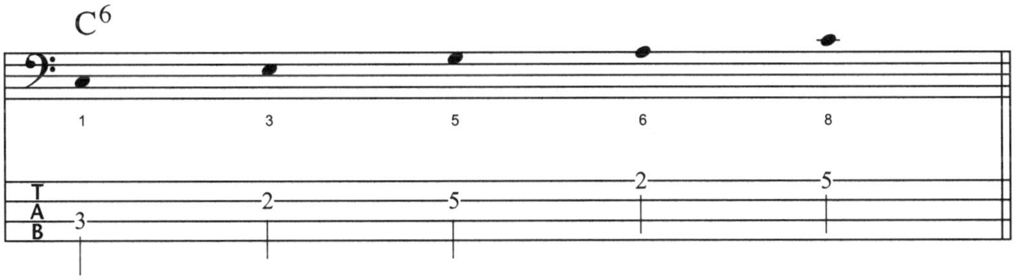

T A B: 3 2 5 3 7

C6

1 3 5 6 8

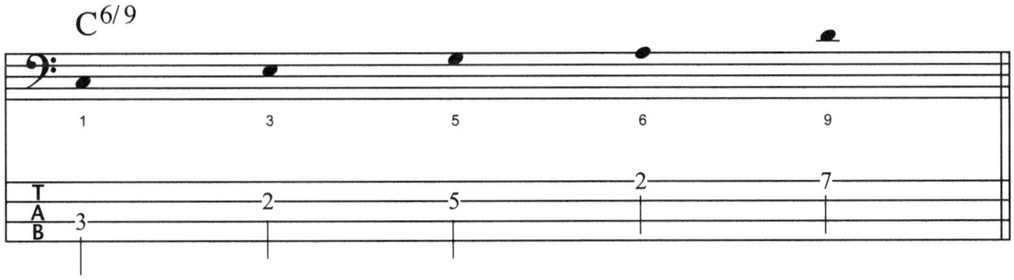

T A B: 3 2 5 2 5

C6/9

1 3 5 6 9

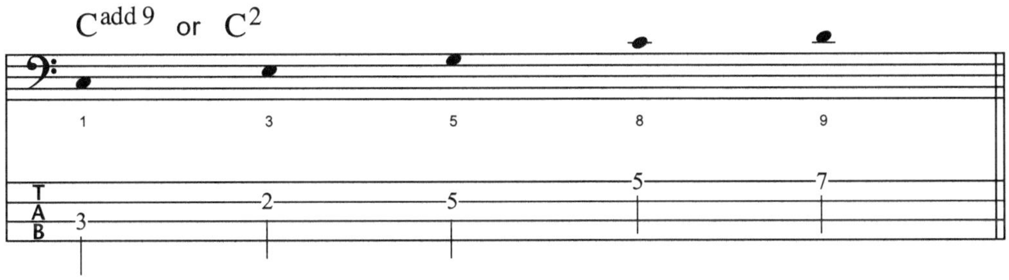

T A B: 3 2 5 2 7

Cadd 9 or C2

1 3 5 8 9

T A B: 3 2 5 5 7

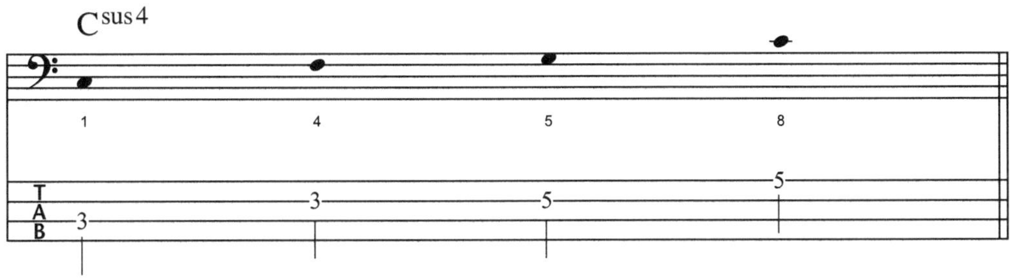

Csus4

1 4 5 8

T A B: 3 3 5 5

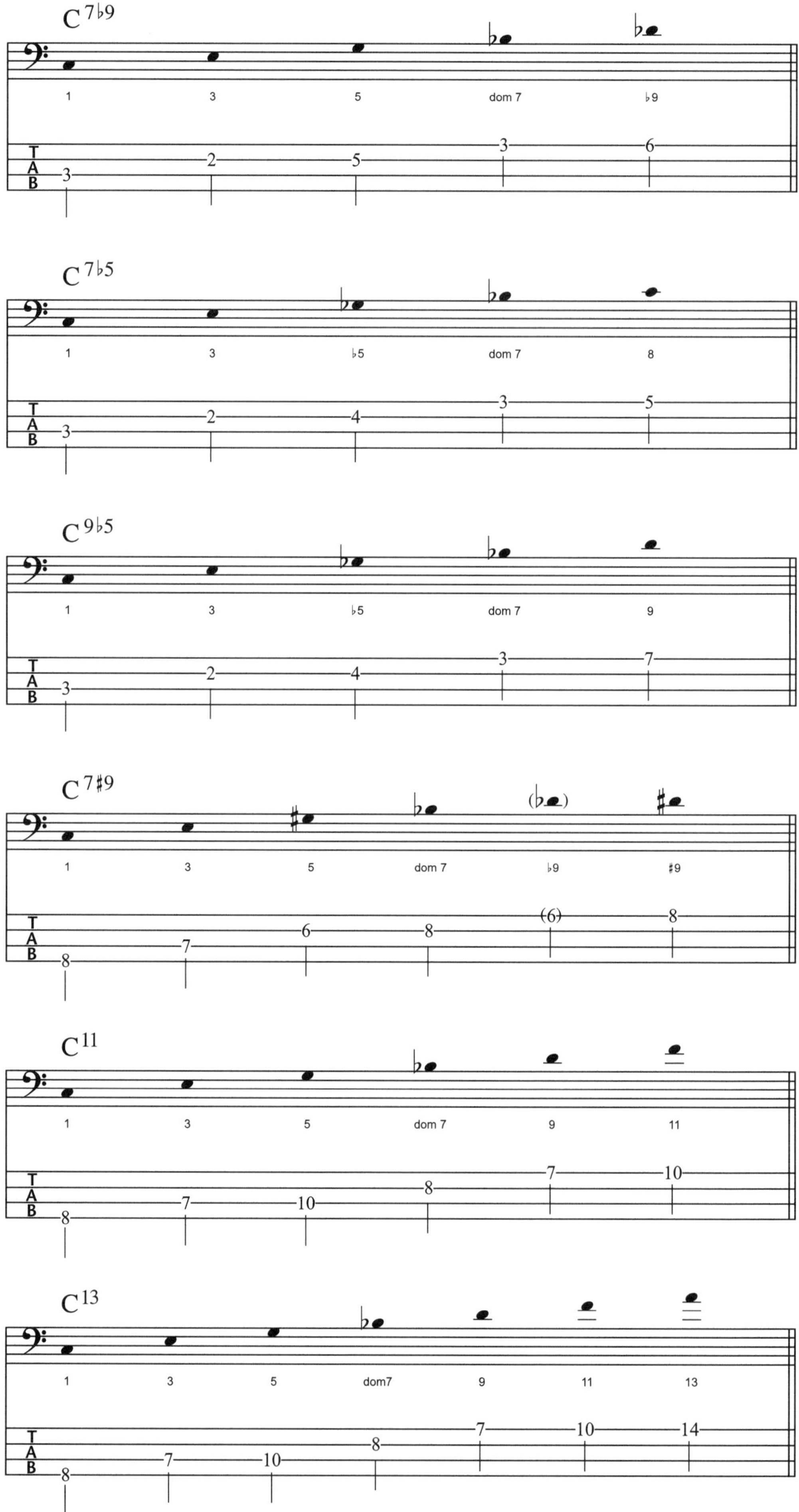
C 7♭9
1
3
5
dom 7
♭9
C 7♭5
1
3
♭5
dom 7
8
C 9♭5
1
3
♭5
dom 7
9
C 7♯9
1
3
5
dom 7
♭9
♯9
C 11
1
3
5
dom 7
9
11
C 13
1
3
5
dom7
9
11
13

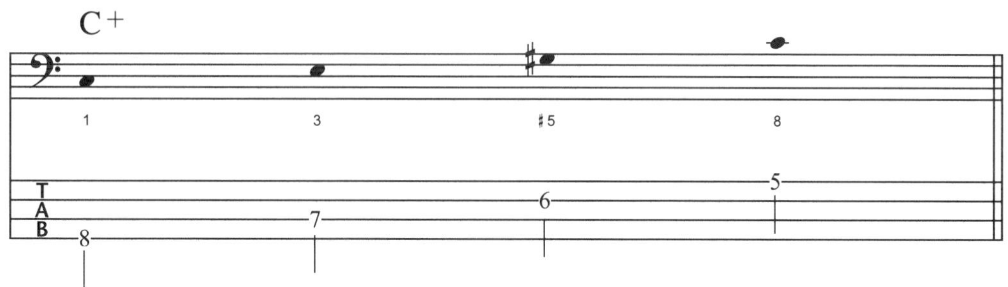

Arpeggios (Minor)

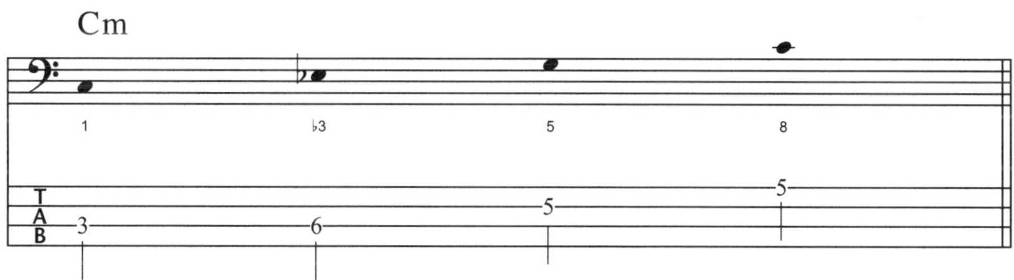

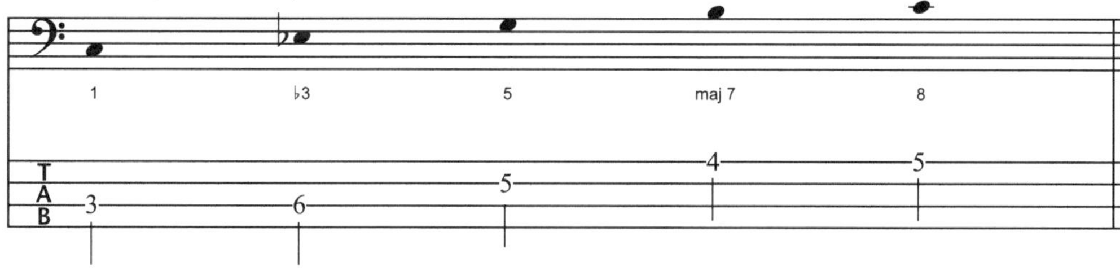

($C^{maj7\flat6}$ scale)
($C^{maj7\flat13}$ chord)

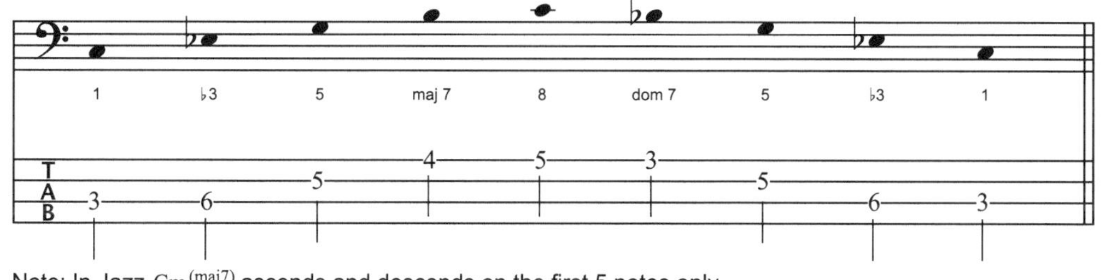

($Cm^{(maj7)}$ ascending)
($Cm^{(inc7)}$ descending)

Note: In Jazz $Cm^{(maj7)}$ ascends and descends on the first 5 notes only.

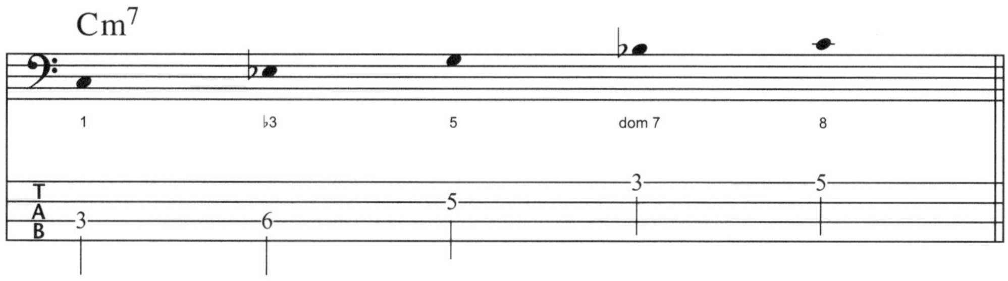

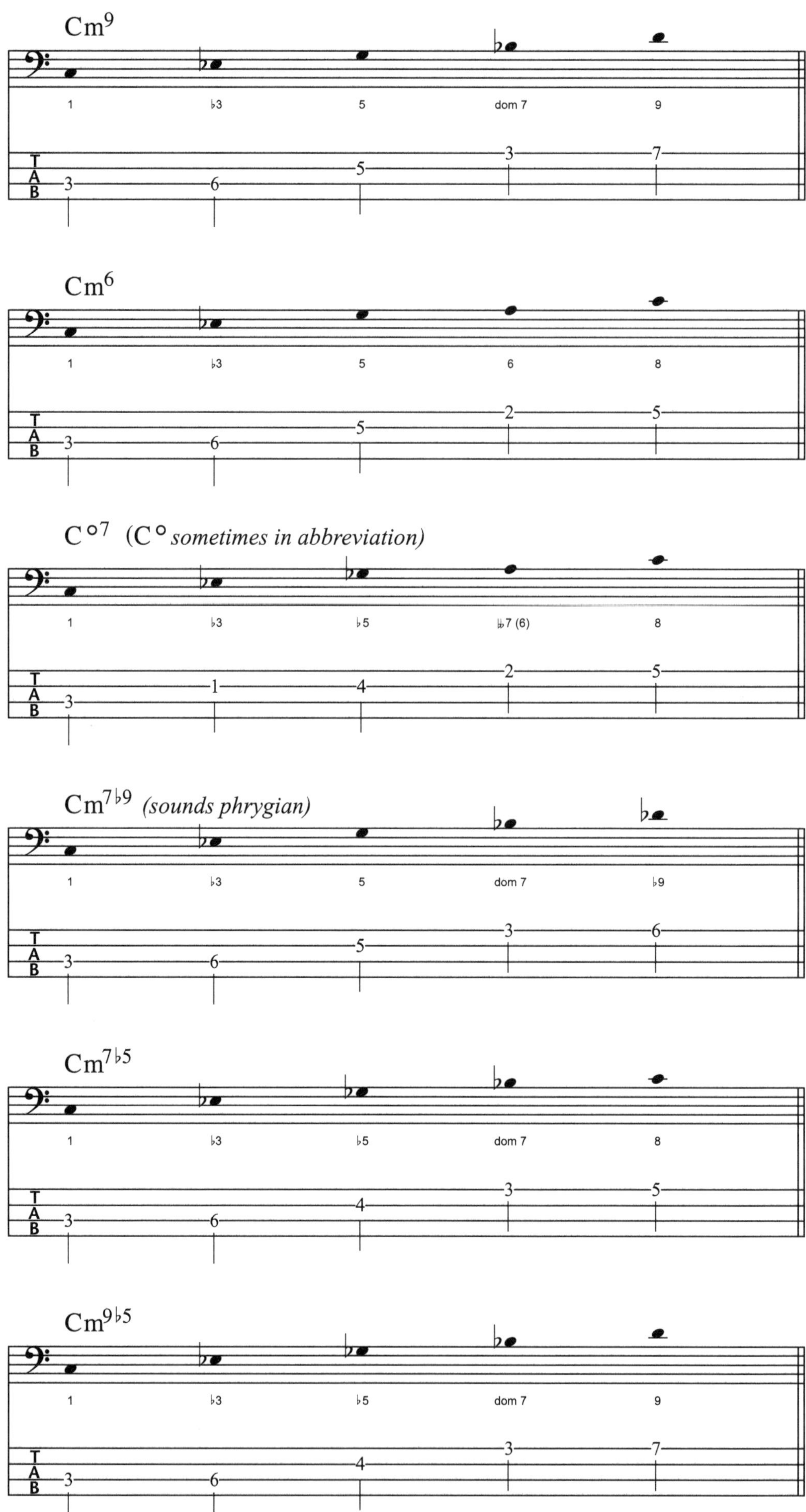
Cm9
1 ♭3 5 dom 7 9
3 6 5 3 7
Cm6
1 ♭3 5 6 8
3 6 5 2 5
C °7 (C ° sometimes in abbreviation)
1 ♭3 ♭5 𝄫7 (6) 8
3 1 4 2 5
Cm7♭9 (sounds phrygian)
1 ♭3 5 dom 7 ♭9
3 6 5 3 6
Cm7♭5
1 ♭3 ♭5 dom 7 8
3 6 4 3 5
Cm9♭5
1 ♭3 ♭5 dom 7 9
3 6 4 3 7

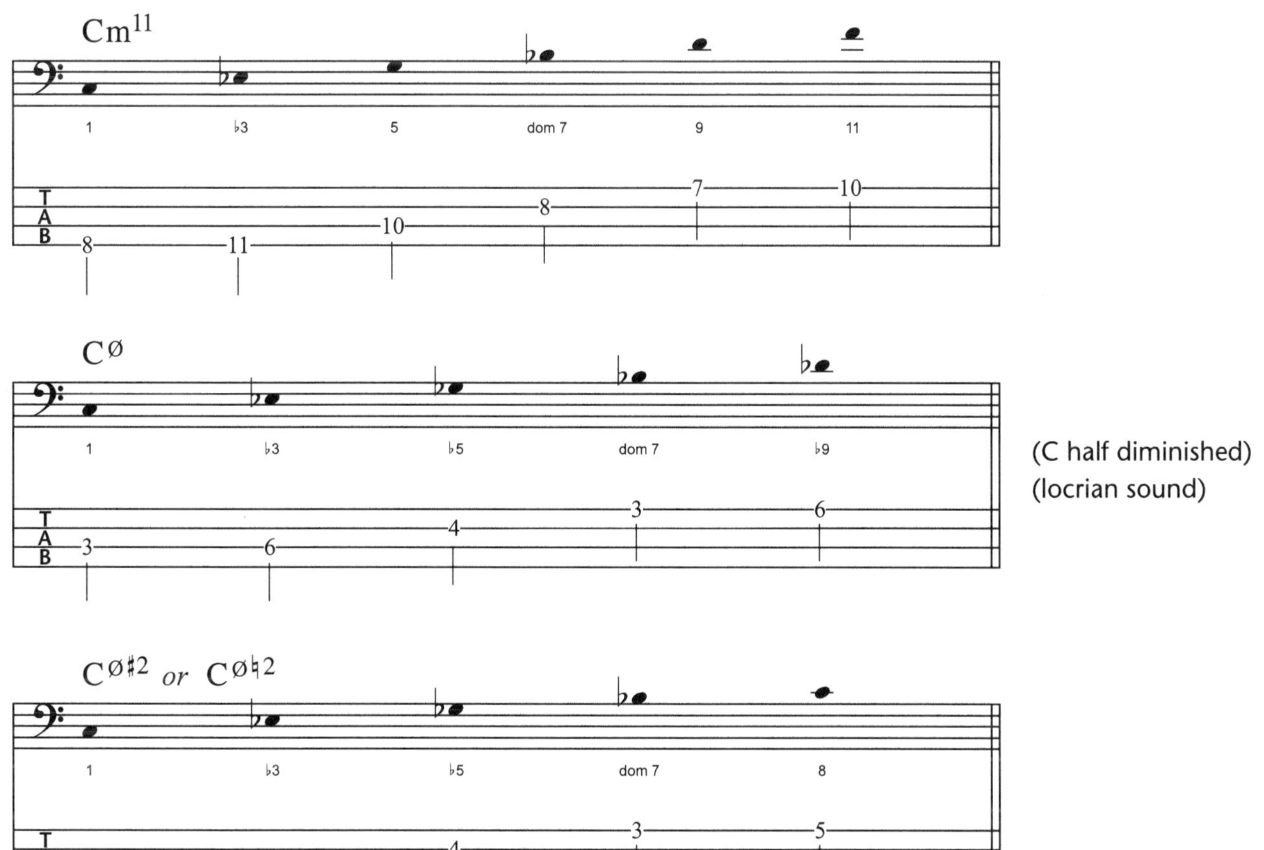
Cm11
1 ♭3 5 dom 7 9 11
8 11 10 8 7 10
CØ
1 ♭3 ♭5 dom 7 ♭9
3 6 4 3 6
(C half diminished)
(locrian sound)
CØ♯2 or CØ♮2
1 ♭3 ♭5 dom 7 8
3 6 4 3 5

Scale Exercises

1

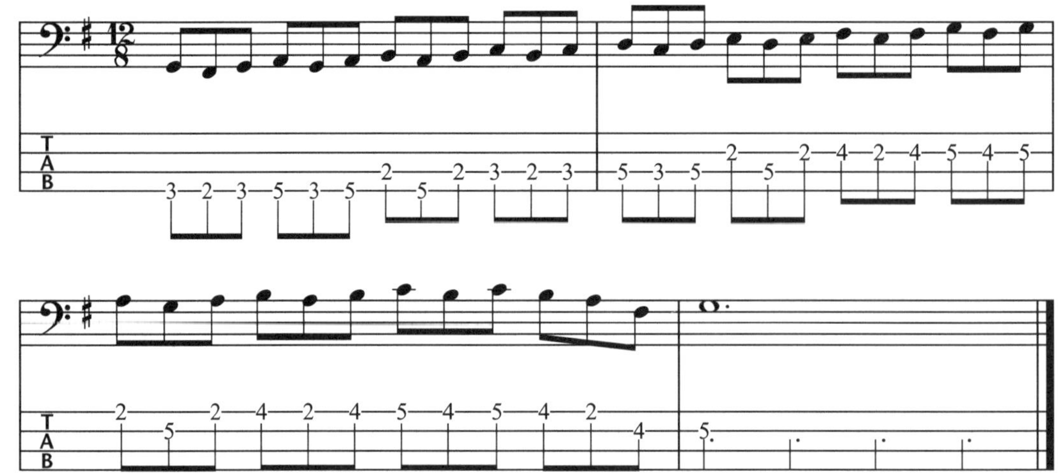

2

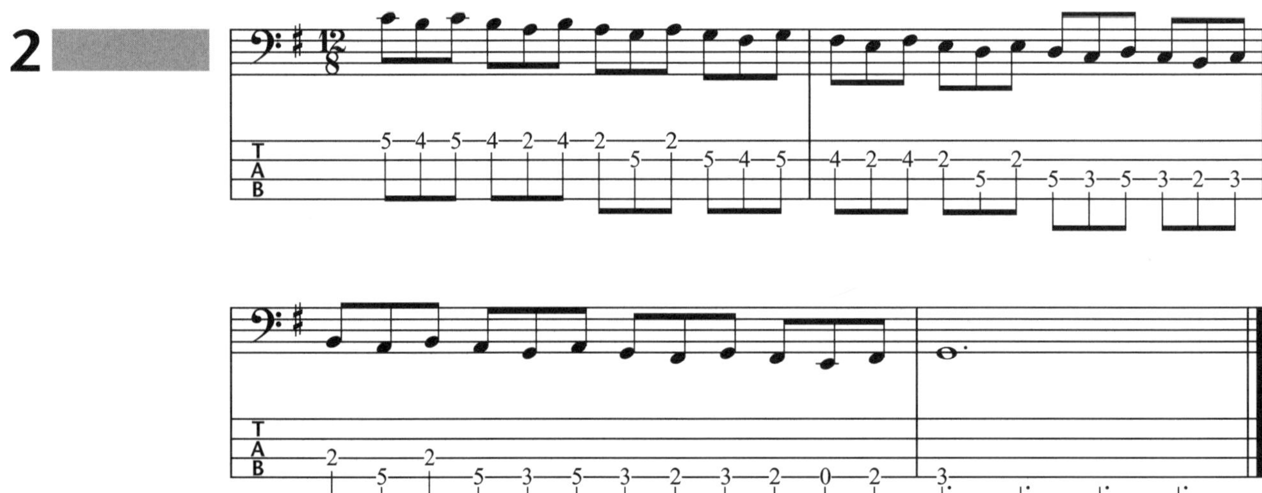

3

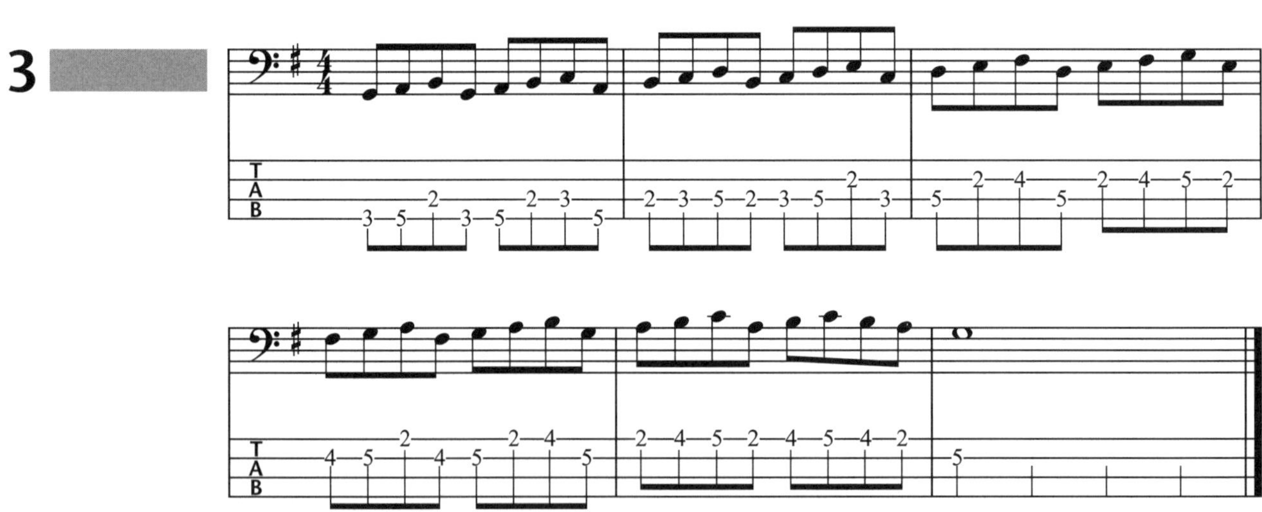

4

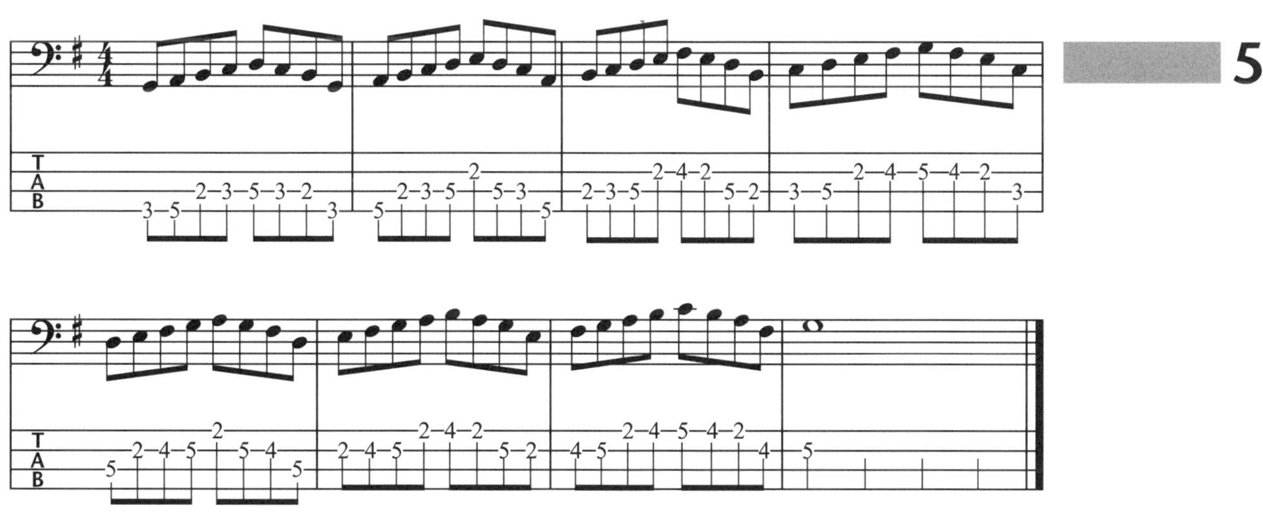

5

6

7

8

9

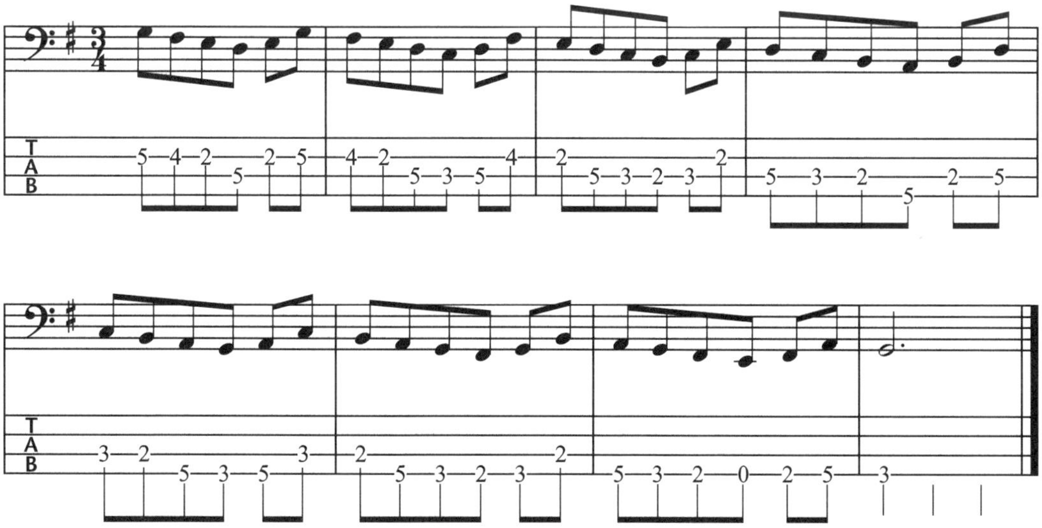

10

11

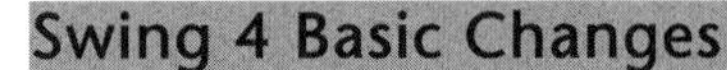

Swing 4 Basic Changes

12

13

14

15

16

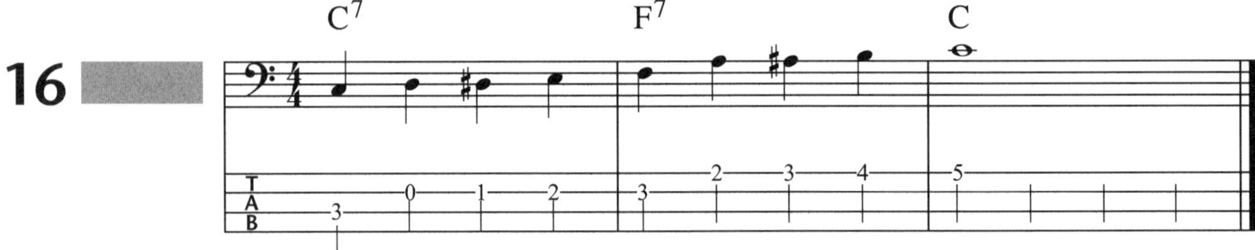

17

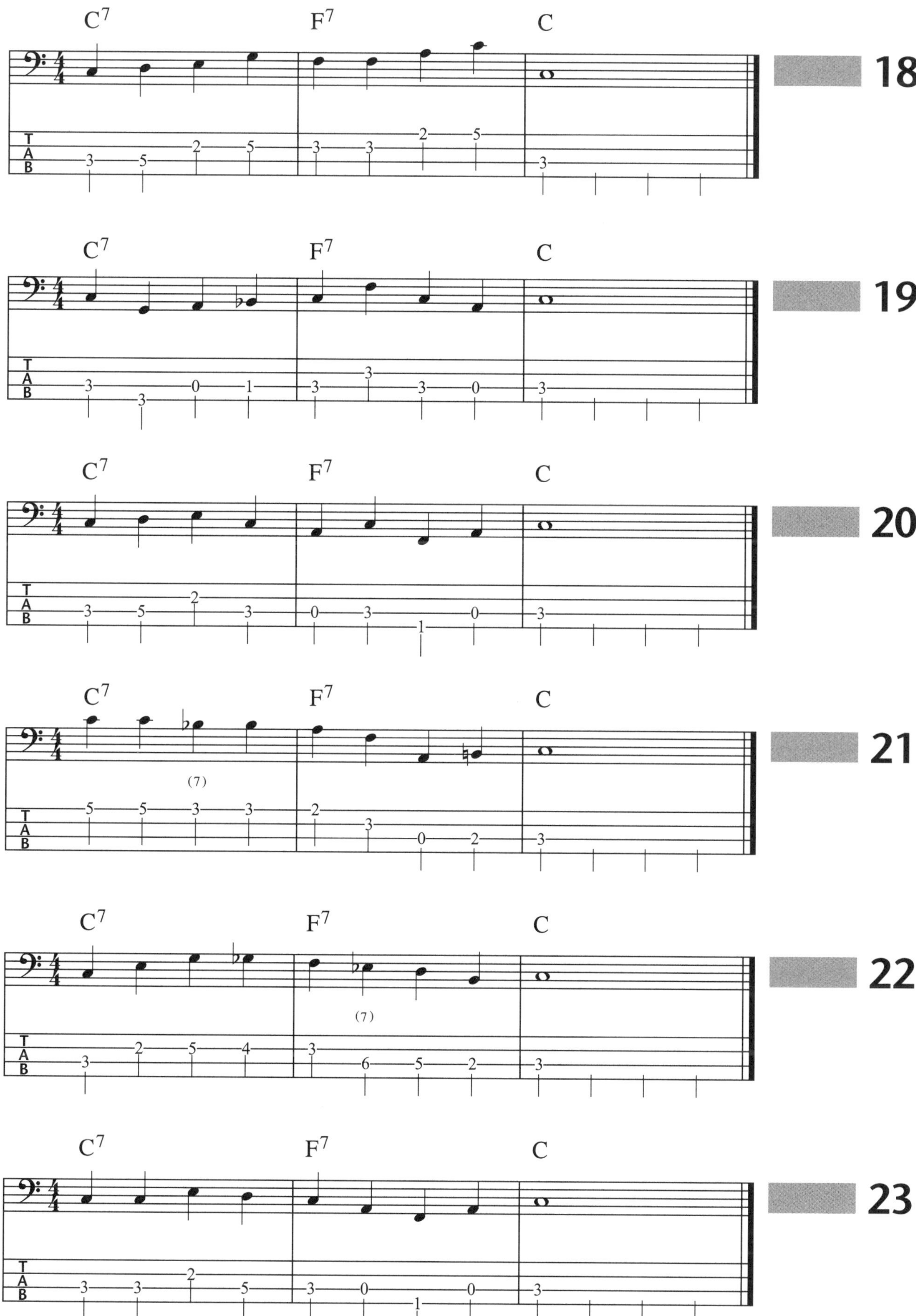
C7
F7
C
18
C7
F7
C
19
C7
F7
C
20
C7
F7
C
21
C7
F7
C
22
C7
F7
C
23

24

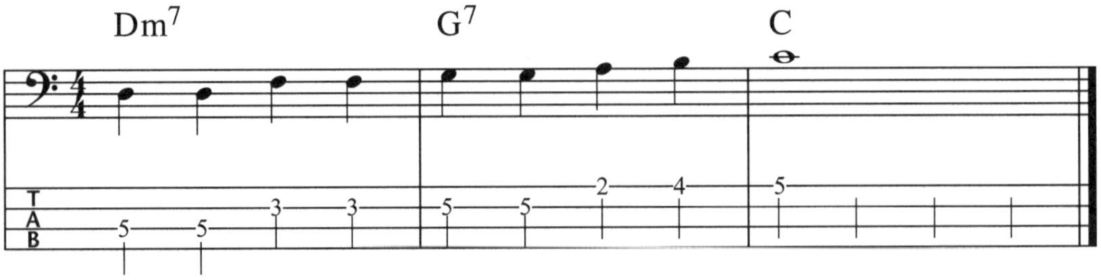

Dm7 G7 C

25

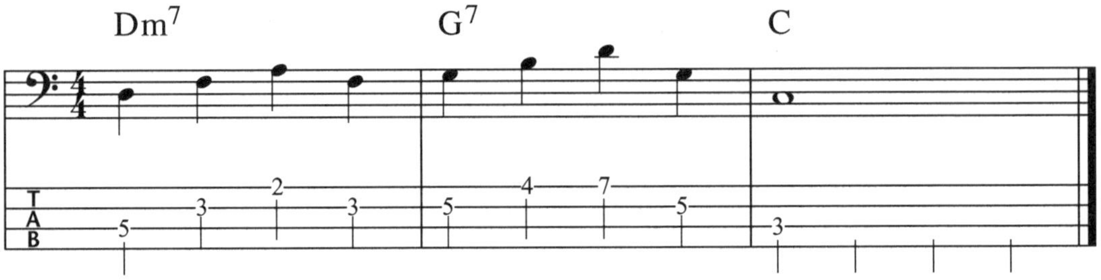

Dm7 G7 C

26

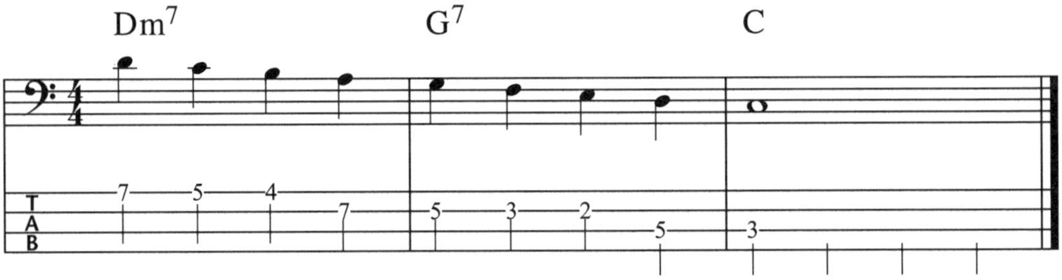

Dm7 G7 C

27

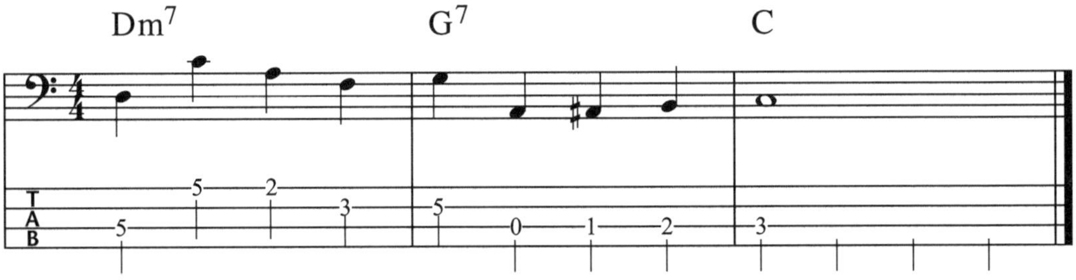

Dm7 G7 C

28

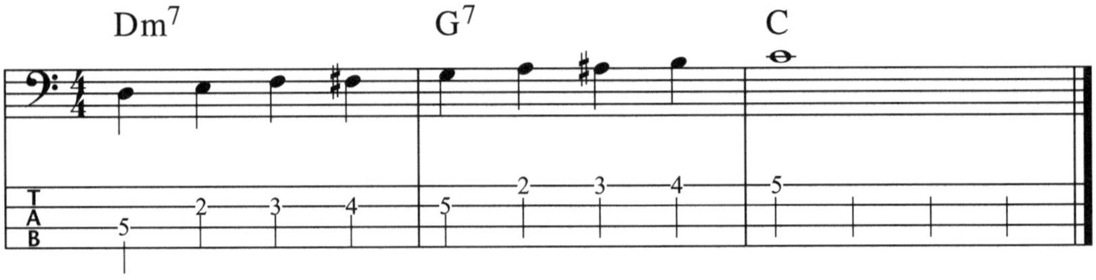

Dm7 G7 C

29

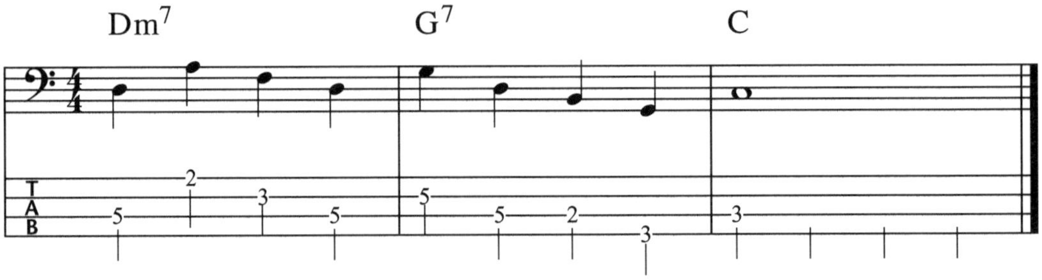

Dm7 G7 C

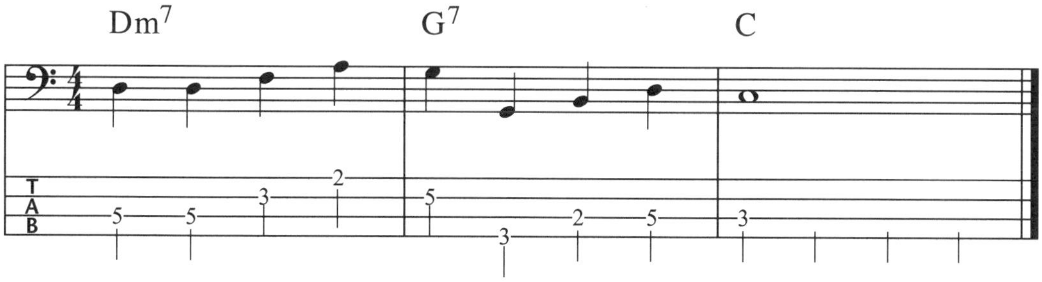

30

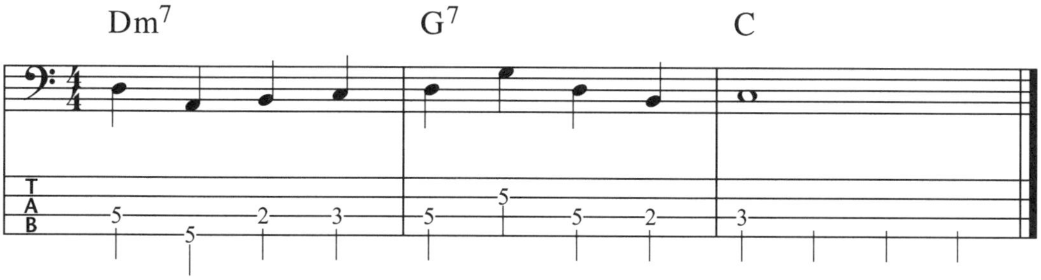

Dm^7 G^7 C

31

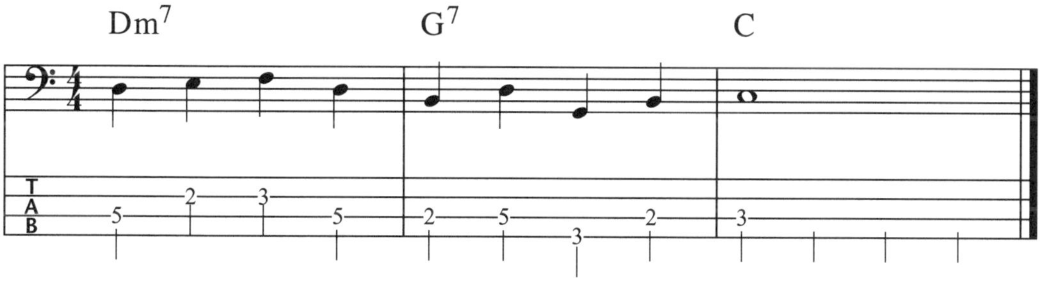

Dm^7 G^7 C

32

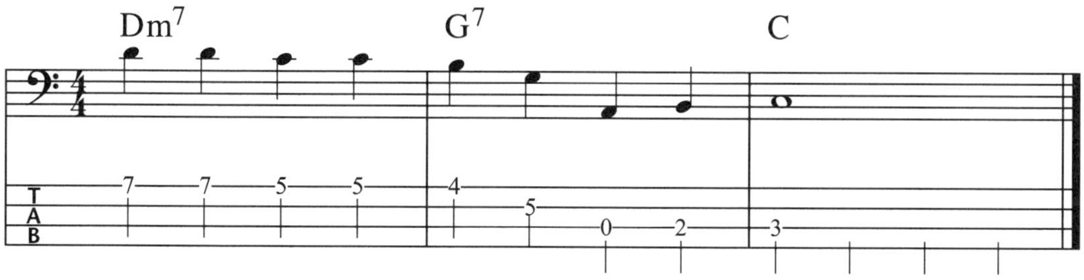

Dm^7 G^7 C

33

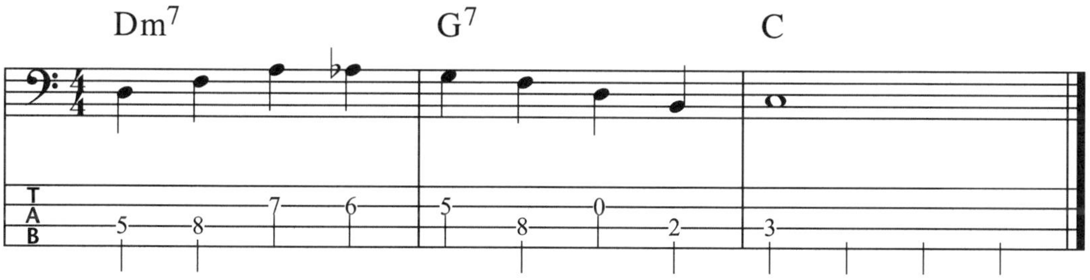

Dm^7 G^7 C

34

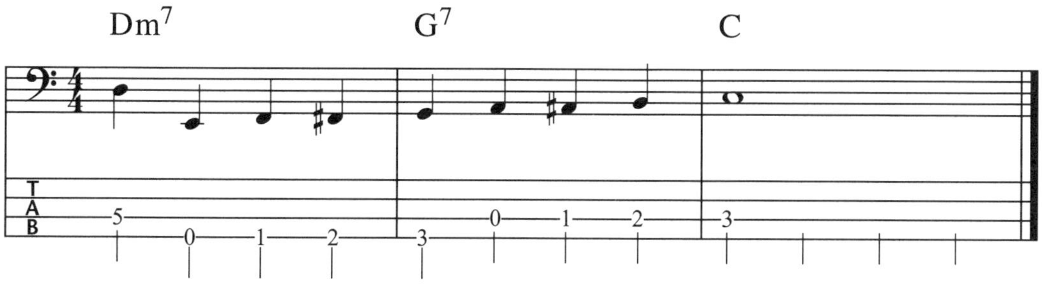

Dm^7 G^7 C

35

Dm^7 G^7 C

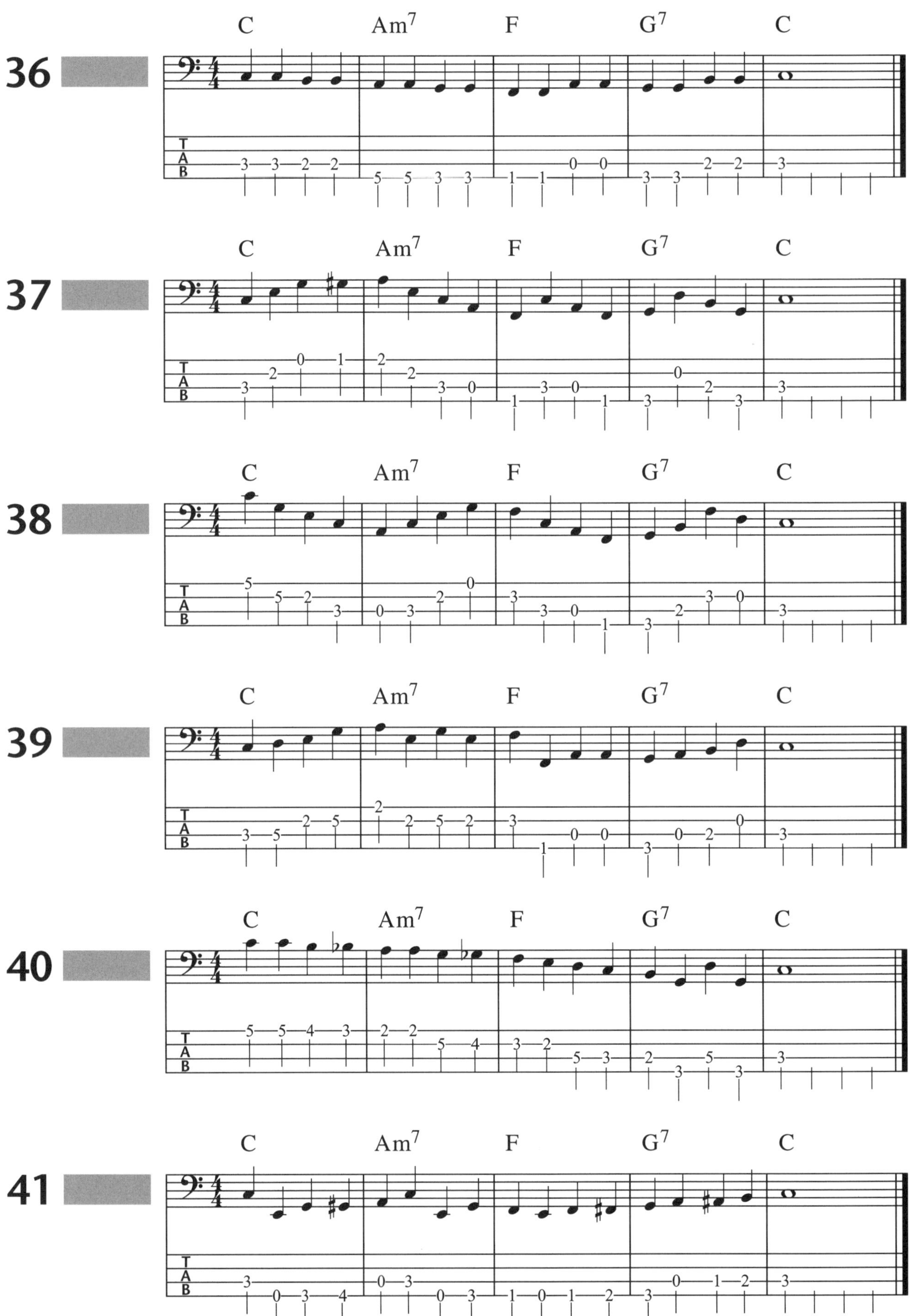
36
C Am7 F G7 C
37
C Am7 F G7 C
38
C Am7 F G7 C
39
C Am7 F G7 C
40
C Am7 F G7 C
41
C Am7 F G7 C

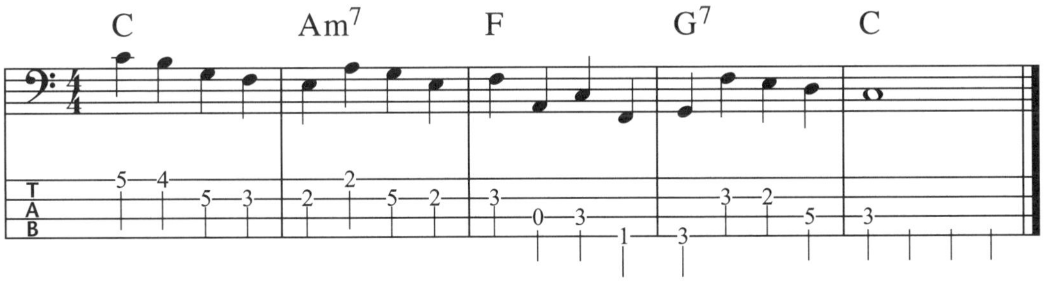

42

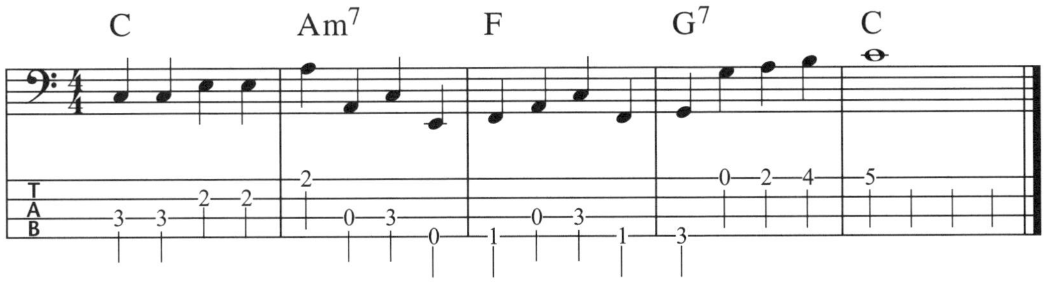

C Am7 F G7 C

43

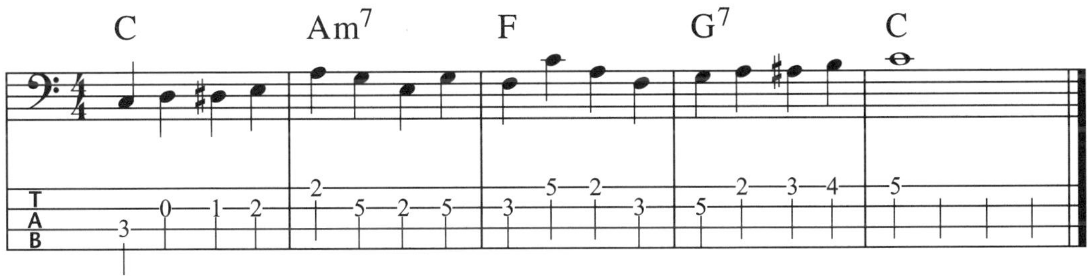

C Am7 F G7 C

44

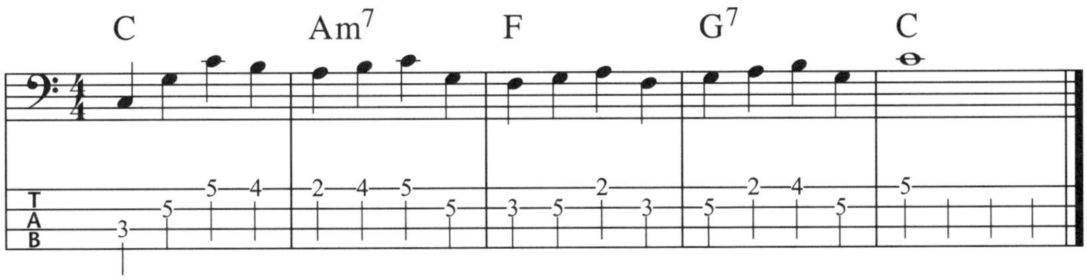

C Am7 F G7 C

45

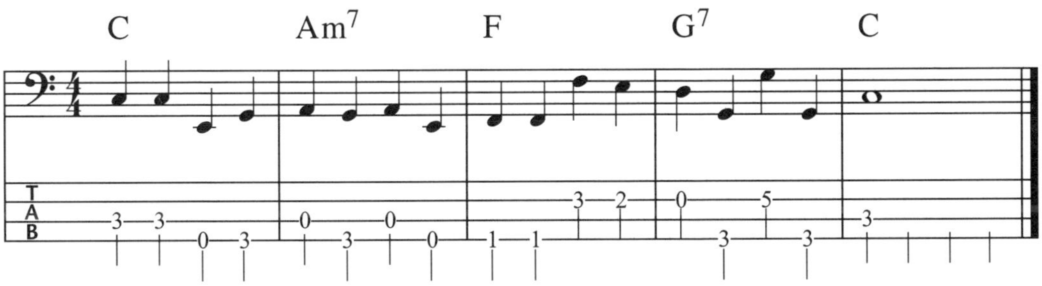

C Am7 F G7 C

46

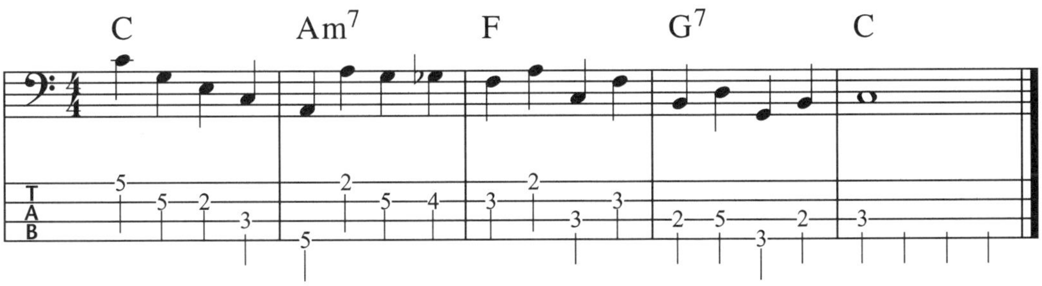

C Am7 F G7 C

47

C Am7 F G7 C

Swing 4 with Chord Extensions

48

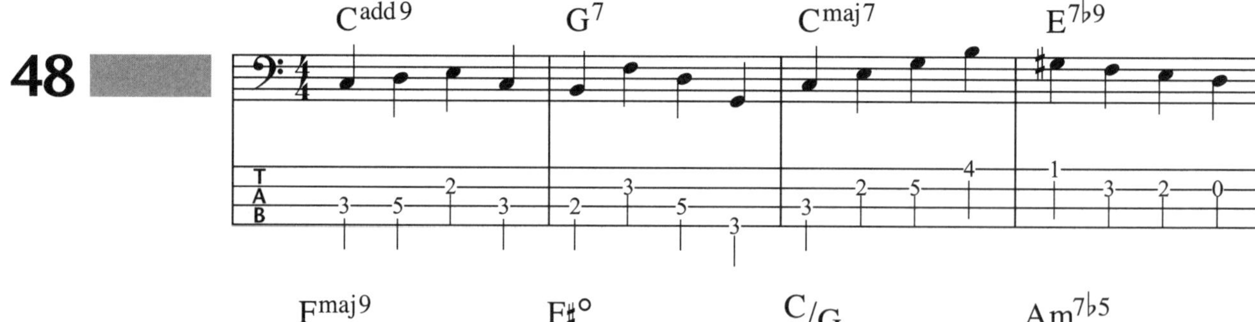

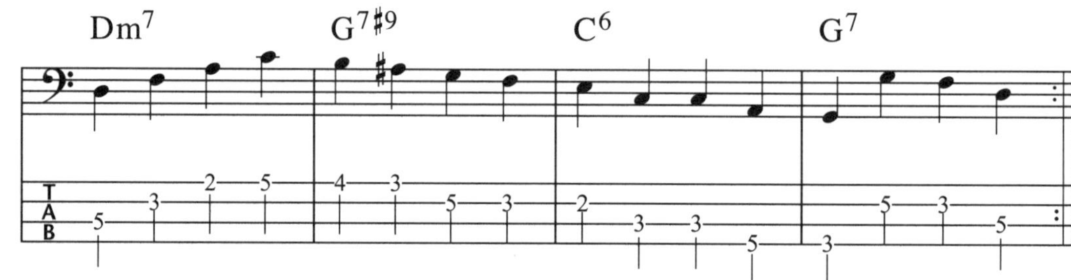

49

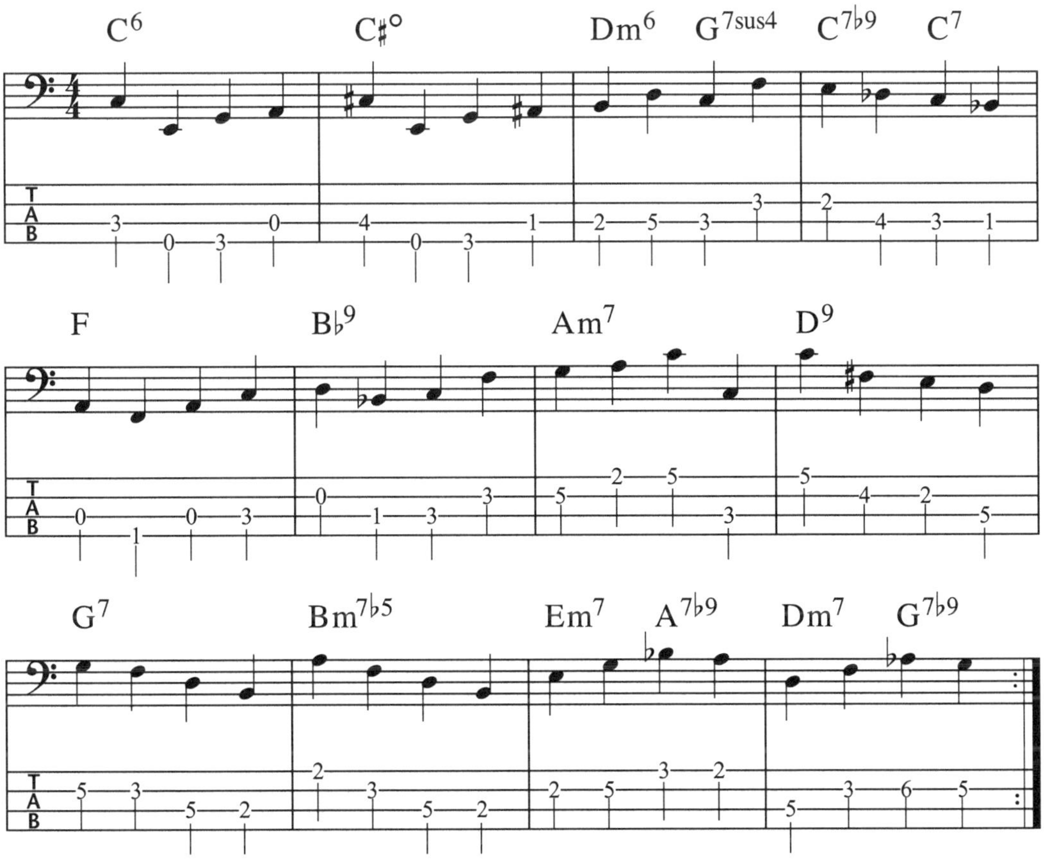

C6 C♯° Dm6 G7sus4 C7♭9 C7
F B♭9 Am7 D9
G7 Bm7♭5 Em7 A7♭9 Dm7 G7♭9
T A B

50

C Dm9 D♯° C/E
Fmaj9 Dadd9/F♯ Gsus4 E/G♯
Am7 Dm7♭5 G7♭9 C Em9 Fm9/G G11
T A B

51

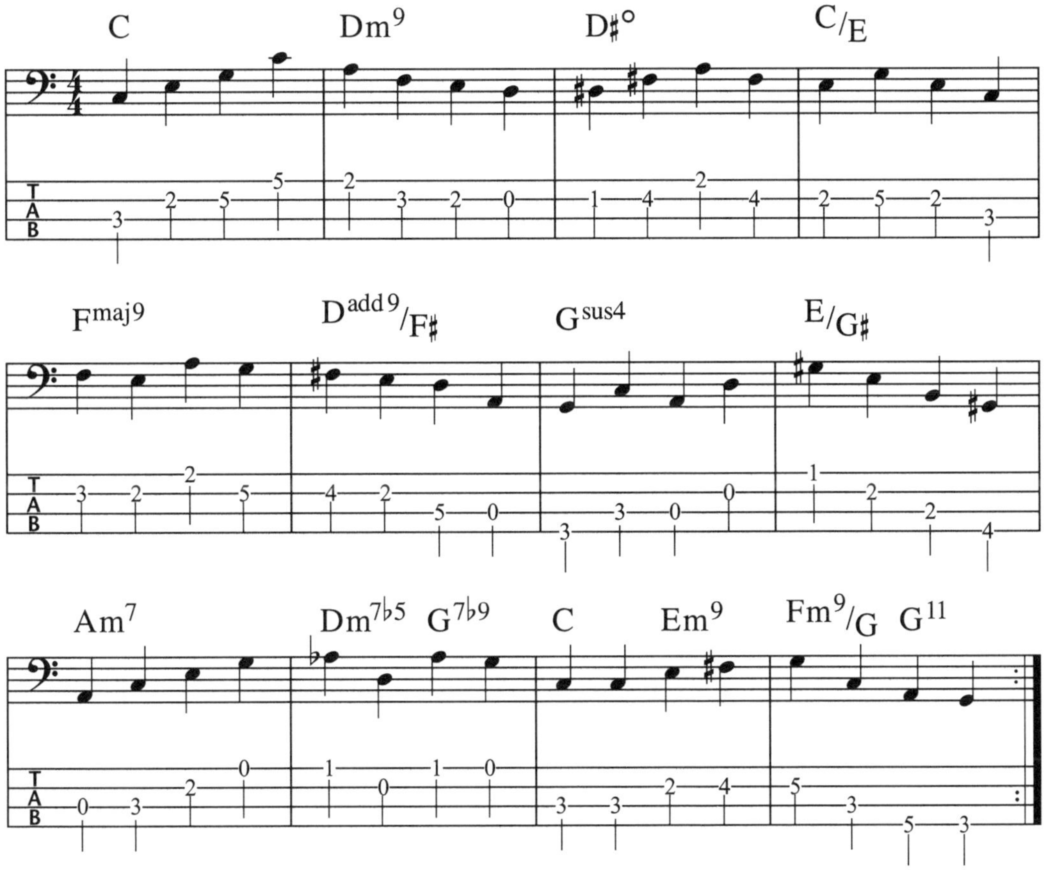

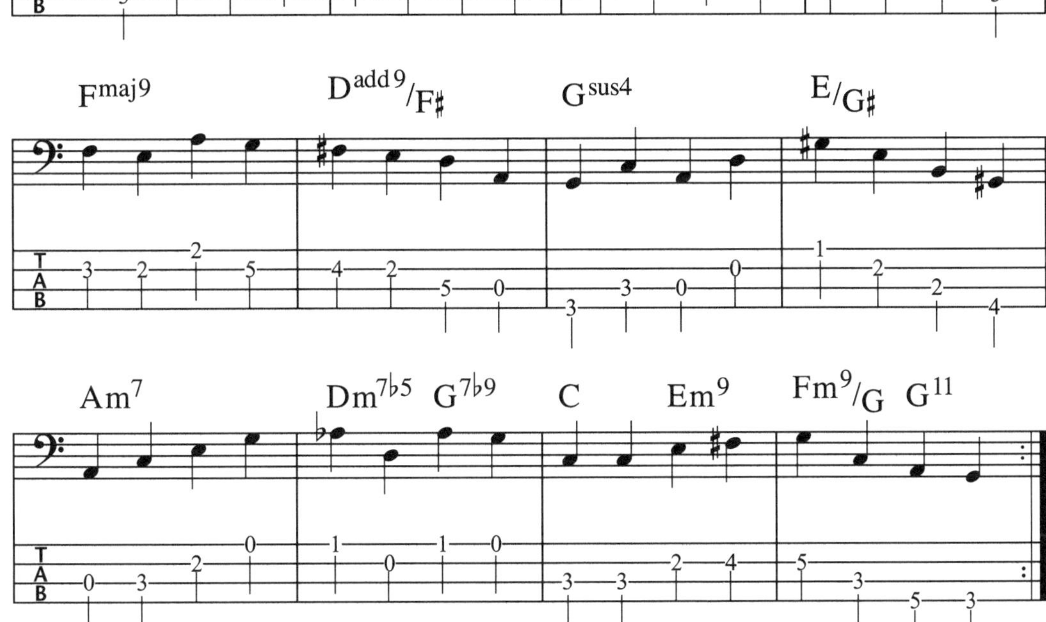

Swing 4 with Passing Notes

52
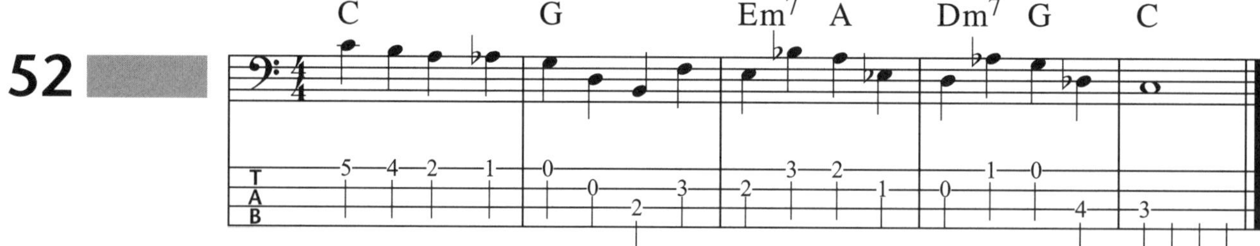

53

54
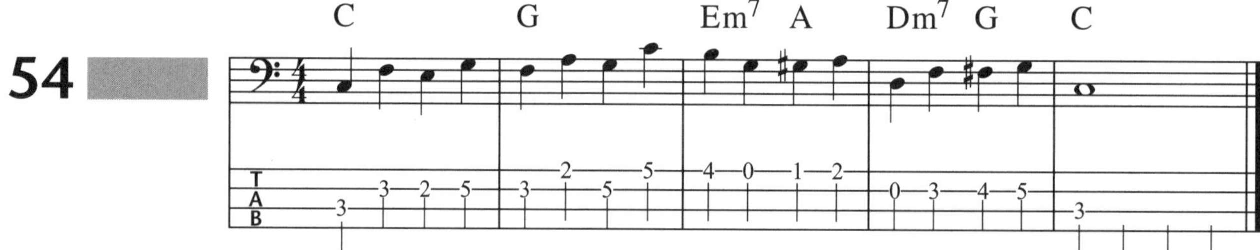

55

56

57
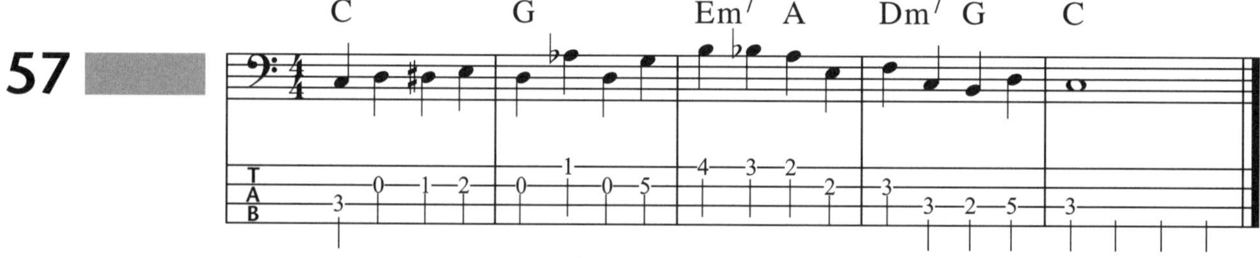

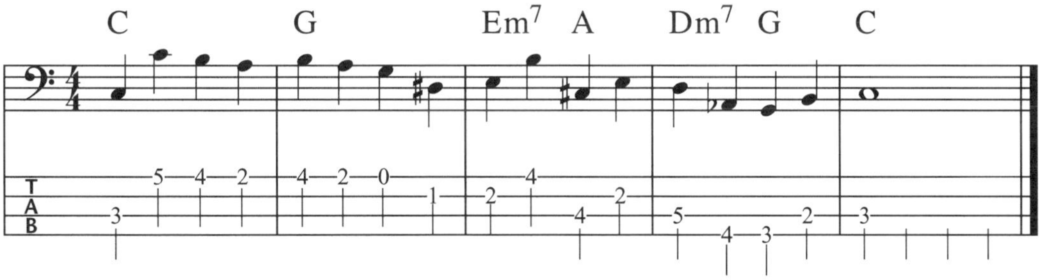

58

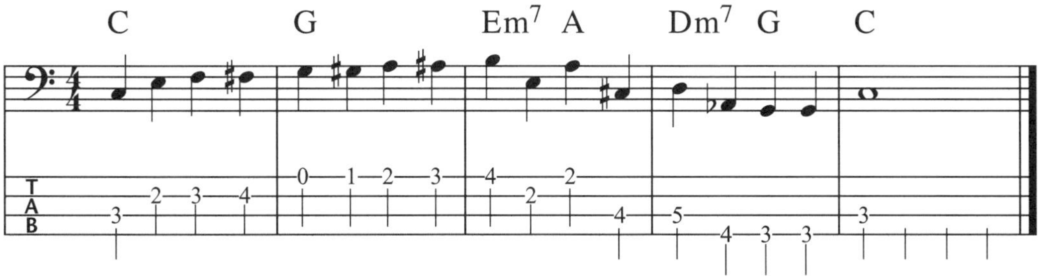

C | G | Em^7 A | Dm^7 G | C

59

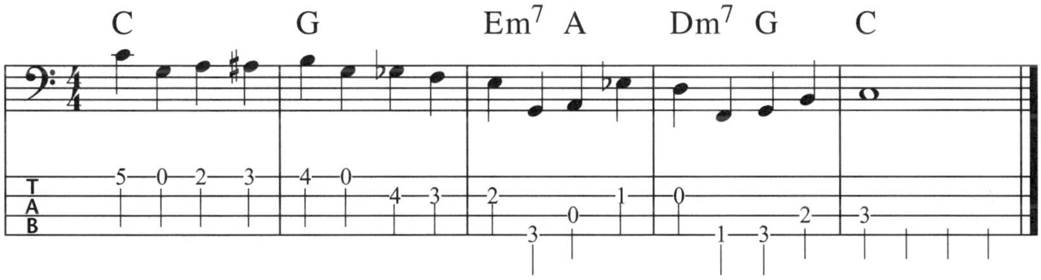

C | G | Em^7 A | Dm^7 G | C

60

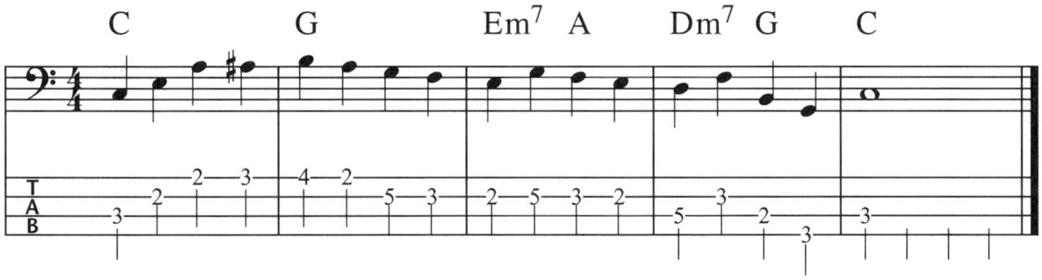

C | G | Em^7 A | Dm^7 G | C

61

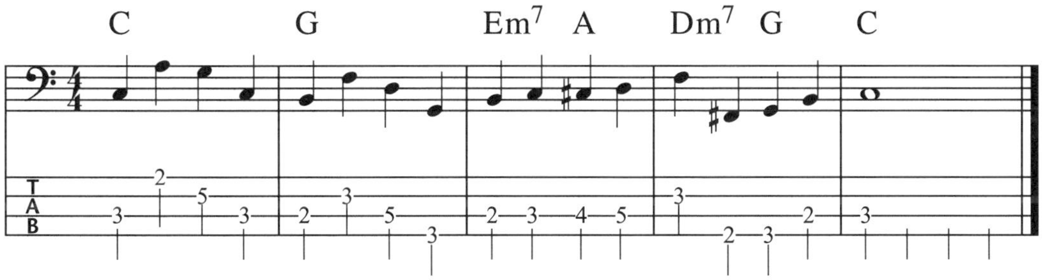

C | G | Em^7 A | Dm^7 G | C

62

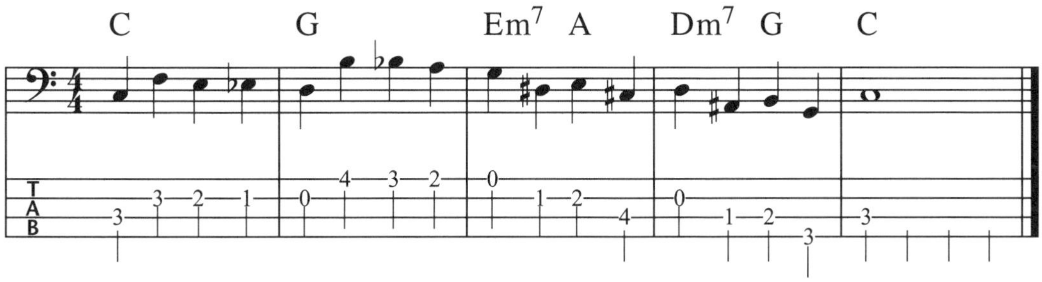

C | G | Em^7 A | Dm^7 G | C

63

C | G | Em^7 A | Dm^7 G | C

Triplet Fills (rhythms used sparingly)

Shuffle or Swing Feel ♩. ♪ = ♩ ♪ (3)

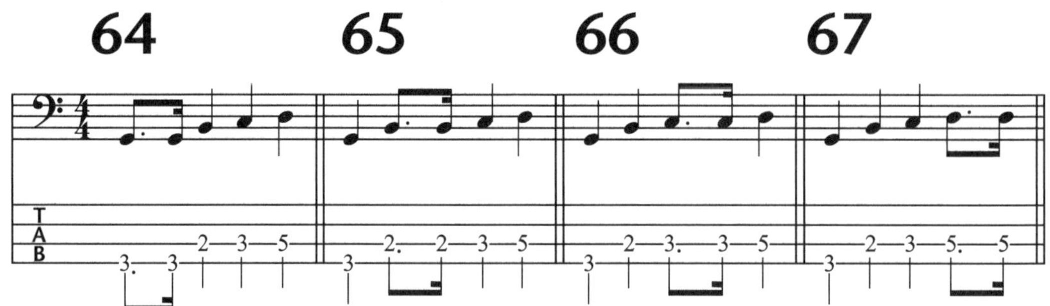

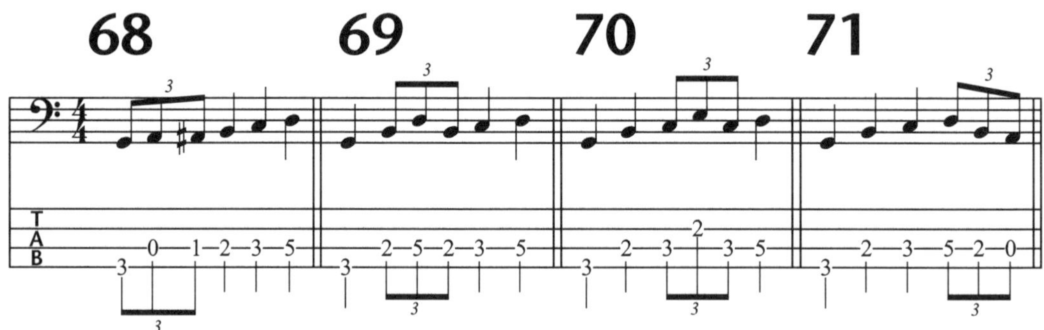

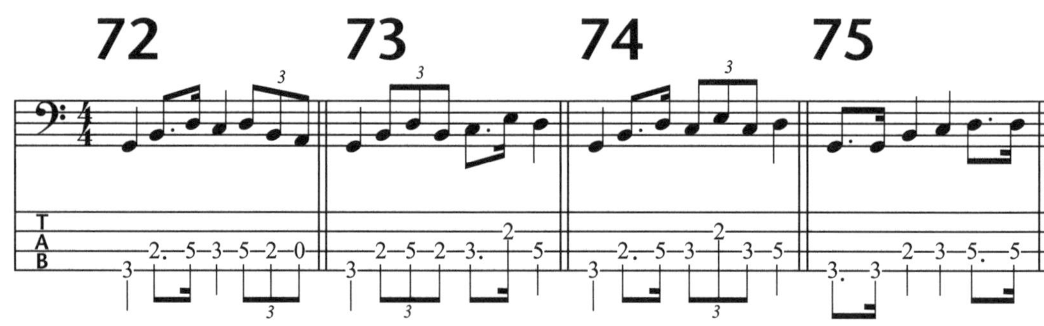

Chord Sequences and Improvisation

Many songs have interesting chord sequences. For a bass player to confidently read a sequence of changes, and either play basic roots or improvised lines, it is important to experience as many alternatives as you can. In this way there will be the minimum surprises on a gig!

Many chord structures are quite regular and predictable. Some you will recognise as being similar to others. Beware of those structures which are deliberately different. Introductions may be unusual, because the writer wants to try some alternative ideas. Endings may also not be what you have seen before.

Watch out too for an irregular number of bars to a verse or chorus. It is very common for songs to be based on a sequence of 8, 12 or 16 bars, but it is not always so. For instance, if a song has a lot of lyrics at the end of a sequence, an extra bar is often added. This allows the singer to get a breath before the next part of the song, and prevents the lyrics from sounding rushed. On the other hand, if a melody finishes well before the end of a regular sequence, it is common for a bar to be taken out. This removes any long embarrassing breaks and prevents the song from stagnating. These techniques are used to keep the attention of the listener.

The following sequences are organised in this way:

Letters	a – g	Contemporary Pop
	h – l	Latin
	m – r	Ballad
	s – v	Jazz 4s

The ideas from the book can be practised using these changes.

Contemporary Pop

a

b

Am7 | Am/G | F9 E9♯5 | Am7

C G | F C | G | ⁒

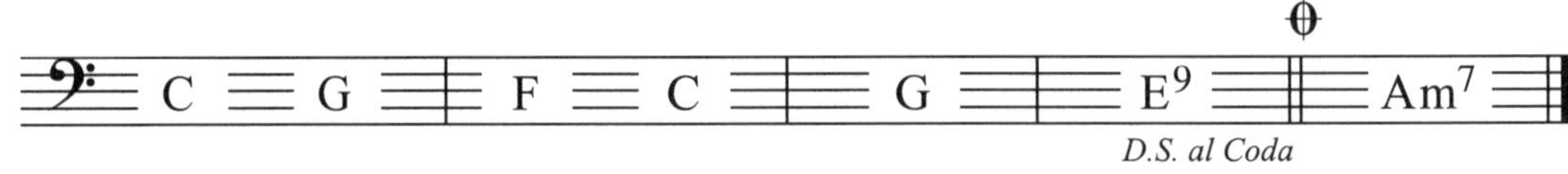

c

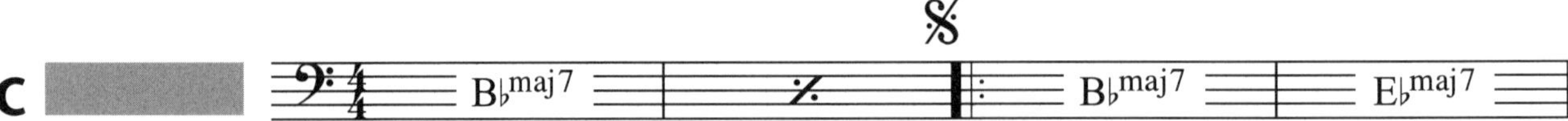

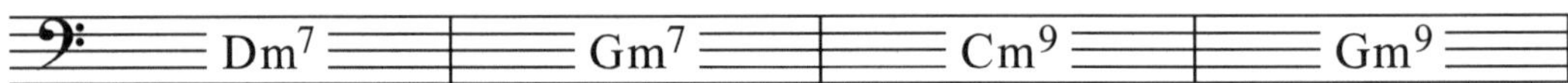

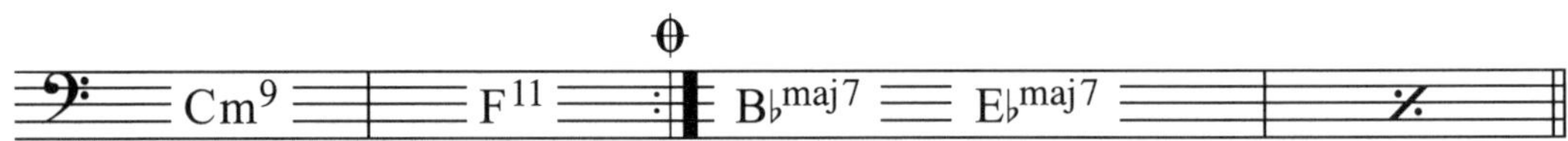

Gmaj7 Cmaj7 | ⁒ | ⁒ | ⁒

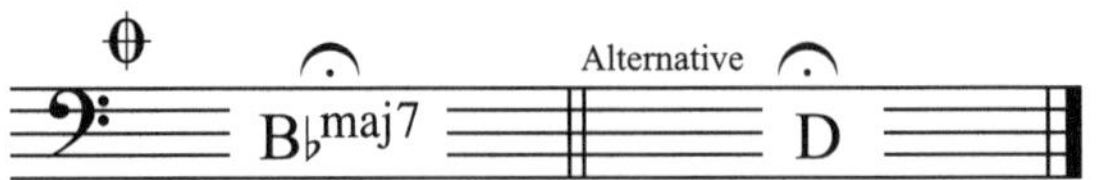

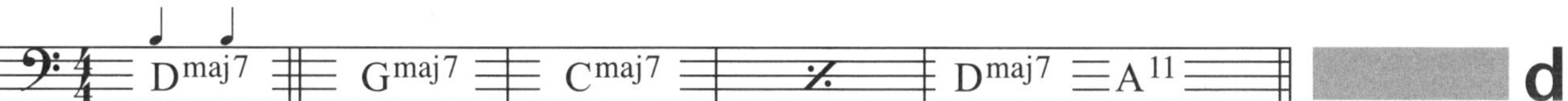

Dmaj7 | G11 | Cmaj7 | Asus4 A7

Gmaj7 | A11 | C9♭5 | B7

E7 | A7 | Dmaj7 | A11

D.C. al Coda

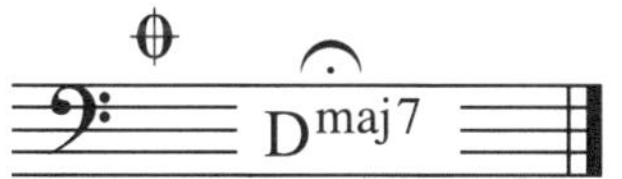

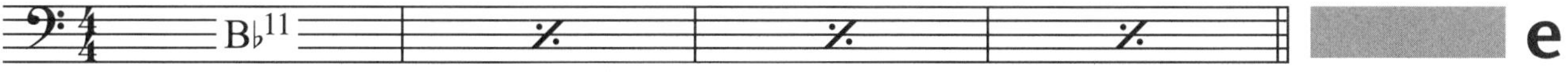

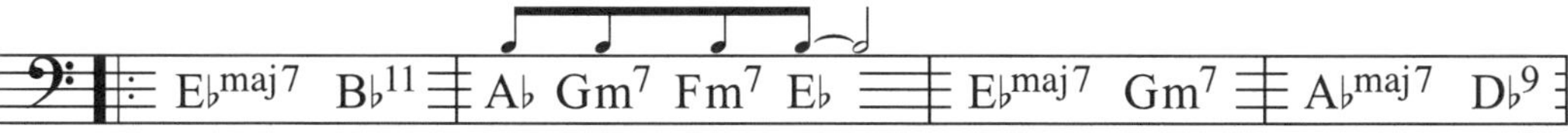

E♭maj7 B♭11 | A♭ Gm7 Fm7 E♭ | E♭maj7 Gm7 | B♭11 E♭ Fm7 Gm7 A♭

A♭maj7 Gm7 Fm7 B♭11 | E♭maj7 | ./.

./. | A♭maj7 Gm7 Fm7 | B♭11 | ./.

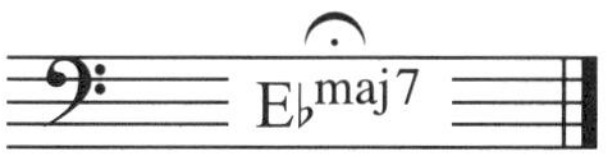

f

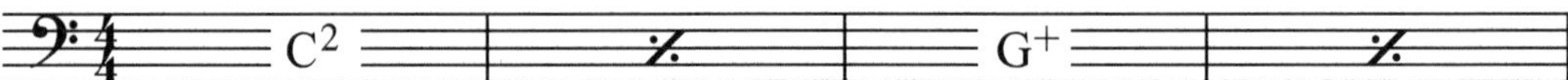

Dm7 | G11 | C2 | Dm7 G11

Cmaj9 | Fmaj7 G11 | Cmaj9 | Dm7 G11

Cmaj9 | Fmaj7 G11 | Bm7 | E9

A | D E11 | Am7 |

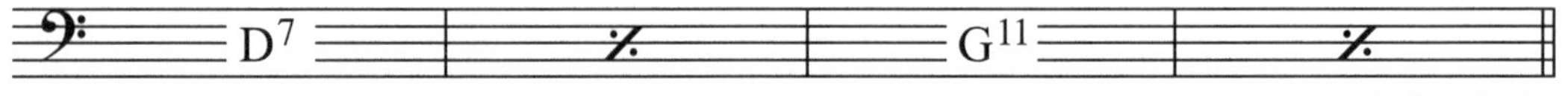

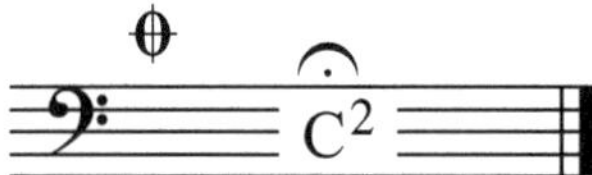

g

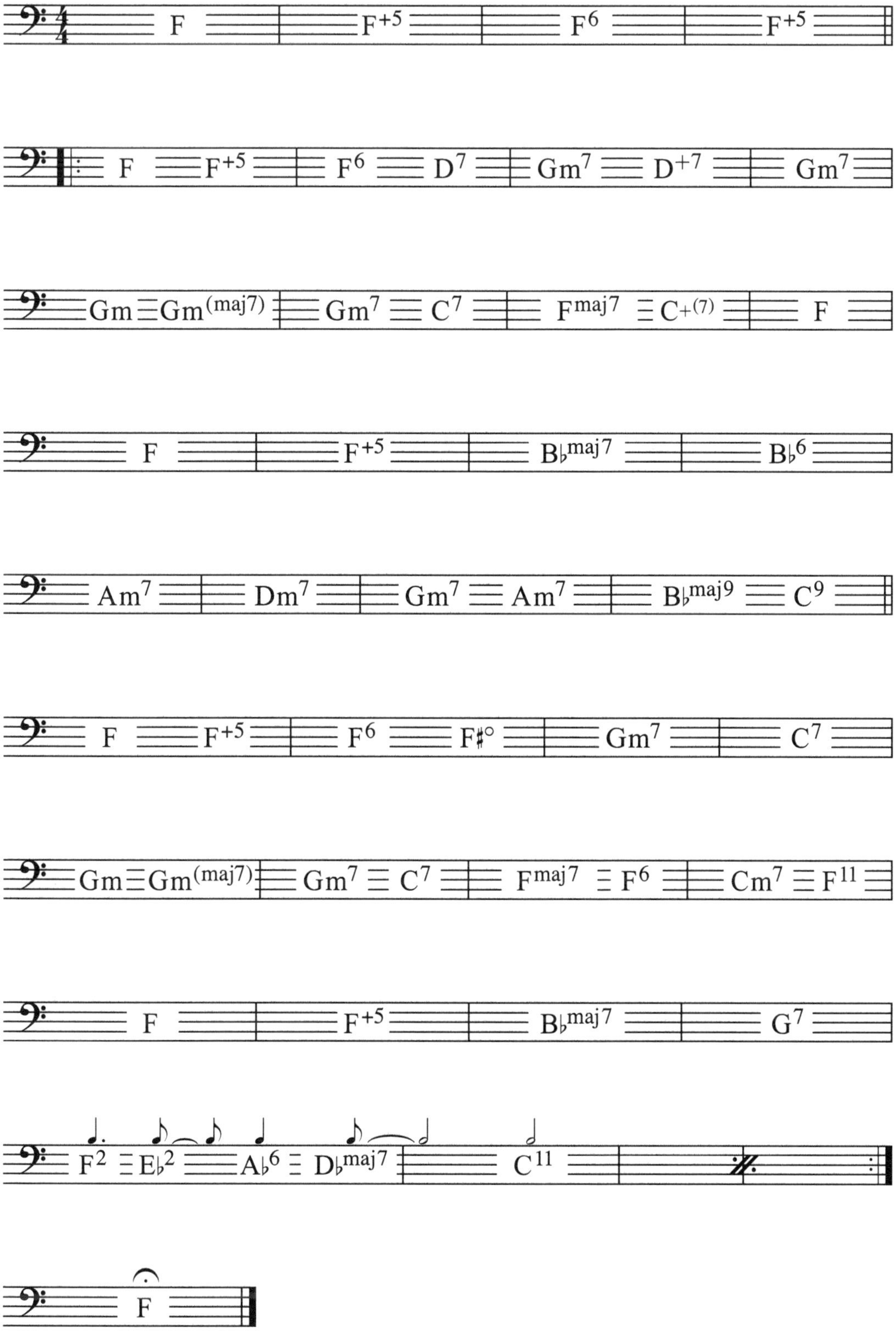

4/4 | F | F^{+5} | F^{6} | F^{+5} ||

|: F F^{+5} | F^{6} D^{7} | Gm^{7} D^{+7} | Gm^{7} |

| Gm $Gm^{(maj7)}$ | Gm^{7} C^{7} | F^{maj7} $C+^{(7)}$ | F |

| F | F^{+5} | $B\flat^{maj7}$ | $B\flat^{6}$ |

| Am^{7} | Dm^{7} | Gm^{7} Am^{7} | $B\flat^{maj9}$ C^{9} ||

| F F^{+5} | F^{6} $F\sharp^{\circ}$ | Gm^{7} | C^{7} |

| Gm $Gm^{(maj7)}$ | Gm^{7} C^{7} | F^{maj7} F^{6} | Cm^{7} F^{11} |

| F | F^{+5} | $B\flat^{maj7}$ | G^{7} |

| F^{2} $E\flat^{2}$ $A\flat^{6}$ $D\flat^{maj7}$ | C^{11} | % :|

| F (fermata) ||

Latin

h

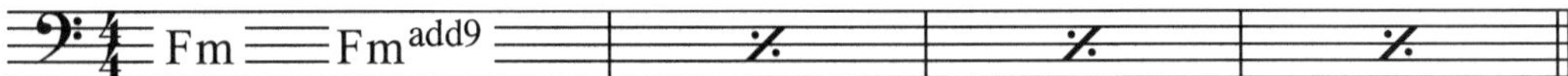

|: Fm7 | A♭7 | D♭maj7 | C9 |

Fm7 | A♭7 | D♭maj7 | C9 ||

Fm Fmmaj7 | Fm7 Fm6 | D♭maj7 | D♭m9 ||

Gm7sus4 | C+(7) || Fm Fmadd9 | ./. |

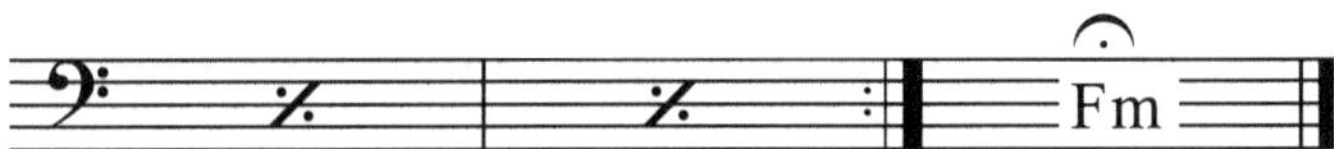

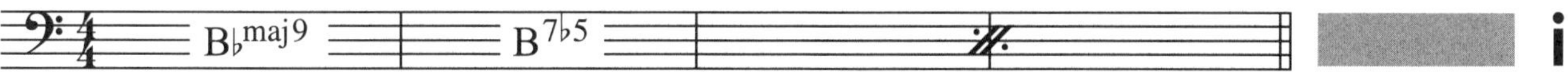

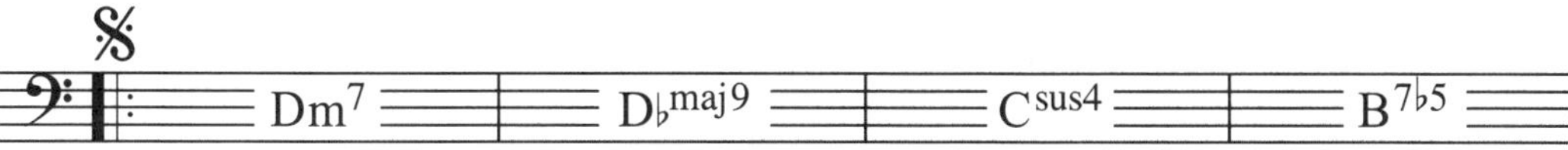

B♭maj9 | D♭maj9 | Csus4 | F7♭5

B♭7 | E♭7 | A♭9 | D♭9

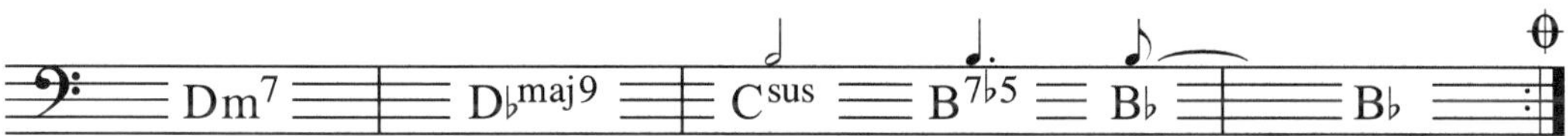

E♭m7 | A♭7 | D♭maj9

D♭m7 | G♭7 | C♭maj9 | C7♭5 F7♭5

D.S. al Coda

B♭

k

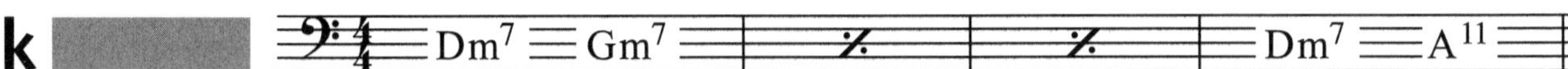

Gmaj7 | Gm7 | F♯m7 | B7

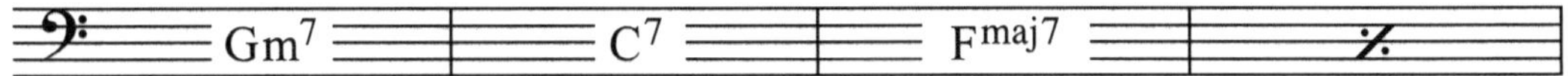

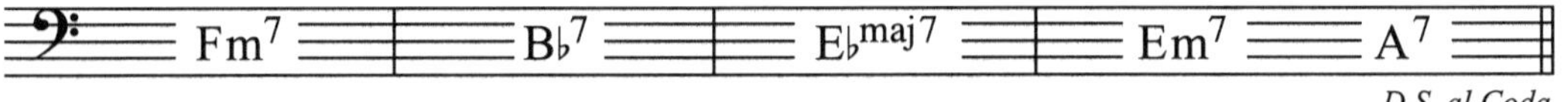

D.S. al Coda senza rep.

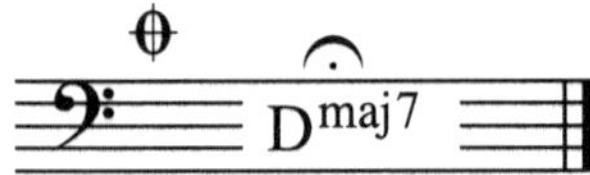

Fmaj9
F♯maj9
Fm9
G9
Gm7
G♭9
Fm7
1.
F♯maj9
2.
F♯maj9
F♯maj7
B9
F♯m9
D9
Gm9
E♭9
Am7
D9♭5
Gm7
C9♭5
D.S. al Coda
senza rep.
Fmaj9
F♯maj9
Fmaj9

Ballad

m

F♯m7 | A/E | Dmaj7 | A/C♯

B7 | D6 D | C♯m7sus4 C♯m7 | F♯m | %

F♯m7 | A/E | Dmaj7 | A/C♯

B7 | D | C♯m7 | %

D C♯m7 B7 | A | %

% | Gmaj7 | Dmaj7

F♯m7

n

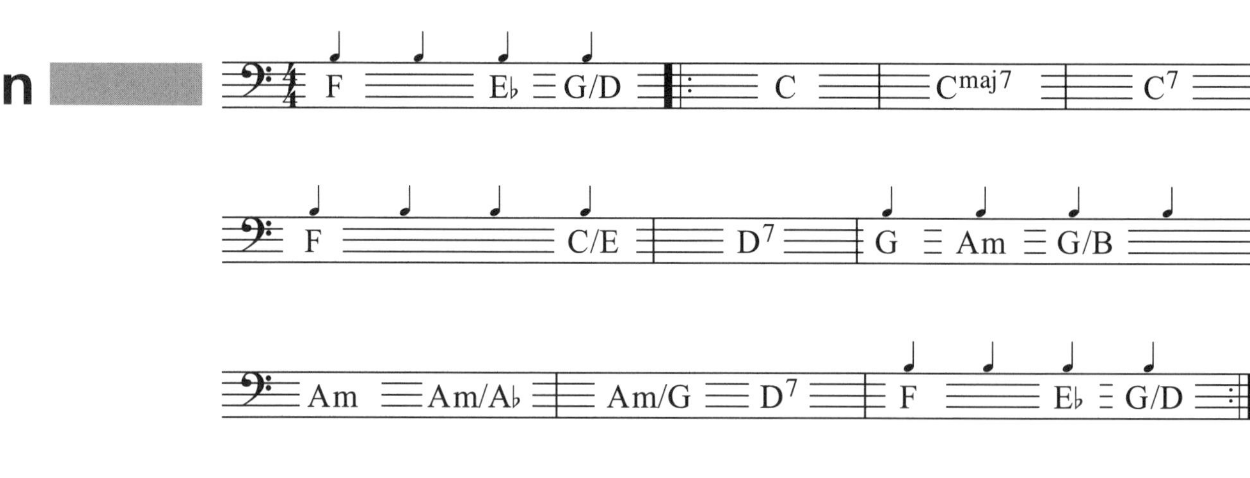

o

Dm7 Am7 | Am7 B♭maj7 | | % ‖ (To Coda)

‖: Dm7 | D11 | Am7 | % |

C7/B♭ | B♭6/9 | A7sus4 | A7 ‖

Dm7 | D11 F7/C | B♭maj7 | % |

B♭11 | Am7 F7sus4 | B♭maj7 | % |

A7 | Dm7 G9 ‖ Fmaj7 | C11 |

% | Fmaj7 | C11 | % :‖

Da Capo al Coda

(Coda) Dm7 (fermata) ‖

p

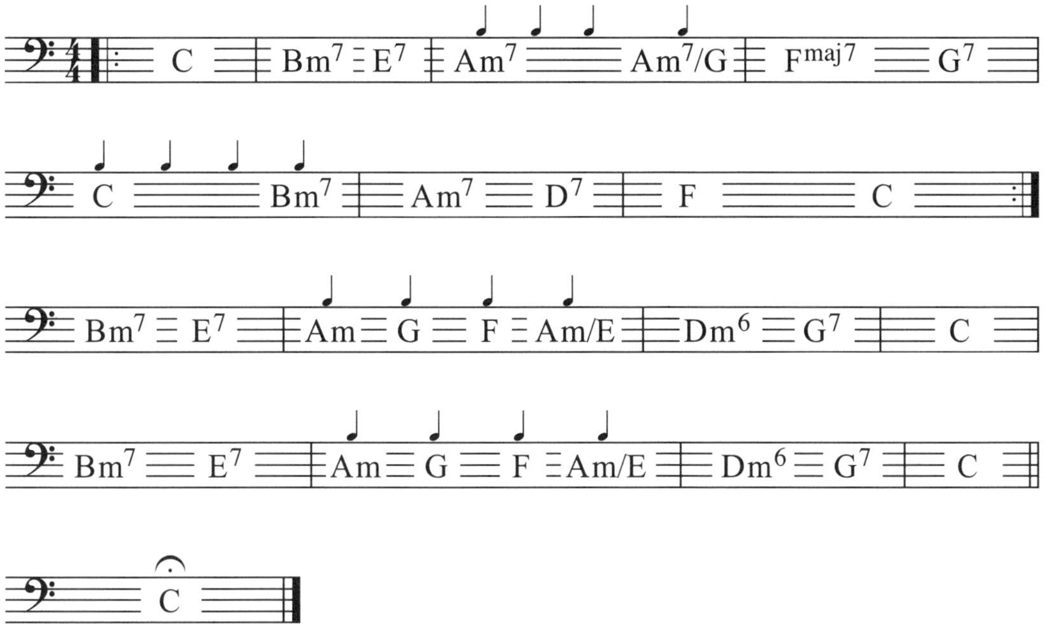

‖: C | Bm7 E7 | Am7 Am7/G | Fmaj7 G7 |

C Bm7 | Am7 D7 | F C :‖

Bm7 E7 | Am G F Am/E | Dm6 G7 | C |

Bm7 E7 | Am G F Am/E | Dm6 G7 | C ‖

C (fermata) ‖

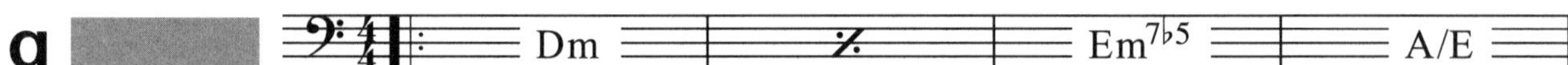

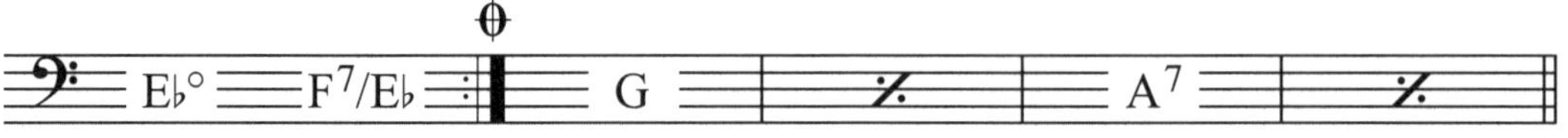

Da Capo al Coda

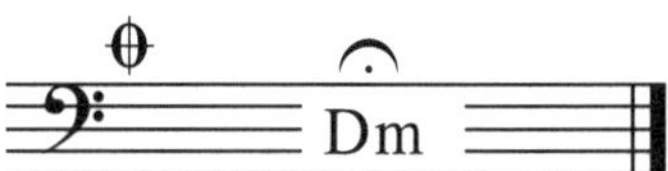

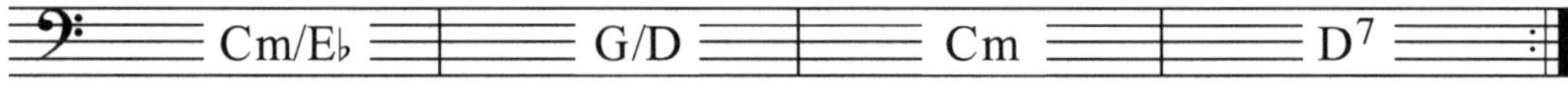

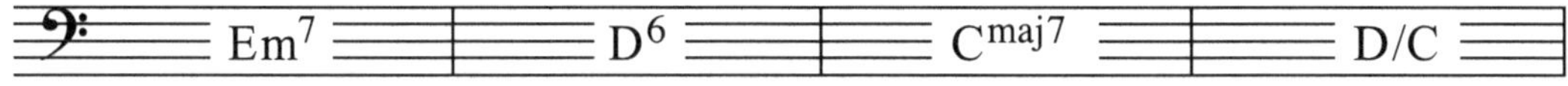

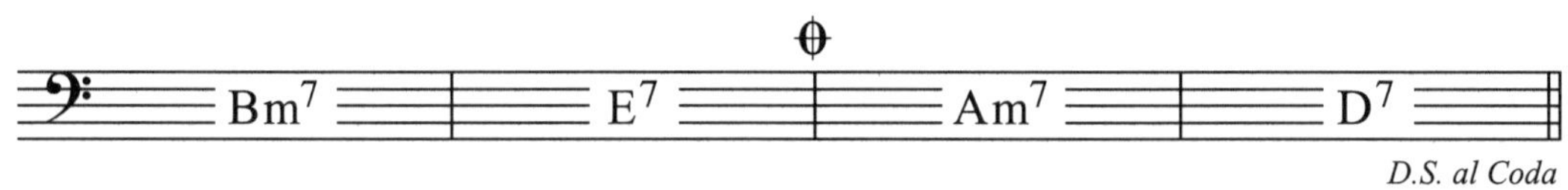

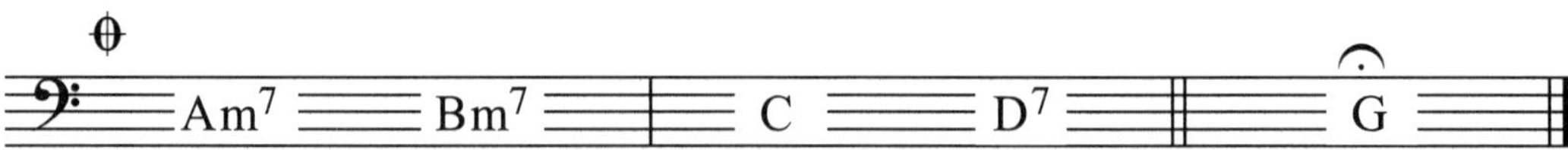

Jazz

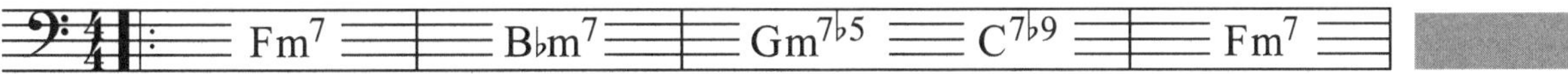

s

F7♭9 | B♭m7 | E♭9 | A♭maj9

D♭maj9 | B♭m7 B♭m6 | G7 | C11 C7

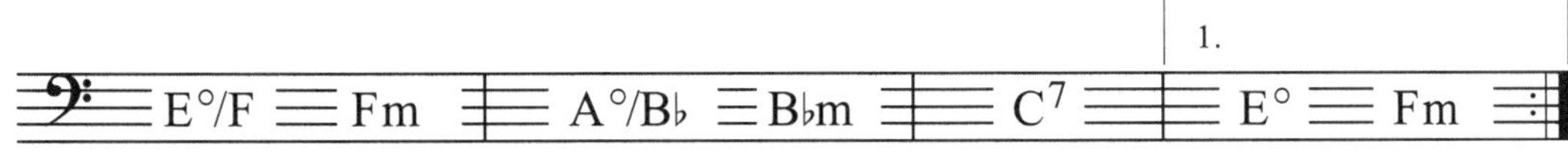

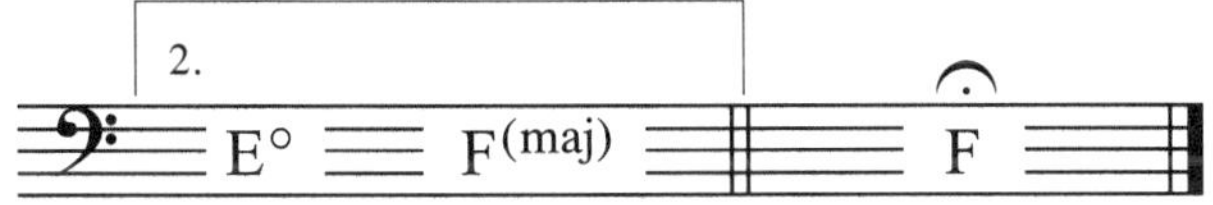

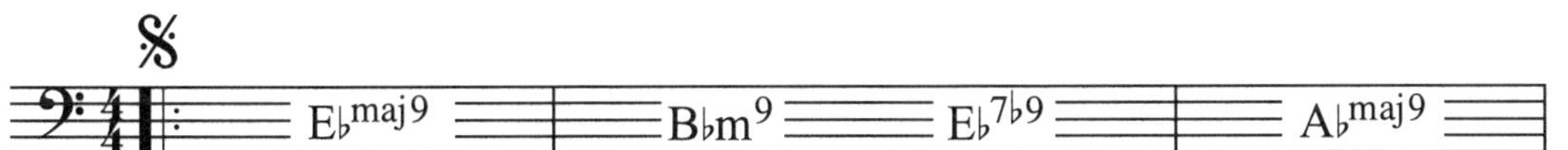

t

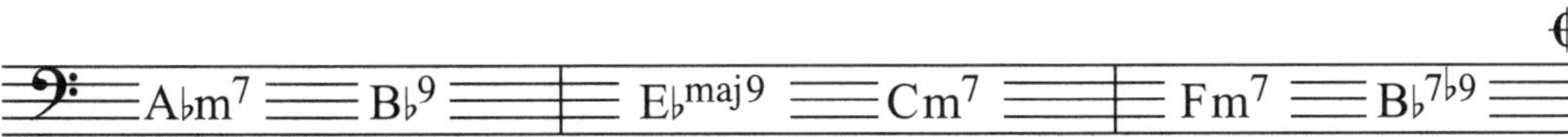

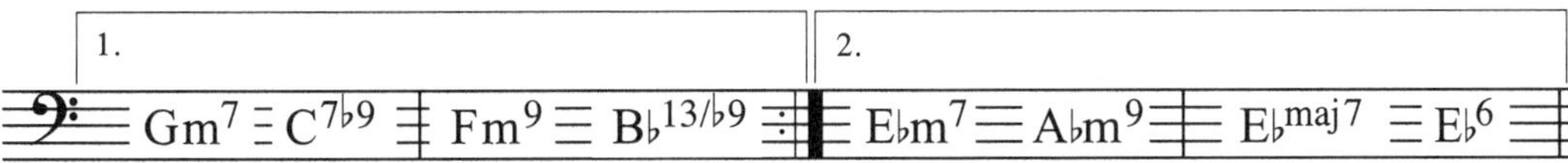

B♭m7 | E♭7♭9 | A♭maj9 | A♭6/9

Am7sus4 D9 | Cm9 F9 | B♭11 | B♭13/♭9

D.S. al Coda senza rep.

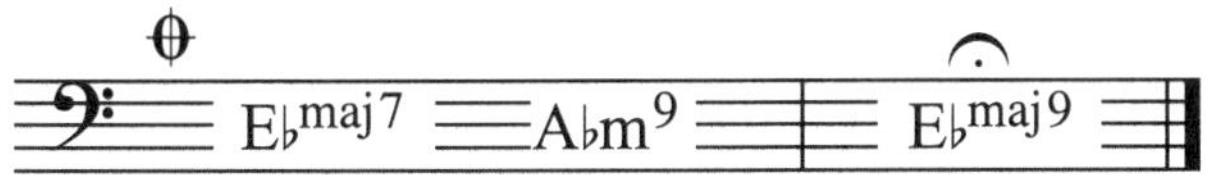

u
F maj7 | D♭° | Dm7 Cm7 F11 | B♭maj7 | Am7 | Gm7 | C11
F maj7 B9 F♯° | Gm9 Csus4/♭9 C9 | Am7 D7sus4/♭9 D9
Gm7 Am7 B♭maj7 C9 | A♭maj7 | Fm7 | G7/♭9/♭5 | C7♭9
Am7 E♭9♭5 D9 | Am7 B♭maj7 Am6 D7 | F/G | G9
B♭m7sus4 | B♭m6 | Am7 | D9 | Gm9 | C7♭9 | Fmaj9

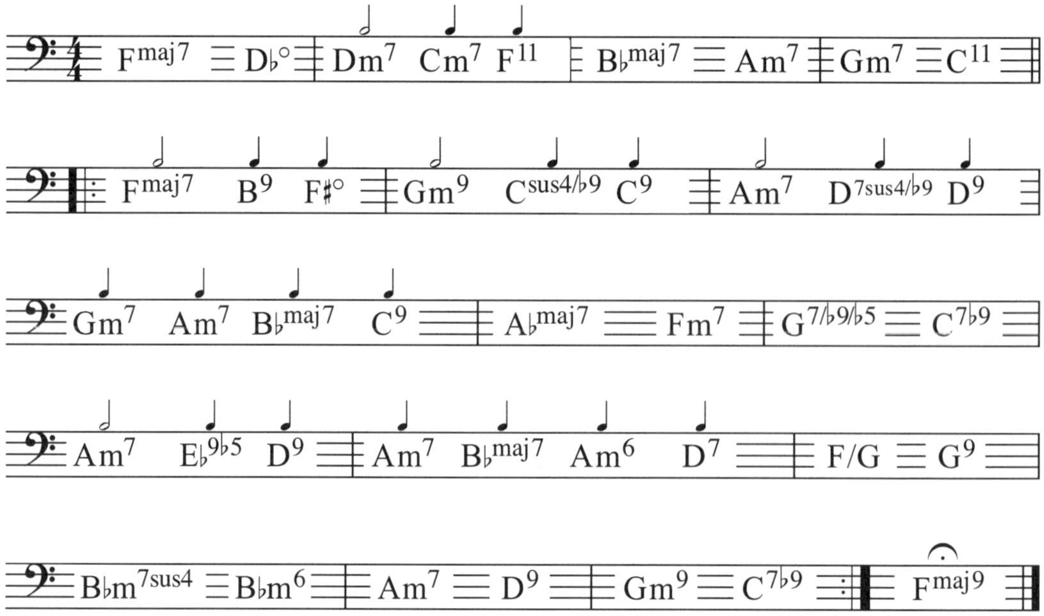

v
F | D7 | G7 | ⁒ 
Gm | C7 | F | Cm B7
B♭ | E♭7 | F | D7
G7 | G7/♯11 | Gm | C7
F | D7 | G7 | ⁒
Eø | A7 | Dm | A7
Dm | A7 | Dm | G♯°
A7 D7 | Gm C7 | F | Gm C7
F

BOOK TWO

Basic Grooves

Riff playing is important together with the knowledge of a wide range of phrases, but the basic grooves are crucial. Most forms of music have a basic groove, pulse or rhythm which drives the beat along. It can be reduced to merely one note in the bar or expanded to 16 notes in the bar. The bass has to play a pulse which forms a rhythmic and harmonic basis for the other instruments.

If a melody is strong and does not need a riff or too much harmonic movement from the bass, then a basic groove will be ideal. It can also be a welcome break from songs which are full of riffs, phrases and complicated patterns. The simplicity of a basic groove can be restful and calming. It can also be insistent and forceful when used as a driving rhythm. It can even steady a complex arrangement.

There are many types of grooves, and the variations are endless. However, there are some which are standard and widely used. This familiarity does not reduce their value or usefulness.

8th Note Basic Grooves

76

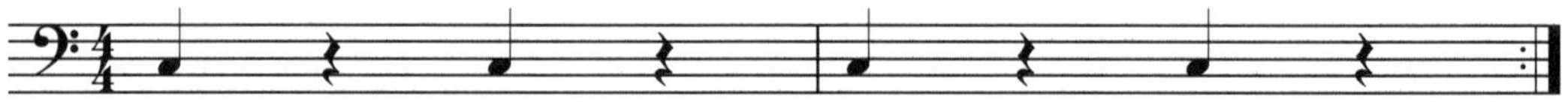

77

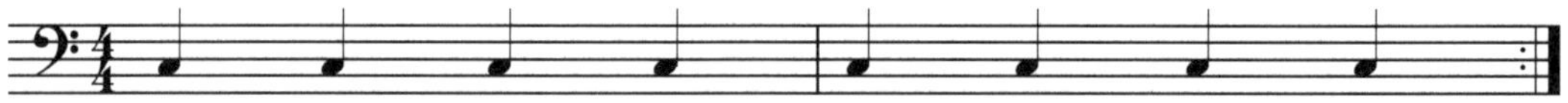

78

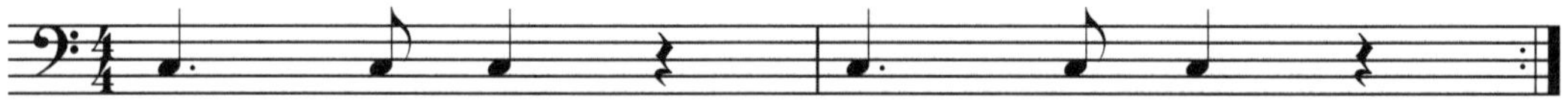

79

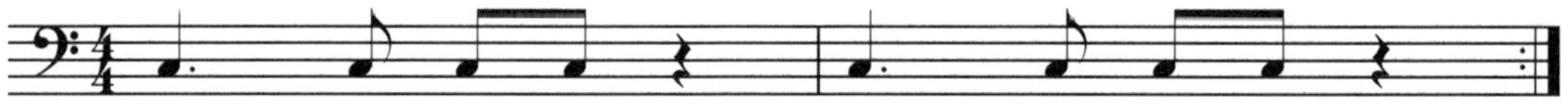

80

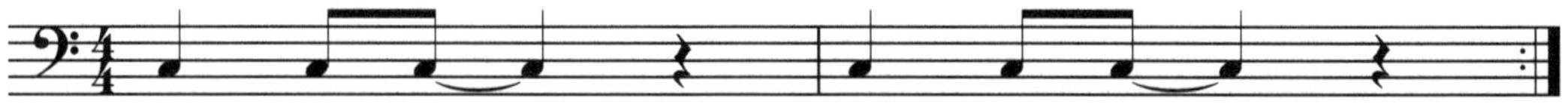

81

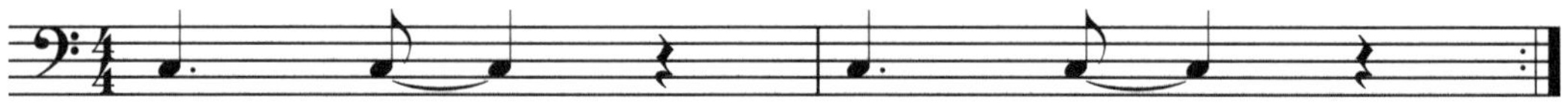

82

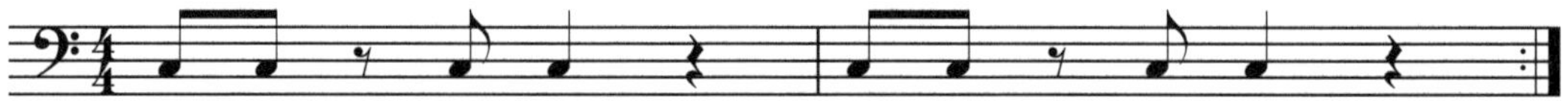

83

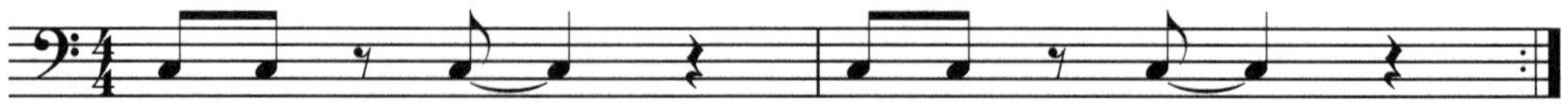

84

85

86

87

16th Note Basic Grooves

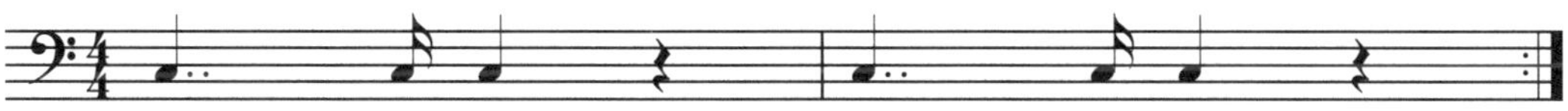

88

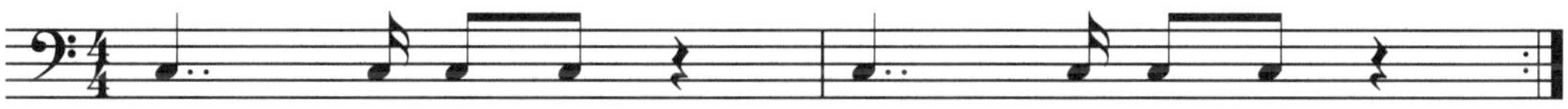

89

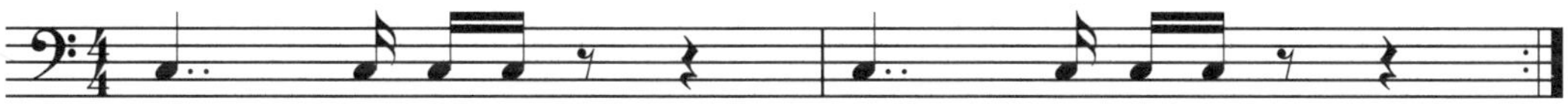

90

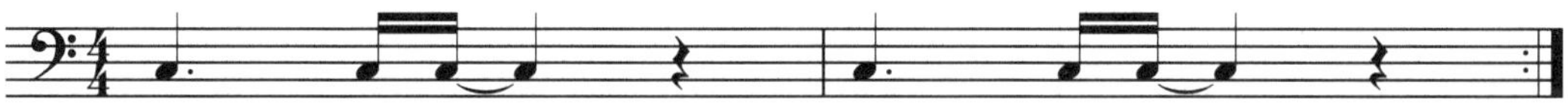

91

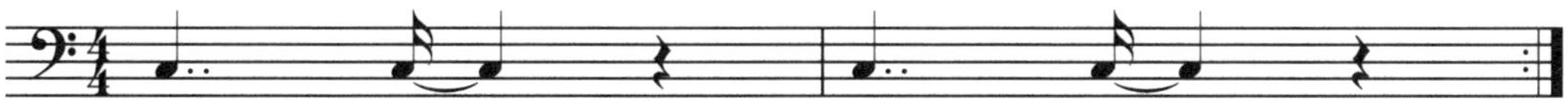

92

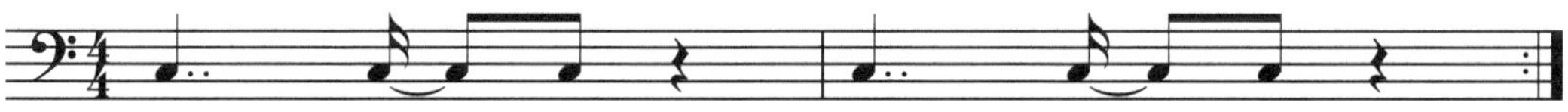

93

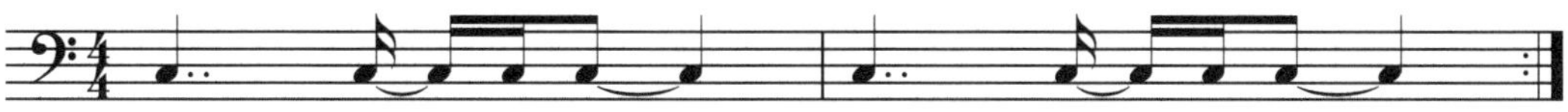

94

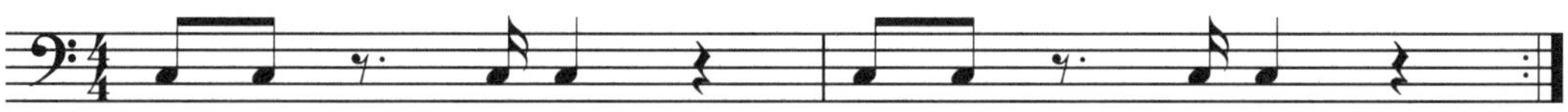

95

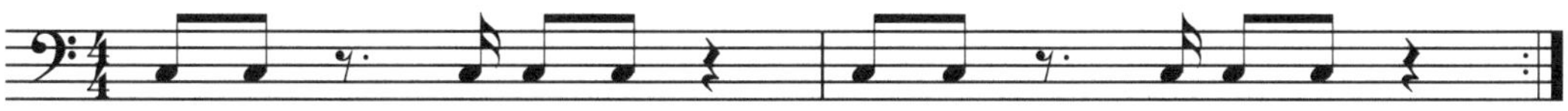

96

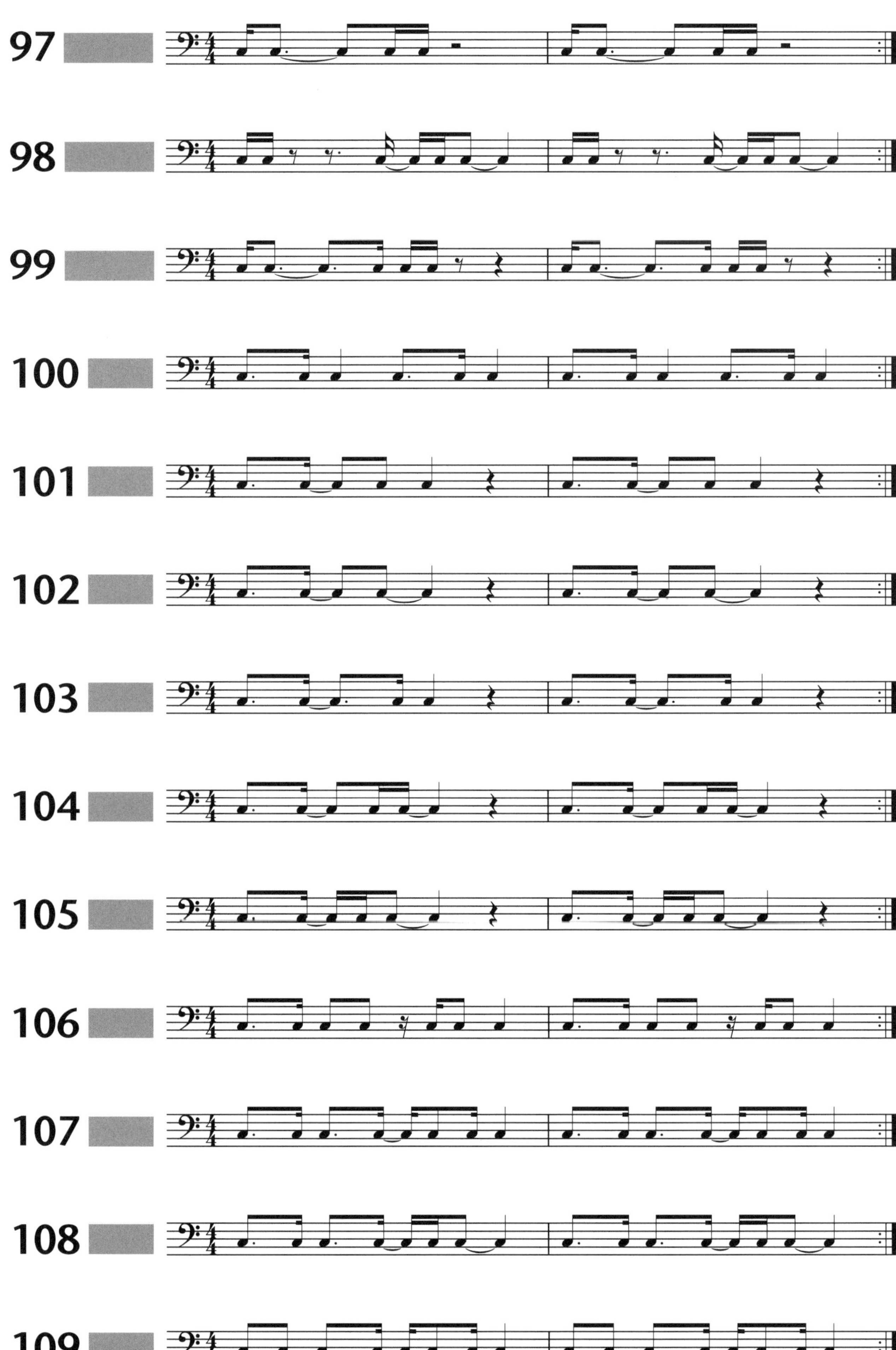
97
98
99
100
101
102
103
104
105
106
107
108
109

110

111

12/8 Shuffle Basic Grooves

112

113

114

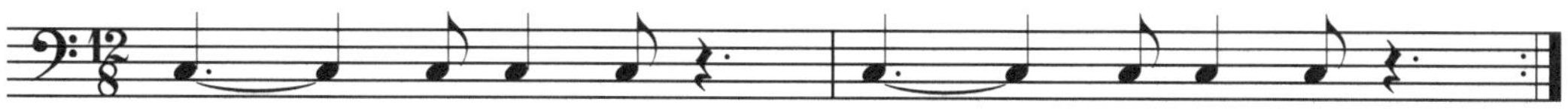

115

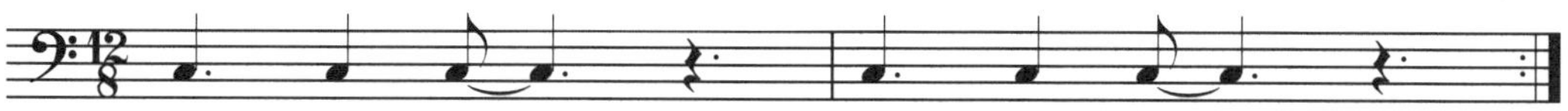

116

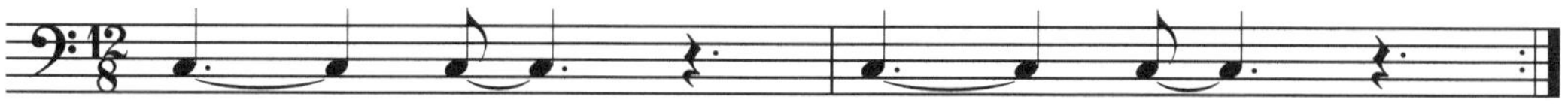

117

118

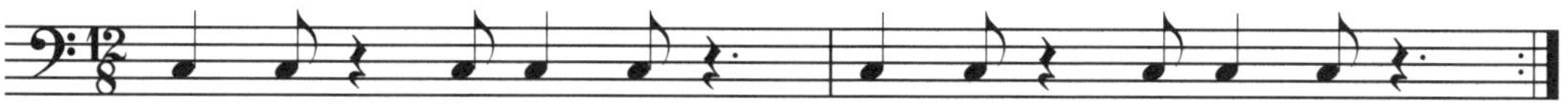

119

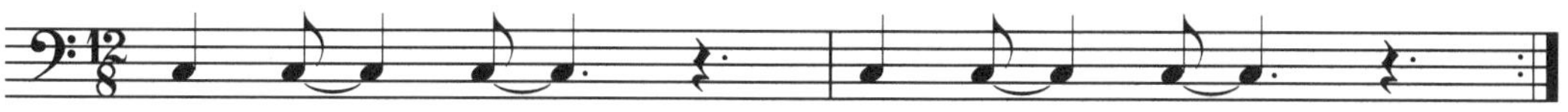

120

121

■ Blues and R & B

Blues music has quite a long history in America and began with acoustic instruments. The double bass would often play 2 or 4 in the bar with a 12/8 swing feel.

As the Blues developed, it maintained certain characteristics. Many Blues bands still use the 12 bar sequence and the 12/8 swing feel or "shuffle" to emphasize the roots their music comes from. It is a well-known rhythm which is popular, traditional and nostalgic. Even though many modern forms of music have had an enormous influence on the Blues, enthusiasts still go back to the original artists to find new inspiration.

When the electric bass was introduced, the role of the bass line changed. Although the guitar and piano were still widely used in riff playing, the bass guitar began more adventurous lines, because it was louder, clearer, easier to play, and created a solid backbone to the band. The other instruments therefore developed slightly different roles. The electric guitar was able to be far more strident, as it had loud support from the bass and drums. Pianists could be more selective in their choice of phrases, because the bass did not need as much rhythmic support.

As the basic Blues chord sequence is quite simple, it became increasingly important for the bass player to find riffs which gave the song an individual quality; something which made each song stand out on its own. Melodies were not always the Blues' strongest point. After all, it is the lyric which most strongly characterises the Blues. Also, since it is based on Folk music, very often a simple melody was regarded as most suitable for allowing the power and free expression of the singer to come through. The bass line, therefore, had to be an integral part of the song, both in its harmonically simple use of notes and in its uncomplicated rhythm. It should not attract any attention away from the singer by being too dominating, but should add enough strength and support to express some individuality.

A tradition of vocal and bass lines evolved. Certain riffs became standard. As other forms of music began to be influenced by the Blues, it too began to absorb other influences. However, basic electric bass riffs are important, and can instantly signal a mood which the musician wants the audience to experience and identify with.

A strong bass riff is often the force which pulls the whole arrangement together. Contemporary Blues artists include Jeff Healey, John Mayall, Albert Collins, Etta James, Paul Rodgers, Alexis Korner, Gary Moore and Robert Cray.
When the Blues became more commercial, audiences wanted to dance more to a straight 8 rhythm. The new Rhythm and Blues artists reached a wider audience. "Hook lines" became more important, as did melodic bass riffs. Howlin' Wolf, B.B. King, Fats Domino, Muddy Waters, Bo Diddley and Ray Charles were all innovators.

R & B was more extrovert, dynamic, driving and exciting. Image was more important, too. Bass riffs tended to remain harmonically simple in the Blues tradition, and the rhythm section would often find a blend of riffs and phrases which would "lock-in" together and drive the beat along. There are also other "shuffle" sections in the book, which give more blues-influenced riffs.
Many artists began using alternative chords, and stretched out certain sections of the 12 bar sequence to give greater variety. As songs became more sophisticated, writers disguised the 12 bar tradition even further to provide a product which became increasingly popular to a wider audience, and also commercially suitable for records, radio, TV and live clubs.

Common 12 bar Blues sequences:

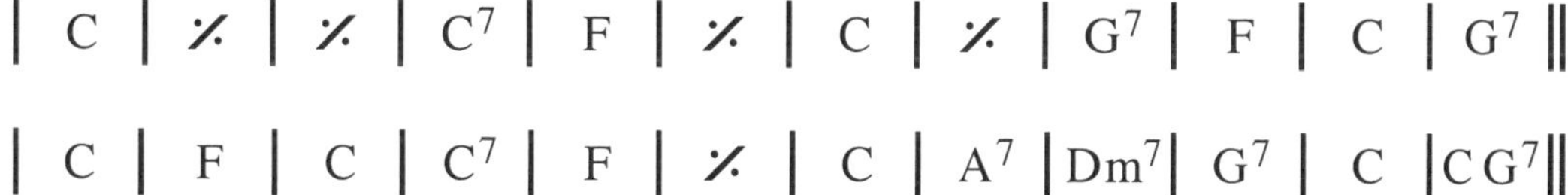

12/8 Blues and R & B (Shuffle Feel)

VERLAG

127
fast
C7

128
CD 1 Track 2
slow
C7

129
fast
C

130
CD 1 Track 3
fast
C F C F C F C

131
medium
C

132
CD 1 Track 3
slow
C7

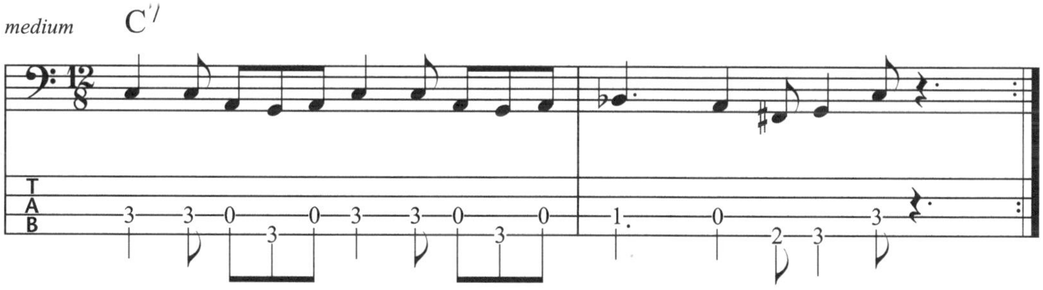

medium
C7
T
A
B

133

CD 1 Track 4

open key
fast
G7
T
A
B

134

open key
medium
G
T
A
B

135

CD 1 Track 4

4/4 Blues and R & B

medium
Gm7
T
A
B

136

CD 1 Track 5

slow
Cm
T
A
B

137

CD 1 Track 5

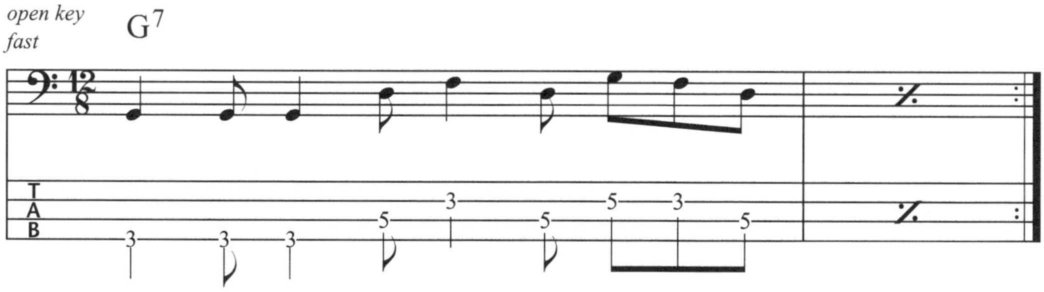

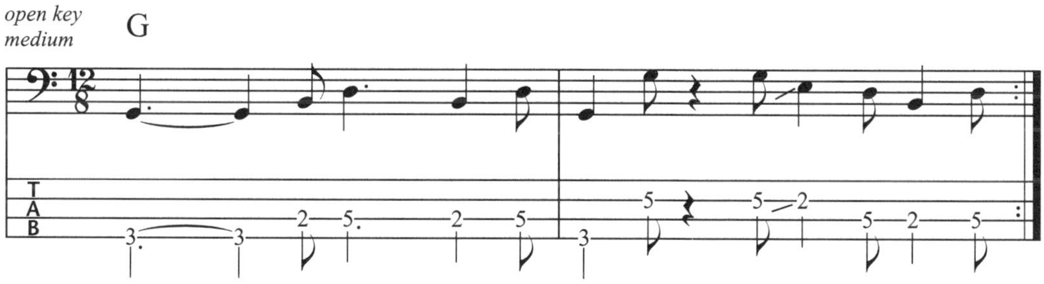

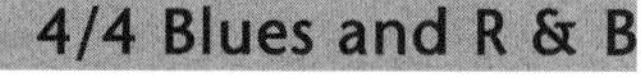

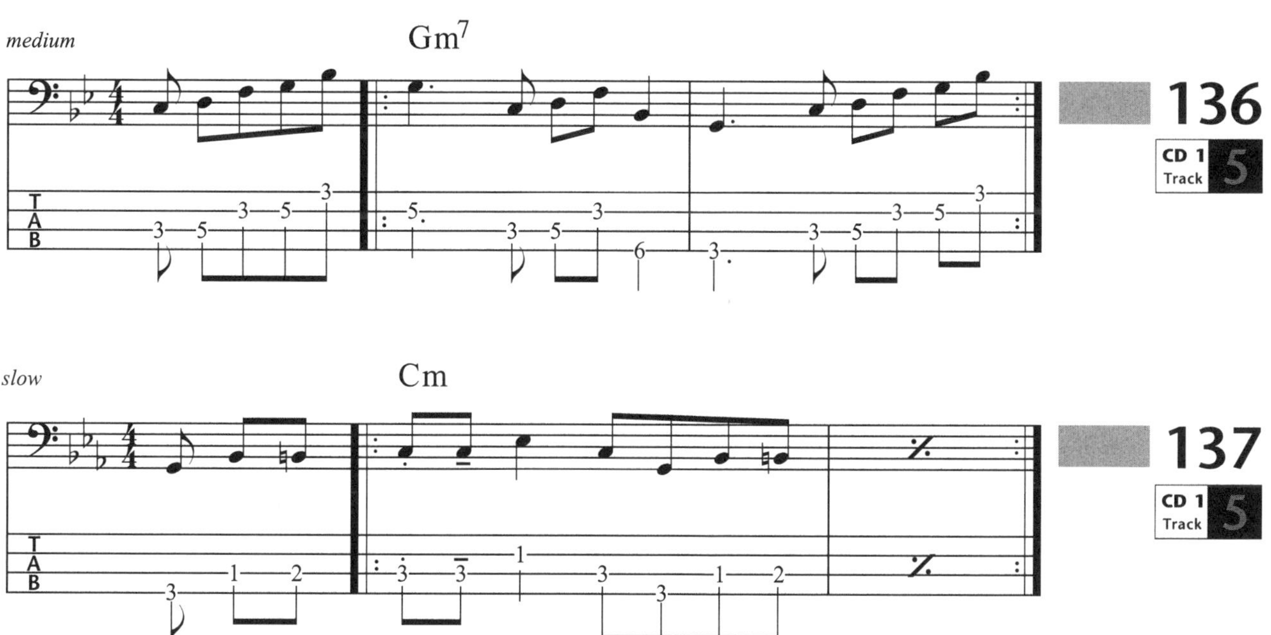

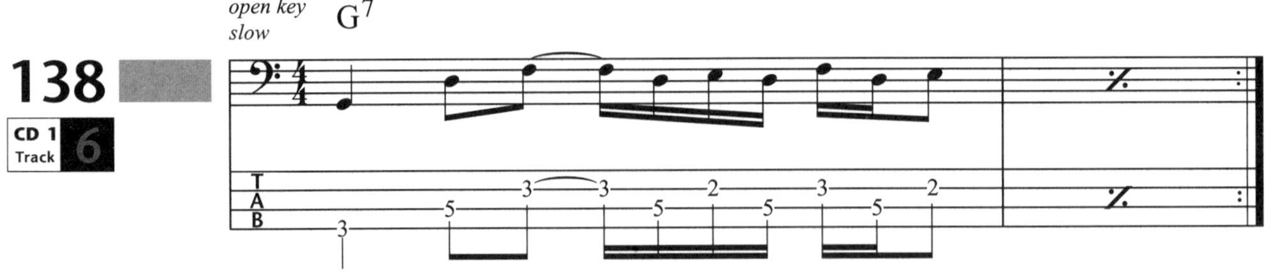
138
CD 1 Track 6
open key
slow
G7

139
slow
Cm

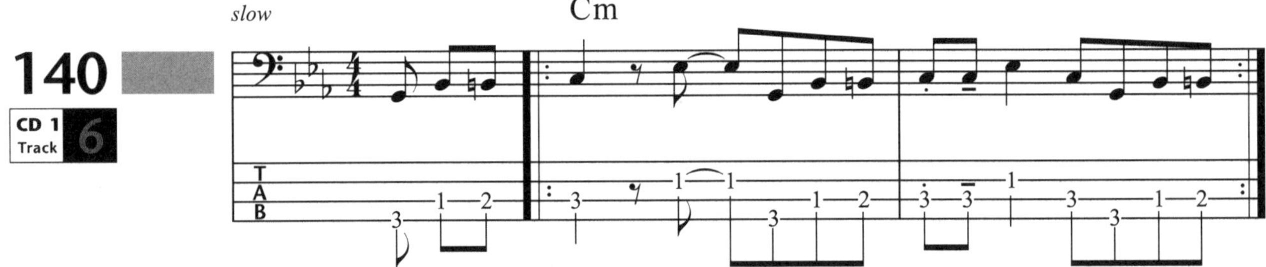
140
CD 1 Track 6
slow
Cm

141
slow
Gm

142
open key
fast
G7

143
medium
C7

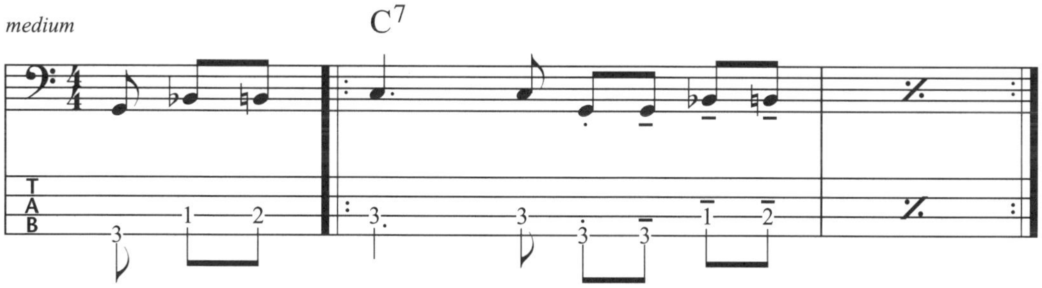

medium
C7
144

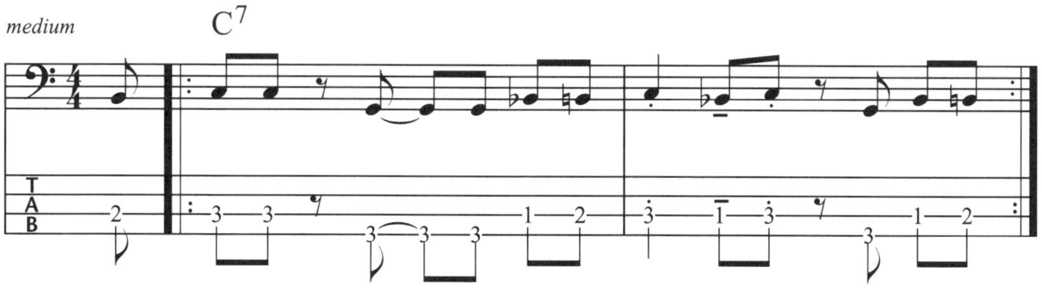

medium
C7
145
CD 1 Track 7

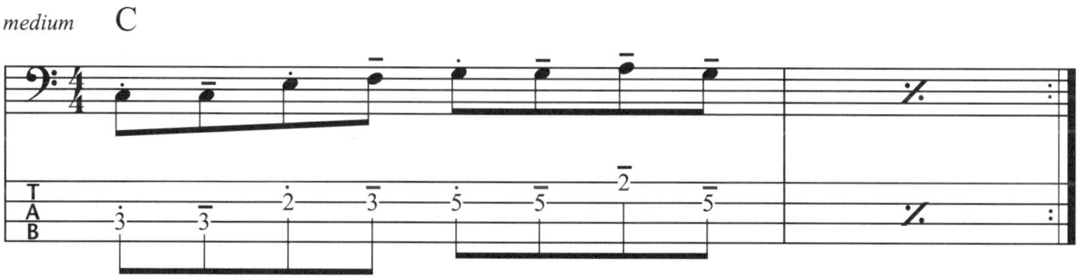

medium
C
146

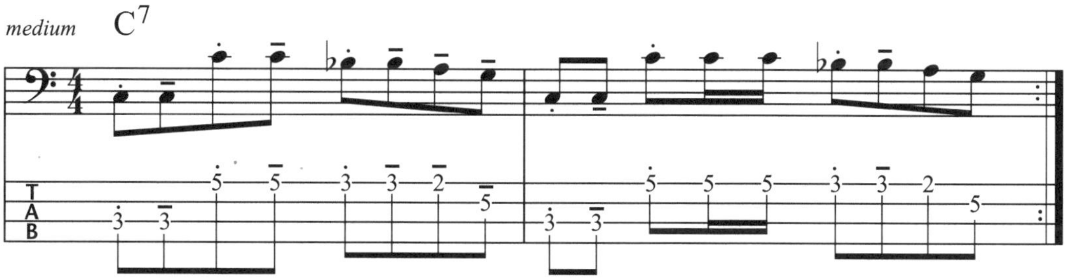

medium
C7
147
CD 1 Track 7

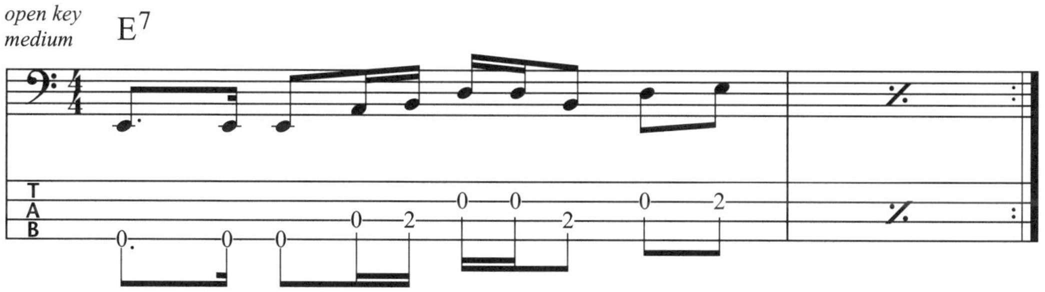

open key
medium
E7
148
CD 1 Track 8

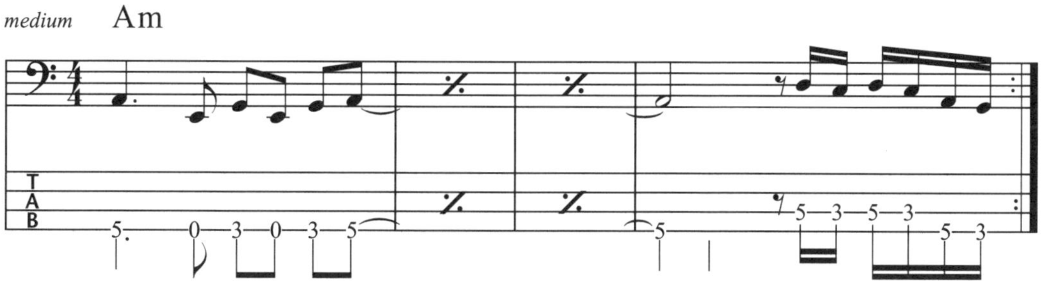

medium
Am
149

medium
Am

150
CD 1 Track 8
T
A
B

medium
Am
151
T
A
B

medium
Am
152
T
A
B

medium
Am
153
T
A
B

Soul

Soul music developed to a large extent from Gospel music. Singers took the harmonic structure of religious black music and changed the lyric to reach a wider commercial audience.

In addition to some basic grooves, Soul bass lines became harmonically more interesting and rhythmically more sophisticated with the influence of African rhythms. Soul is dance music, and the bass had to adapt to different roles. Many James Brown songs have bass lines which follow the staccato quality of the vocal and brass phrases. Otis Redding liked to vary the vocal rhythm of a song, so the bass lines tended to be simpler and steadier. Marvin Gaye sang very melodically, and the bass lines became flowing and more melodic.

Stax Records had in-house rhythm sections which set up solid, simple, but driving backing tracks, and this suited their many different singers. The overall variety of soul styles became large. The most important ingredients were a good "hook-line", a solid beat, and an interesting bass line which made people want to dance.

Bass lines became even more melodic as Jazz influences crept in. James Jamerson, Chuck Rainey and Carol Kaye all stamped their influence on Soul music. As Jazz and Blues artists started to cross over, the boundaries between Jazz, Blues, R & B, Gospel and Soul became more blurred when each form of music influenced the other.

Rock music today has been influenced by just about every type of popular music. Soul bass lines, however, have done a great deal to make Rock music more interesting. Other bass players who made a big contribution include Willie Weeks, Bootsie Collins, Jerry Jemmott, Wilton Felder, Bernard Edwards, Gordon Edwards and Donald "Duck" Dunn.

Soul

All examples are medium tempo unless other wise stated.

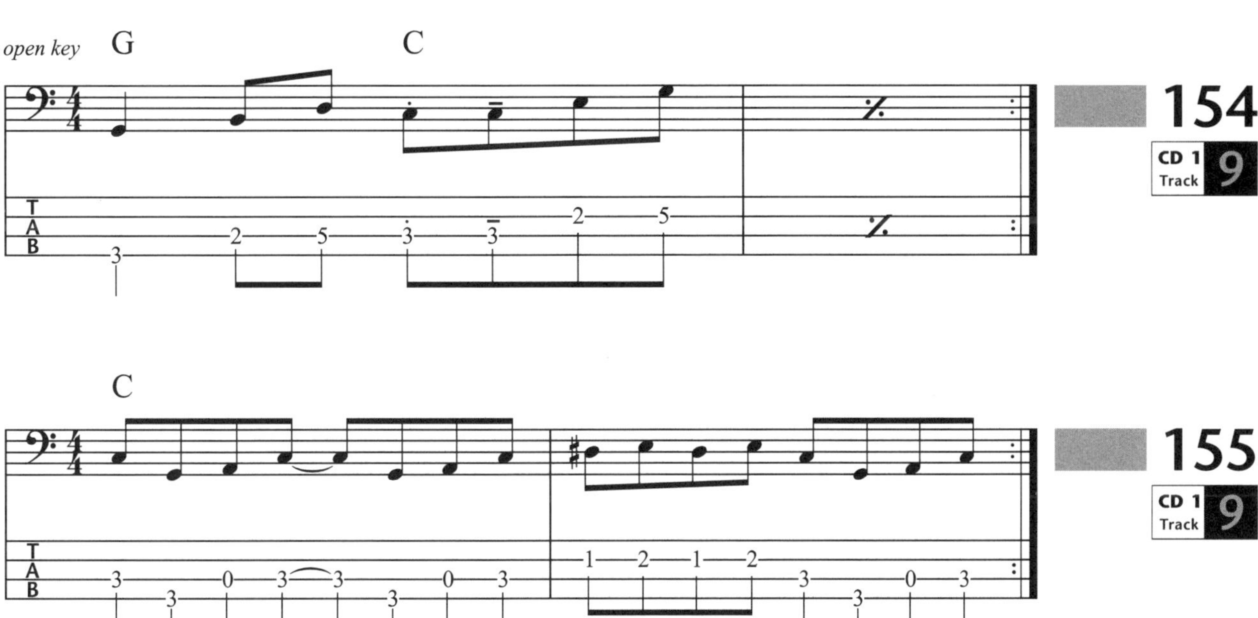

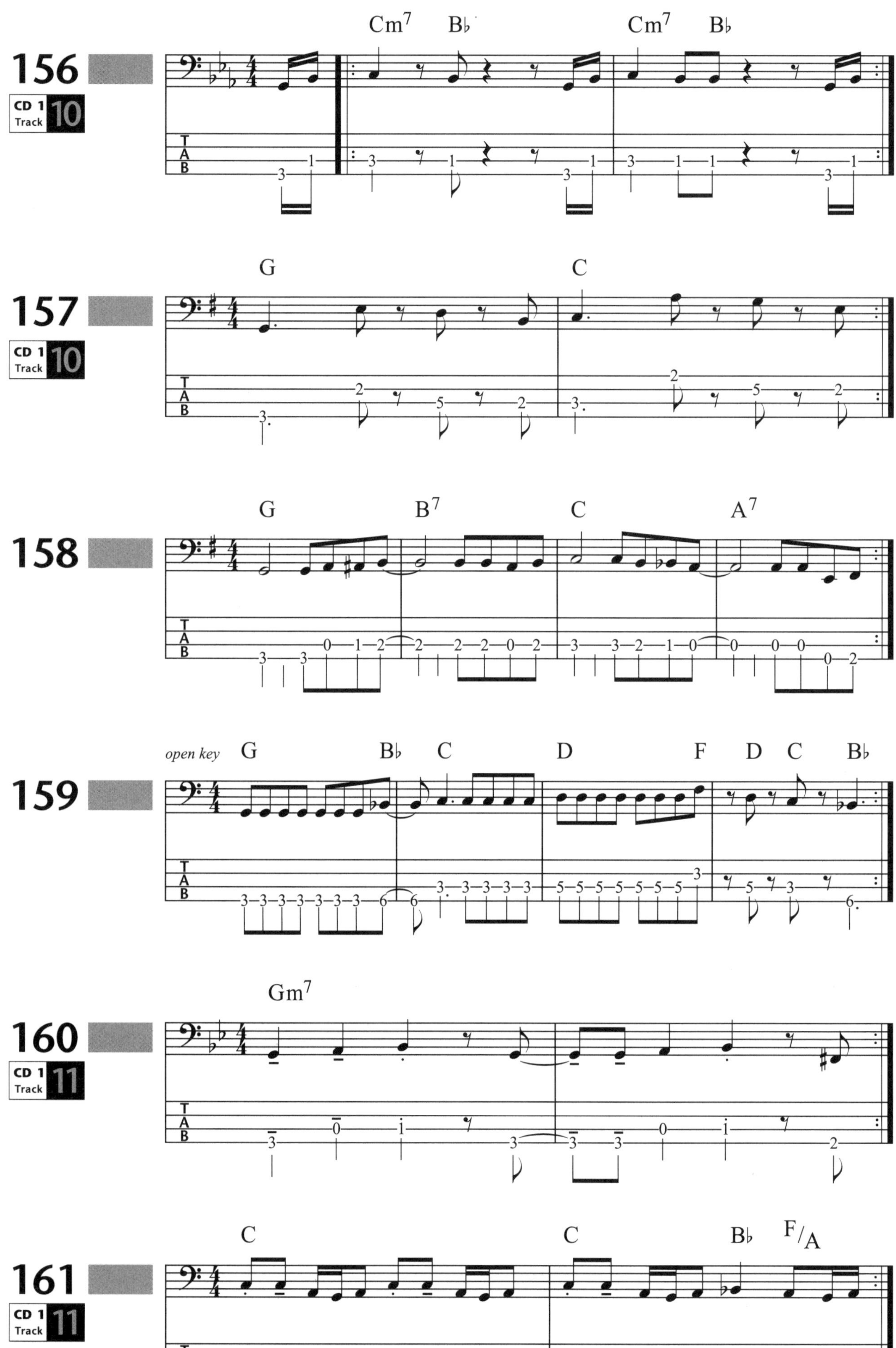
156
CD 1 Track 10
Cm7 B♭ Cm7 B♭
157
CD 1 Track 10
G C
158
G B7 C A7
159
open key G B♭ C D F D C B♭
160
CD 1 Track 11
Gm7
161
CD 1 Track 11
C C B♭ F/A

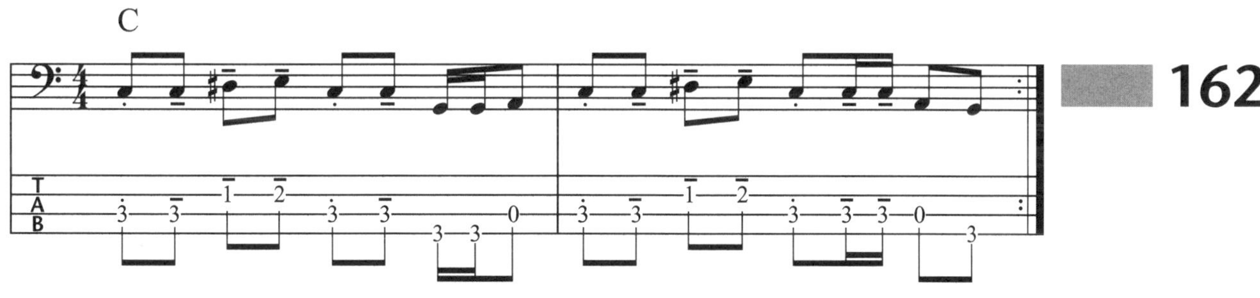
C
162

open key
G
F
C
163

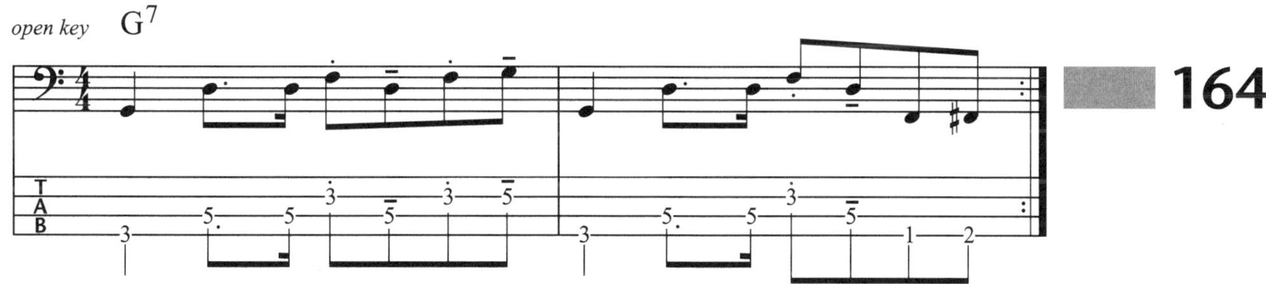
open key
G7
164

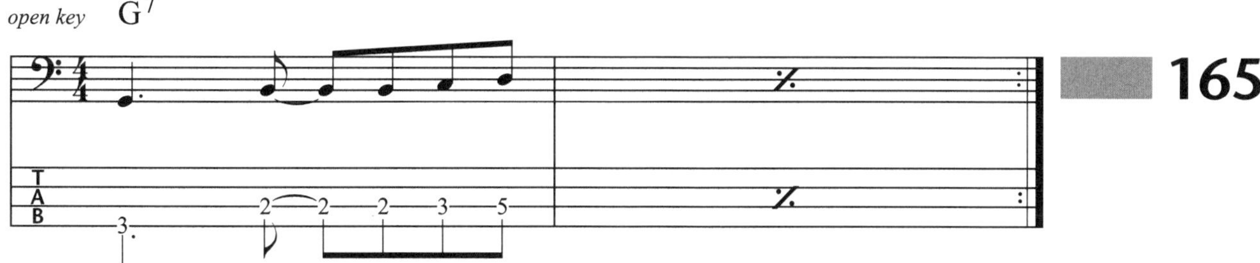
open key
G7
165

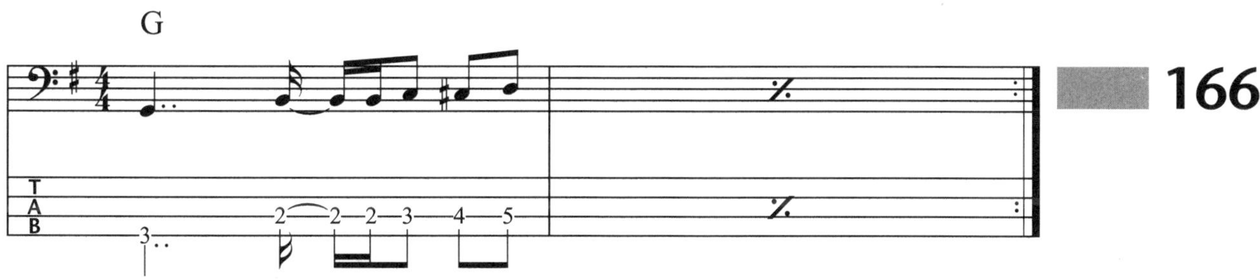
G
166

open key
Gm7
167

168 CD 1 Track 12

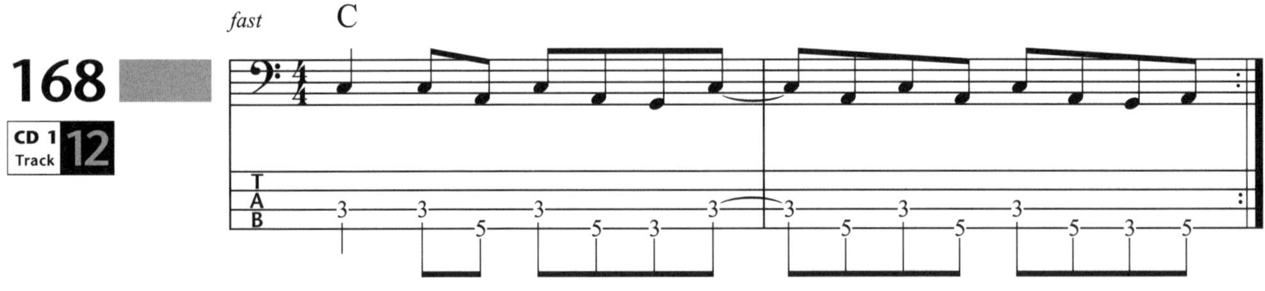

169

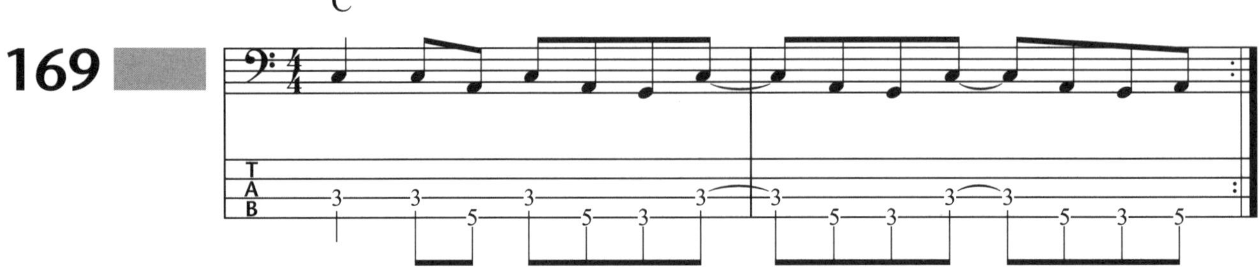

170

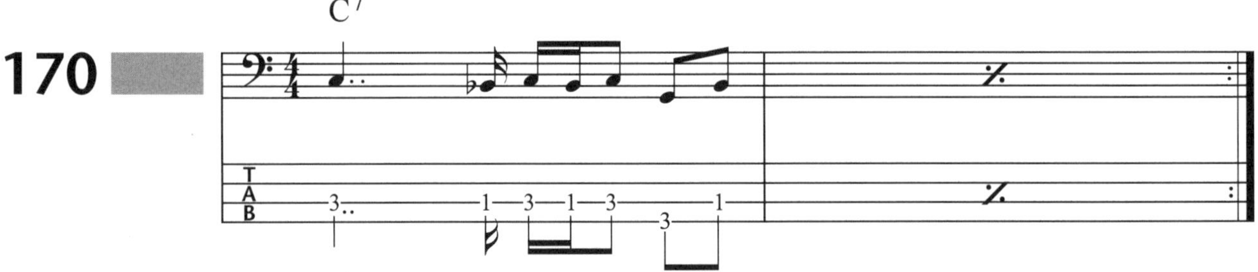

171

172

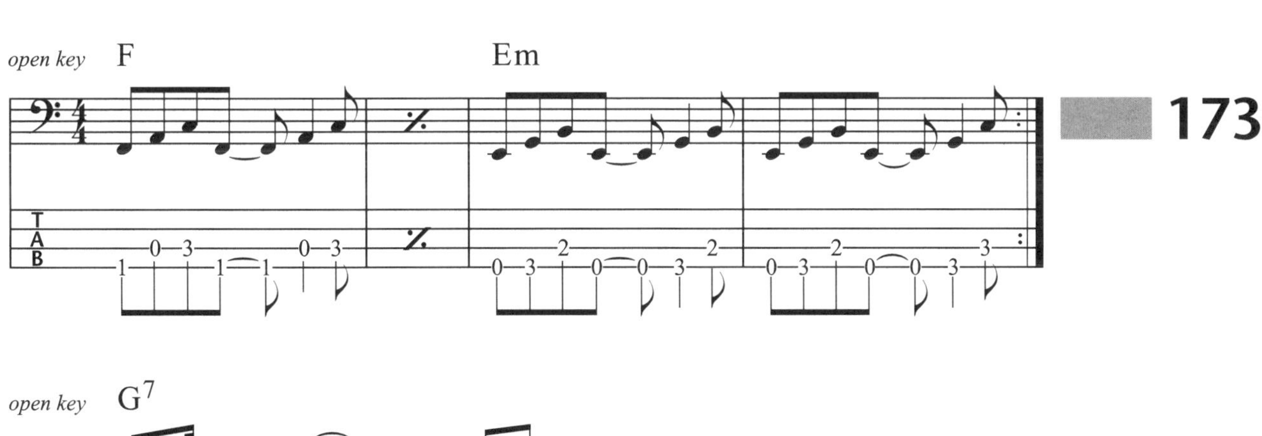
open key
F
Em
173

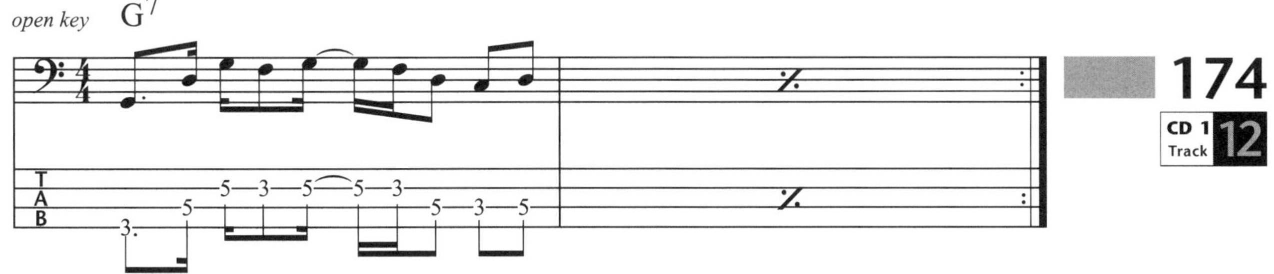
open key
G7
174
CD 1 Track 12

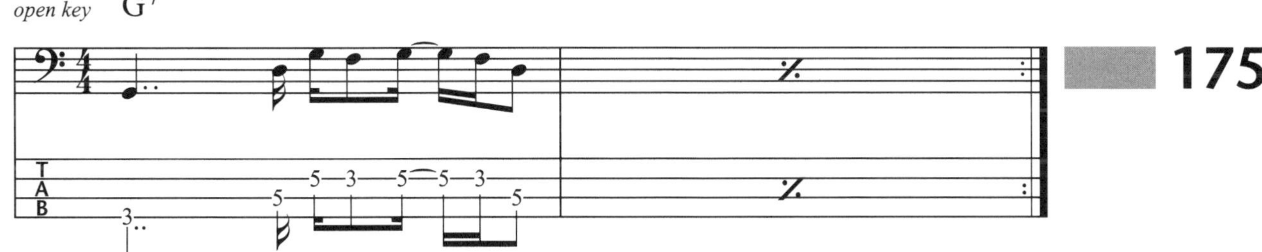
open key
G7
175

C
C/E
F
F/G
176

open key
Cm9
177

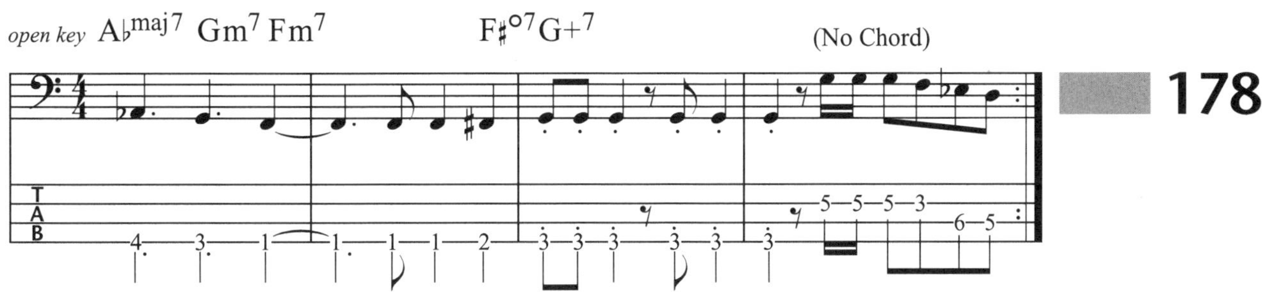
open key
A♭maj7 Gm7 Fm7
F♯°7 G+7
(No Chord)
178

179
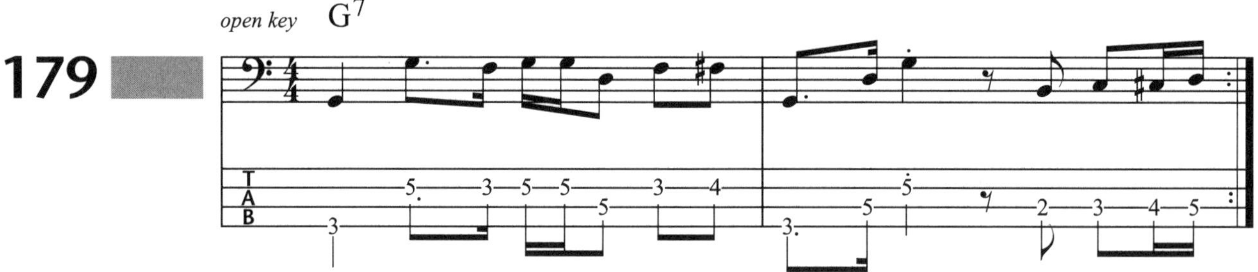
open key
G7
T
A
B
3
5
3
5
5
5
3
4
3
5
5
2
3
4
5

180

open key
G7
T
A
B
3
5
3
5
3
5
3
4
5

181
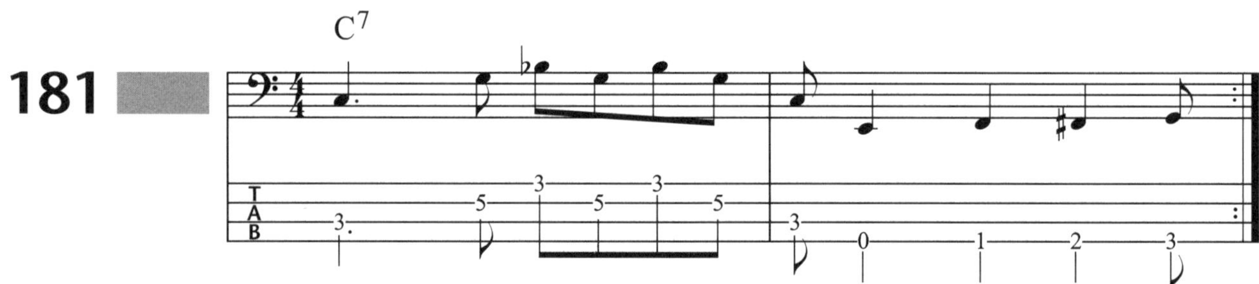
C7
T
A
B
3
5
3
5
3
5
3
0
1
2
3

JAMES JAMERSON and Motown

(Supremes, Four Tops, Temptations, Marvin Gaye)

One of Motown's most famous bass players was James Jamerson. He came from Detroit where his original instrument was the double bass. Consequently, when he began on the bass guitar, he tended to play it rather like a double bass. Notes tended to be legato (long), firmly played, rhythmic and often improvised in the Jazz tradition. In fact, many of his ideas were based on polyrhythmic walking bass lines. He mainly played at the bottom end of the instrument, letting as much of the string vibrate as possible. He often used open strings. His right hand played the strings mostly with the first finger, and only used the second when absolutely necessary. This enabled him to play very evenly, deliberately and cleanly so that his bass lines would "swing". He used a deep tone, rather like a double bass, so that his sound would project from beneath the band and not compete with frequencies occupied by other instruments. He used heavier rather than lighter strings for a fuller sound on his Fender Precision bass.

His approach was to find an original line from a modified basic groove. Very rarely did you hear that same riff used again in another song. Therefore, each song had a "personality" or individual quality. He tried to make each one "swing" in its own way. He was never afraid to ad lib or expand basic ideas. If the song needed something extra, he would liven up the backing track. He used a variety of musical concepts, but at the same time never really moved much above the 5th fret. This contained approach (as opposed to using the whole fingerboard) was counterbalanced by the sophisticated, rhythmic patterns he set up. He always related his lines to the overall feel of a song, and when improvising, always kept the rhythm of the melody in mind, and used vocal pauses to set up the next phrase. He seemed to capture the mood of a lyric. He was a very sympathetic accompanist, who always supported any changes of tonality, feel and mood.

Dynamically, he tended to play at one level; maybe this was more to do with commercial aspects of the record, and the need to hear his bass lines clearly through poor quality car and jukebox speakers.

In the following examples, "unison" means "tutti". This is where the bass line is played together with other instruments. In some cases chords are not played. This is indicated by a chord symbol in brackets, e. g. (C^7).

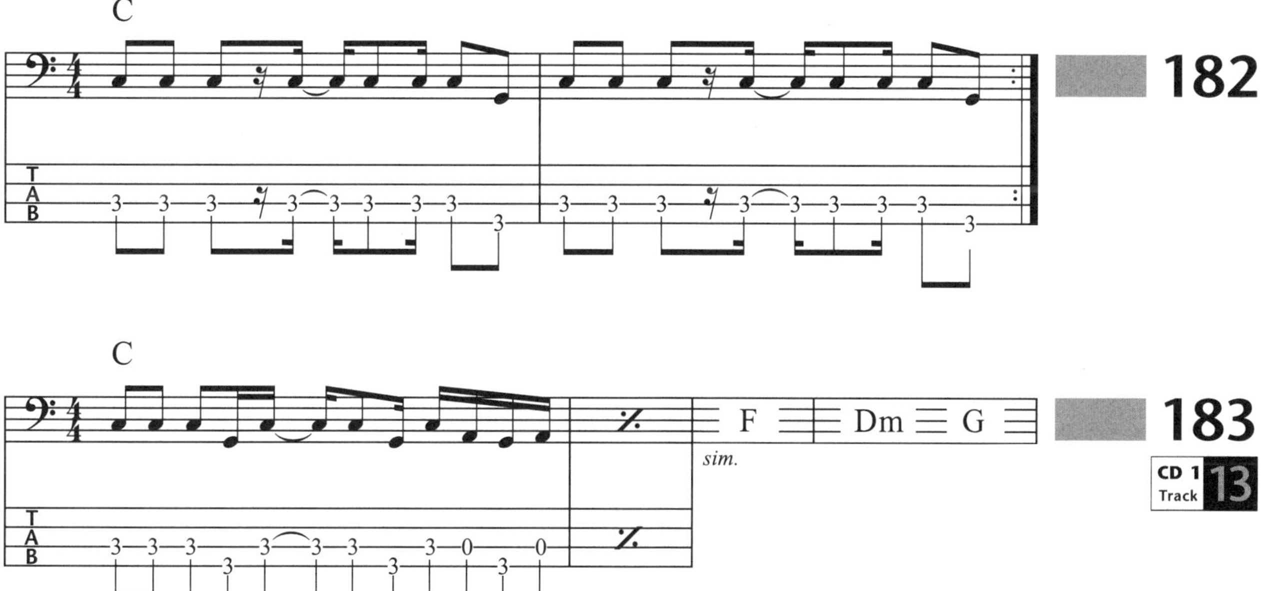

184

185

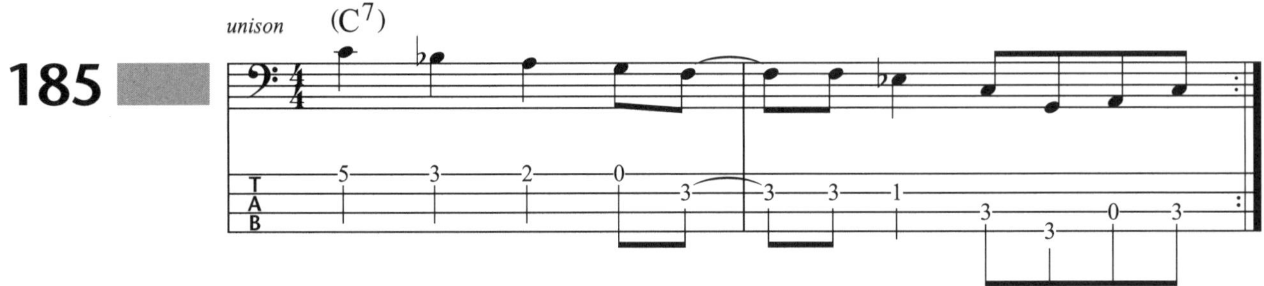

186

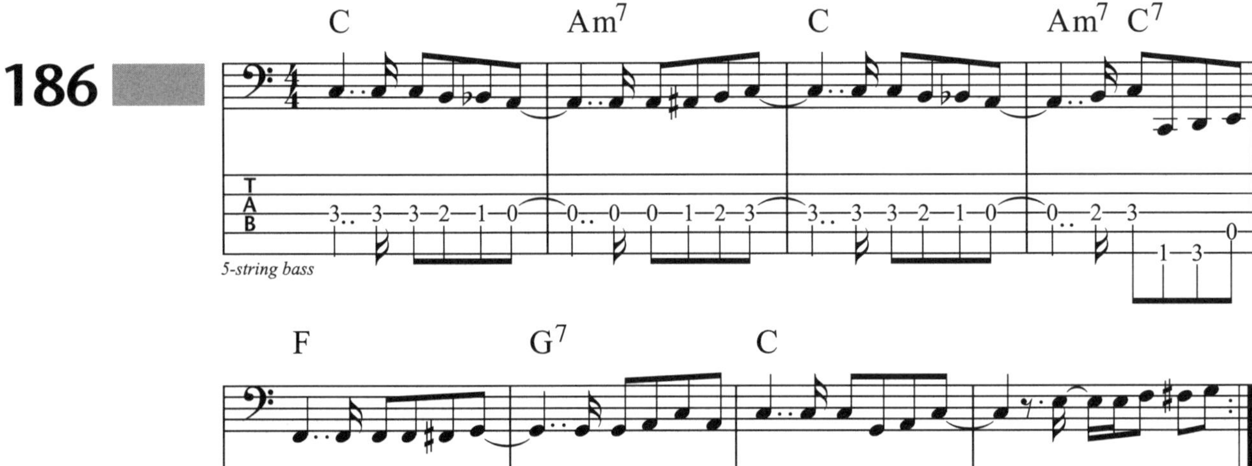

187

CD 1 Track 13

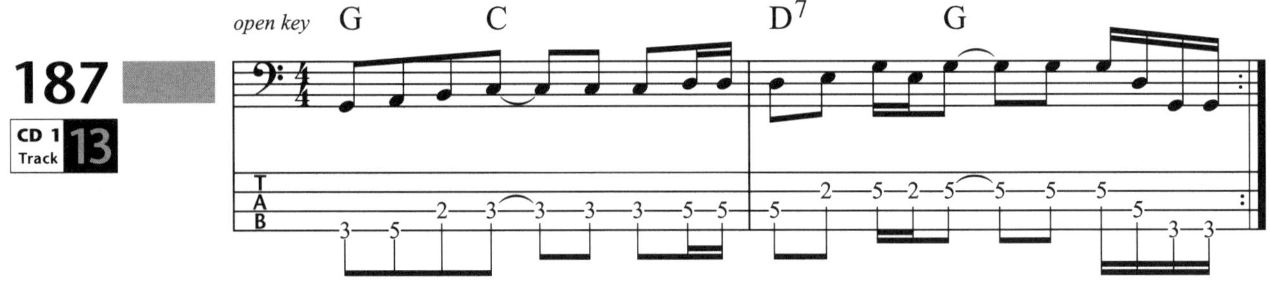

188

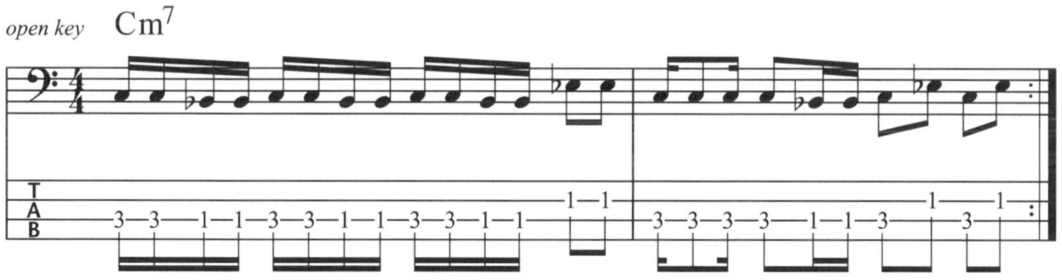

open key Cm7

189

CD 1 Track 14

open key Dm7

190

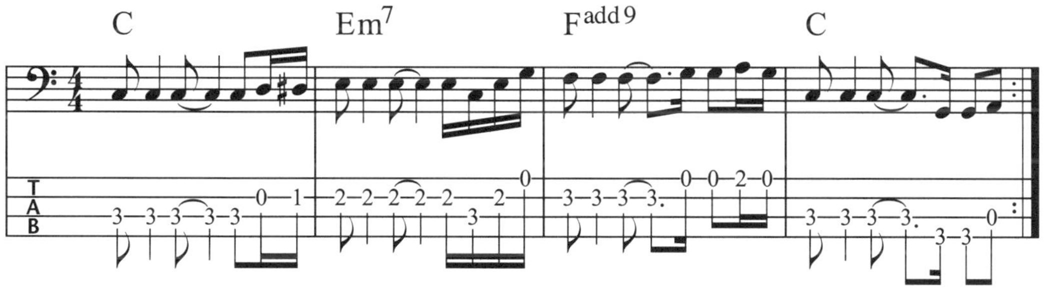

C Em7 Fadd 9 C

191

CD 1 Track 14

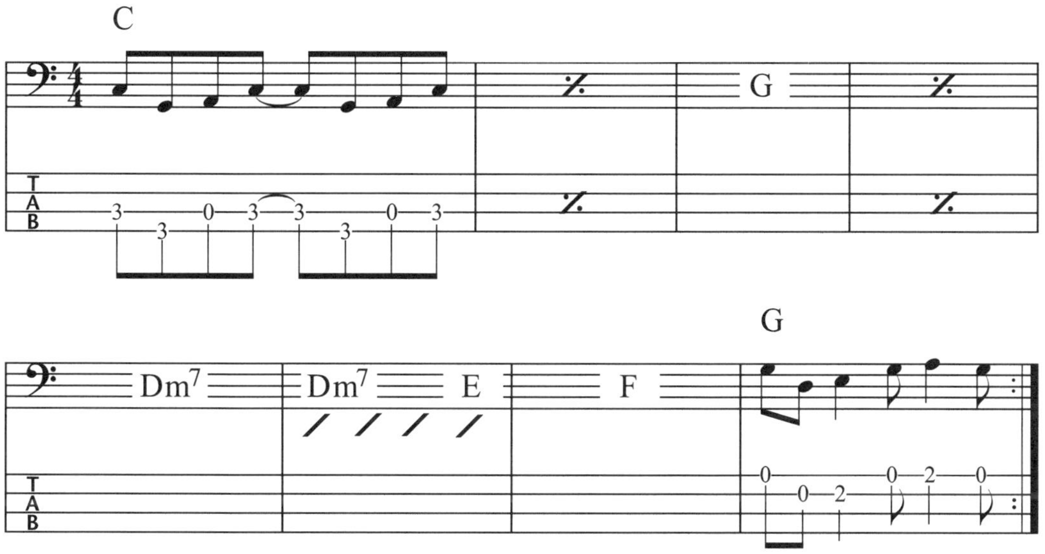

C G

192

Dm7 Dm7 E F G

open key D7 G F

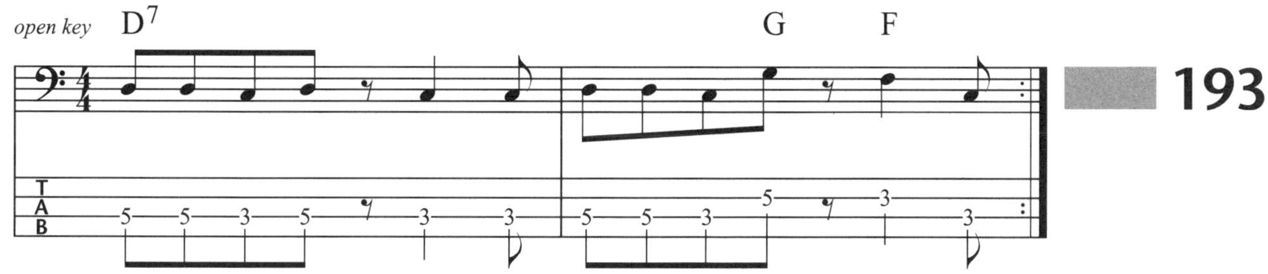

193

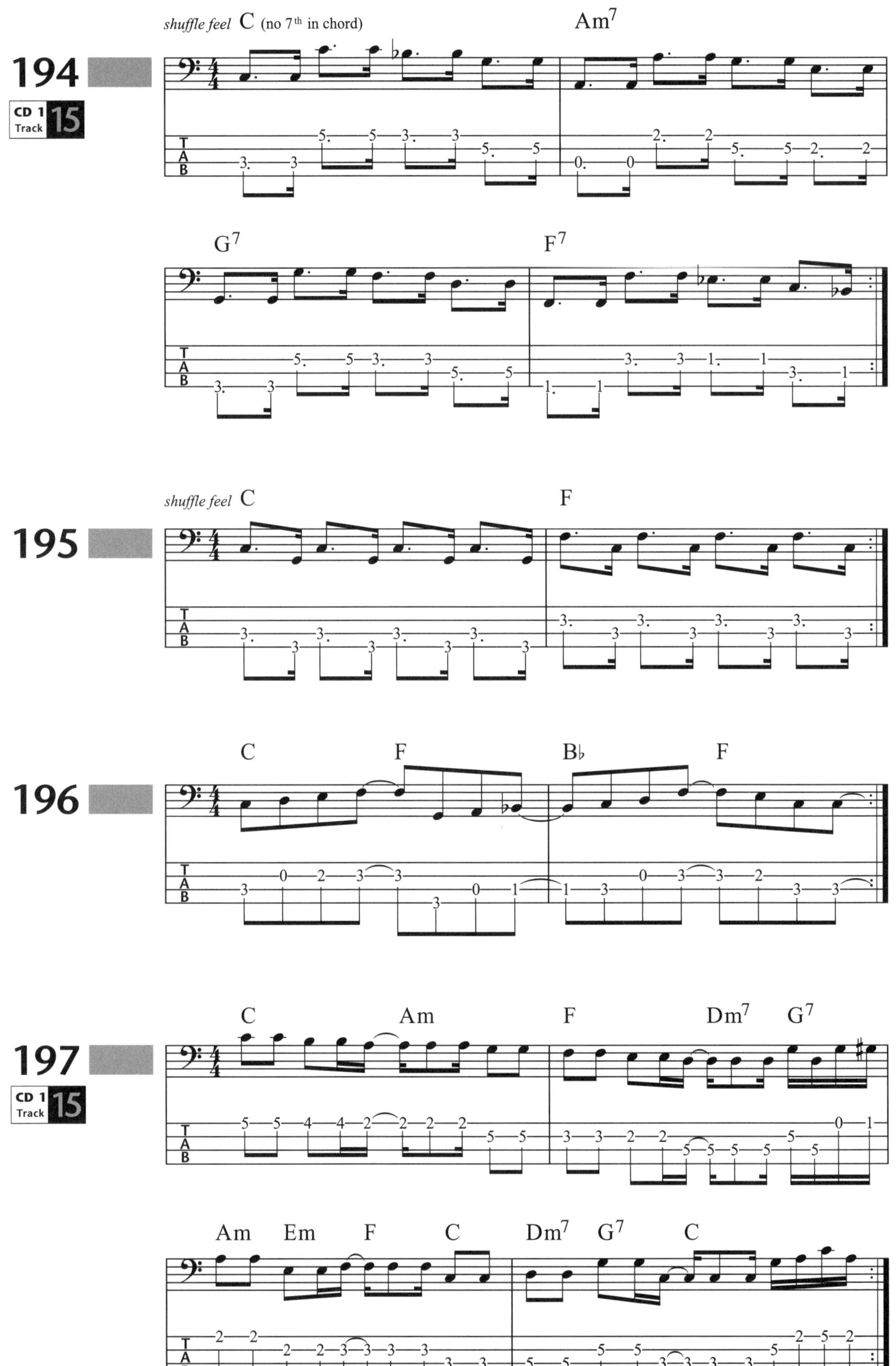
194
CD 1 Track 15
shuffle feel C (no 7th in chord)
Am7
G7
F7
195
shuffle feel C
F
196
C
F
B♭
F
197
CD 1 Track 15
C
Am
F
Dm7
G7
Am
Em
F
C
Dm7
G7
C

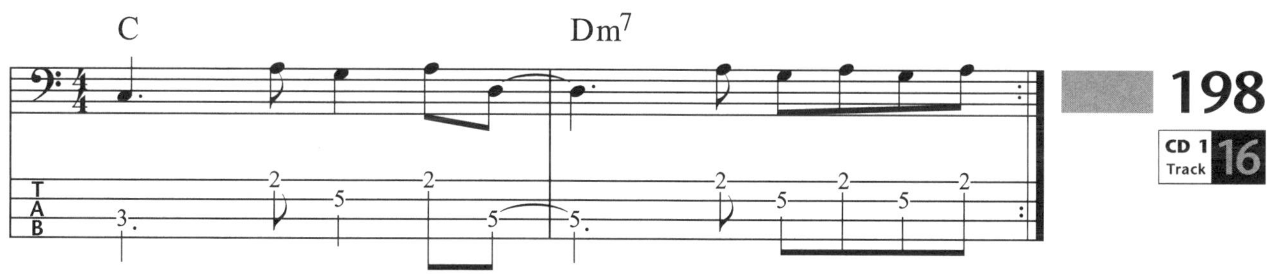
C
Dm7
198
CD 1 Track 16

C
199
B♭
C

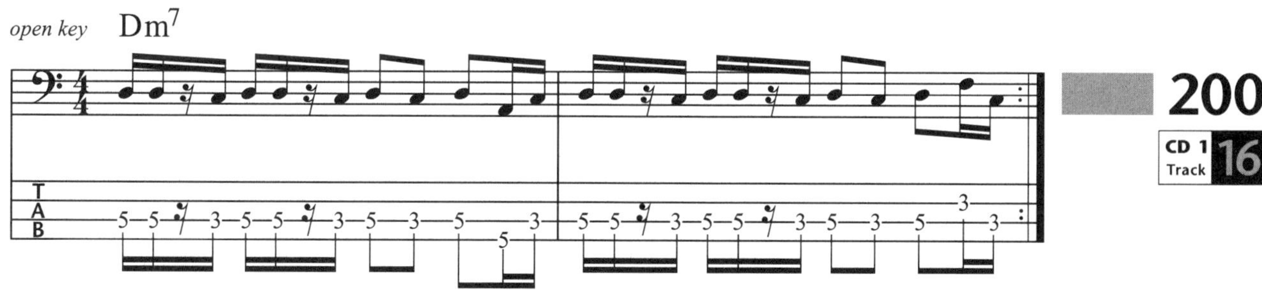
open key
Dm7
200
CD 1 Track 16

C
201
B♭

Bass Fills

202

203
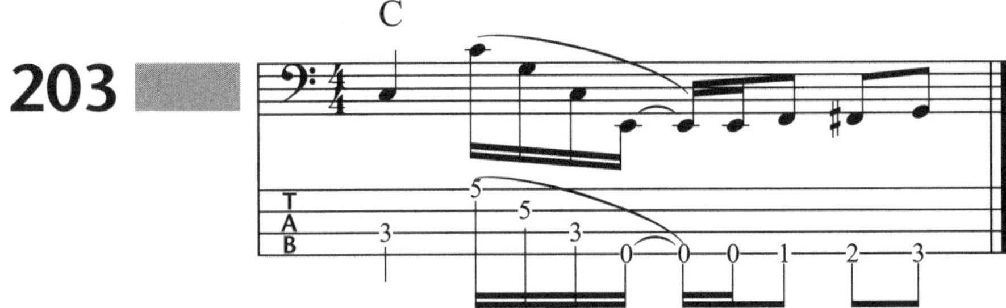

204

205

206

207

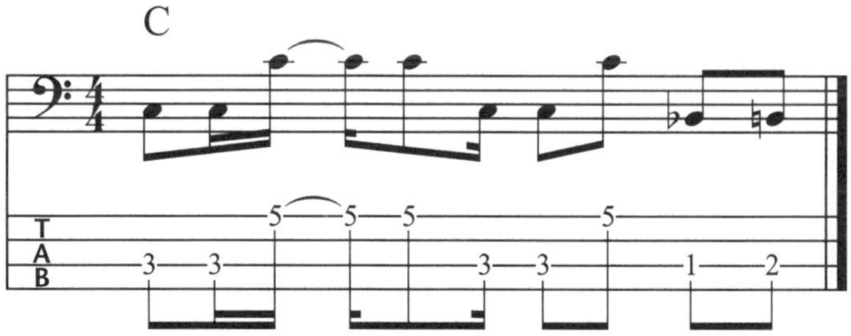

C

208

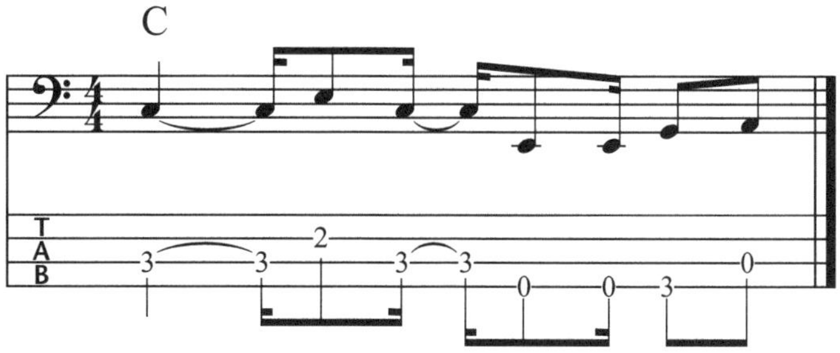

C

209

C

210

C

211

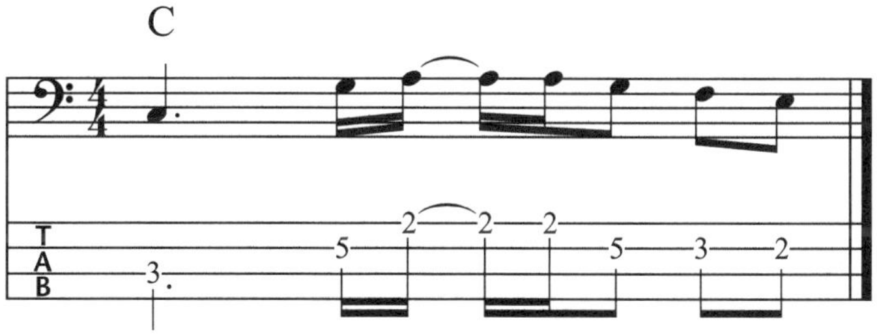

C

212

C

213

■ CHUCK RAINEY and Atlantic Records

(Aretha Franklin, Quincy Jones, Steely Dan)

Chuck Rainey really came to be noticed internationally when working in New York for Atlantic Records. He is a very sophisticated and clever musician who weaves in and out of styles, sounds and techniques. Many producers wanted him to play Motown sound-alikes or Soul riffs, and some put him in a Pop mould. He played unusual Jazz lines and subtle rhythmic patterns too. His approach to the bass guitar was to play it more like a guitar than a double bass. In some ways he let the amplification do some of the hard work, and allowed certain subtle guitar characteristics to creep in. For instance, he would play a series of roots and fifths then gliss from the bottom of the instrument to the top, ending above the 12th fret with a 7th or 3rd note harmony.

He used a deep tone on his Fender Precision, and ensured that the bass always made a firm sound which blended with the bass drum. Although his sound is full and round, it is always clear. Sometimes he used damping to shorten notes, so that a busier pattern would sound more percussive. At other times he used long notes to maximise the feeling of space created in a song.

Rhythmically he had some very interesting ideas. For instance, he would set up a simple riff and then, as the rhythm section took over the momentum, begin a sort of "bubble" bass line. He "seemed" to be playing 16 notes to the bar, but as he used a variety of damped, clipped and understated notes, the lines sounded both relaxed and exciting, without being overbearing. He liked to use short glisses, too. A slide of a tone was common, returning to the original note to complete the phrase.

He had several styles which were unusual. One was a way of playing with his right hand which involved his fingers actually striking the strings against the frets. (See the paragraph called "Right Hand Tapping", BOOK ONE.)
This gave a crisper start to the note, but as it was not plucked, the follow-through was almost a "hollow" sound. In another style he used chordal effects and harmonies, concentrating less on riffs, but more on the harmonic content of the sequence. He could also either drive the rhythm section along, or sit on the back of the beat. His accompaniment was always sympathetic to singer, song and rhythm section. He would often go for the simple and unusual, because subtlety made all the difference to the overall feel. He was never afraid to play simply, especially when someone else was featured.

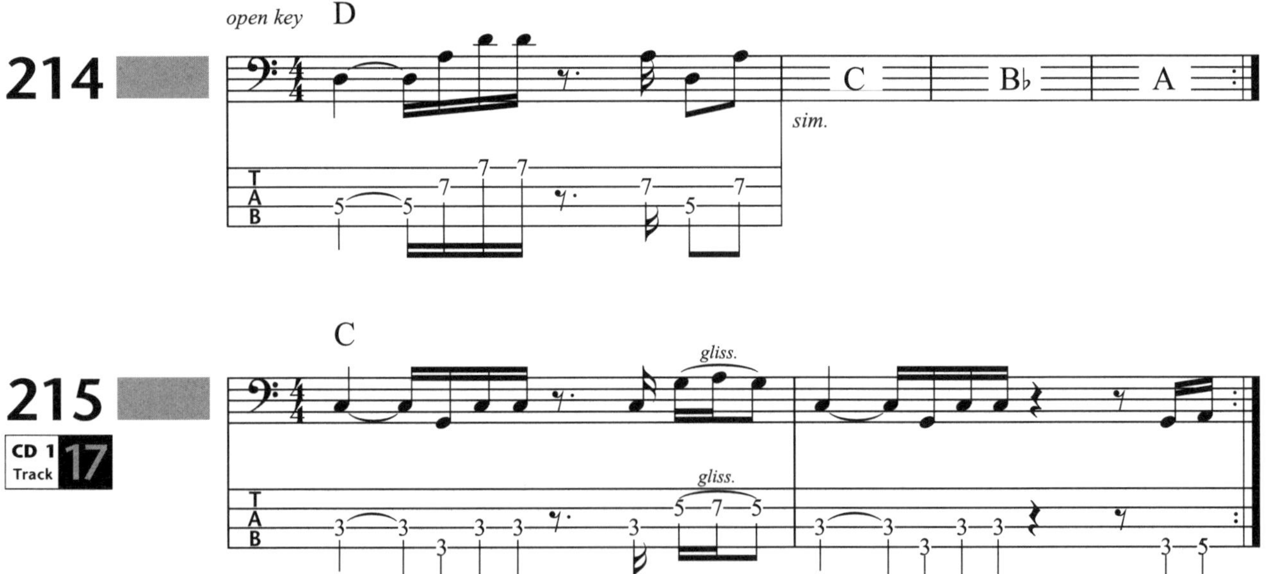

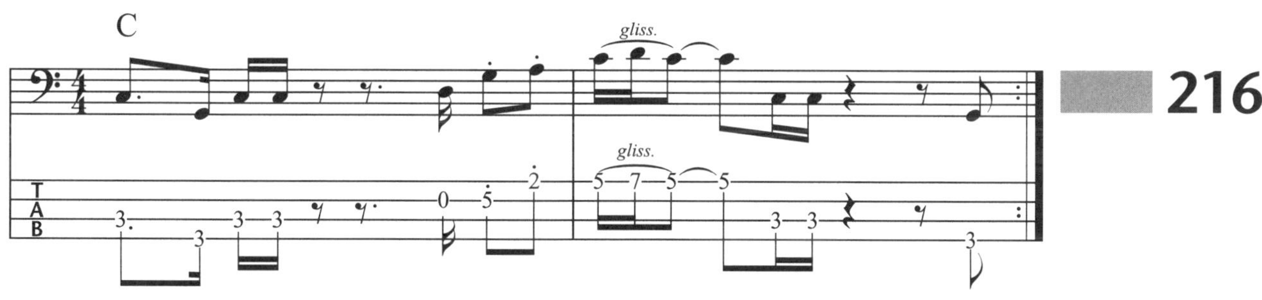

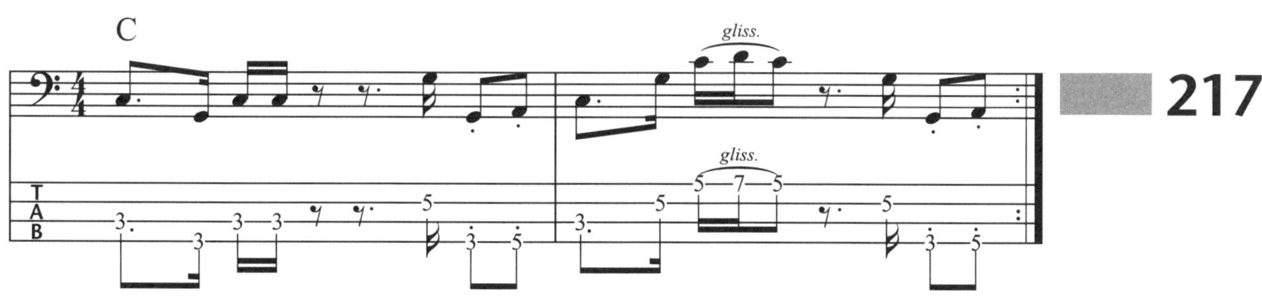

open key G7

219

CD 1 Track 17

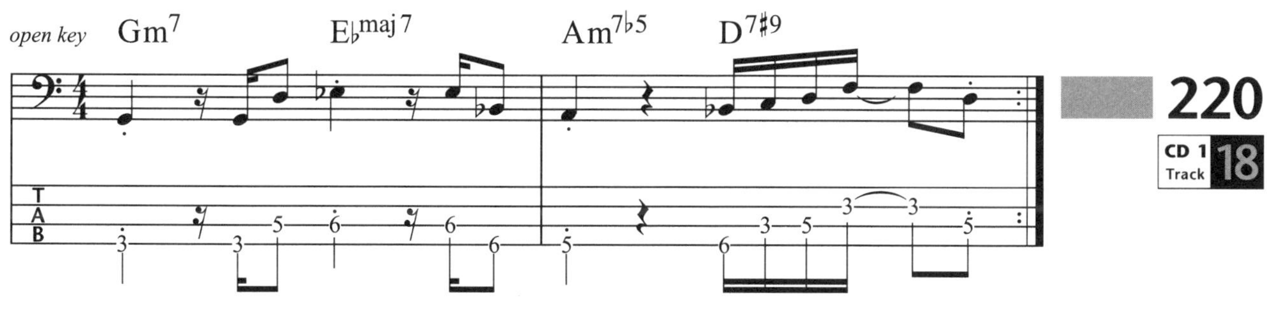

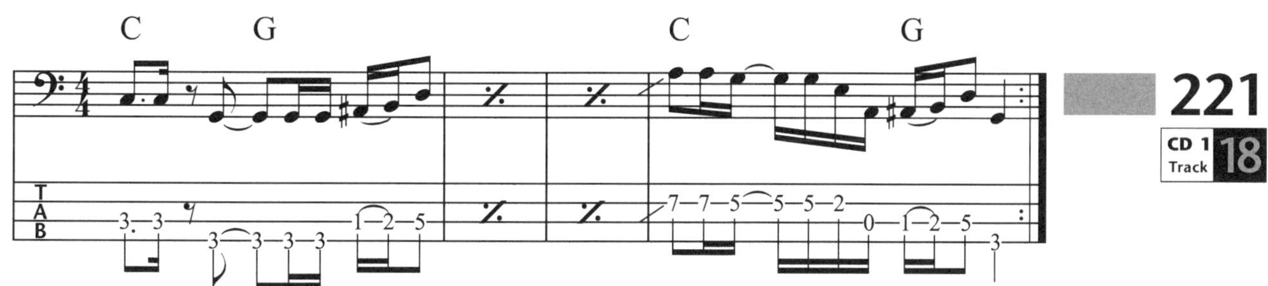

222

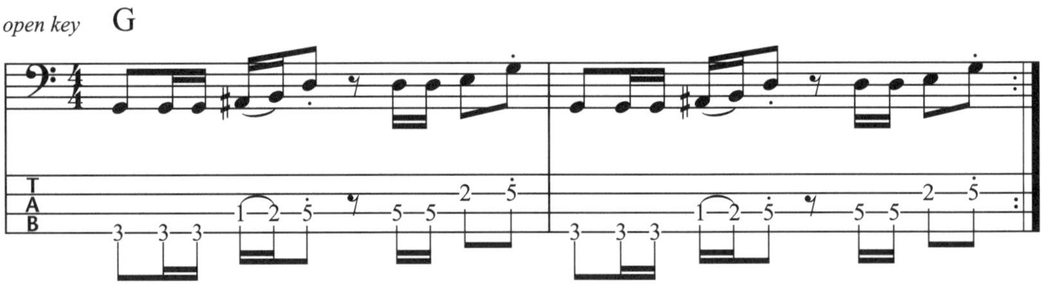

open key G

223

CD 1 Track 19

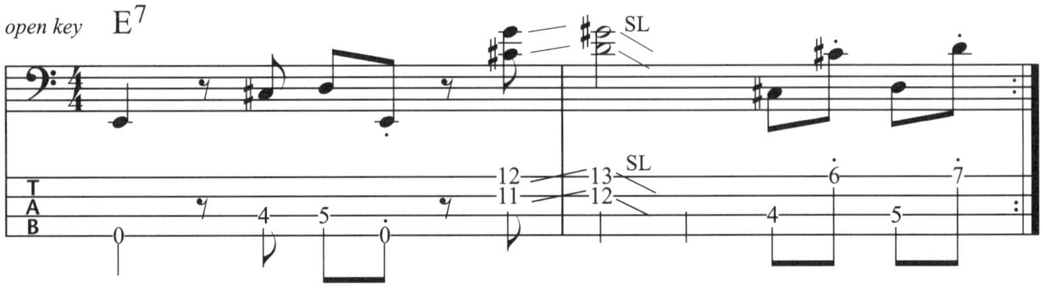

open key E7

SL

224

CD 1 Track 19

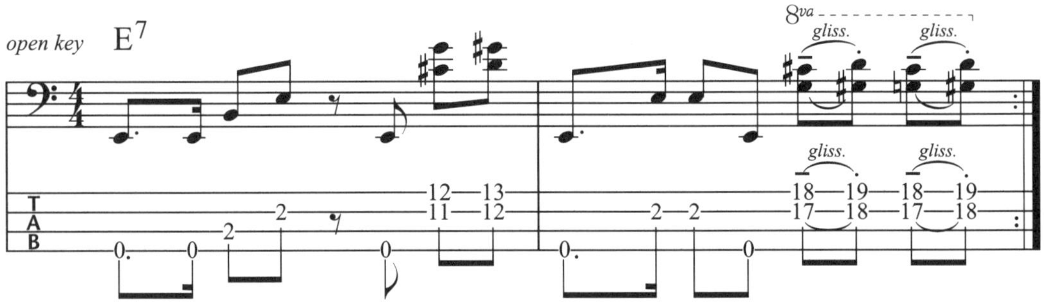

open key E7

8va gliss. gliss.

225

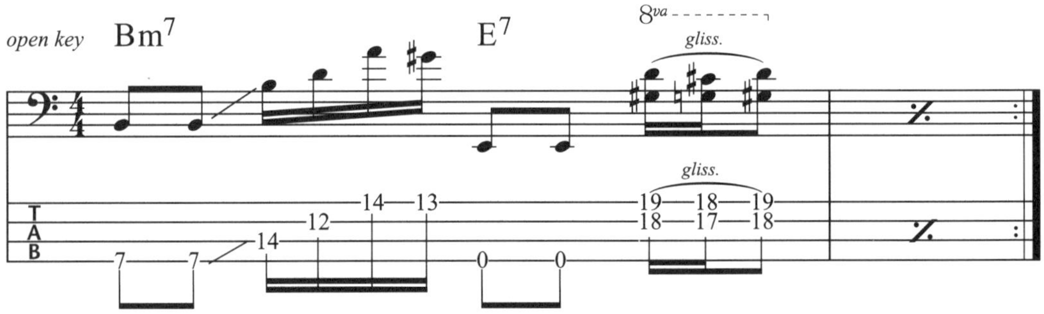

open key Bm7 E7

8va gliss.

226

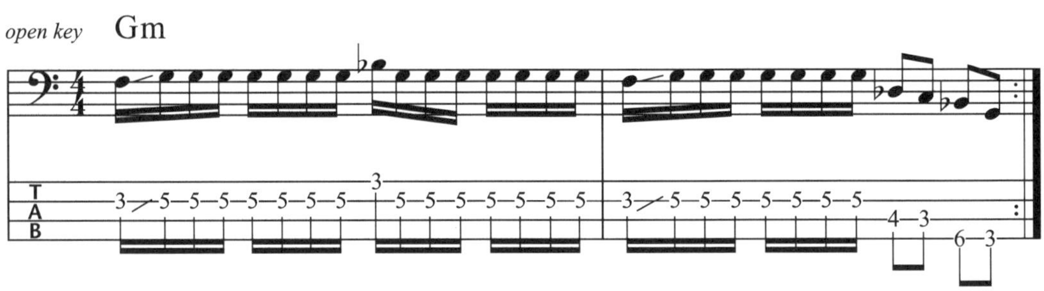

open key Gm

227

CD 1 Track 20

C

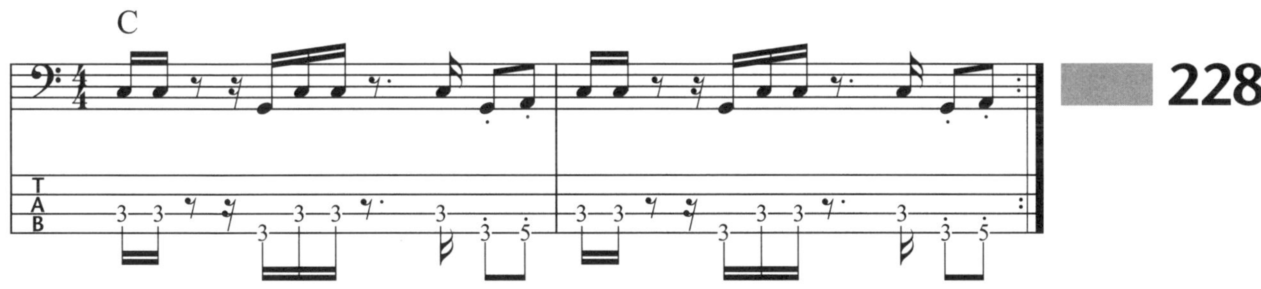

228

229

CD 1 Track 20

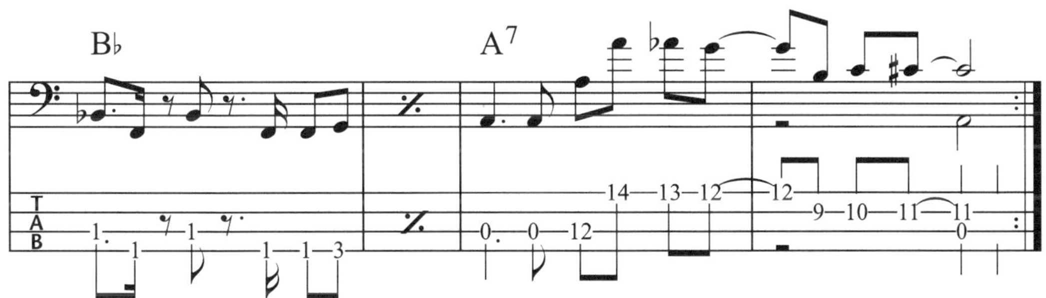

■ JAMES BROWN and Funk

His most recognisable soul style involved a basic funk rhythm and a series of chants and repeated vocal phrases. His famous "take it to the bridge" signal would often lead to the only other variation of the original feel.

He relied less on melody and more on rhythm. Therefore, the bass lines had to be basic one or two bar riffs, to provide the repetitive background for his vocal effects. Anything too complex or harmonically adventurous would have interfered with this style. As his vocal delivery was often clipped and shouted, the backing tended to be jerky and staccato. It is an African based style.

These bass riffs were designed to be exciting and to make people want to dance. The hypnotic repetition and the tight relationship between bass, drums and guitar provided a solid, driving feel. Whereas other bands played on the beat to make it relaxed, his musicians tended to push into the beat a lot more, anticipating notes and throwing accents around. This energetic style made you restless, edgy and want to move with the off-beat rhythms. His approach was aggressive, and the bass lines were played equally aggressively in repeated bursts of energy. He found his audience in the excitable black inner city communities. "I'm black and I'm proud" was the chant of the day, and aggressive repetition and rhythmic excitement got the message across. The roots of the music lay in Blues, Gospel and Jazz, but with a new dance element introduced. It was extrovert, brash and showy.

The bass player had to set up a firmly played, solid bass line on which everything relied. The riffs had to be interesting enough to stand being repeated dozens of times, yet simple enough for other members of the band to add their phrases. Bands like Tower of Power took it a stage further later on, and incorporated the staccato style into their more complex songs and arrangements.

230
CD 1 Track 21

231

232
CD 1 Track 21

233

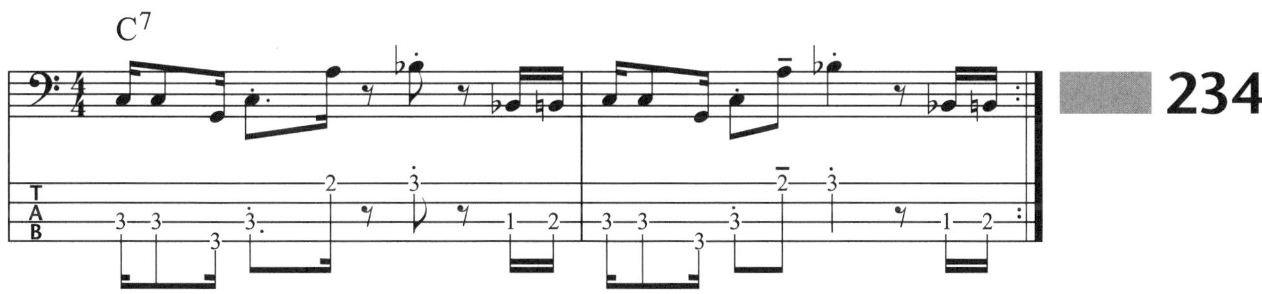

234

235

236

237

CD 1 Track 22

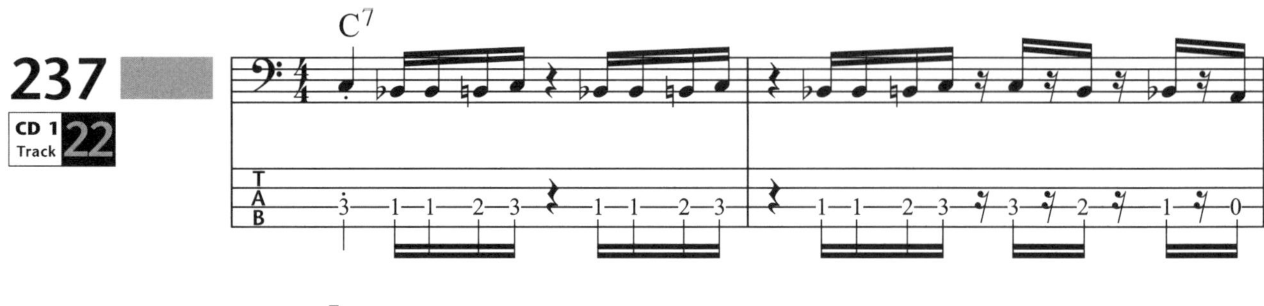

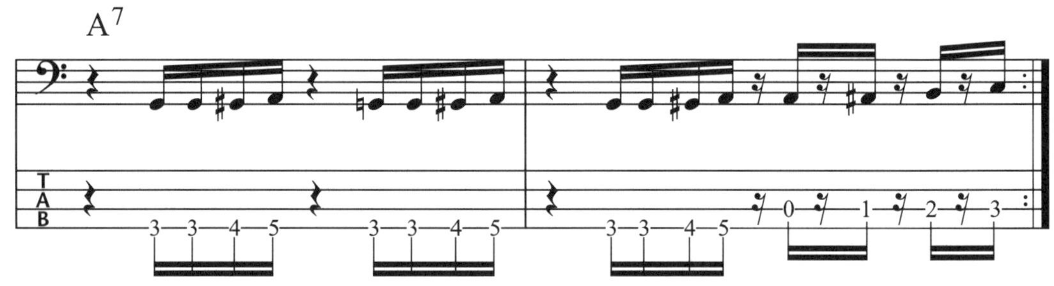

238

239

240

CD 1 Track 22

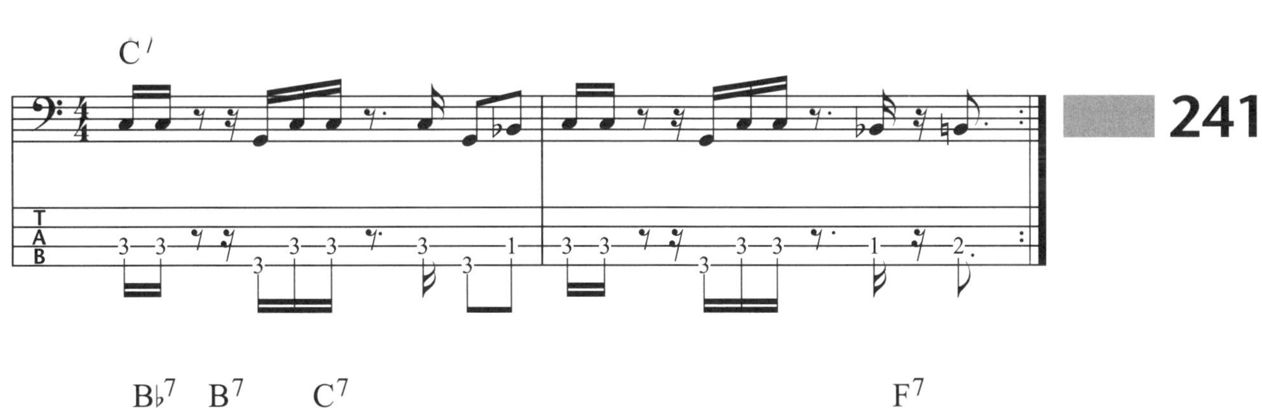
C7
241
T
A
B

B♭7
B7
C7
F7
242
T
A
B

open key
Cm7
243
T
A
B

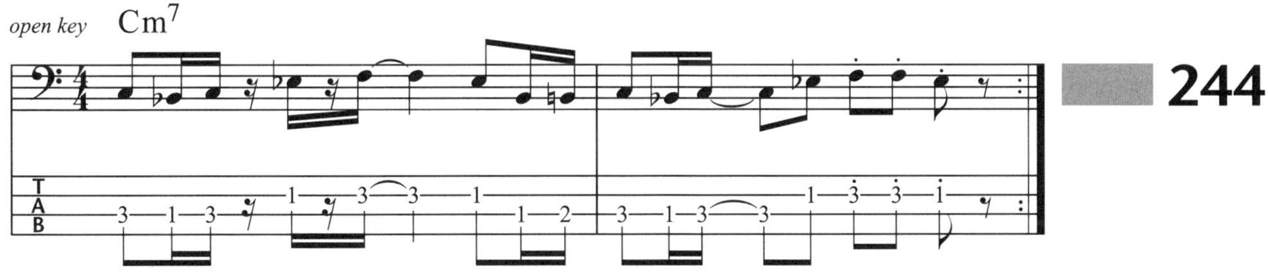
open key
Cm7
244
T
A
B

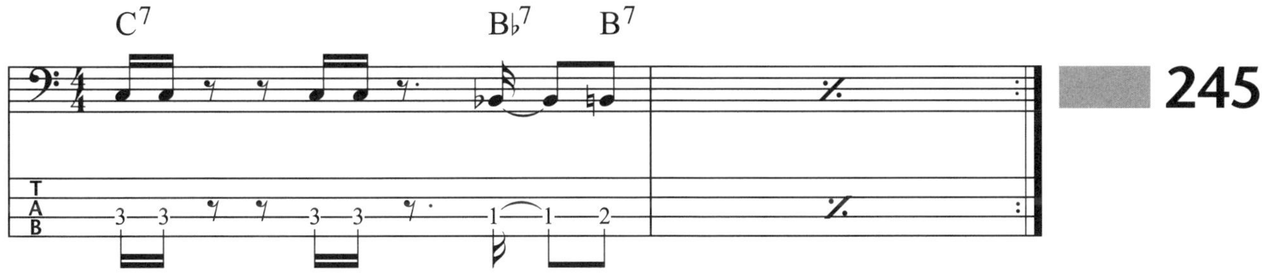
C7
B♭7
B7
245
T
A
B

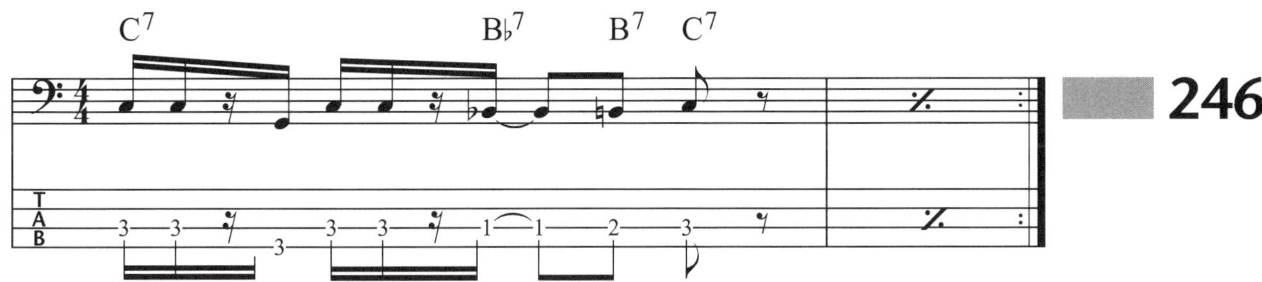
C7
B♭7
B7
C7
246
T
A
B

247

248

249

250

251

CD 1 Track 23

252

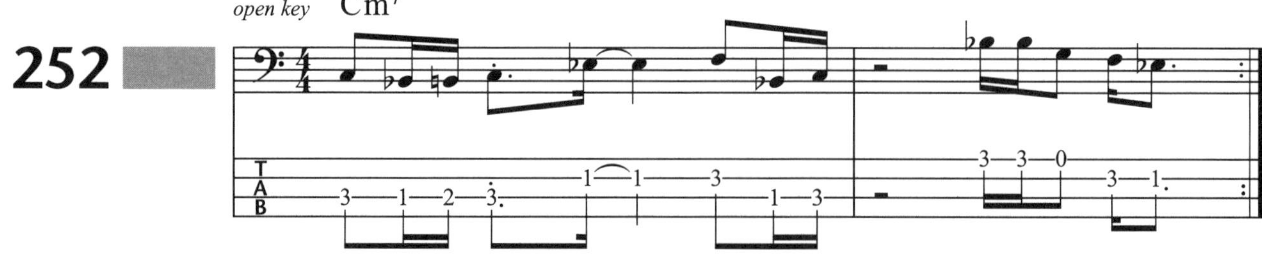

open key C B♭

F B♭ G7

253
CD 1 Track 23

open key F7 F♯7 G7 F7 F♯7

254

open key E7

255
CD 1 Track 24

open key E7

256

open key Em7 E7/G♯ A9

257
CD 1 Track 24

■ STANLEY CLARKE

Stanley Clarke rose to fame through working with Chick Corea in the Jazz world and many popular singers like Aretha Franklin. His own particular brand of bass guitar playing was very stylised. He was one of the first to use the very bright sound which active circuits made available. In fact it became a trademark. He could produce such a clear and distinct sound that his solos became almost guitar like in their complexity and clarity.

He tends to play the strings quite hard for several reasons. Firstly, he is also a double bass player who has long, strong fingers, and he likes to play aggressively. Secondly, he uses quite light strings for a thinner, clearer lead tone. His exciting style often consists of a series of fast runs, which crescendo in a flamenco style strumming. He has many interesting ideas (including his use of the piccolo bass guitar), and one musical example is his use of open string roots combined with moving harmonies higher up the instrument. Mark King of Level 42 also began using this style, which was first explored by Chuck Rainey and Carol Kaye (of Motown and Quincy Jones fame). Larry Graham, too, incorporated it into his slap style.

See from the examples how effective it is when chord progressions allow the use of open strings.

258 CD 1 Track 25

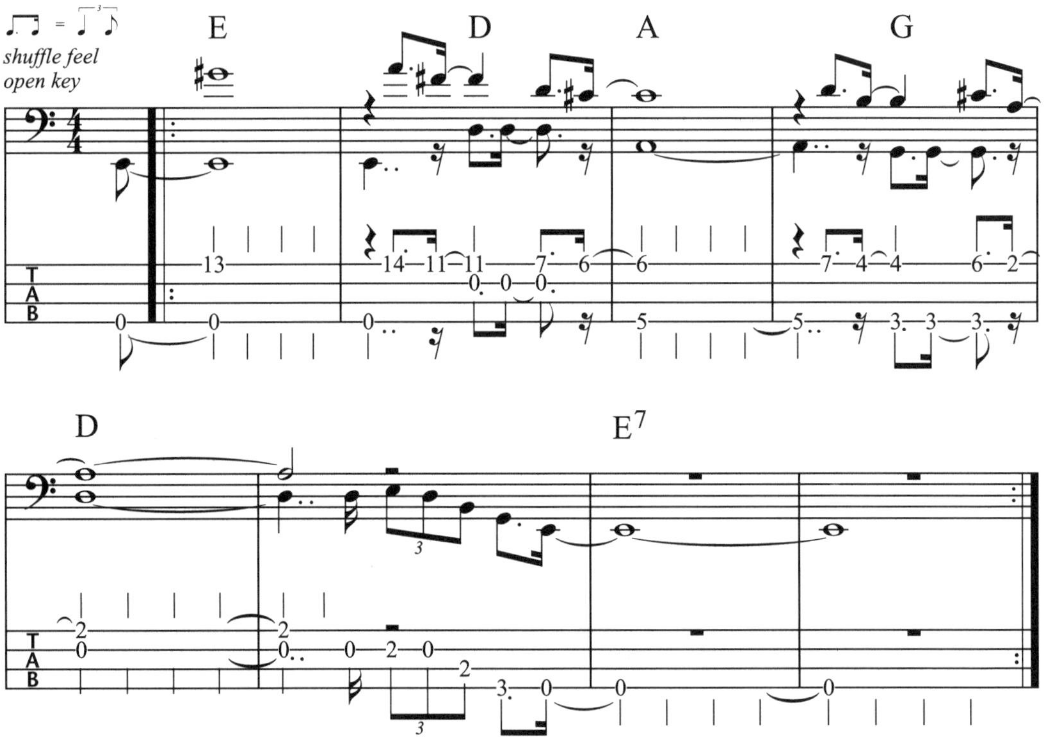

shuffle feel
open key

E D A G

D E7

259 CD 1 Track 25

shuffle feel
open key

E7

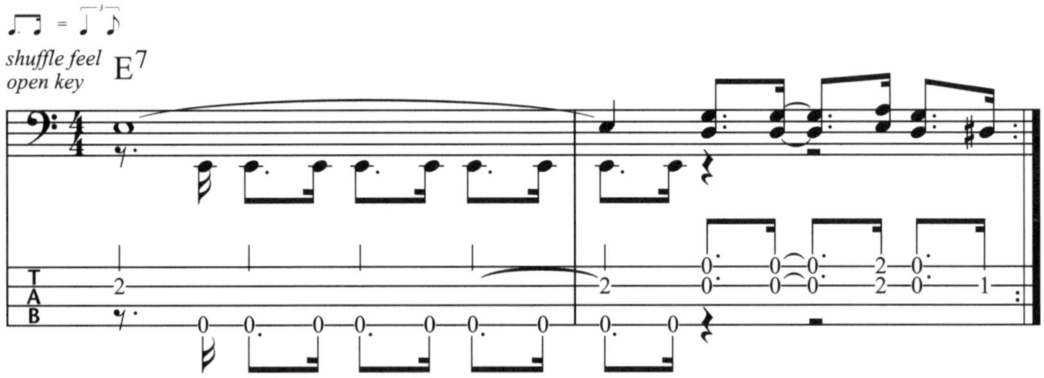

260
CD 1 Track 26

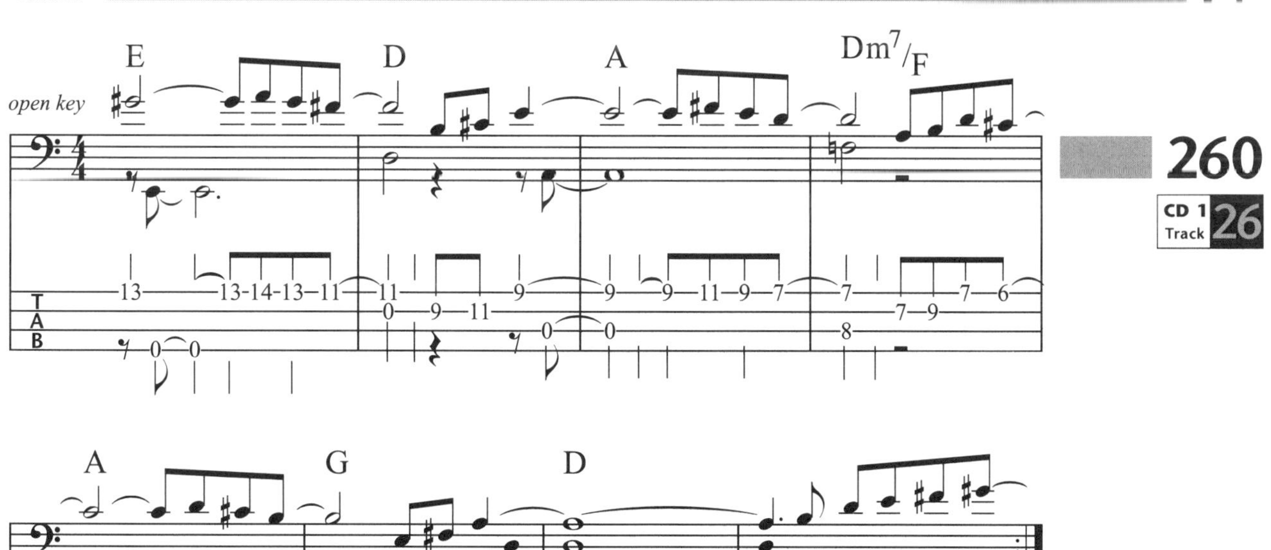

261
CD 1 Track 26

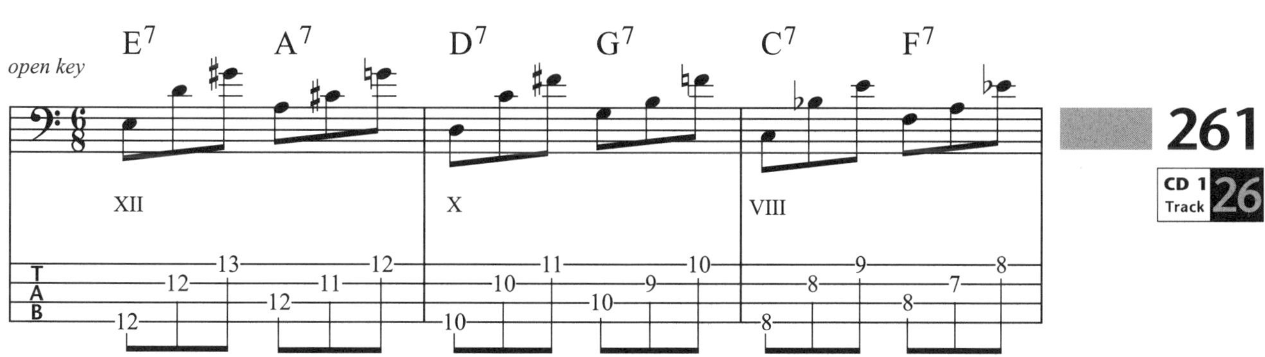

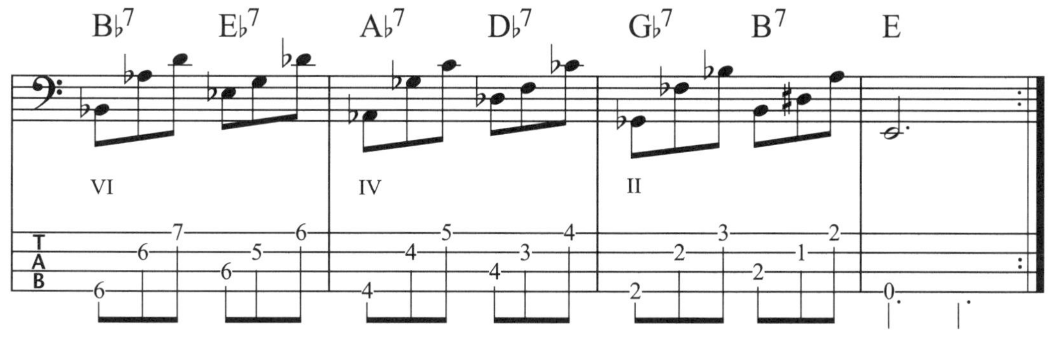

262
CD 1 Track 27

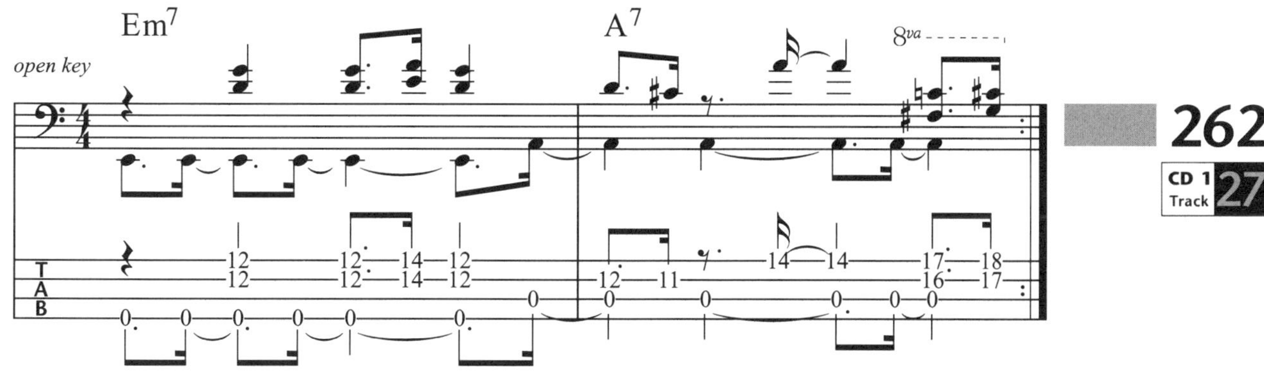

263

CD 1 Track 27

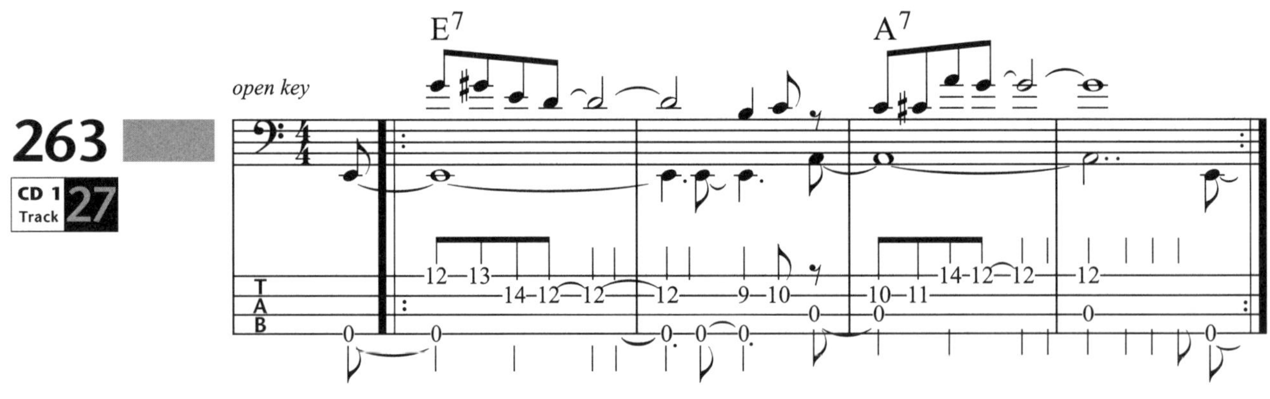

264

CD 1 Track 28

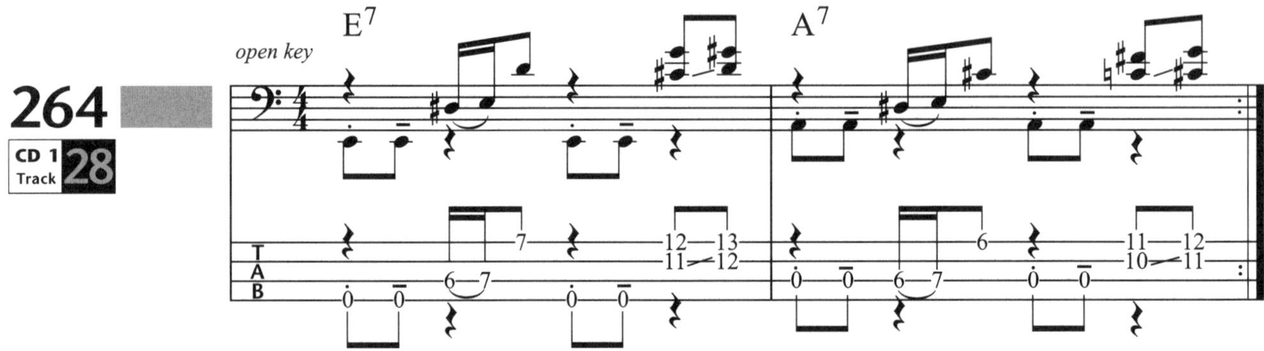

265

CD 1 Track 28

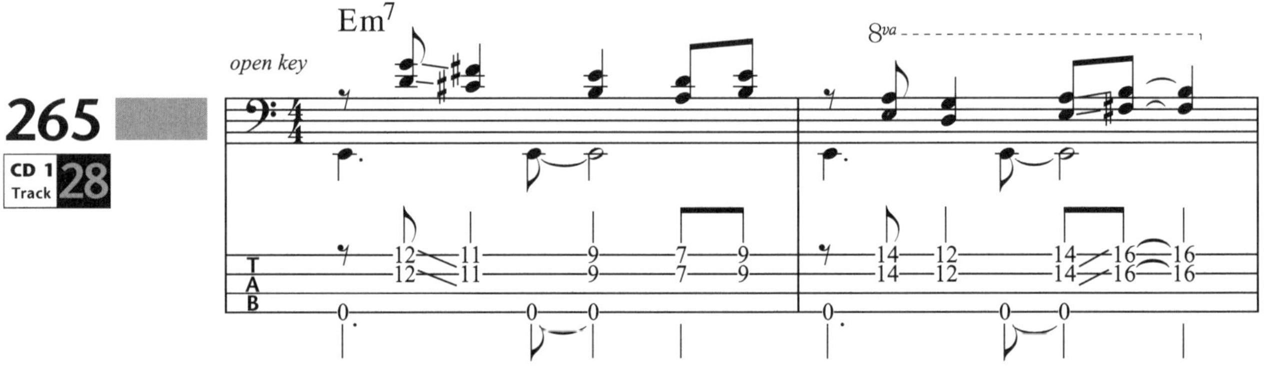

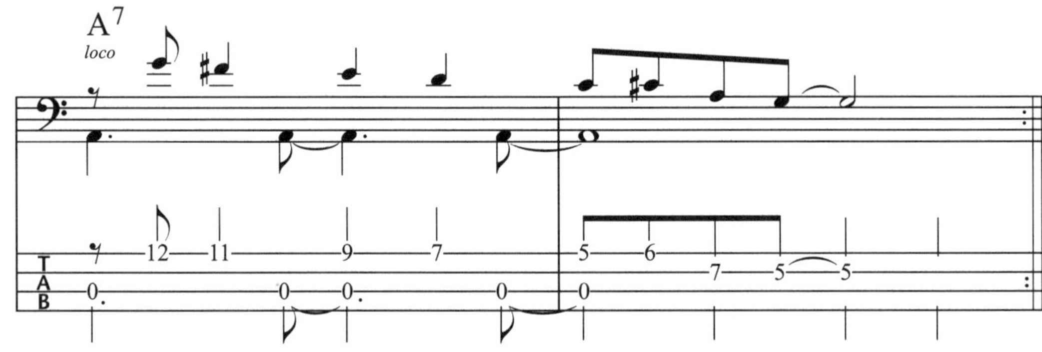

Rock

Rock music is a form which covers a huge range of different styles and influences. It is the most commercially successful type of music, and the name is used to describe other dramatic styles which have been influenced by Rock itself e.g. Jazz-Rock.

Names of styles can be misleading, as artists are often labelled with the latest trend. For instance, Tina Turner started as an R & B artist, became a Soul singer, and ended up as a Rock star. Her basic approach is still the same!

Some Rock bass playing originally had an R & B feel, e.g. early Chuck Berry records. By using a 2 or 4 feel on the double bass, a solid back beat from the drums, and a guitar or piano to add a sense of urgency, performers like Little Richard were able to be more dramatic. Bass guitar playing changed with Rock and Roll to become heavier. Elvis' music, for instance, which started out with a country feel, was greatly helped by songwriters like Leiber and Stoller. They were not traditionalists, but as young composers eager to find a different sound, they tried many ways of developing new ideas. Elvis' producers used Pop, Blues, Gospel, R & B, Soul, Country and Rock feels, and even foreign songs with English lyrics.

Buddy Holly developed from a Country Music background, and even experimented with R & B based rhythms, as used by Bo Diddley. Jerry Lee Lewis was developing a steady, driving rhythm behind his energetic performance. As electric guitars became more dominant, many new areas were explored. Guitarist Eric Clapton played a Chicago Blues style, but adapted and extended it for a Rock trio called Cream. The group's bassist, Jack Bruce, developed his style from Blues and Jazz roots. His Rock playing became more experimental, as he often moved away from basic riffs and improvised his accompaniment. Jimmy Hendrix played a vast range of styles from the unusual to the outrageous, and because of Mitch Mitchell's often complex Rock drum style, it was necessary for Noel Redding to play fairly simple patterns of solid riffs and steady 8th notes on the bass.

Rock styles include Soft Rock (Crosby, Stills & Nash), Folk Rock (Pentangle), Acid Rock (Velvet Underground), Glam Rock (Kiss), Funk Rock (Earth, Wind & Fire), Punk Rock (Sex Pistols), Rock Fusion (Frank Zappa), Jazz Rock (Blood, Sweat & Tears), Latin Rock (Santana), Country Rock (Canned Heat), Heavy Metal (Guns & Roses), Psychedelic Rock (Jimmy Hendrix), Heavy Rock (Deep Purple) and Rock & Roll (Elvis).

Generally speaking, Soul had a black majority audience and Rock had a white majority. Obvious exceptions like Little Richard had an enormous influence on bands like The Beatles. They adopted certain black vocal techniques so that styles became more mixed. Chuck Berry was greatly influenced by R & B but managed to find a white Rock audience.

The Rolling Stones are an R & B influenced band, and have never moved away from that. As many of their songs are based on 12 bar Blues, they retain the strong hook-line, simple bass and drum patterns, and rhythm guitar riff playing.

When it came to heavier bands, the biggest like Led Zeppelin were white. Although they were influenced by The Blues, R & B etc., the style was very different. John Paul Jones' bass lines were not based on Soul and dance music. White Rock seemed to aim more at concert and festival audiences. It sometimes became so heavy and loud that the music was intended to overwhelm the audience with a tidal wave of volume, drama and excitement.

The "Heavy Metal" groups of today base much of their style on Led Zeppelin; hence the play on words. Bass players often hammer out an 8th note rhythm, and rely on the overall level of excitement than fussing about each note or phrase. A wall of electronic sound became fashionable as a result.

Bands like The Who had tremendous imagination and talent. They showed that a Rock band could play dance music, power music, ballads and even the Rock opera "Tommy". John Entwistle varied his bass style enormously.

The group Chicago had many Jazz influences, including their use of brass instruments, but their songs and concerts were loud and in the Rock tradition. The Beatles wrote melodic songs with interesting lyrics and drew inspiration from many sources. They never relied on loud volume to achieve excitement. They went for certain distorted effects in their productions, but these were not overstated.
Paul McCartney's bands have since been very musical and never out of control with distortion or volume. This is perhaps to do with his own musical roots. His Rock bass lines, though, are always well-considered.

Some generalisations that you can make about Rock music are that it has a strong sense of energy, drama, spectacle and self-image. Much of Rock is deliberately designed to shock and be outrageous. It is larger than life. Excitement is most important and many performers display great sexuality.

If the bass lines become too fussy, energy is dissipated in detail rather than concentrated in the driving rhythm, which should be a basic groove pattern.

For the purposes of detailing some of the many influences in Rock bass guitar playing, I have created four sections. Each one has a variety of Rock riffs.

"Straight 8th Note Feel" riffs show some of the ways the bass can drive the beat along with a simple rhythm.

"Syncopated 8th Note Feel" riffs show how patterns can be broken up within the bar to produce more variation.

"16th Note Feel" riffs are all strong phrases which are broken up with the use of 16th notes (semiquavers) and more sophisticated polyrhythms. These particular riffs tend to be repeated without ad libs or variation. They are strong riffs, which make a major contribution to the overall composition. Ad libs would tend to alter the feel and not support the singer or soloist in the right way.

The riffs are all played firmly and positively. Depending on the accompaniment, it is possible to make them work in very different circumstances. The important thing about finding a suitable bass line is that the riff should have the right feel, it should be as simple, dynamic or melodic as the material suggests, and if possible, it should have some characteristics which set it apart from other riffs.

"Shuffle feel" riffs have a different groove. Many bands specialise in this particular style, and bass lines can vary enormously. Some use simple one-note rhythms which are full of energy, e.g. Status Quo, while others mix energy with harmonic movement. This style is reminiscent of the Blues and R & B from years before.

Straight 8th Note Feel

open key G7

266

CD 1 Track 29

open key G7

267

C

268

C

269

C

270

C7

271

CD 1 Track 29

272

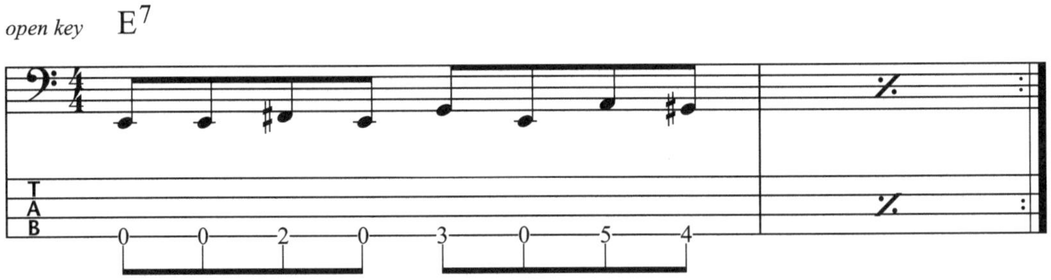
open key
E7
T
A
B

273

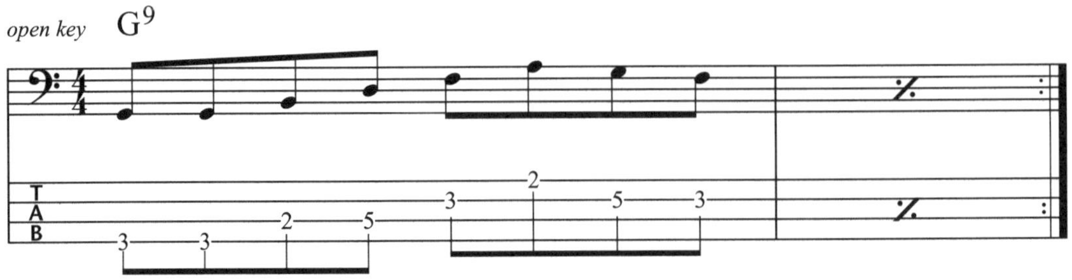
open key
G9
T
A
B

274

CD 1 Track 30

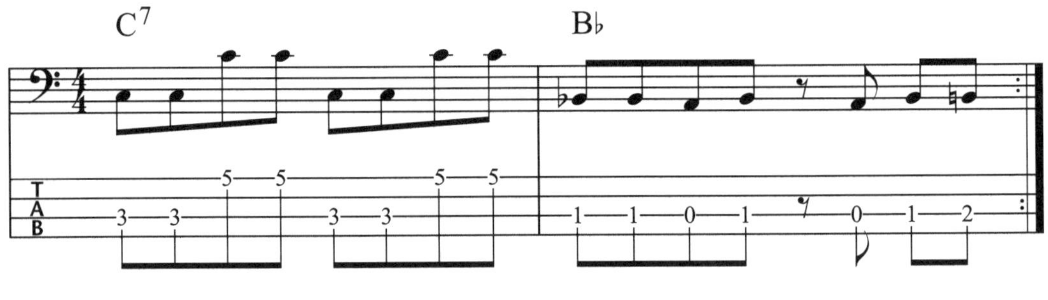
C7
B♭
T
A
B

275

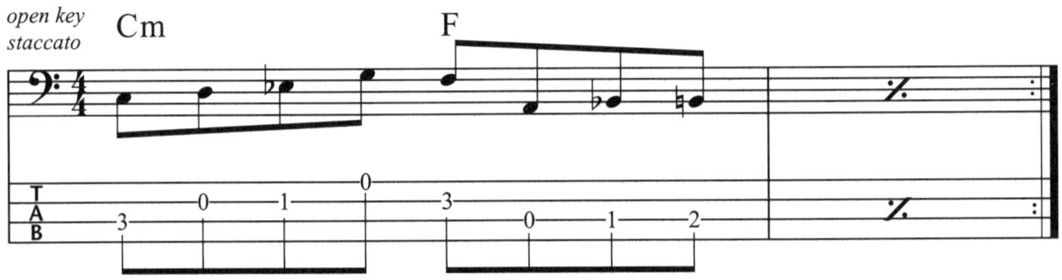
open key
staccato
Cm
F
T
A
B

276

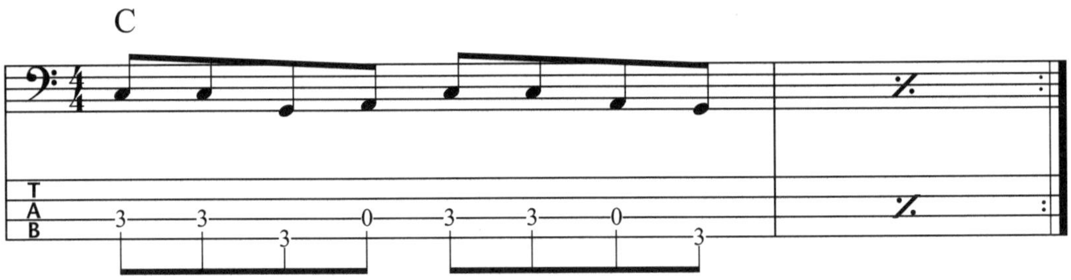
C
T
A
B

277

open key
G7
T
A
B

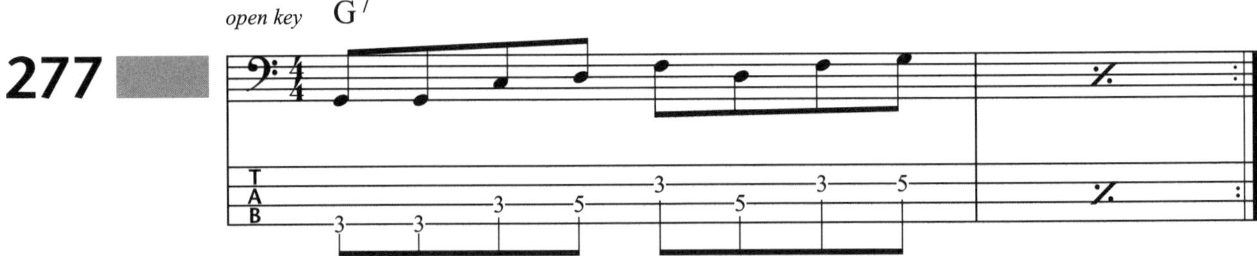

open key
G7
278
CD 1 Track 30

open key
G7
279

C
F
G7
280

open key
F
G
F
G
F
281

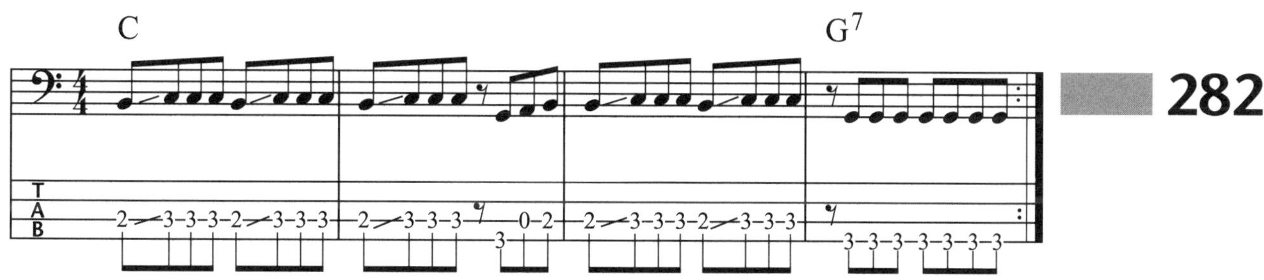
C
G7
282

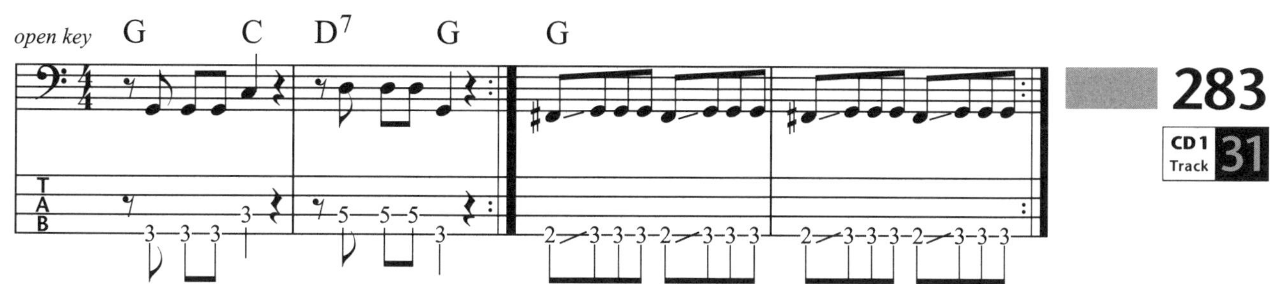
open key
G
C
D7
G
G
283
CD1 Track 31

284

CD 1 Track 31

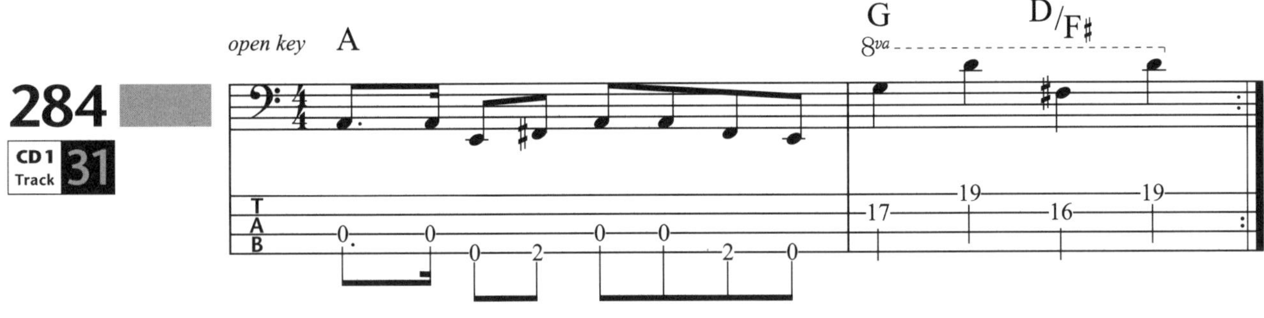

285

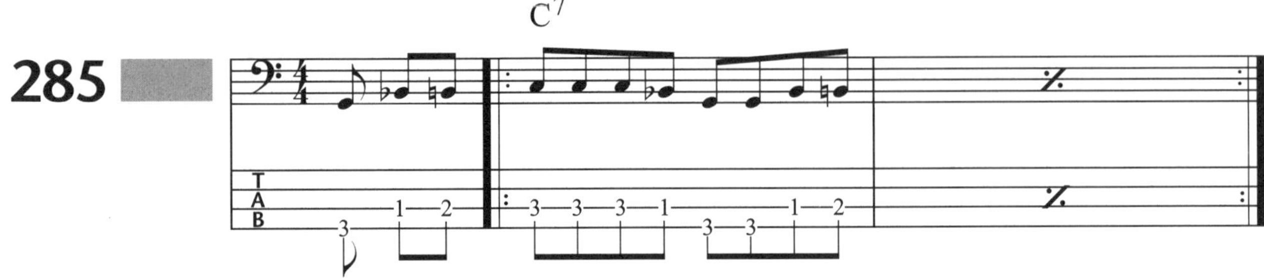

286

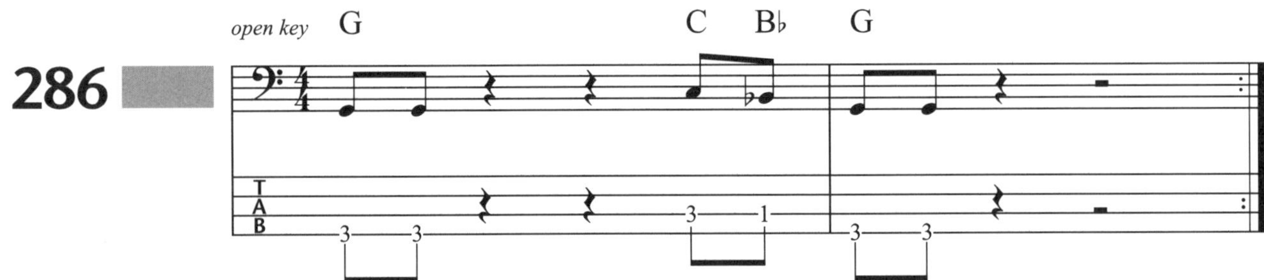

287

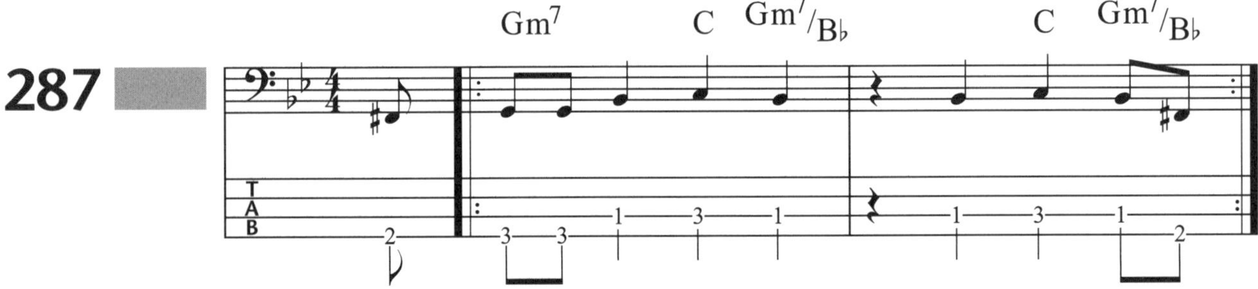

288

289

Syncopated 8th Note Feel

open key unison
G7

290
CD1 Track 32

Dm7

291
CD1 Track 32

Gm7 Cm7 D7

292
CD1 Track 33

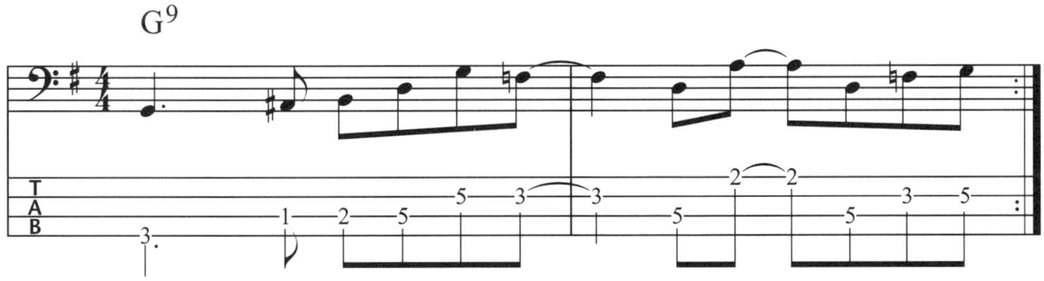

G9

293
CD1 Track 33

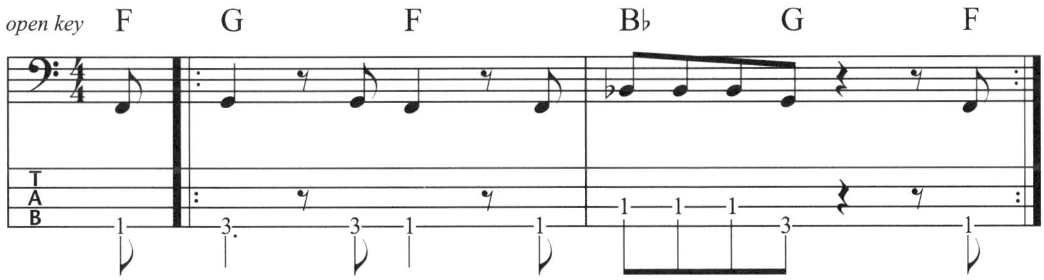

open key
F G F B♭ G F

294

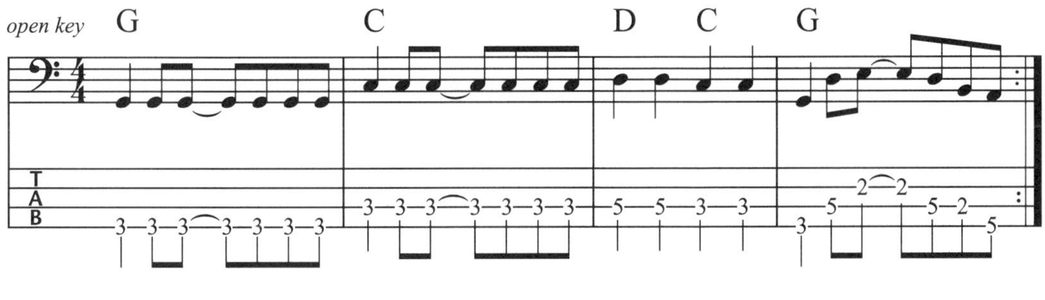

open key
G C D C G

295

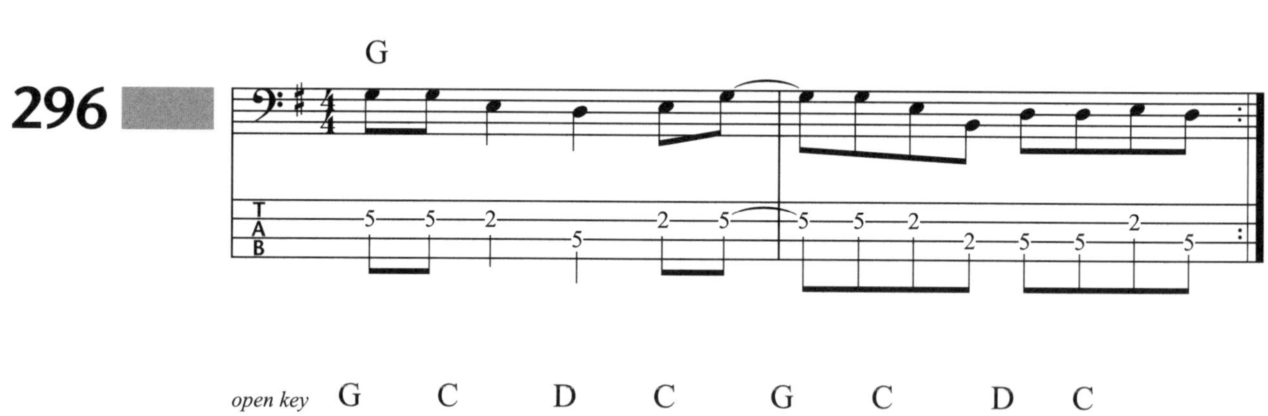
296
G

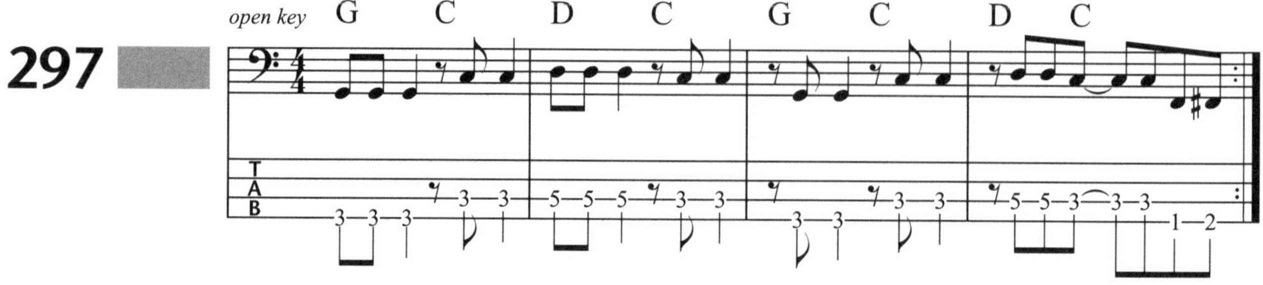
297
open key
G C D C G C D C

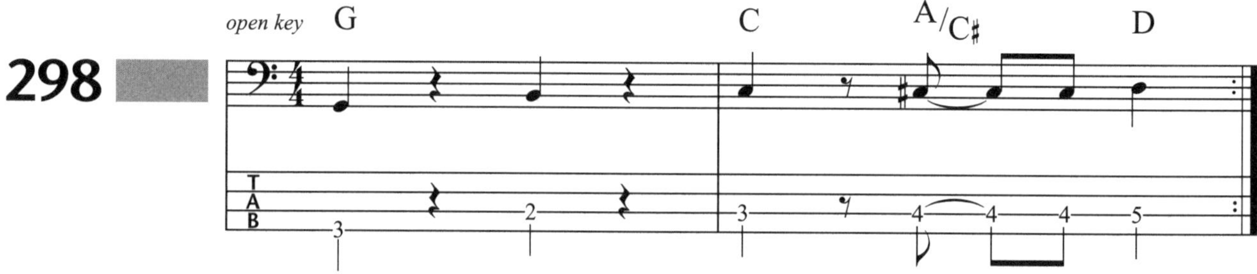
298
open key
G C A/C♯ D

299
CD 1 Track 34
open key
G7

300
open key
B♭add 9 (B♭2)

301
open key
G7

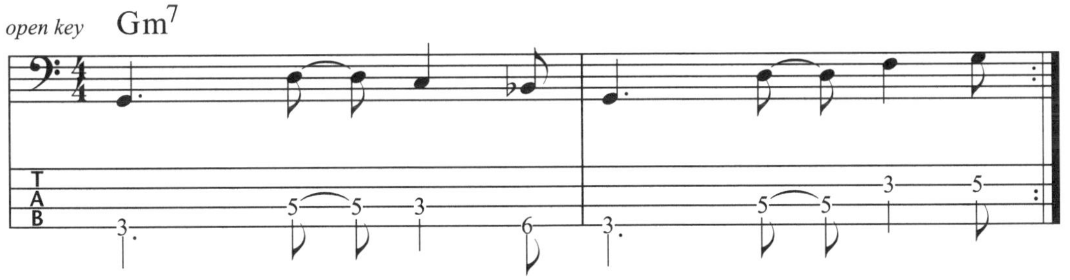
open key
Gm7
T
A
B

302

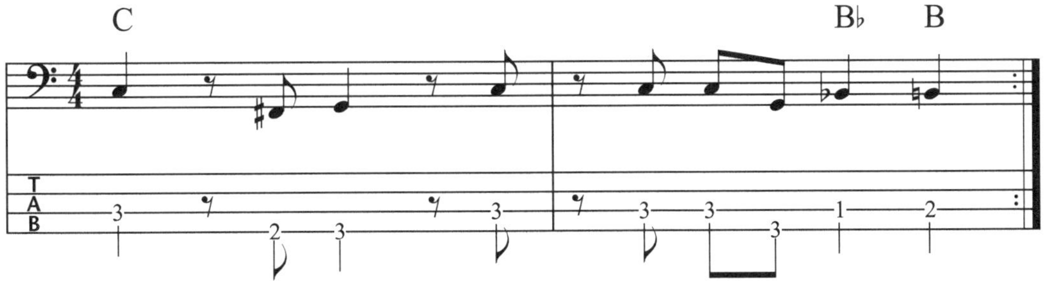
C
B♭
B
T
A
B

303

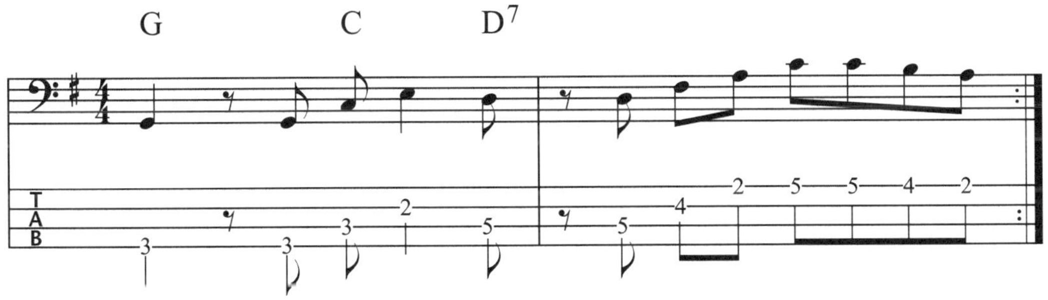
G
C
D7
T
A
B

304

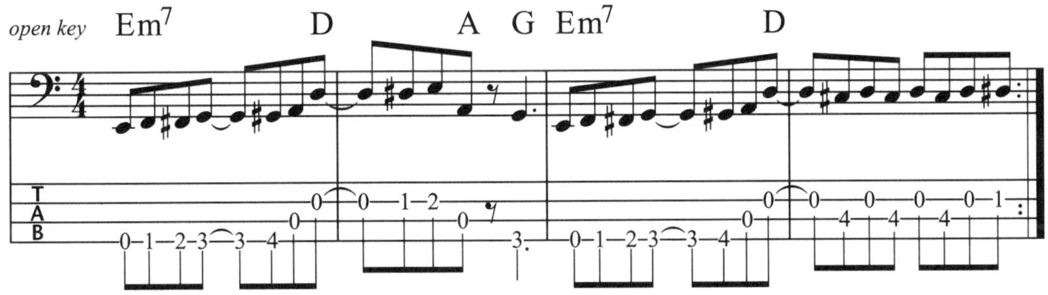
open key
Em7
D
A
G
Em7
D
T
A
B

305

CD 1 Track 34

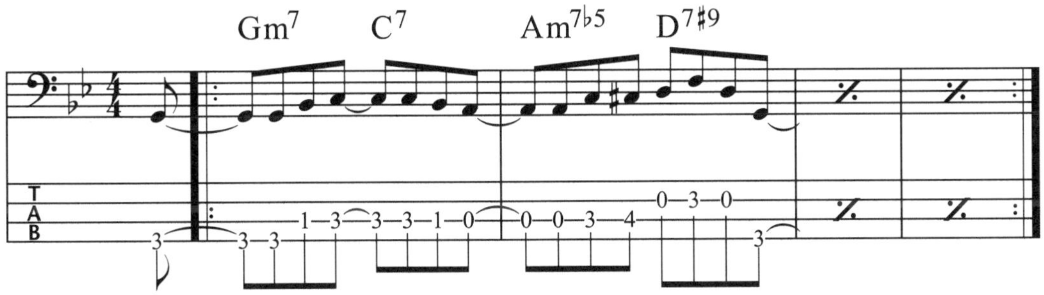
Gm7
C7
Am7♭5
D7♯9
T
A
B

306

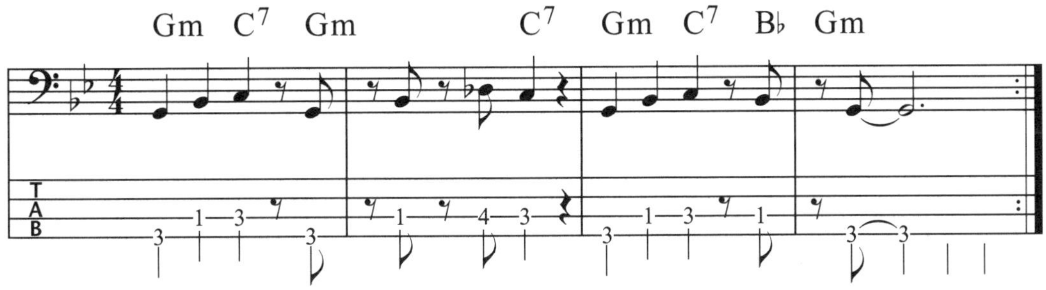
Gm
C7
Gm
C7
Gm
C7
B♭
Gm
T
A
B

307

308

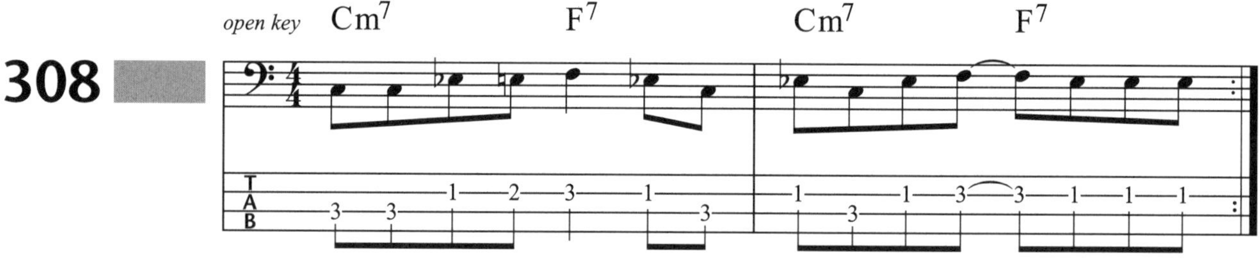

309

310

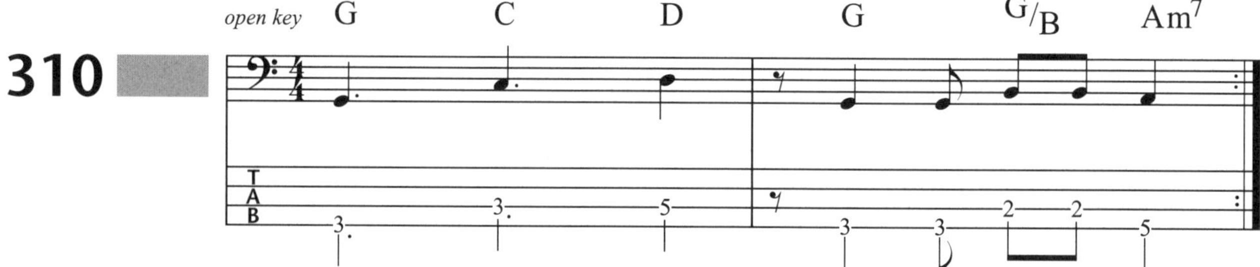

311

312

16th Note Feel

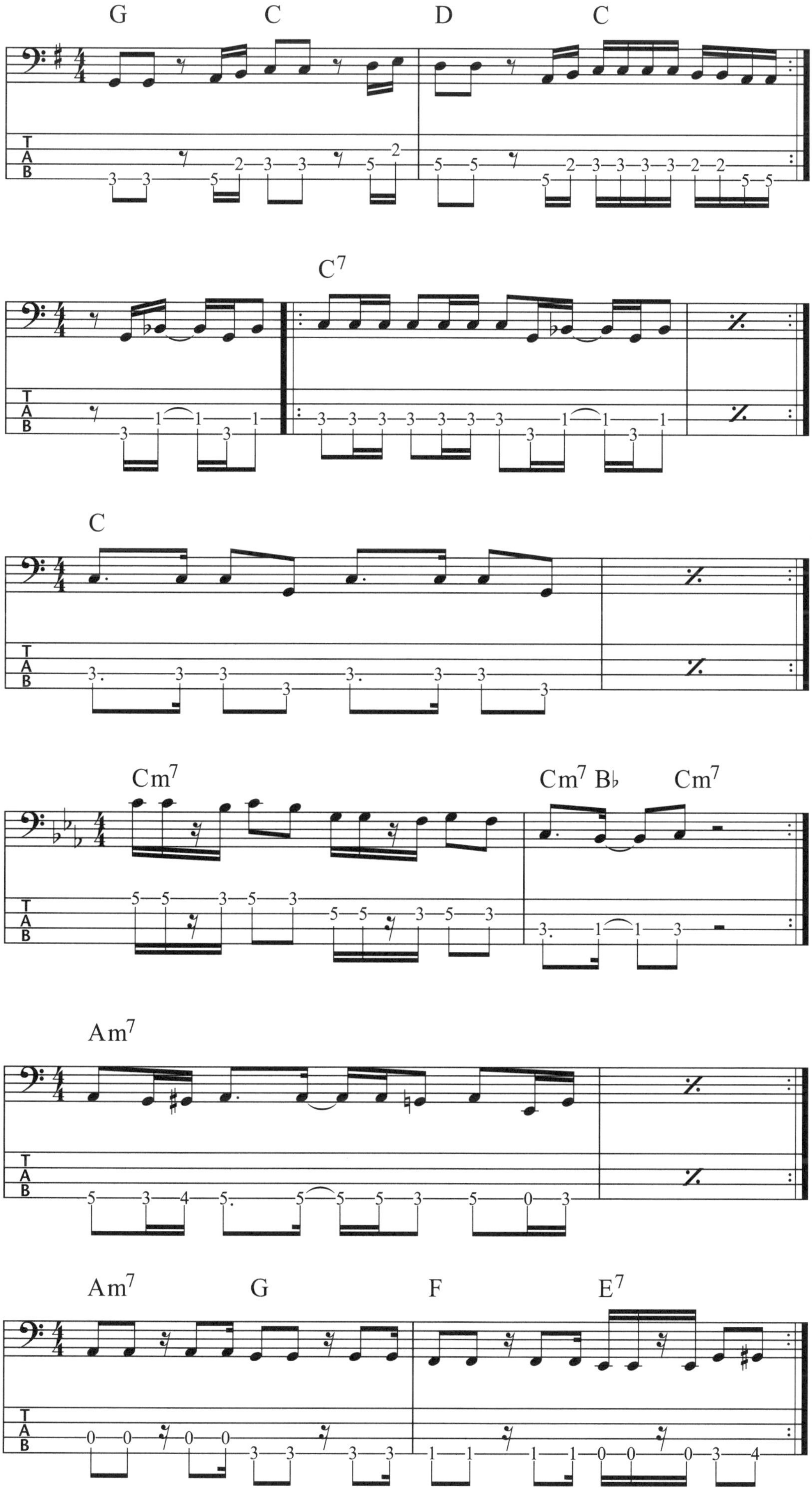

G C D C

313

C7

314

CD1 Track 35

C

315

Cm7 Cm7 B♭ Cm7

316

CD1 Track 35

Am7

317

Am7 G F E7

318

319

320

CD 1 Track 36

321

322

323

324

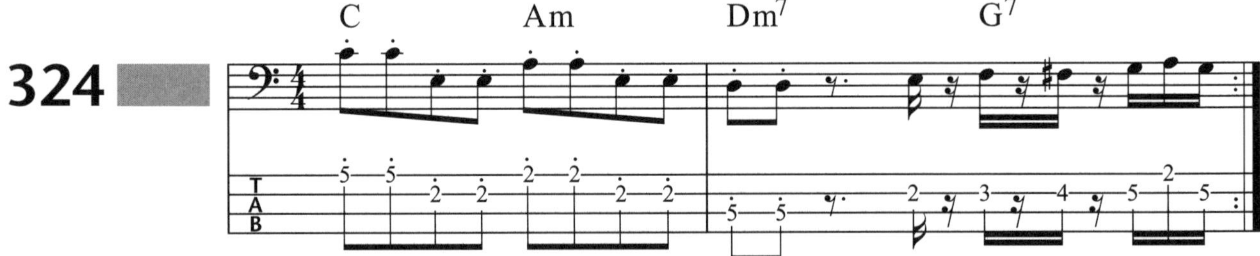

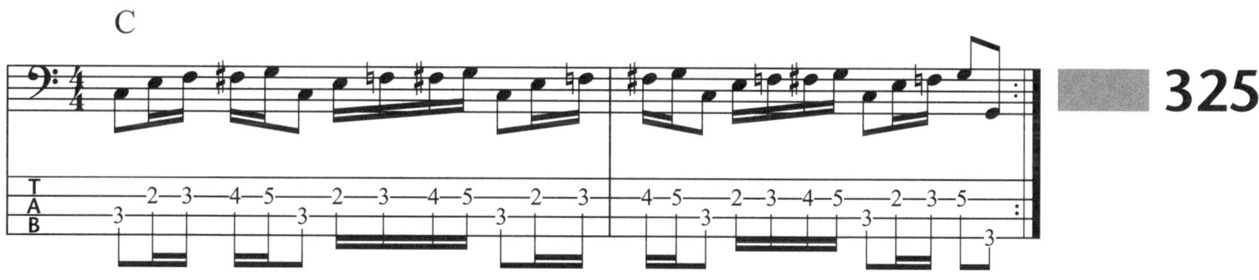
C
325

C7
326
CD 1 Track 36

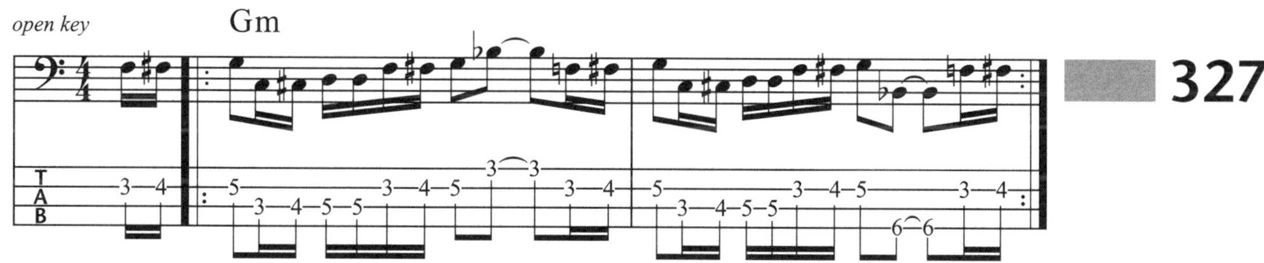
open key
Gm
327

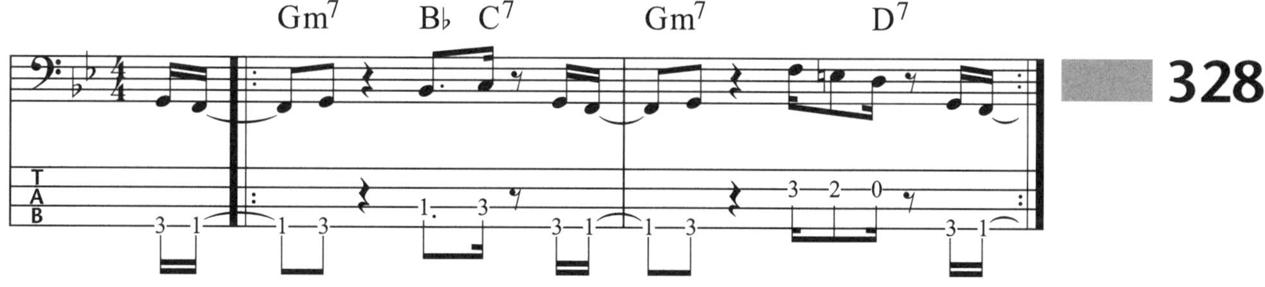
Gm7
B♭
C7
Gm7
D7
328

C7
329

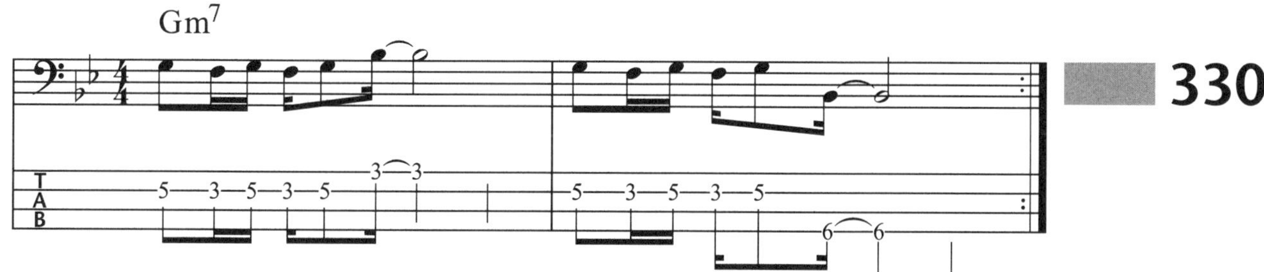
Gm7
330

331
CD 1 Track 37

332

333
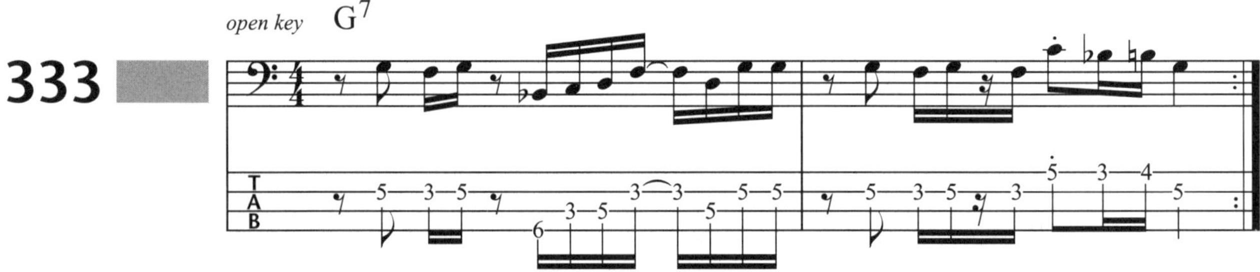

334

335
CD 1 Track 37
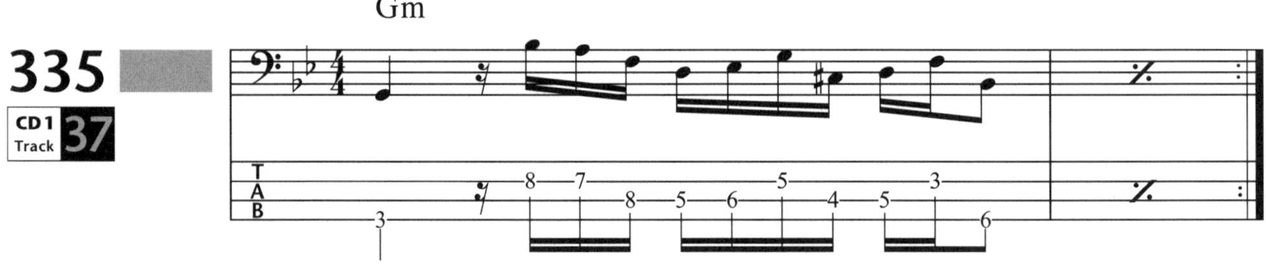

336

Shuffle Feel

open key G7

337
CD 1 Track 38

open key G7

338

open key G7 F

339

open key G7

340

C

341
CD 1 Track 38

open key G7

342
CD 1 Track 39

343

344

345
CD1 Track 39

346
CD1 Track 40

347

348
CD1 Track 40

BOOK THREE

■ Latin Music

Latin music has a variety of influences and traditions. It is rhythmically very sophisticated. Most rhythms are derived from dances, of which there are a large number.

Rhythms are created by drums, agogos, claves, cabasas, tambourines, shakers, cuicas, whistles, vibra-slaps, guiros, etc. In fact, tuned instruments are often played so rhythmically that they double as percussion effects.

Bands tend to be small in size and are concentrated on the rhythm section and a fairly simple front line. Chord structures are often totally different from classically based European and North American Jazz and Blues. Some Spanish music, for instance, uses a series of modes, which are the result of Moorish, African and Arabic influence. When the Spanish, Portuguese, Africans, French and English spread their cultures to other parts of the world, these styles were then blended with local influences to produce further variations. As a result, many bass lines consist largely of roots beneath changing modes. Many Latin bass lines are very similar to African ones.

As much of Latin music is rhythm based and layered with percussion instruments playing complex cross-patterns, it is traditional for the bass to play harmonically simple lines. Roots and fifths are very common, as they anchor the rhythm section down and allow the soloists greater freedom with the melody. The percussion section use a solid bass line as a reliable foundation, and then experiment with polyrhythms. When bassists became tired of providing simple on-the-beat support, they began anticipating certain accents to phrase with other members of the percussion section. Even downbeats are left out sometimes. In fact, often the majority of bass accents are off the beat.

Cuban, Brazilian, Puerto Rican, Haitian and many other Latin styles have quite differing bass traditions. Some use triplet lines across an even quaver rhythm, while others sit squarely on beat 1, 3 and 4. Some anticipate every first beat and complete the bar with a simple pattern, while others have a downbeat followed by polyrhythms. One thing in common with all Latin music is that the bass plays a steady constant rhythm with tireless consistency.

From Cuba came the Rumba and its variations Guaracha and Mambo. The bass in the Rumba plays on the beat. The feel in Mambo is often off the beat and stresses the after beats. A slower variation of Mambo is the Cha Cha. Bolero originated from Spain in 3/4 time, but became 4/4 time in middle South America. Haiti produced Merengue and Habanera. From Argentina came the Tango. Venezuela introduced the Valse Créole (a cross-breeding of Spanish and Viennese Waltzes).

Middle South America also produced Montuño, La Balanga, Bajon, Pachanga, Beguine and La Cumbia. Trinidad was the birthplace of Calypso music.

Brazil was influenced by Africans from the Zambesi and Congo, and produced Samba. The exciting Rio festival music is famous for La Batucada, which is a drum feature. Bossa Nova is a slower variation of Samba. The Carioca also came from Brazil.

USA
New York
Bahamas
Mexico
Cuba
Haiti
Dominican Rep.
Belize
Honduras
Jamaica
Guatemala
El Salvador
Nicaragua
Costa Rica
Panama
Trinidad
Venezuela
Guyana
Surinam
Guiana
Colombia
Ecuador
Peru
Brazil
Bahia
Bolivia
Rio
Paraguay
LATIN AMERICA
Argentina
Chile
Uruguay
Pacific
Atlantic

African rhythms are sometimes used in their basic forms, but are treated with Latin harmonies. Reggae came from the West Indies, and because of its commercial success has begun to be influenced by Western Rock music.

Salsa is a mixture of Puerto Rican Cha Cha and Cuban Rumba. Mixed with Jazz, it became popular in New York, where some people claim it was started by immigrant musicians.

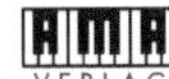

Latin Styles

Cha Cha 1.

349

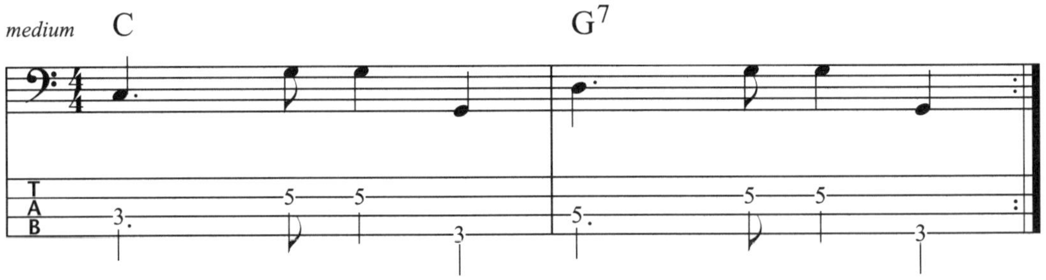
medium
C
G7
TAB

Cha Cha 2.

350

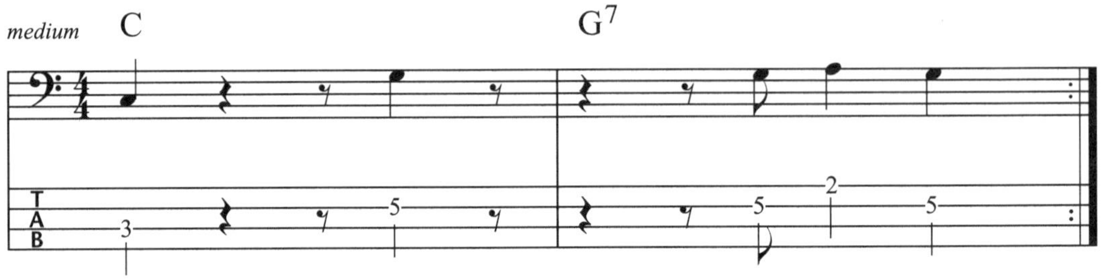
medium
C
G7
TAB

Cha Cha 3.

351

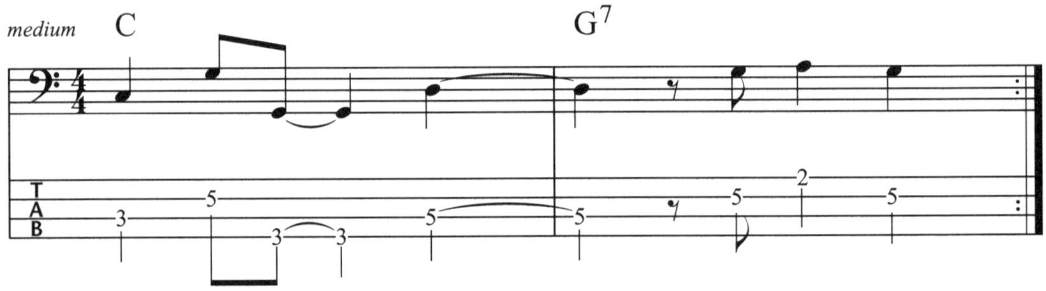
medium
C
G7
TAB

Cha Cha 4.

352

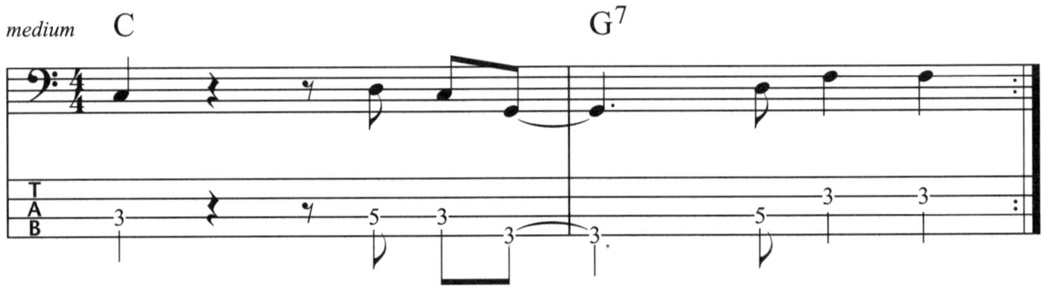
medium
C
G7
TAB

Cha Cha 5.

353

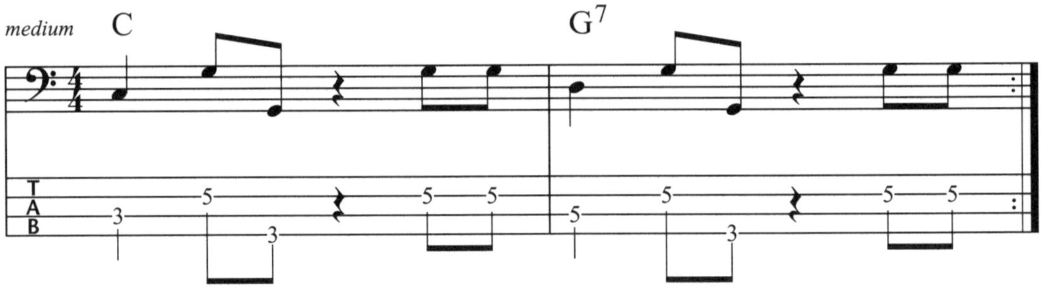
medium
C
G7
TAB

Cha Cha 6.

354

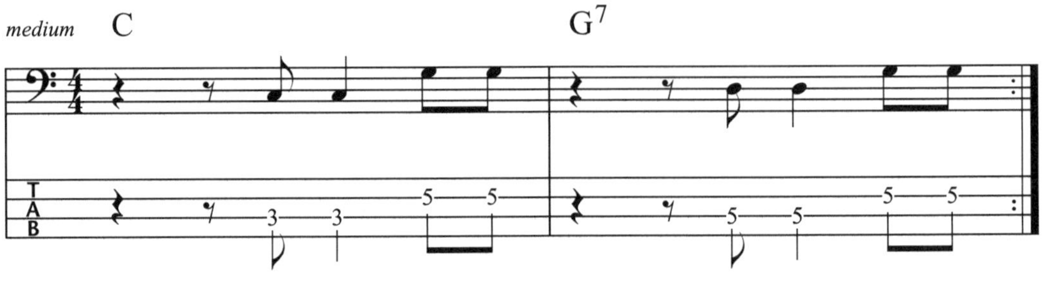
medium
C
G7
TAB

medium G7 Cm

Tango 1. 355

medium G7 Cm

Tango 2. 356

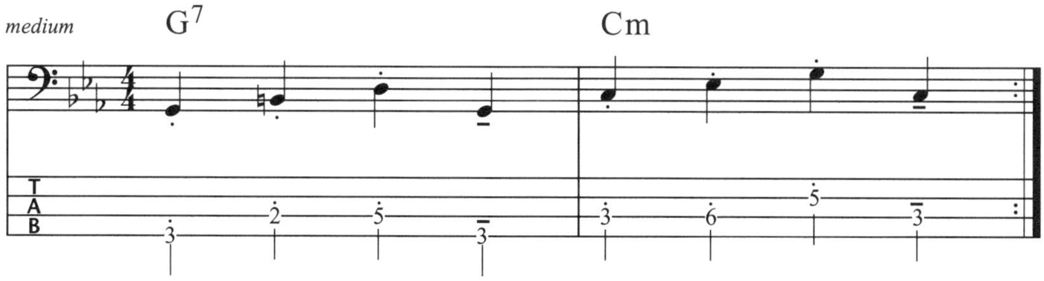

medium G7 Cm

Tango 3. 357

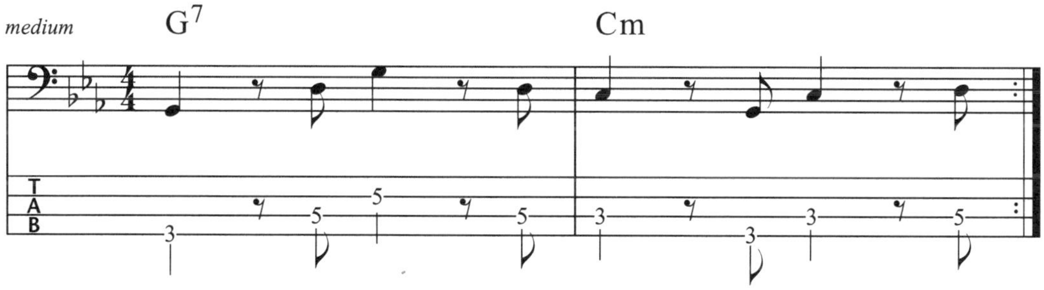

medium G7 Cm

Tango 4. 358

medium G7 Cm

Tango 5. 359

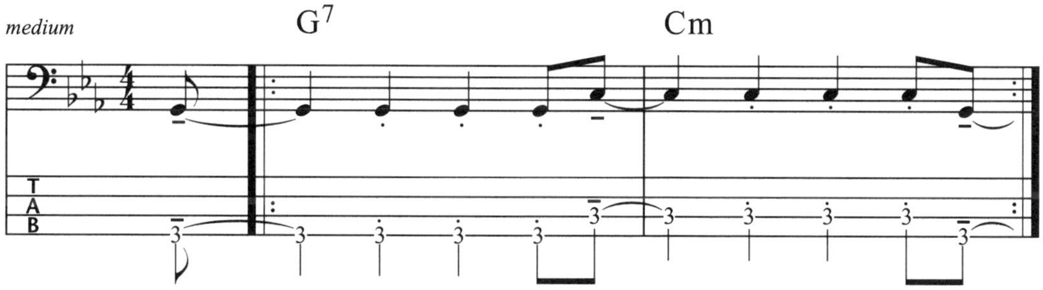

2 feel/fast 4 F C7

Montuño 1. 360

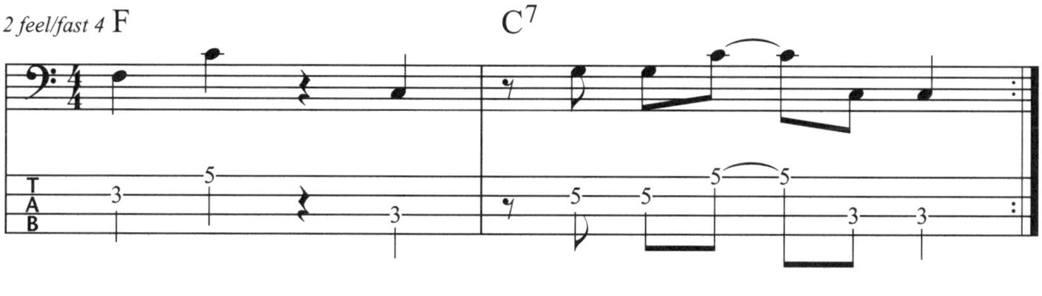

Montuño 2.

361

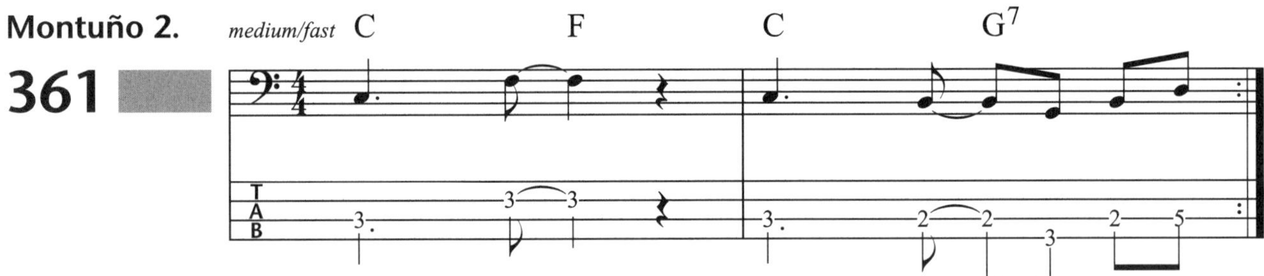

Montuño 3.

362

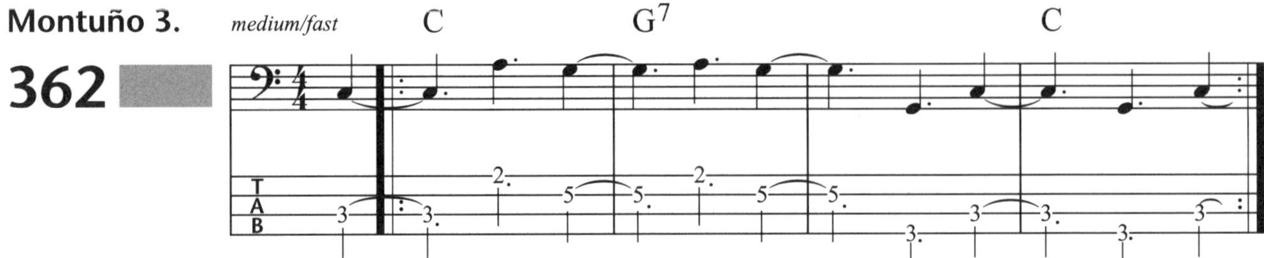

Merengue 1.

363

Merengue 2.

364

Merengue 3.

365

Rumba 1.

366

Rumba 2.

367

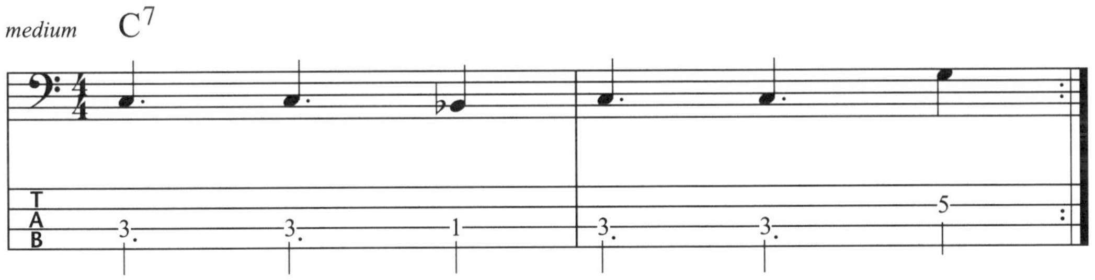
medium
C7

Rumba 3.

368

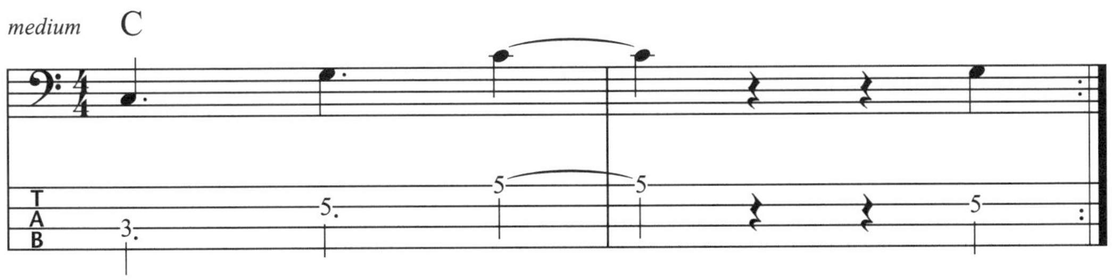
medium
C

Calypso 1.

369

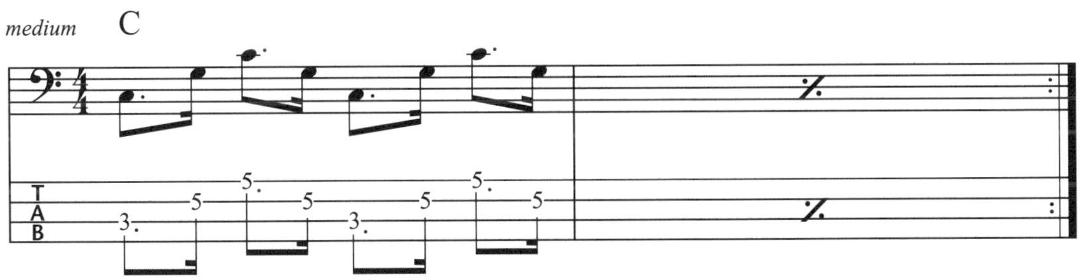
medium
C

Calypso 2.

370

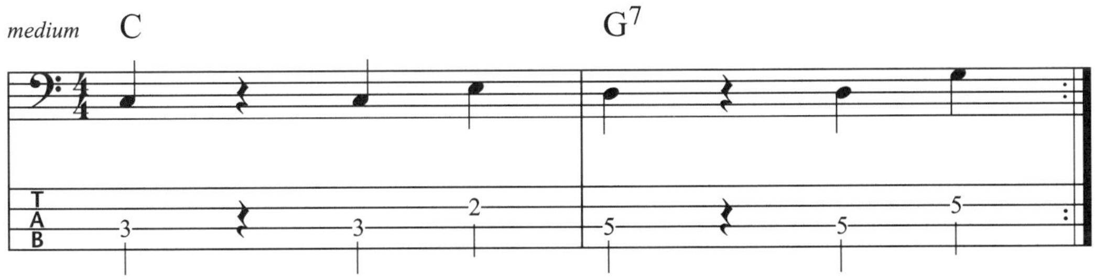
medium
C
G7

Calypso 3.

371

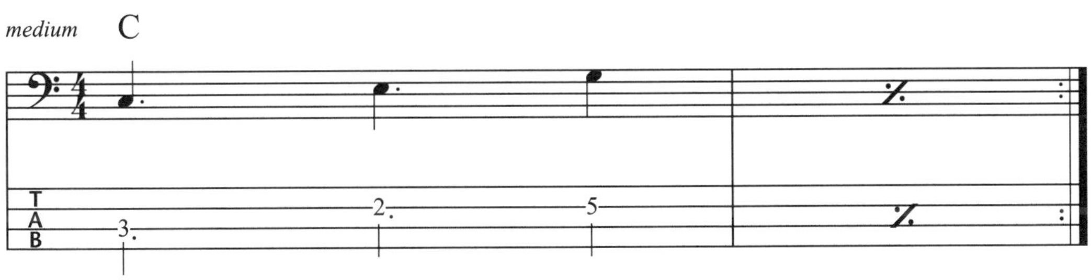
medium
C

Calypso 4.

372

medium
C
F
C
G7

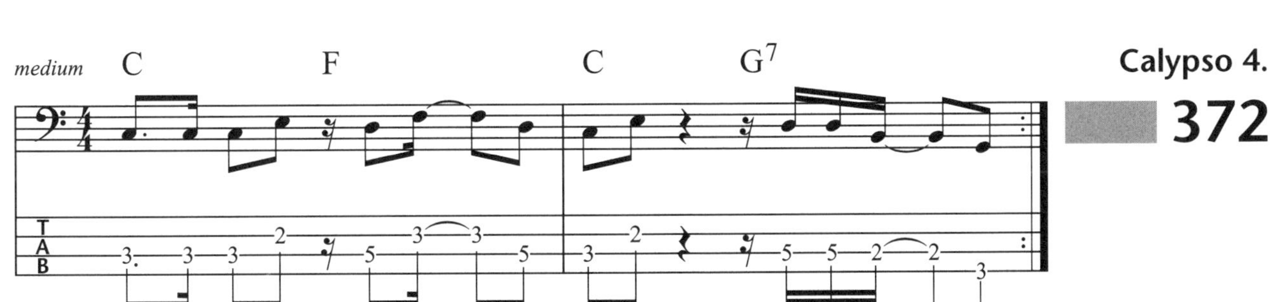

Calypso 5.

373

Bajon 1.

374

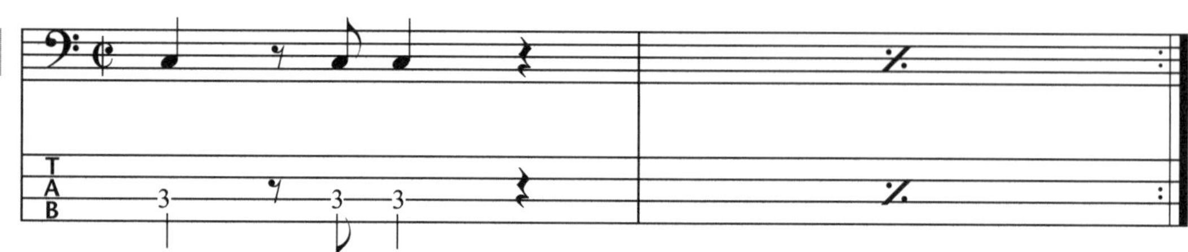

Bajon 2.

375

Mambo 1.

376

Mambo 2.

377

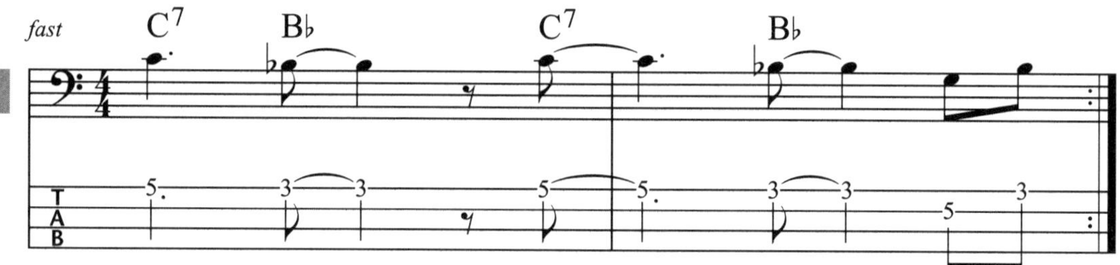

Mambo 3.

378

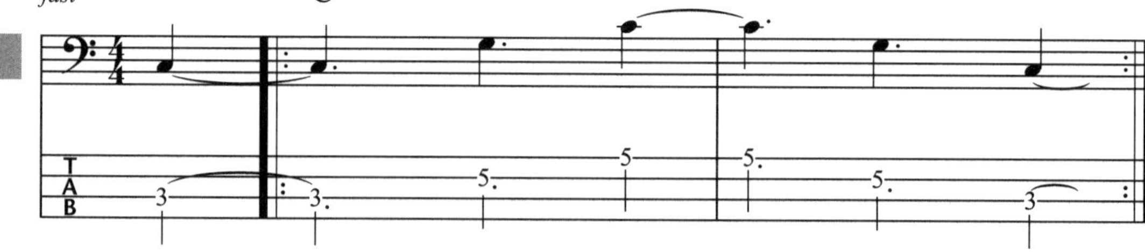

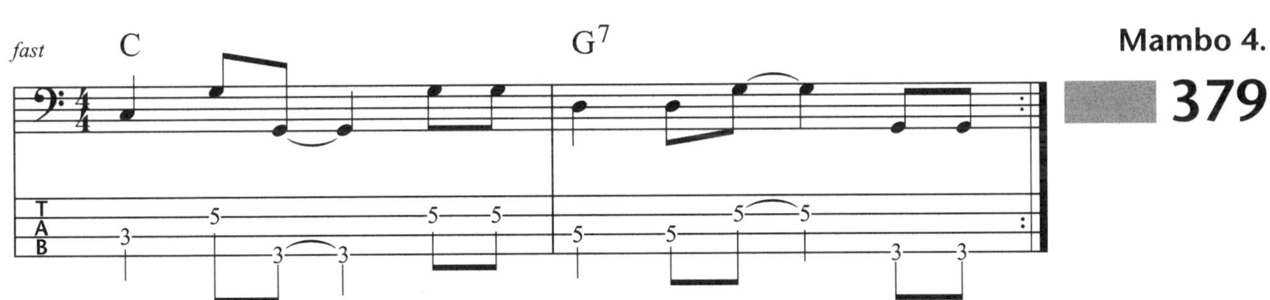
fast
C
G7
Mambo 4.
379

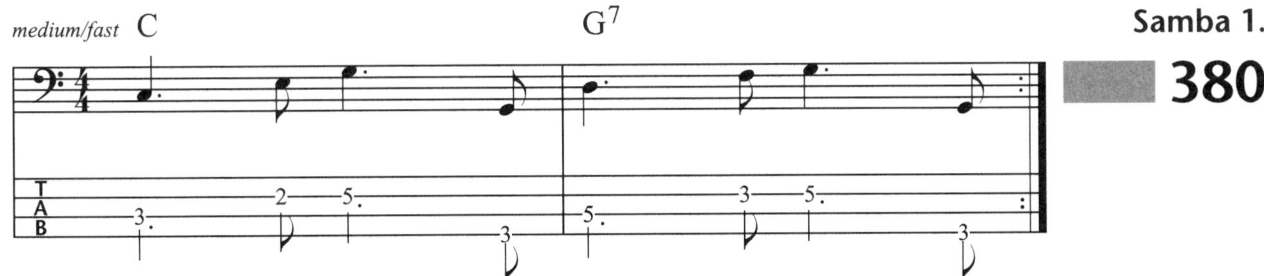
medium/fast
C
G7
Samba 1.
380

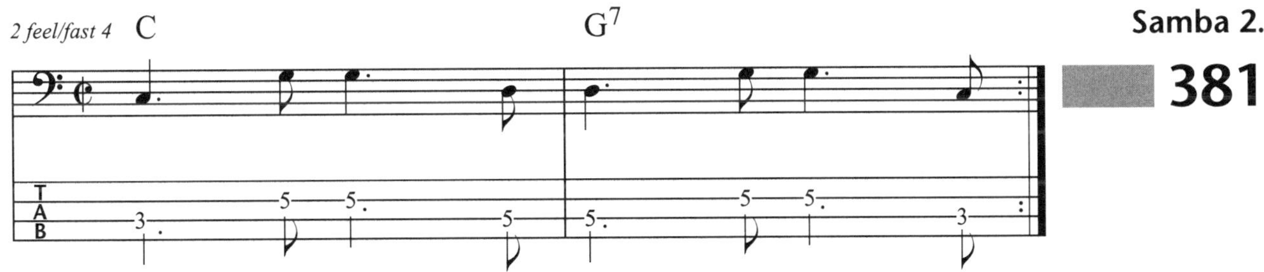
2 feel/fast 4
C
G7
Samba 2.
381

2 feel/fast 4
C
Samba 3.
382

medium
C
Bossa Nova 1.
383

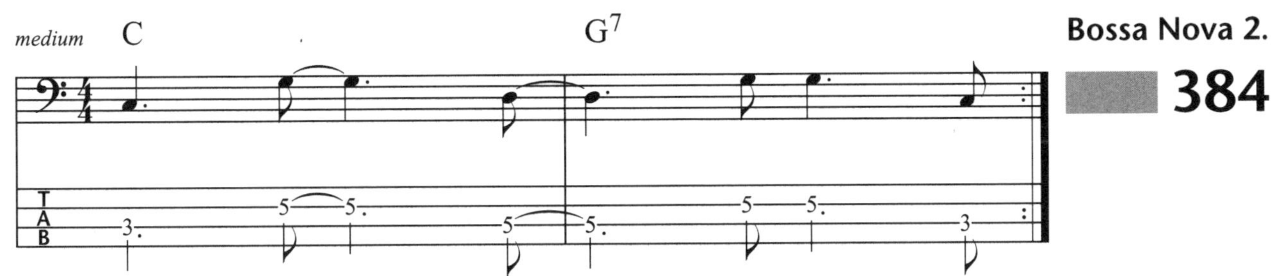
medium
C
G7
Bossa Nova 2.
384

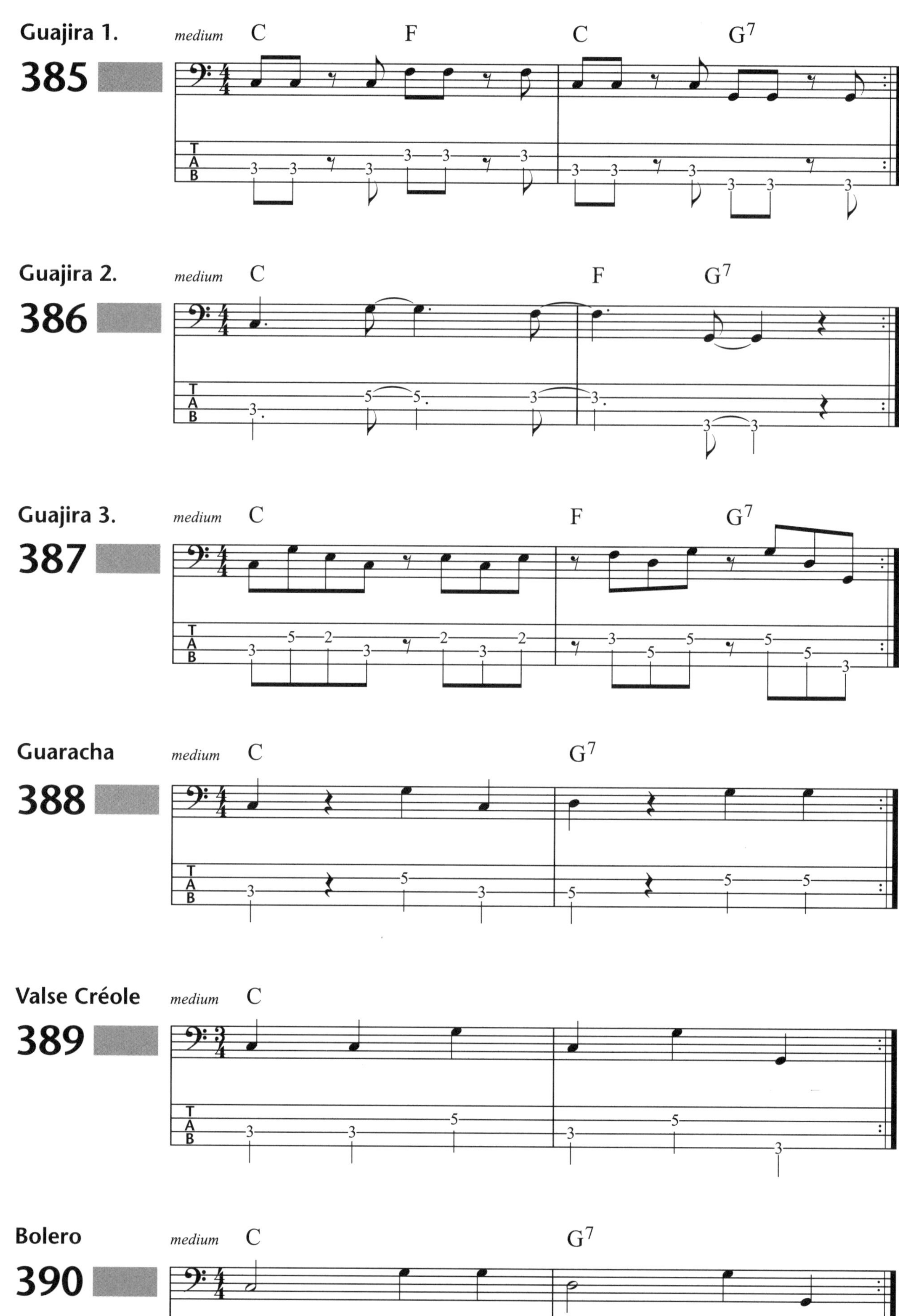
Guajira 1.
385
medium
C F C G7
Guajira 2.
386
medium
C F G7
Guajira 3.
387
medium
C F G7
Guaracha
388
medium
C G7
Valse Créole
389
medium
C
Bolero
390
medium
C G7

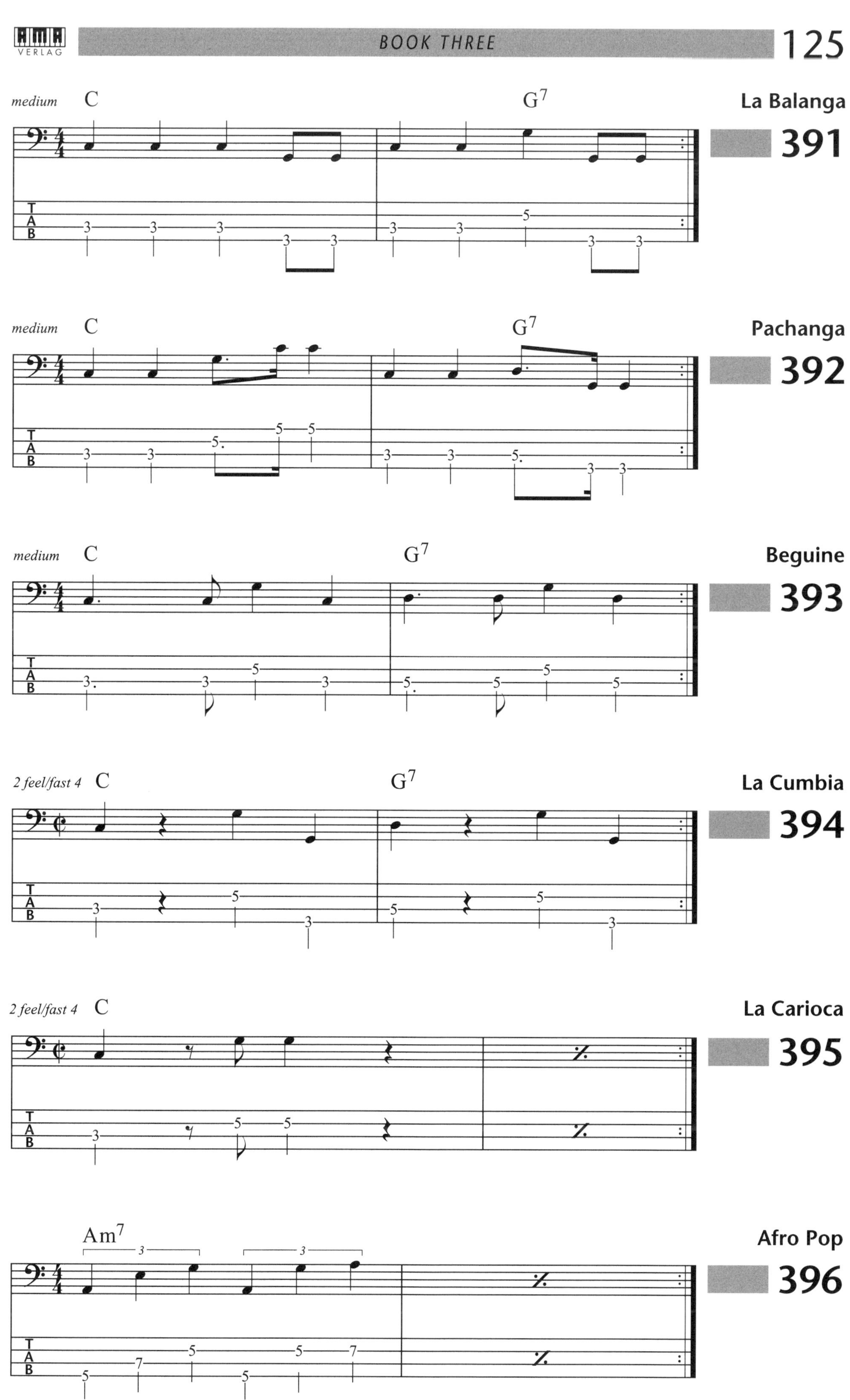
medium
C
G7
La Balanga
391
medium
C
G7
Pachanga
392
medium
C
G7
Beguine
393
2 feel/fast 4
C
G7
La Cumbia
394
2 feel/fast 4
C
La Carioca
395
Am7
Afro Pop
396

Lambada

397

Salsa

398

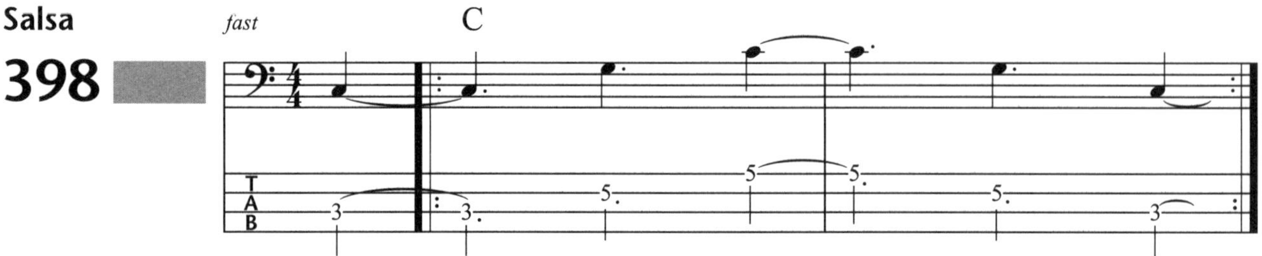

Nanigo

399

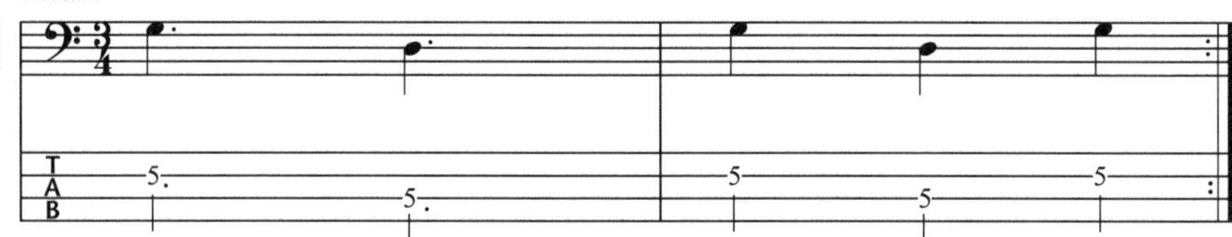

Latin Riffs

There are literally thousands of riffs used in Latin music. With a wide variety of feels to choose from, they also blend even 8th notes with triplets. When these are crossed by further rhythms, the possibilities are endless. The big problem with writing Latin bass lines down is that simple notation does not convey the way that they are played, or in what context. Only a full score can show the accompanying instruments and which rhythms they are playing. Many patterns will be played simply at first, and then expanded and improvised around during the chord sequences. There are half time feels and double time feels.

Some patterns are fairly basic to the whole arrangement and feel of the piece, and are good riffs to start with. Of course, bass lines are interchangeable with different rhythm backings and tempos. Often a tune will be based on a simple 2- or 4-in-the-bar feel.

fast G Am7

400 CD 1 Track 41

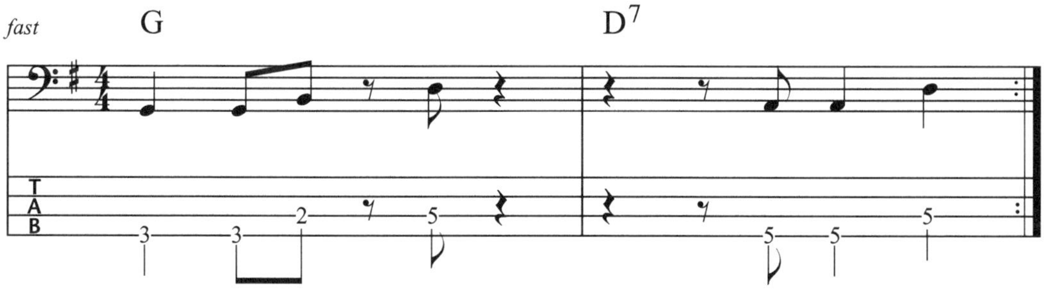

fast G D7

401 CD 1 Track 41

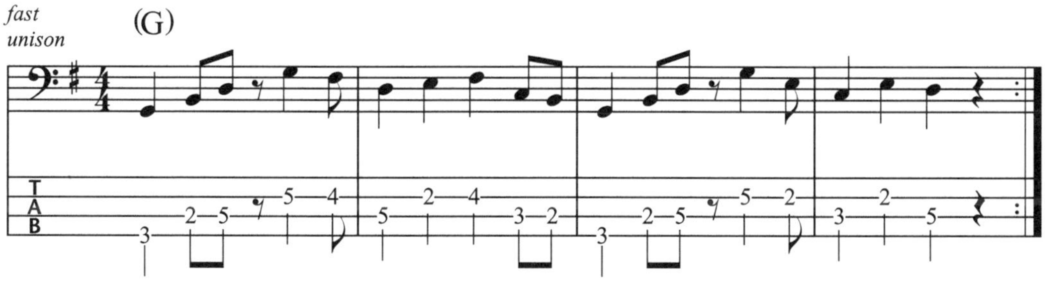

fast unison (G)

402 CD 1 Track 42

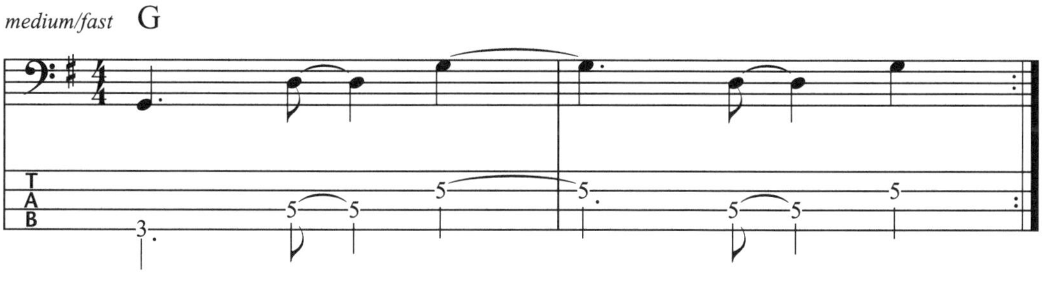

medium/fast G

403

medium G
404
CD 1 Track 42
medium G C
405
CD 1 Track 43
medium C G7
406
medium/fast G D7
407
CD 1 Track 43
medium G D7
408
fast G C
409
CD 1 Track 44

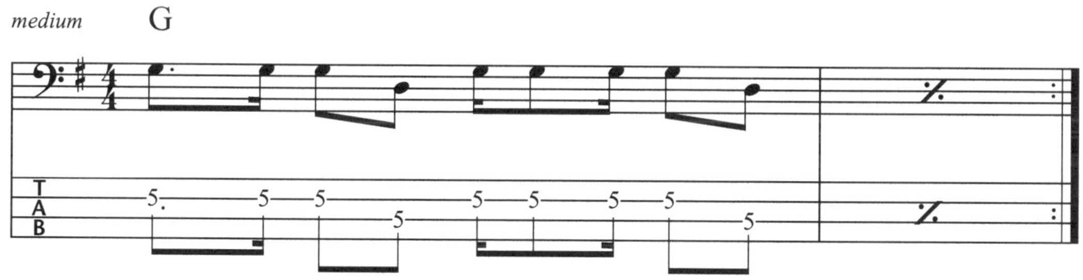

medium G

410

open key fast G

411

CD 1 Track 44

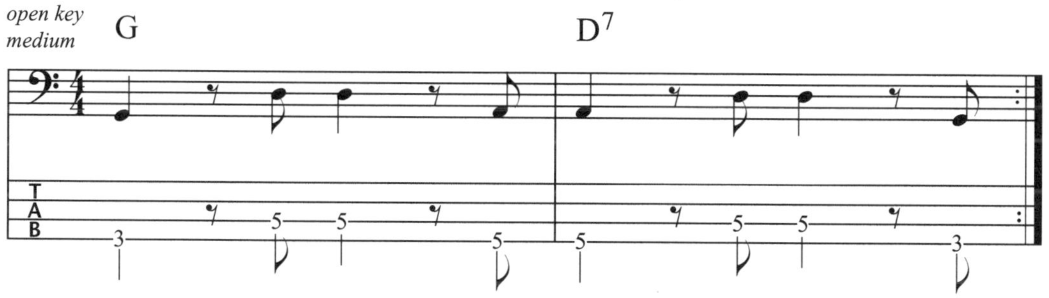

open key medium G D7

412

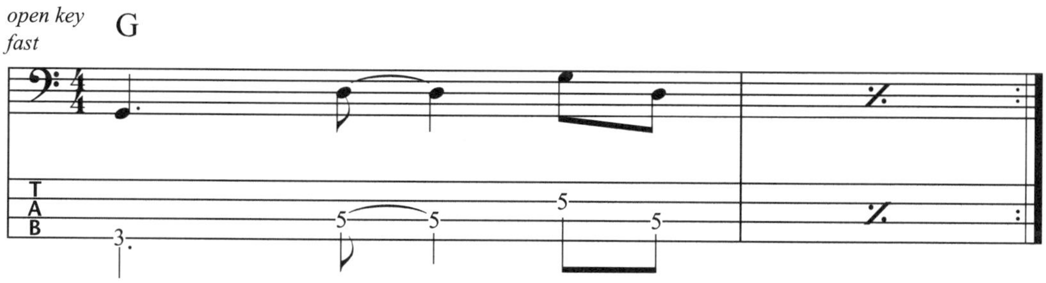

open key fast G

413

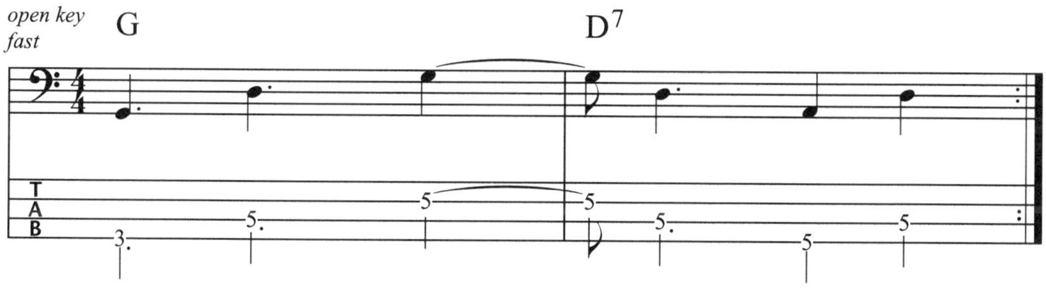

open key fast G D7

414

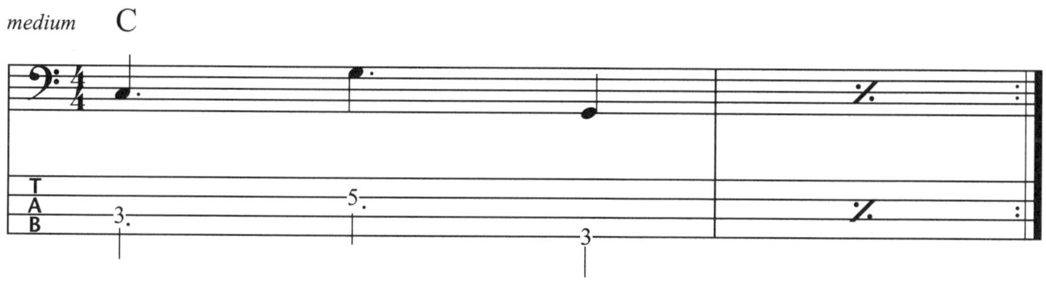

medium C

415

Double Time Latin Riffs

416
CD 1 Track 45

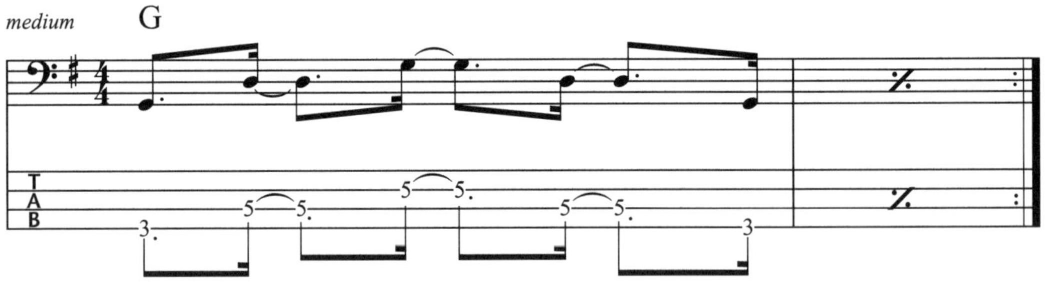

medium G

417

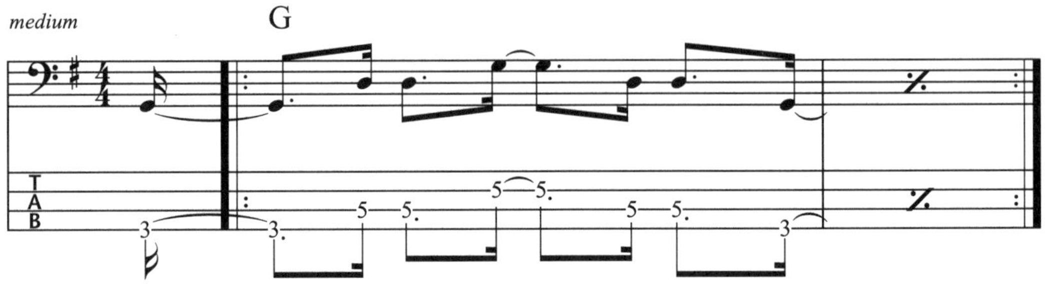

medium G

418
CD 1 Track 45

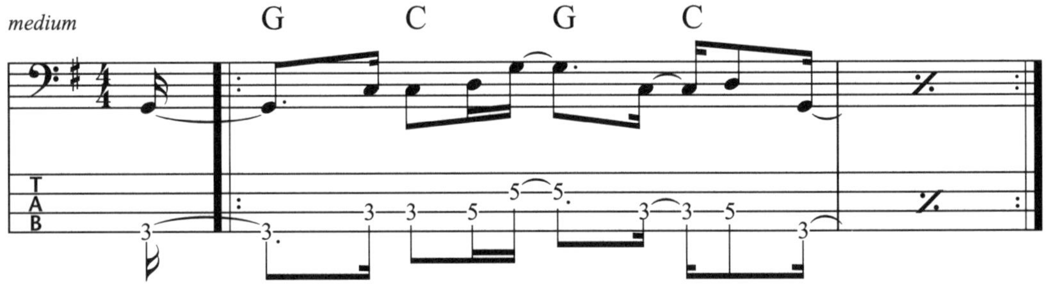

medium G C G C

419
CD 1 Track 46

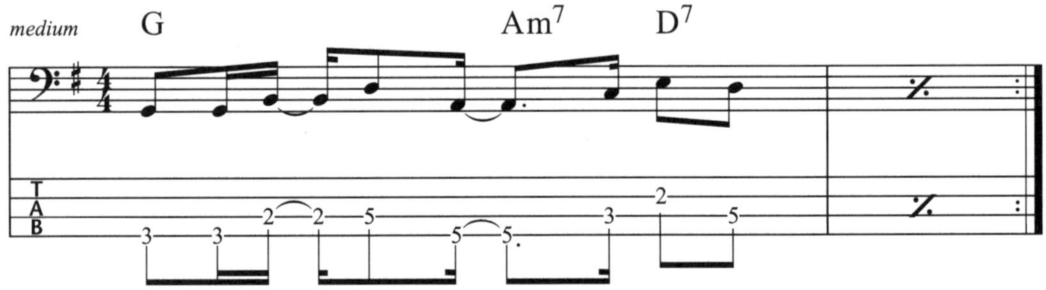

medium G Am7 D7

420
CD 1 Track 46

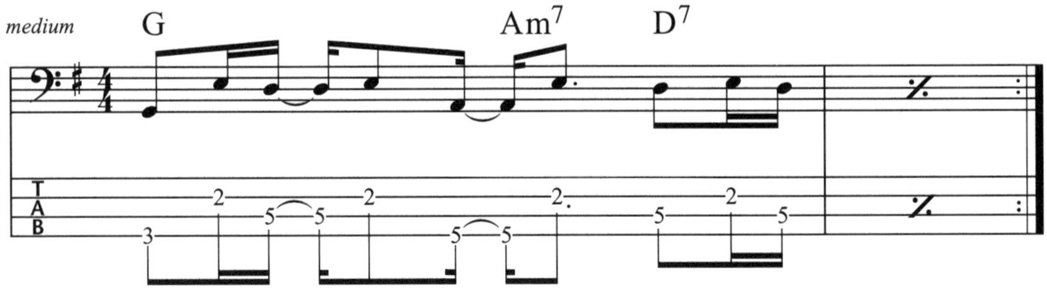

medium G Am7 D7

421
CD 1 Track 47

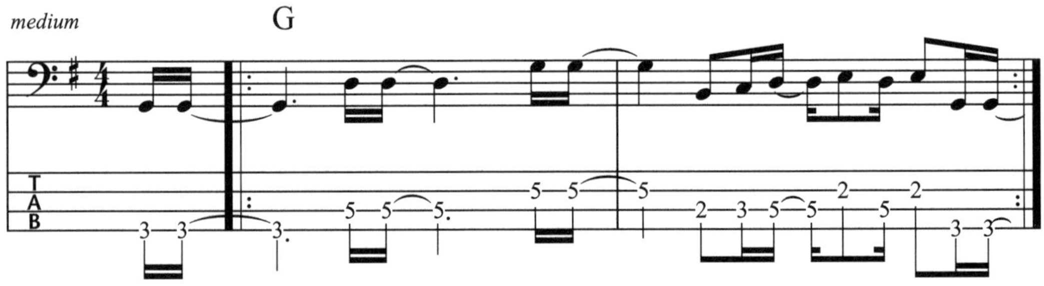

medium G

422 CD 1 Track 47

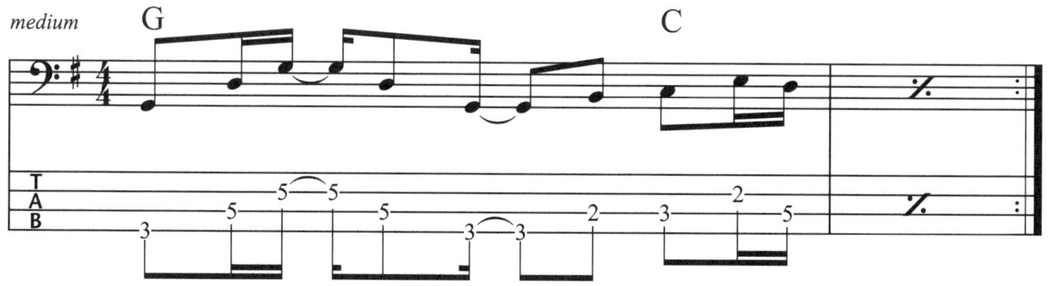

medium

G — G7 — C

423

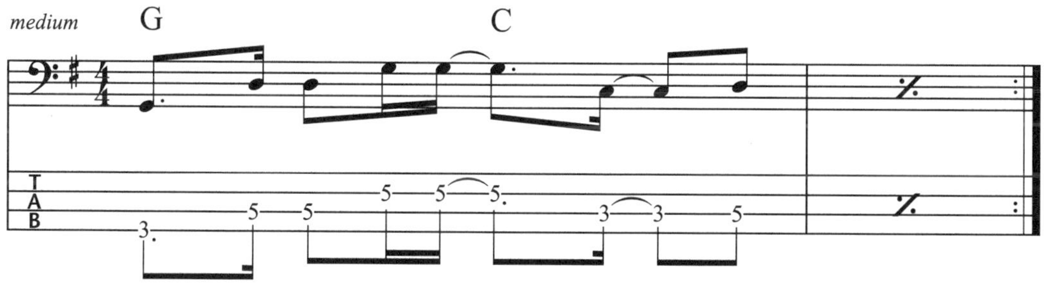

medium

G — C

424

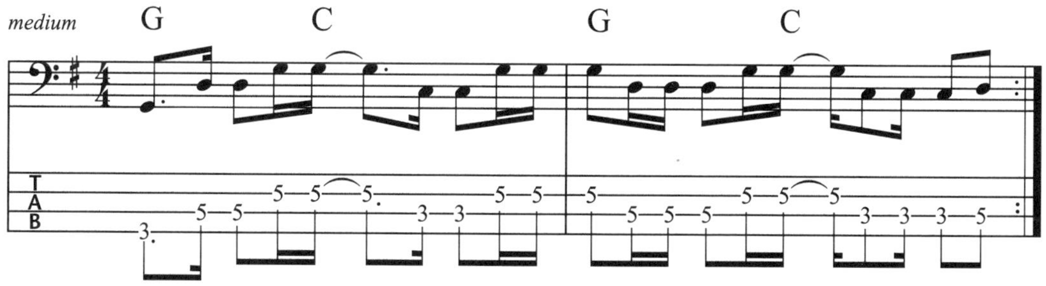

medium

G — C

425 CD 1 Track 48

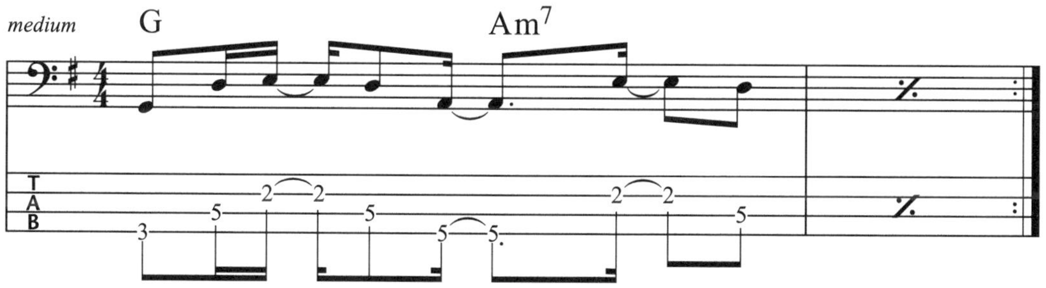

medium

G — C — G — C

426 CD 1 Track 48

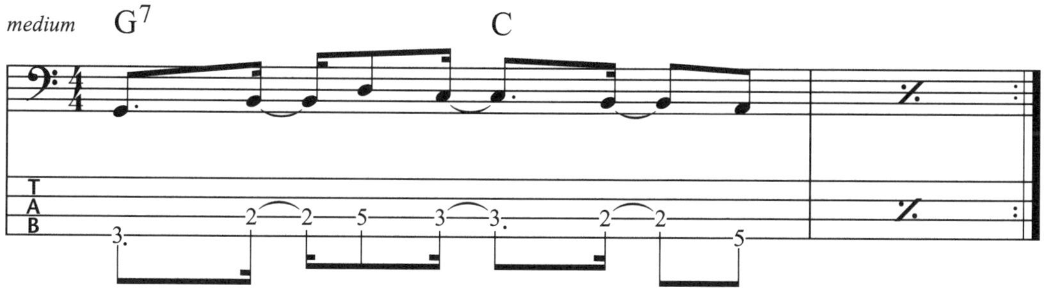

medium

G — Am7

427

medium

G7 — C

Latin Riffs – Salsa

428
fast D

429
fast D

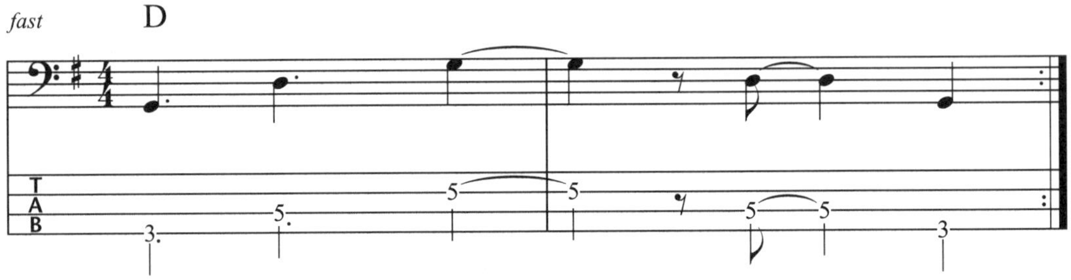

430
CD1 Track 49
fast D

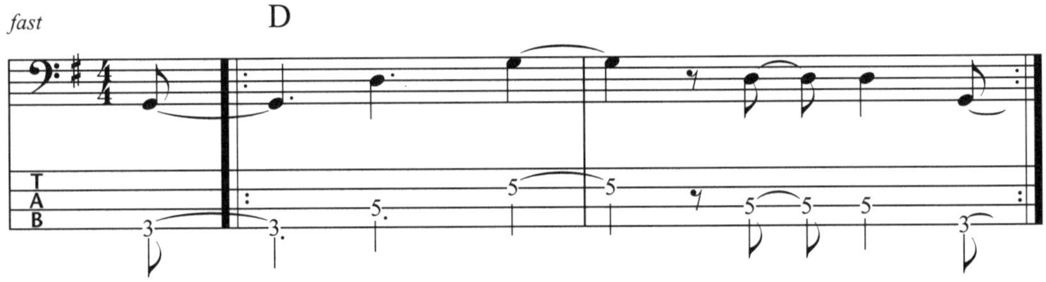

431
fast D

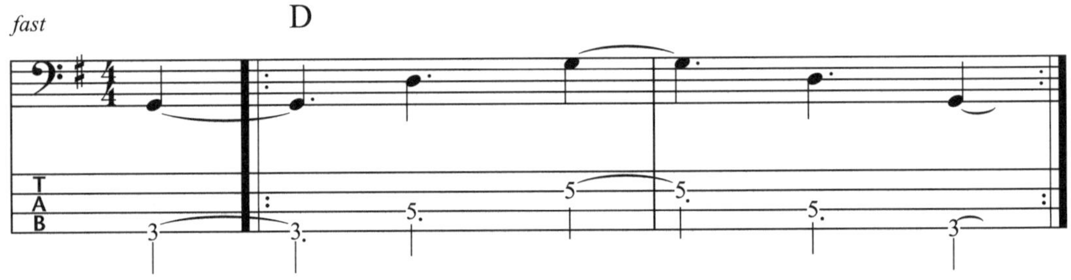

432
CD1 Track 49
fast G Em G D^7

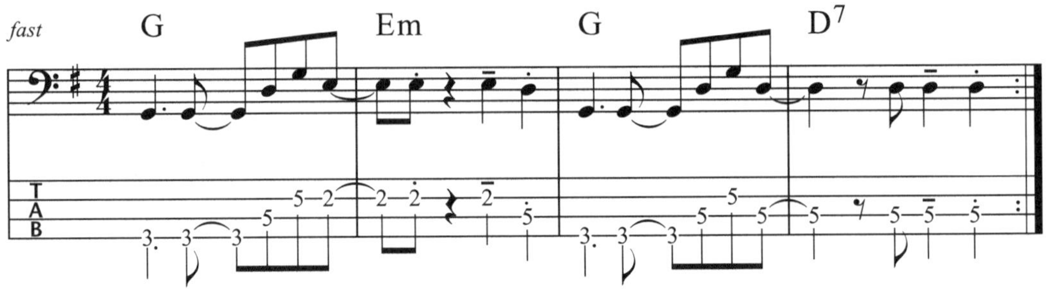

433
2 feel/fast 4 G^7 C

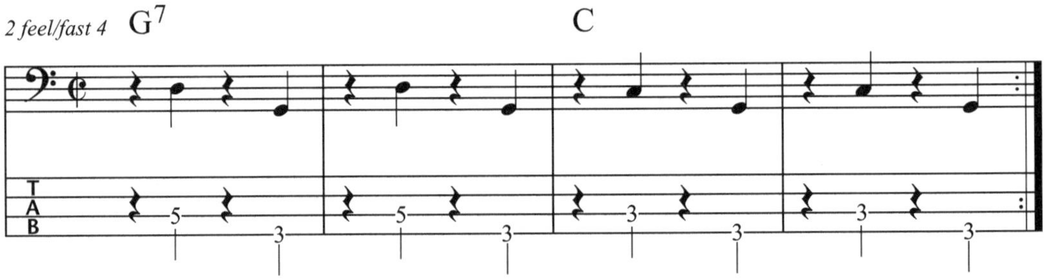

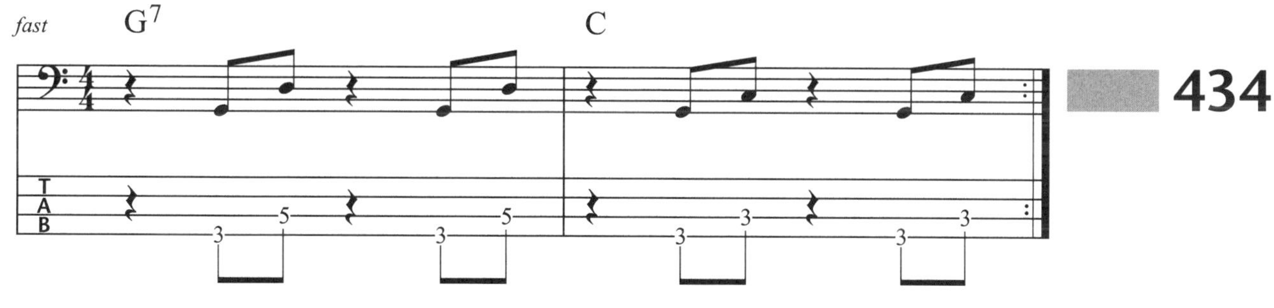
fast
G7
C
434

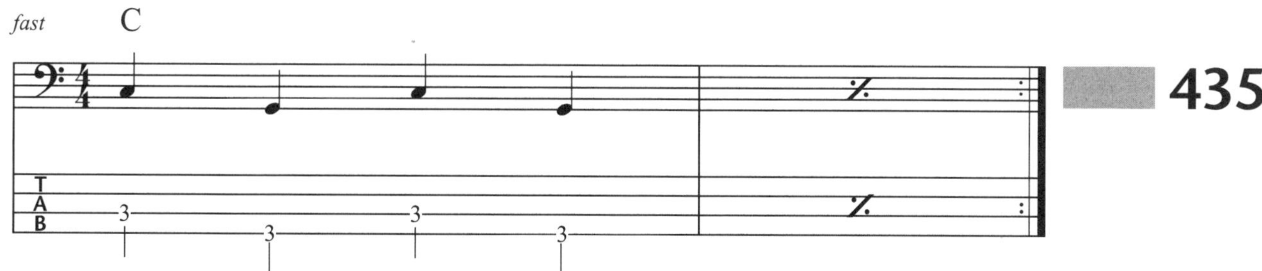
fast
C
435

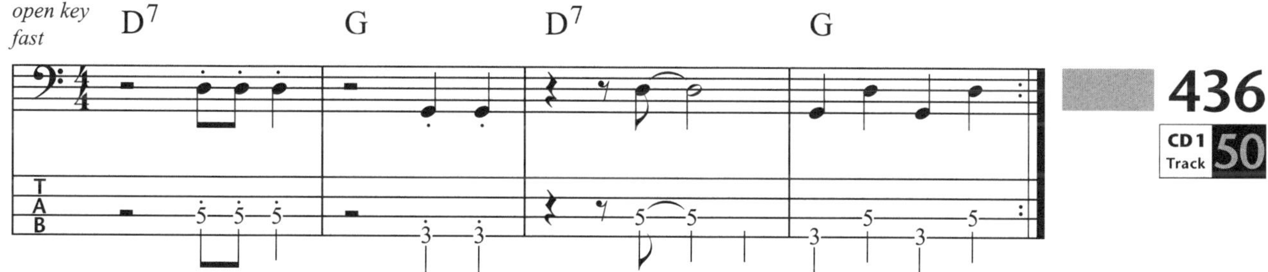
open key
fast
D7
G
D7
G
436
CD 1
Track 50

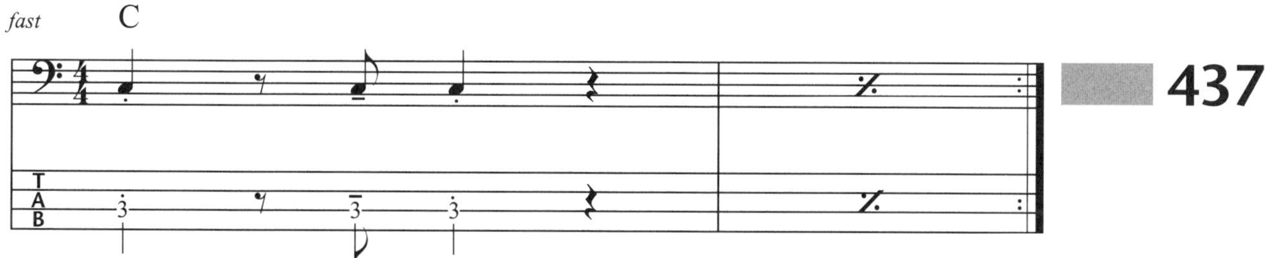
fast
C
437

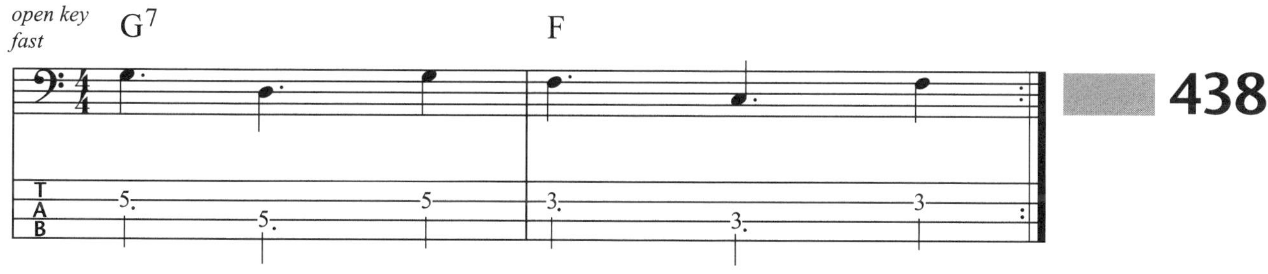
open key
fast
G7
F
438

open key
fast
G7
F
439
CD 1
Track 50

440

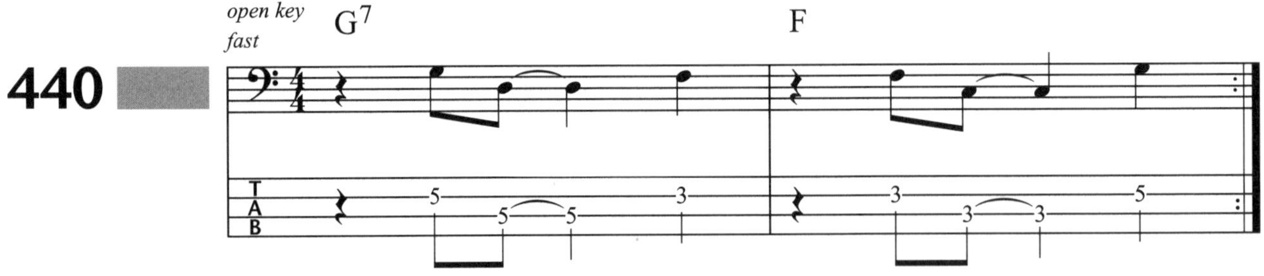

441

442
CD 1 Track 51

443
CD 1 Track 51

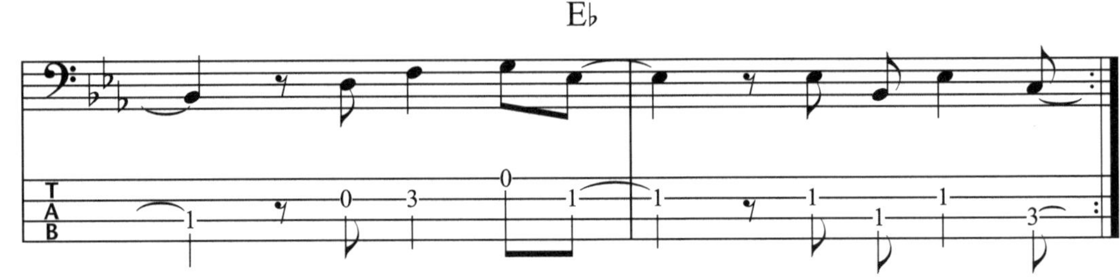

444

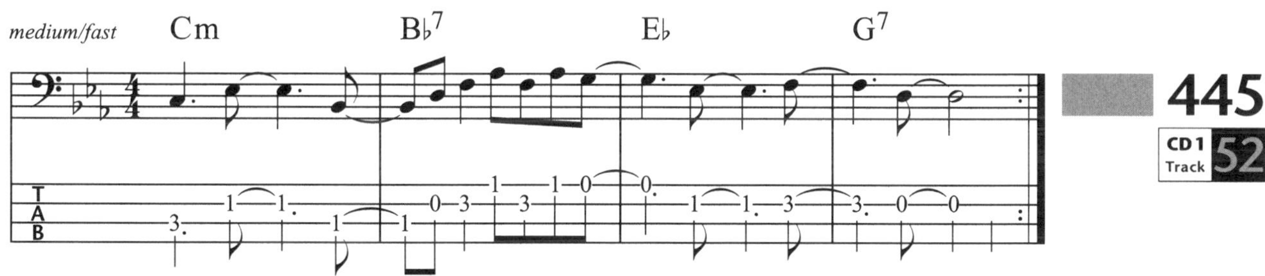
medium/fast
Cm
B♭7
E♭
G7
445
CD 1 Track 52

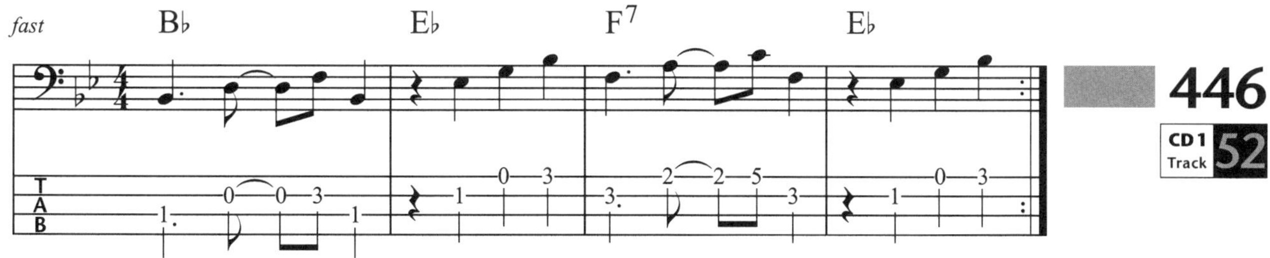
fast
B♭
E♭
F7
E♭
446
CD 1 Track 52

fast
C7
447

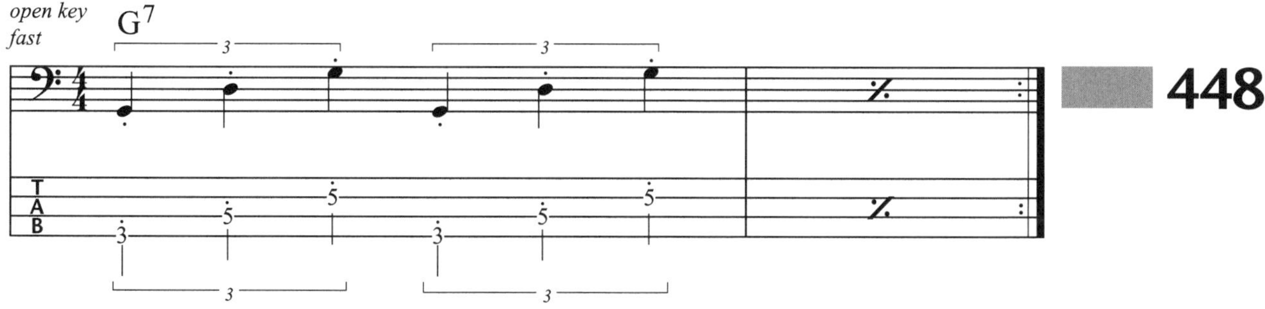
open key
fast
G7
448

Spanish Flamenco

Gipsy music has been influential in Spain for centuries. The southern people of Andalucia have adopted the race as their own. In fact, when the Spanish government wanted to rid the country of gipsy workers hundreds of years ago, a local landowner adopted the entire tribe, and christened them all with his name so that they could remain. Having spread all over Europe, their history is complex, but their music is steeped in pride, precision, colour and fiery passion. Flamenco guitars thrash out dancing patterns, and basses drive the band along with assorted rhythms and relentless grooves.

The most famous Flamenco musicians are Manitas de Plata, The Gipsy Kings, Paco de Lucia and Los Reyes.

449

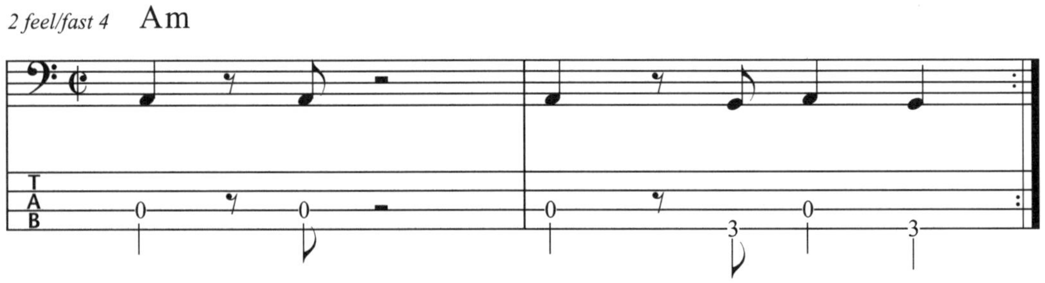

2 feel/fast 4 Am

450

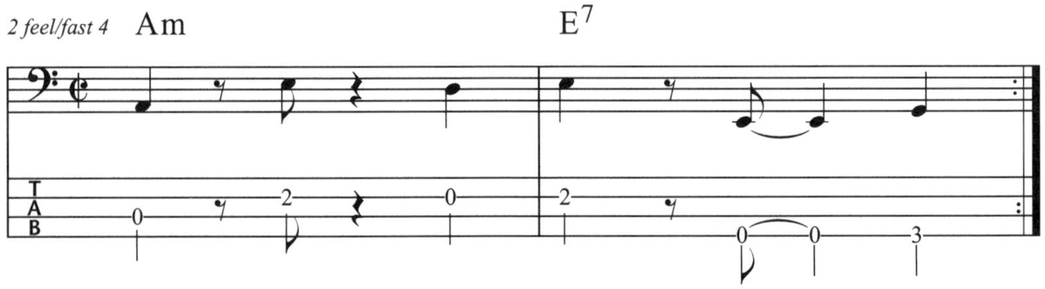

2 feel/fast 4 Am E7

451

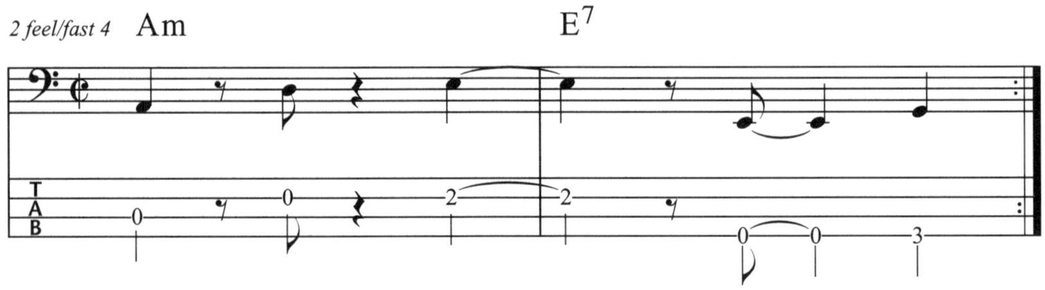

2 feel/fast 4 Am E7

452

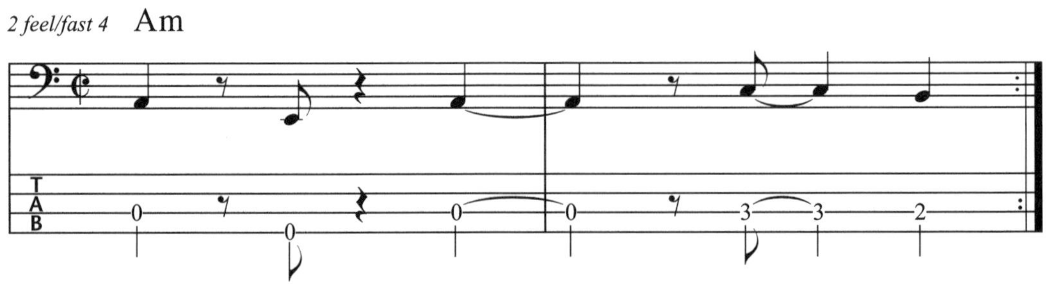

2 feel/fast 4 Am

open key
2 feel/fast 4
A7
453

open key
2 feel/fast 4
A
454

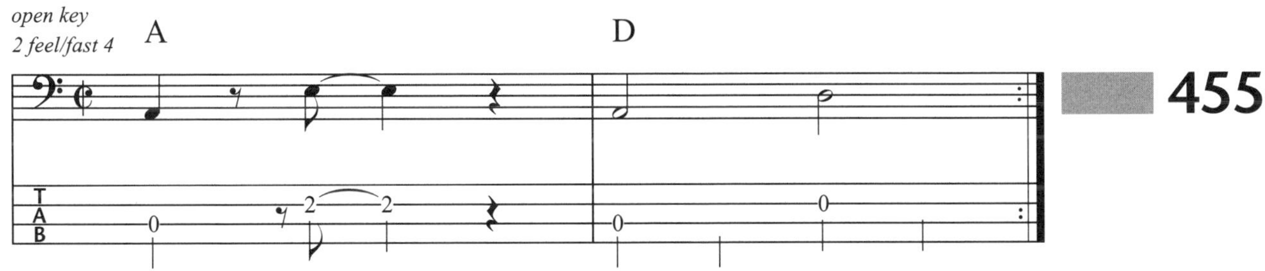
open key
2 feel/fast 4
A
D
455

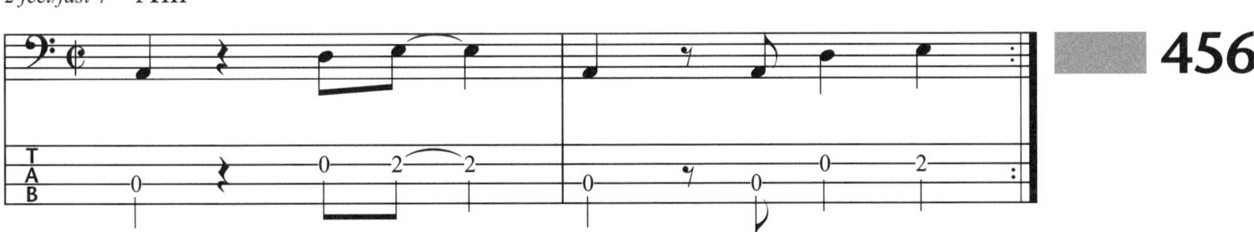
2 feel/fast 4
Am
456

open key
2 feel/fast 4
A
457

open key
2 feel/fast 4
A
458

459

460

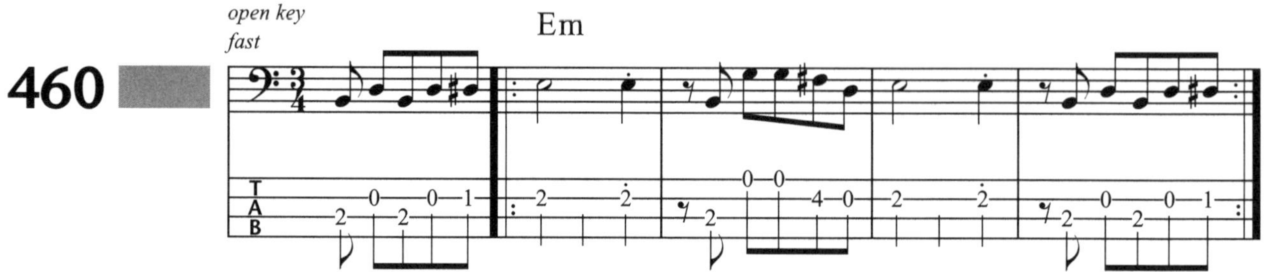

Mexican Mariachi

Mariachi is influenced mainly by Spanish music. Spanish guitars, vihuelas, trumpets, violins, light percussion and a guitarron (acoustic bass guitar) accompany the balladiers, who sing romantic songs or clap and stamp to fast tempo music. Some of the dances are even Scottish based! It is festival music.

Tempos are very varied and time signatures are based on 12/8, 3/4 and 4/4. Rhythms within the bar can be a blend of even 8th notes and triplets. The Viennese Waltz is common. Rhythm sections play a feel which is full of bounce and makes the music really swing for dancing. Mariachi is from an Indian word which refers to the wooden platform on which the dancers performed.

medium D7 G

461

fast G

462

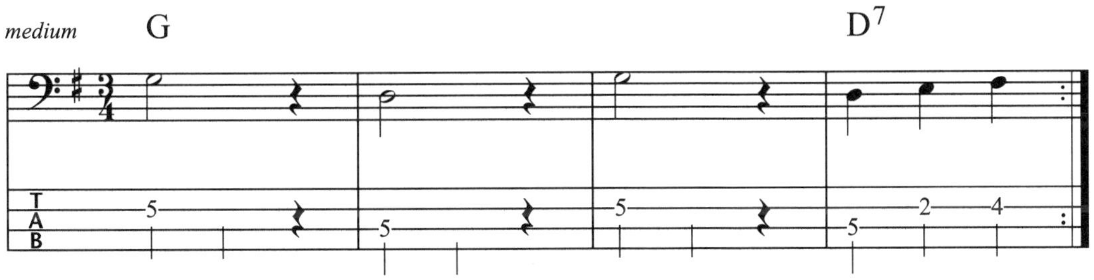

medium G D7

463

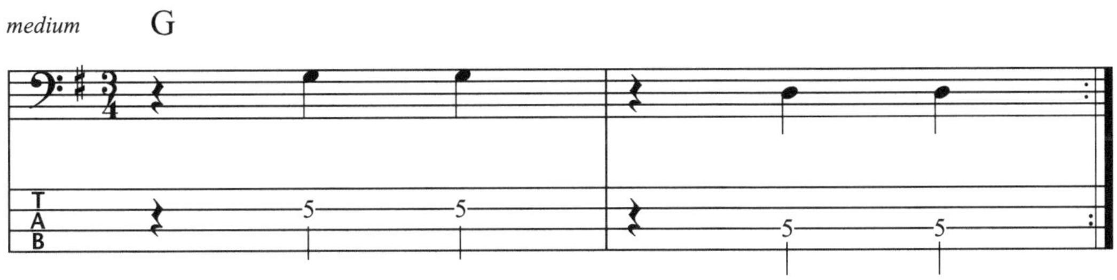

medium G

464

465

466

467

468

469

470

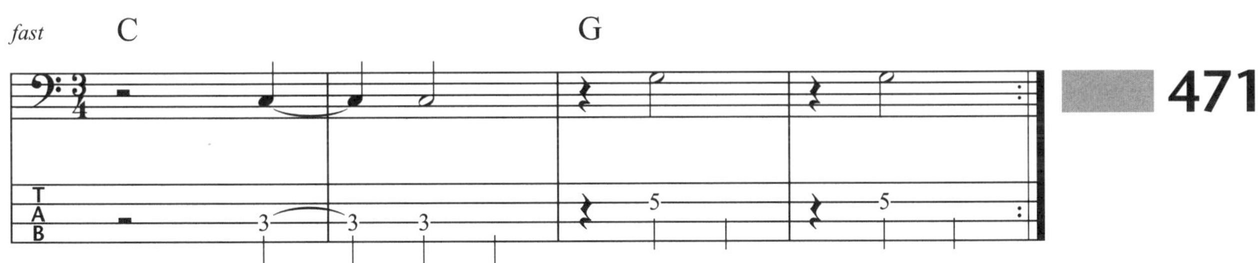
fast
C
G
471

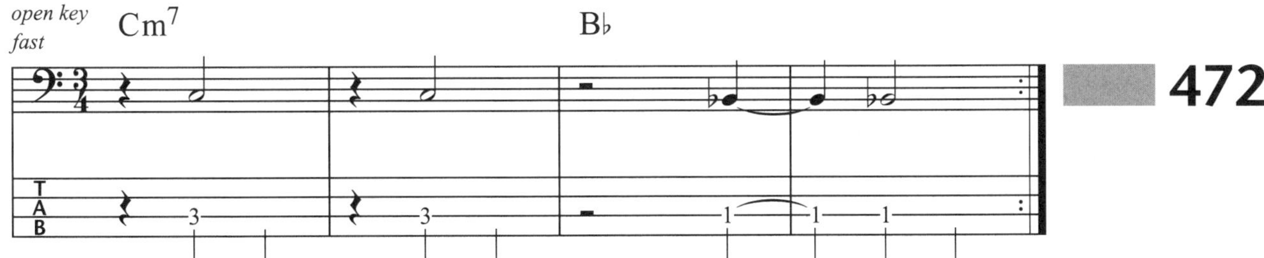
open key
fast
Cm7
B♭
472

fast
C
473

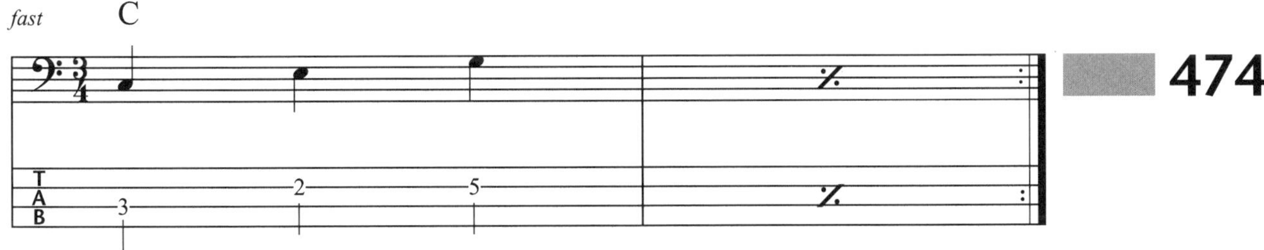
fast
C
474

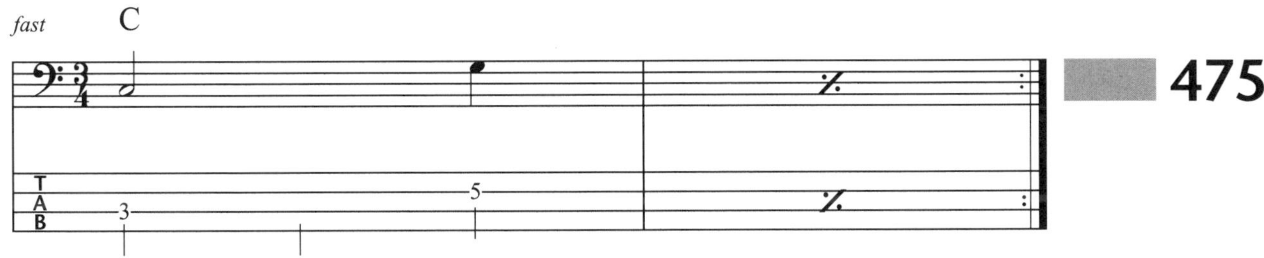
fast
C
475

fast
C
G7
476

477

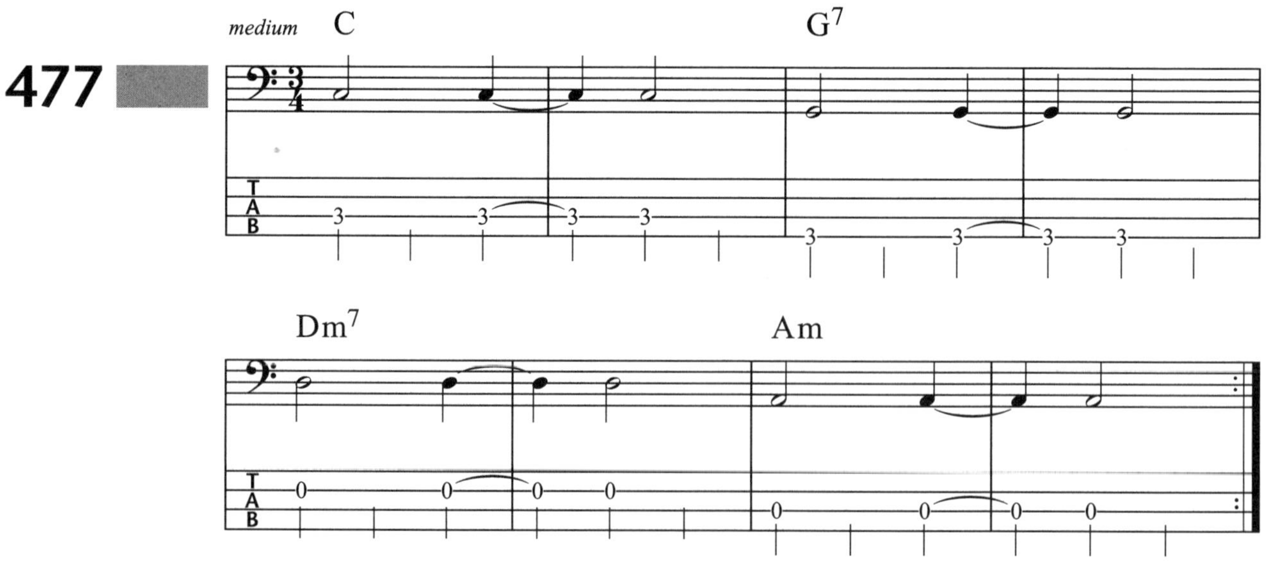

478

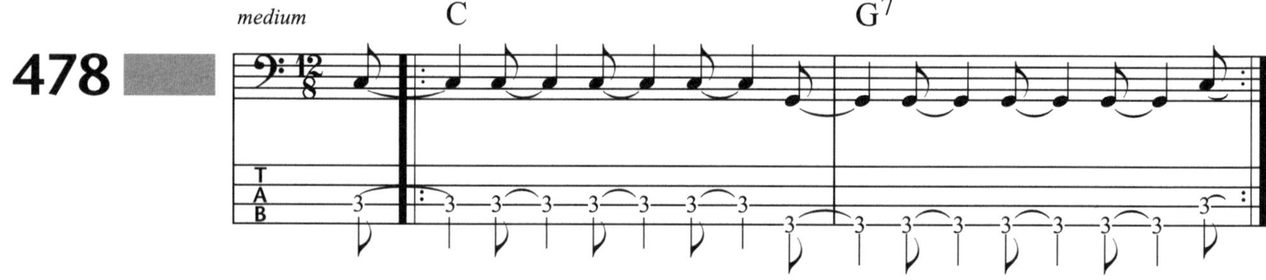

479

480

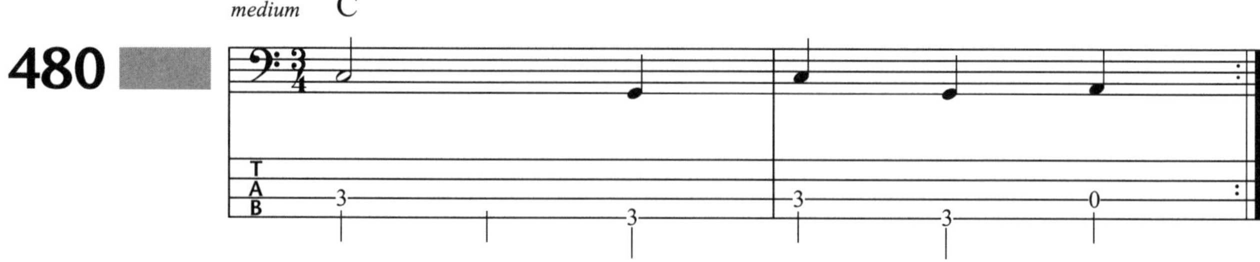

Cuban Mambo

Mambo in Cuba was a product of the pre-revolution era. Some of the next generation rejected this form of music and produced more of the rock-based Salsa music. Mambo became, and still is, a very popular form of dance music.

Tito Puento, José Fajardo, Tito Rodriguez, Tico All-Stars, Charlie Palmieri and Celia Cruz are some of the leaders of this style. The rhythm section traditionally consists of Conga drums leading the whole band, supported by double bass and piano.

Mambo is basically an African rhythm. Slaves introduced their music to Cuba, where it was influenced by native rhythms which were used in jungle rituals and ceremonies.

It became modified through the years and then spread to the USA, where it fused with Jazz and Bop. Jazz leaders like Stan Kenton, Dizzy Gillespie, Duke Ellington and Woody Herman all used Mambo influences in their music to produce a more modern, dance-based Jazz, which was often more commercially successful and attracted a wider audience than the traditional big band swing arrangements.

Mambo stresses the off-beats, whereas the Rumba, its predecessor, is more on the beat. Mambo is much looser and Jazz orientated. The Cha Cha is a variation of this.

Famous Mambo bassists include Israel "Cachao" Lopez, his son Orlando "Cachaito" Lopez, Ignacio Pineiro and Joseito Beltran.

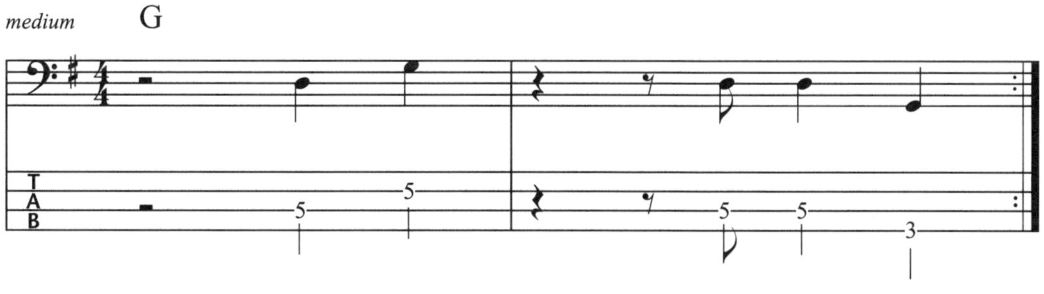

medium G

481

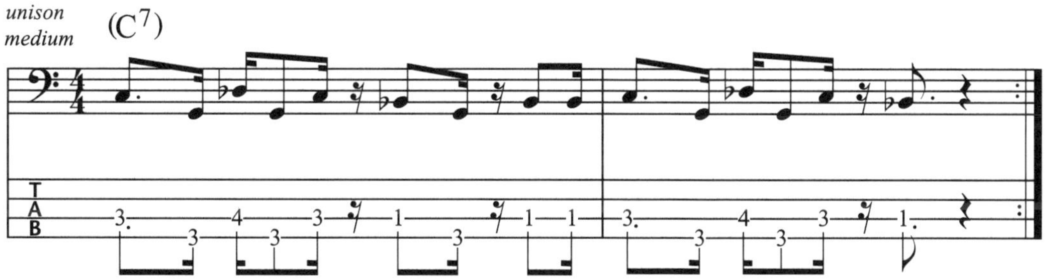

unison
medium (C7)

482

CD1 Track 53

medium G7 C

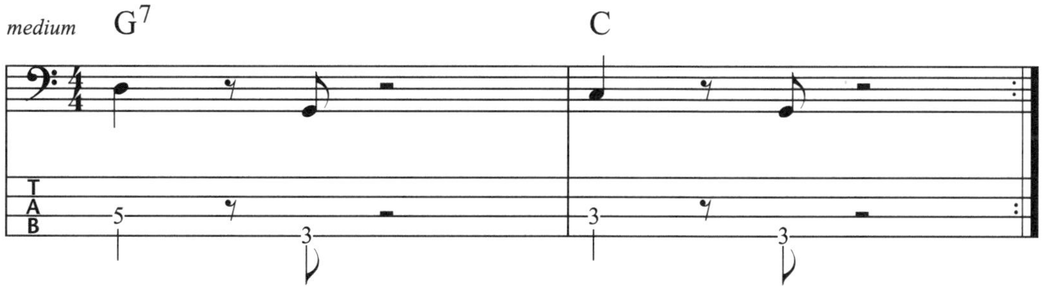

483

484
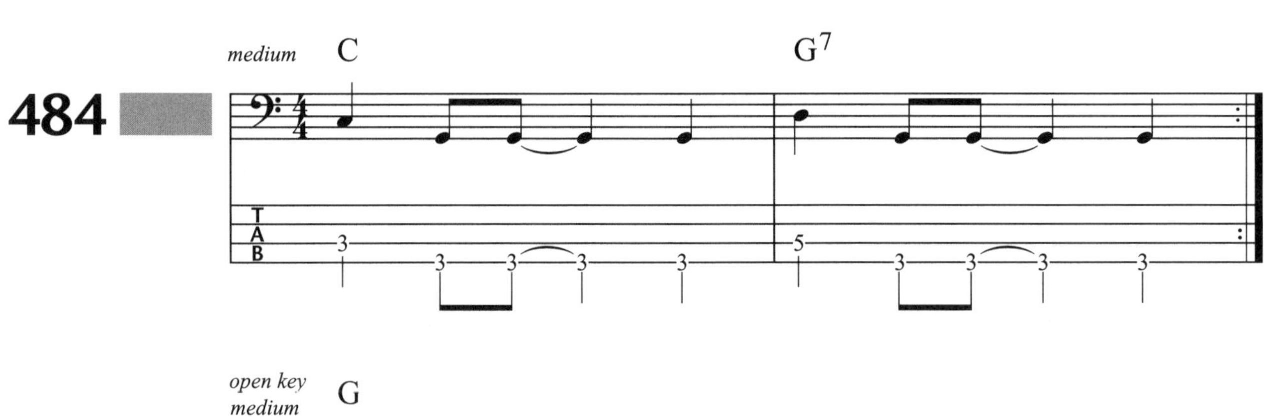

485

486
CD 1 Track 53

487
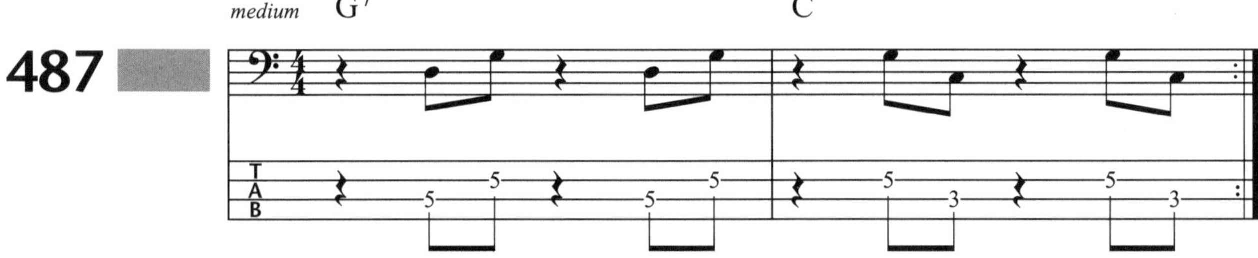

488
CD 1 Track 54
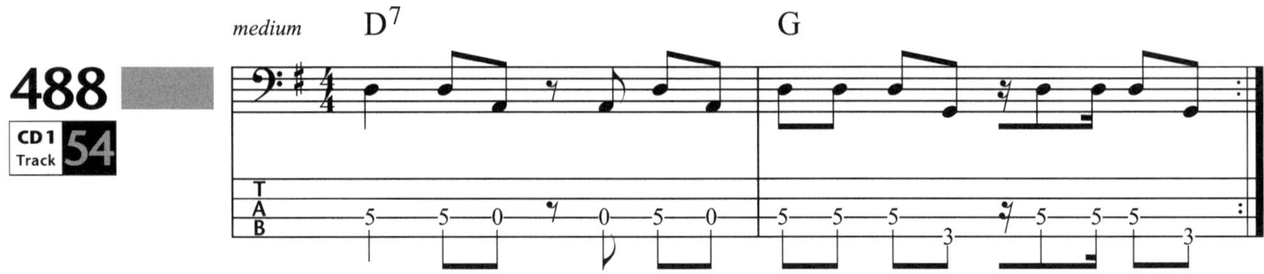

489
CD 1 Track 54
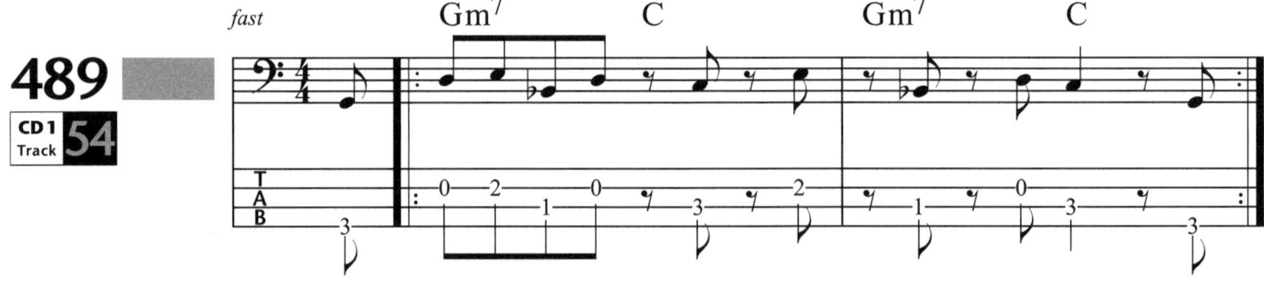

fast
G
490

fast
Gm
491
CD 1 Track 55

open key
medium
G
492

open key
medium
G
493

medium
C
494

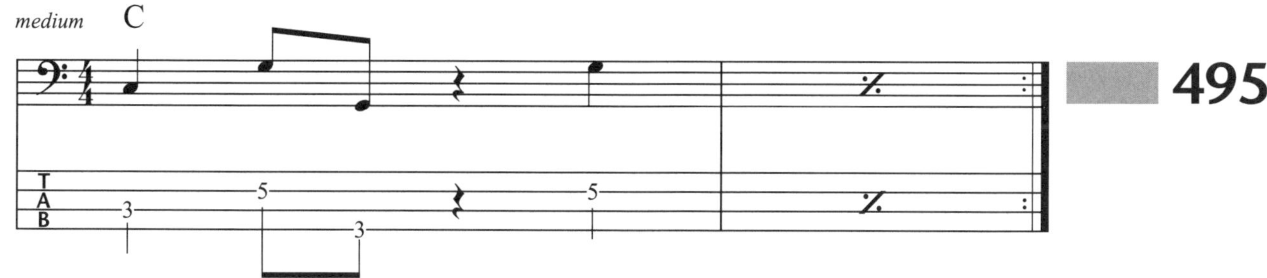
medium
C
495

496
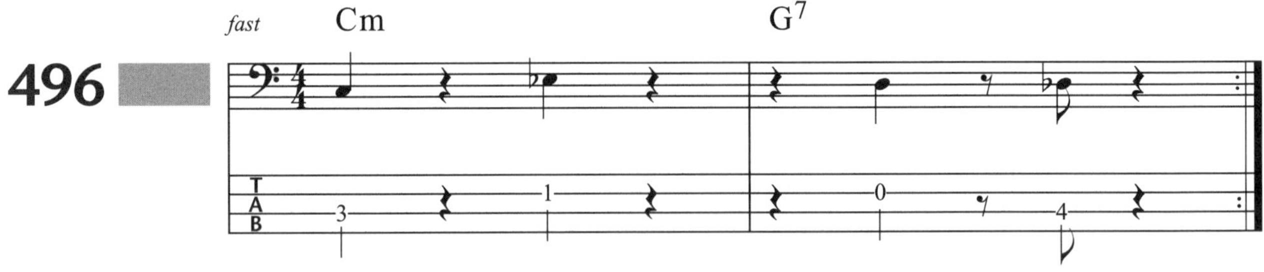

497

498
CD 1 Track 55

499

500

501

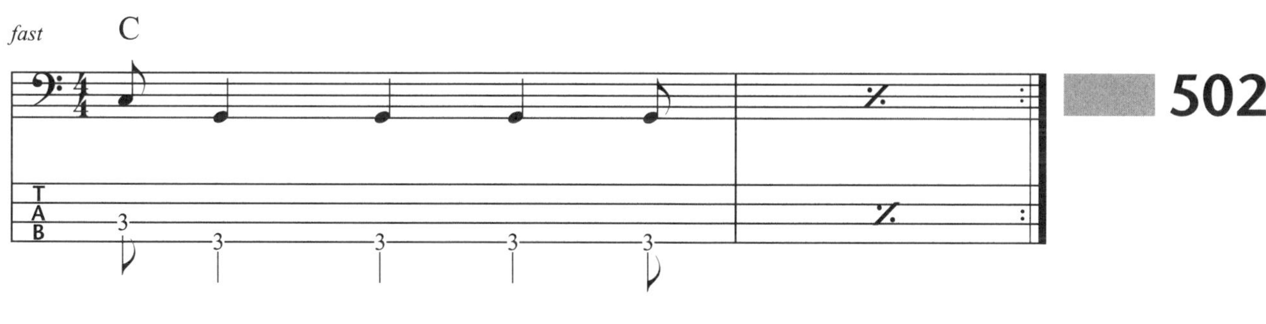
fast
C
502

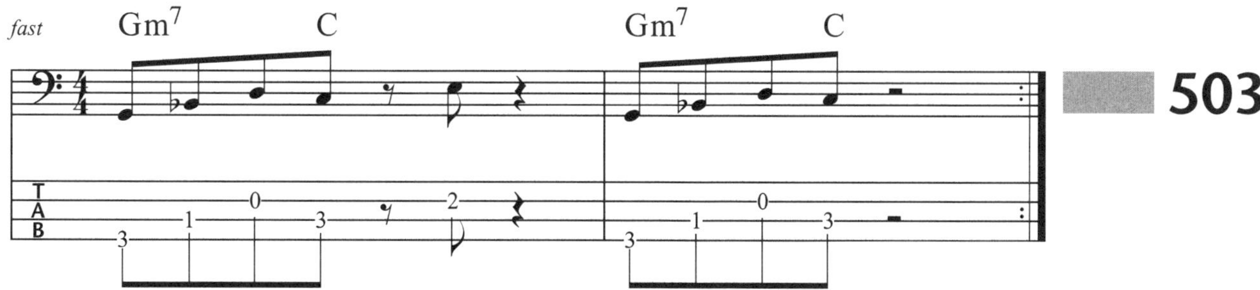
fast
Gm7
C
Gm7
C
503

medium/fast
C7
504

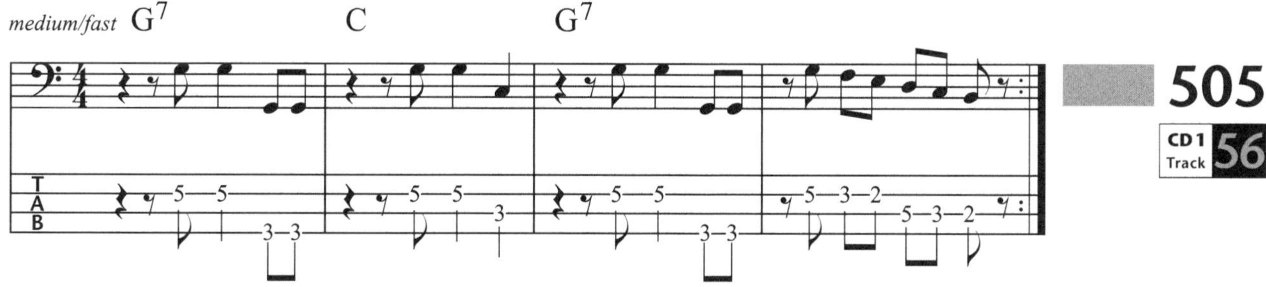
medium/fast
G7
C
G7
505
CD 1 Track 56

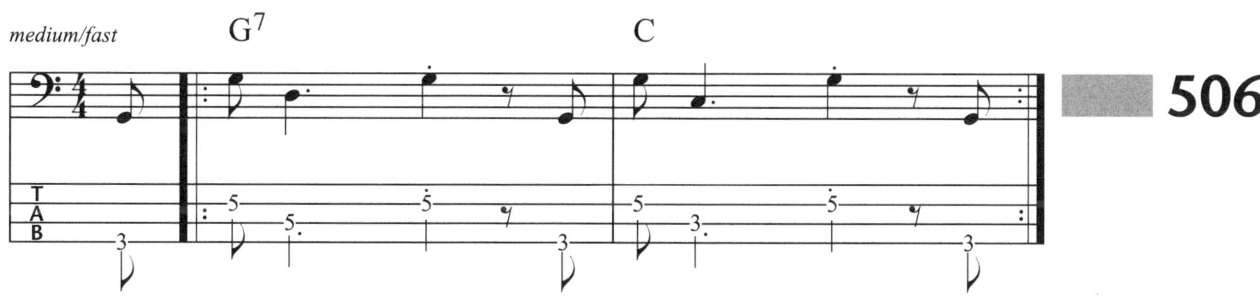
medium/fast
G7
C
506

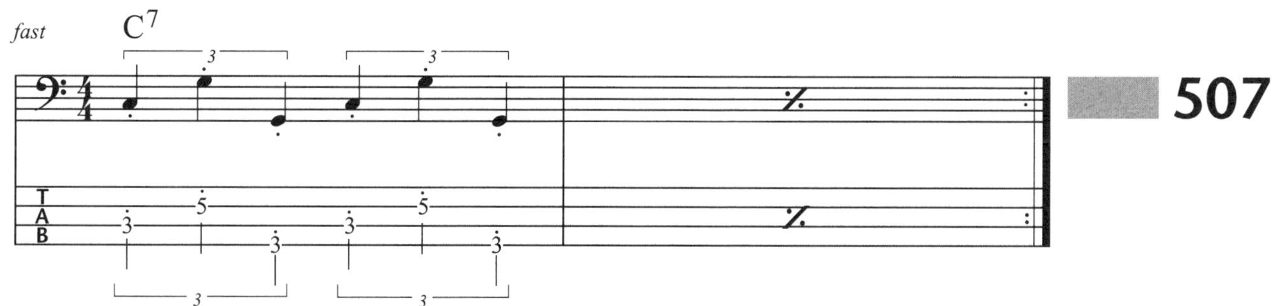
fast
C7
507

■ Cuban Rock

Cuba has remained largely isolated from the rest of the world. However, it has still received music from outside, and consequently, maintained its musical contact. Their music has developed uniquely and the Cubans have produced some very interesting ideas. With the relaxation of trading restrictions, their music has only recently begun to become available.

Many Cubans emigrated to America, and mixed their brand of dance music with the contemporary scene in Florida. Gloria Estefan and the Miami Sound Machine were a very successful band, who incorporated Cuban rhythms into their arrangements. Silvio Rodriguez is a well-known Cuban singer who has taken his "Nueva Trova" (new song) music all over South America, and even played to audiences of around 90,000 in Chile. Other well-known Cuban performers are Sindo Garay, Los Van Van, Noel Nicolla, Pablo Milanes and the Jazz Group "Irakere". Much of Cuba's popular dance music is called Salsa, which was exported to New York, and then spread elsewhere to produce variations in other countries. Contemporary Cuban bass players include Silvio Vergara, Juan Formell, Carlos Del Puerto, Felipe Cabrera, Feliciano Arrango, Carlitos Puerto Jnr, Angel De Jesus, Charles and Jorge Reyes.

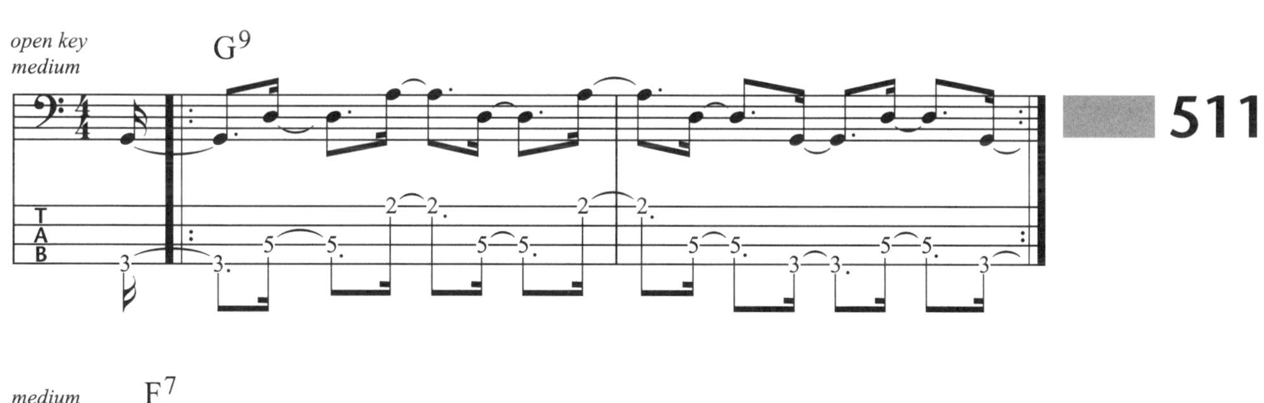

511

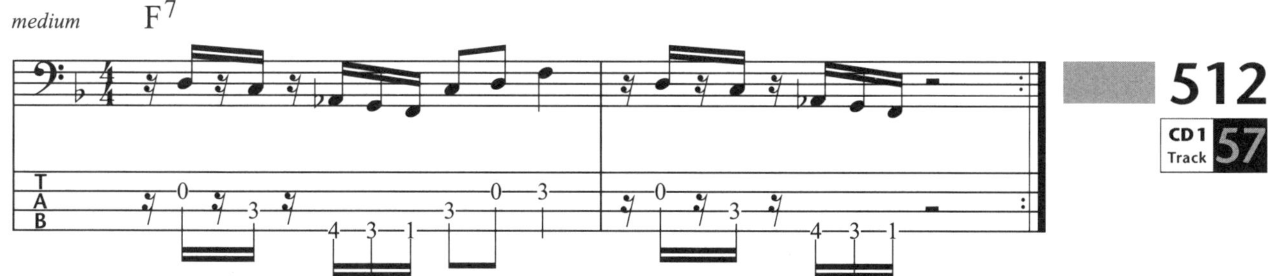

512
CD 1 Track 57

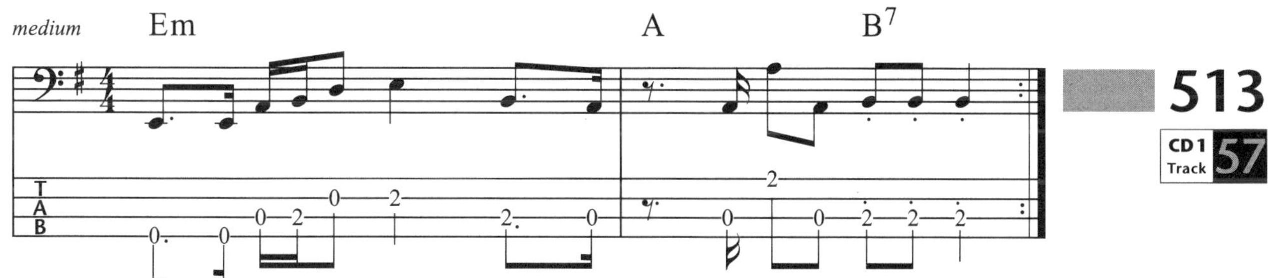

513
CD 1 Track 57

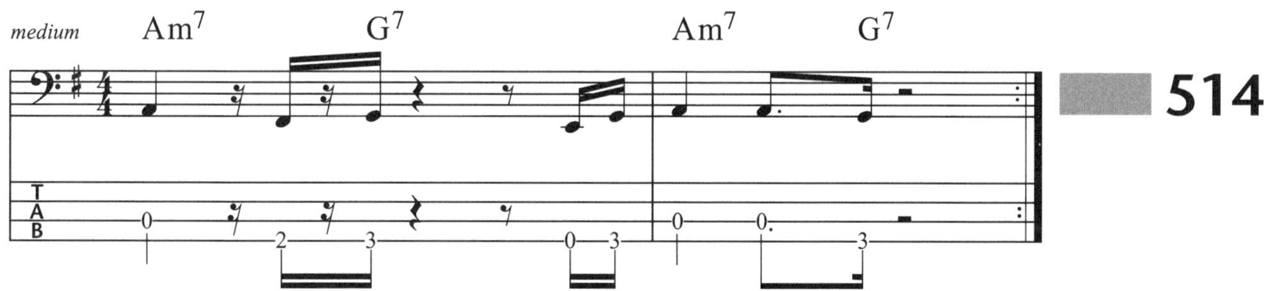

514

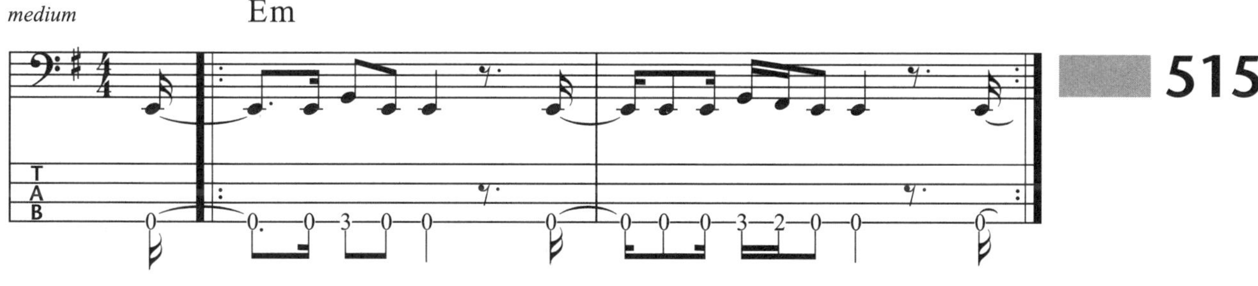

515

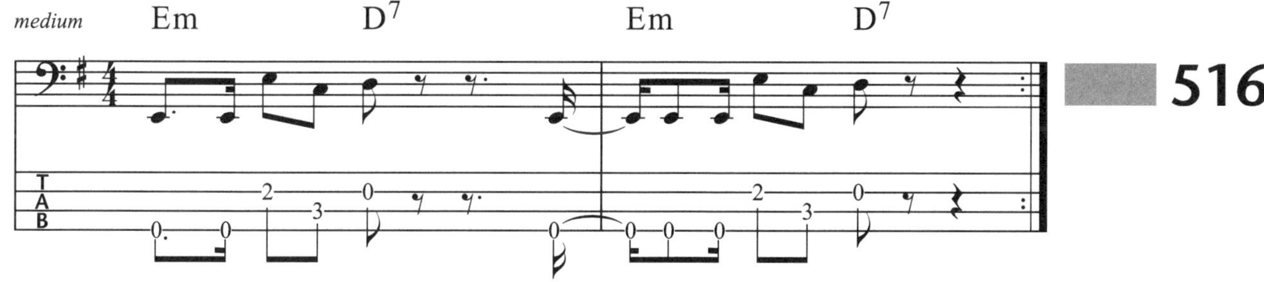

516

517
CD 1 Track 58
medium
Em
A
B7

518
CD 1 Track 58
medium
F♯m7
B7

519
open key
medium
Em

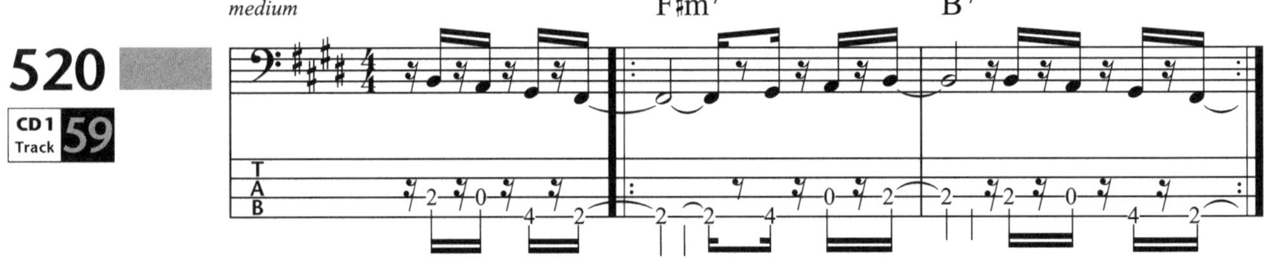
520
CD 1 Track 59
medium
F♯m7
B7

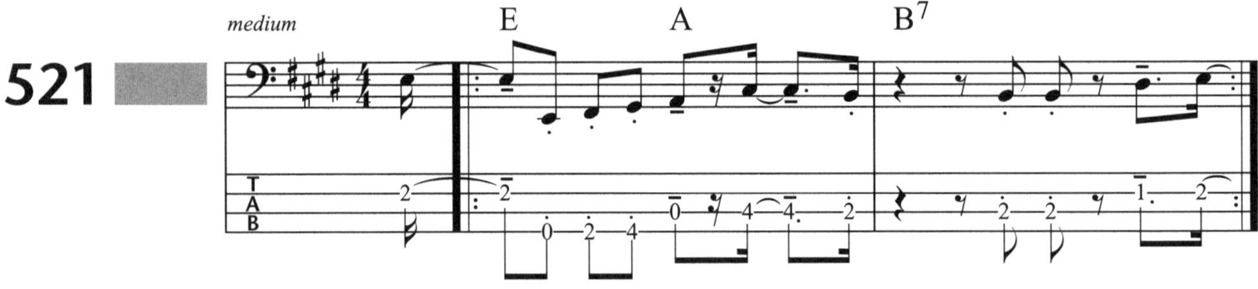
521
medium
E
A
B7

522
open key
medium
E7
D7

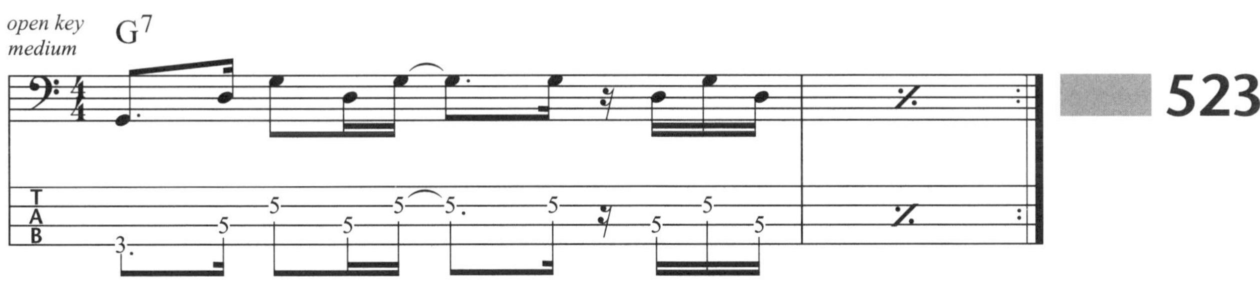
open key
medium
G7
523

medium
E
F♯m7
B7sus4
524

open key
medium
G
525

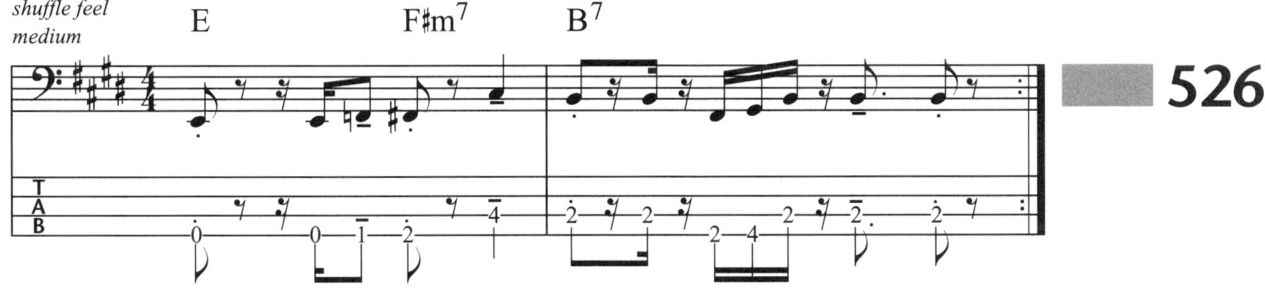
shuffle feel
medium
E
F♯m7
B7
526

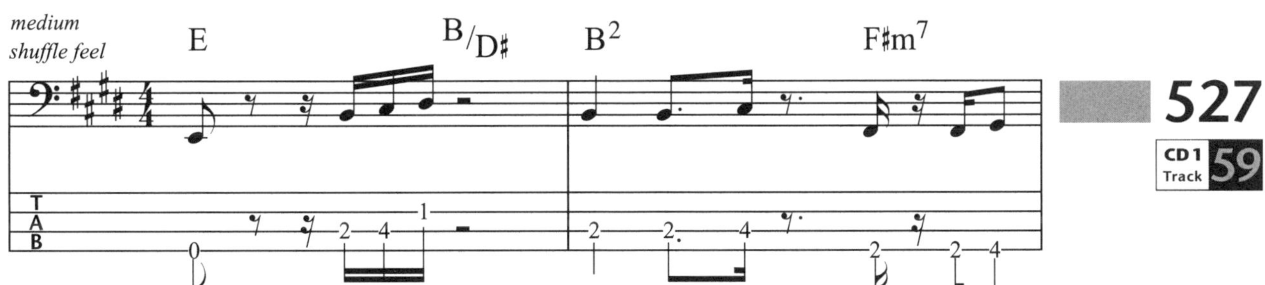
medium
shuffle feel
E
B/D♯
B2
F♯m7
527
CD 1 Track 59

A
B7
E
A
A/B

528
medium
shuffle feel
Fm7
Gm7
C7
T
A
B

529
medium
C7
F7
T
A
B

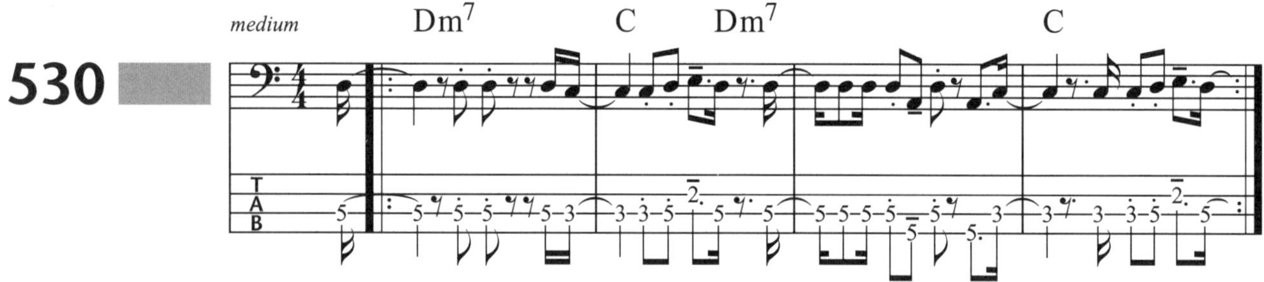
530
medium
Dm7
C
Dm7
C
T
A
B

531
open key
medium
Dm7
T
A
B

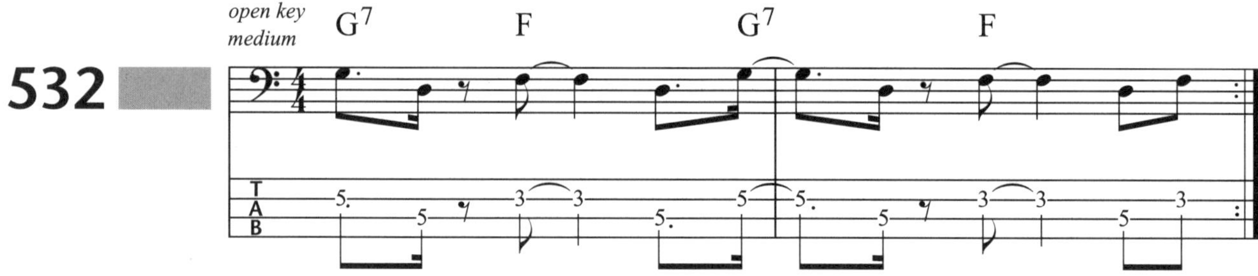
532
open key
medium
G7
F
G7
F
T
A
B

533
CD1
Track 60
medium
Gm7
Am7
Cm7
Gm7
T
A
B

534

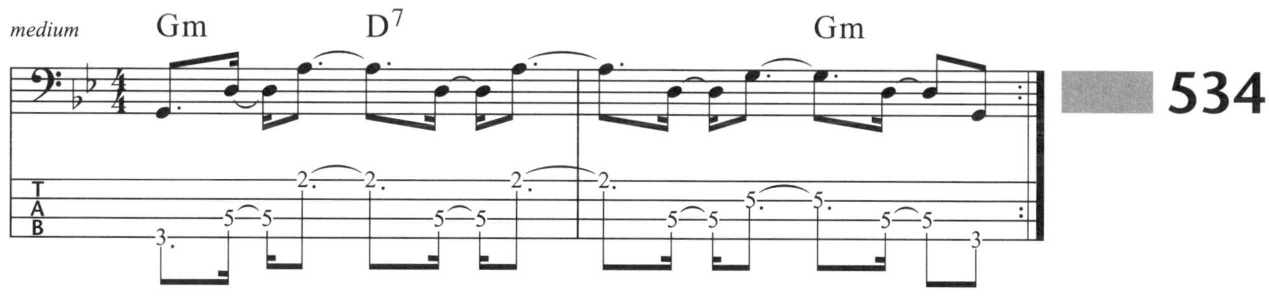

535

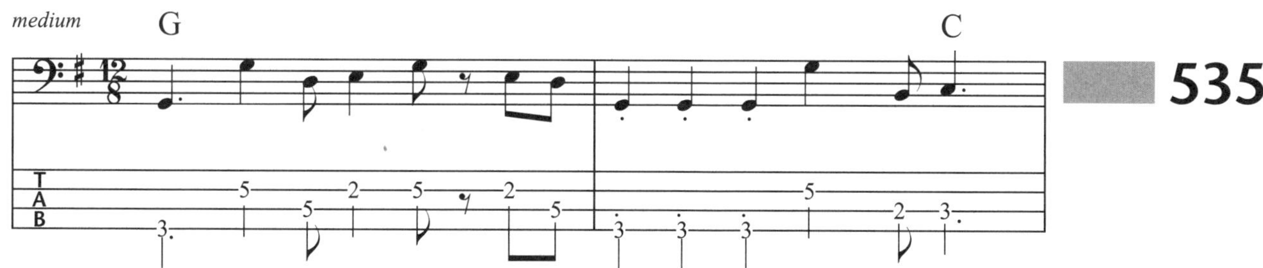

536

CD 1 Track 60

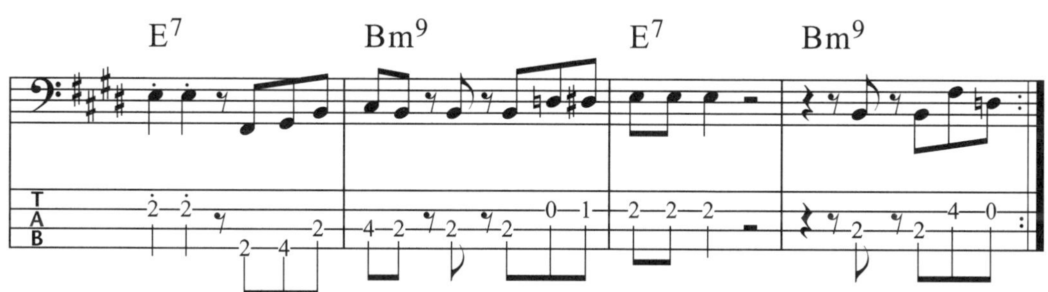

Jamaican Reggae

Reggae comes from Jamaica in the West Indies. Its biggest star was Bob Marley. He led Reggae to international popularity and made it successful throughout the world. Many rhythms are African dance-based and quite hypnotic. The bass is usually deep and dominating, although it is sometimes played more lightly in ballads and in a 4 beat "skip" feel.

In the Latin tradition, bass lines are varied and can be complex. Straight even rhythms, triplets, shuffles, 4 in-a-bar swing, 8th and 16th note feels are all used, but usually with a simple rhythm section line up. The bass guitar mainly plays solid riffs and the drums keep a steady rhythm. They provide an interesting background for songs which can be either full of space or rhythmically complex. Harmonically the music is simple in the African tradition.

Reggae also has many concepts. Either the music has a constant insistent rhythm, or it can be full of unexpected gaps which create a sense of calm. Spaces can also have the effect of leaving a motif unresolved, so the listener is constantly waiting for the resolution or answering phrase. Where the downbeat is deliberately unplayed, the emphasis can be shifted away from the beginning of the bar, allowing the phrase to be spread over several bars. Reggae riffs often have a question and answer shape to them.

Some of the many varieties of Reggae are performed by Maxi Priest, Third World, UB 40, Eddy Grant, Peter Tosh, Ziggy Marley, Jimmy Cliff, Black Uhuru, Inner Circle, Burning Spear, Dennis Brown, Big Youth, Gregory Isaacs, The Maytals and Cocoa Tea.

Even Feel

537

medium
Cm
538
CD 1 Track 61
F7

medium
Cm
539

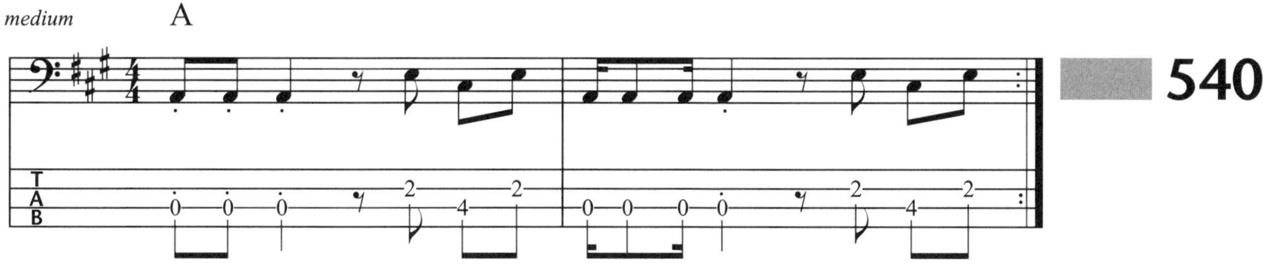
medium
A
540

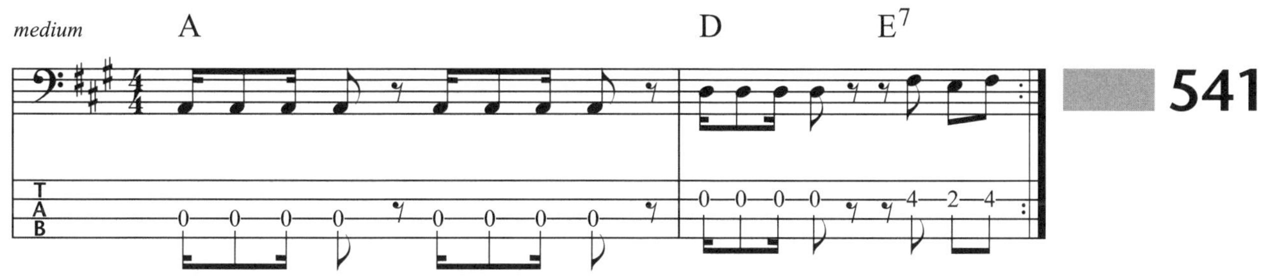
medium
A
D
E7
541

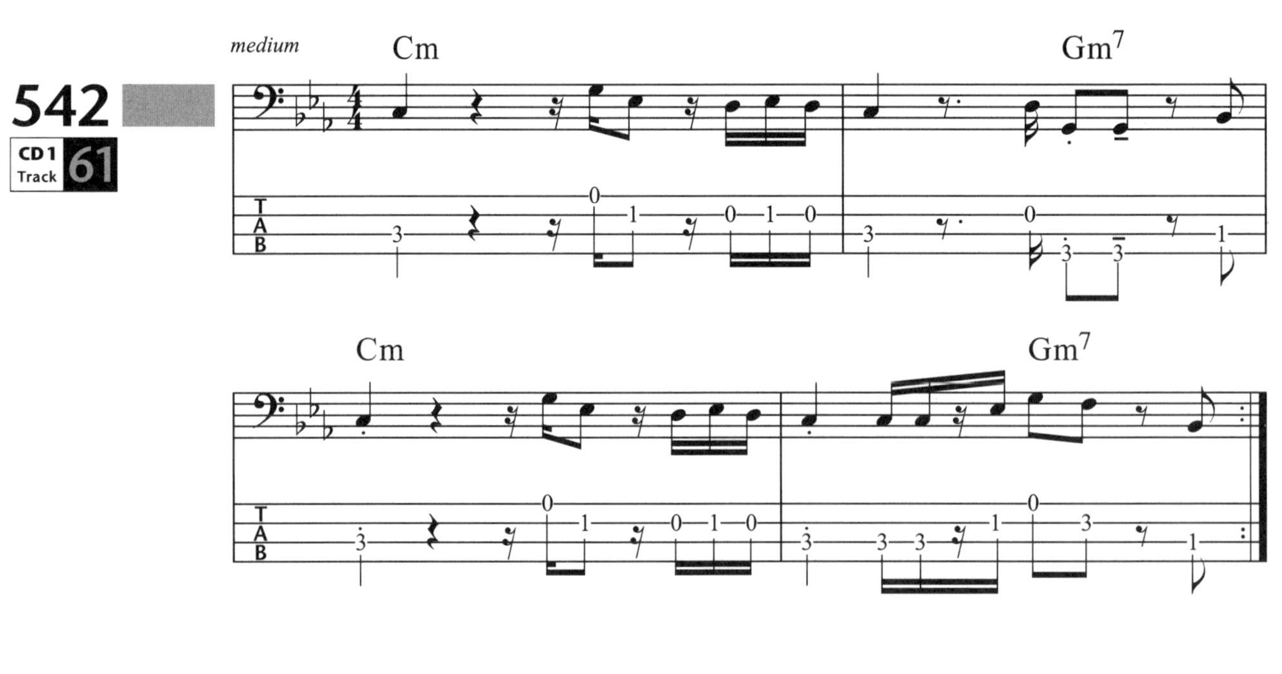
542
CD 1 Track 61
medium
Cm
Gm7
Cm
Gm7

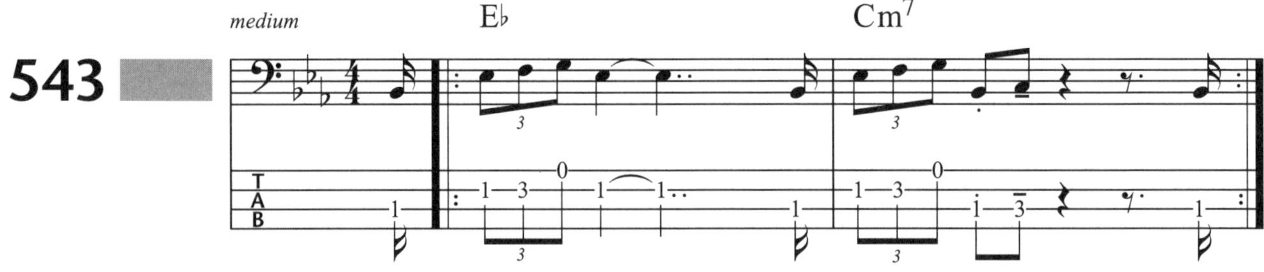
543
medium
E♭
Cm7

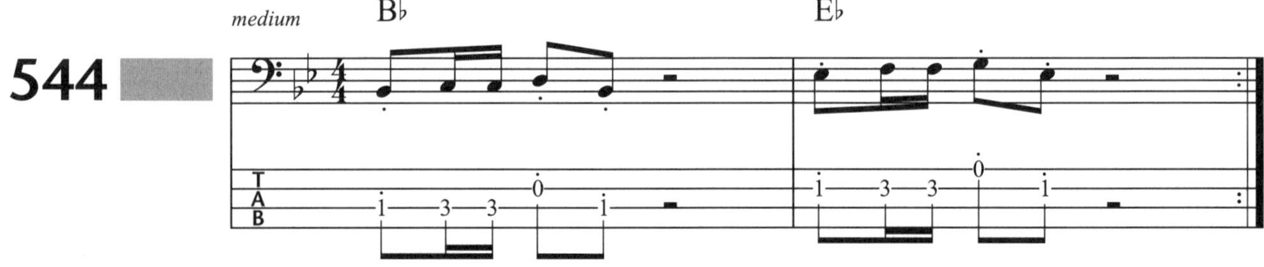
544
medium
B♭
E♭

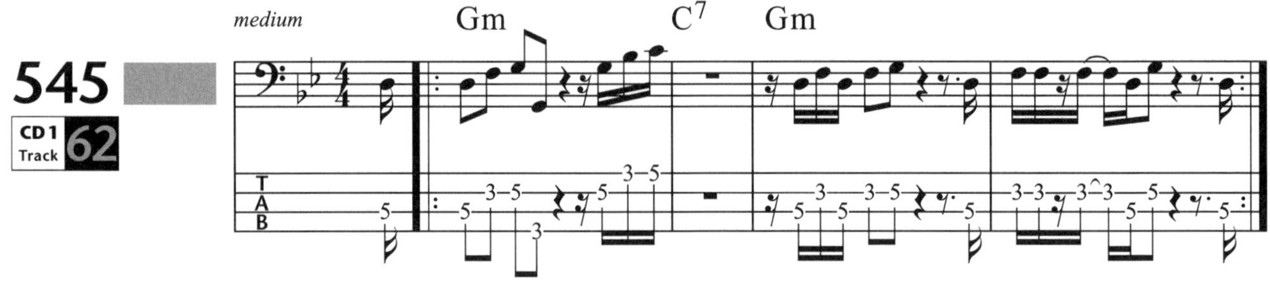
545
CD 1 Track 62
medium
Gm
C7
Gm

546
open key
medium/fast
A7

open key medium

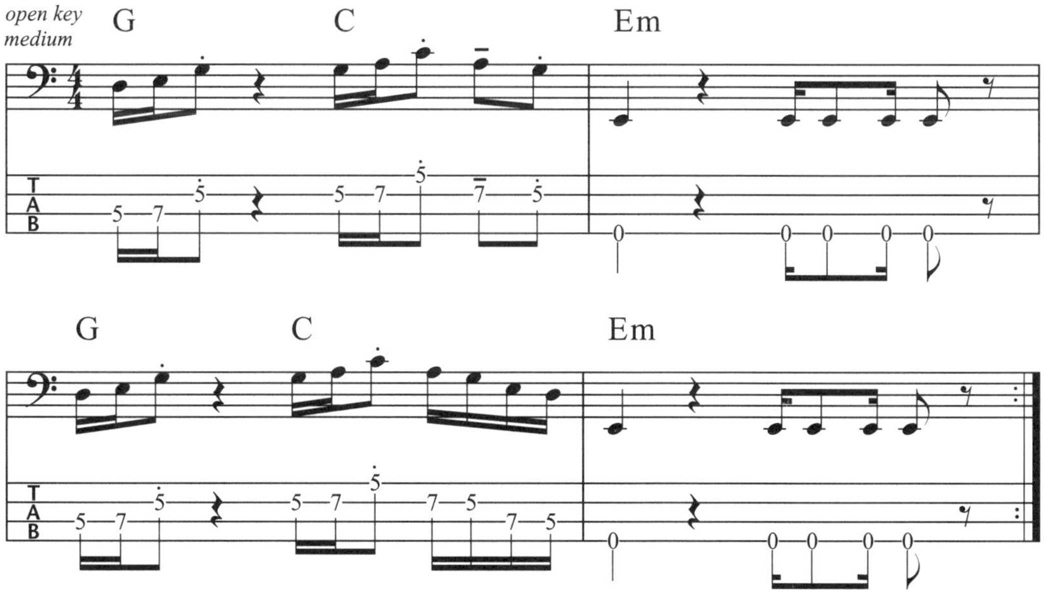

G C Em

G C Em

547

open key medium

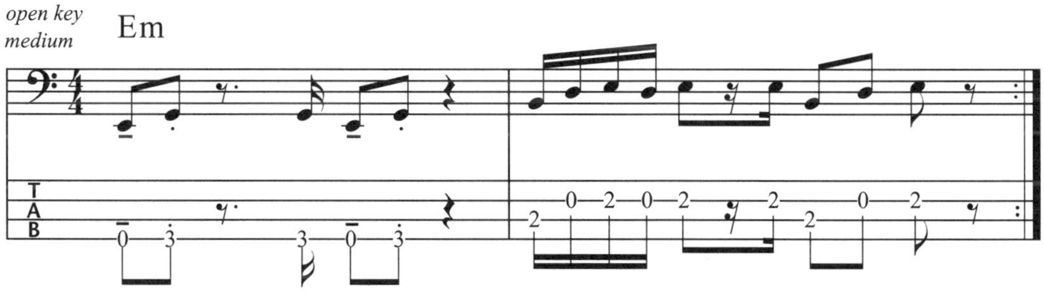

Em

548

medium

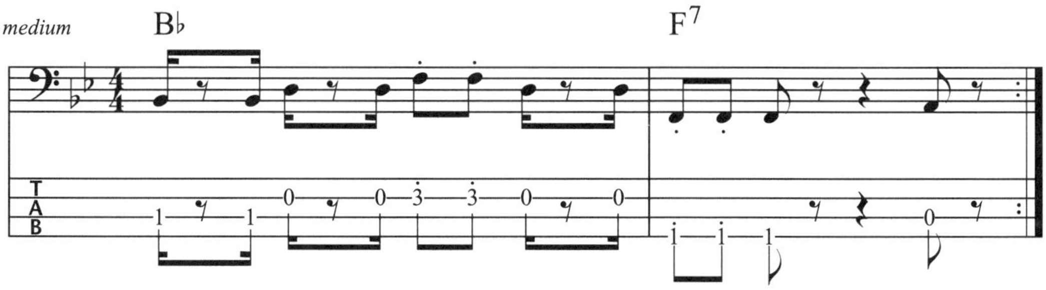

B♭ F7

549

medium

F C

B♭ F

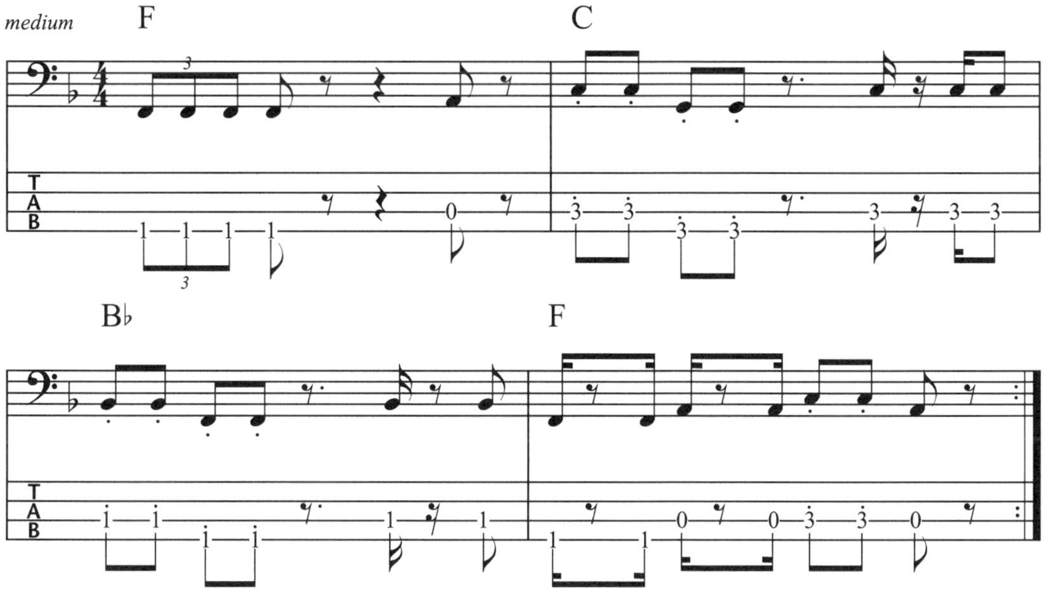

550

CD 1 Track 62

551
CD 1 Track 63

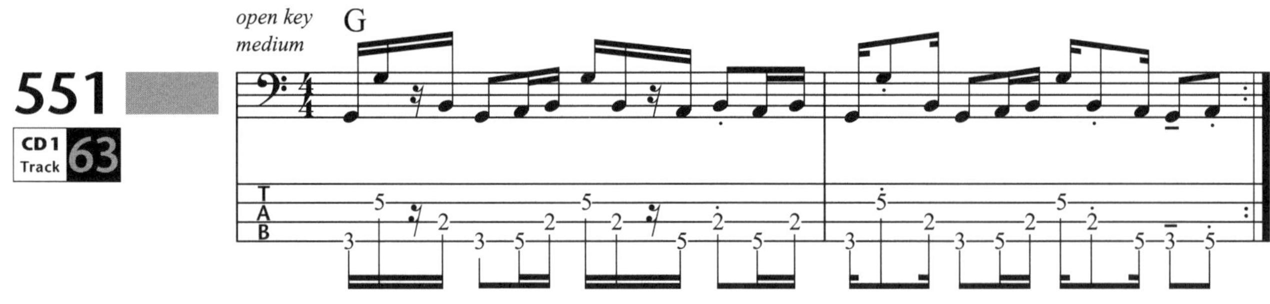

552

553

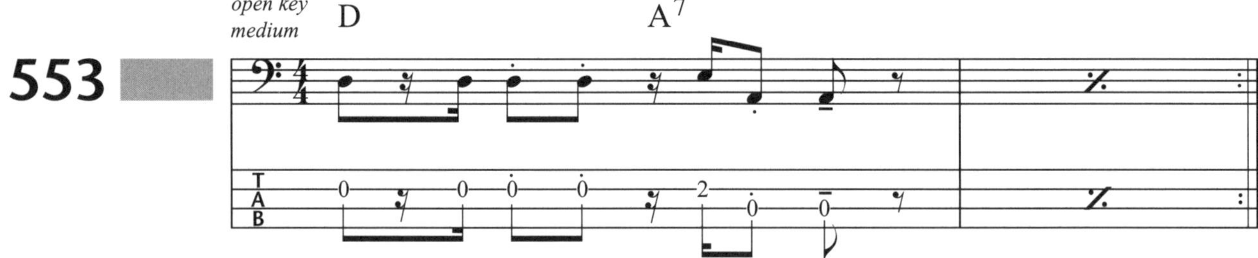

554

555

556

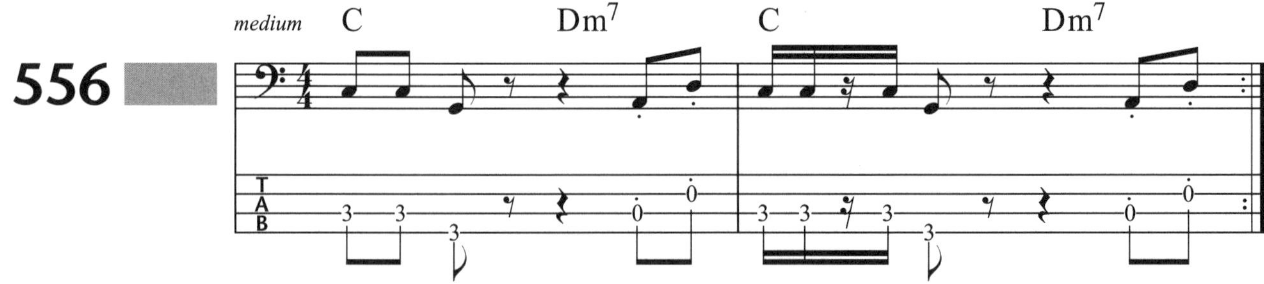

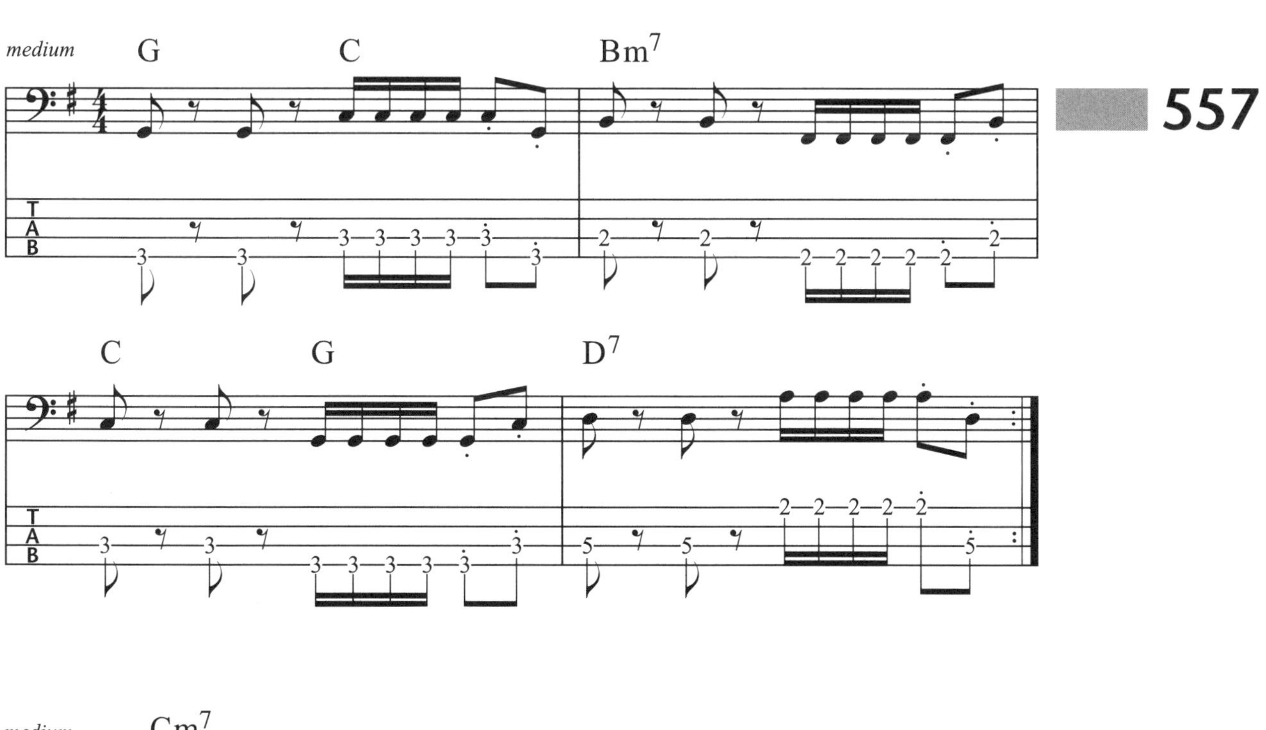
medium
G
C
Bm7
557
C
G
D7

medium
Cm7
558

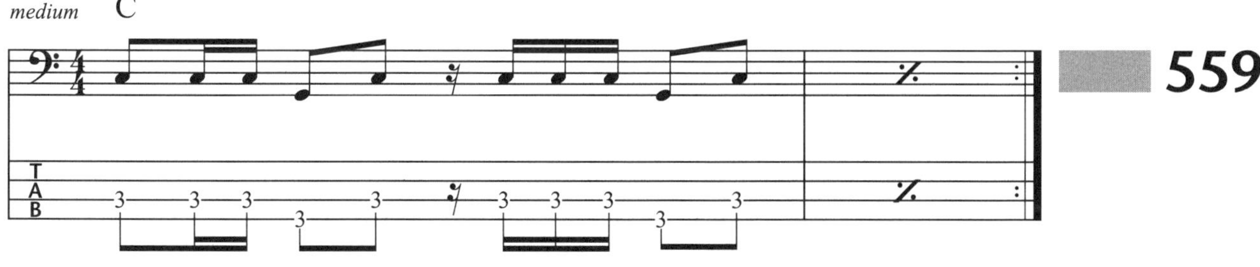
medium
C
559

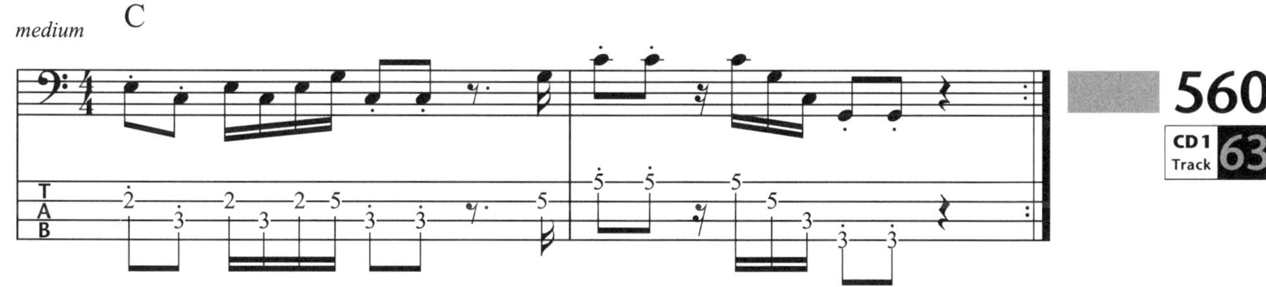
medium
C
560
CD 1
Track 63

561

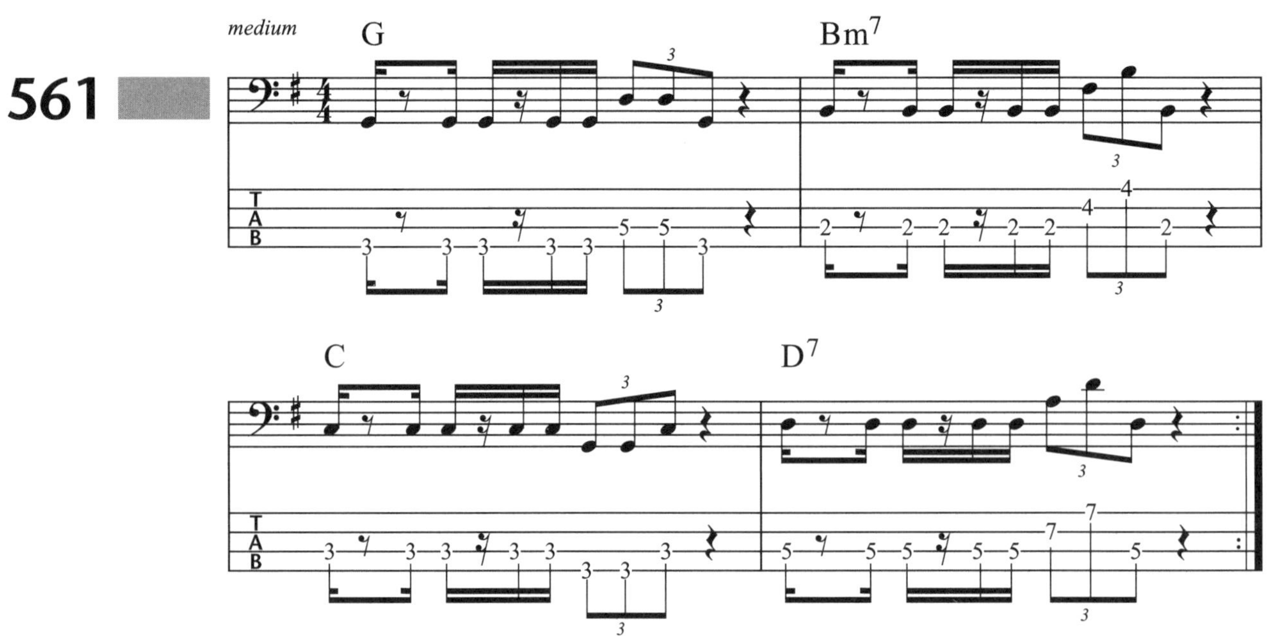

562

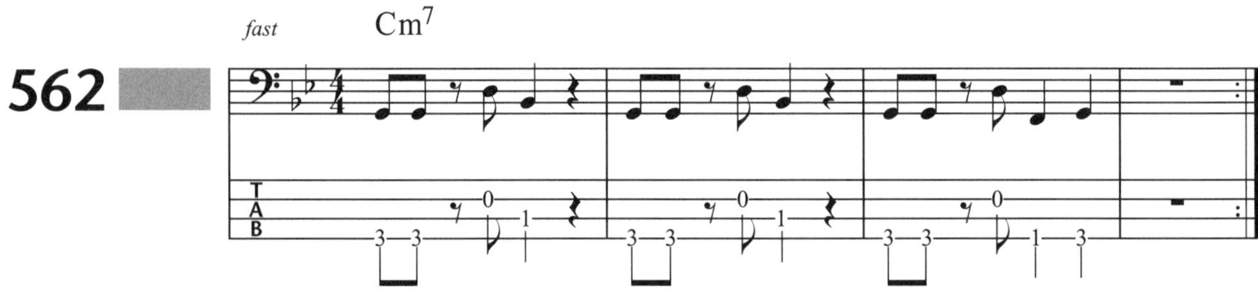

563

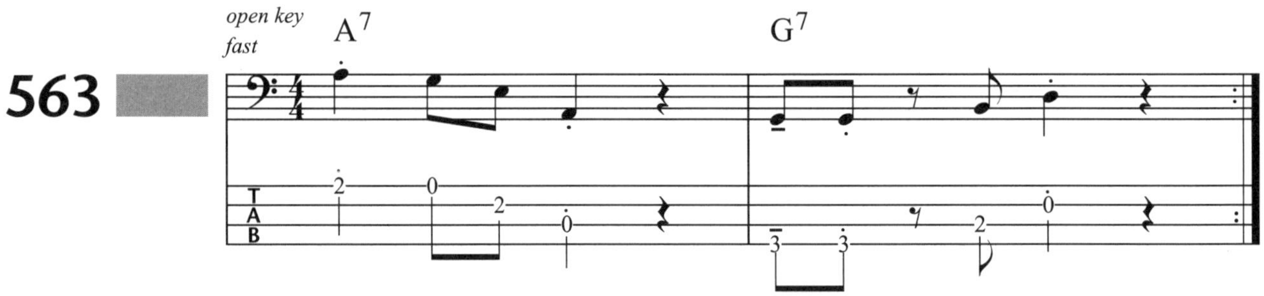

564

CD 1 Track 64

fast
Bm7
565

Em7
G

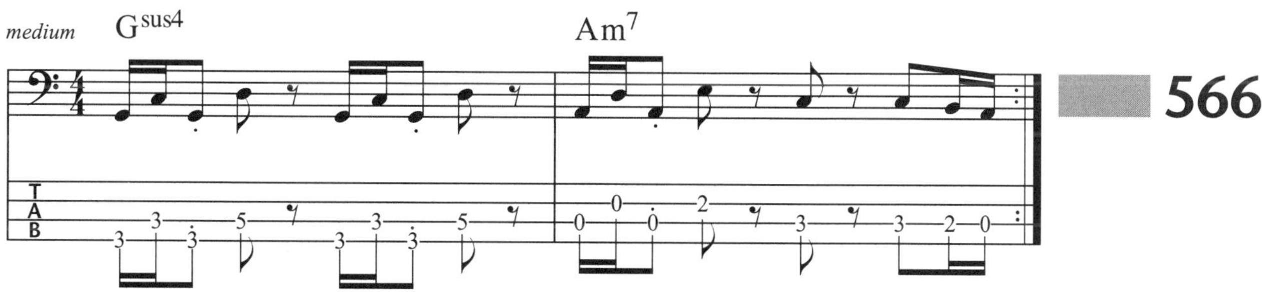
medium
Gsus4
Am7
566

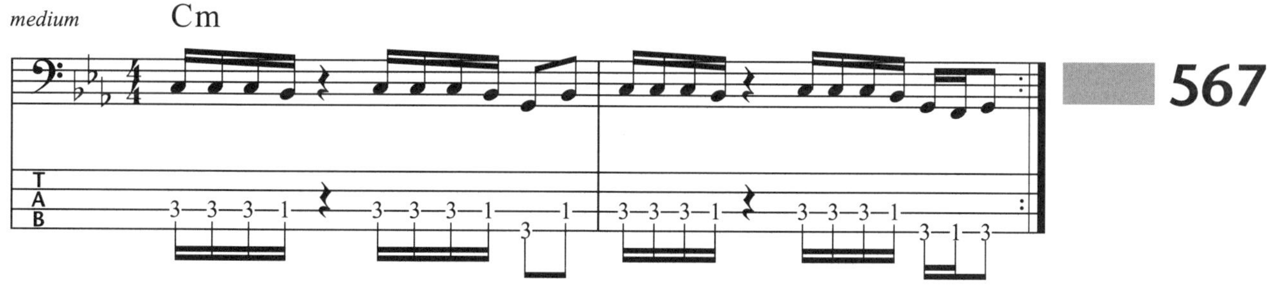
medium
Cm
567

medium
Bm
568

569

CD1 Track 64

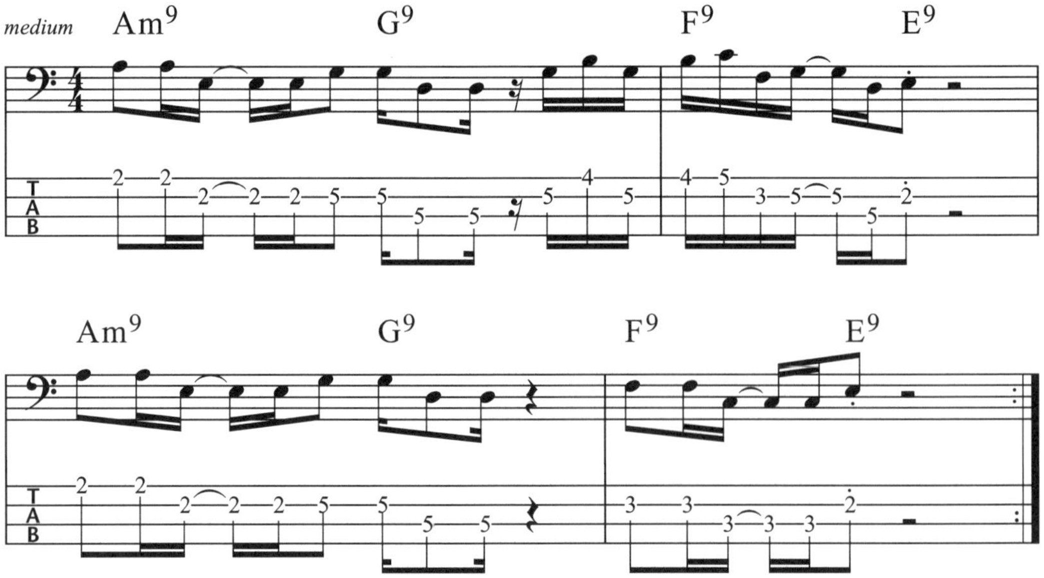
medium
Am9
G9
F9
E9
Am9
G9
F9
E9

570

open key
fast
Dm7
G7sus4
Dm7

571

medium
A
D
F♯m
Bm7

572

fast
B♭6
Cm7
B♭6

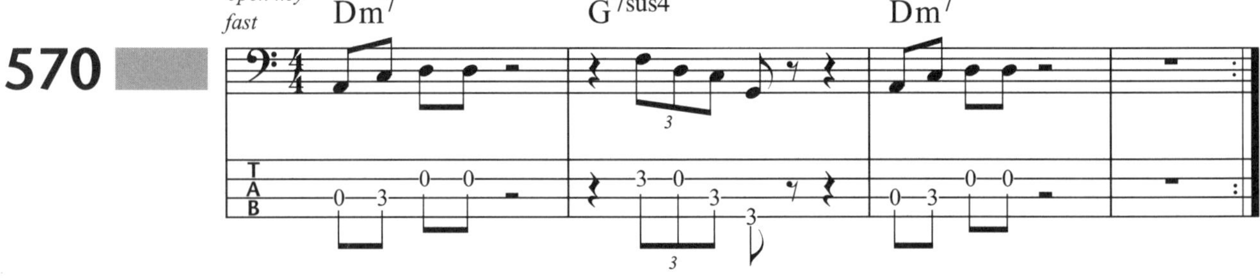

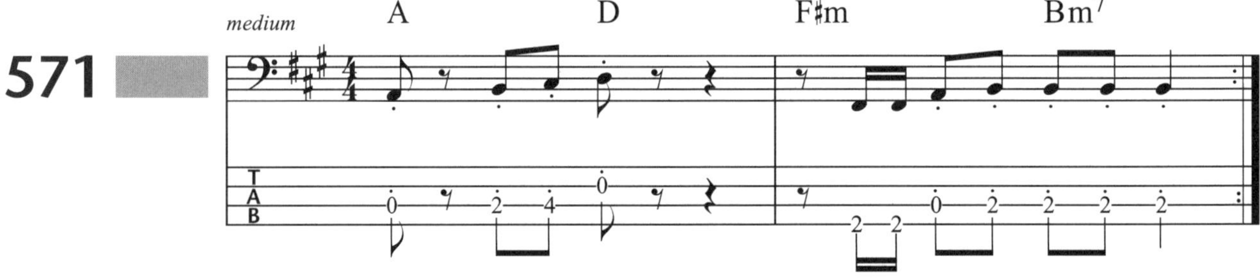

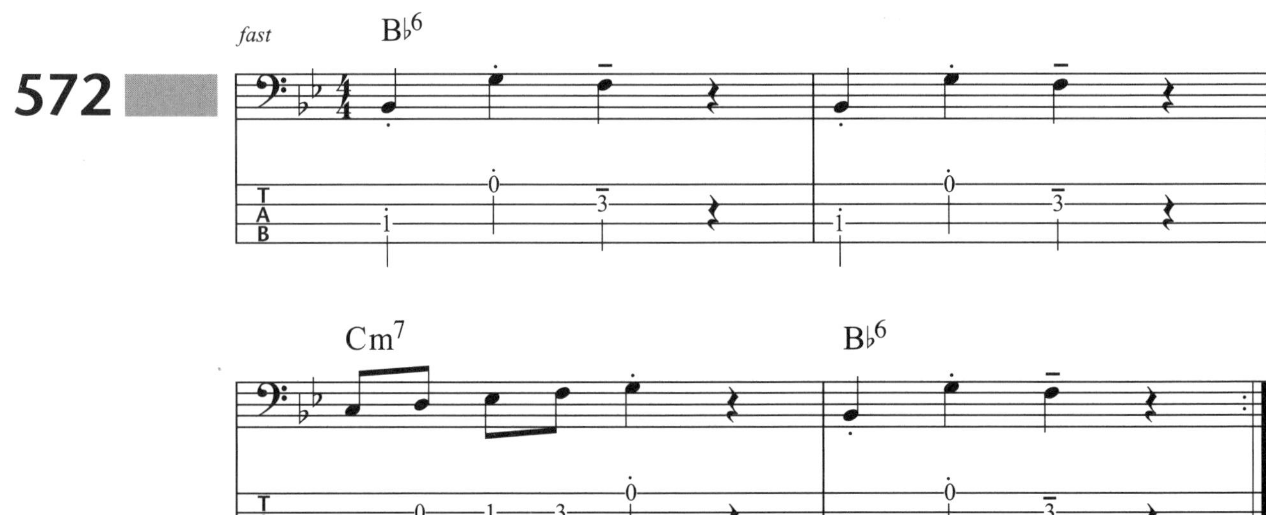

Even Feel, No Downbeat

573

CD 1 Track 65

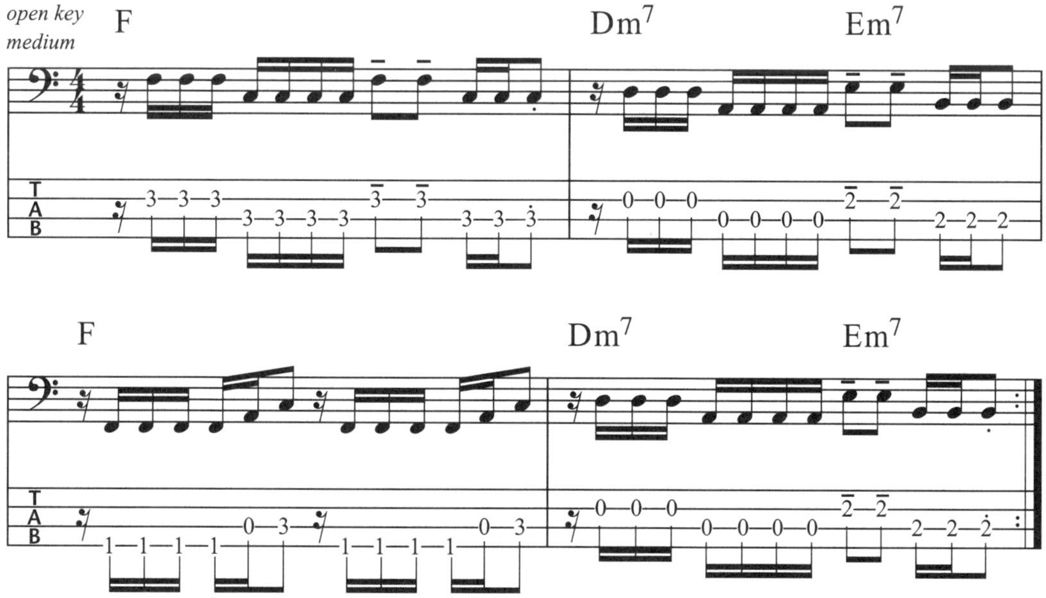

574

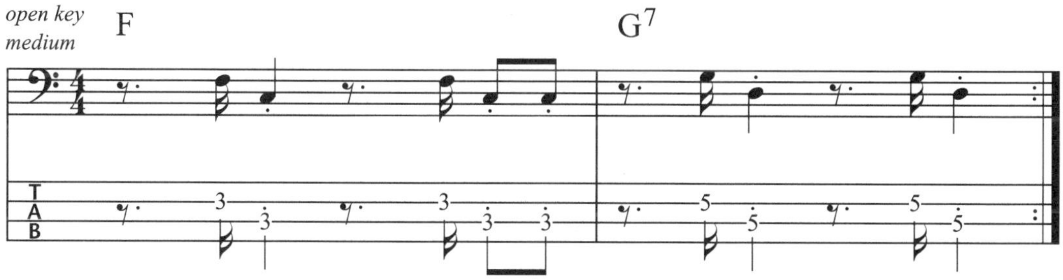

575

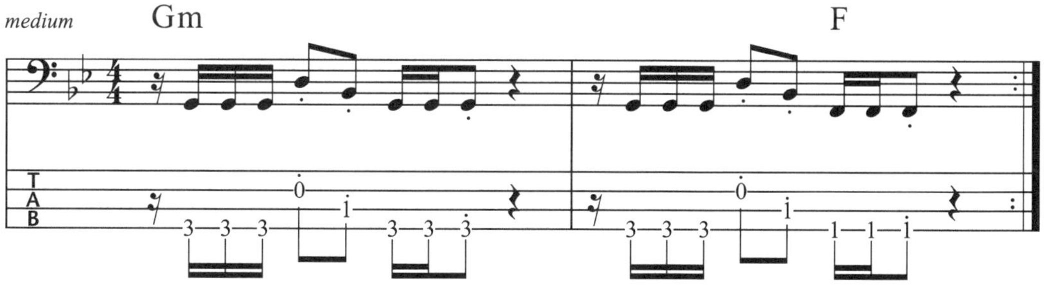

576

CD 1 Track 65

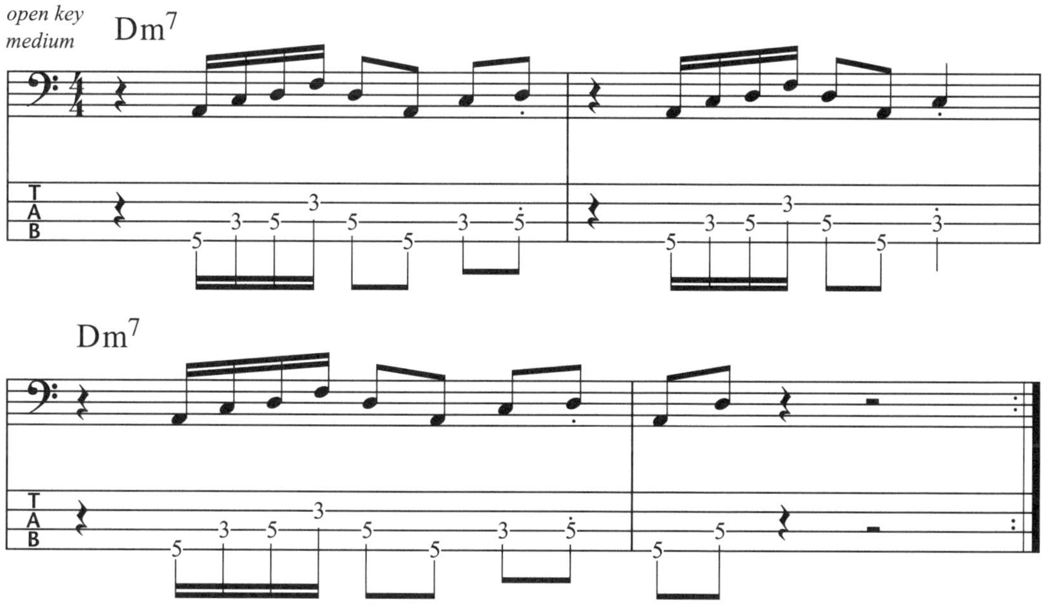

medium
G
Am7 D7
577
CD 1 Track 66
medium
G
Am7
G
Am7
578
medium
C
579
medium
B♭
580
CD 1 Track 66
open key
medium
Em
D
Em
D
581
CD 1 Track 67
open key
medium
Gm7
582
CD 1 Track 67

583

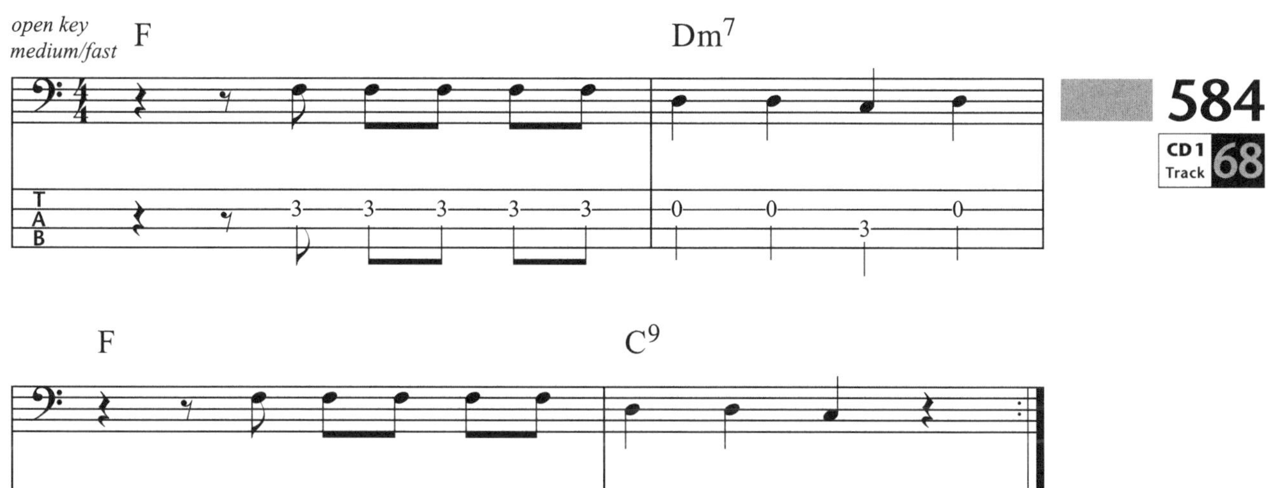

584

CD1 Track 68

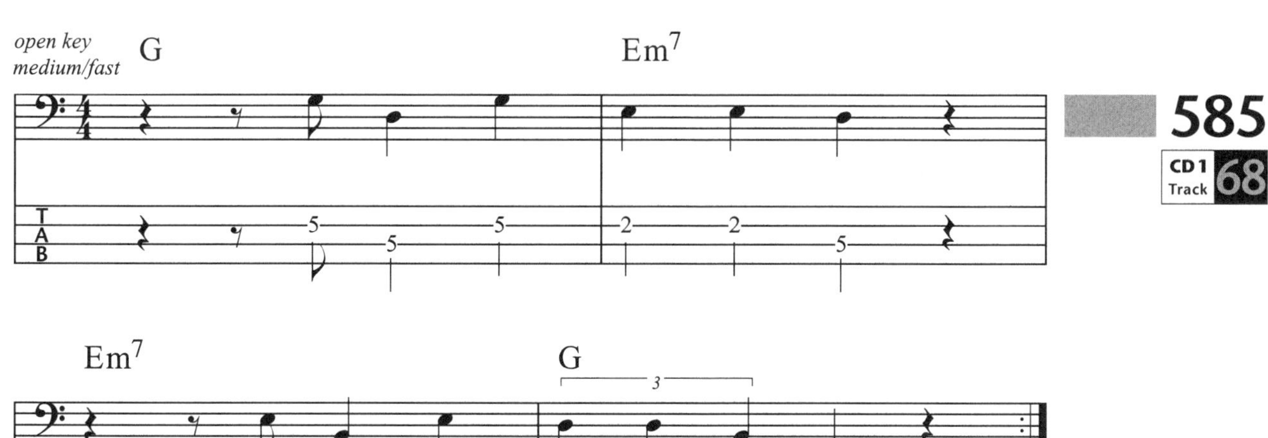

585

CD1 Track 68

Shuffle Feel

586

CD1 Track 69

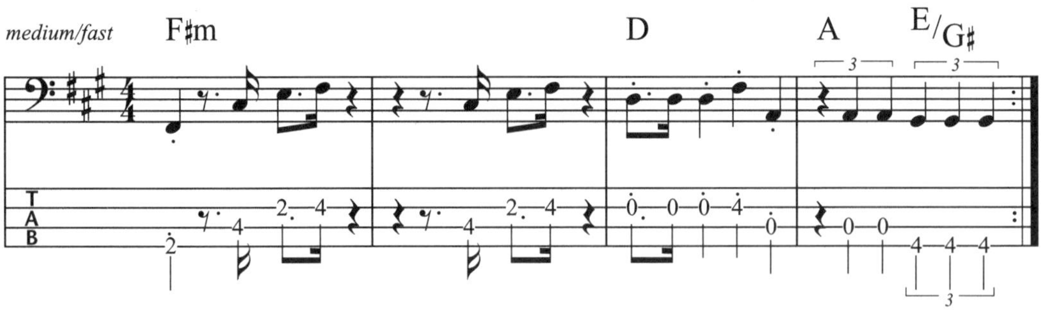
medium/fast
F♯m
D
A
E/G♯

587

CD1 Track 69

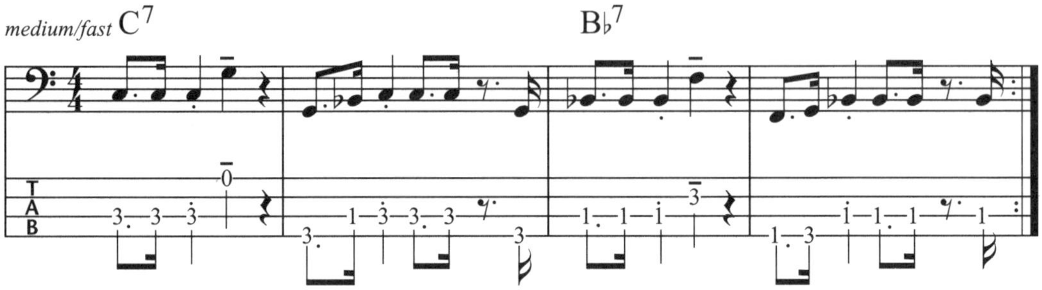
medium/fast
C7
B♭7

588

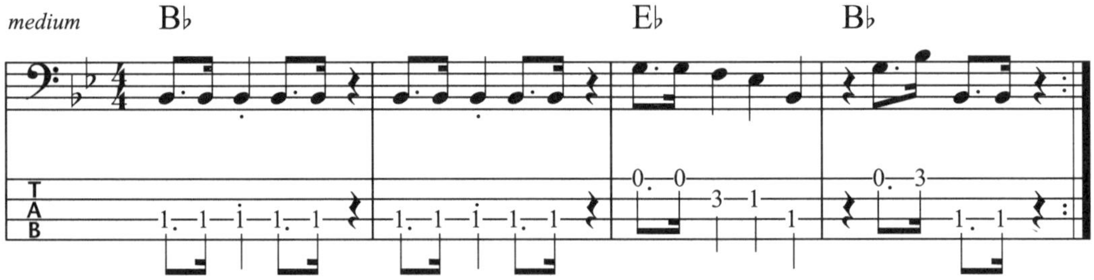
medium
B♭
E♭
B♭

589

CD1 Track 70

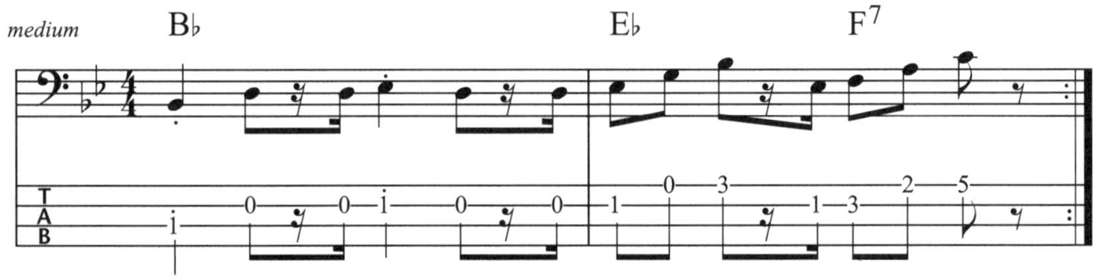
medium
B♭
E♭
F7

590

CD1 Track 70

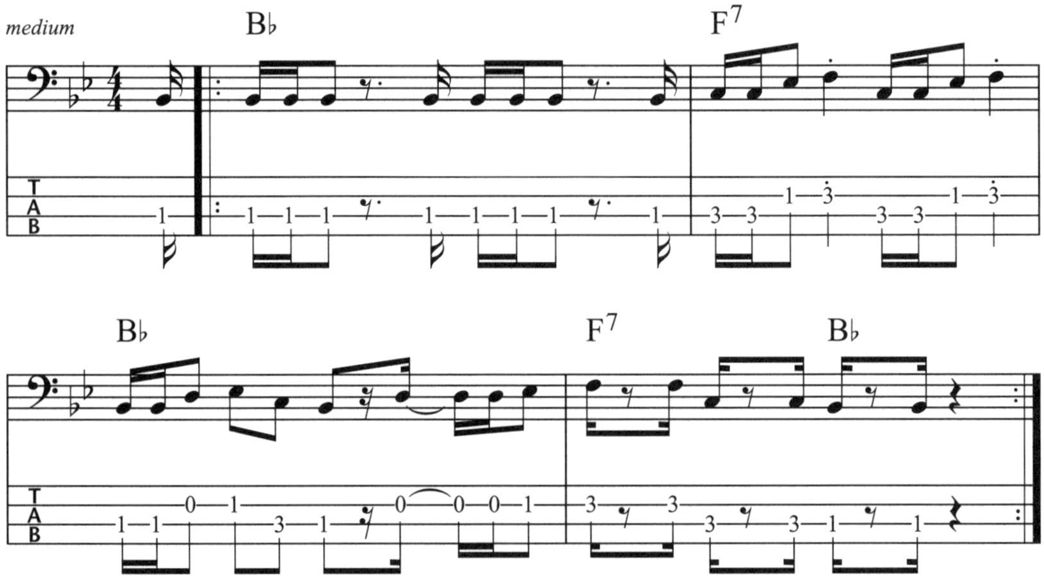
medium
B♭
F7
B♭
F7
B♭

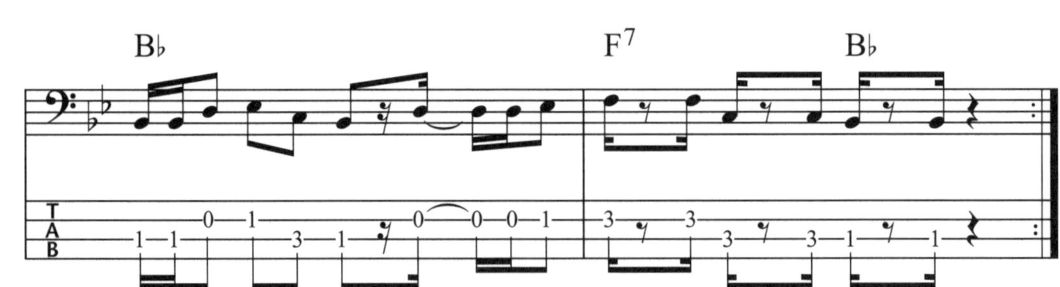

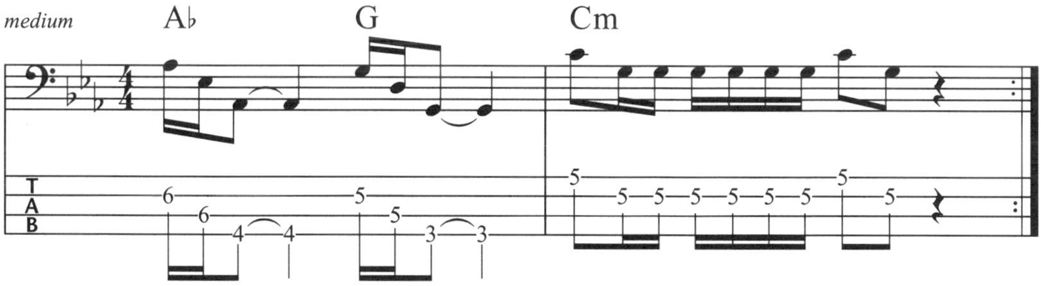
medium
A♭
G
Cm
T
A
B

591

CD 1 Track 71

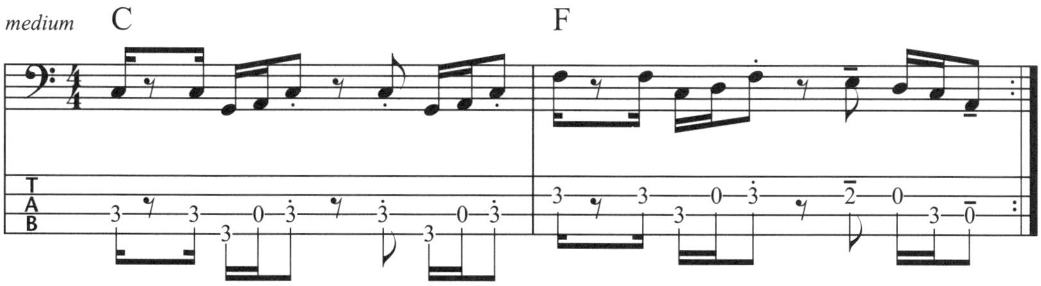
medium
C
F
T
A
B

592

CD 1 Track 71

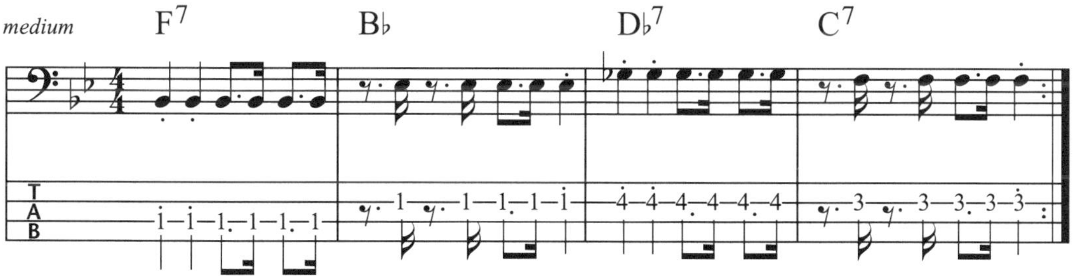
medium
F7
B♭
D♭7
C7
T
A
B

593

CD 1 Track 72

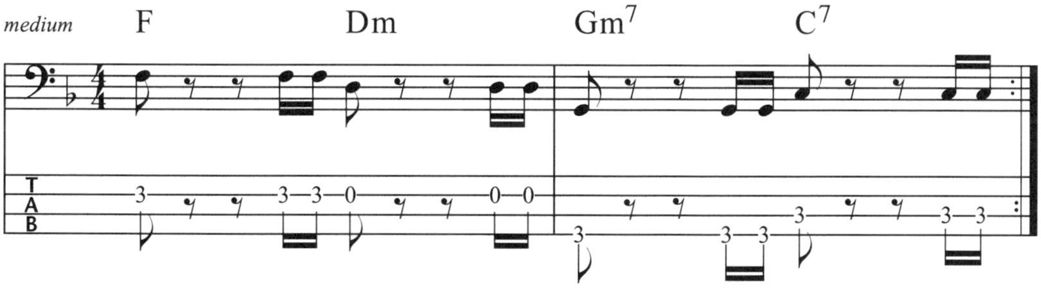
medium
F
Dm
Gm7
C7
T
A
B

594

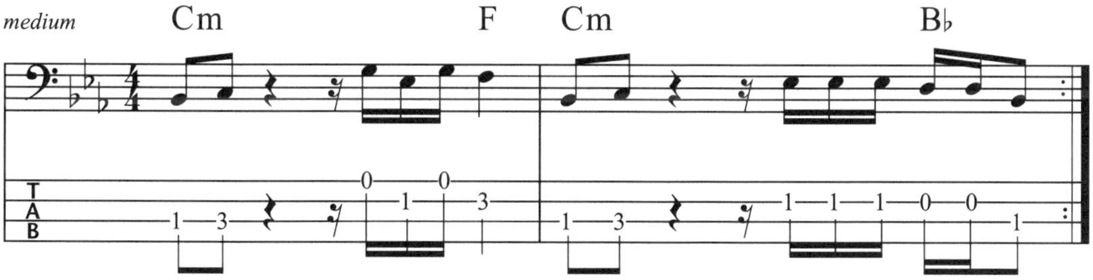
medium
Cm
F
Cm
B♭
T
A
B

595

CD 1 Track 72

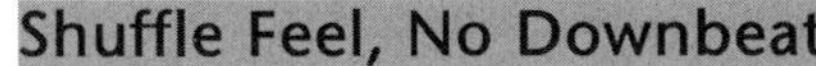

Shuffle Feel, No Downbeat

596
CD 1 Track 73

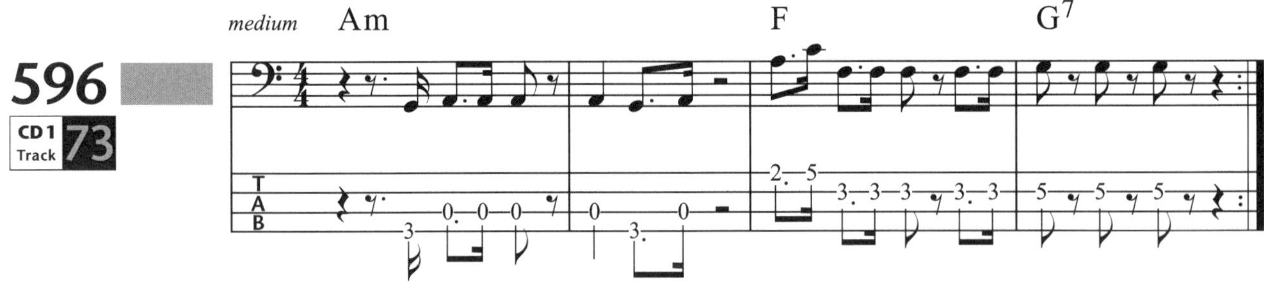

597
CD 1 Track 73

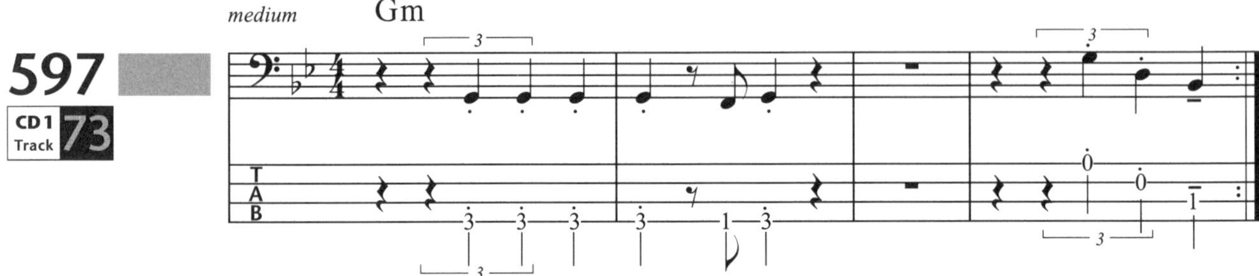

598
CD 1 Track 74

599
CD 1 Track 74

600
CD 1 Track 75

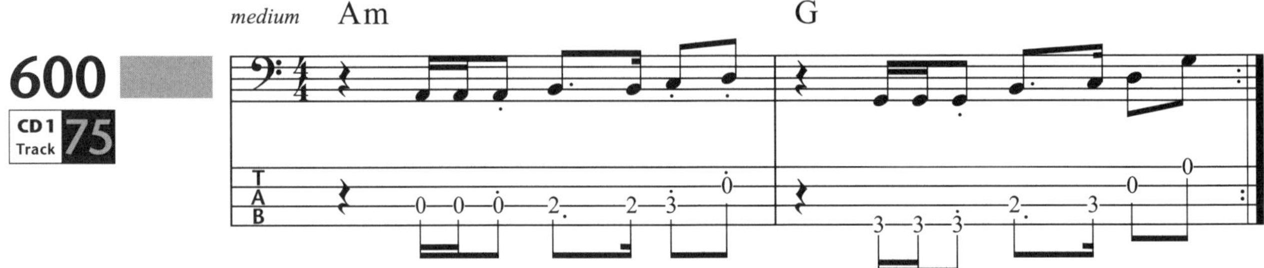

601
CD 1 Track 75

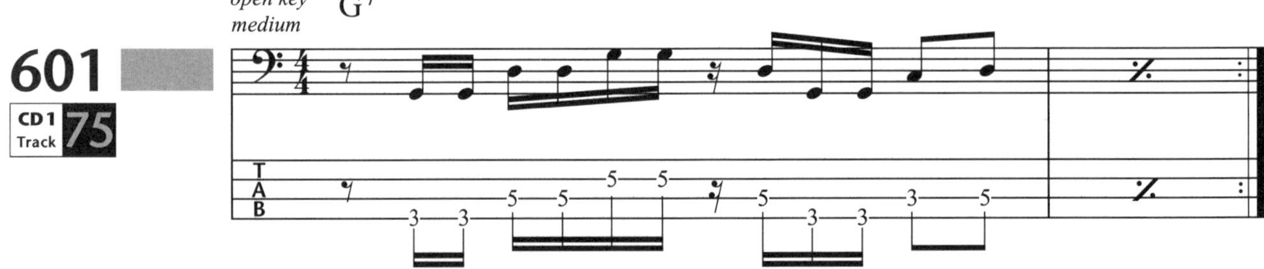

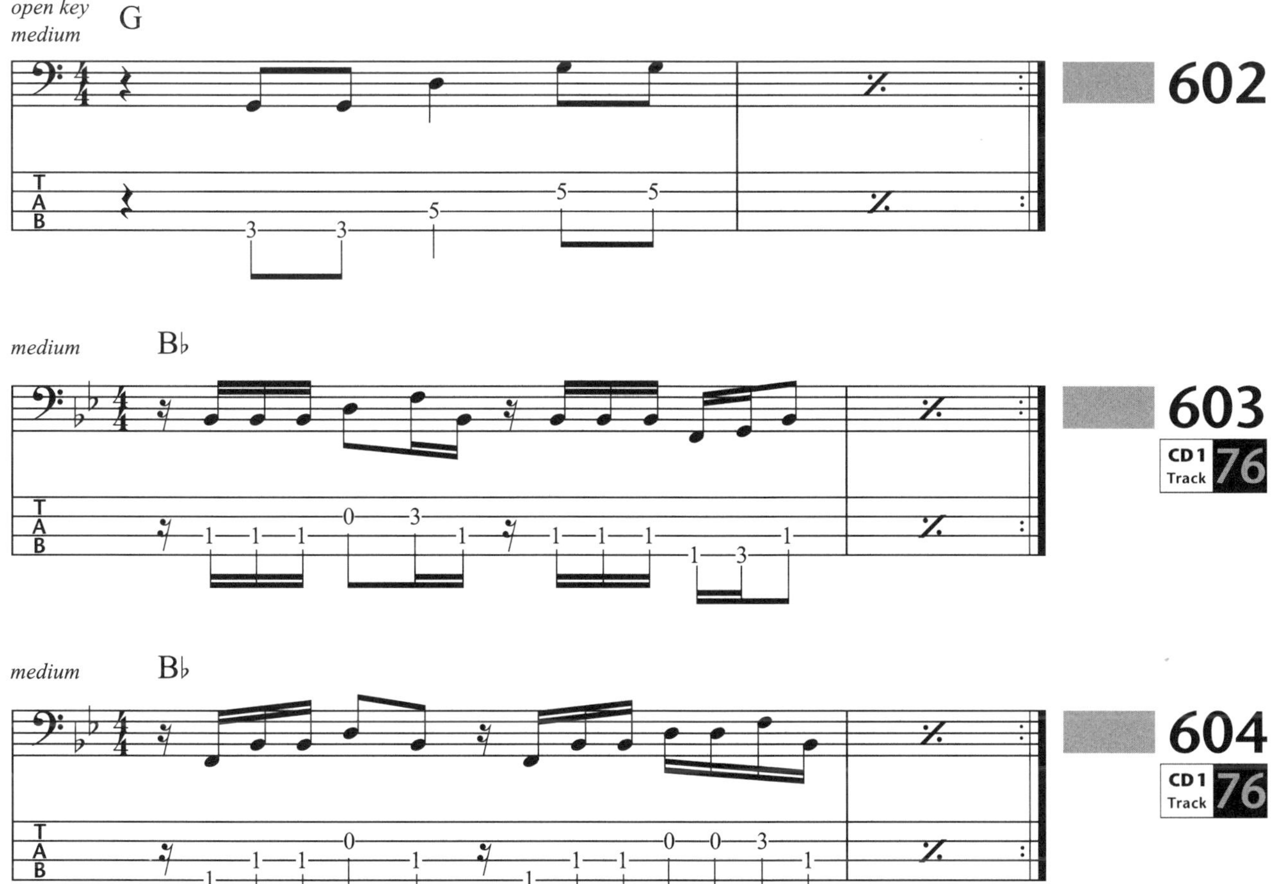
open key
medium
G
602
medium
B♭
603
CD1 Track 76
medium
B♭
604
CD1 Track 76

Colombia

Colombia has many varieties of musical style and rhythm including Cumbia, Vallenato, Salsa, Son Caribeno, Paseo, Pasieto, Paseje, Porro and Gaita. Many of these styles and dances have originated from its Caribbean coast.

Some of the best-known artists are Los Corraleros, The Latin Brothers, Los Inmortales, La Sonora Dinamita, Joe Rodriguez, La Integracion, German Carremo, Alfredo Gutierrez and Luis Enrique Martinez.

These are all artists whose styles range from roots music to dance, but who concentrate on strong melodies which appeal to an audience who love to sing. Emphasis is put on entertainment and getting people together for a good time.

605

606

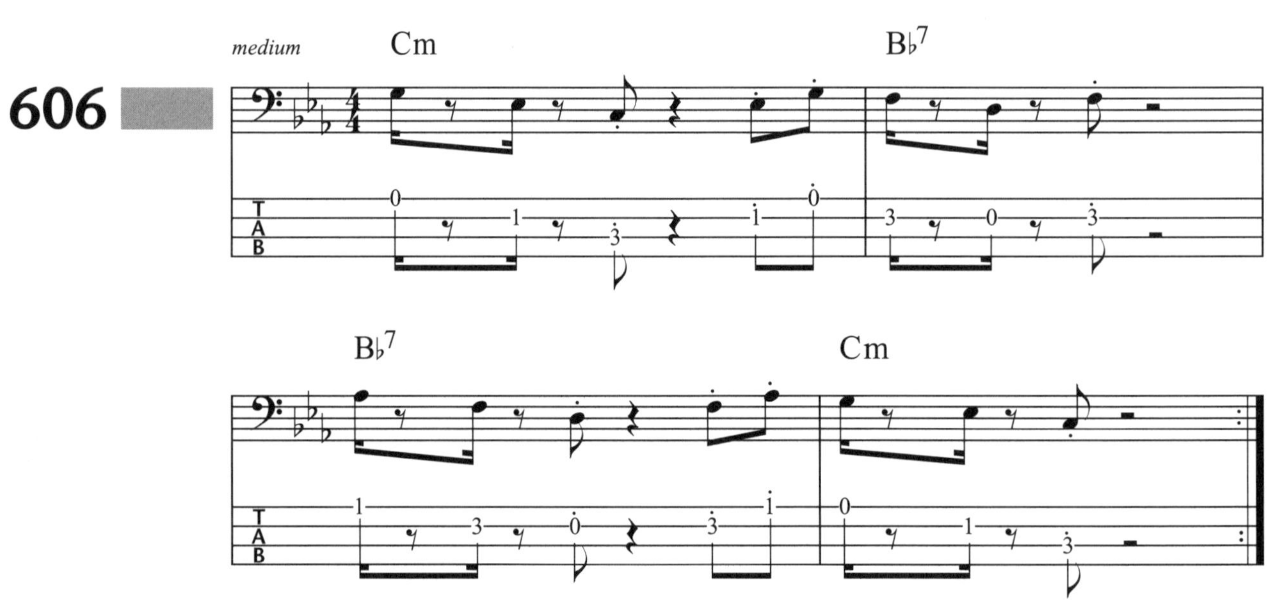

607

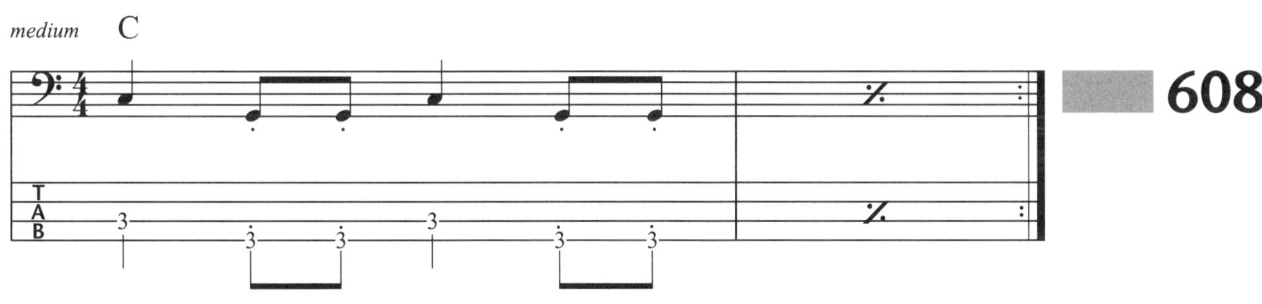

608

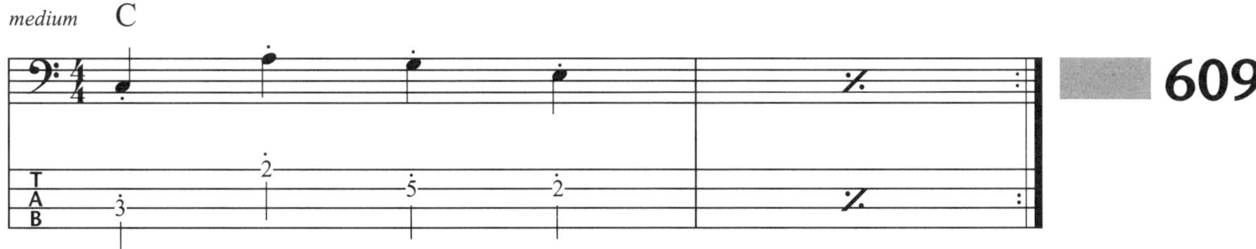

609

610

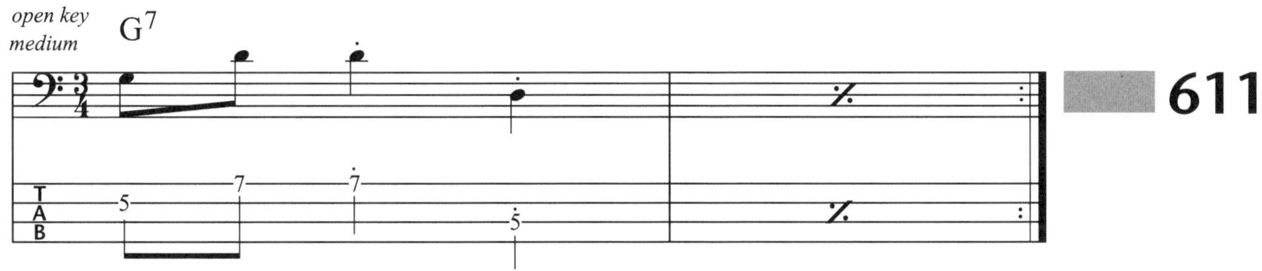

611

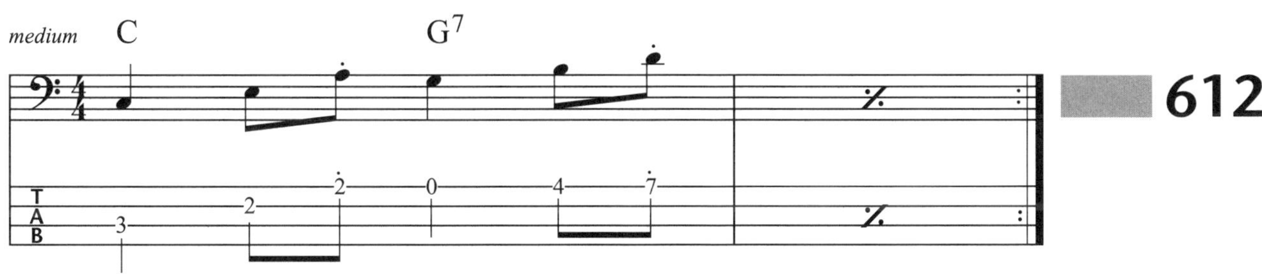

612

613

Brazilian Samba

Sambas are played in 4/4 time. Bass guitars are used to play quite simple patterns when the percussion rhythms are complex. Many rhythms contrast 8th and 16th note feels, 12/8 shuffles and triplets spread across the bar. Instruments used include the drum kit, congas, bongos, maracas, guiro, cowbell, pandeiro, wooden agogos, claves, cabasa, cuica, boimbau and caxixi, agogo bells, triangle, tambourine, whistle and vibra-slap. The instruments come from different countries and bring their various qualities and influences with them.

When the rhythms are complex, the bass is not always used. At times the bass line is provided by a Spanish guitar playing very intricate ideas, which are played very accurately. The lightness of the bass line, therefore, does not weigh the percussion section down or dominate the rhythm. The percussion section is assisted by drums and another Spanish guitar, which is strummed.

Many of the songs change chords constantly in the European tradition, but often with an African rhythm. Bass lines are therefore improvised to a large degree by the Spanish guitar, but some riffs are basic to a particular song. The guitarist has tremendous freedom to play around with the rhythms of the song, and consequently they are very exciting. Tempos can be fast, but the bands always play very tightly.

Although harmonically simpler than Jazz, many of the rhythms played are in two different time signatures at the same moment, i.e. 4/4 and 12/8. They can be more complex than their more regular counterparts, which concentrate separately on either even rhythms or triplet ones.

medium C

614

medium C

615

medium C

616

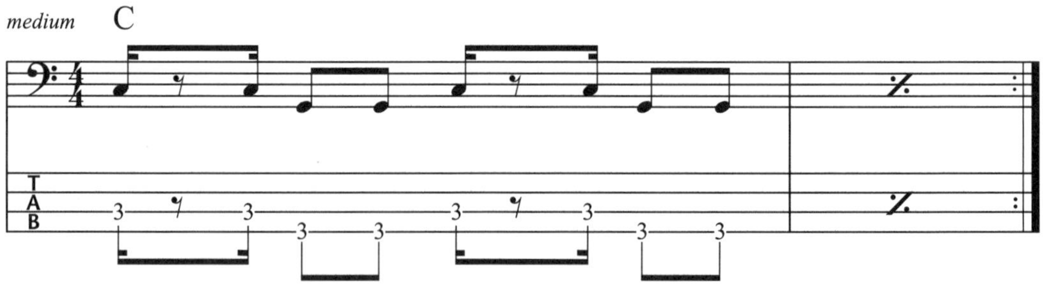

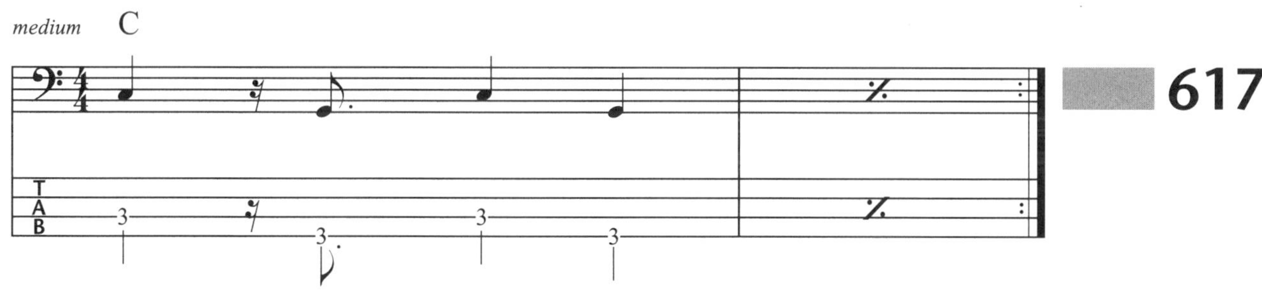
medium
C
617

medium
C
618

medium
C
619

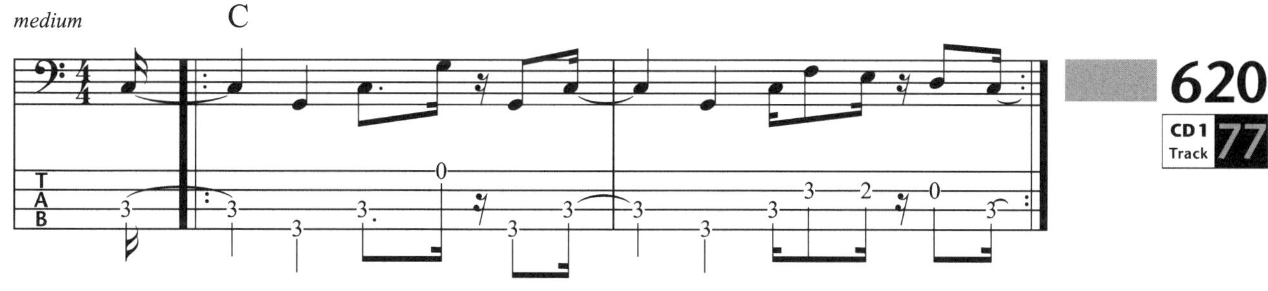
medium
C
620
CD 1 Track 77

medium
C
621

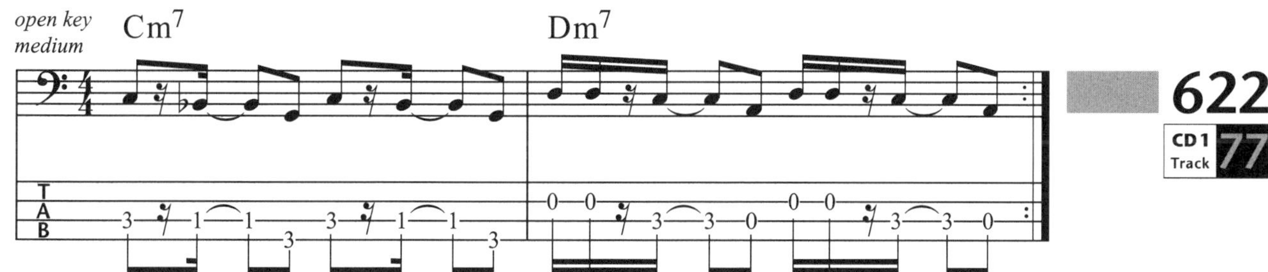
open key
medium
Cm7
Dm7
622
CD 1 Track 77

623

624
CD 1 Track 78

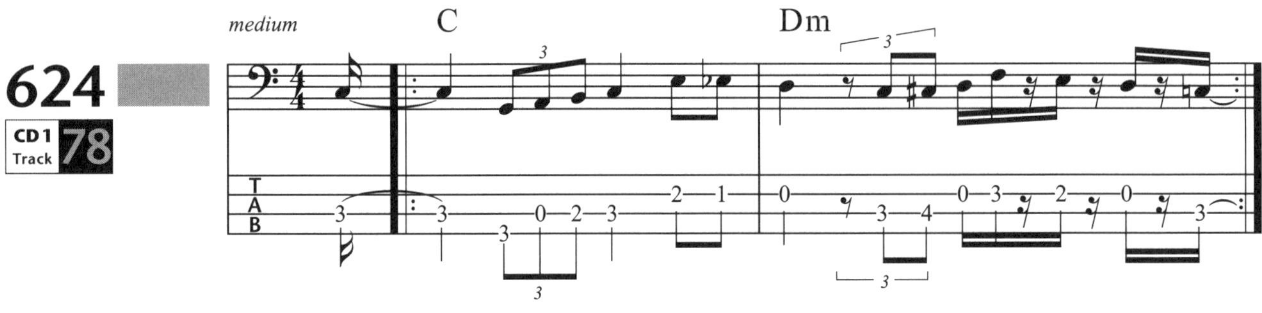

625
CD 1 Track 78

626
CD 1 Track 79

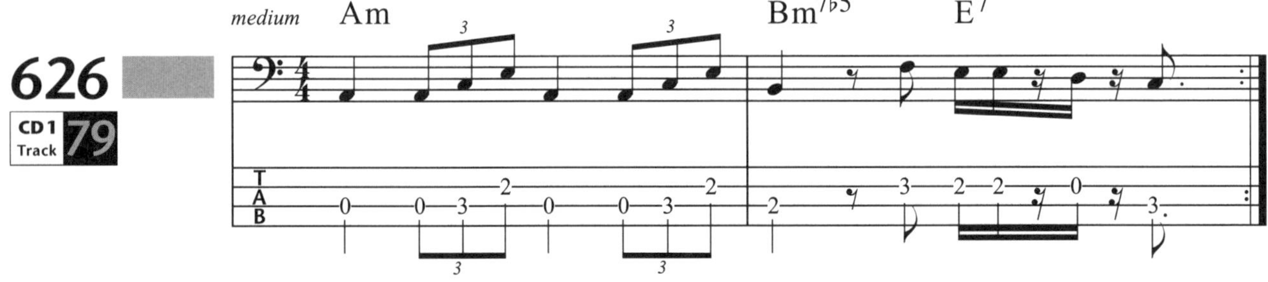

627
CD 1 Track 79

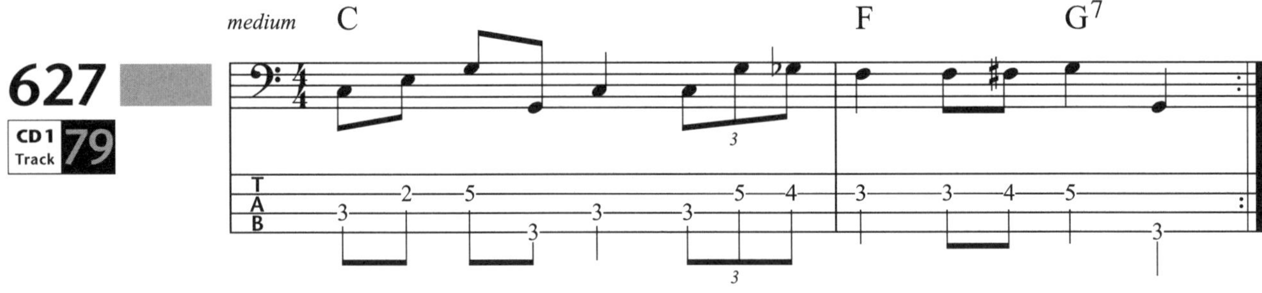

628

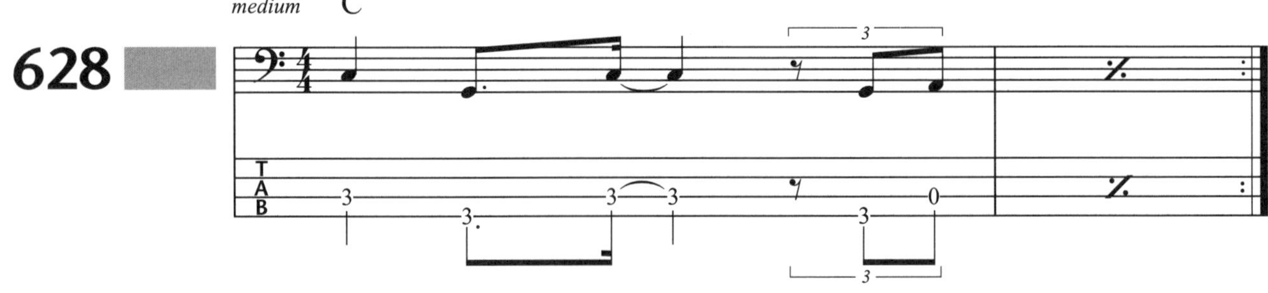

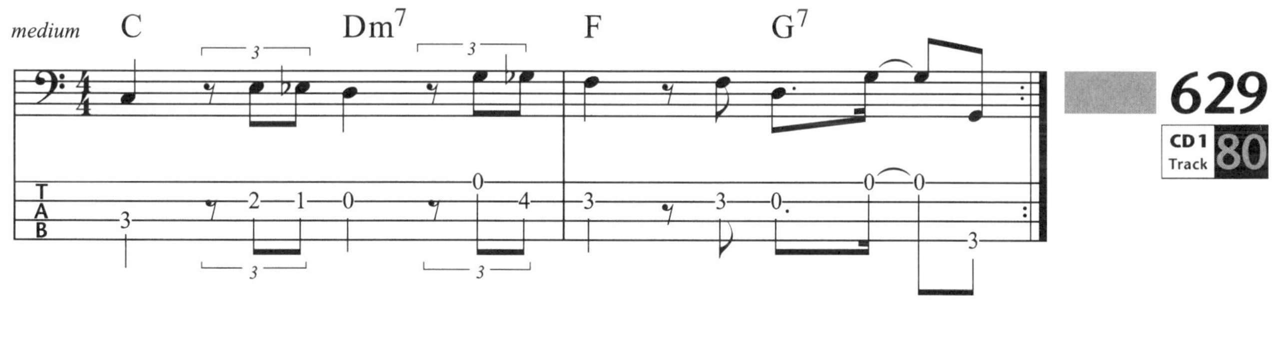
medium
C
Dm7
F
G7
629
CD 1 Track 80

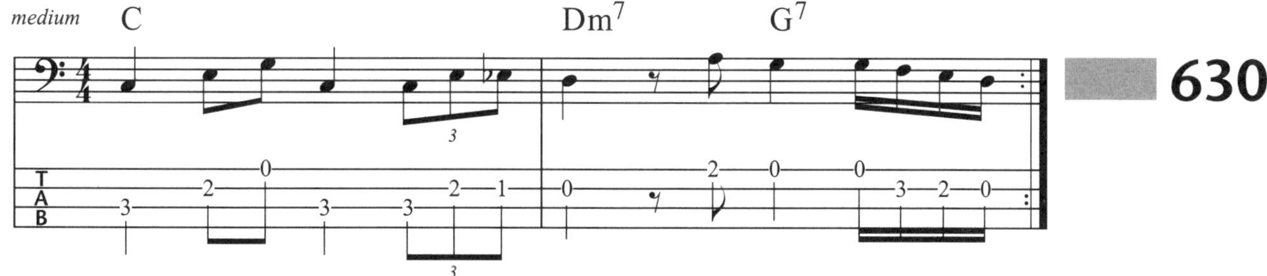
medium
C
Dm7
G7
630

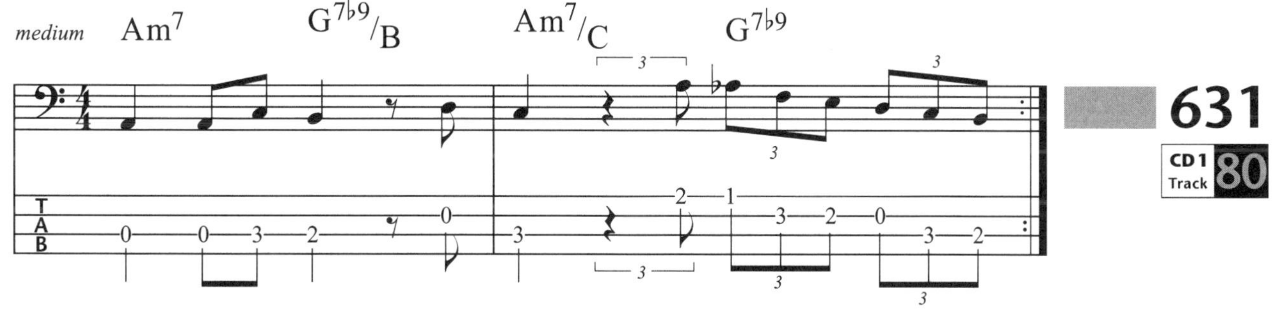
medium
Am7
G7♭9/B
Am7/C
G7♭9
631
CD 1 Track 80

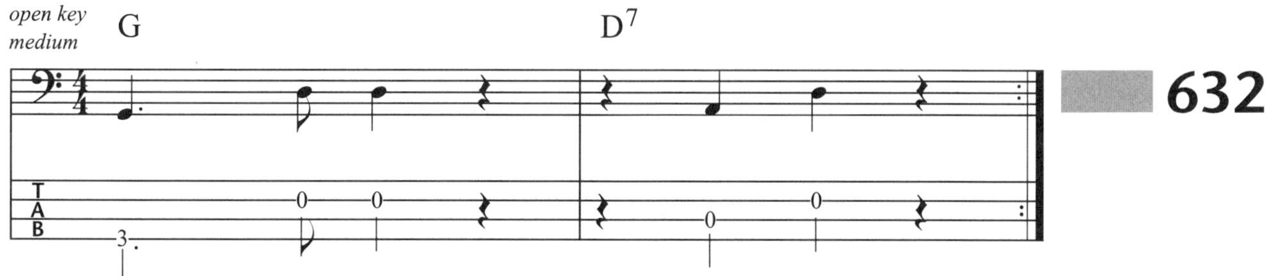
open key
medium
G
D7
632

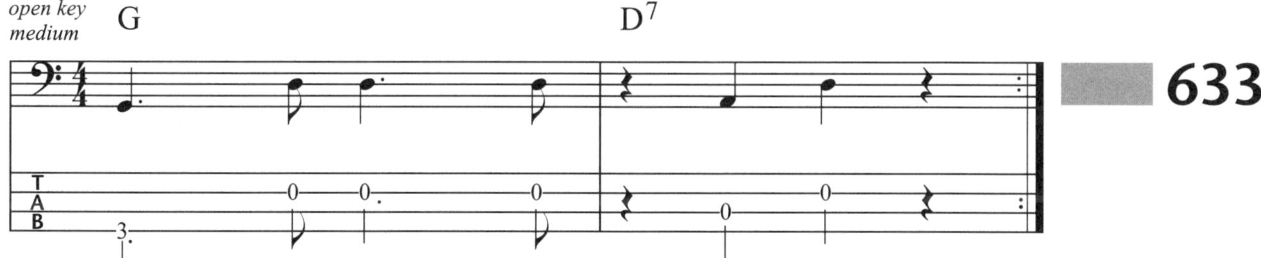
open key
medium
G
D7
633

■ Peru, Ecuador, Chile, Bolivia

Music from these countries is very much oriented towards Folk Music. Traditionally they have used quite simple rhythms played on acoustic instruments, with small numbers of people in each band. The bass lines are played on guitar, drums and harp, or even wind instruments like pan pipes. Double basses are sometimes used, but some of the most interesting lines come from other instruments, which do not limit themselves to a 2 or 4 beat feel quite so much.

medium Am G Am

634

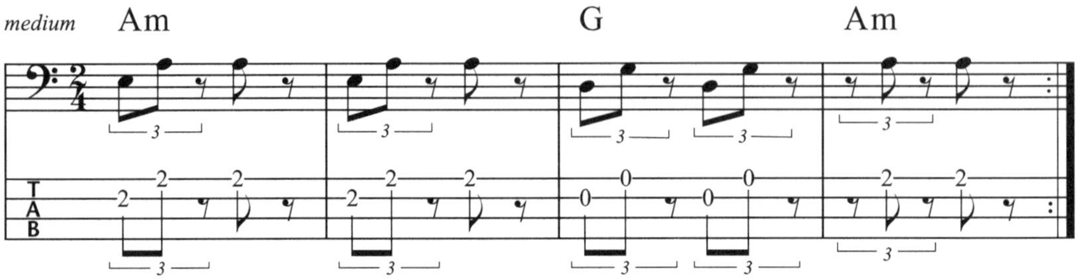

open key
medium Dm7

635

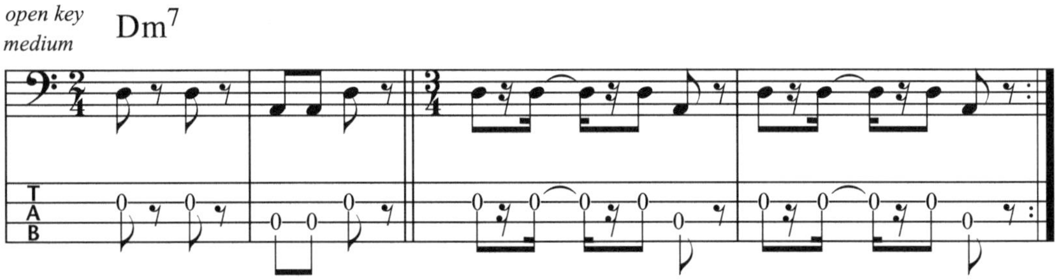

open key
medium F

636

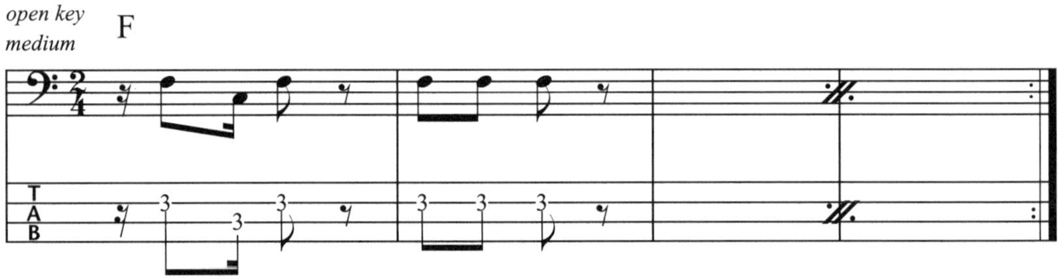

open key
medium Dm7

637

medium C Am

638

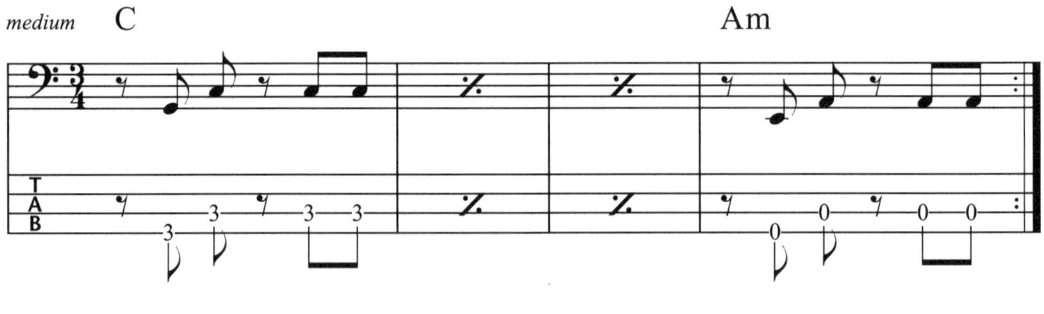

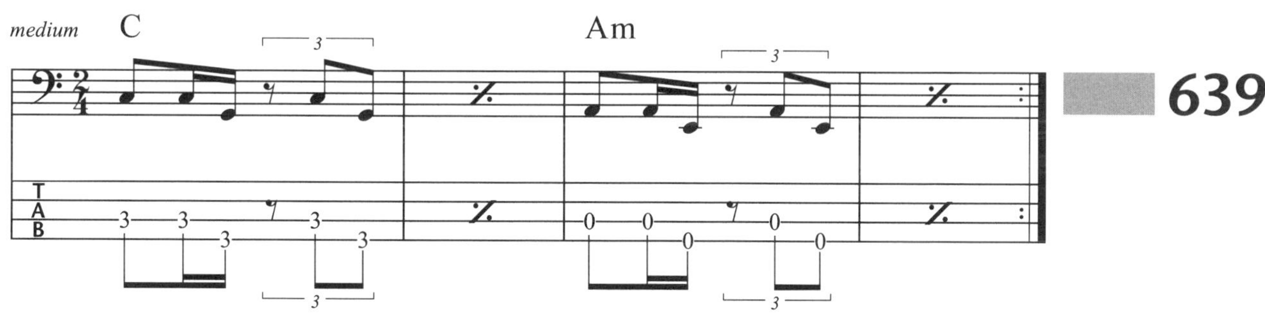

639

640

641

642

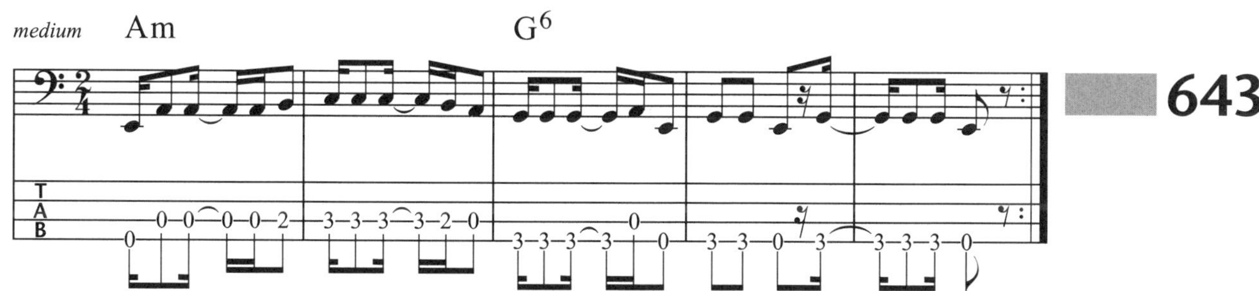

643

644

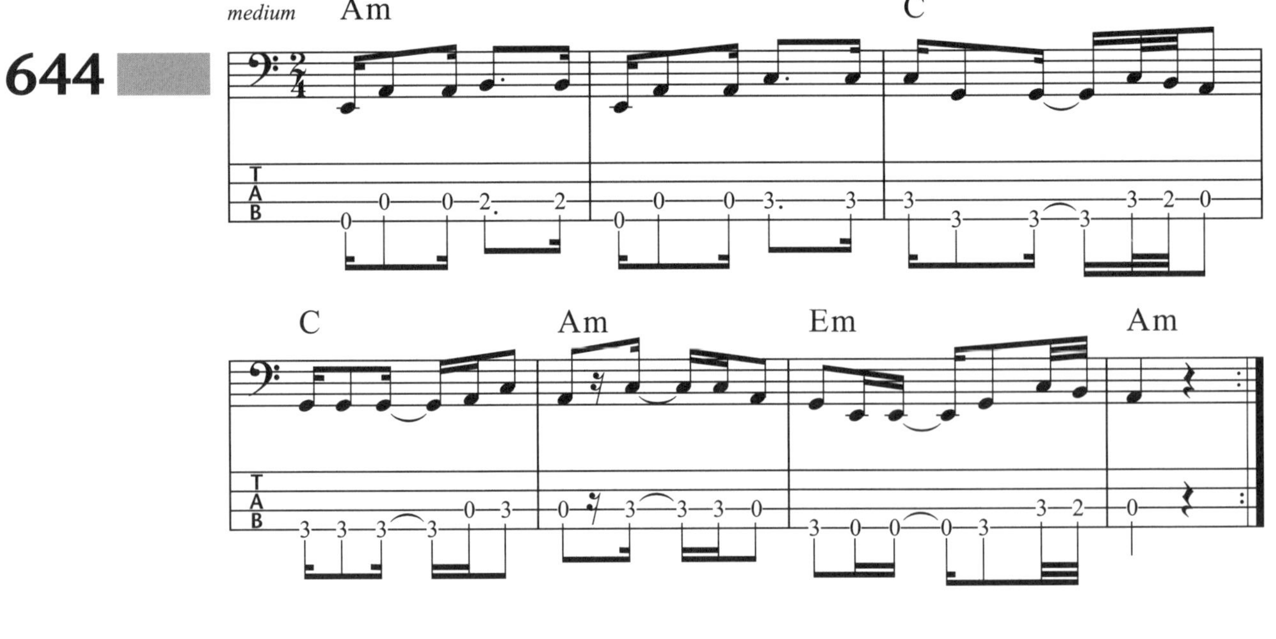

645

646

A variation of ex. 645.

BOOK FOUR

Africa contains many different countries and cultures. Consequently, the variety of music throughout Africa is enormous. You often hear people describe ethnic styles as "African", which indicates that there is an underlying common link between these differing forms of music. However, each African country developed musical styles, melodies and rhythms of their own and these are peculiar to that region.

African influences spread with the advent of the slave trade. Each company involved in the slave trade had a contract with a particular part of the world which needed cheap labour. They would choose a part of Africa to exploit and ship people from that particular region to this other overseas country. Therefore, each overseas country very often obtained slaves from a specific part of Africa.

As a result, strong musical influences from the African country of origin were absorbed by each overseas country. This is one reason why various kinds of African music have developed independently in many countries, especially when mixed as a "fusion" with the musical cultures of the new country. The subsequent crossovers are numerous.

Although information was traditionally not written down in Africa, their ability to remember huge amounts of information is legendary. For instance, the history of many tribes was taught to selected individuals who became the "cultural keepers". They could recite, word for word, information which stretched back for generations. Often this recitation could last for 3 days or more! They, therefore, developed the power of memory, whereas today we tend to store information on paper or computers. Our present day ability to remember things is comparatively poor.

Often, cultured historians were musicians who travelled the country looking for a place to play. Not much has changed there! As everyone knew that these musicians were independently minded and did not involve themselves personally in local politics or business, their opinions were regularly sought in quarrels or disputes. Many musicians, therefore, became arbiters or "honourary judges". Can you imagine today a US court asking a touring Rock band to give a judgement on whether Microsoft has broken any Antitrust laws? Maybe times have changed afterall!

■ African Music

African music has had a worldwide influence. Riffs can be based on tuned percussion rhythms, vocal chants, or double-time drum pulses with many anticipated notes. Percussion sections play almost hypnotically, and the bass lines are often ones which can be repeated for long periods of time, but have enough rhythmic content to keep them varied and musical. Sometimes just one riff is played throughout. At other times there may be 3 or 4 riffs which make up the various sections.

Africa is a massive continent and the styles of music vary enormously. Africa's influence on black American music, White Rock music, Latin American, etc., is obvious. Africa's dance music is rich with rhythms which were not previously used in Europe and the USA. It is very sophisticated and musicians now often use instruments with the latest technology. Harmonically the music is modal, but influences are crossing over in every country.

Some of the best-known artists are Koffi Olomide (Republic of Congo), Abdul Tee Jay's Rokoto (Sierra Leone), Toure Kunda (Senegal), Soul Brothers (South Africa), Mahlathini and Mahotella Queens (South Africa), King Sunny Ade (West Africa), Thomas Mapfumo (Zimbabwe), Kalambya Sisters (Kenya), Cheb Kader (Algeria), Chaba Fadela (Algeria), Ali Hassan Kuban (Upper Egypt), Salif Keita (Mali), Kante Manfila (West Africa), Kanda Bongo Man (Republic of Congo), Pierre Akendengues (Gabon), Audrey Motaung (South Africa) and Johnny Clegg (South Africa).

African Riffs

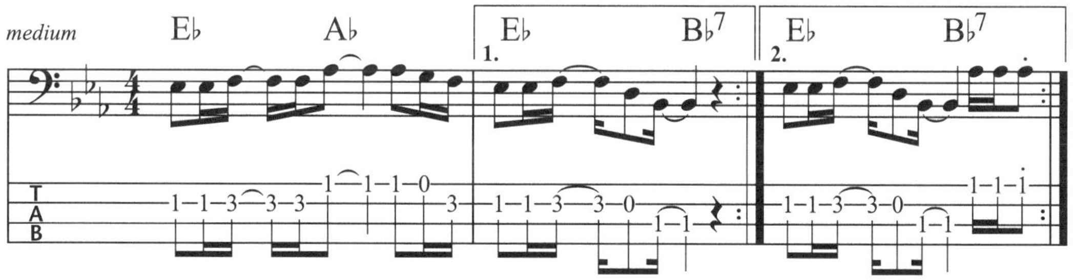

medium — E♭ A♭ | 1. E♭ B♭7 | 2. E♭ B♭7

647 CD1 Track 81

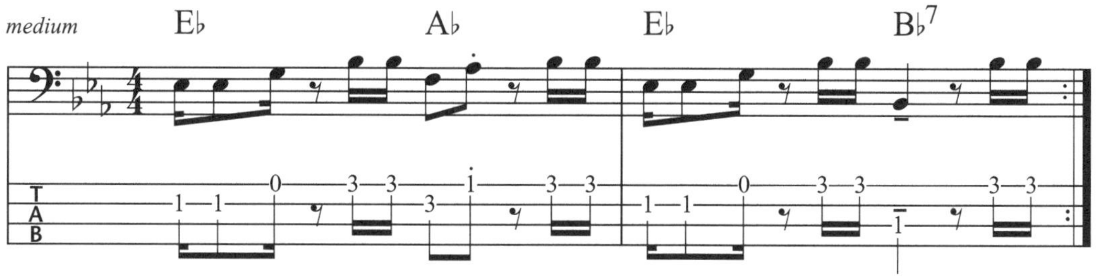

medium — E♭ A♭ | E♭ B♭7

648

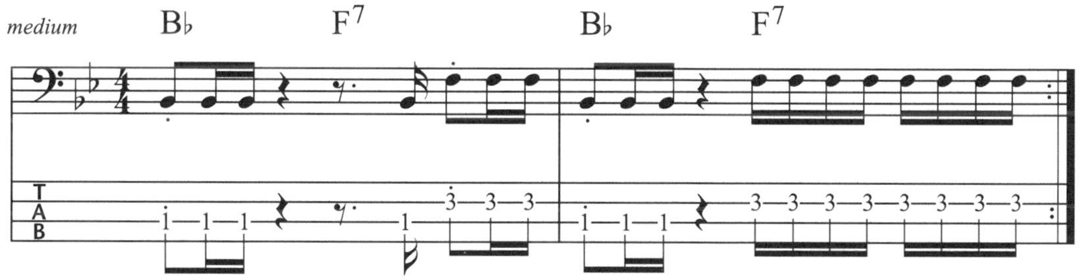

medium — B♭ F7 | B♭ F7

649

medium — Gm

650 CD1 Track 81

Gm

medium — B♭ | F7

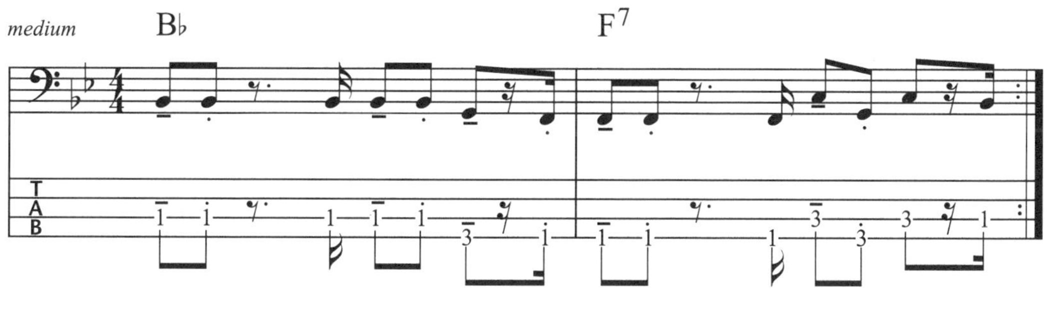

651

652
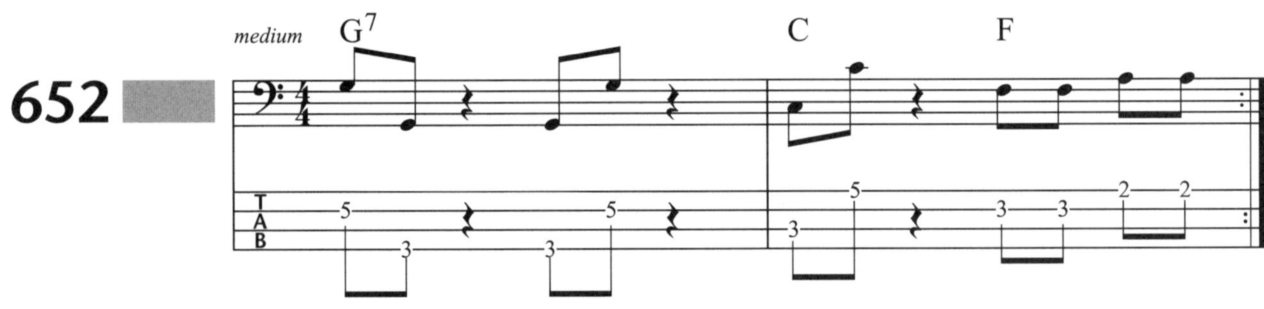

653

654
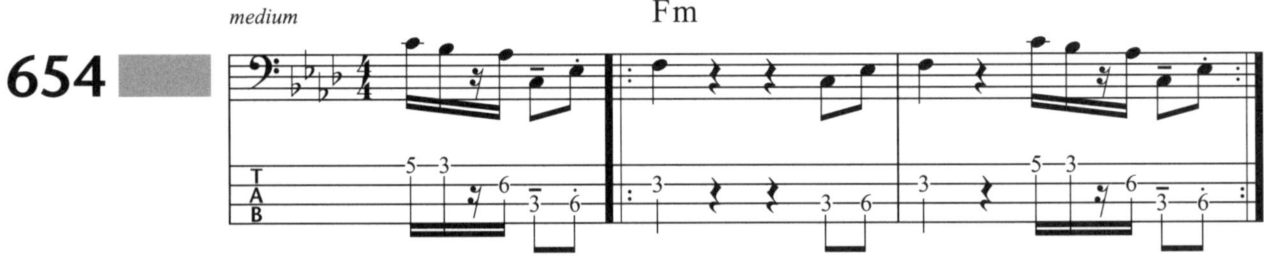

655
CD 1 Track 82

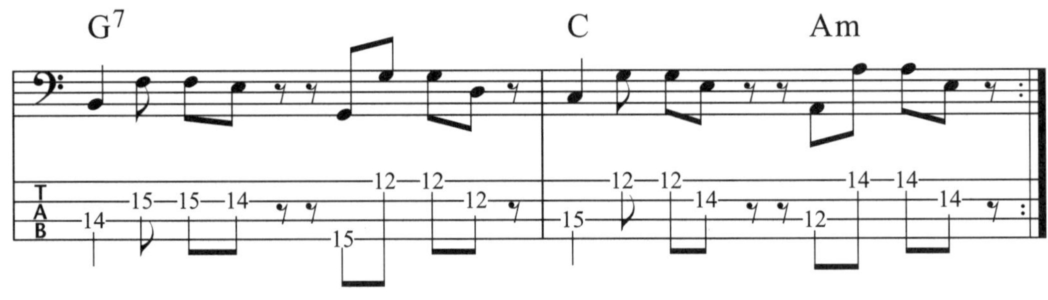

656

medium
Am7
657

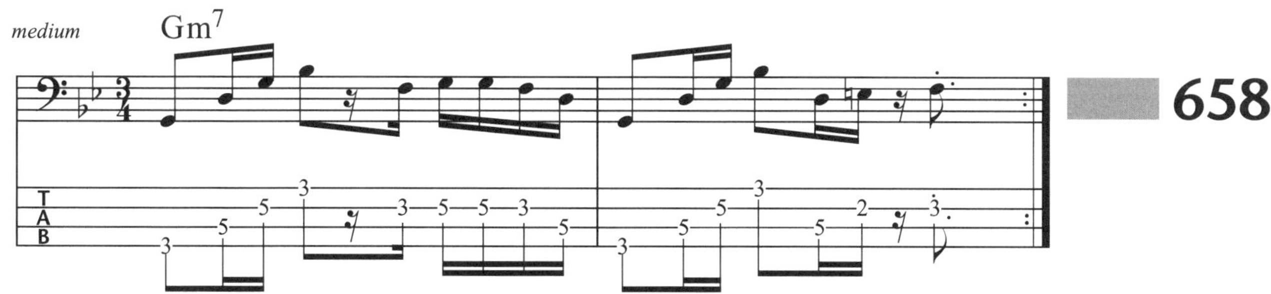
medium
Gm7
658

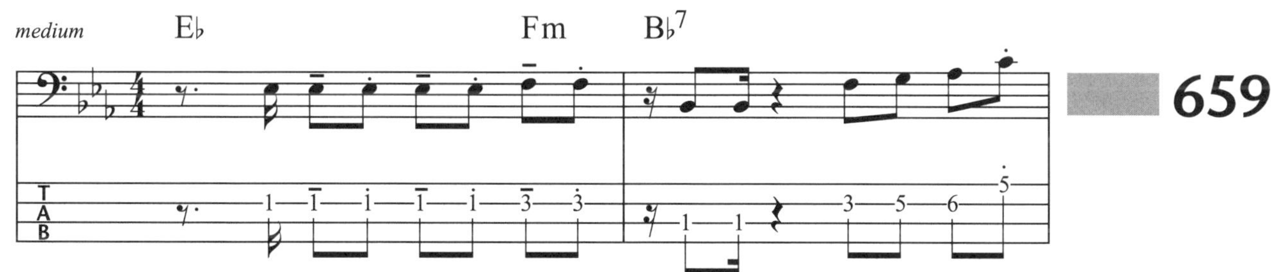
medium
E♭
Fm
B♭7
659

E♭
Fm
B♭7

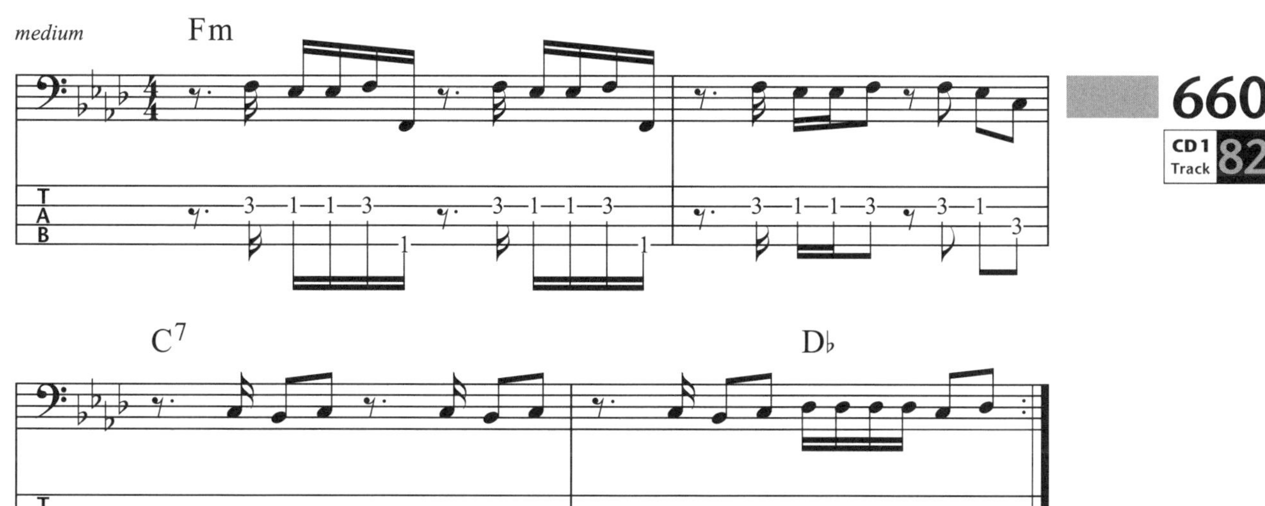
medium
Fm
C7
D♭
660
CD 1 Track 82

661

662

663

664

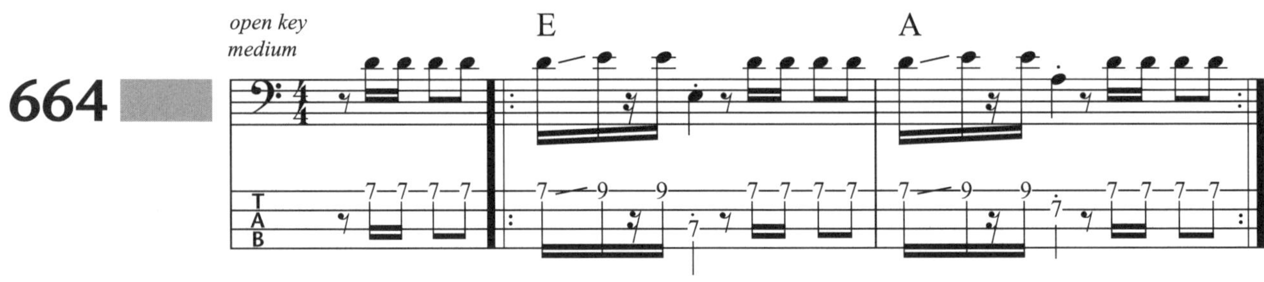

665

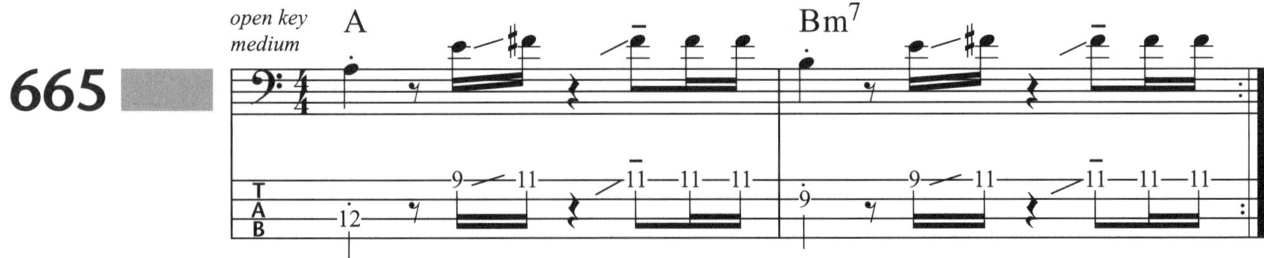

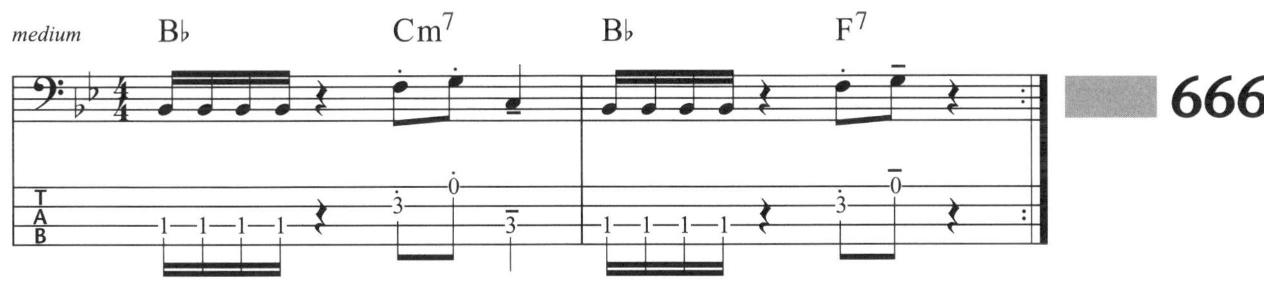

666

667

CD 1 Track 83

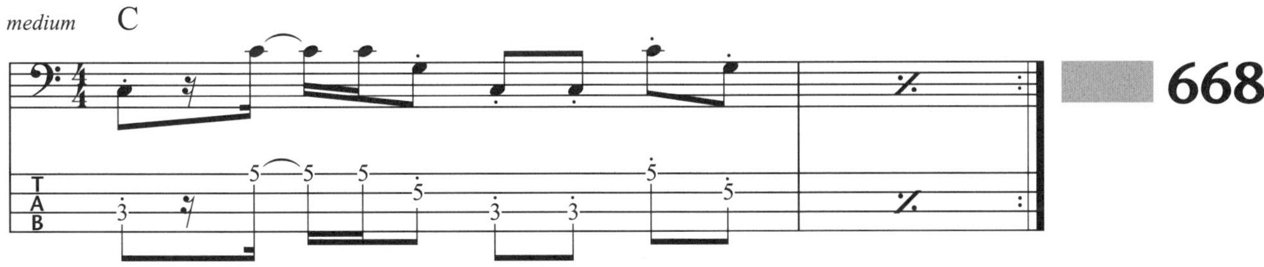

668

669

670
CD 1 Track 83
medium/fast
Gm7

671
medium
Gm7
C7
Gm7
C7

672
fast
Gm

673
fast
Gm7

674
medium
Gm7
C7
D7
Gm7

675
medium
Gm7
C9
F
Gm7

open key
medium
staccato
G9

676

G9
D7

medium
Cm

677

medium
Dm

678

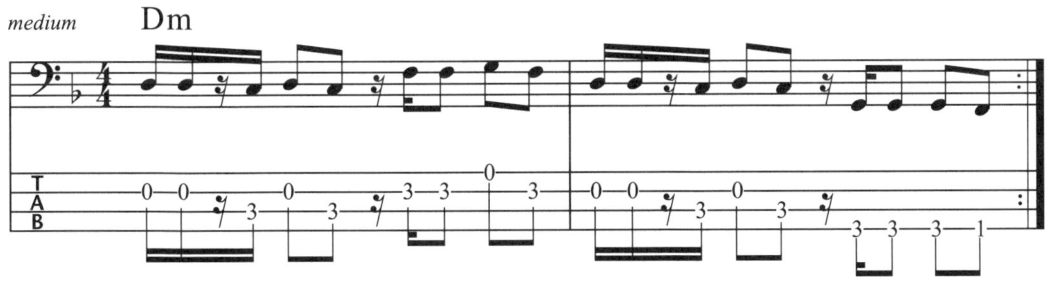

medium
Gm7

679

medium
Dm7

680

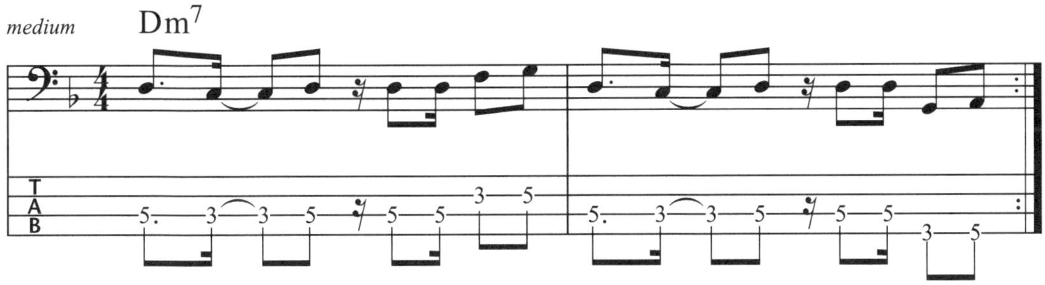

open key
medium
Dm7

Dm7

open key
medium
Em
G

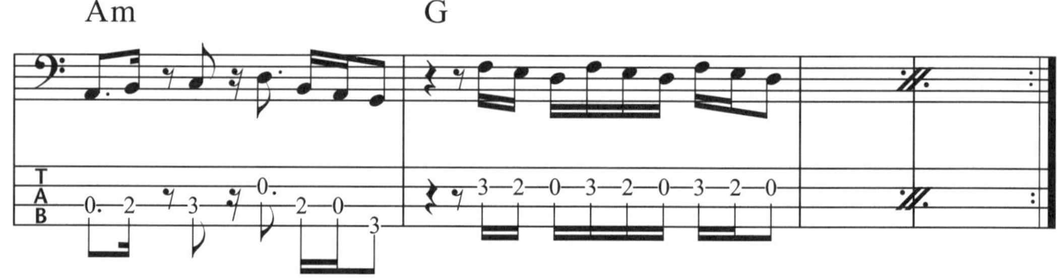
Am
G

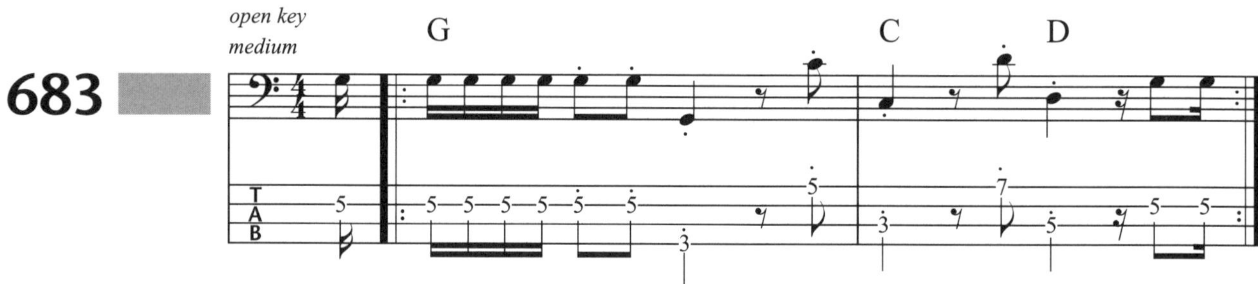
open key
medium
683
G
C
D

open key
medium
684
G7

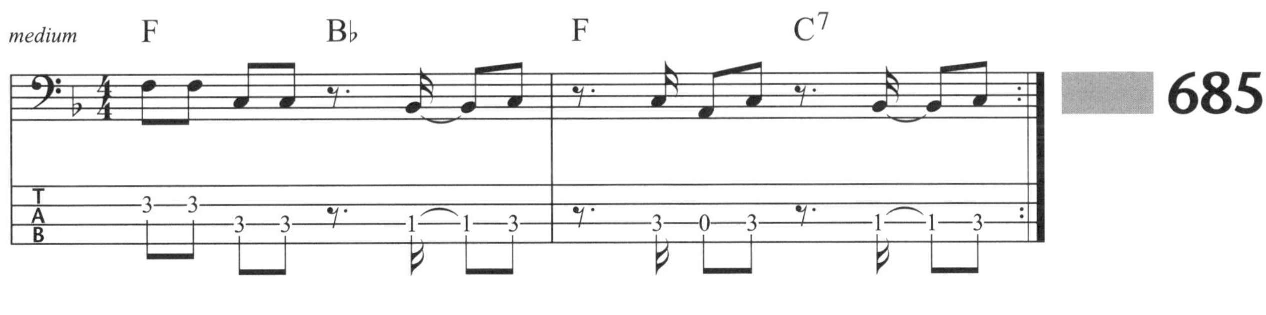

medium
F
B♭
F
C7
685

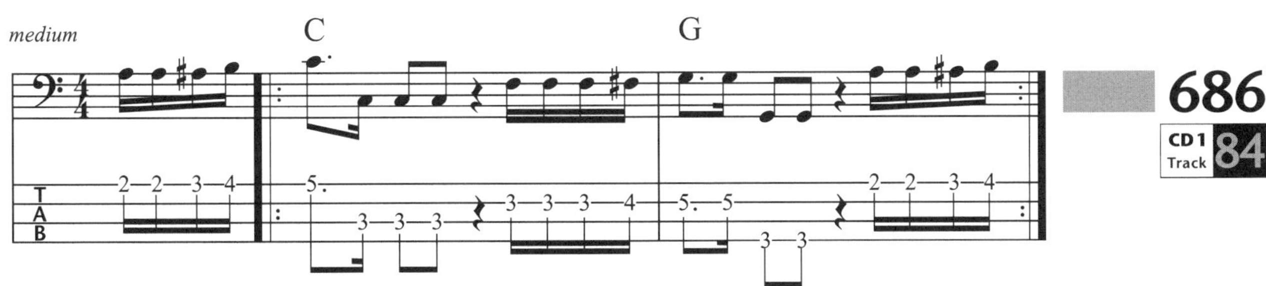

medium
C
G
686
CD 1 Track 84

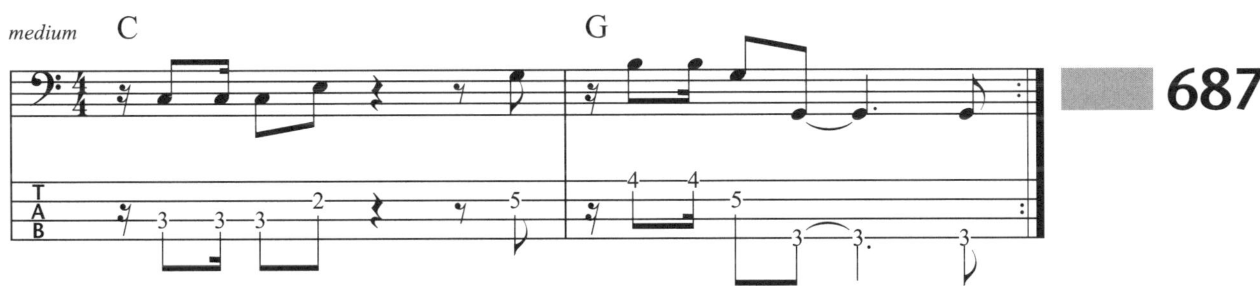

medium
C
G
687

medium
C
G7
688

medium
C
G7
689
CD 1 Track 84

690
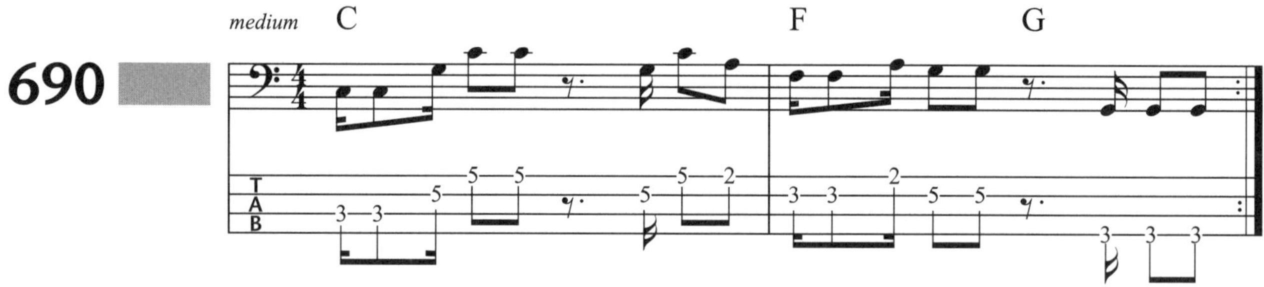

691

692
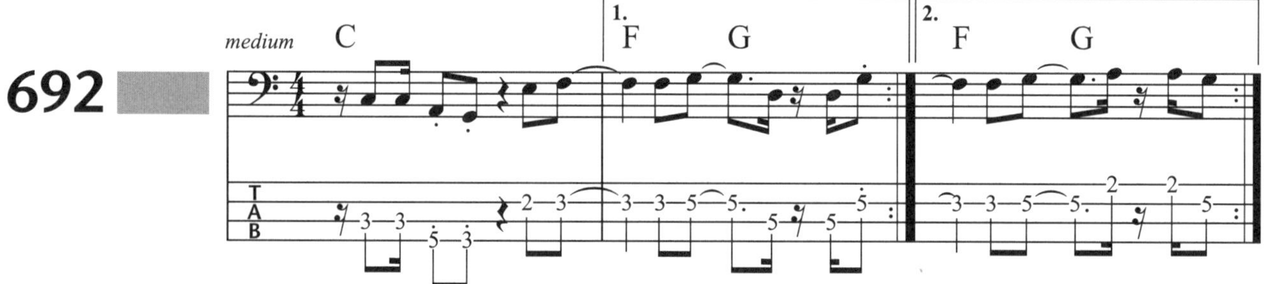

693
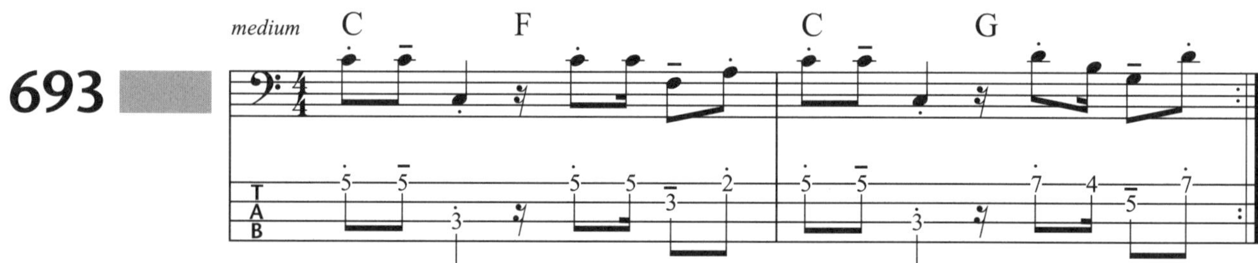

North Africa & The Middle East

The Arabic style of music is not as forceful as the African drum dominated variety. As the acoustic instruments which play the tune and accompaniment are relatively quiet, the percussion is played much more subtly. Bass guitars were, unfortunately, not in vogue during the evolution of Middle Eastern and Turkish music, but I have adapted some lines which are close to authentic drum patterns, and also ones which follow lines played by other instruments having a similar role to the bass.

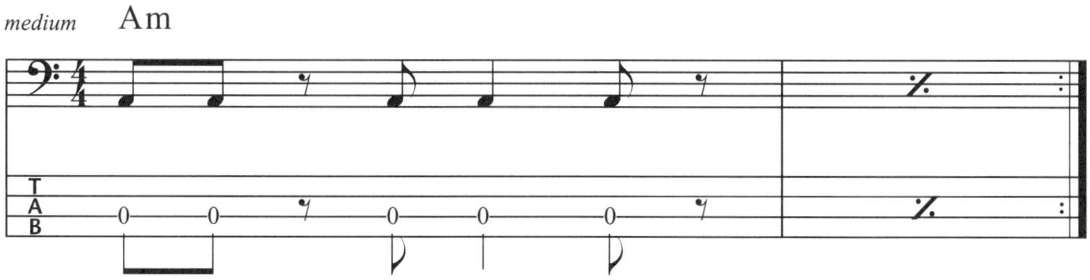
medium
Am
T
A
B
0 0 0 0 0

694

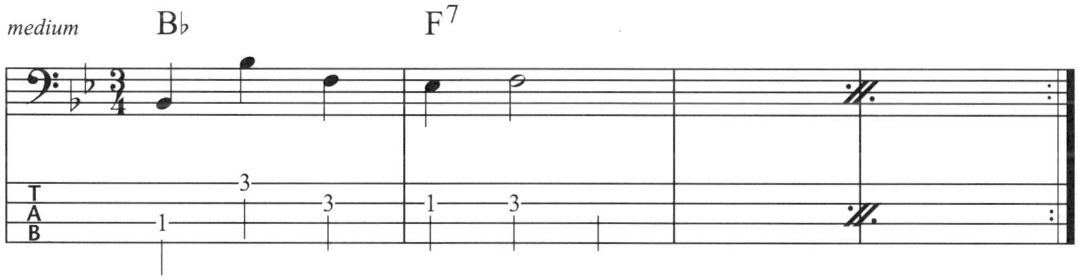
medium
B♭
F7
T
A
B
1 3 3 1 3

695

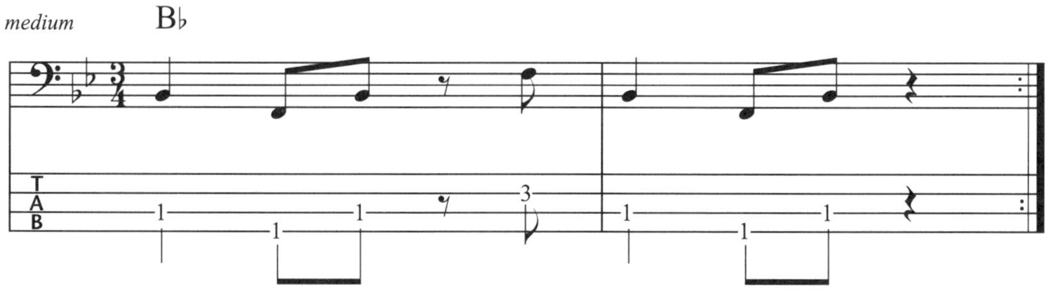
medium
B♭
T
A
B
1 1 1 3 1 1 1

696

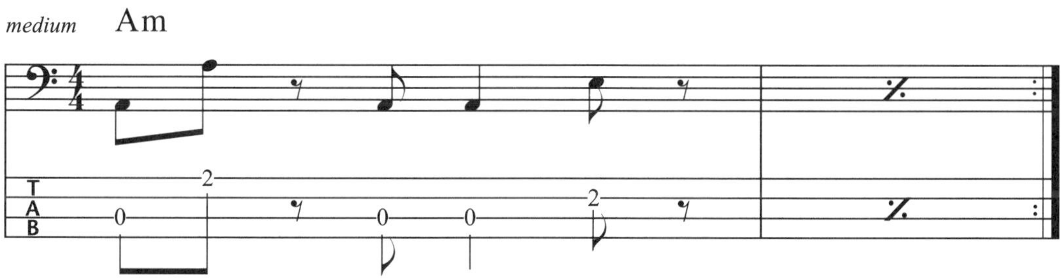
medium
Am
T
A
B
0 2 0 0 2

697

CD1 Track 85

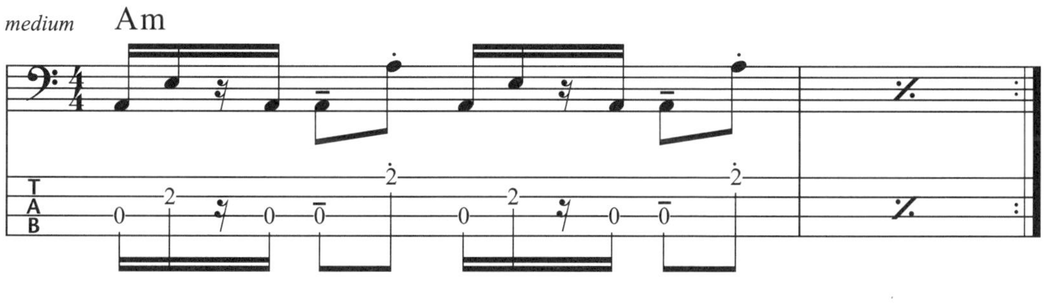
medium
Am
T
A
B
0 2 0 0 2 0 2 0 0 2

698

CD1 Track 85

AMA
VERLAG

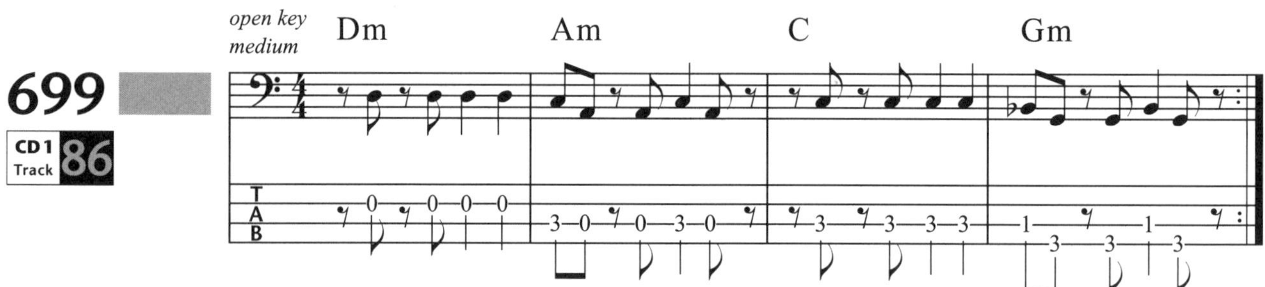
699
CD1 Track 86
open key
medium
Dm
Am
C
Gm

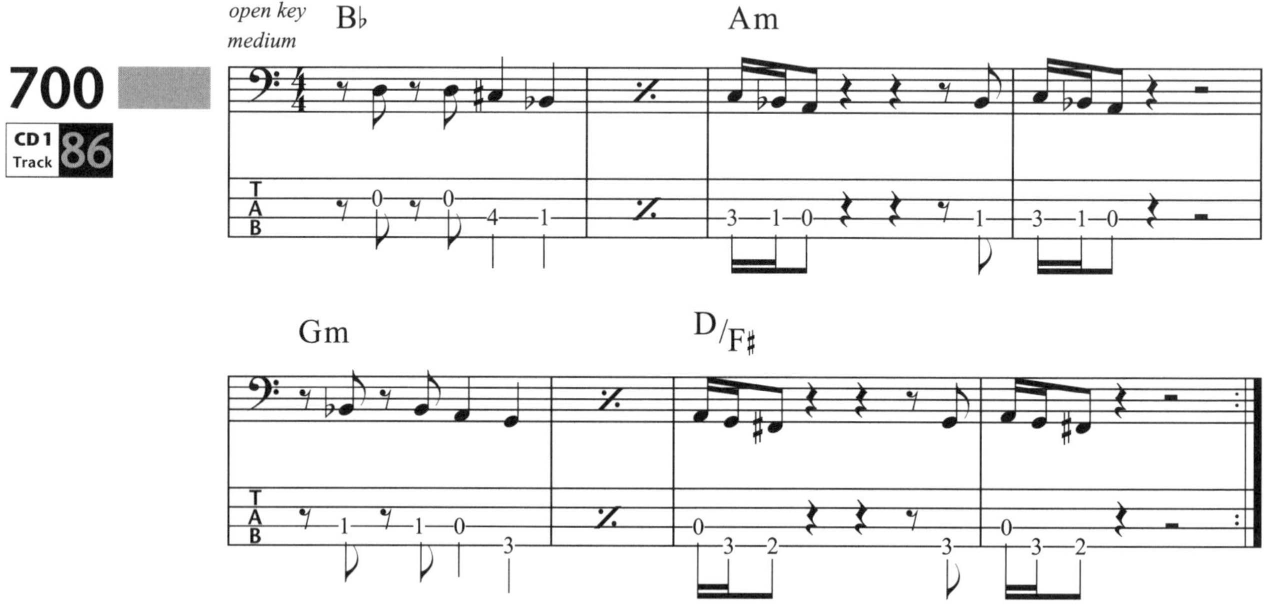
700
CD1 Track 86
open key
medium
B♭
Am
Gm
D/F♯

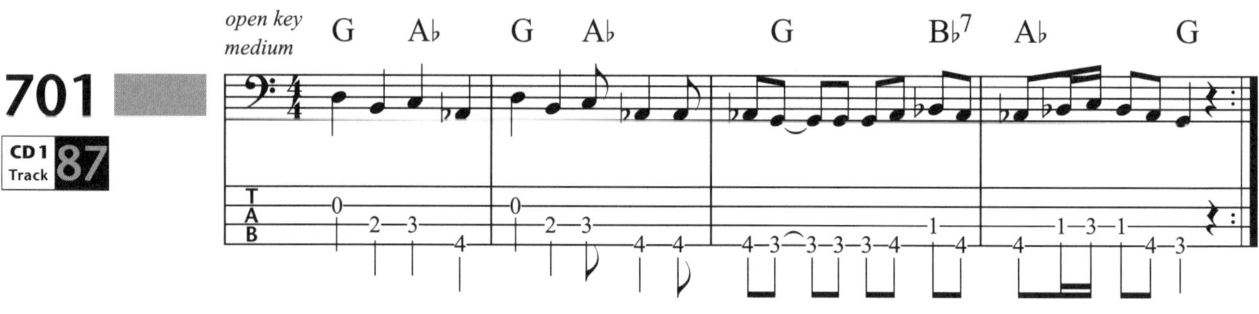
701
CD1 Track 87
open key
medium
G
A♭
G
A♭
G
B♭7
A♭
G

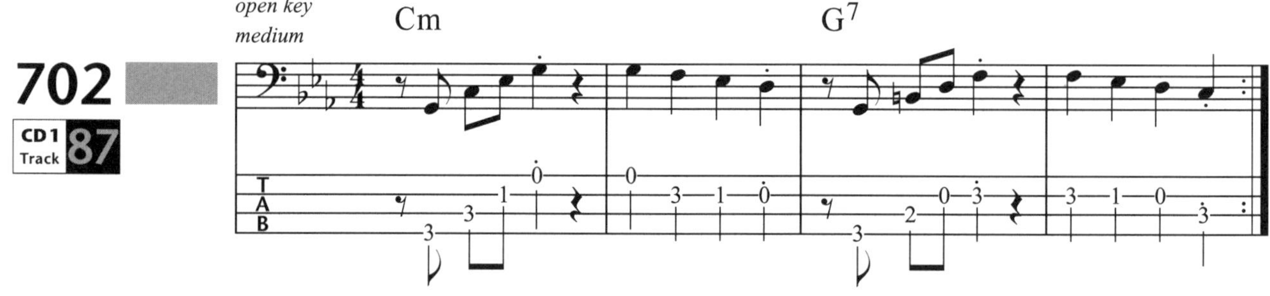
702
CD1 Track 87
open key
medium
Cm
G7

open key
medium/fast

703
CD 1 Track 88

open key
medium

704
CD 1 Track 88

Somalia

Somalia is an East African nation, and has been influenced by its neighbours Ethiopia and Kenya, and from across the sea by the Arabic nations and their Islamic culture. The British and Italians divided up the country later on, before it became independent.

Musically, Somalia also draws on influences from Tanzania, Sudan and Muslim North Africa. Some of its instruments come from countries like Egypt and Lebanon, but the six-string guitar is also widely used, as it now is in the whole of Africa. Portable harmoniums and small keyboards are a feature of their music, and probably came from India. The modern Japanese keyboards are the latest influence.

Songs are sung in various languages including Swahili, Bantu, Chimina and Somalian dialects. Most Somalian musicians are part-timers and their "proper" jobs are shoemaking, carving, etc. Many musicians are in the army and police force, and they have some fine dance bands. Most songs are about success and failure in love and romance.

705

medium C

706

CD1 Track 89

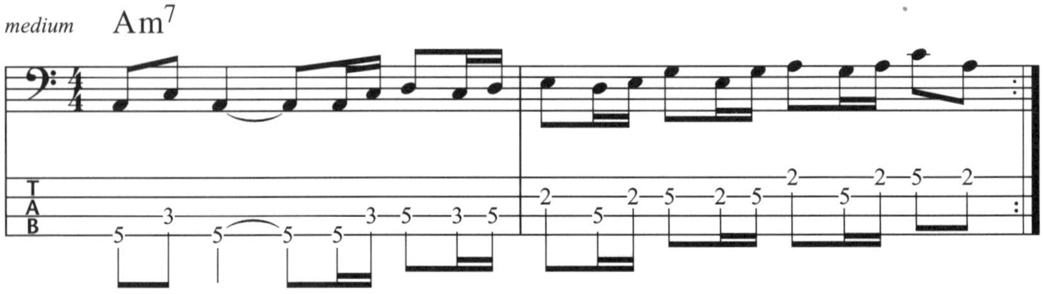

medium Am7

707

CD1 Track 89

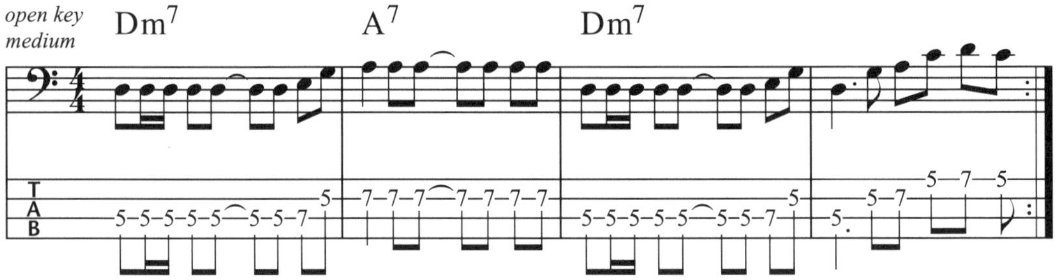

open key *medium* Dm7 A7 Dm7

708

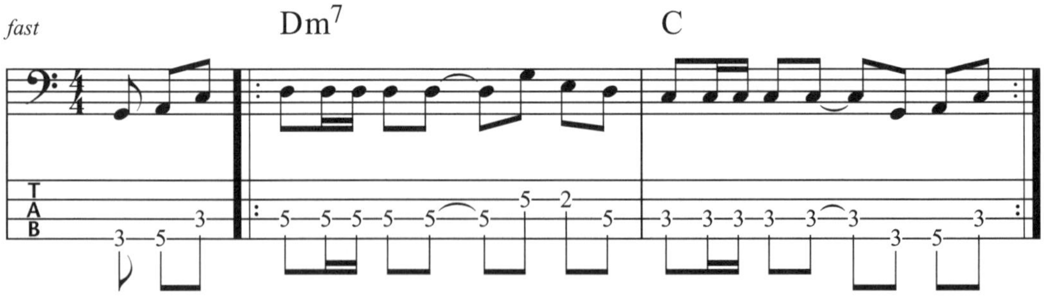

fast Dm7 C

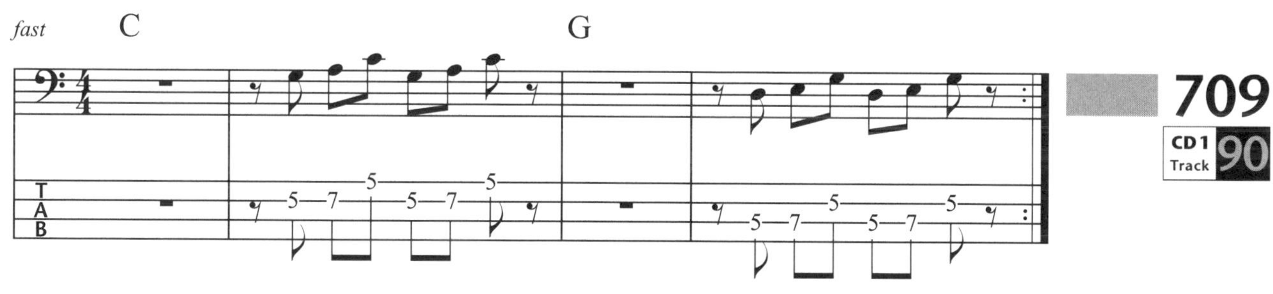
fast
C
G
709
CD 1 Track 90

fast
C
710

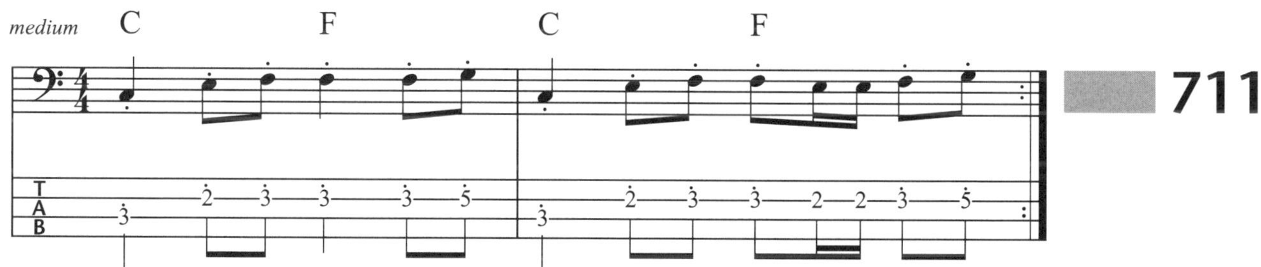
medium
C
F
C
F
711

open key
medium
F
712
CD 1 Track 90

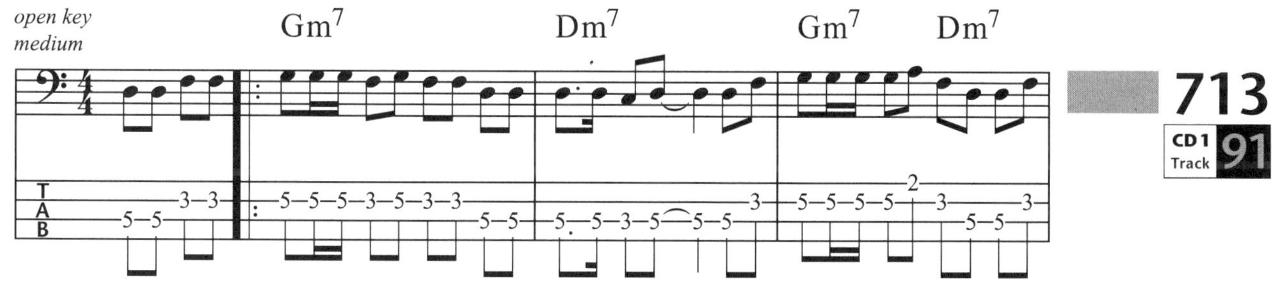
open key
medium
Gm7
Dm7
Gm7
Dm7
713
CD 1 Track 91

Gm7
Dm7
Gm7
Dm7

714

CD 1 Track 91

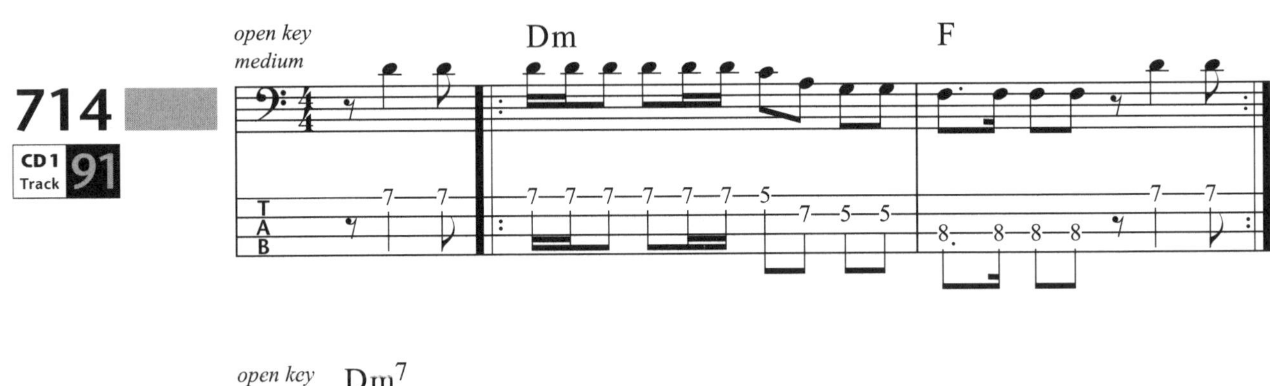

715

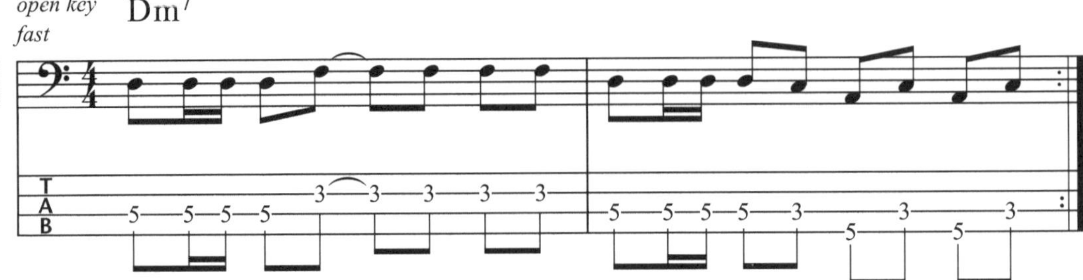

716

717

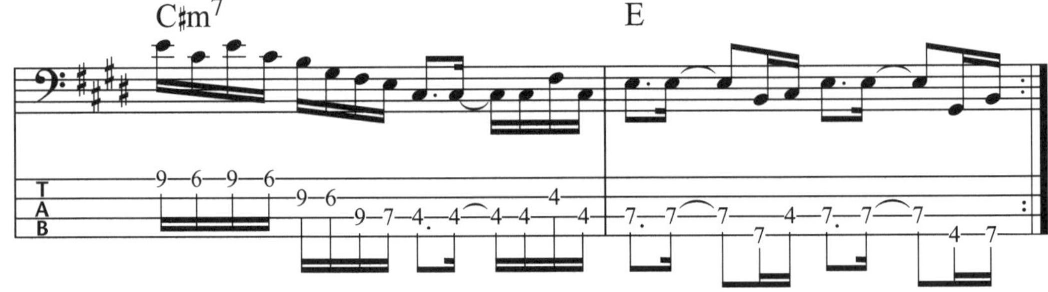

Mali

Many male Mali singers are "Jalis", the inheritors and carriers of the culture of the sophisticated Manding Empire, which dates back to the 13th century. Jalis are hereditary musicians, diplomats, arbitrators and moral and political counsellors. They are the oral "librarians" and the culture's memory. They are considered to have great wisdom, experience and healing power. Traditionally they are not paid with money for their performances, but receive gifts from the people whose hearts and souls have been uplifted. They are great musical improvisers and can have very rich voices. One particular singer who has made a big impact in Africa is Kassy Mady.

Many other singers deal with more contemporary social issues, human problems and political ideals. One of these modern female vocalist/composers is Nahawa Doumbia. Her lyrics are very much about "today", and she works with contemporary rhythm sections and massed voices. It is very dance orientated music.

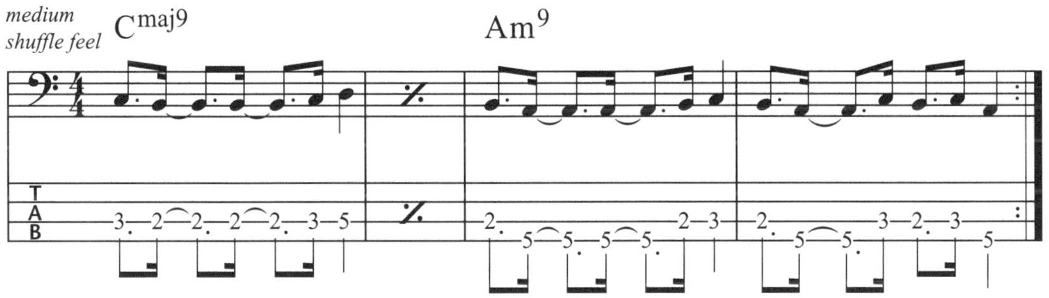

medium shuffle feel Cmaj9 Am9

718 CD 2 Track 1

medium shuffle feel C6

719

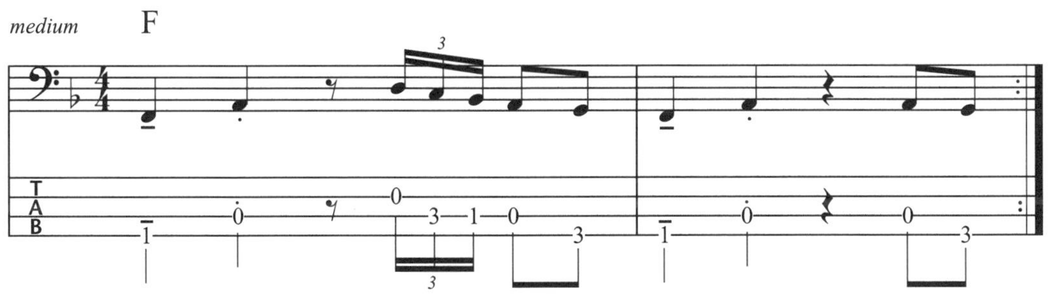

medium F

720

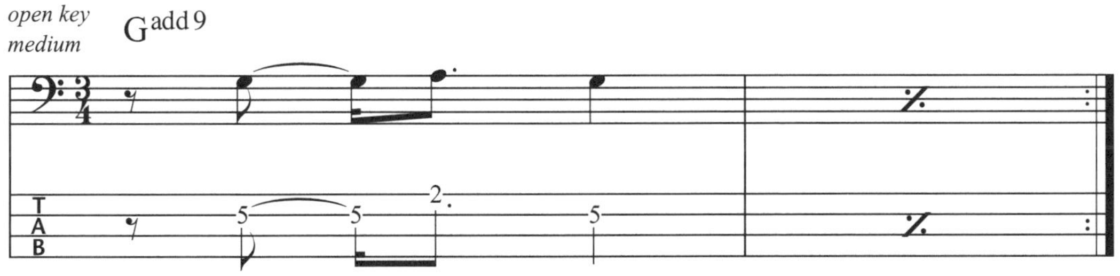

open key medium Gadd9

721

722

723
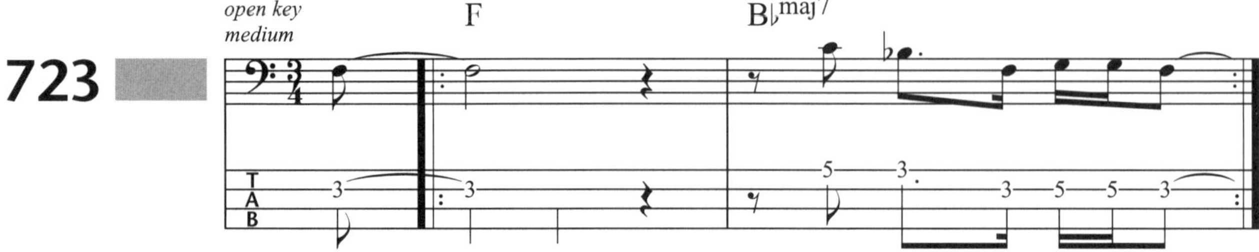

724

725
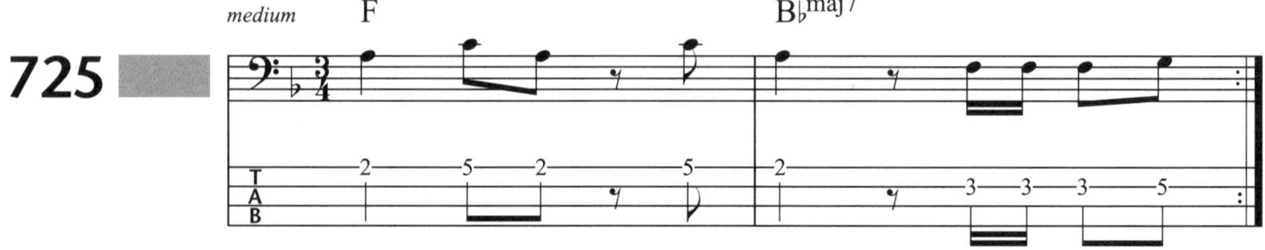

726
CD 2 Track 1

727
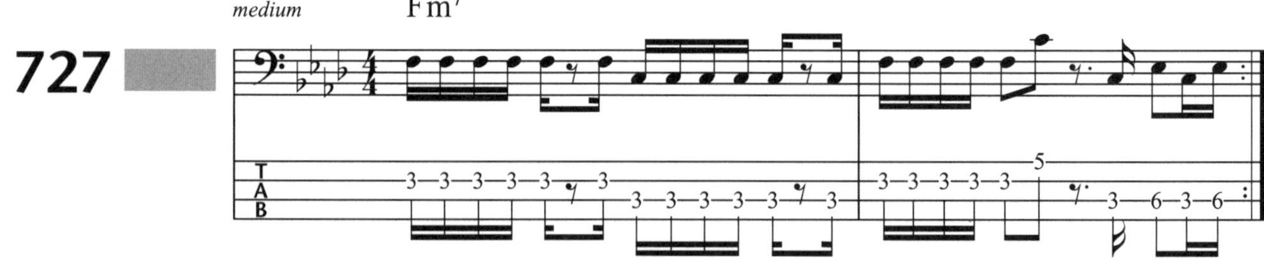

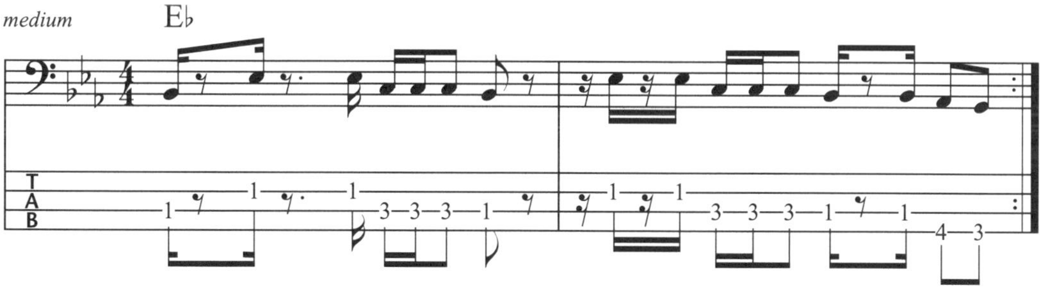

medium
E♭
T
A
B

728
CD 2 Track 2

medium
Fm7
T
A
B

729
CD 2 Track 2

medium
Em7
D
T
A
B
Em7
D
T
A
B

730
CD 2 Track 3

medium
D7
T
A
B

731

medium
Bm
T
A
B

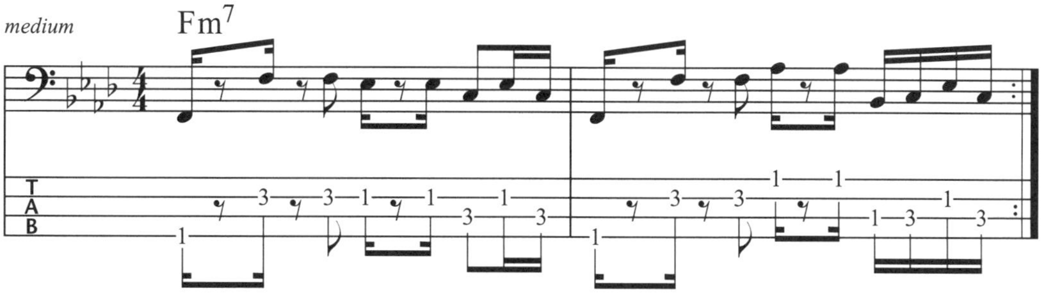

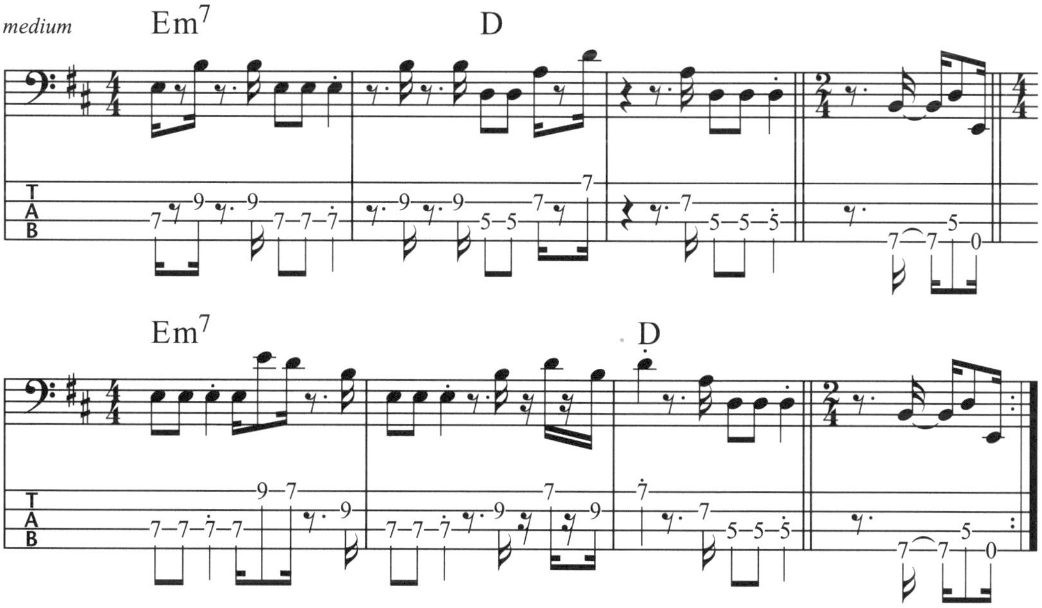

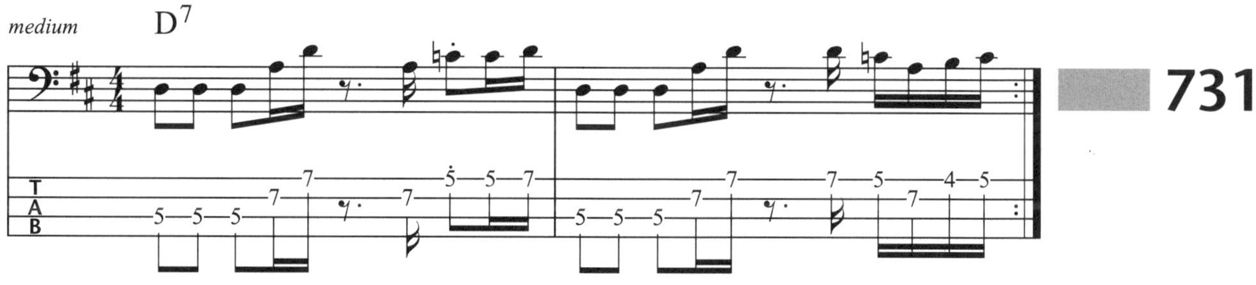

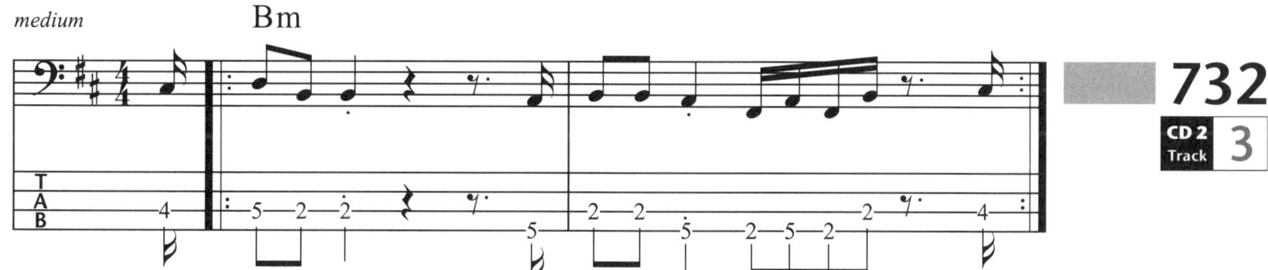

732
CD 2 Track 3

733
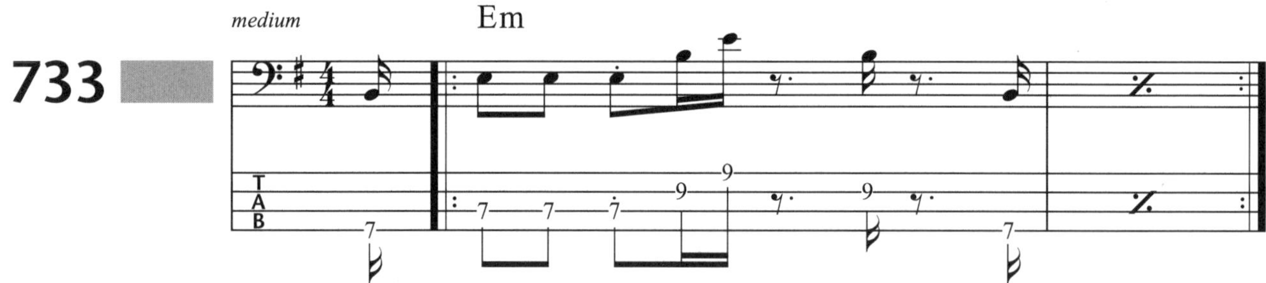

734

735

736
CD 2 Track 4

737

738

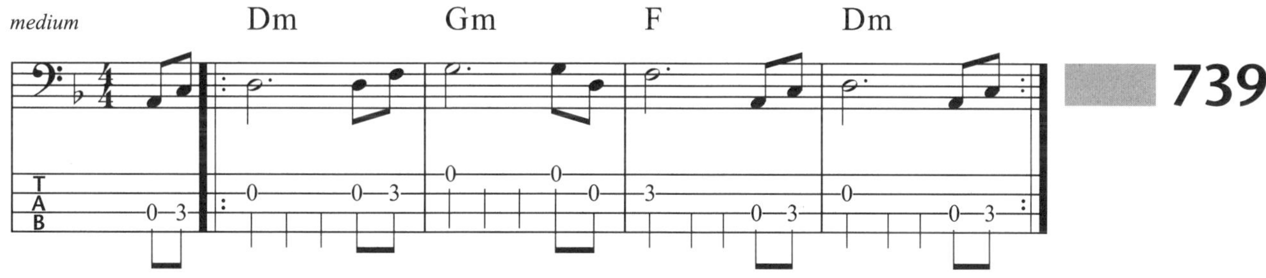

739

740

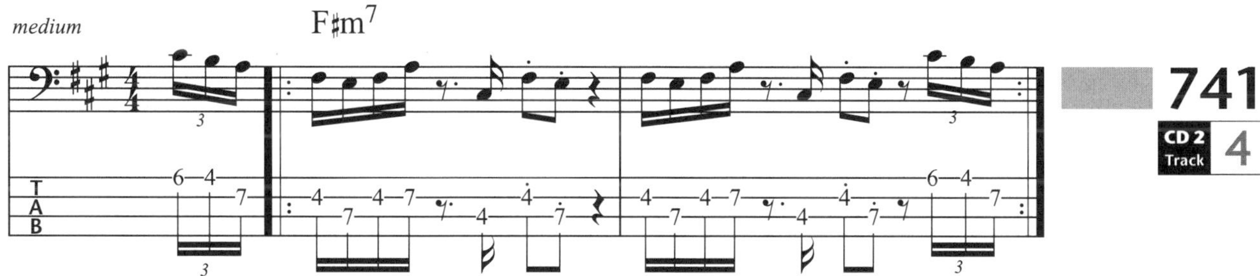

741
CD 2 Track 4

■ Guinea

As a result of presidential support in the 70's, music was subsidized as part of a revolution in the arts. Consequently, musicians were able to concentrate on their work and greatly progress in their quest for new forms of expression. Their presence was greatly felt in West Africa, and particularly neighbouring Mali. They became musical ambassadors of the Guinea culture in Europe also, especially France. Some of the best known artists are Ousmane Kouyate, Les Ambassadeurs, Manfile Kante, Salif Keita and Kaba Kante.

Chord sequences are quite sophisticated and draw on American and European music. Trying to reach a wider audience, modern musicians have softened the hard driving dance rhythms to produce a different feel altogether. It is almost jazz-like with its floating patterns. The songs consist more of chord progressions than just simple riffs, but the motif is still the basis of these popular songs, whether it is taken up by a bass, drum pattern or chord progression.

742 *medium* C F G7

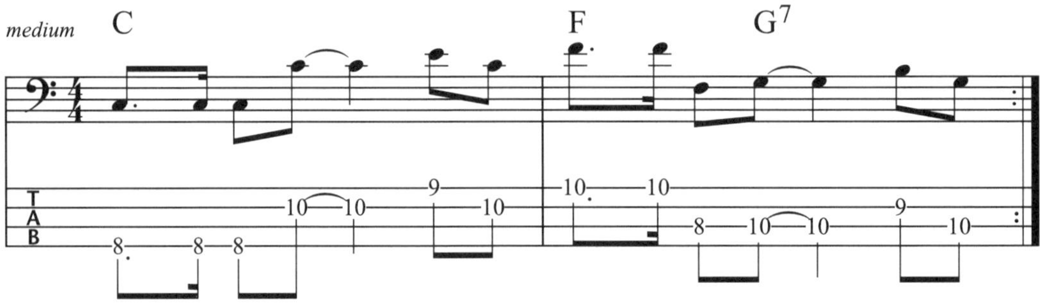

743 CD 2 Track 5 *medium* C G 8va

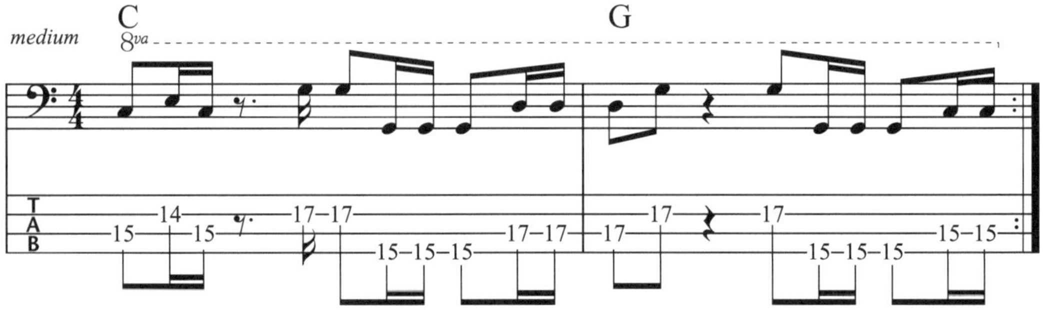

744 *medium* C G 8va

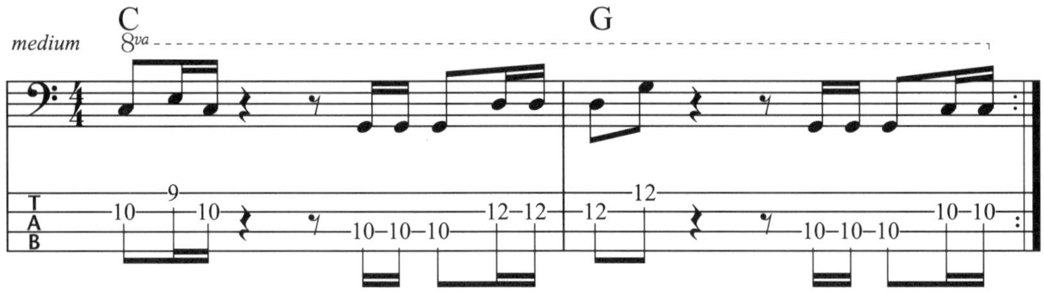

745 CD 2 Track 5 *open key* *medium* Dm7 A7

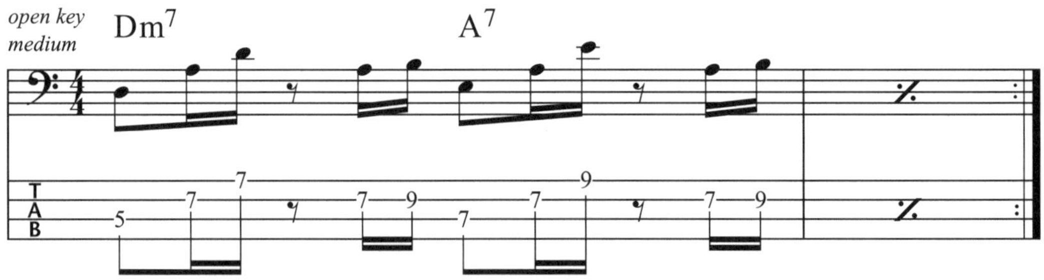

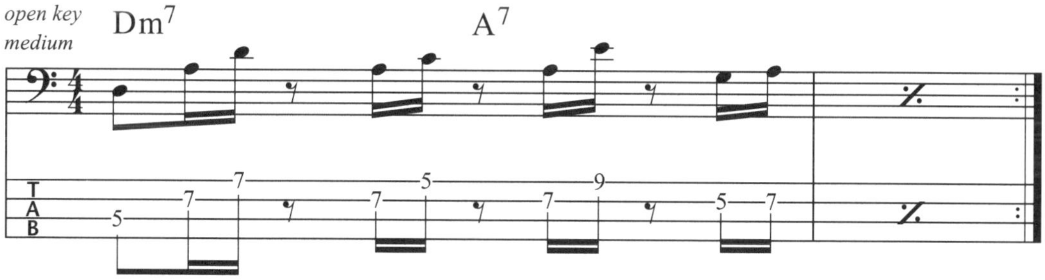

open key
medium
Dm7
A7

746

open key
medium
G7
F

747

medium
C7
C
B♭

748

CD 2 Track 6

medium
C
B♭

749

medium
C

750

medium
C
Dm
Am
G7

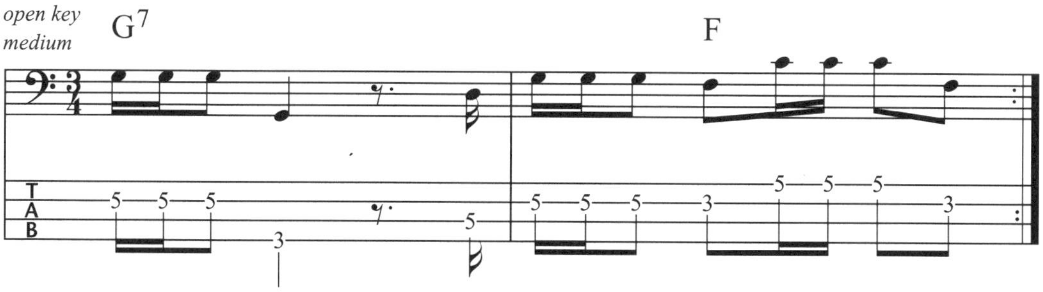

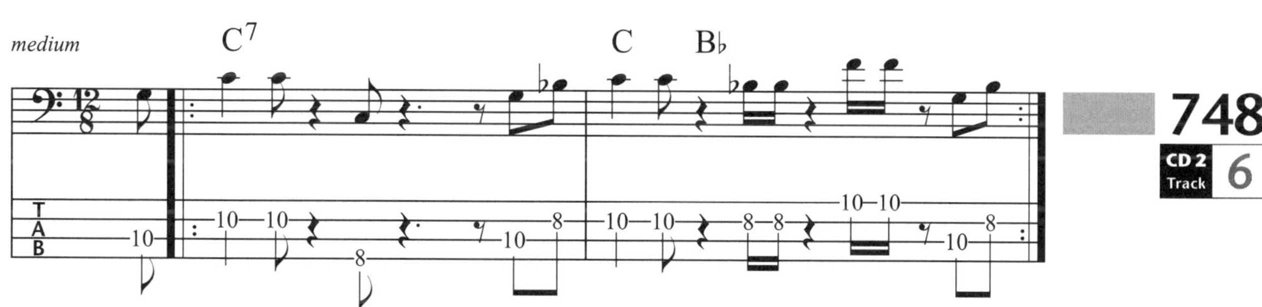

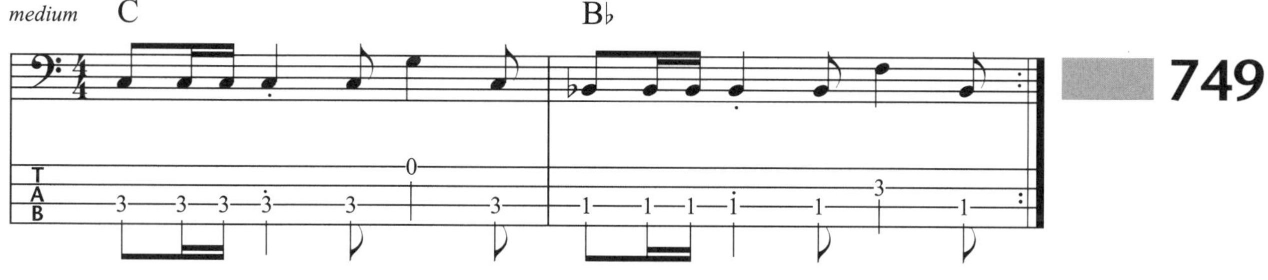

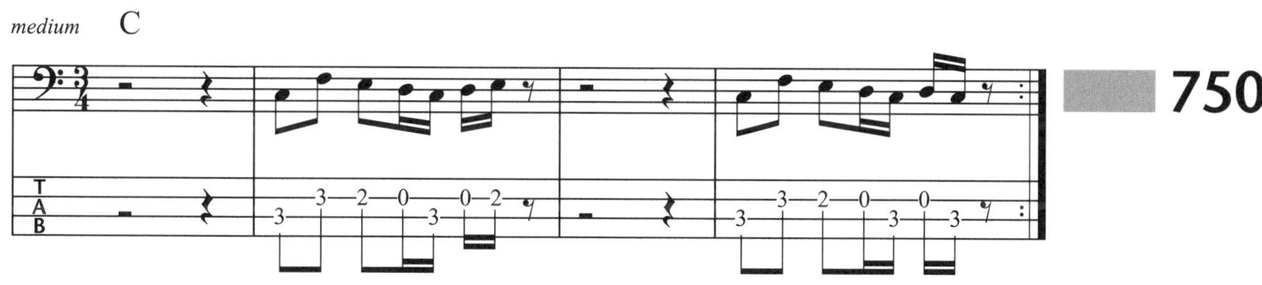

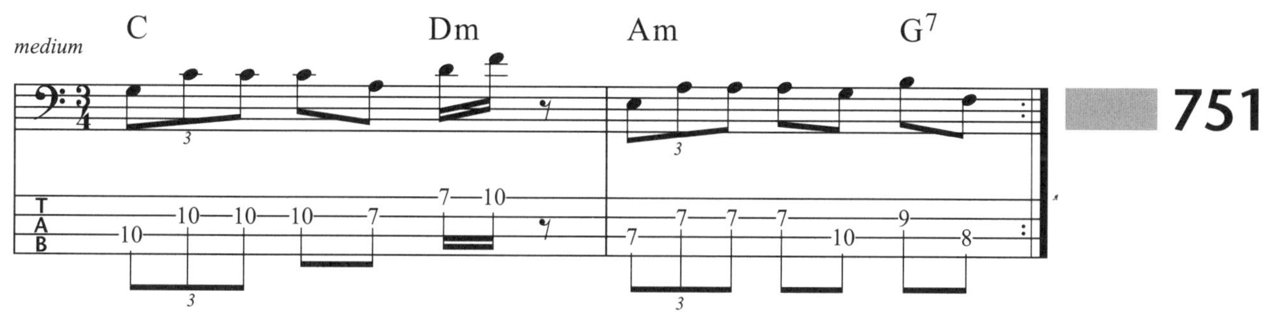

751

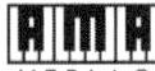

AMA VERLAG

752

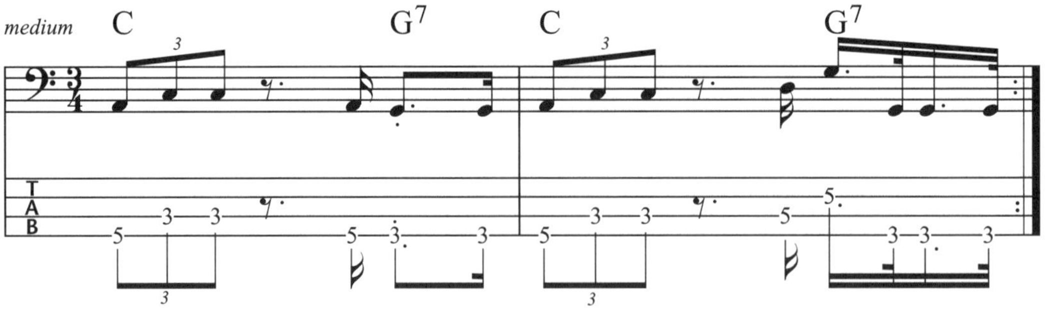
medium
C
G7
C
G7
T
A
B

753

CD 2 Track 6

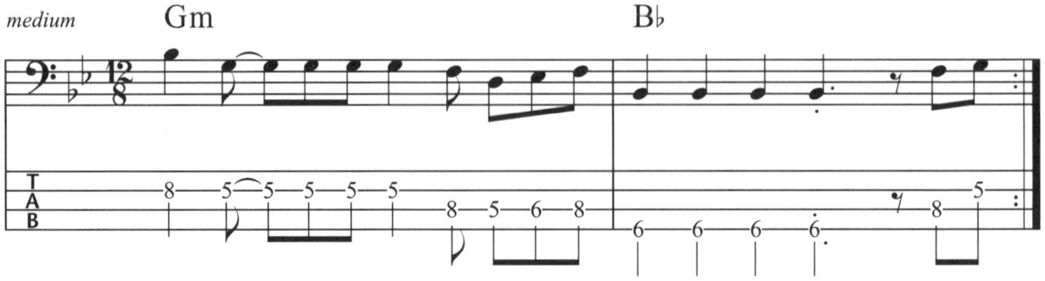
medium
Gm
B♭
T
A
B

754

CD 2 Track 7

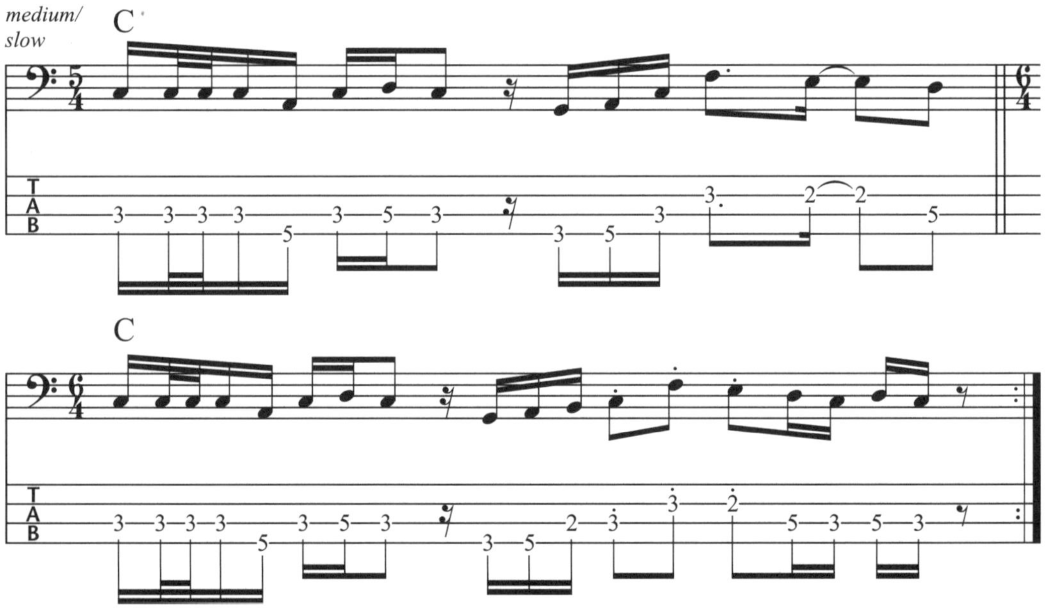
medium/
slow
C
C
T
A
B

755

CD 2 Track 7

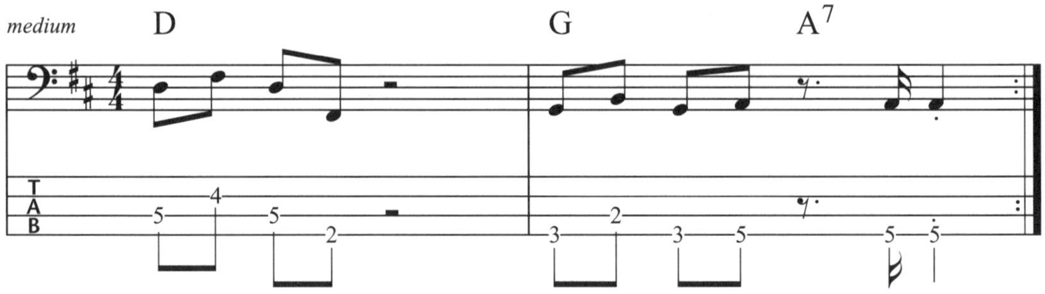
medium
D
G
A7
T
A
B

756

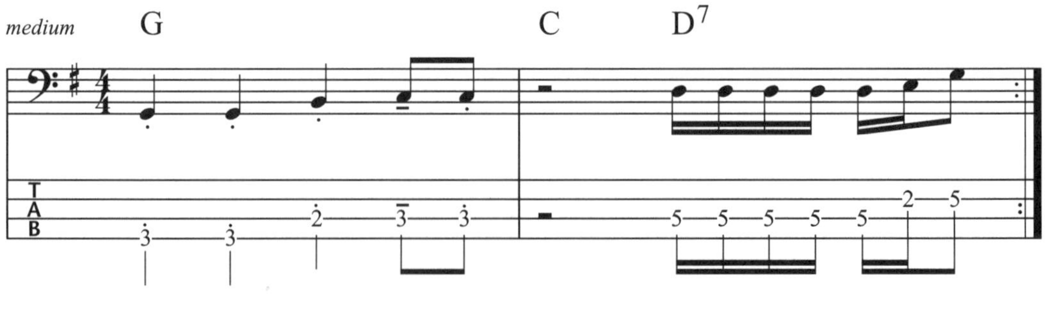
medium
G
C
D7
T
A
B

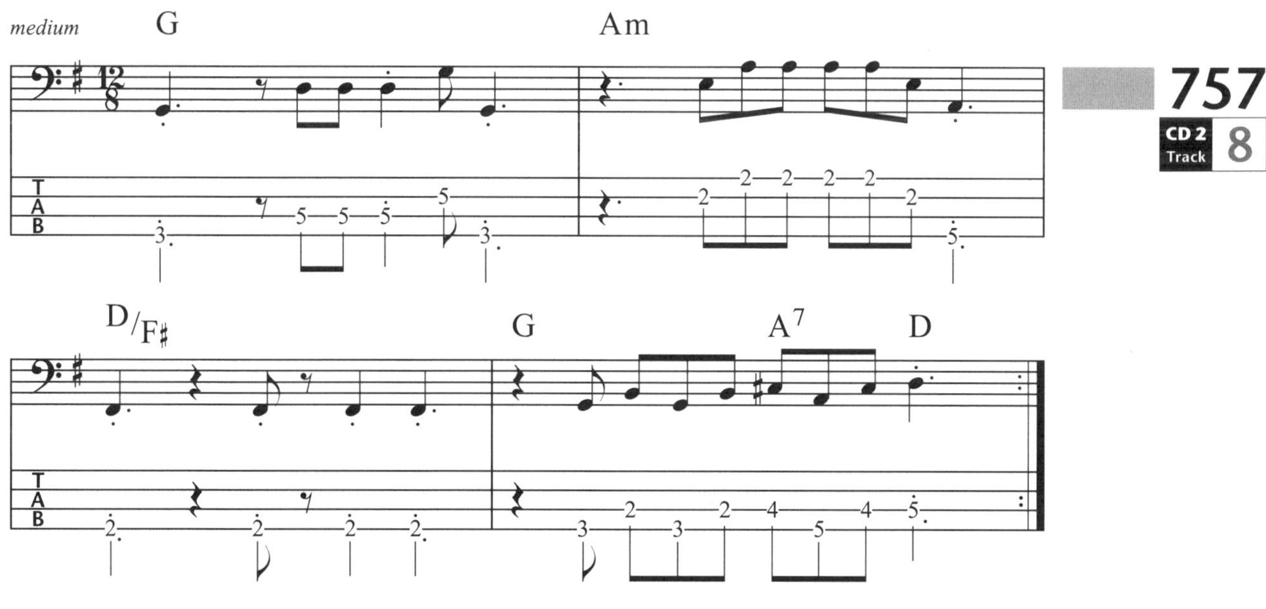

medium
G
Am
757
CD 2 Track 8
D/F♯
G
A7
D

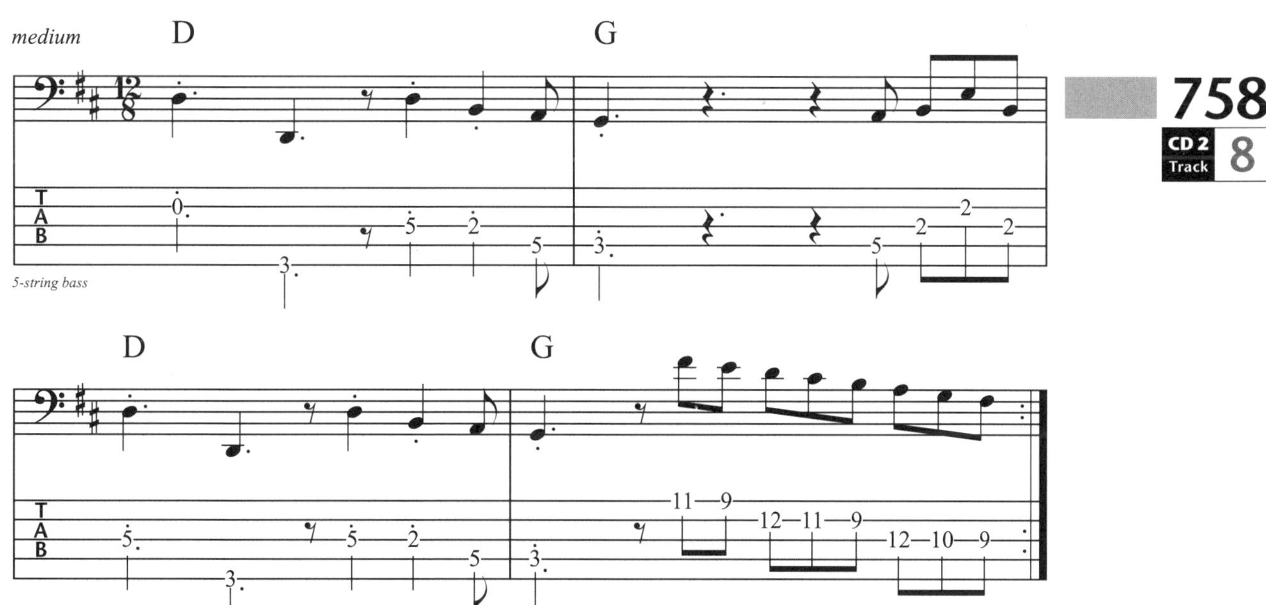

medium
D
G
758
CD 2 Track 8
5-string bass
D
G

medium
shuffle feel
G7
C
759

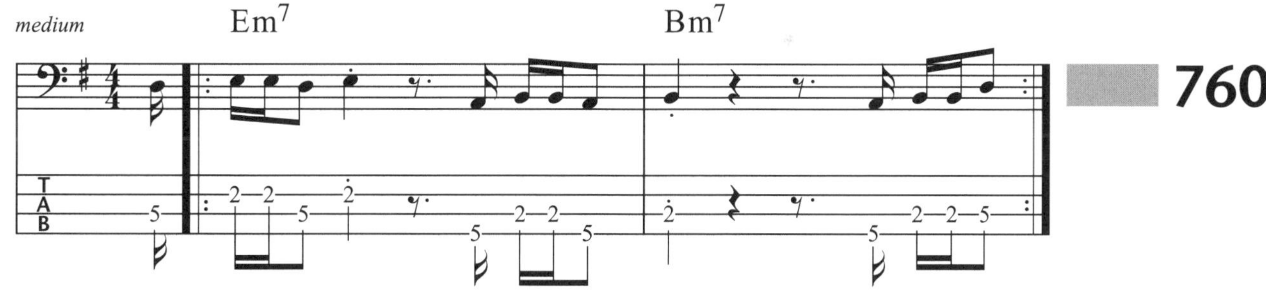

medium
Em7
Bm7
760

761

762

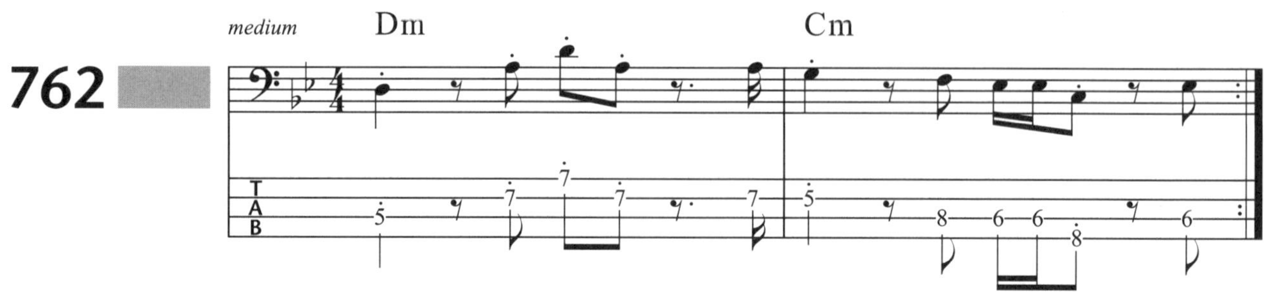

Cameroon

One of the leading bands from Cameroon is Tetes Brulees, who have revived Bikutsi music, which is a primeval rhythm from the forests of West African Cameroon. Another popular style is called Zouk. The sound is raw and exciting, with fast rhythms and guitars playing dancing patterns. The vocals can be almost "punk-like".

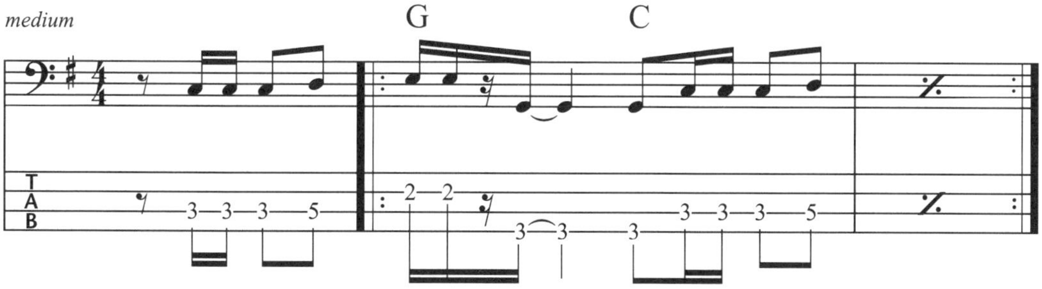

medium G C

763 CD 2 Track 9

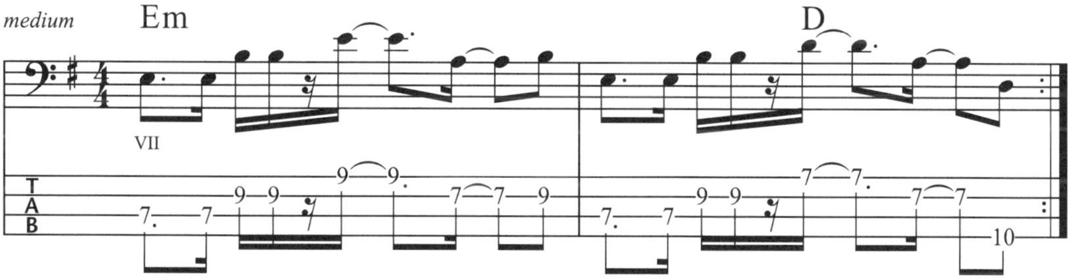

medium Em D

VII

764 CD 2 Track 9

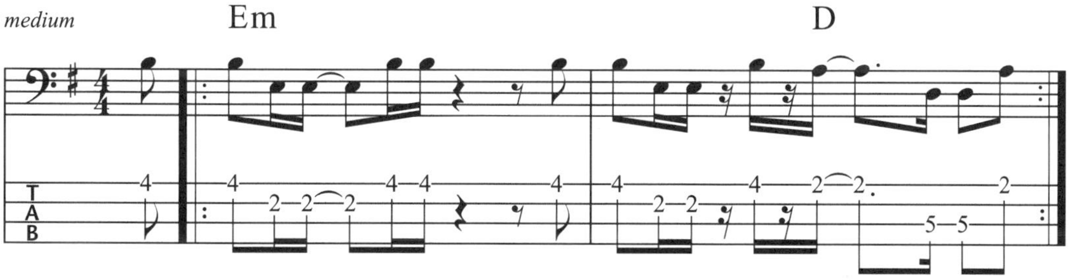

medium Em D

765 CD 2 Track 10

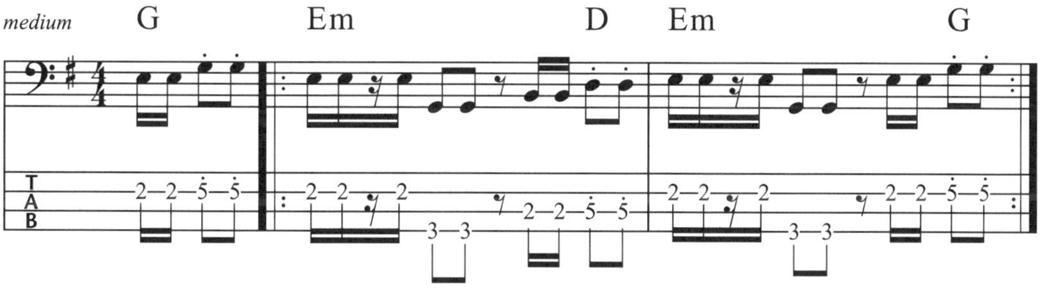

medium G Em D Em G

766

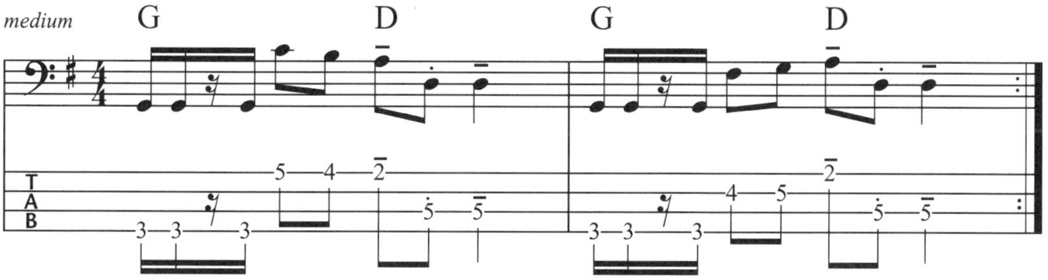

medium G D G D

767

768

CD 2 Track 10

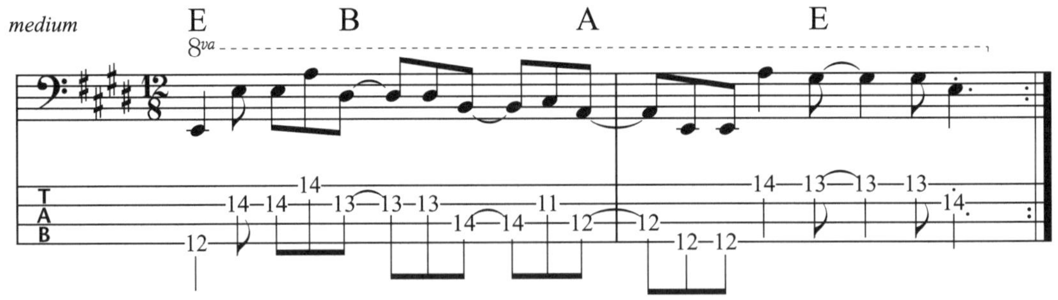

medium

E B A E

8va

769

CD 2 Track 11

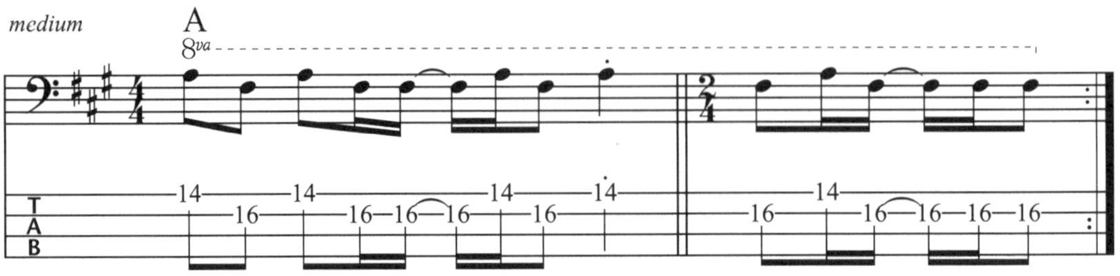

medium

A

8va

770

CD 2 Track 11

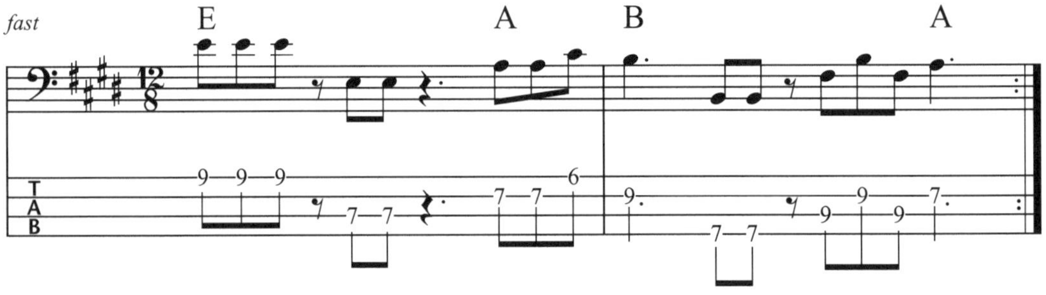

fast

E A B A

771

CD 2 Track 12

medium

E B

A B E

772

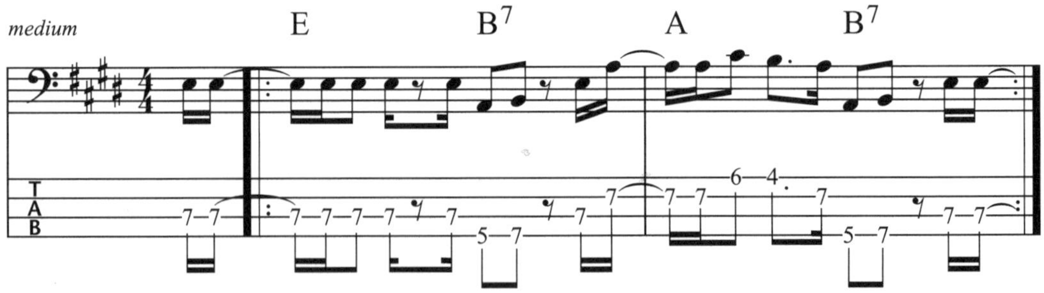

medium

E B7 A B7

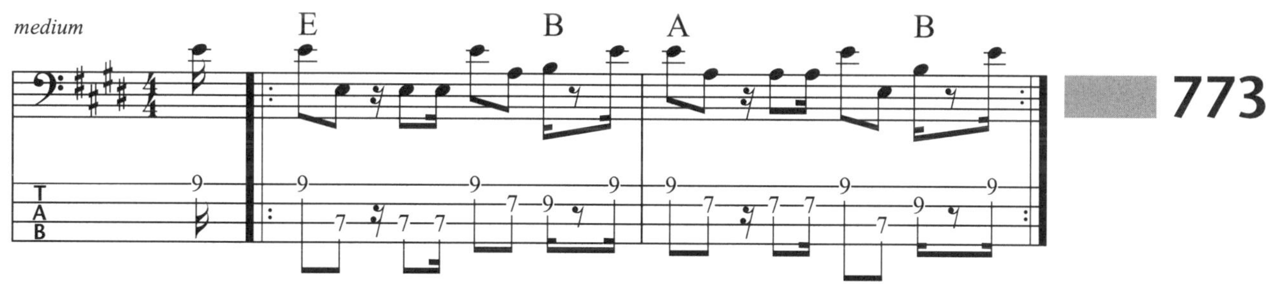

773

774

CD 2 Track 12

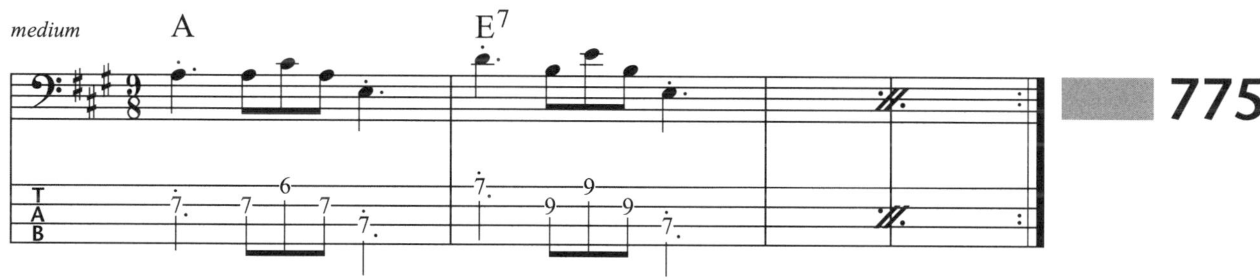

775

Republic of Congo (Zaire)

Many musicians from the Republic of Congo have become big stars. Koffi Olomide, for instance, is very contemporary in his high-tech approach and ballad style vocals. Other well-known names are Franco, Ray Lema, Papa Wamba, Sam Mangwana, Empire Bakuba, 4 Etoiles, Kanda Bongo Man, Kass Kass, Jean Papy Ramazani and Palle Kalle, and Nyboma. Their music is very commercial and dance orientated. A riff will dominate the whole composition with perhaps one or two variations. The bands are very tight and imaginative. The rhythms they play are designed to keep the music exciting, and they are great believers in the "live sound" which keeps their audience dancing. Brass figures help to punctuate instrumental passages, and the general feel is very positive and driving.

776

777

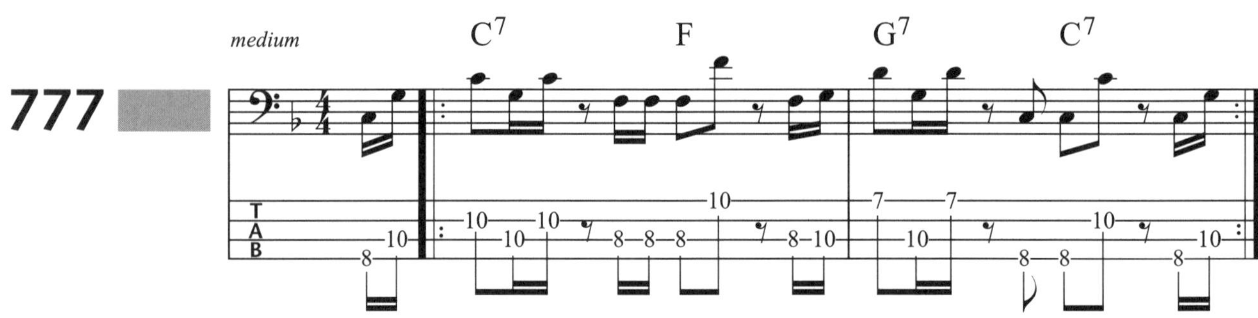

778

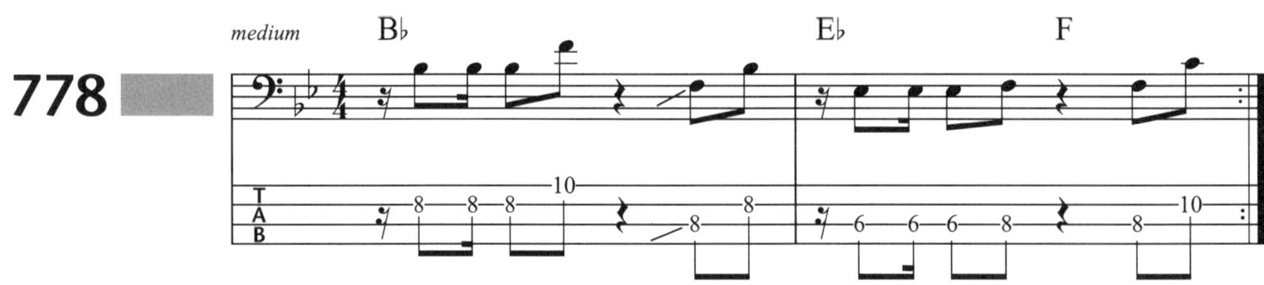

779

CD 2 Track 13

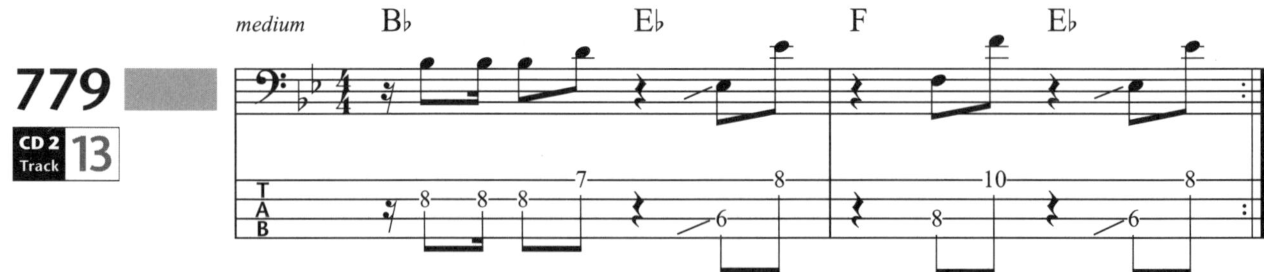

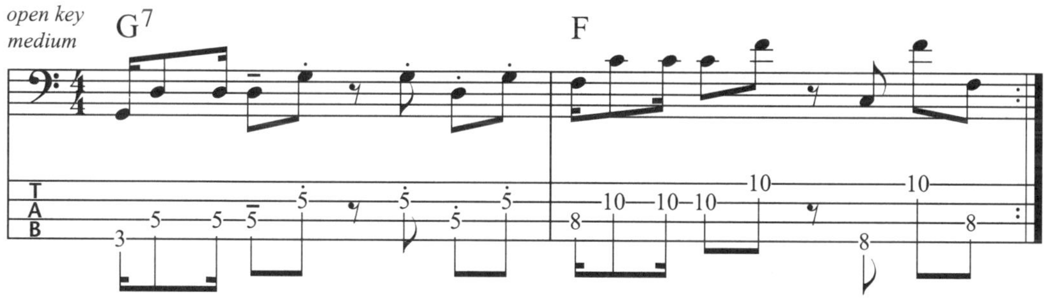

open key
medium
G7
F

780

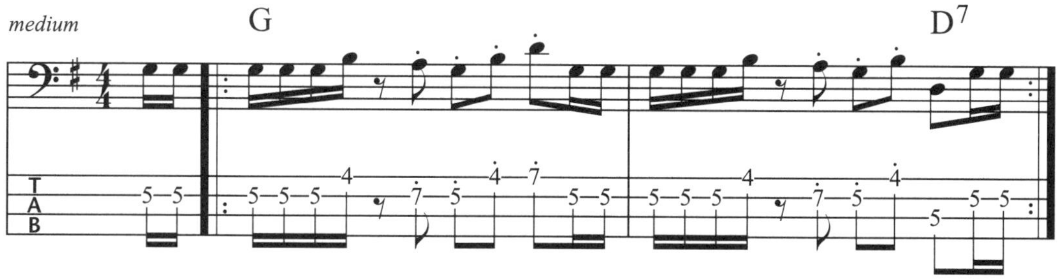

medium
G
D7

781
CD 2 Track 13

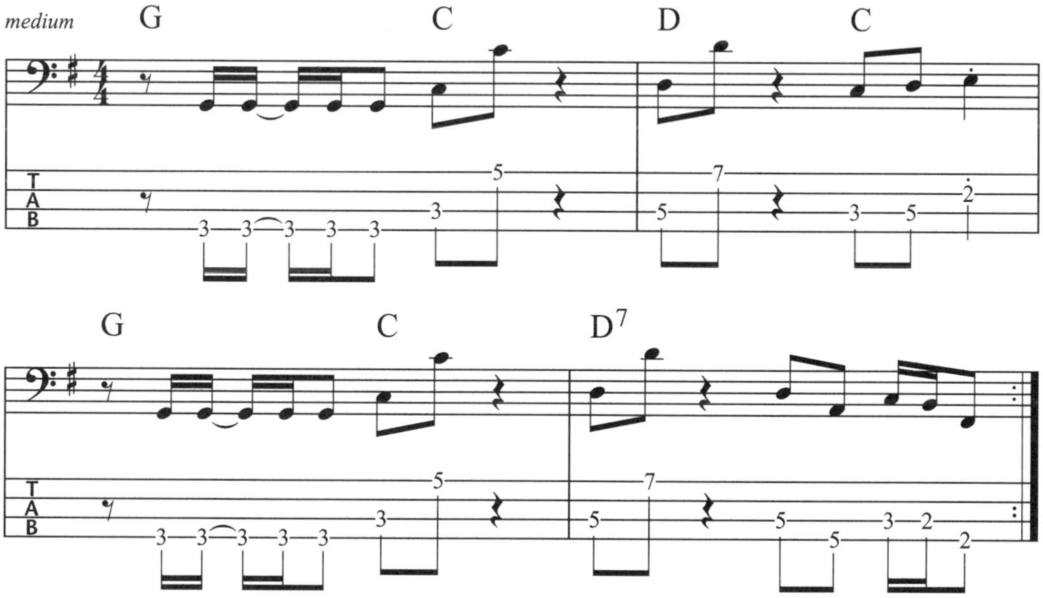

medium
G
C
D
C
G
C
D7

782
CD 2 Track 14

medium
G
C
D7

783

medium
D
G
A
G

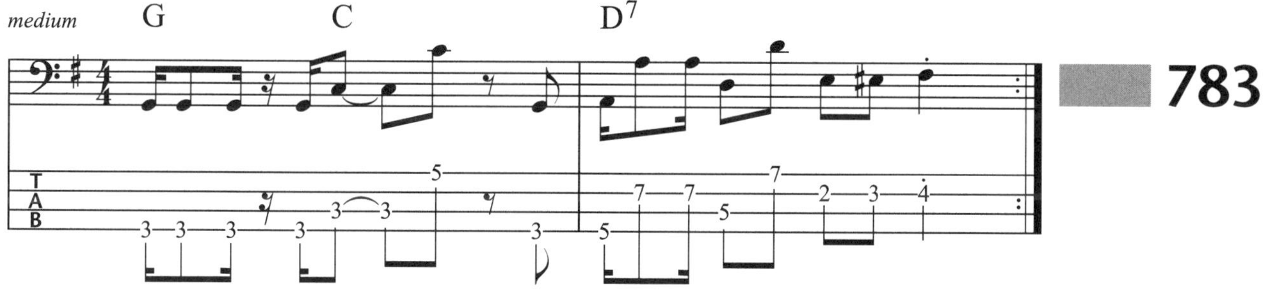

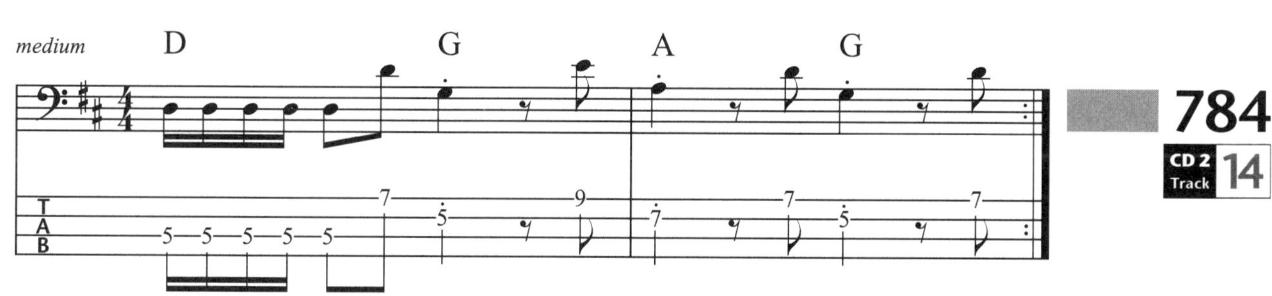

784
CD 2 Track 14

785

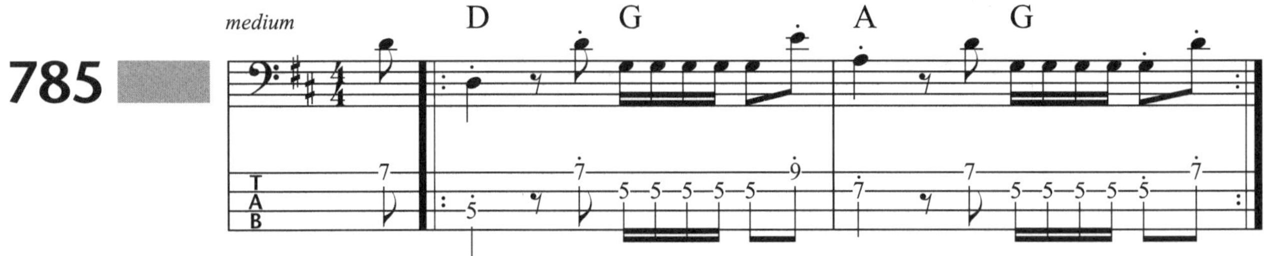

786

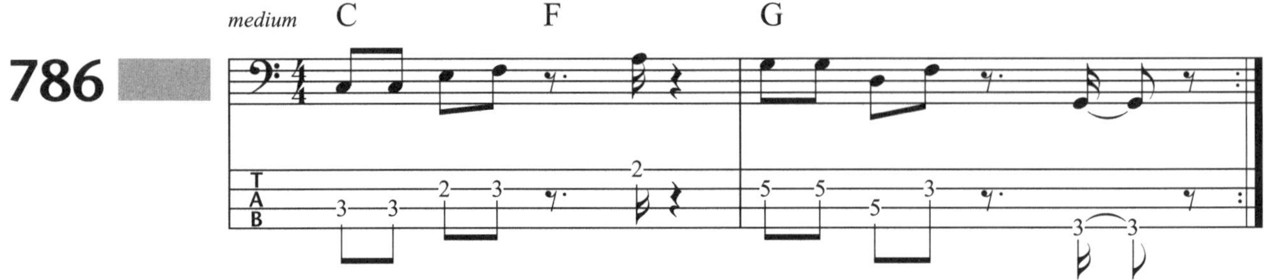

787

788

789

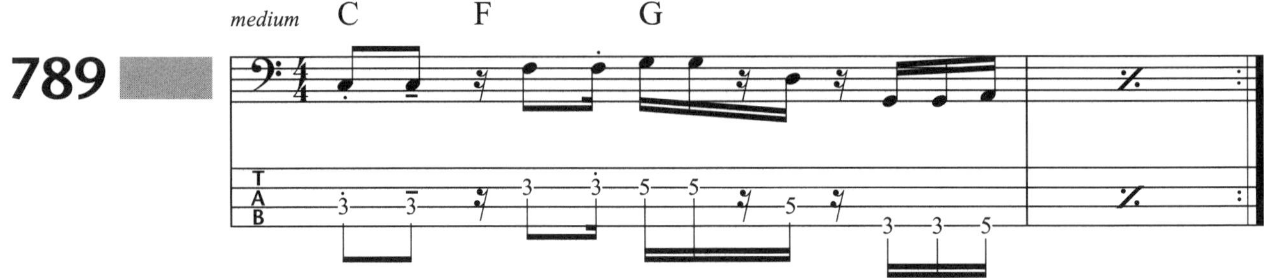

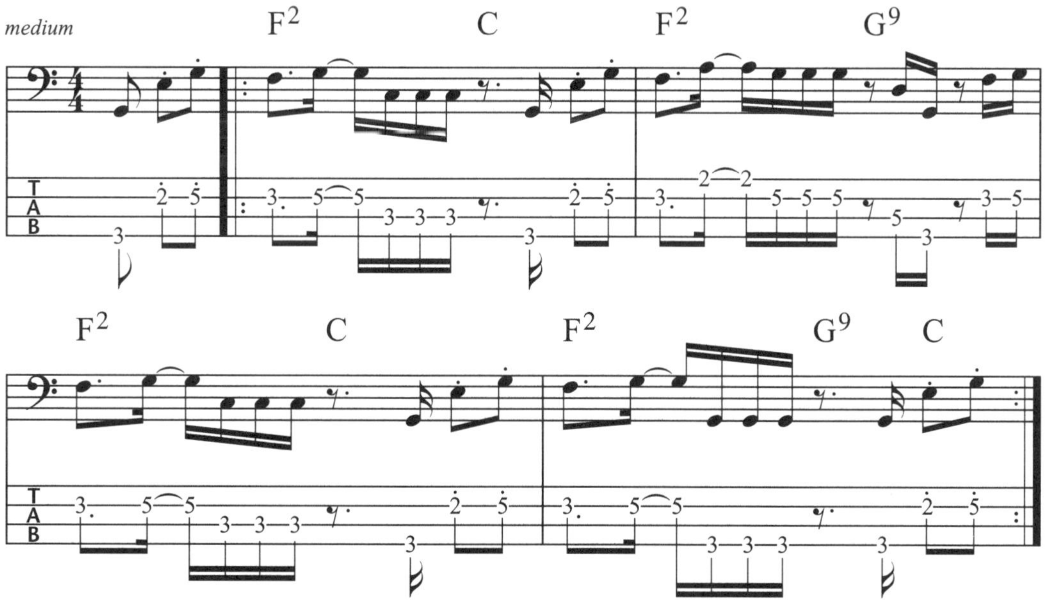
medium
F2
C
F2
G9
F2
C
F2
G9
C

790

CD 2 Track 15

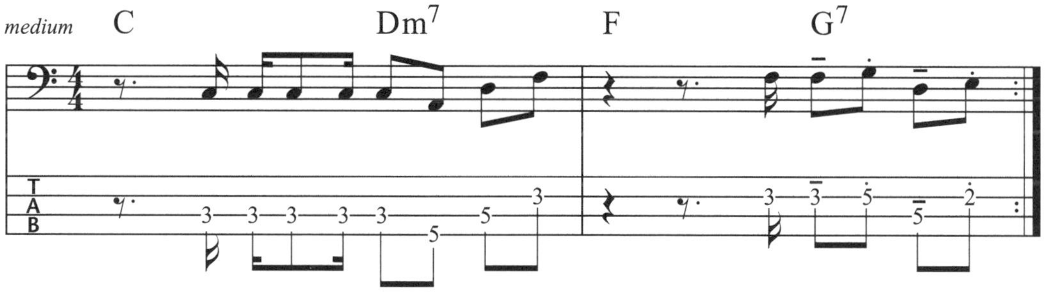
medium
C
Dm7
F
G7

791

CD 2 Track 15

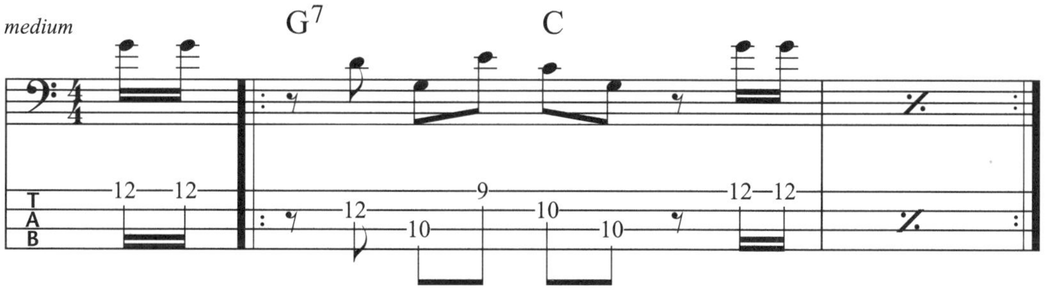
medium
G7
C

792

CD 2 Track 16

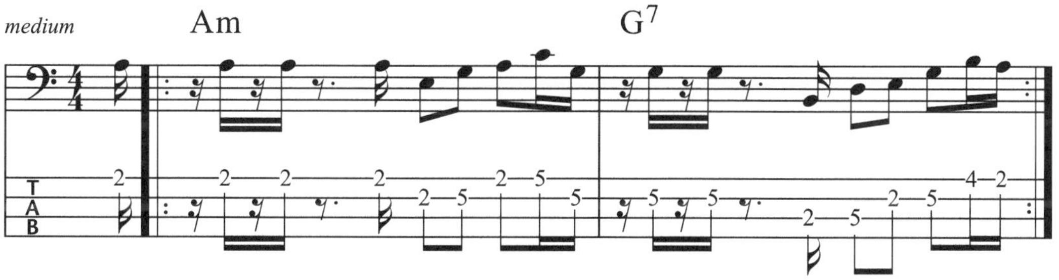
medium
Am
G7

793

CD 2 Track 16

medium
C
F
G7
F

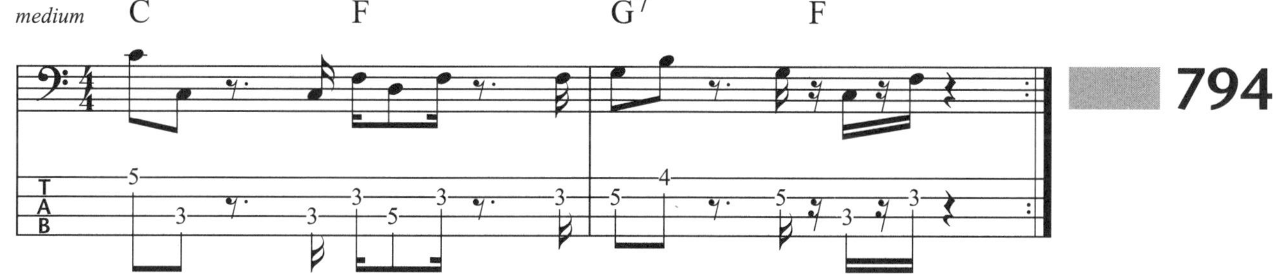

794

Zimbabwe

One particularly good artist from Zimbabwe is John Chibadura. His music is traditional, in so far as his lyrics are about pain, suffering, love, happiness, family and friends, fortune and misfortune, tragic loss to the community, and the binding spirit.

His modern dance style has some great rhythm section feels, and mixed in with up-tempo grooves are some marvellous bass lines. Generally he looks for a groove on a simple chord sequence. The bass player has great freedom to incorporate arpeggio patterns above the 10th fret, and this creates a different feel because it is an octave higher than normal. Some patterns are guitar-like in their approach, although harmonically the chords are only major and minor triads. There are many cross-patterns, and occasionally a blend of related chords played simultaneously, which provide enough variety to keep the music interesting.

The music is not brash or showy, but reflective. It has the bitter-sweet feel of being driving dance music with a soft vocal.

795 CD 2 Track 17

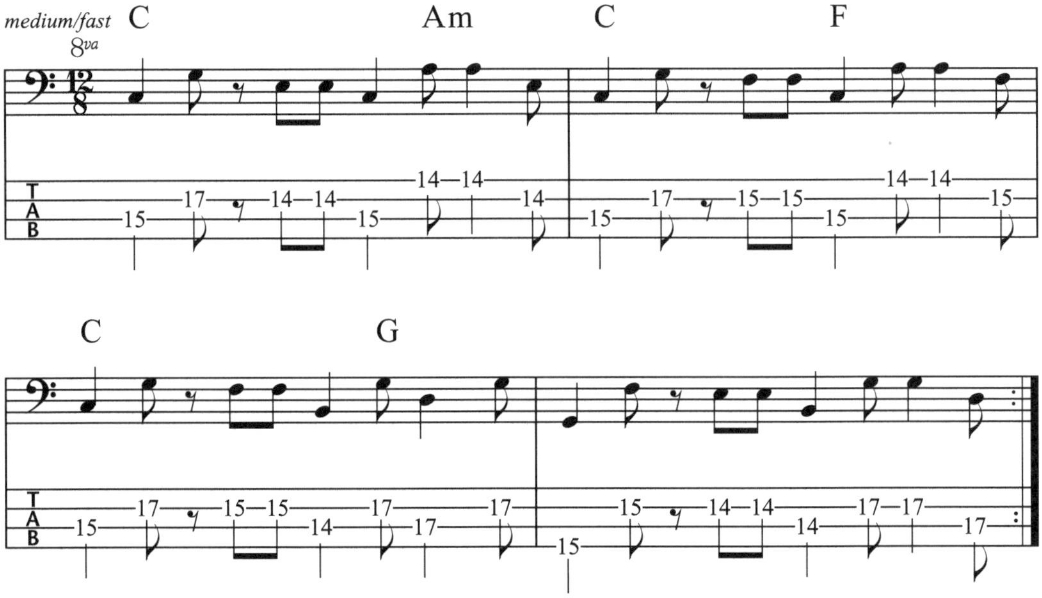

medium/fast 8va

C Am C F

C G

796 CD 2 Track 17

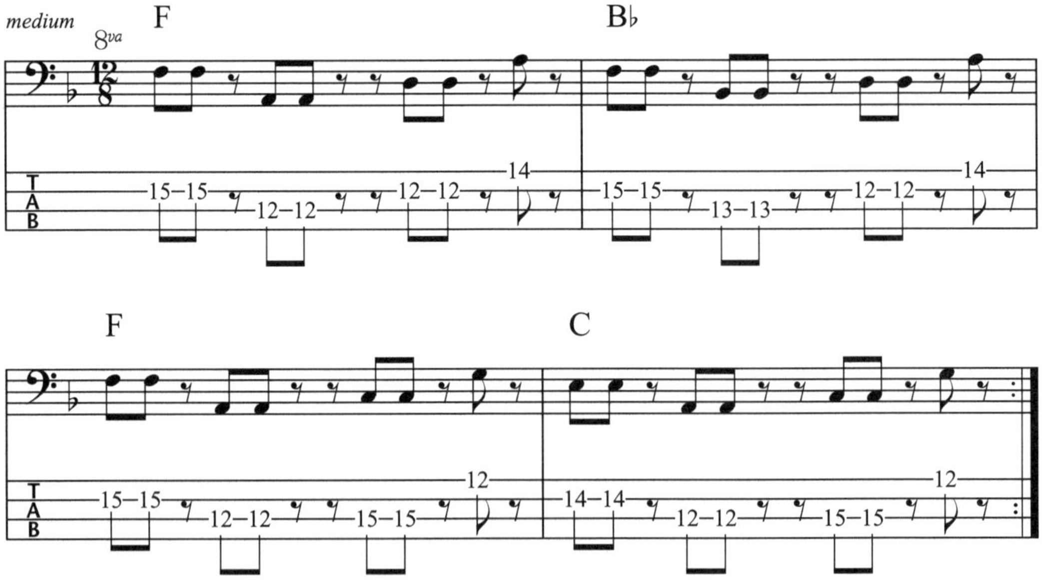

medium 8va

F B♭

F C

medium
E♭
B♭
E♭
A♭
B♭
797
CD 2
Track
18

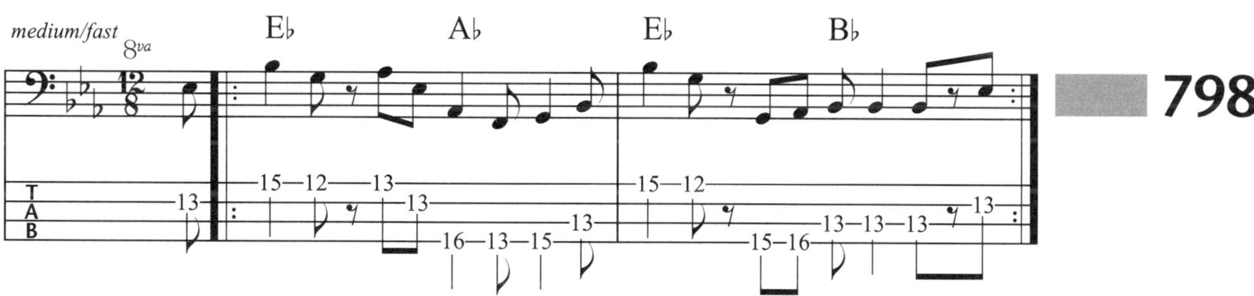
medium/fast
8va
E♭
A♭
E♭
B♭
798

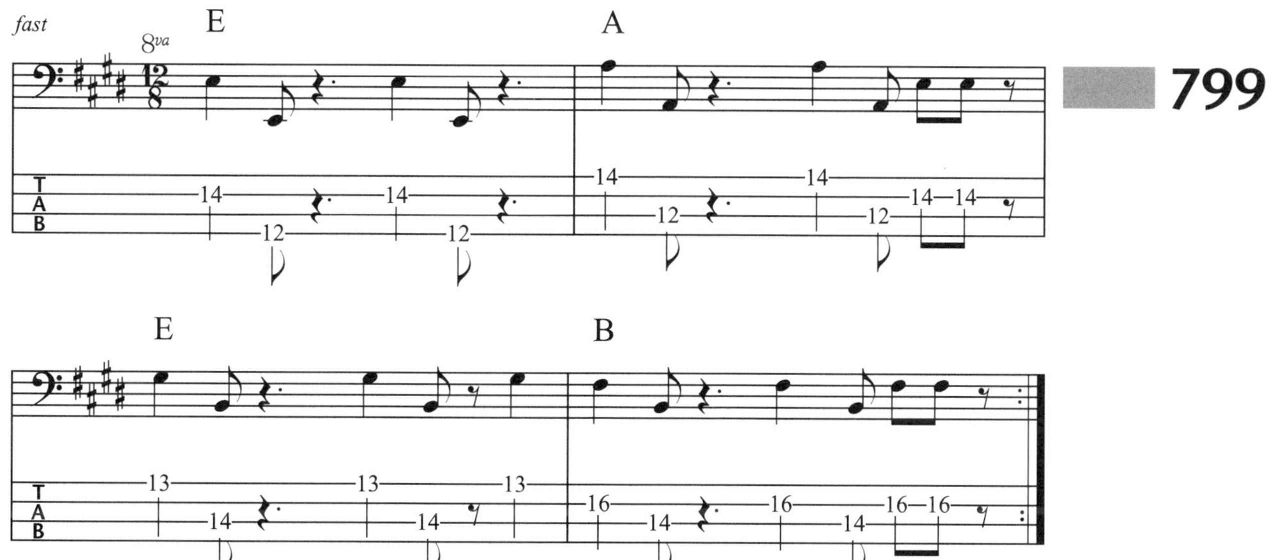
fast
8va
E
A
E
B
799

800
CD 2 Track 18

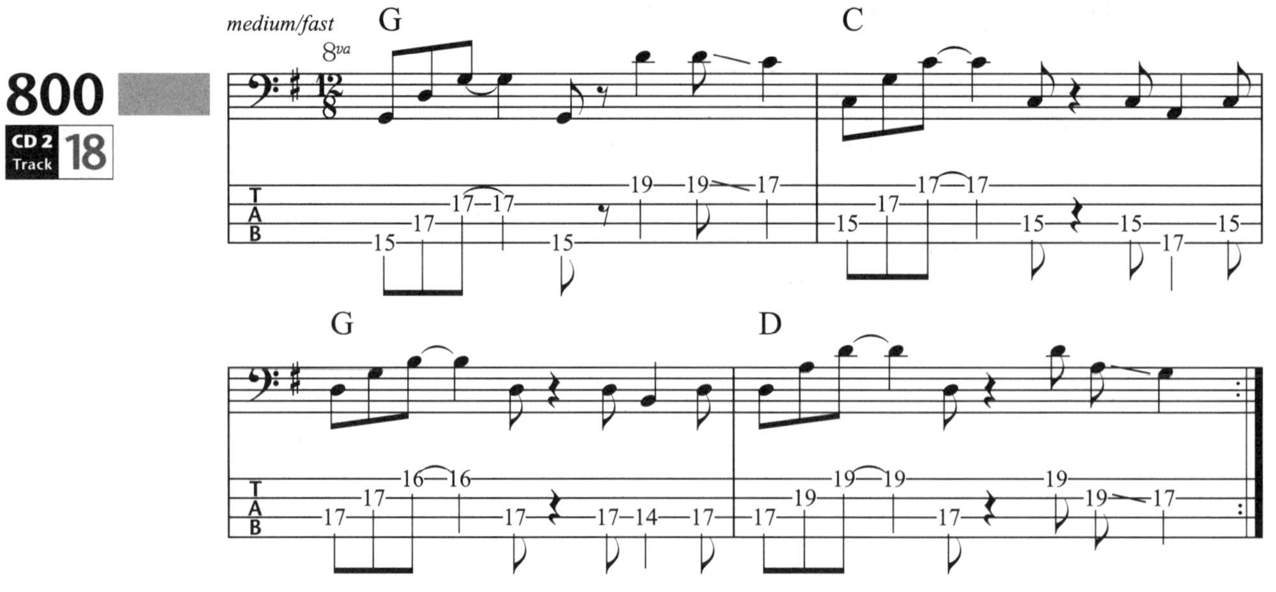

801

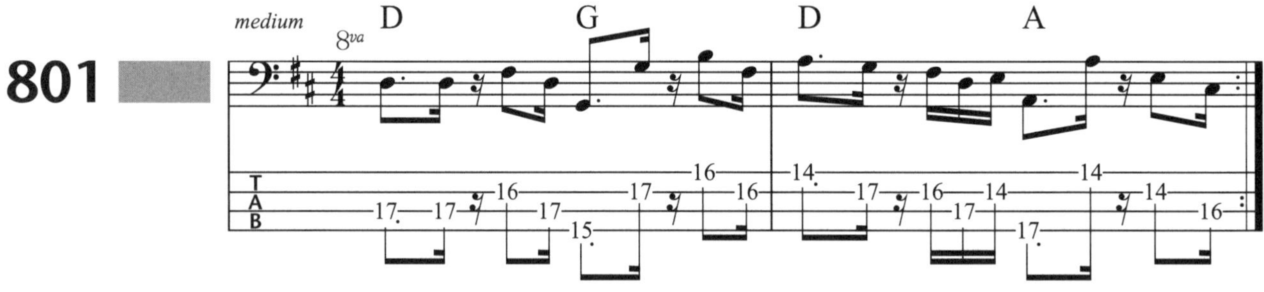

802

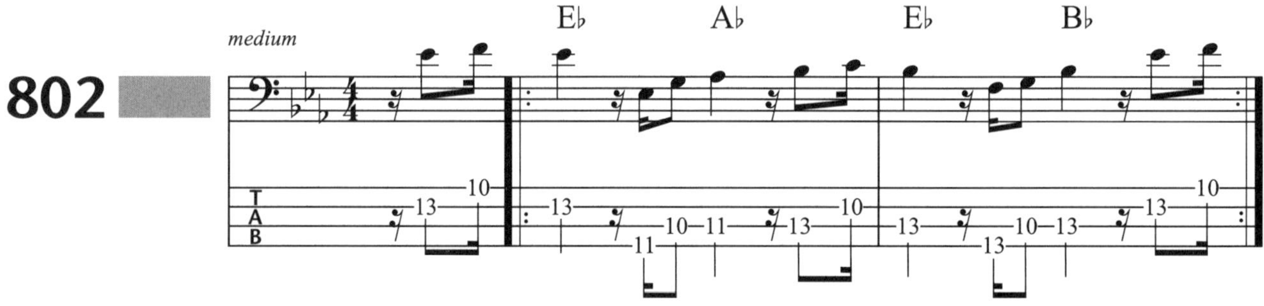

803
CD 2 Track 19

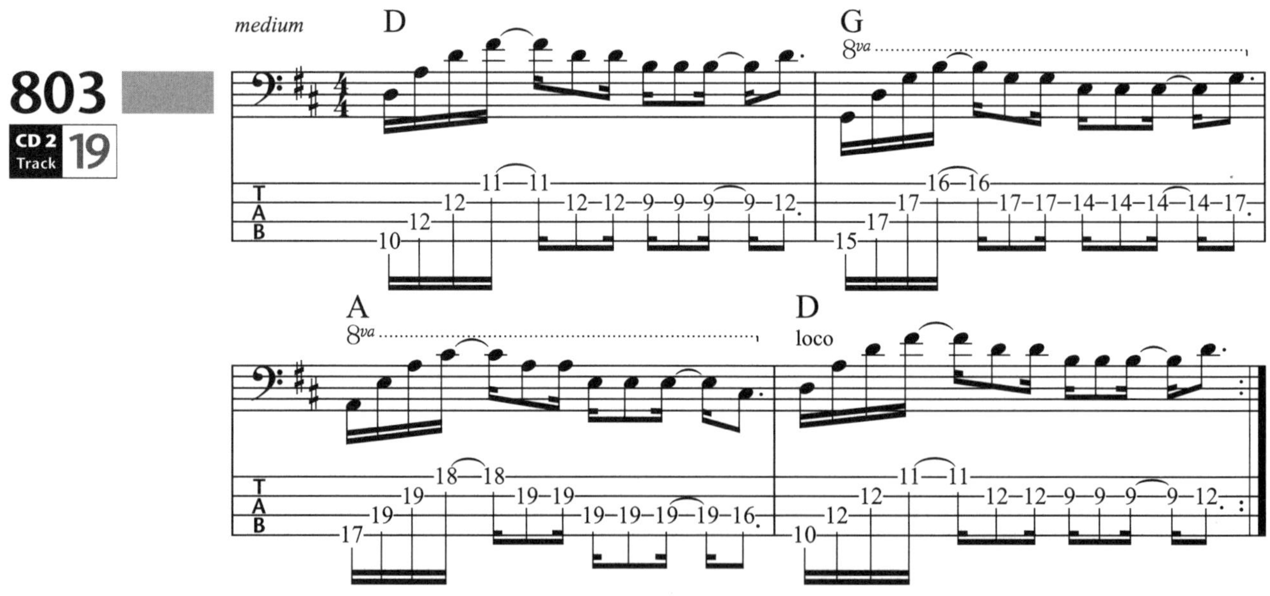

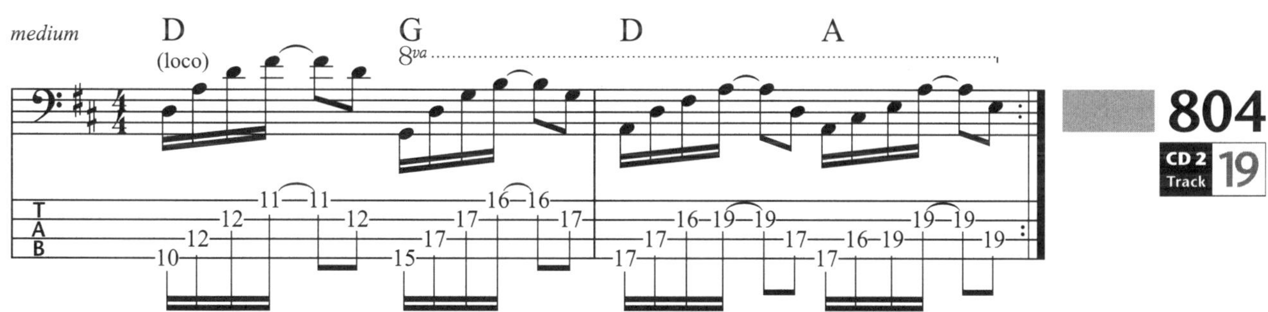
medium
D
(loco)
G
8va
D
A
804
CD 2 Track 19

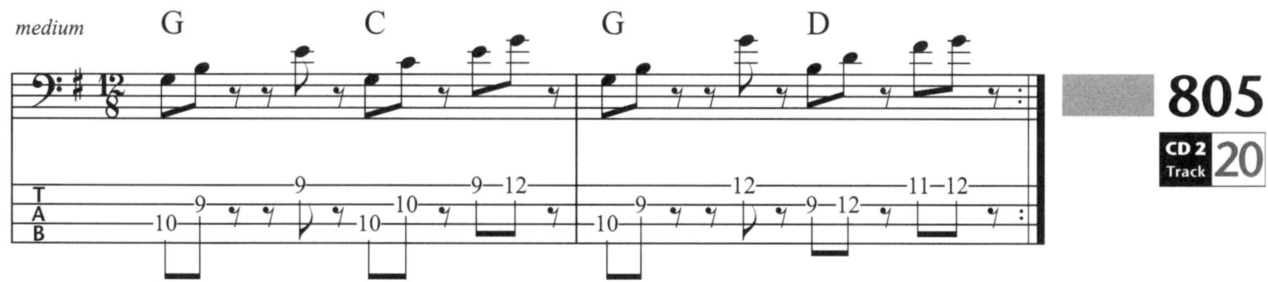
medium
G
C
G
D
805
CD 2 Track 20

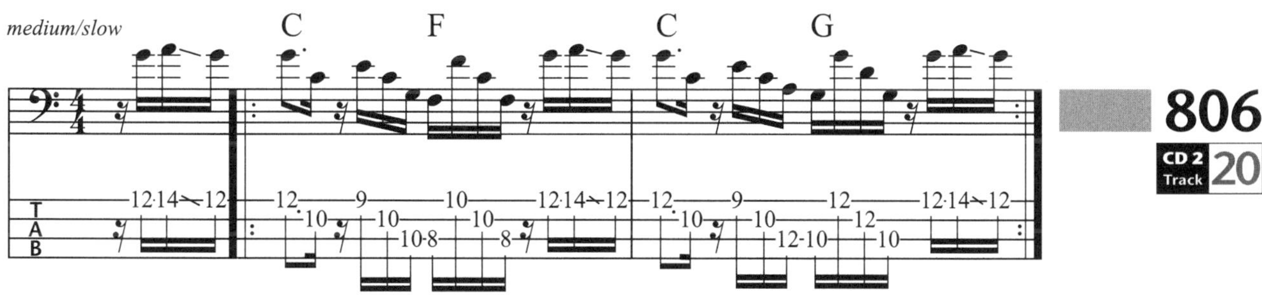
medium/slow
C
F
C
G
806
CD 2 Track 20

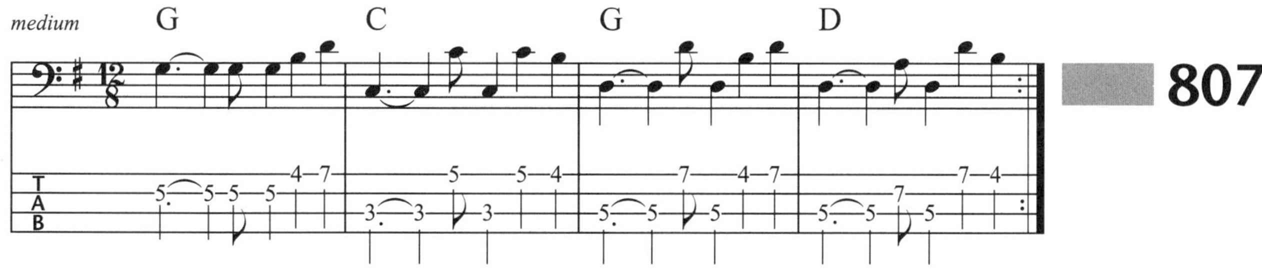
medium
G
C
G
D
807

South Africa & Soweto

Mahlathini (as previously mentioned) is one of the most famous grass roots musicians of Soweto, Johannesburg. His style of vocals is called "Mbaqanga" (township). His popularity has grown and influenced other bands since the 1950's. The harder vocal sound he uses is called "Mgqashiyo". The music combines city sounds with traditional roots and praise songs, although American Jazz and Blues of the 1960's helped influence local music too.

Many lyrics are sung in Zulu for their own people, but also in English for a wider audience. Songs are mostly dominated by one bass riff, with a couple of occasional variations. Harmonically it is quite simple, but the hypnotic repetition of phrases and the insistent beat provide a strong background for the often adventurous singers.

Other bands from Soweto include Alexandra Black Mambazo, Ladysmith Black Mambazo, The Makgona Tsohle Band, Amaswazi Emvelo, Johnson Mkhalali, Dilika, Jozi, Malombo and Abafakasi.

open key
medium
G C D7 G C D7
812

medium
A C D A
C D C D C D
813

medium
G E G F♯m E G
E F♯m G
814
CD 2 Track 21

medium
D D/F♯ G A7
815

816

817

818

819

820

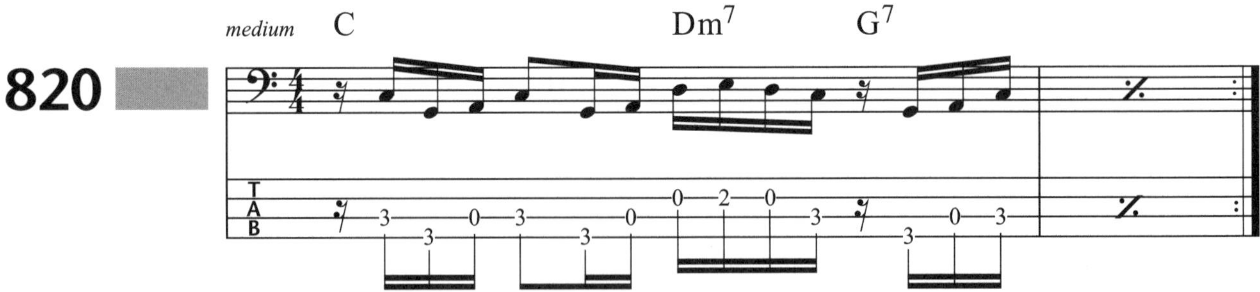

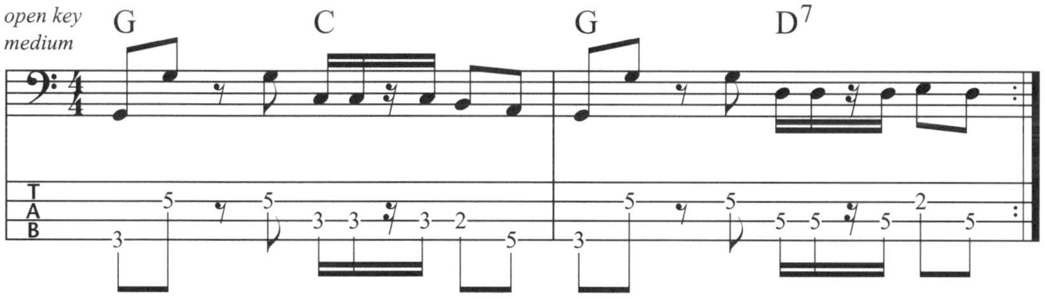

open key
medium
G
C
G
D7

821

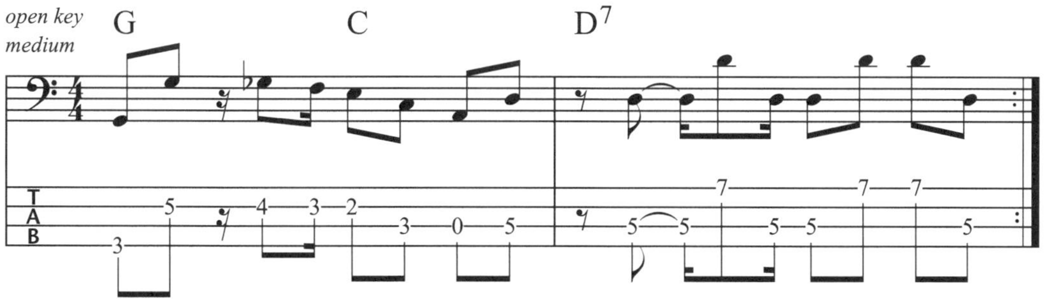

open key
medium
G
C
D7

822

CD 2 Track 21

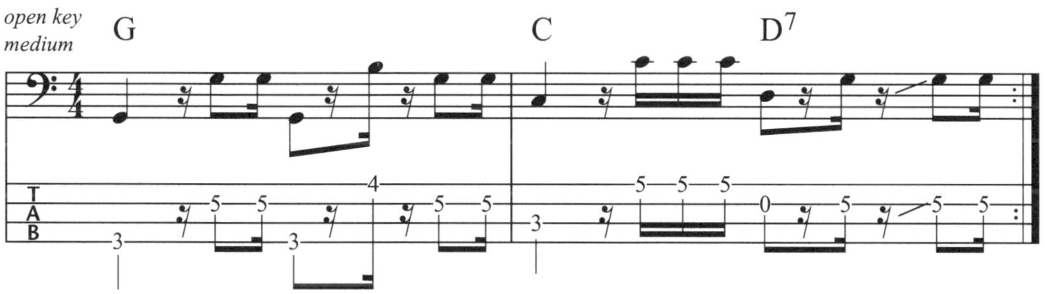

open key
medium
G
C
D7

823

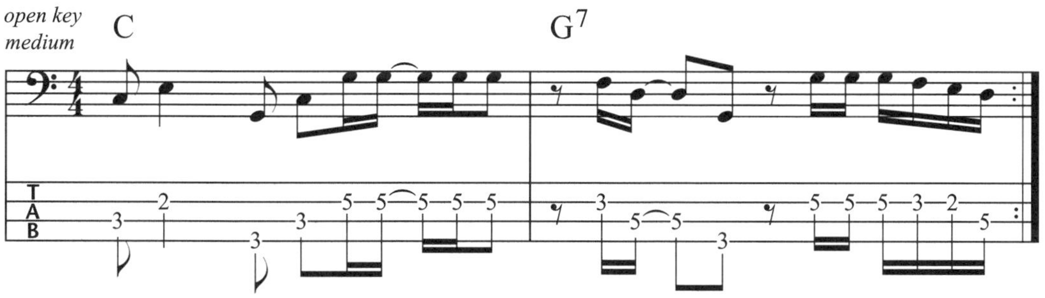

open key
medium
C
G7

824

CD 2 Track 22

medium
C
F
G7

825

medium
C
F
C
G7

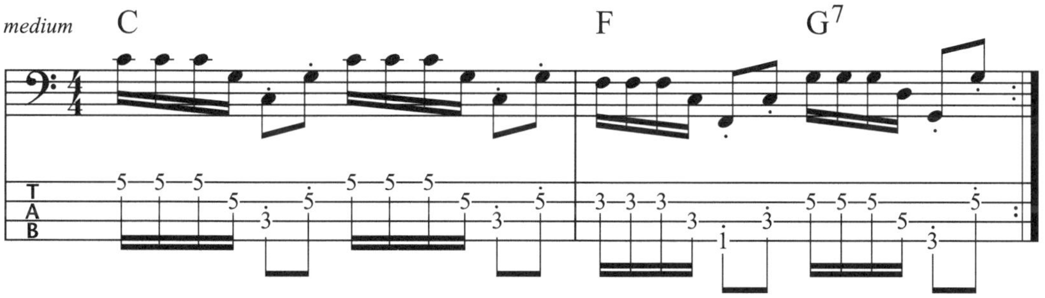

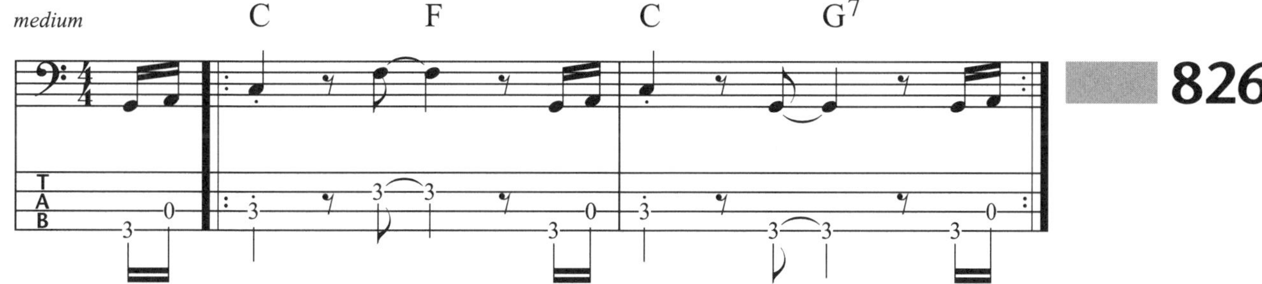

826

827

CD 2 Track 22

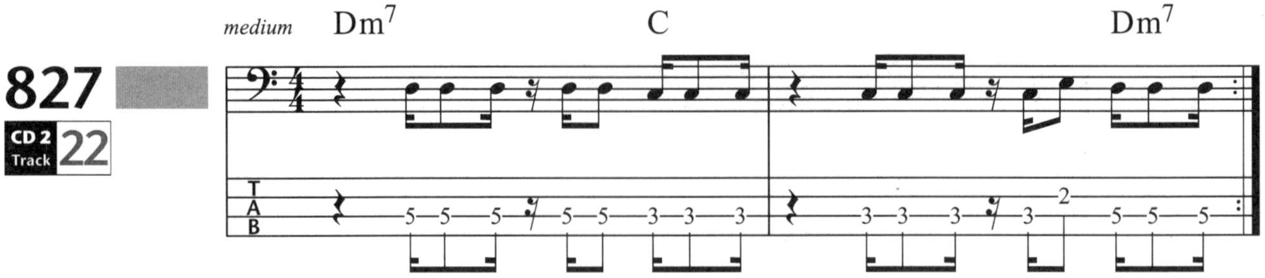

828

CD 2 Track 23

829

CD 2 Track 23

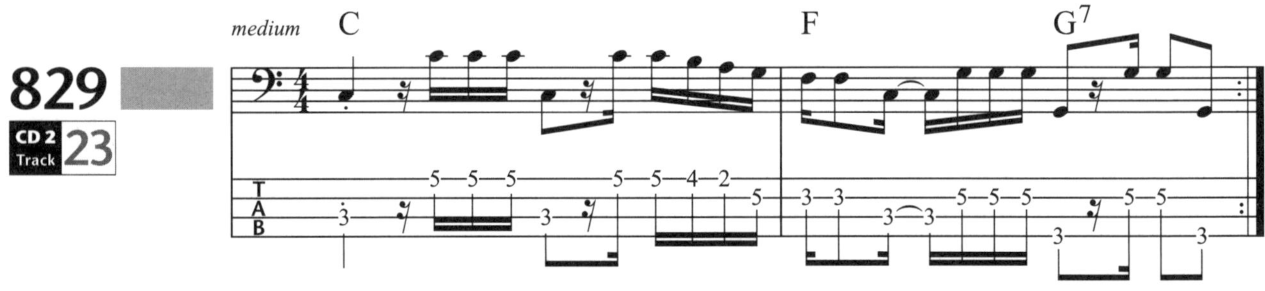

830

CD 2 Track 24

Note: In bar 3, tone ♮f is a "Blue Note".

medium

C F G7

831

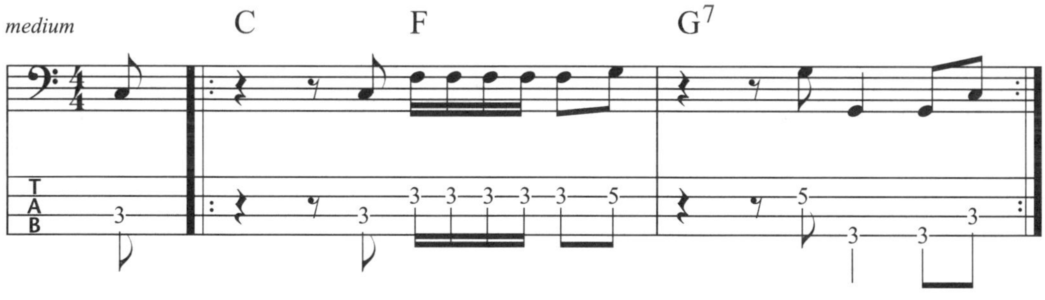

medium

G7 C G D7

832

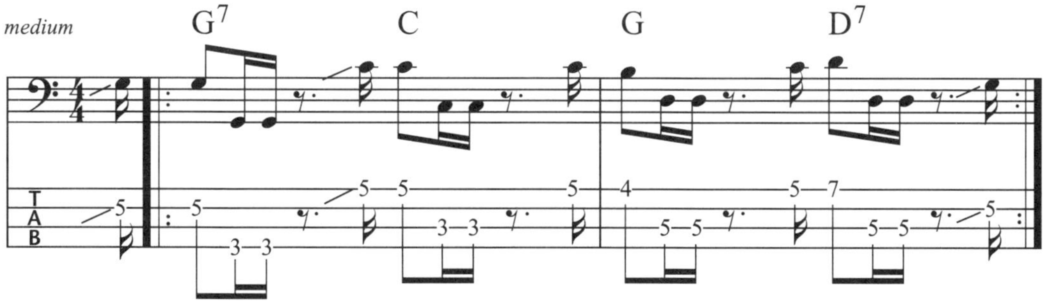

open key
medium

G7 C G D7

833

open key
medium

G C G

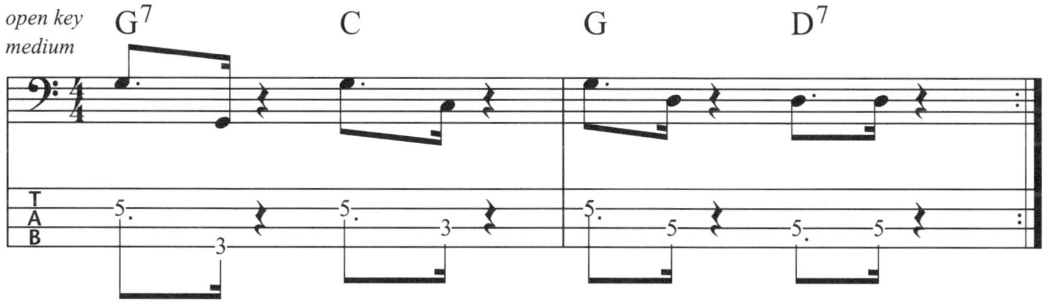

834

CD 2 Track 24

5-string bass

C Em

D7 G/B D7 G D7

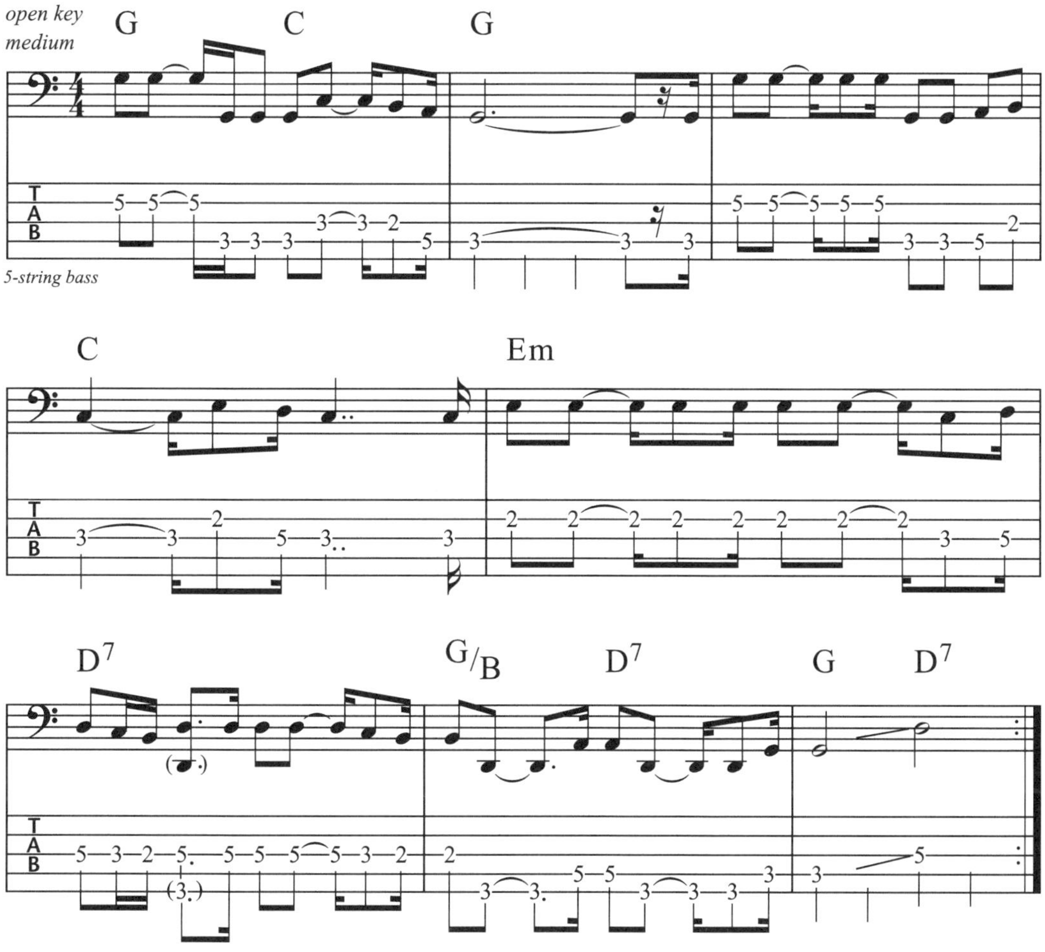

835

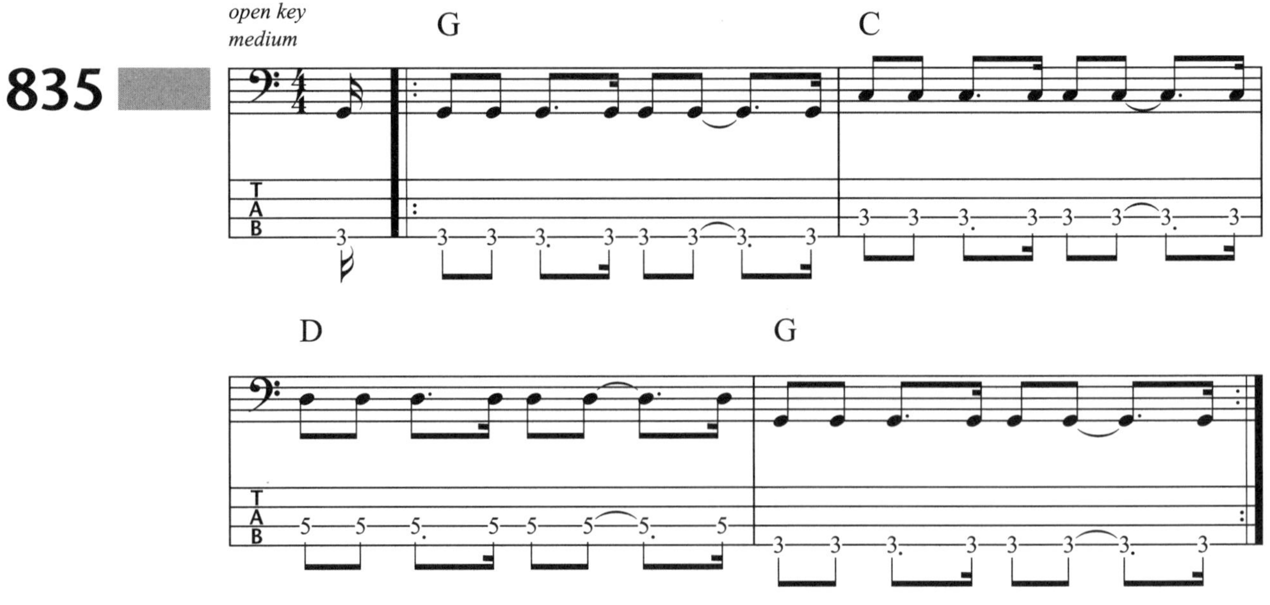
open key
medium
G
C
D
G
T
A
B

836

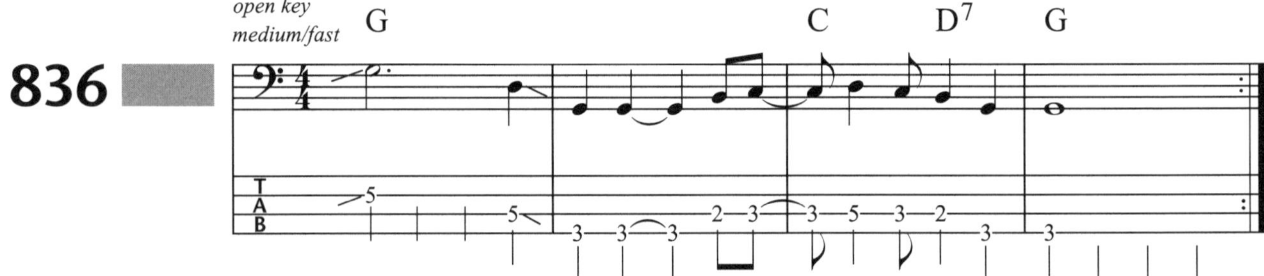
open key
medium/fast
G
C
D7
G
T
A
B

837

open key
fast
G
C
D7
T
A
B

BOOK FIVE

■ Boogie Lines

Boogie lines developed from pianists inventing ways of playing a walking bass line with the left hand. Boogie was based on a 4-in-the-bar walking bass line, but with the thumb repeating each beat of the bar an octave up, it became a more exciting 8-notes-to-the-bar rhythm.

When transcribed for the guitar, musicians tended to leave out the octaves, because it was difficult for the hand holding the plectrum to keep jumping across the strings. It sounded far smoother and convincing to play the same note twice. As boogie piano players became more skilful and were seeking new and more complex lines, they mixed octaves with 8th note running bass lines. Guitar players incorporated these changes into their repertoires also. Bass players tended to play a swing 4 and omit the subtle running lines.

When the bass guitar came along, it was possible to play 8 notes to the bar and make it swing. Later on, when Larry Graham began the slap boogie style, he followed many of the old-fashioned left hand piano riffs, which suddenly took on new life and sounded very hip. By changing the technique of his right hand, the first finger was able to strike notes an octave higher than his thumb, and therefore it became possible for a bass player to make these boogie octave jumps.

In reality tempos vary from medium to fast.

841
CD 2 Track 25

842

843
CD 2 Track 25

844

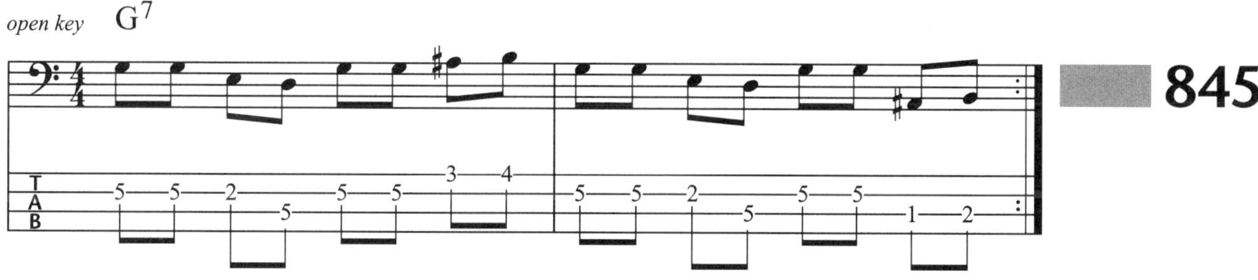

845

846
CD 2 Track 26

847

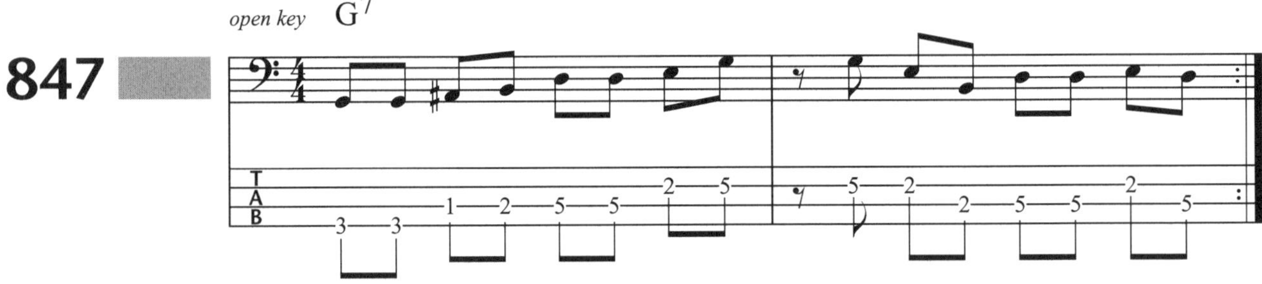

848

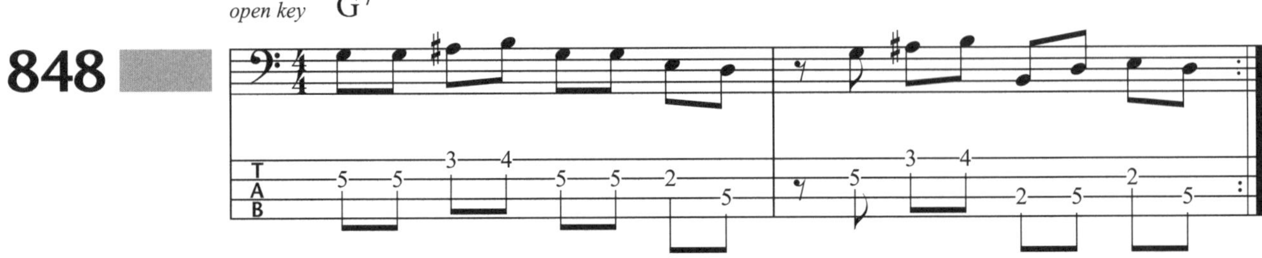

849

CD 2 Track 26

850

LARRY GRAHAM & MARK KING – Slap Bass

The slap bass style was first used on the double bass by players like Chubby Jackson. The most difficult problem for an acoustic bass player was being heard above the volume of the band, so the most sought-after players were often either the loudest or the ones who somehow cut through. By pulling the string hard and then releasing it to slap against the fingerboard, it created not only a brighter, more definite sound, but also a different feel.

When bass guitarists began developing this style, they did not know at first how to play contemporary music tastefully. Consequently, slap bass did not really emerge until Larry Graham popularised it in the 70's with Sly and the Family Stone, and Graham Central Station.

He used various approaches. He borrowed and developed old-fashioned octave boogie lines which were based on a swing 4 feel, but with the octave note added between each downbeat, producing a new 8th note feel. The thumb slaps the bottom strings against the frets at the top end of the fretboard, and the first finger is placed underneath the first or second string, pulled back and released, so that the string "pops" against the frets. In this way each note is given a hard metallic edge.

Larry Graham also based many of his moving bass lines on the boogie lines which guitarists had developed. This style relied on the thumb pumping out an 8th note feel as it hit the strings against the fretboard. It is a dynamic and exciting feel, which redeveloped what would otherwise have been a discarded, old-fashioned style. Other bass players then emerged to take the style in other directions. One notable musician is Mark King of Level 42 fame, who developed a highly flexible technique. It became possible for him to play such complex patterns that he practically provided all the percussion section too! His playing gave a kind of bubble or "popping" effect. He uses light strings to gain the maximum effect with the minimum effort, and consequently has a thinner sound than the heavier gauge used by the innovators.

The bass line, though still important, became part of the overall percussion effect he achieved. With the emergence of the synthesizer, it was possible to have an electronic bass line running simultaneously, as he played along with and added to the overall pattern. As a vocalist, it took the pressure off him having to play an exact, predetermined bass line and gave him greater overall flexibility. This all contributed to an exciting show, which even involved him flying through the air on wires whilst playing a solo!

The danger of a thin bass sound is that it no longer fulfils the fundamental role of the traditional bass guitar. However, if covered by another instrument, this approach can lead to a different concept.

There are many variations emerging: for instance, some people are using the first and second fingers in conjunction to pull the strings, producing a more flexible technique and a whole new set of phrases and possibilities.

In the following examples, the first finger "pop" is indicated by a "P". Where the left hand fingers hammer onto the next note, this is indicated by a curved tie line, e.g. ♪‿♪ .
A slide is indicated by a sloping straight line, e.g. ♪╱♪.

Slap (Beginners)

851

852

853
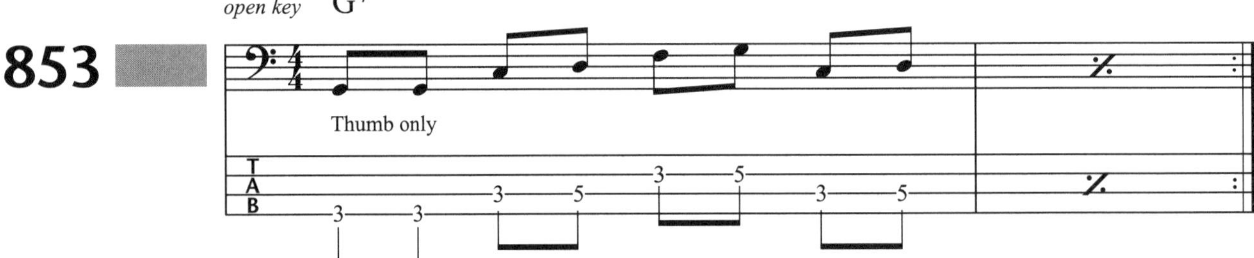

854
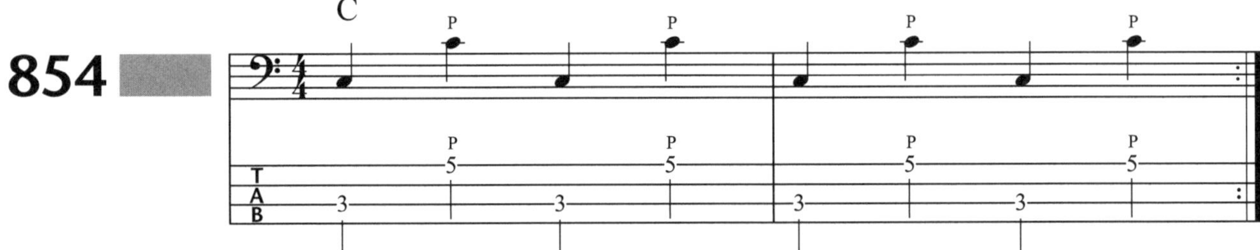

855
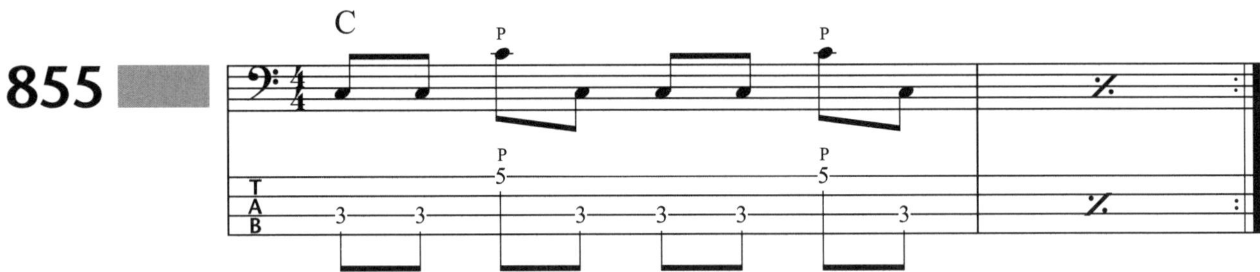

856
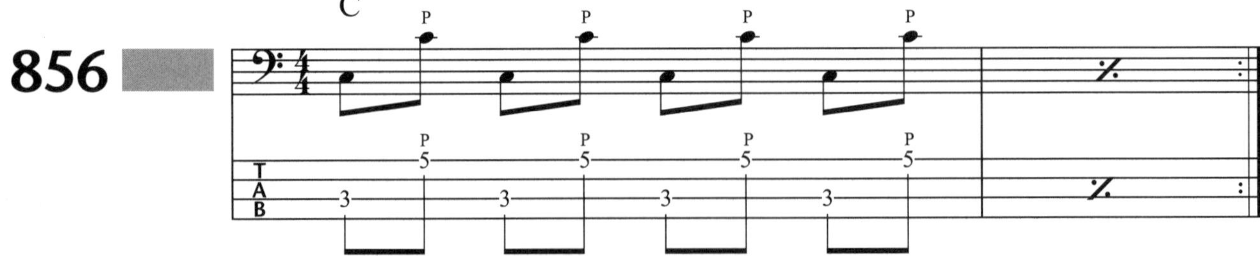

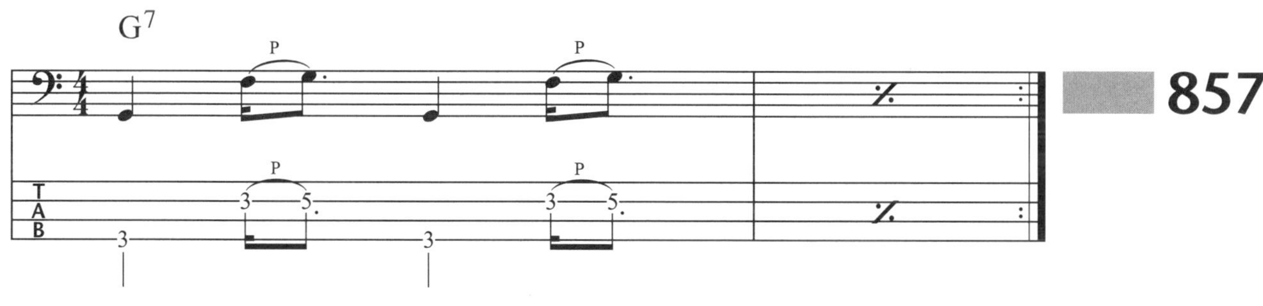
G7
857

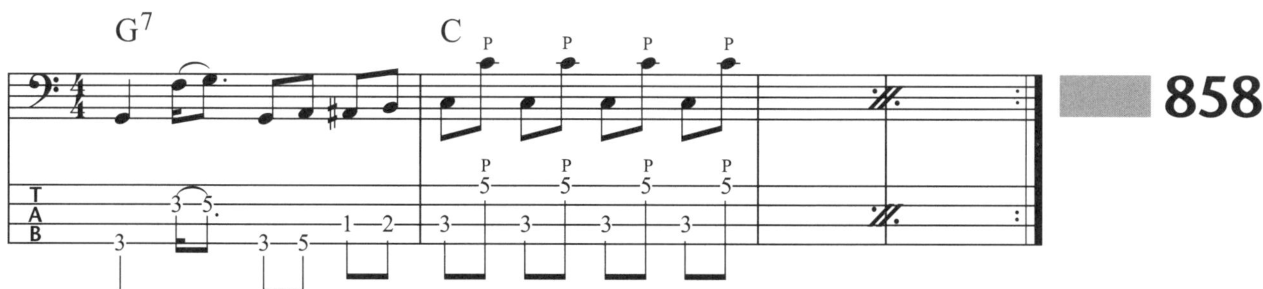
G7
C
858

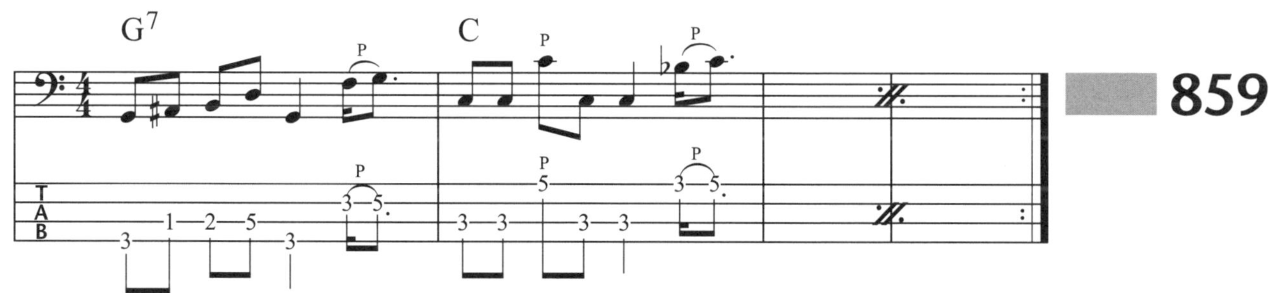
G7
C
859

C
860

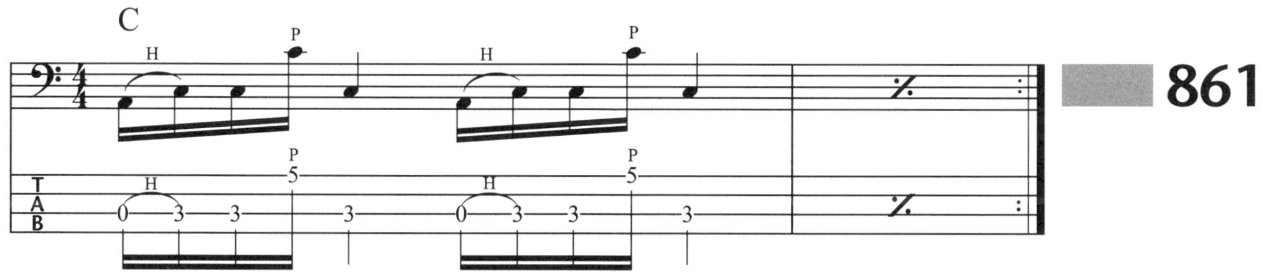
C
861

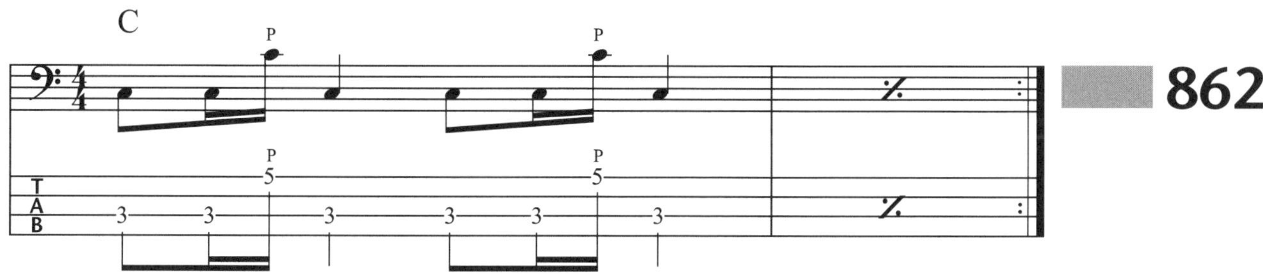
C
862

Larry Graham – Slap (Boogie)

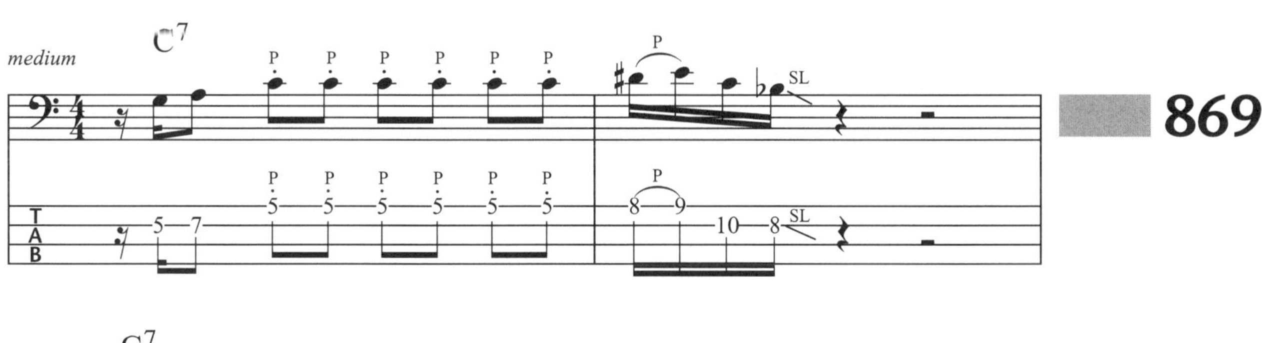
medium
C7
869

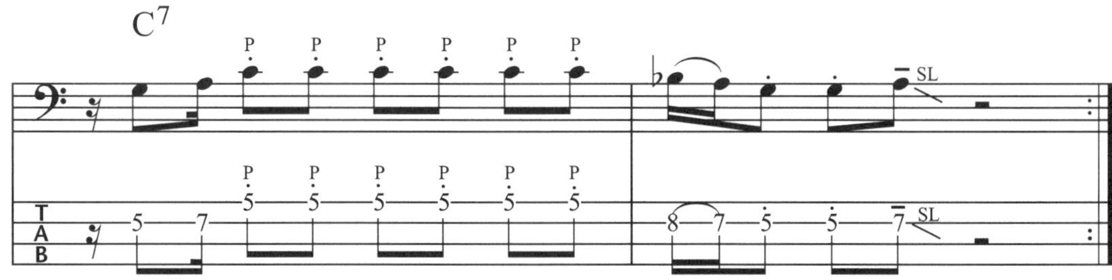
C7

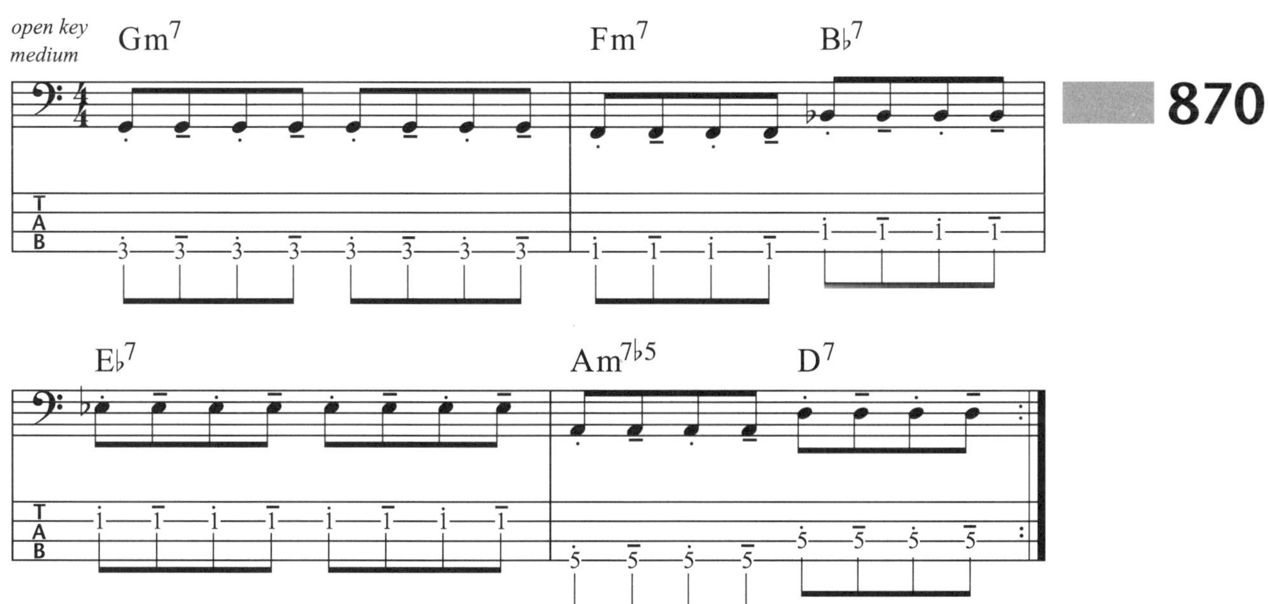
open key
medium
Gm7
Fm7
B♭7
870
E♭7
Am7♭5
D7

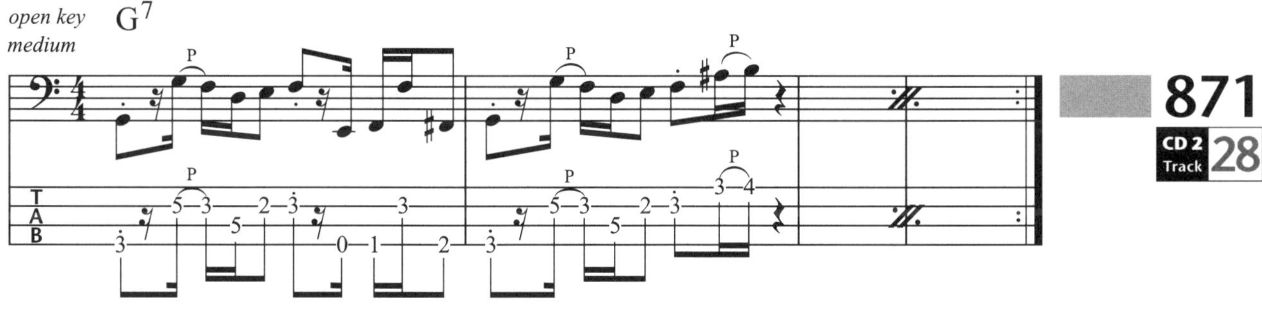
open key
medium
G7
871
CD 2 Track 28

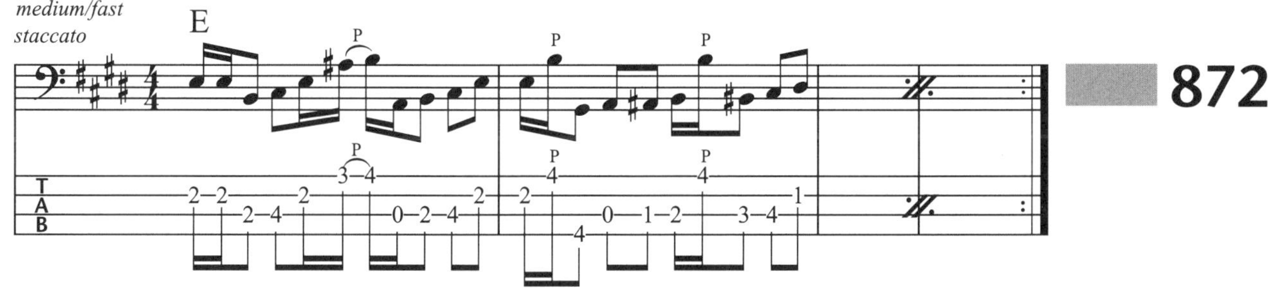
medium/fast
staccato
E
872

873

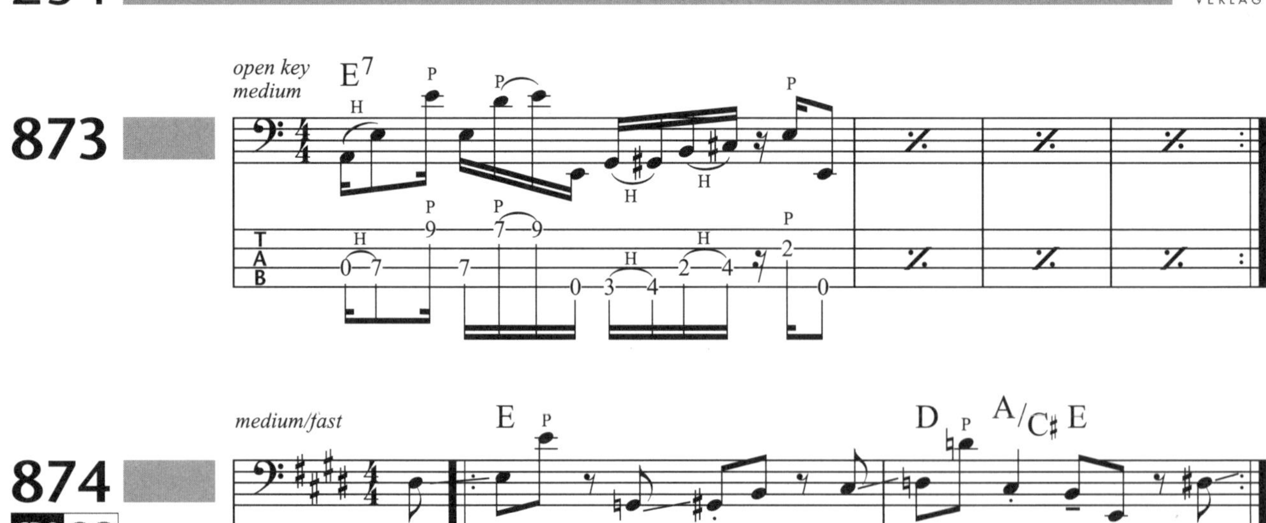

874
CD 2 Track 28

875

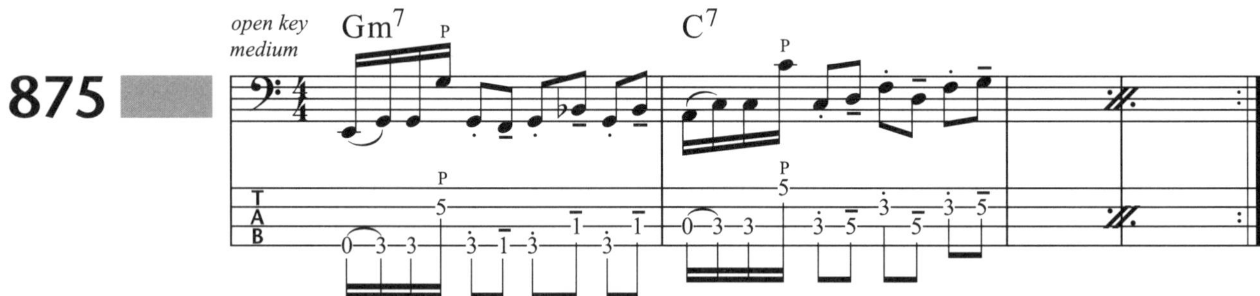

876
CD 2 Track 29

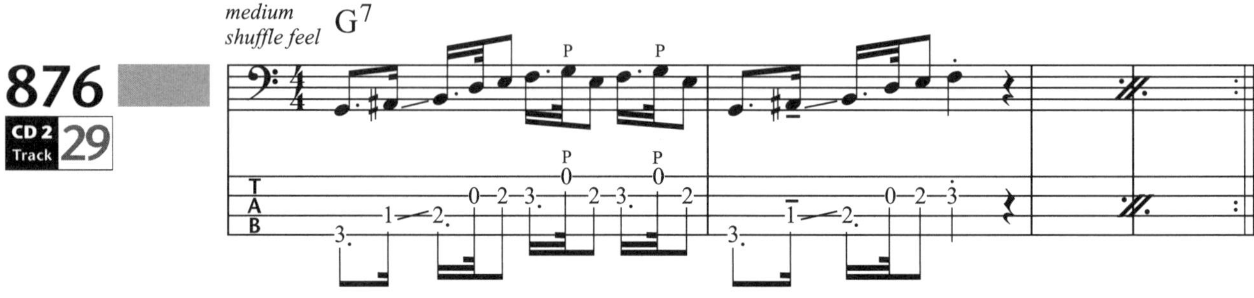

877
CD 2 Track 29

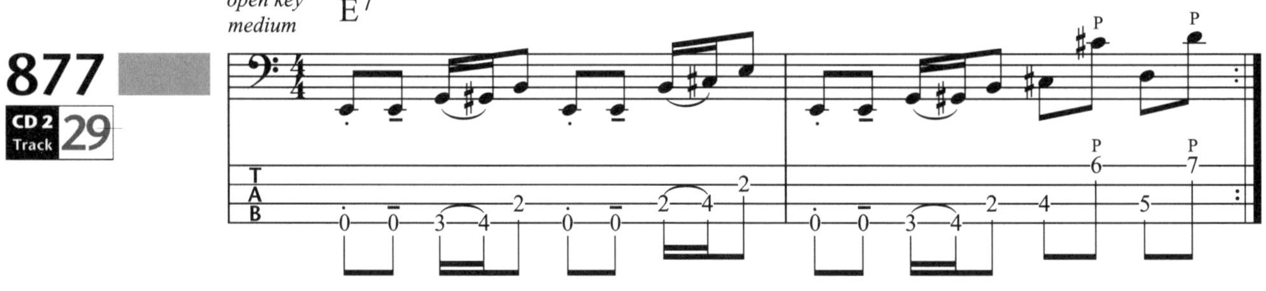

878

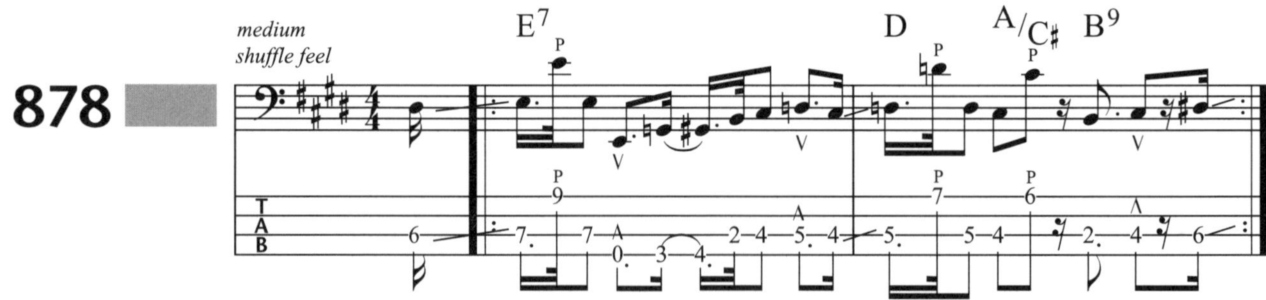

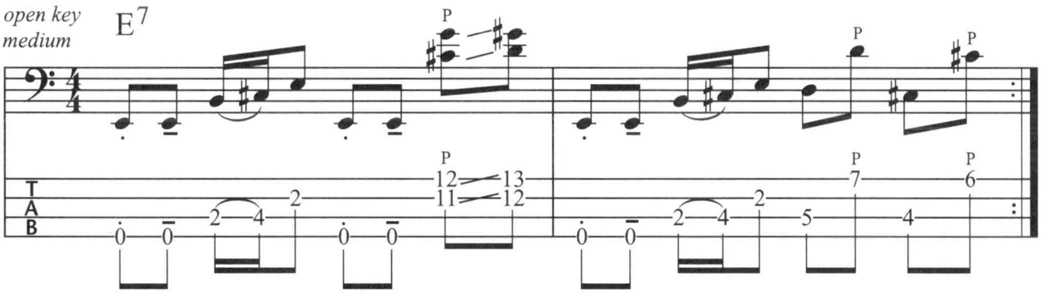

open key
medium
E7

879

CD 2 Track 30

open key
medium/fast
E7

880

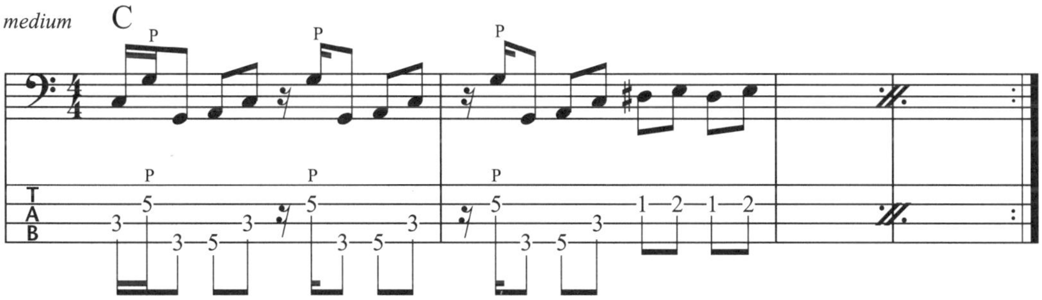

medium
C

881

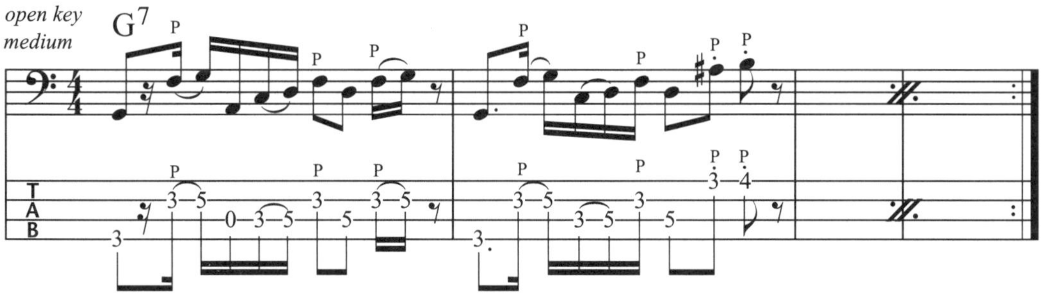

open key
medium
G7

882

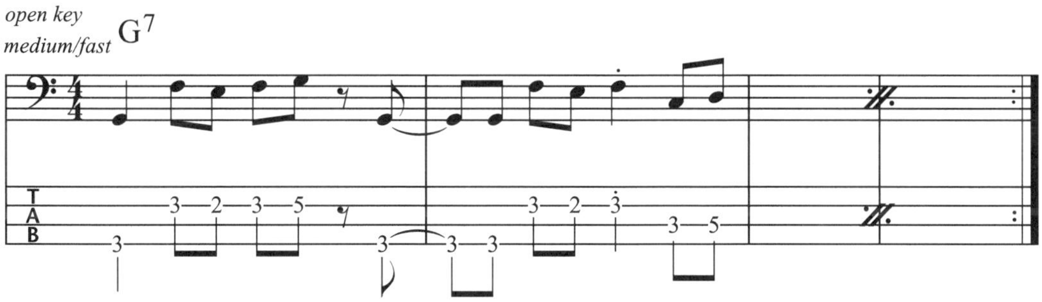

open key
medium/fast
G7

883

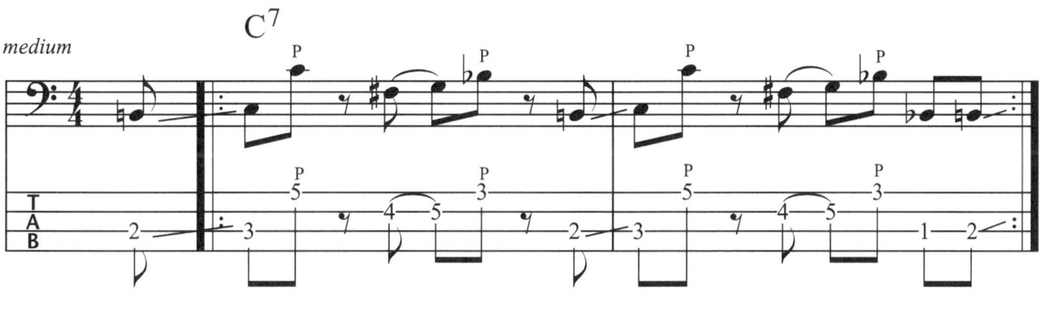

medium
C7

884

885

886

CD 2 Track 30

Mark King – Slap (Popping)

medium

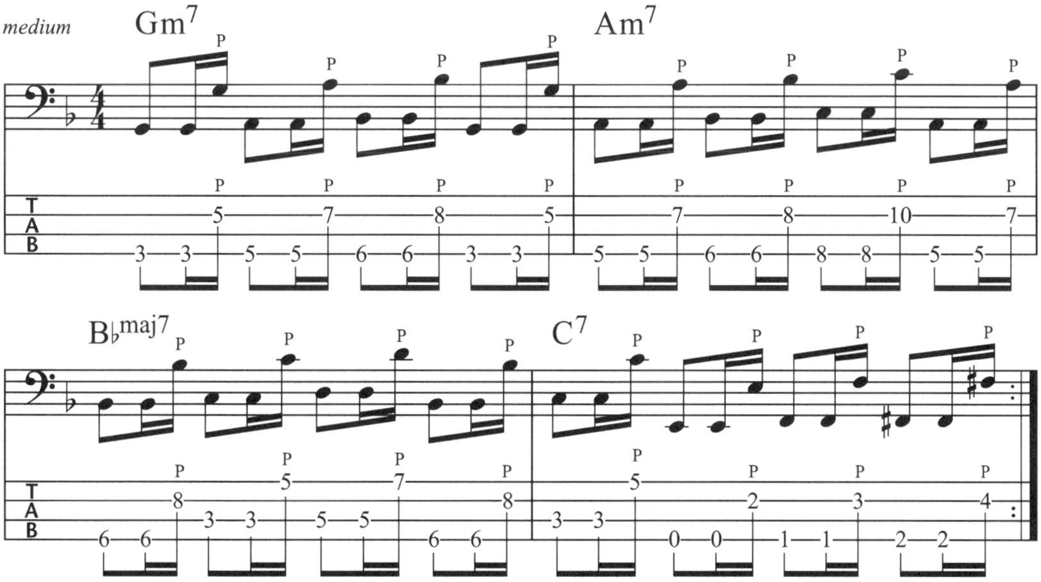

Gm7 Am7

887

CD 2 Track 31

B♭maj7 C7

open key medium

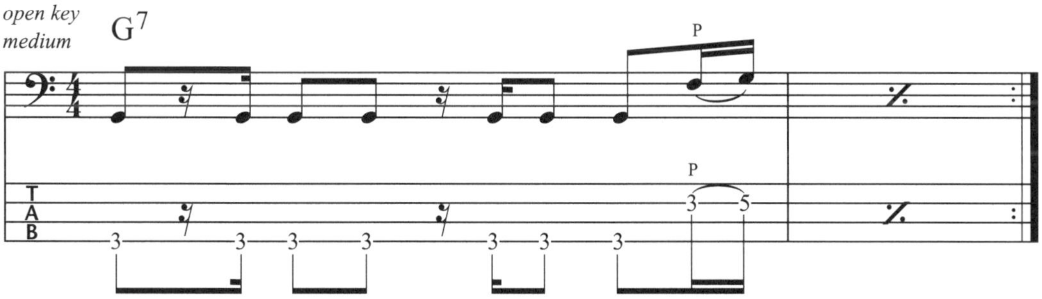

G7

888

medium

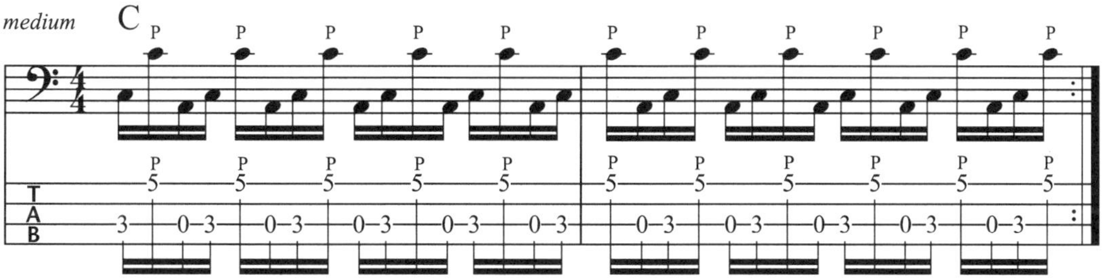

C

889

CD 2 Track 31

open key medium

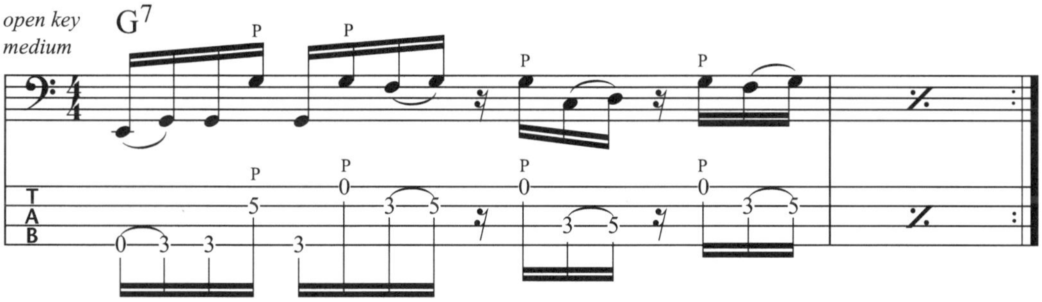

G7

890

open key medium

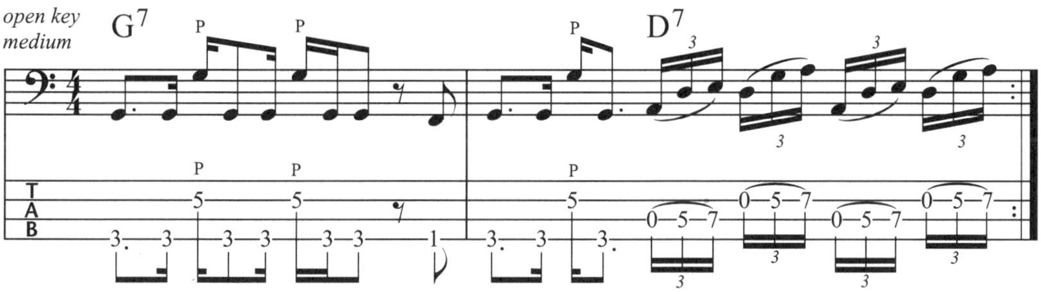

G7 D7

891

892
CD 2 Track 32

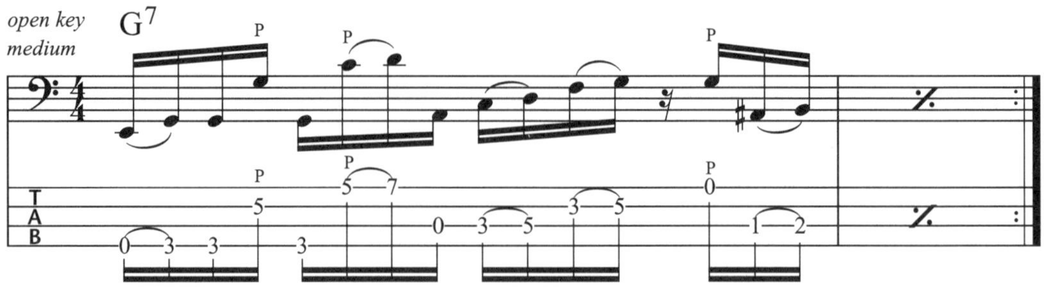

open key
medium
G7

893
CD 2 Track 32

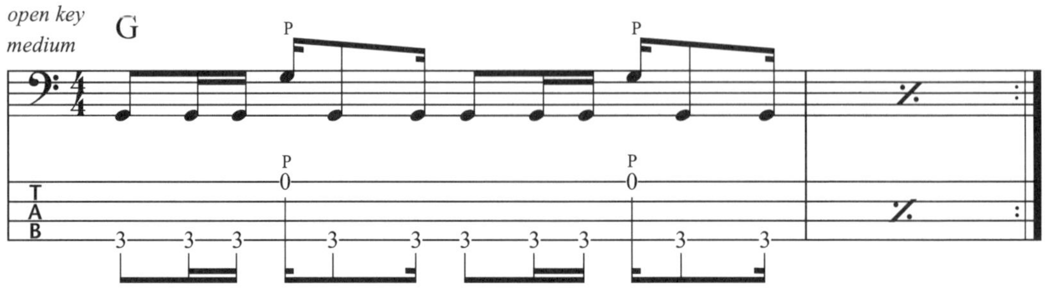

open key
medium
G

894
CD 2 Track 33

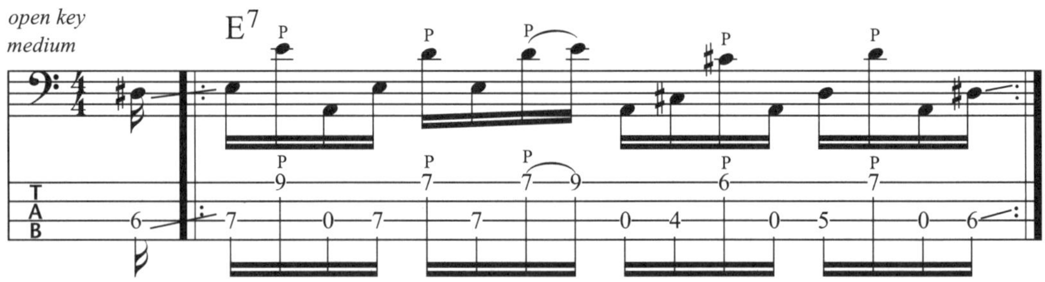

open key
medium
E7

895

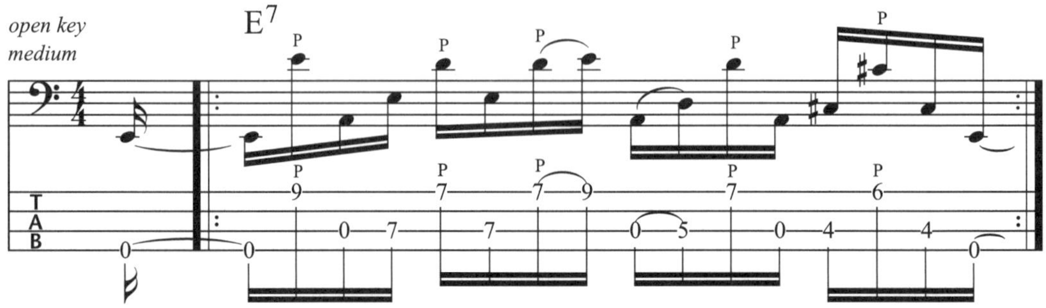

open key
medium
E7

896
CD 2 Track 33

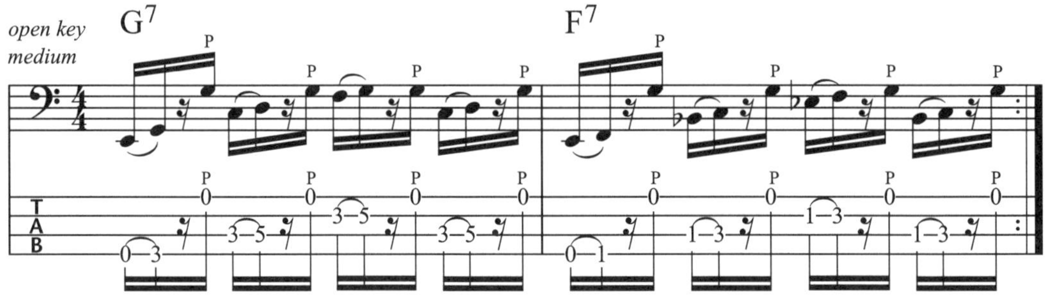

open key
medium
G7 F7

897
CD 2 Track 34

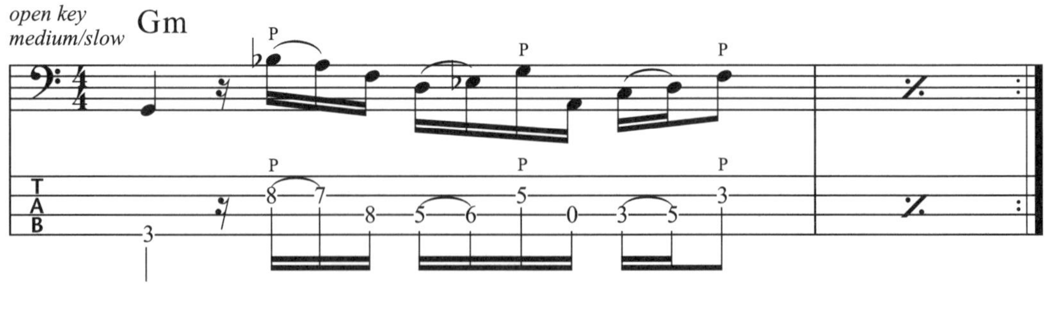

open key
medium/slow
Gm

open key
medium

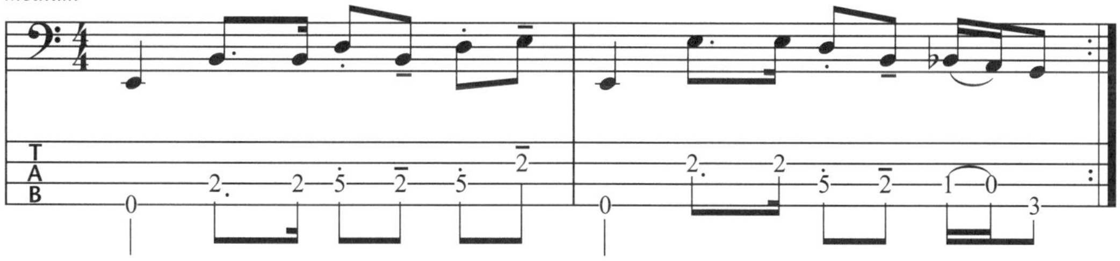

E7

898

open key
medium

G7

899

open key
medium

Dm7

900

open key
medium

G7

901

CD 2 Track 34

■ JACO PASTORIUS – Fretless Bass

The fretless bass guitar was rather unknown and underdeveloped until Jaco Pastorius appeared. He joined Weather Report and instantly found a wider audience.

His solo album catapulted him to the forefront of bassists worldwide. Suddenly much of what was being played by other musicians became old-fashioned and outdated. Whereas others had a traditional dull, woolly sound, he managed to combine strength, depth and clarity. Many bassists were still struggling to play interesting Jazz solos, and fumbling about trying to get a decent solo sound with a fluent technique. Jaco suddenly appeared with a sound so new and rich that sometimes just one note sufficed. In the Ron Carter double-bass tradition, it was possible to give a single legato note a crescendo, glissando, vibrato and diminuendo. His approach was Jazz based, although he understood and played Rock, R & B and Soul. Often he would find a melodic line to support the front line rather than a riff. These lines would weave in and out of the main theme, moving with or against the rhythmic pattern. They would also vary from low, legato sounds to middle and high harmonies, which sang out and added to the melody and harmonies being played by other instruments. When it came to soloing, he really astounded everyone. His solo album featured his fretless version of Donna Lee, a Charlie Parker alto saxophone piece. This was a totally new approach. His technique was so advanced that he could tackle the most complex horn lines, and maintain the harmonic shape without the need for chordal backing. Rhythmically he was solid and had a good sense of time.

A whole new world also opened up when he began exploiting harmonics, which had largely been ignored up to that point. Bassists were aware of them, but did not know that you could actually use them to play tunes and chord changes. Harmonics had only really been used previously for tuning up purposes.

The effect he had on the bass community was astonishing. People were rushing out to buy fretless basses, ripping out existing frets and filling the gaps with plastic wood, planing down fretboards, changing pick-ups, experimenting with new strings, practising furiously, and trying to find out how he made this extraordinary sound. Several basic changes emerged. Instead of regarding the left hand as being fairly static and concentrating on moving "across" the strings, the fretless bass allowed the player to think in terms of also moving more fluently up and down the neck. Jaco moved from low E's through a series of scales, arpeggios and flowing lines to the highest notes on the instrument with ease and "seamless" dexterity, so that the audience was not aware of the changes of position. Some of the most resonant notes are actually to be found in the middle of the instrument, which meant that a new approach had to be found to concentrate on these areas and exploit those sounds. Glisses and vibrato could be exploited as never before, and this marked a new era in developing a different approach. Glisses are indicated by a sloping straight line, e.g. ♪╱♩ .

Riffs

902 CD 2 Track 35

903 CD 2 Track 35

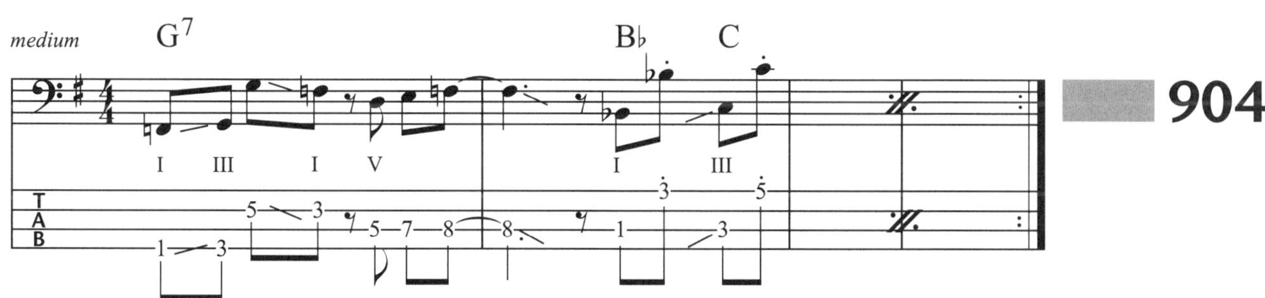

904

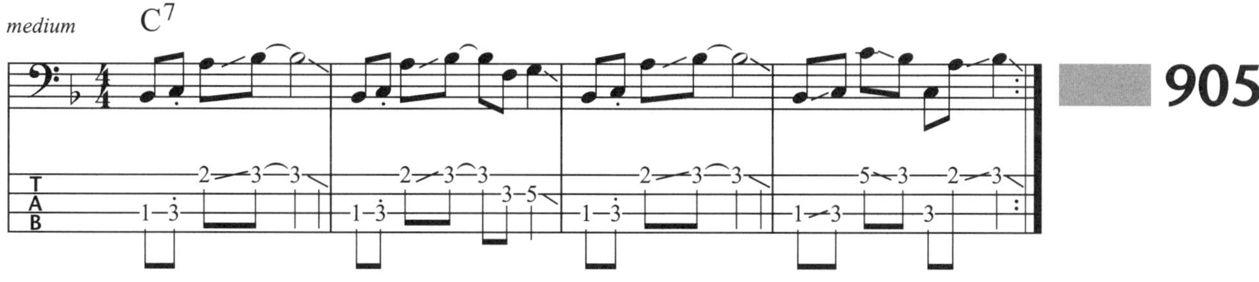

905

906

907

CD 2 Track 36

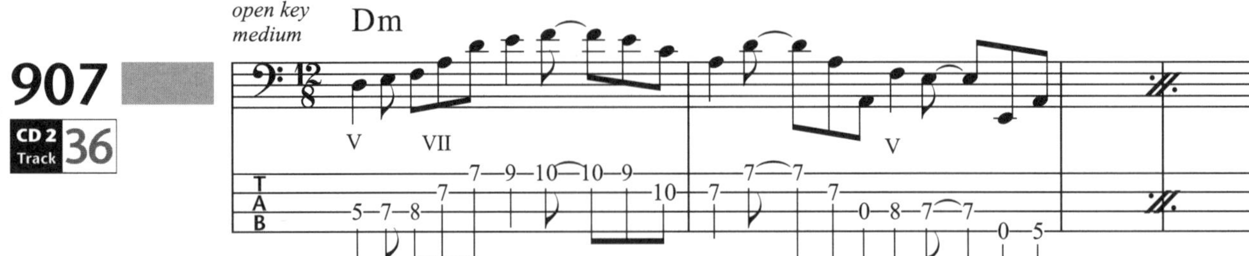

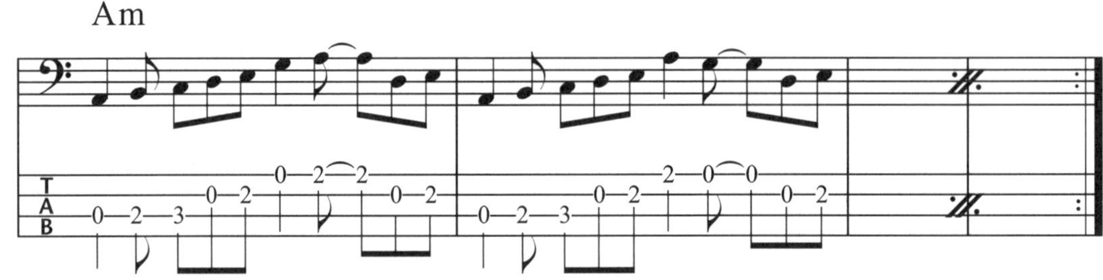

908

CD 2 Track 36

909

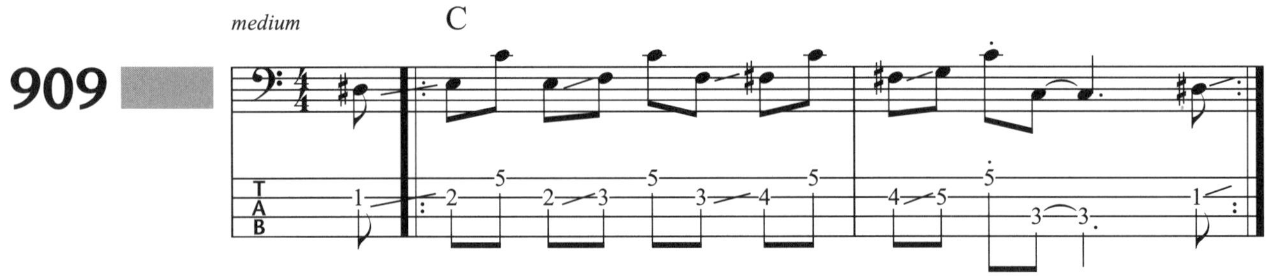

910

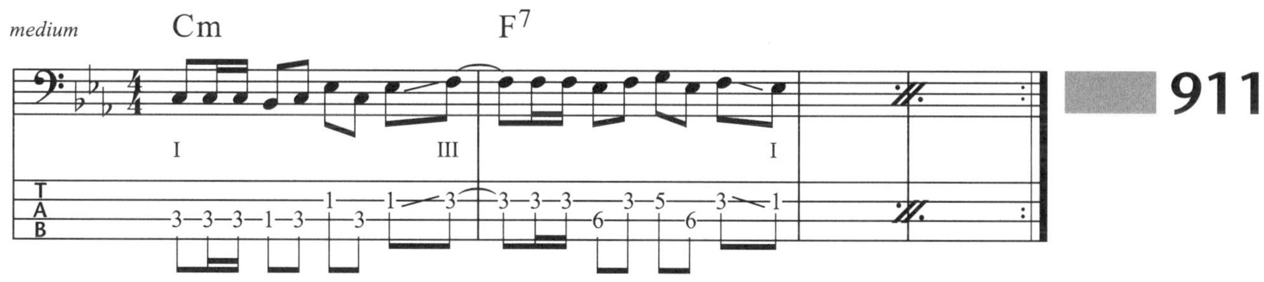
medium
Cm
F7
I
III
I
911

slow
Cm
III
V
III
912
CD 2 Track 37

open key
medium
F
I
III
V
VII
IX
913
CD 2 Track 37

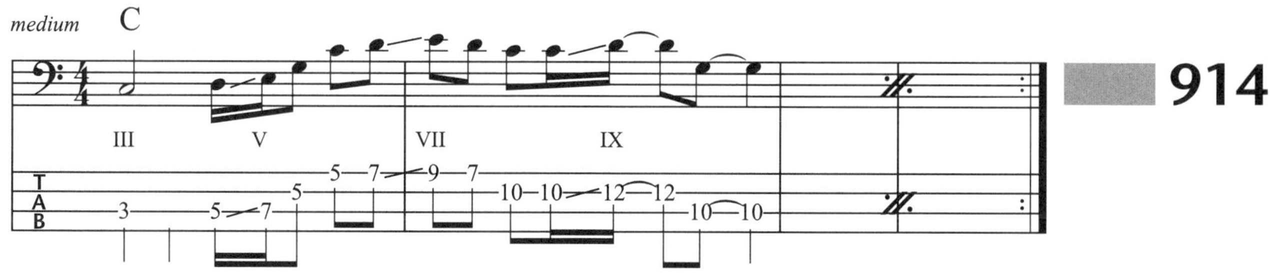
medium
C
III
V
VII
IX
914

shuffle feel
medium
Gm
I
III
I
III
915

B♭
medium/slow
XII
X
VII
V
III
I
916
CD 2 Track 38

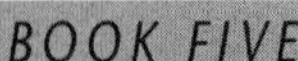

917
CD 2 Track 38
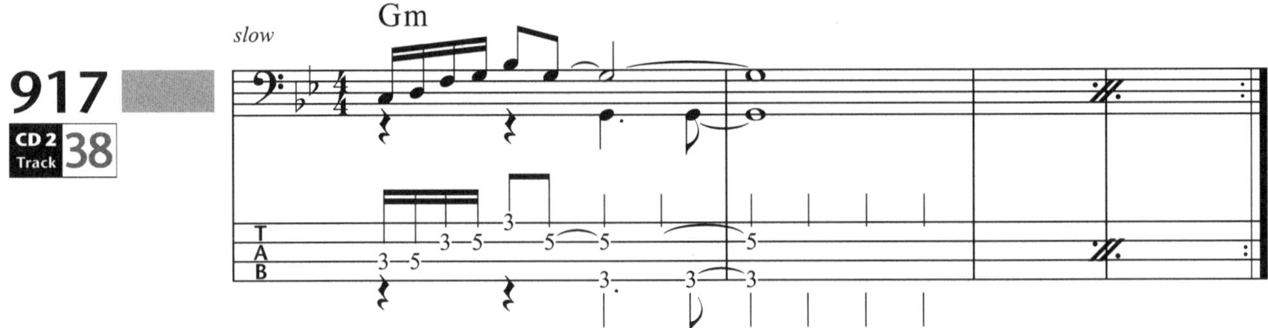

918
CD 2 Track 39

919
CD 2 Track 39

920
CD 2 Track 40
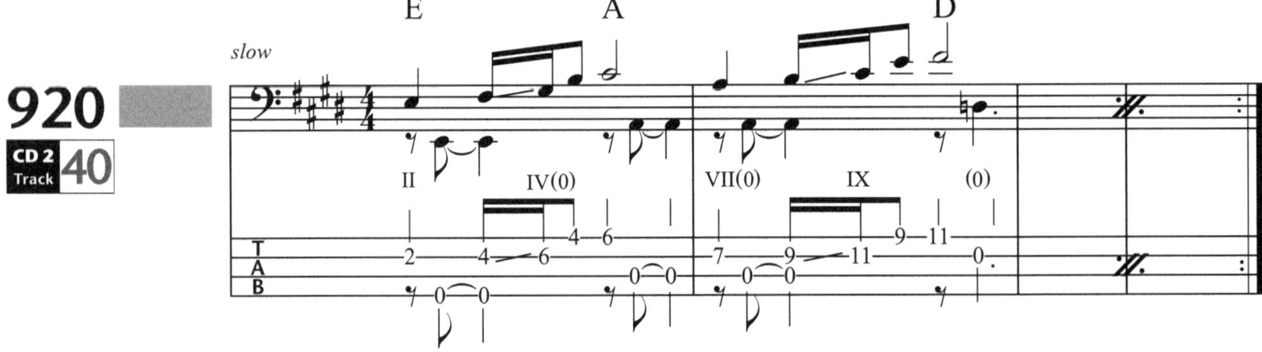

921
CD 2 Track 40
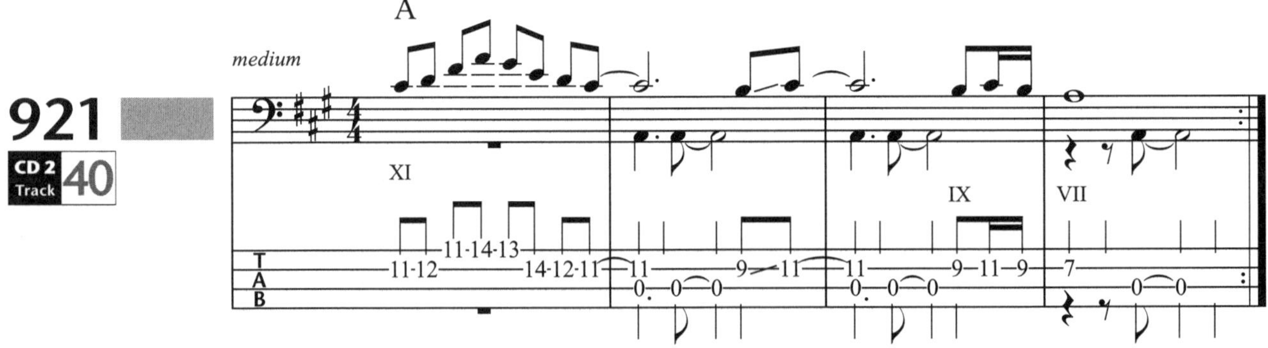

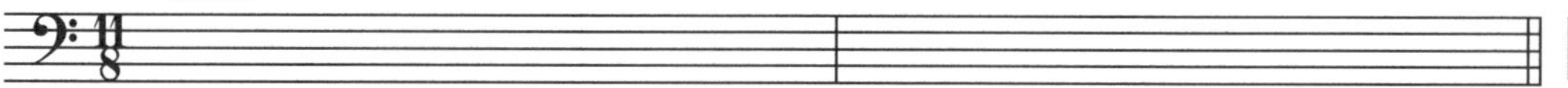

open key
medium

Gmaj7
ad lib.

CD 2 Track 41

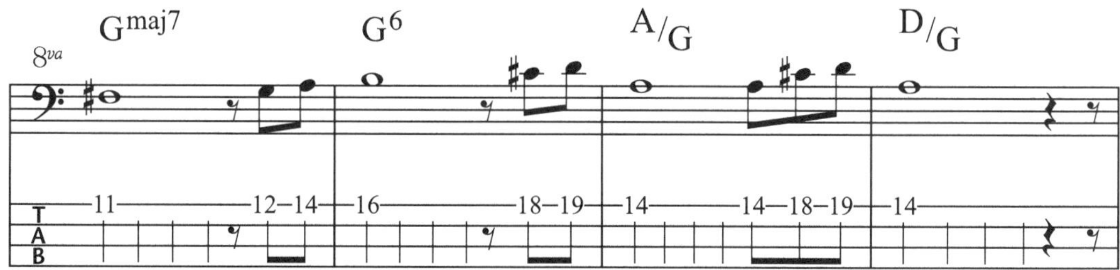

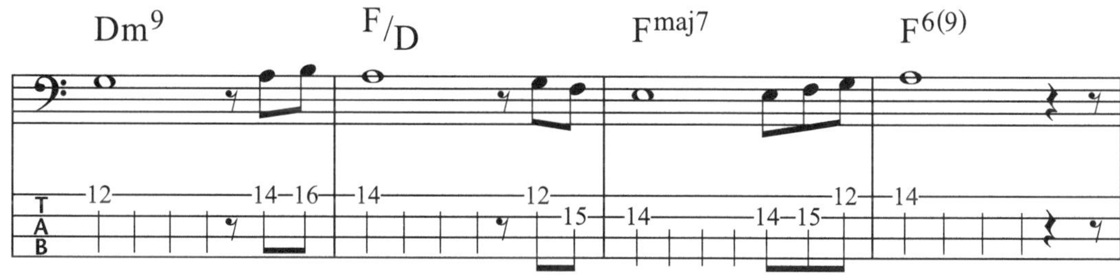

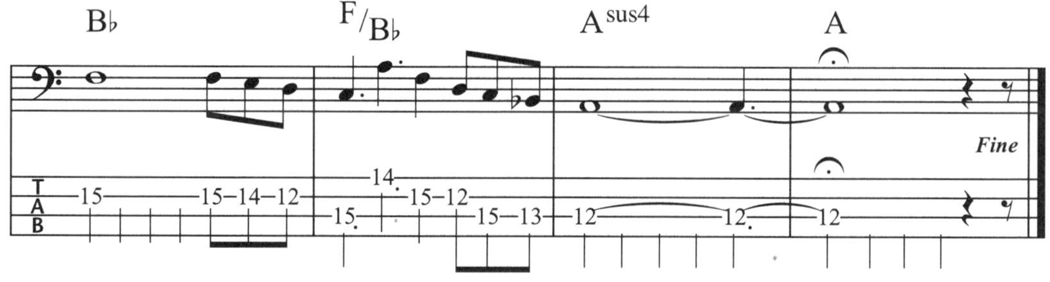

Note: Some phrasing may be altered slightly during performance. Slides and hammer-ons may be added to assist phrasing.

923

CD 2 Track 42

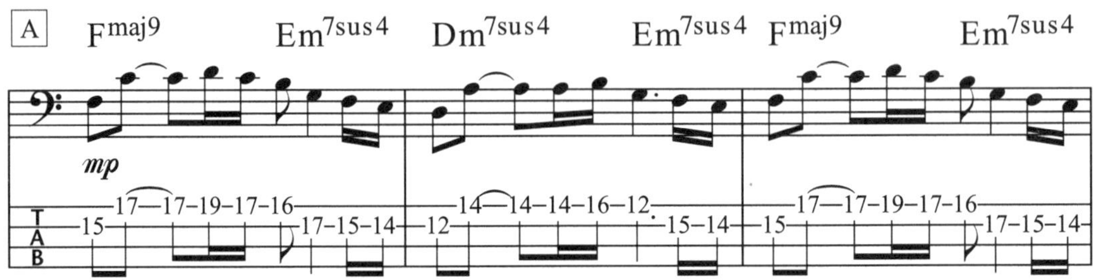

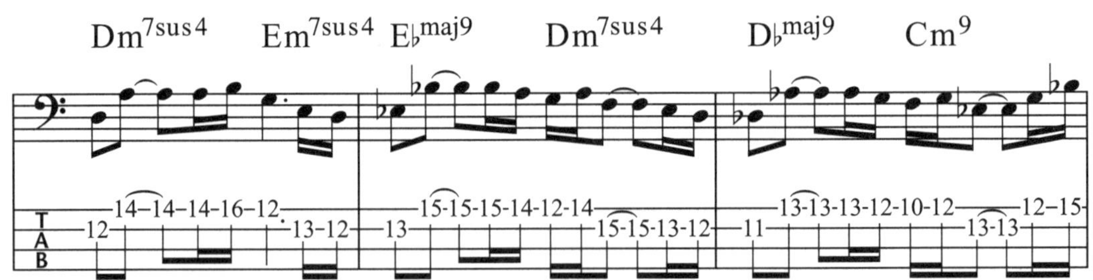

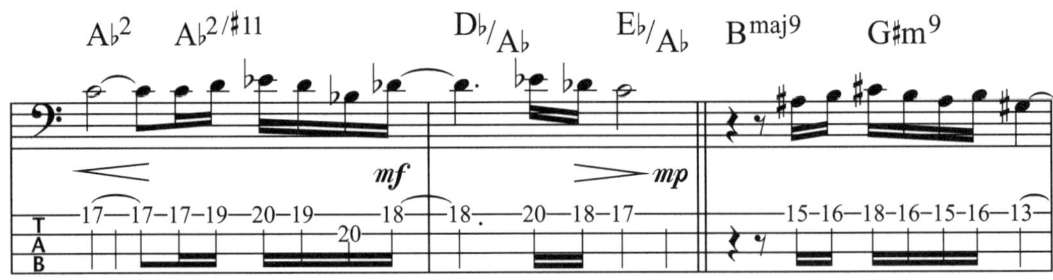

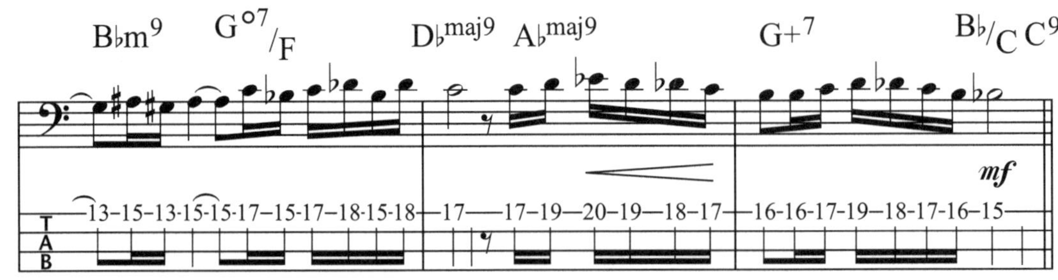

B
Am G F G Em F C♯/B
mf

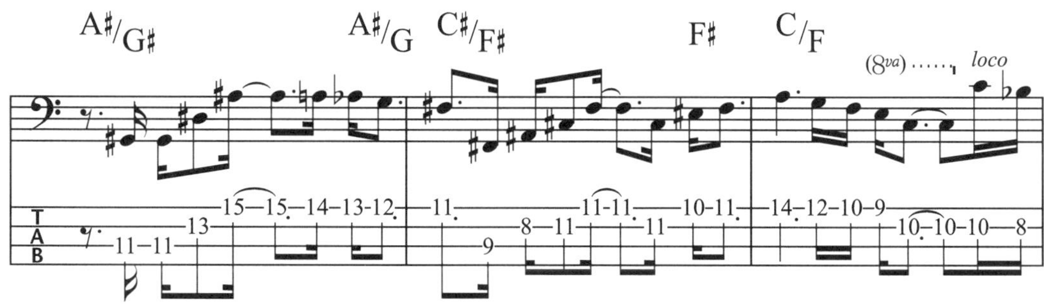
A♯/G♯ A♯/G C♯/F♯ F♯ C/F
(8va) loco

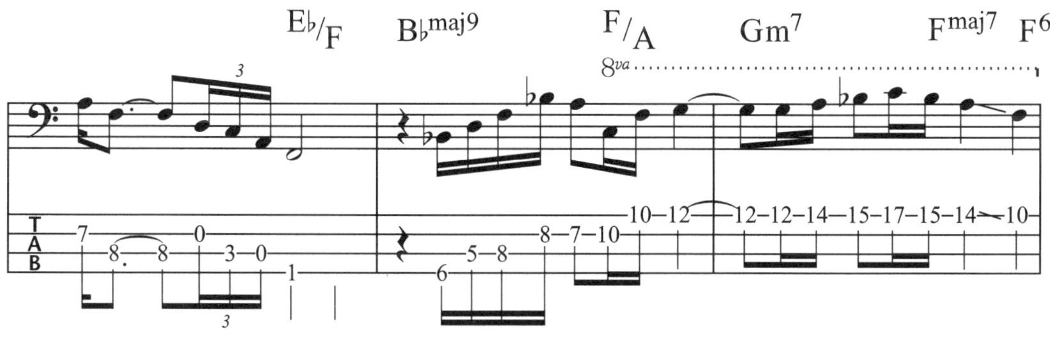
E♭/F B♭maj9 F/A Gm7 Fmaj7 F6
8va

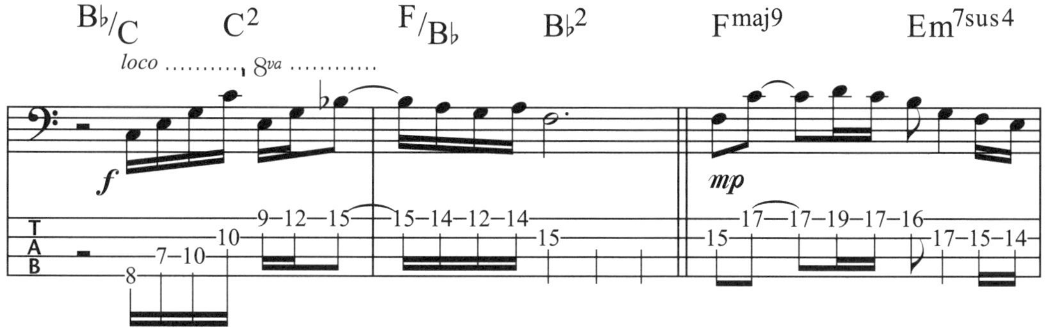
B♭/C C2 F/B♭ B♭2 Fmaj9 Em7sus4
loco 8va
f
mp

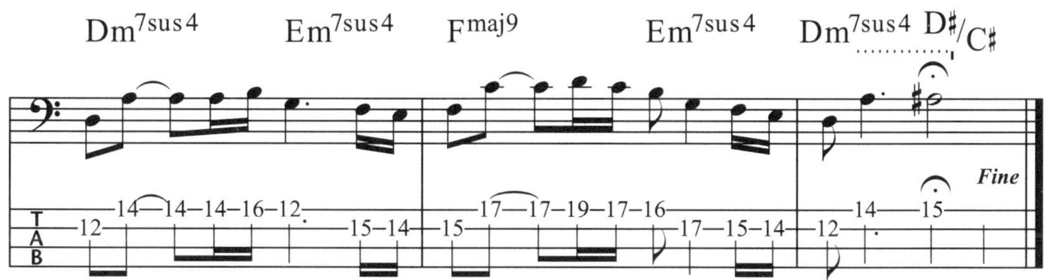
Dm7sus4 Em7sus4 Fmaj9 Em7sus4 Dm7sus4 D♯/C♯
Fine

924

CD 2
Track 43

open key
♩ = 69
D♭/D
ad lib.
E♭/D♭
E/C
F/B
p

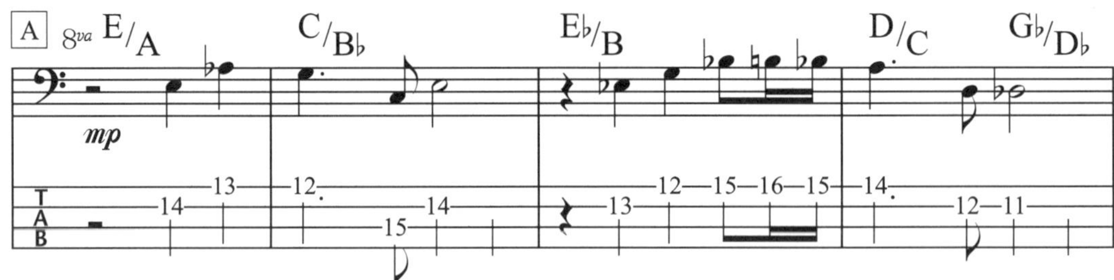
A
8va
E/A
C/B♭
E♭/B
D/C
G♭/D♭
mp
T
A
B
14 13 12 15 14 13 12 15 16 15 14 12 11

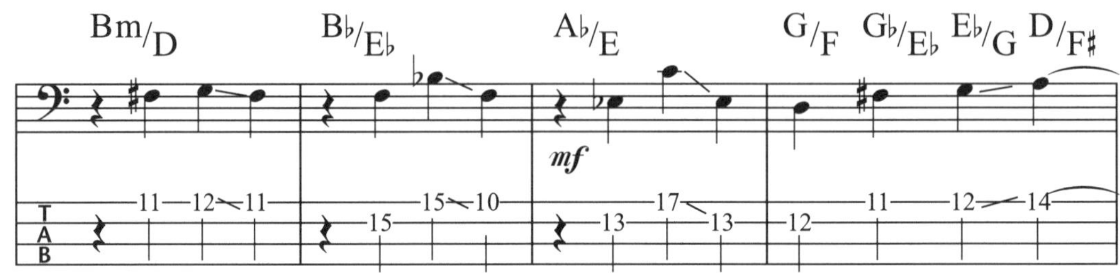
Bm/D
B♭/E♭
A♭/E
G/F
G♭/E♭
E♭/G
D/F♯
mf
T
A
B
11 12 11 15 15 10 13 17 13 12 11 12 14

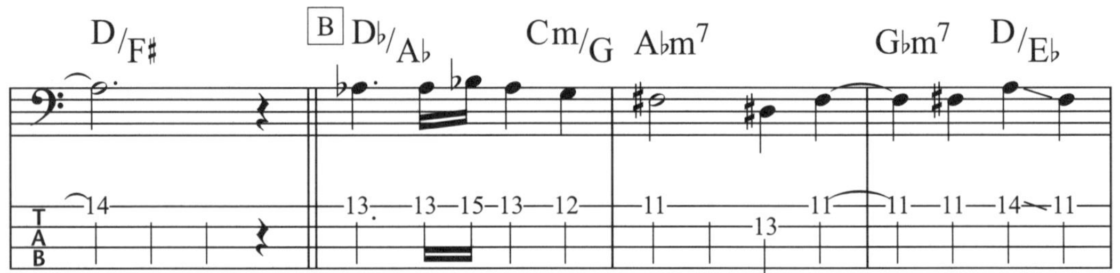
D/F♯
B
D♭/A♭
Cm/G
A♭m7
G♭m7
D/E♭
T
A
B
14 13 13 15 13 12 11 13 11 11 11 14 11

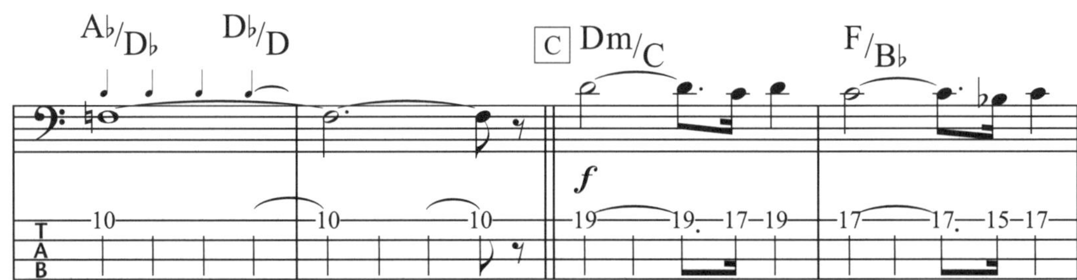
A♭/D♭
D♭/D
C
Dm/C
F/B♭
f
T
A
B
10 10 10 19 19 17 19 17 17 15 17

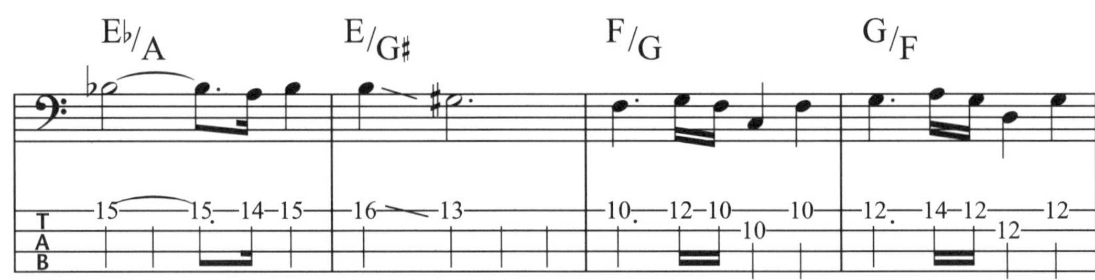
E♭/A
E/G♯
F/G
G/F
T
A
B
15 15 14 15 16 13 10 12 10 10 10 12 14 12 12 12

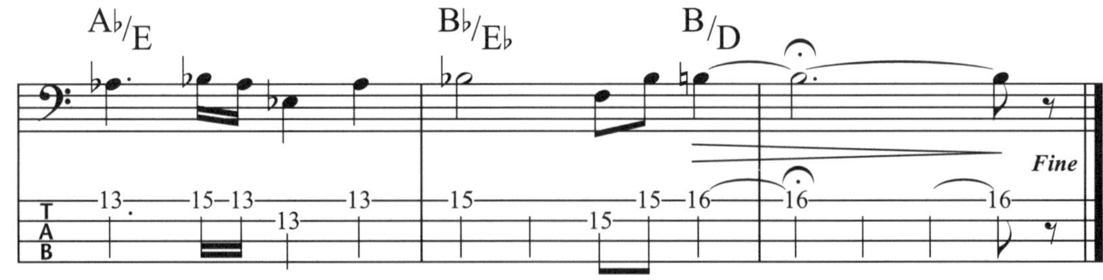
A♭/E
B♭/E♭
B/D
Fine
T
A
B
13 15 13 13 13 15 15 15 16 16 16

Note: Some phrasing may be altered slightly during performance. Slides and hammer-ons may be added to assist phrasing.

925

CD 2 Track 44

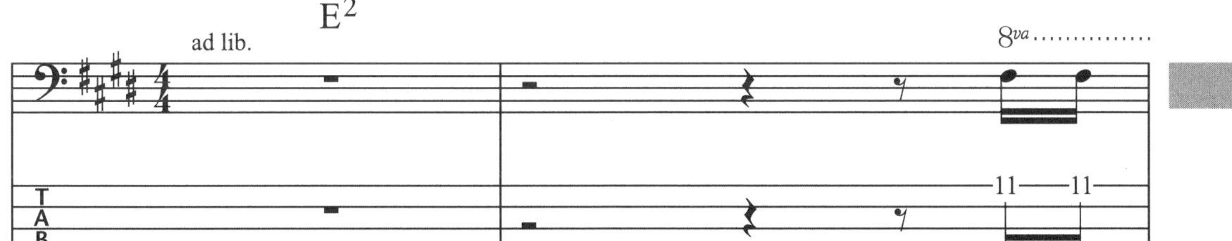

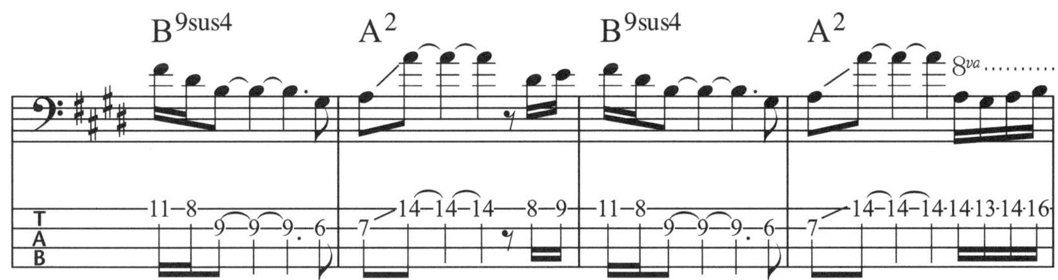

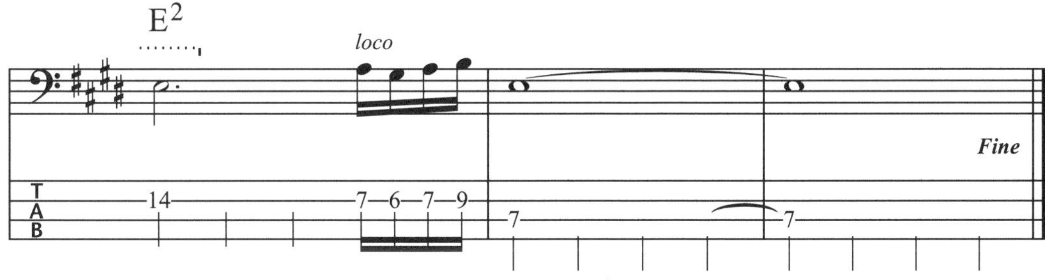

Natural Harmonics

(See section at beginning of book., p. 13)

All strings have natural harmonics. For instance, a string is able to vibrate in 2 equal lengths if you place a finger lightly on it at the 12th fret. The harmonic sounds an octave above the open string. Different harmonics are found at other intervals e.g.; 4th, 5th, 7th, 9th frets, and it is possible to have as many as 30 harmonics on one string. Similar notes occur in various places on different strings. The advantage of this is that in certain positions it is easier to play a natural bass note together with harmonics. Of course, once you play several harmonics together, the chordal possibilities are numerous.

There are probably hundreds of chords available on the bass guitar. The simple truth of the matter is that you would have to make a huge effort to master all of these. Without regular practice it would be easy to forget a great deal.

The reality is that most bass players only want to know a few of the most important chords, which they can play at an appropriate time. This may be very occasionally. As the bassist explores his own ideas, he will discover patterns, chords and tunes to suit himself.

Jaco Pastorius was the master and innovator of the style. He did not approach it academically, but made his discoveries through trial, error, patience and talent. Even his simplest harmonic ideas had great effect when tastefully blended with subtle moving lines and lovely melodies. He also discovered some very unusual voicings. Harmonics can be equally successful on fretted or fretless basses.

To play a harmonic, place a finger of the left hand gently on the string, say, over the 5th fret. Pluck the string with the right hand, then quickly remove the left hand finger. In this position, the harmonic sounds two octaves above the open string.

Chordal Harmonics

A

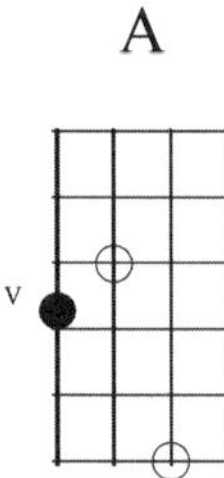

A7

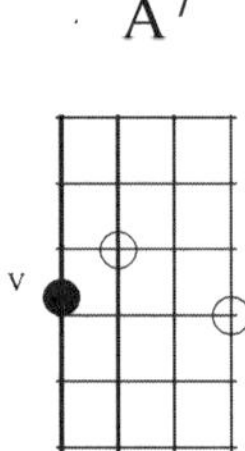

A6(9)

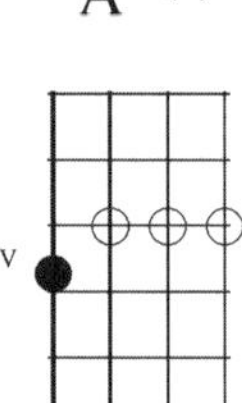

A4

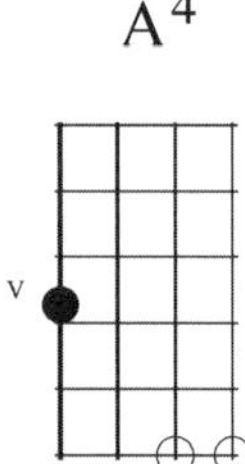

A#maj7

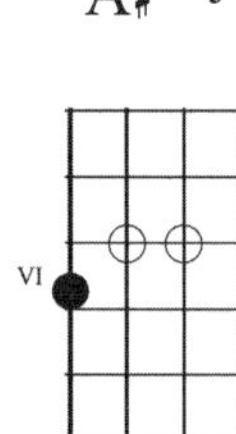

A#6

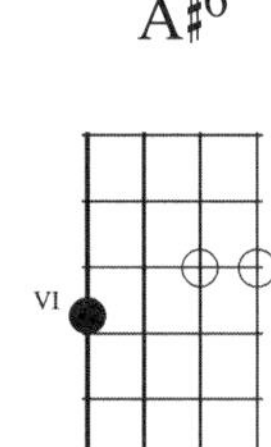

A#(♭5)

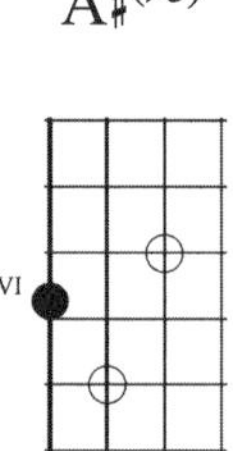

B^{add9}

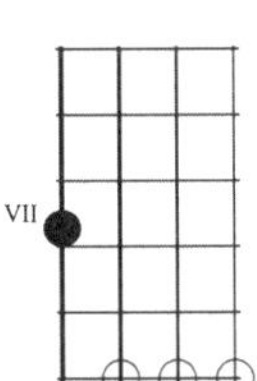

G^{2}/B

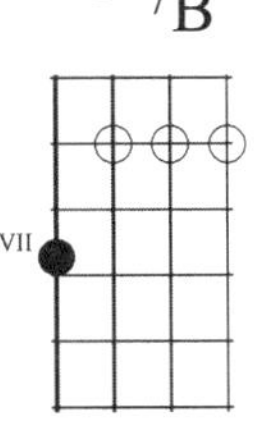

Bm^{7}

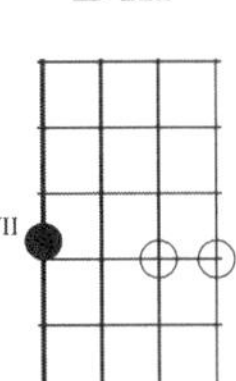

C^{2}

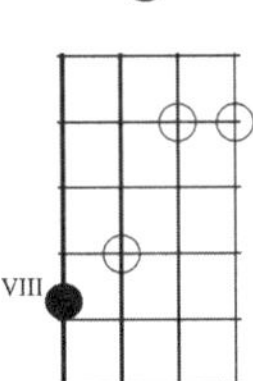

$C^{6(9)}$

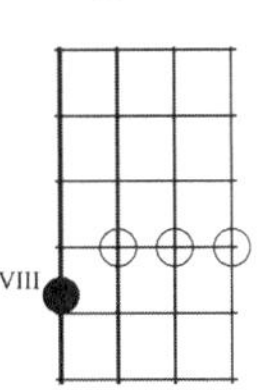

$C^{maj7(6)}$

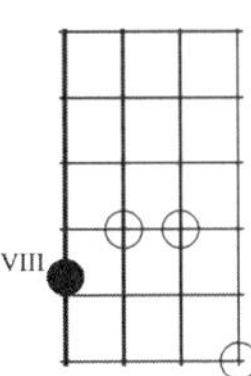

$A/C\sharp$

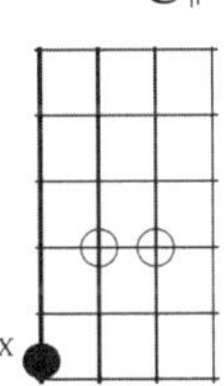
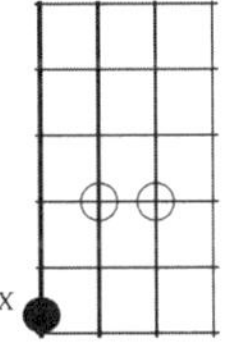

D

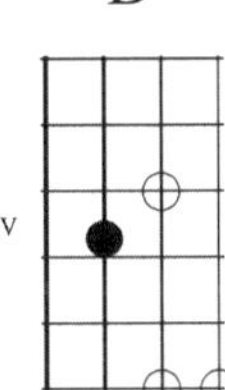

D^{4}

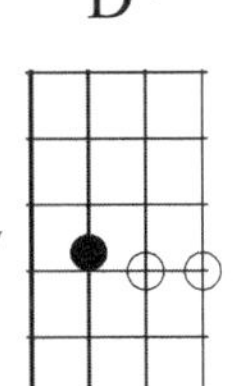

D^{6}

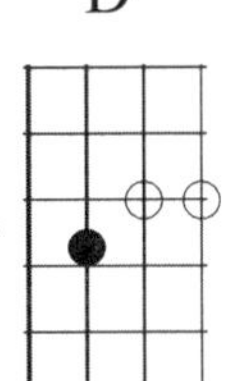

D^{maj7}

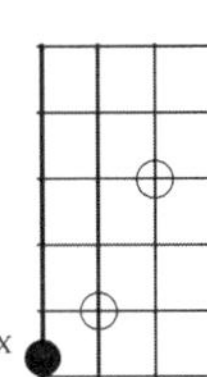

$D\sharp^{maj7}$

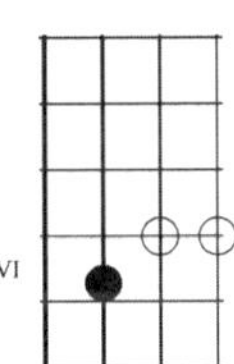

$D\sharp^{(\flat 5)}$

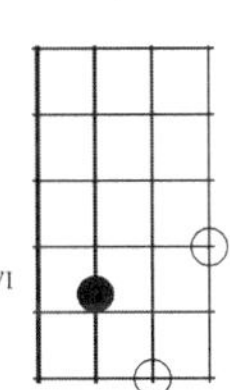

$D\sharp^{7}$

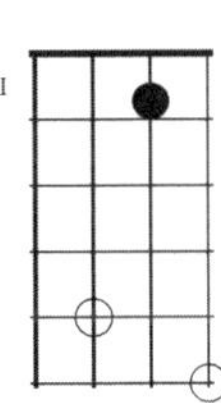

$B/D\sharp$

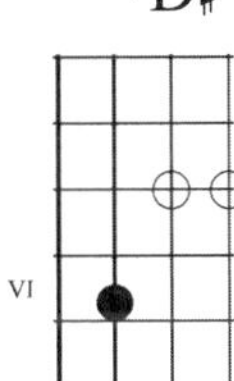

E^{2}

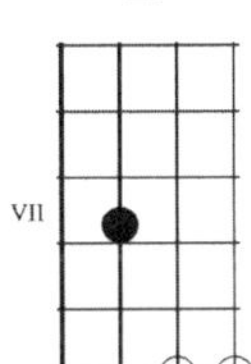

$E^{7(4)}$

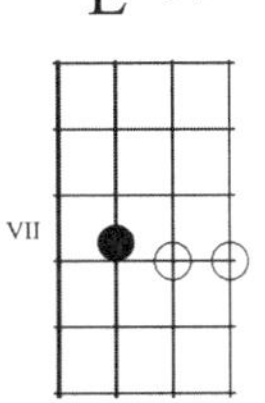

Em^{7}

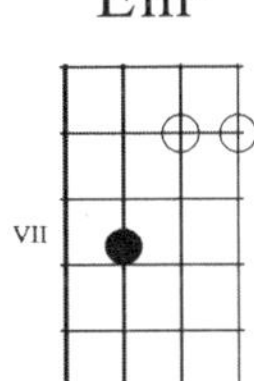

F^{2}

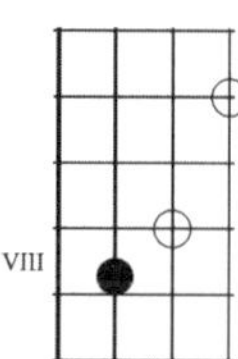

F^{6}

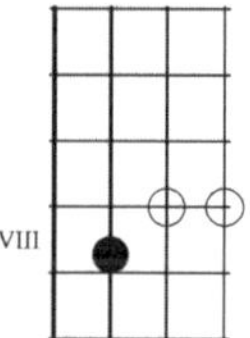

$F\sharp^{4}$

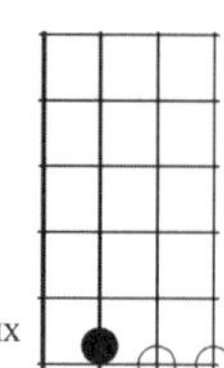

D/F♯

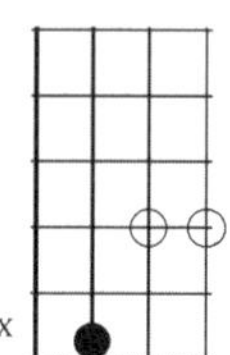

G^{2}

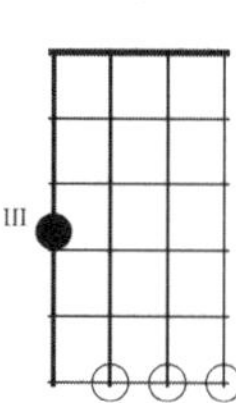

G^{maj7}

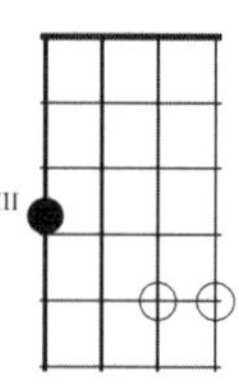

$G^{6(9)}$

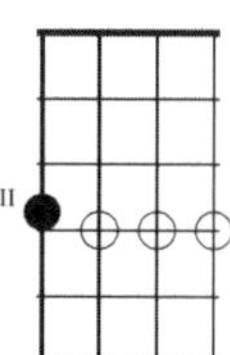

$G\sharp^{maj7}$

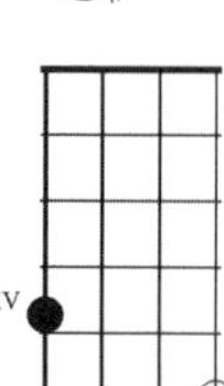

$G\sharp^{7(4)}$

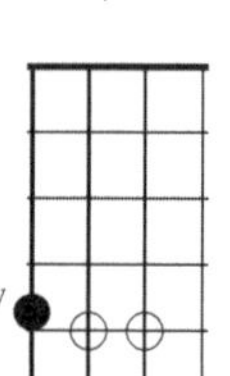

$G\sharp m^{7}$

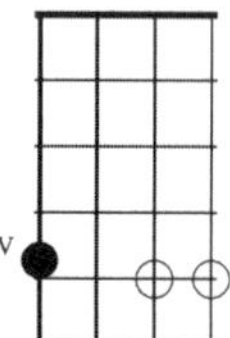

Arpeggio Chord Progressions with Harmonics

926

4/4 |: C^{2} | G^{2}/B | $B\flat^{maj7(6)}$ | G^{2}/B :|

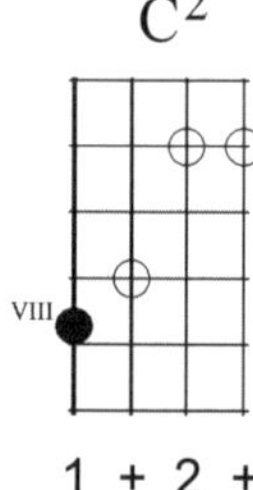

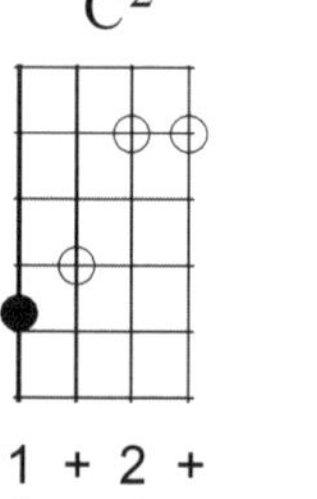

1 + 2 +
3 + 4 +

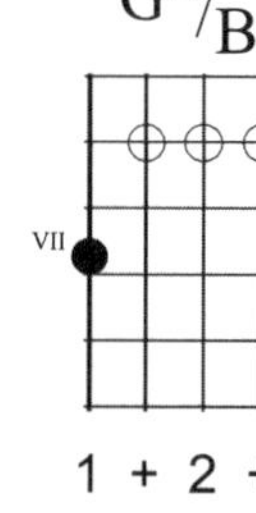

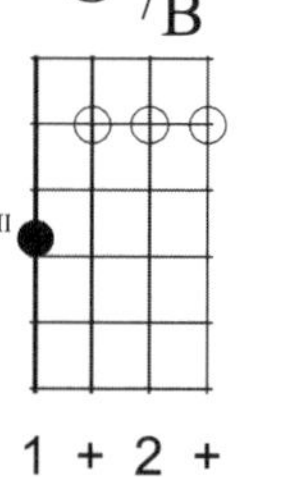

1 + 2 +
3 + 4 +

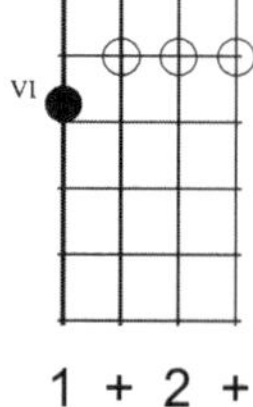

1 + 2 +
3 + 4 +

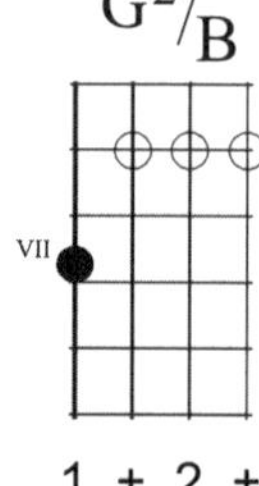

1 + 2 +
3 + 4 +

927

CD 2 Track 45

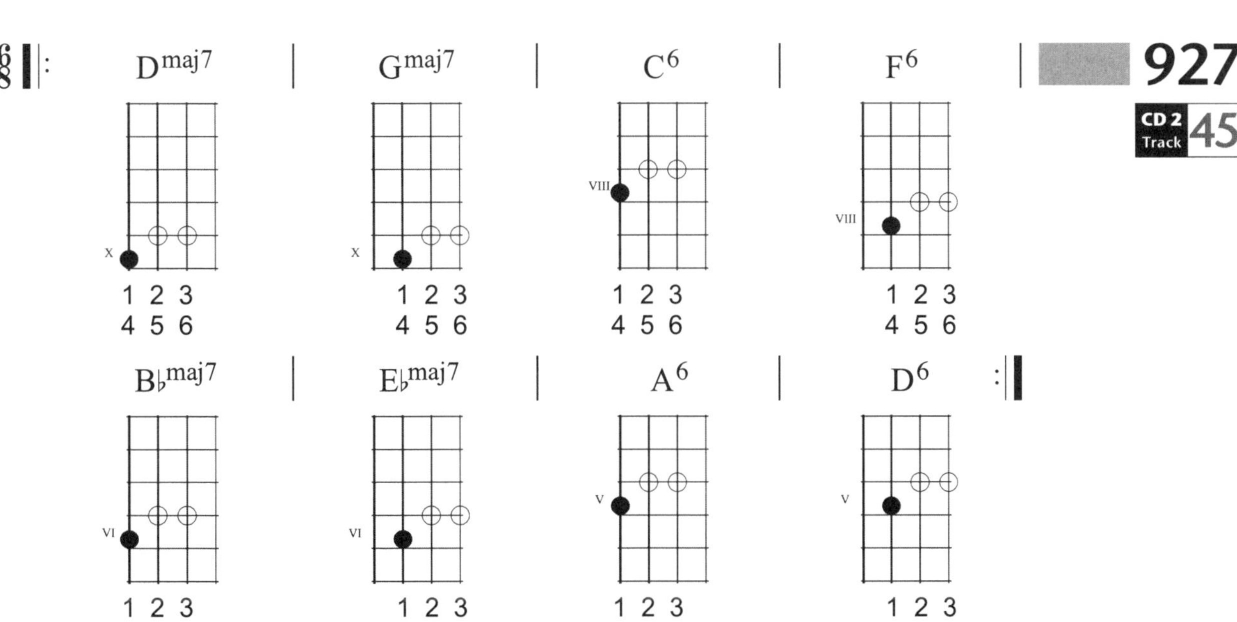

928

CD 2 Track 46

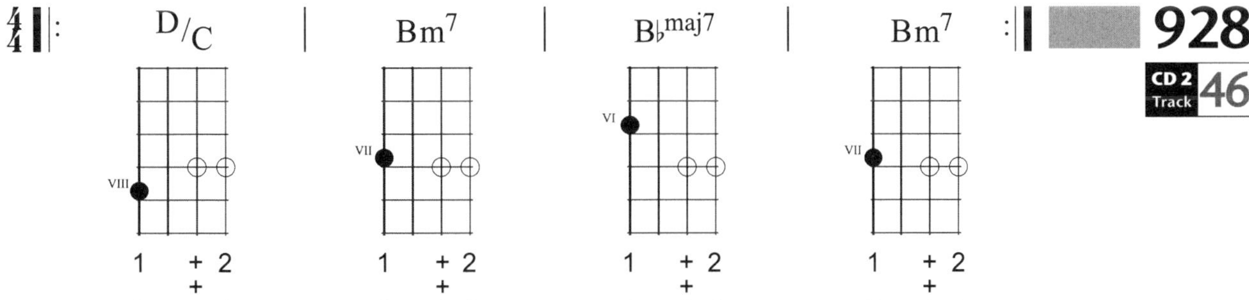

929

CD 2 Track 46

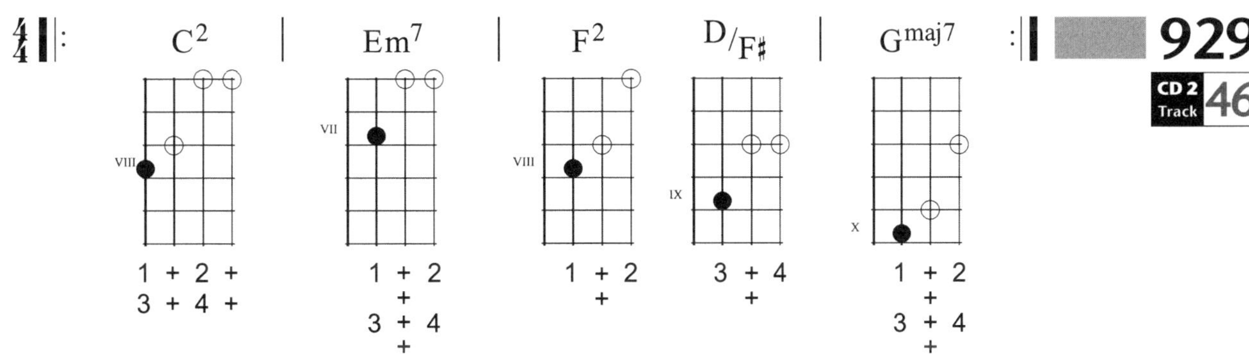

930

CD 2 Track 47

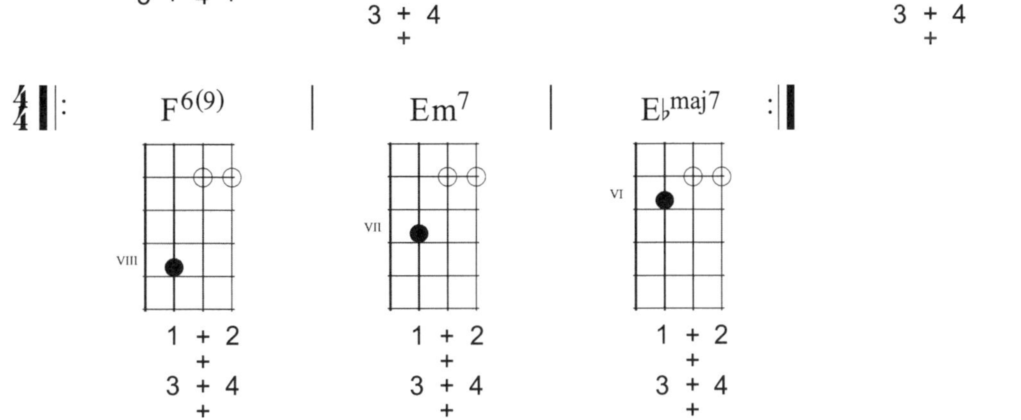

■ Synthesizer Bass

One particular new development which revolutionised the bass line was the computer. It enabled a rhythmic pattern to be programmed-in and played exactly the same each time. Whereas bass players had been deliberately adding the human touch by varying phrases and riffs to maintain interest, the sequencer created a new feel.

These patterns were often played faster and more accurately than would have been possible for most musicians. With the incessant driving beat, they became very popular.

It is important for the modern bass player to blend with electronic dance tracks, and to be able to create a feel similar to the sequencer.

Some riffs are useful when added to the repertoire, as they add a machine-like quality which had previously been unexplored.

As synthesizers are programmed-in on dance tracks, it is essential for the live bass guitar line to be played as accurately as possible, with a hard, mid-range, driving sound, and where necessary with great technical skill. Therefore, technique becomes an essential ingredient to allow constant, repetitive, effortless playing. Stamina is the only way to keep this sequencer feel going.

In reality tempos vary from medium to medium/fast.

931

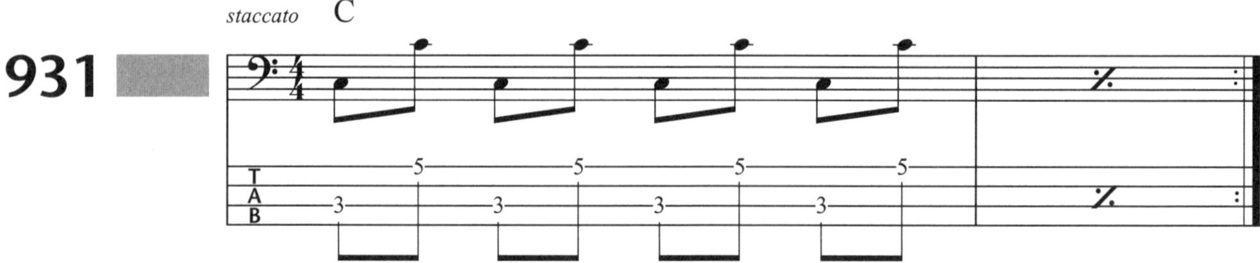

932

CD 2 Track 48

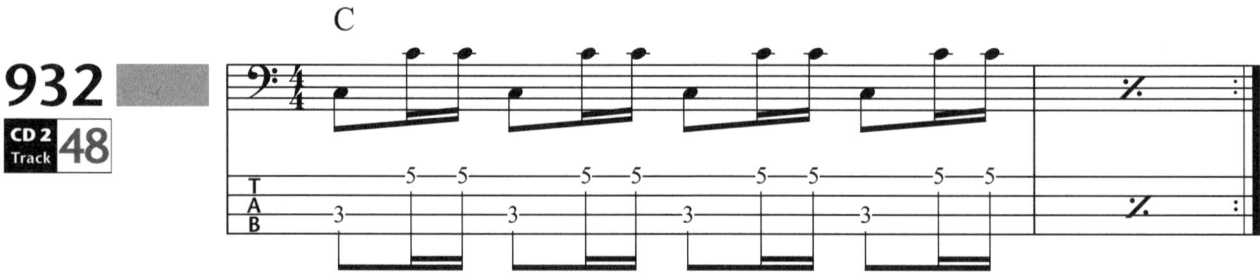

933

C
934

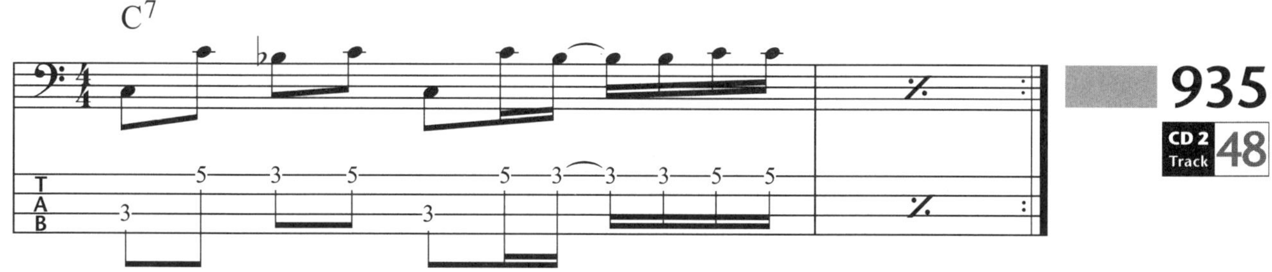
C7
935
CD 2 Track 48

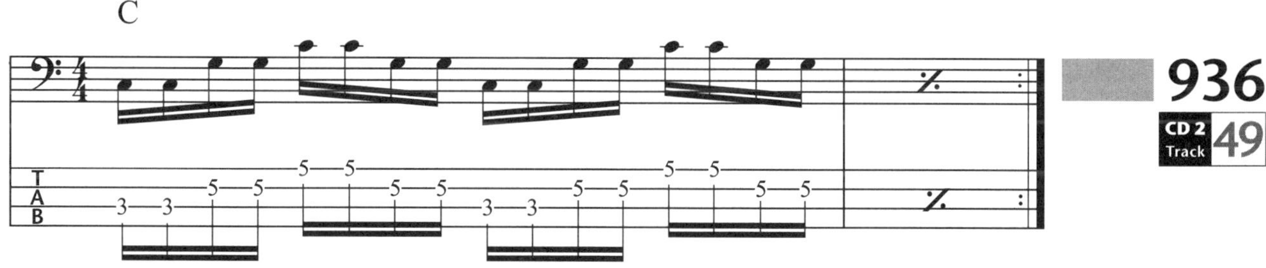
C
936
CD 2 Track 49

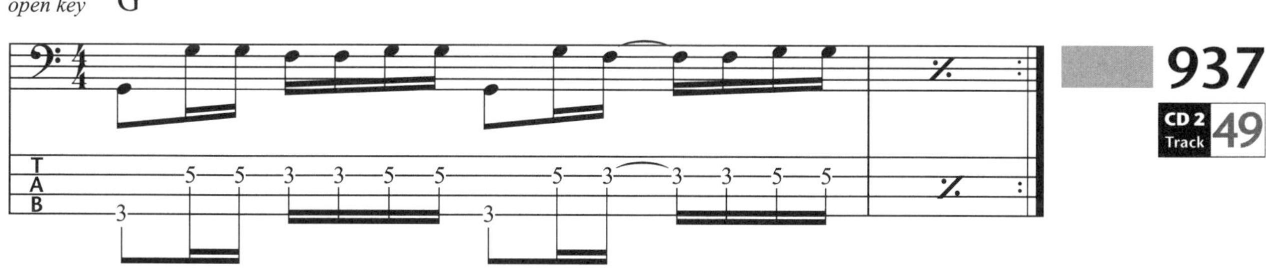
open key
G7
937
CD 2 Track 49

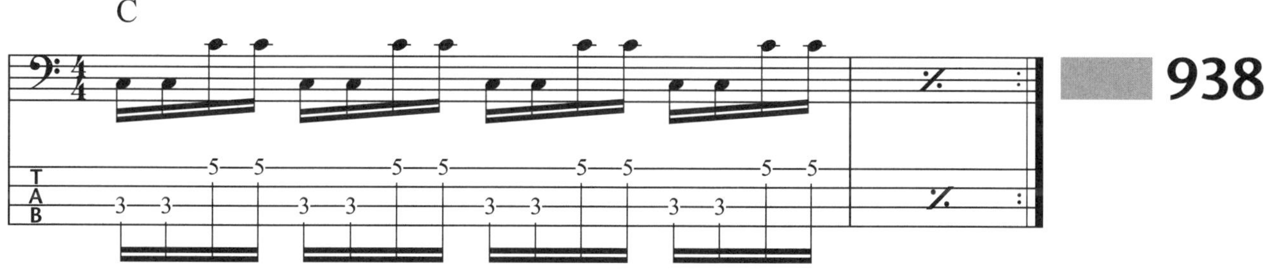
C
938

C7
939

VERLAG

940
open key
Dm7

941
C7

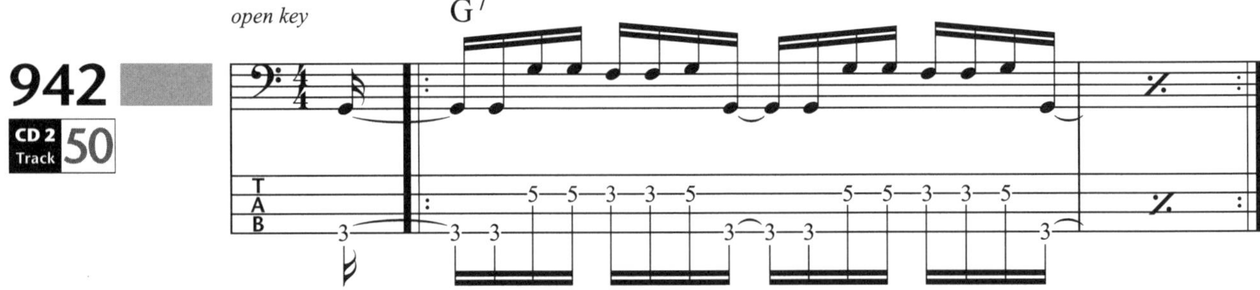
942
CD 2 Track 50
open key
G7

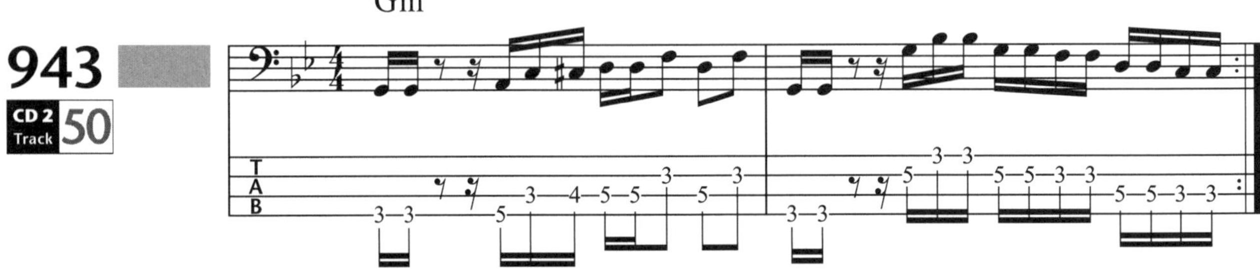
943
CD 2 Track 50
Gm

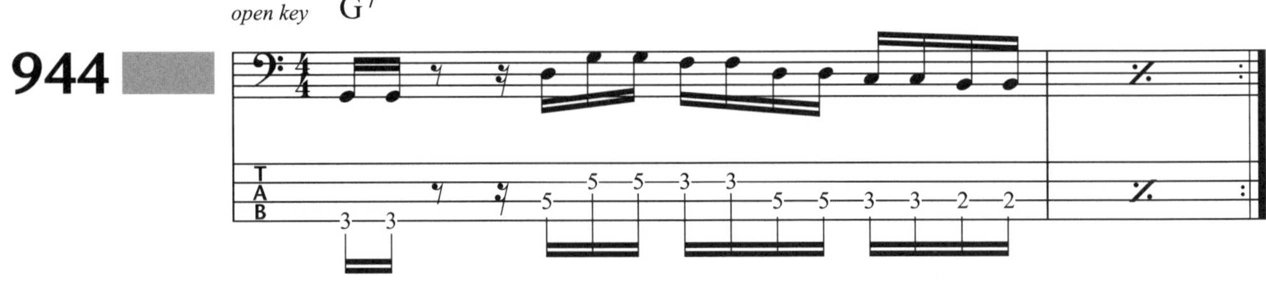
944
open key
G7

945
open key
G7

open key G7

946

CD 2 Track 51

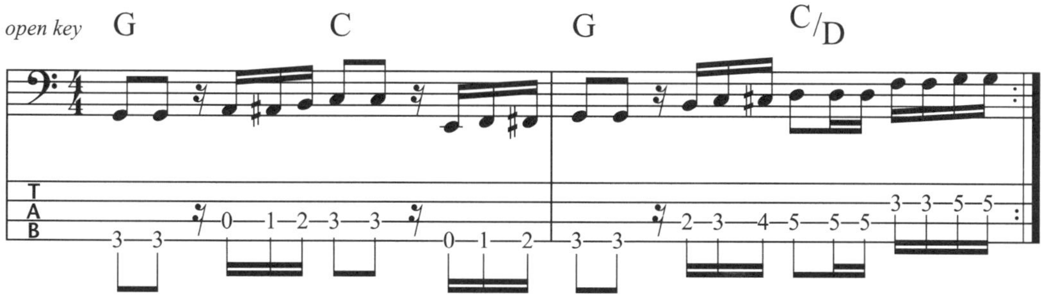

open key G C G C/D

947

CD 2 Track 51

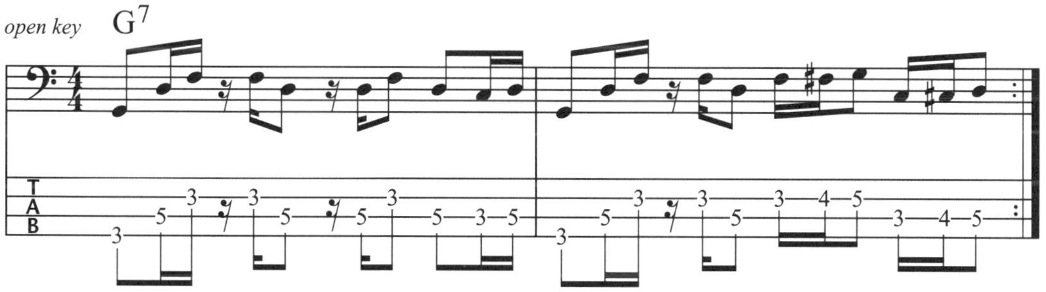

open key G7

948

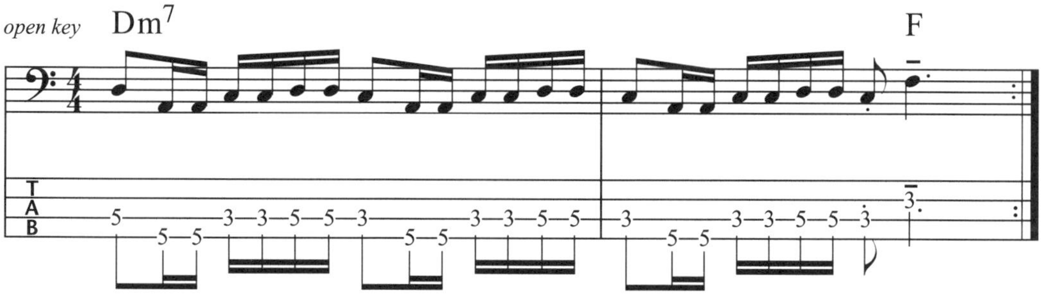

open key Dm7 F

949

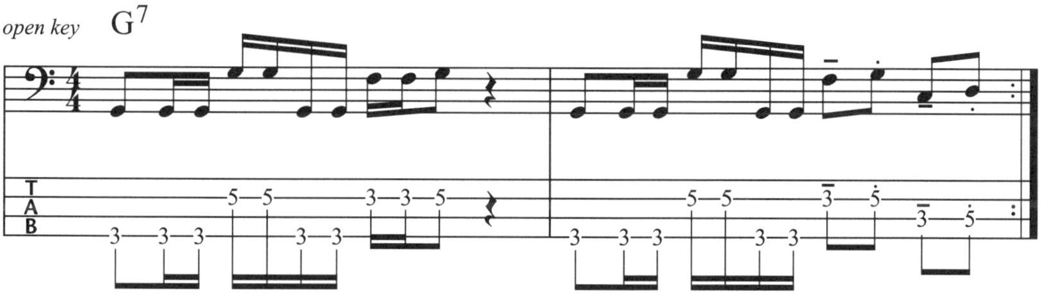

open key G7

950

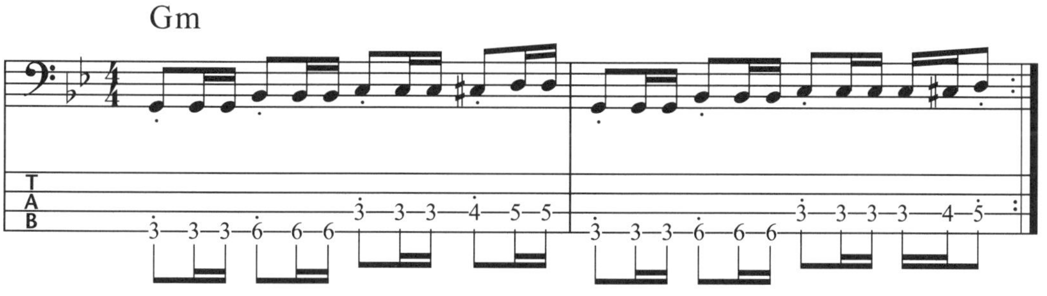

Gm

951

952

953

954

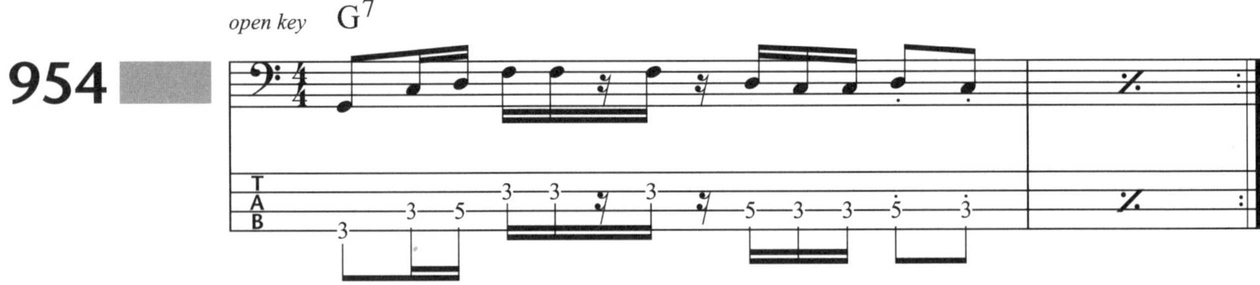

Modern Riffs – Jazz & Progressive Lines ■

With the history of the bass guitar now stretching back over 45 years, developments have inevitably led to the breaking down of purism within each musical style. There were times in the past when it was essential for the bass player to play within a "Soul" or "Rock & Roll" framework. At other times, if he did not maintain a swing 4 feel, musicians could not cope.

A Blues band would not put up with an imaginative Jazz bassist or a "slap" player. Heavy Rock bands did not want the influence of computers to replace the "live" feel. A strident fretless bass was not accepted by Latin bands at first. So it took a while before these and other changes happened.

As more music is recorded for discs, CDs, DVDs, cassettes, videos, TV, radio, etc., the important quality which all musicians seek is freshness. Something which seems new. The simplest way to achieve this is to borrow from another style. For instance, if you take a Reggae feel and put it into a Rock idiom, you have invented "White Reggae".

The most important feature in music is the quality of the composition. It does not matter how much a record producer plays with sound effects and loops, what makes a record commercial is the basic tune or message in the lyric which people can relate to. When a bass player is accompanying someone, he has to keep an open mind as to which notes and styles may best be used. The problem with inventing a new style is that it takes time for audiences to relate to it. If the music is not instantly recognisable as being based on a particular style, record companies are not going to spend money on a product which will only appeal to a minority. However, when a new style catches on, they sign bands up by the dozen.

Many groups have members from different countries. Cross-influences give another dimension to their music. Others try to create something new by either further developing a particular style, or producing new sounds by using the latest technology.

Many of the names which are used for these trends are for convenience only. They do not necessarily signal the dawning of a new musical era or an important breakthrough. Half the time they are labels created to provide a strong commercial angle for selling records!

The reality of the situation is that there are thousands of musicians who are doing the best job they can within the circumstances. Occasionally a bass player will develop a style which somehow sets him apart. It may not be any particular record which gets him noticed, but it may simply be that over a period of time he has played many interesting bass lines with well-known artists. People then begin to look out for his name on album covers and concert advertisements.

Many of the bass players who have led the creative field during the last decade are ones who experiment with Jazz. Jazz Rock, Jazz Funk and Jazz Fusion are now considered old-fashioned terms, but this is loosely what their music has developed from. The most notable players in America are Marcus Miller, John Patitucci, Jeff Berlin, Anthony Jackson, Abraham Laboriel, Will Lee, Jimmy Haslip, Louis Johnson and Paul Jackson.

England also has a strong contemporary music scene and is developing some fine musicians. In the following examples, there are many bass phrases which I have developed during my own experimentation with feels and grooves. If you have studied this book, you will recognise certain influences.

I have approached these riffs in various different ways. First of all I completely changed my right hand technique (watch my "Complete Bass Player" video. It's an "A-Z of Bass Guitar Techniques"). I play in a similar fashion to Spanish guitar players, and this enables me to view modern music from a different angle, which provides the rhythm section with a fresh set of ideas.

Another approach I have used is to mix a staccato Funk style with Latin rhythms (no. 965). Mixing Rock 8th notes with Latin style anticipation notes can give the drummer a chance to play some interesting patterns too (no. 967). Bursts of short phrases give a sense of energy (no. 969). Fast 16th notes developed in a different way give a "bubble-feel" and have the energy of a sequencer (no. 970). An octave pattern works well when phrases are slightly broken up and glisses are added (no. 971). A simple one-note phrase can alter subtly when the first beat in the bar is played early (no. 973). By playing a phrase with greater energy than expected, a new sense of urgency results (no. 974). Slurring notes can provide more variety when the repeated phrase in bar 8 changes the accent from the on-beat to the off-beat (no. 975).

Stressing beats 2 and 3 alters the emphasis in the bar (no. 976). Just 2 notes repeated rhythmically over a 2 bar phrase can be quite exciting (no. 977). A Latin style phrase provides more urgency with a series of 16th note pushes into the beat (no. 979). Leaving out beat 1 changes the momentum in a bar (no. 980). An answer phrase can begin a beat early (no. 983). By varying the length of notes, a 2-bar phrase can appear to lose momentum, but still stay in tempo (no. 984). A 6-beat pattern is more unusual when it begins on beat 3 (no. 985). Starting on the beat before the main downbeat gives the bar space to breathe (no. 986). Even beginning a riff 2 beats early can seem logical (no. 987). A Rock shuffle, walking bass line "drives" when played fast (no. 990). Playing a long note in the repeat of a riff gives the phrase breathing space (no. 992). A simple 16th-note phrase can be answered by one which has no downbeats, except for the resolution at the end of the second bar (no. 993). The bass can even play a kind of rhythm guitar riff, which gives another alternative feel (no. 995).

Modern Riffs

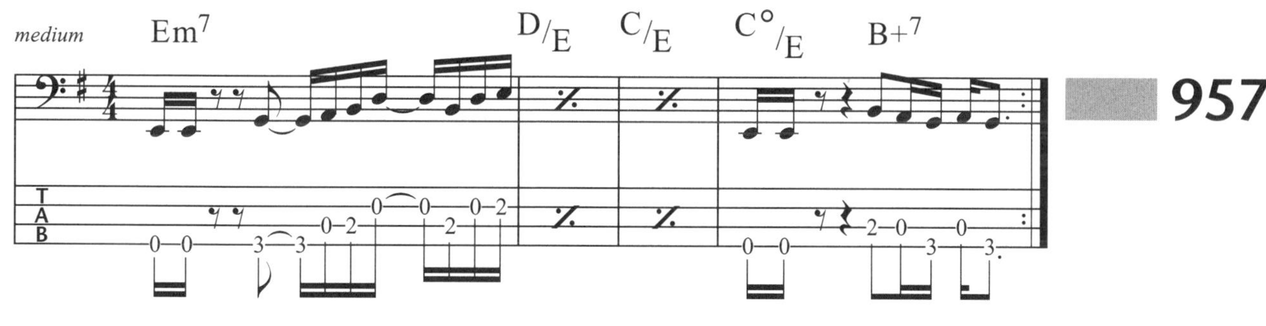
medium
Em7
D/E
C/E
C°/E
B+7
957

medium
Emaj9
G♯m7/C♯
F♯m7/B
958

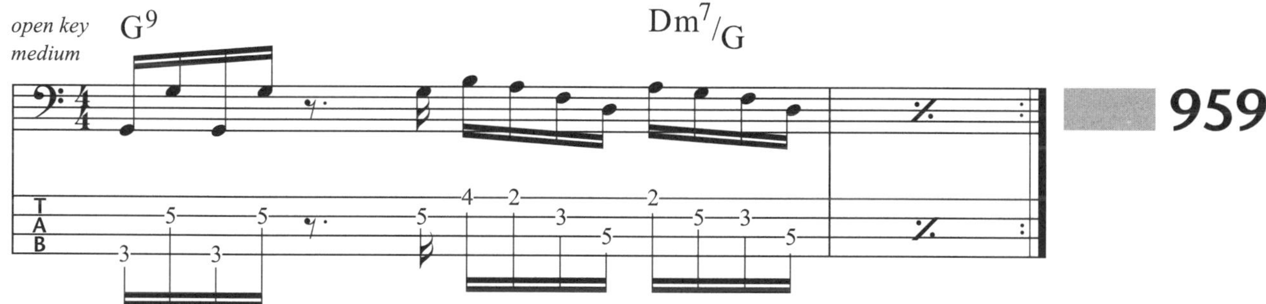
open key
medium
G9
Dm7/G
959

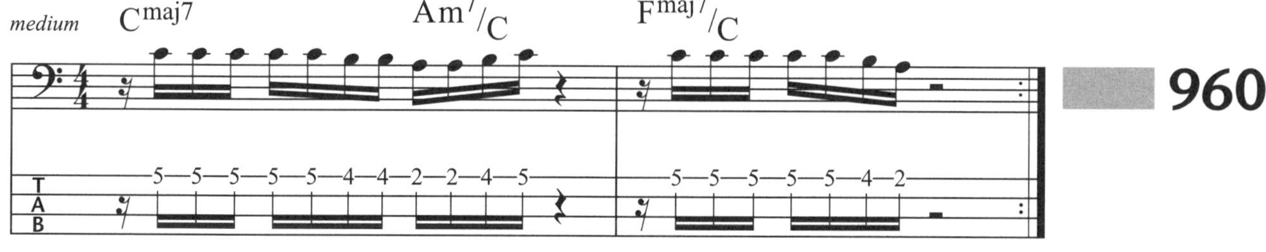
medium
Cmaj7
Am7/C
Fmaj7/C
960

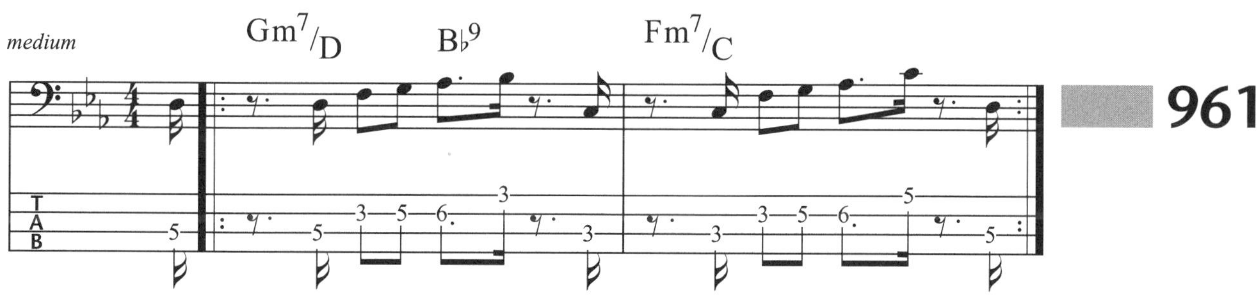
medium
Gm7/D
B♭9
Fm7/C
961

medium
B♭m7/E♭
A♭/E♭
962

967 alternative chords see No. 999, section B, bars 1-4

968 alternative chords see No. 999, section B, bars 9-12

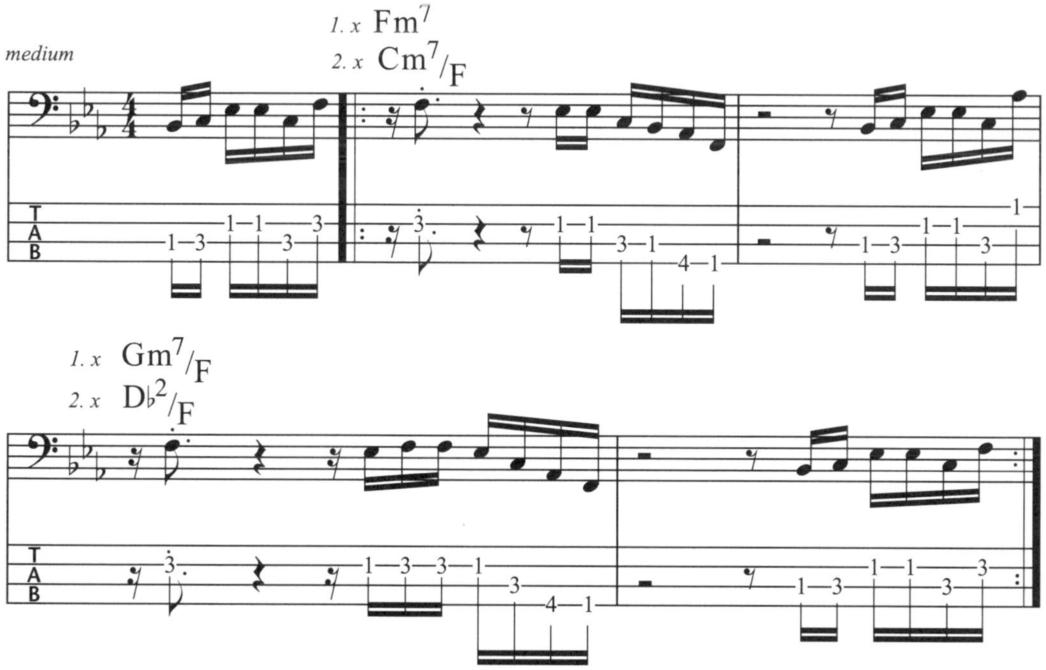

969

medium

1. x Fm7 — 2. x Cm7/F

1. x Gm7/F — 2. x D♭2/F

alternative chords see No. 996, bars 1-5

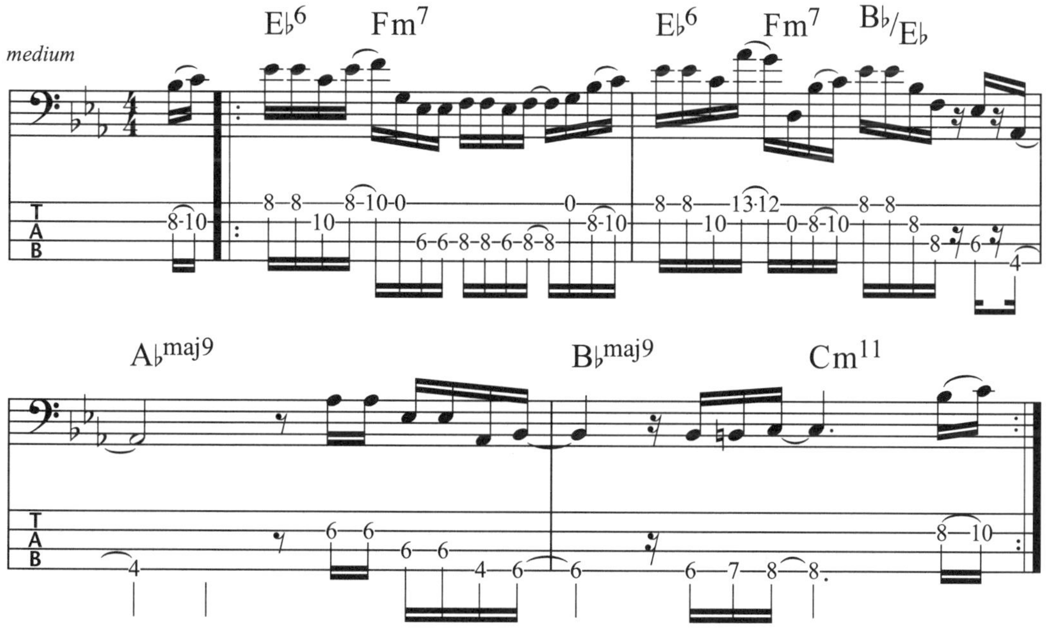

970

medium

E♭6 Fm7 E♭6 Fm7 B♭/E♭

A♭maj9 B♭maj9 Cm11

alternative chords see No. 996, section A, bars 1-4

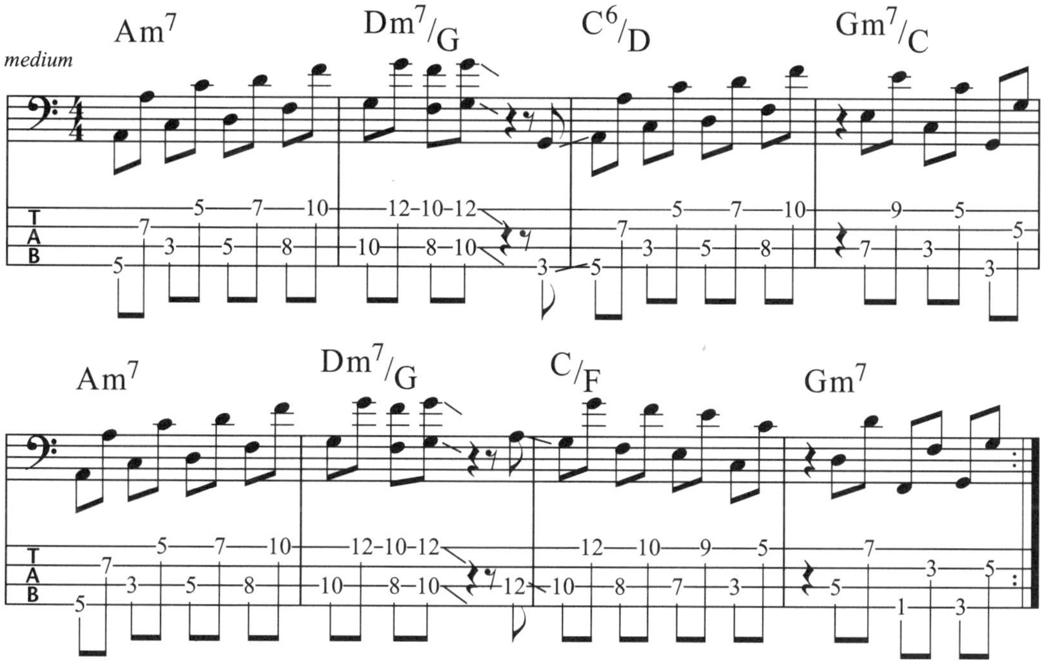

971

medium

Am7 Dm7/G C6/D Gm7/C

Am7 Dm7/G C/F Gm7

alternative chords see No. 996, section B, bars 1-8

972

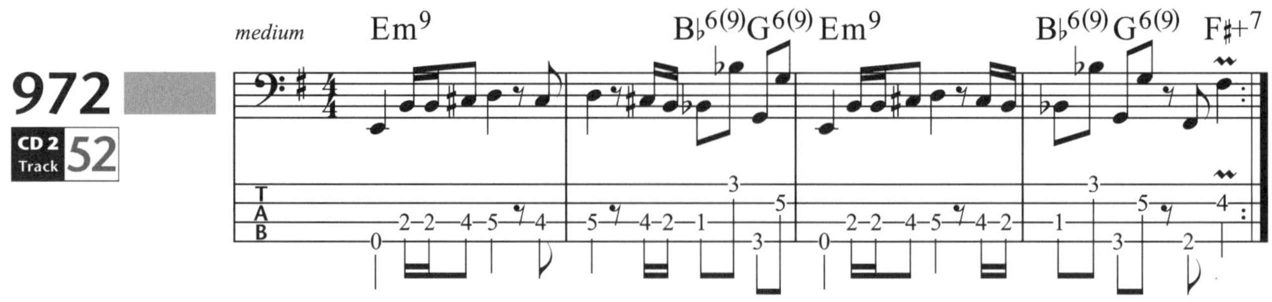

973

974

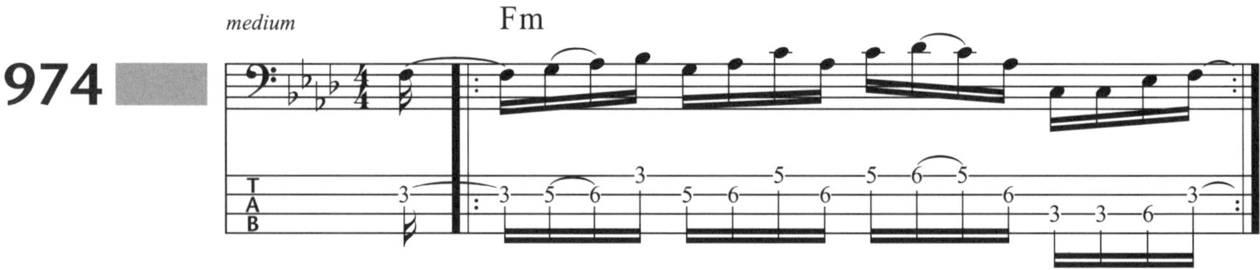

975

976

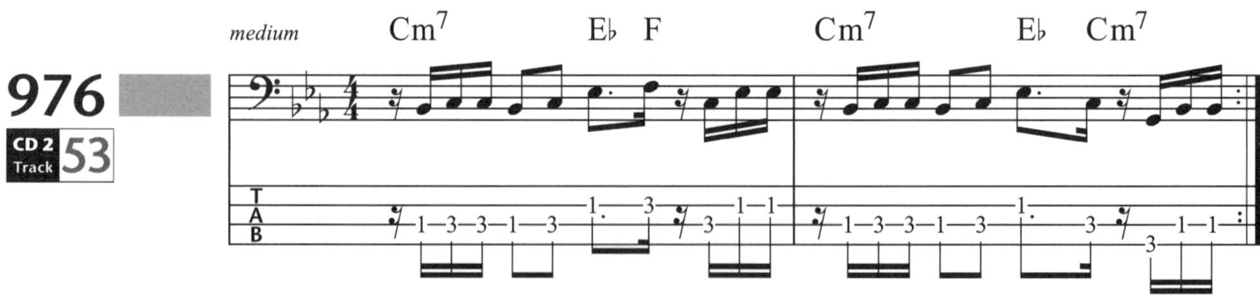

medium Cm7 Gm7/C B♭m7/E♭

977 CD 2 Track 54

medium Cm7 F/C

978 CD 2 Track 54

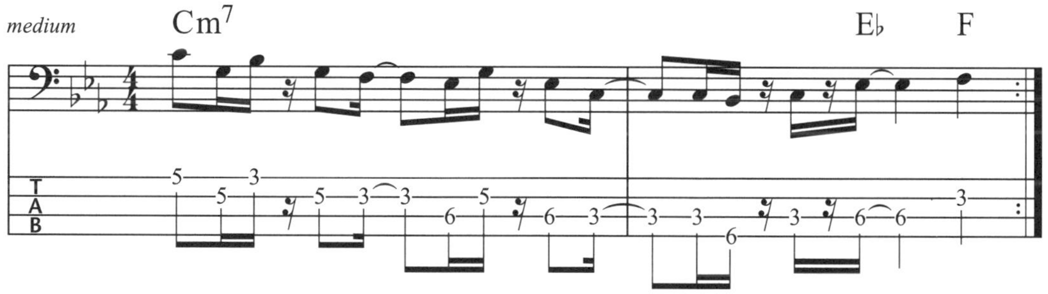

medium Cm7 E♭ F

979 CD 2 Track 55

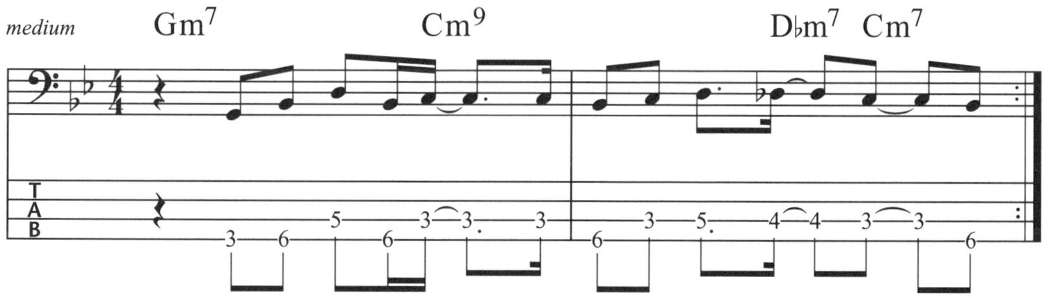

medium Gm7 Cm9 D♭m7 Cm7

980 CD 2 Track 55

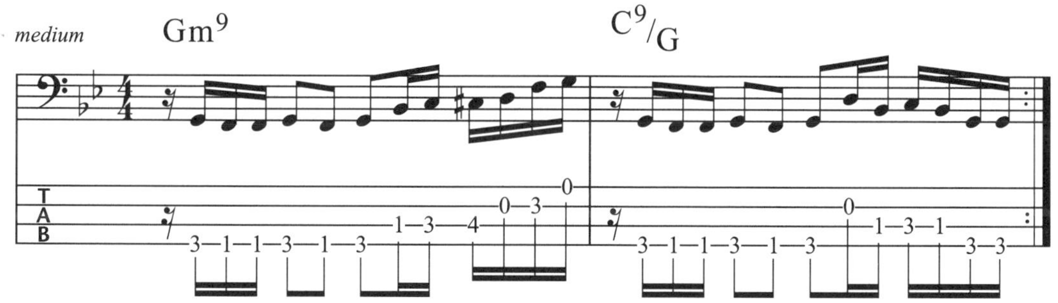

medium Gm9 C9/G

981 CD 2 Track 56

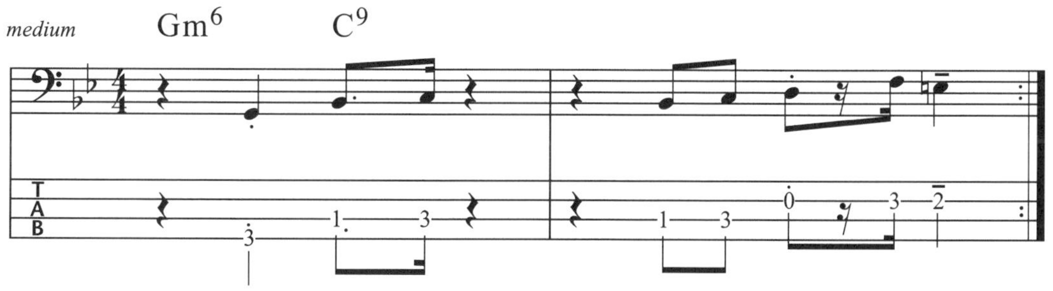

medium Gm6 C9

982 CD 2 Track 56

medium
Cm7
E♭/F
983
CD 2 Track 57
open key medium
G9
Gm7
G9
Gm7
984
CD 2 Track 57
open key medium
G9
Gm9
985
CD 2 Track 58
open key medium
G9
Fm9
F♯9
G9
G9
Fm9
986
CD 2 Track 58
medium/slow
Cm9
Dm9
987
CD 2 Track 59
open key medium
Cm7
B♭maj7/F
Cm7/E♭
B♭maj7/F
988
CD 2 Track 59

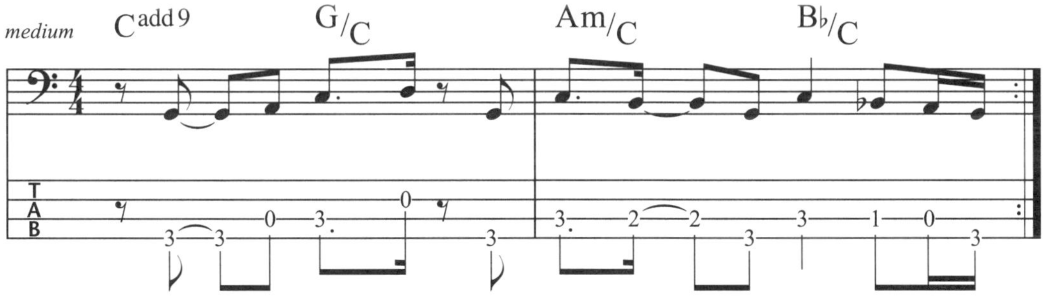

medium
Cadd9 G/C Am/C B♭/C
T A B

989
CD 2 Track 60

open key
fast (1/2 feel)
Dm7/G Fmaj7 Em7 Dm7 Cmaj7
T A B

990
CD 2 Track 60

open key
fast (1/2 feel)
Dm7/G Fmaj7 Em7 Dm7 Dm7/G
T A B

991
CD 2 Track 61

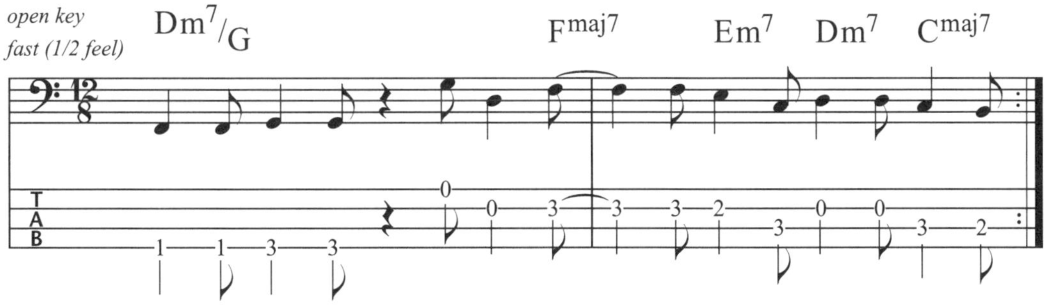

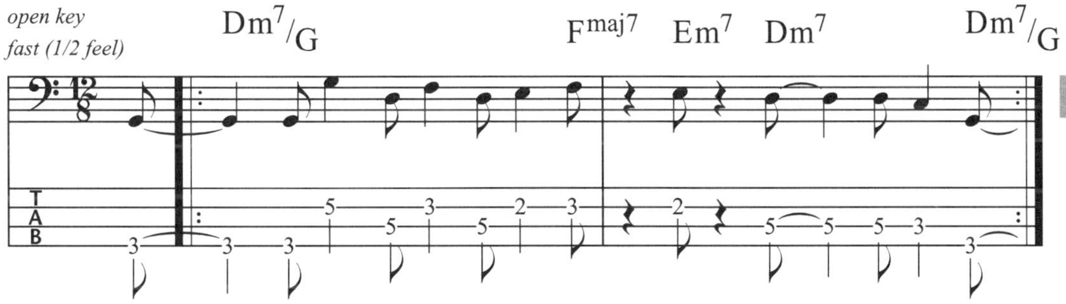

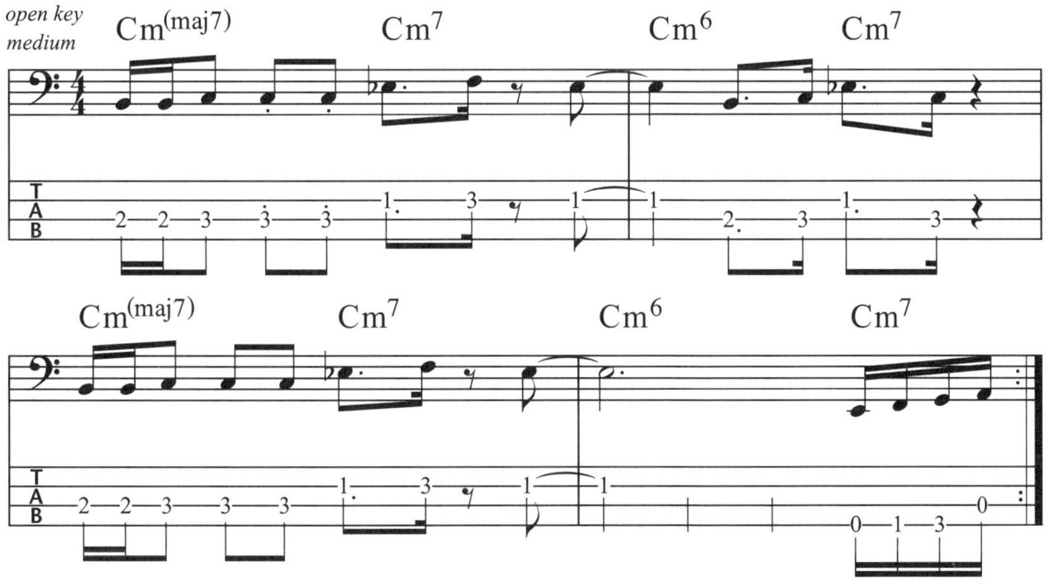

open key
medium
Cm(maj7) Cm7 Cm6 Cm7
Cm(maj7) Cm7 Cm6 Cm7
T A B

992
CD 2 Track 61

open key
medium
G9 B♭6(9) C9
T A B

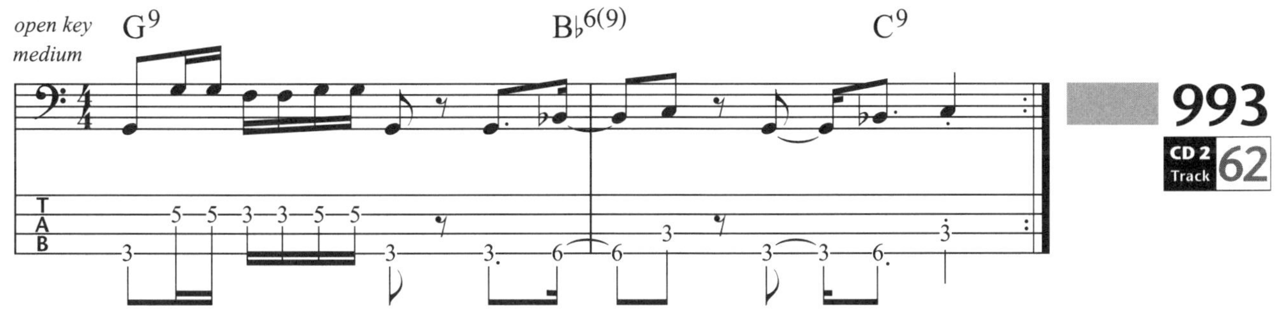

993
CD 2 Track 62

994

CD 2 Track 62

medium
B♭maj9
Gm9

995

CD 2 Track 63

open key
medium
G6
Dm7/G

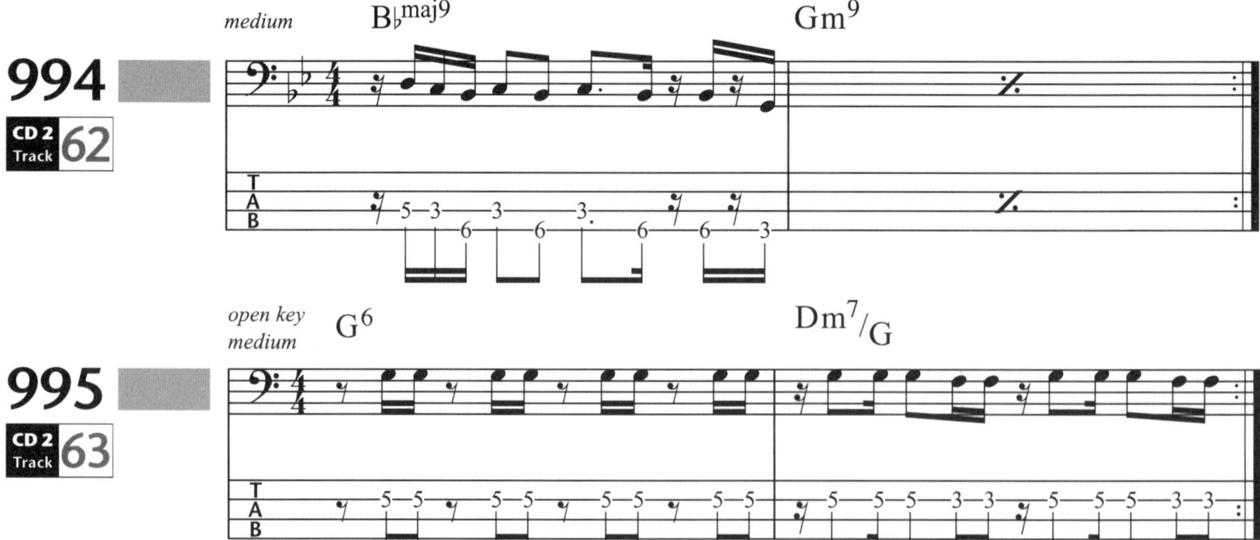

Jazz & Progressive Lines

Note: Some phrasing may be altered during performance in response to what other instruments are playing and what feels right to improvise at the time.

996

CD 2 Track 64

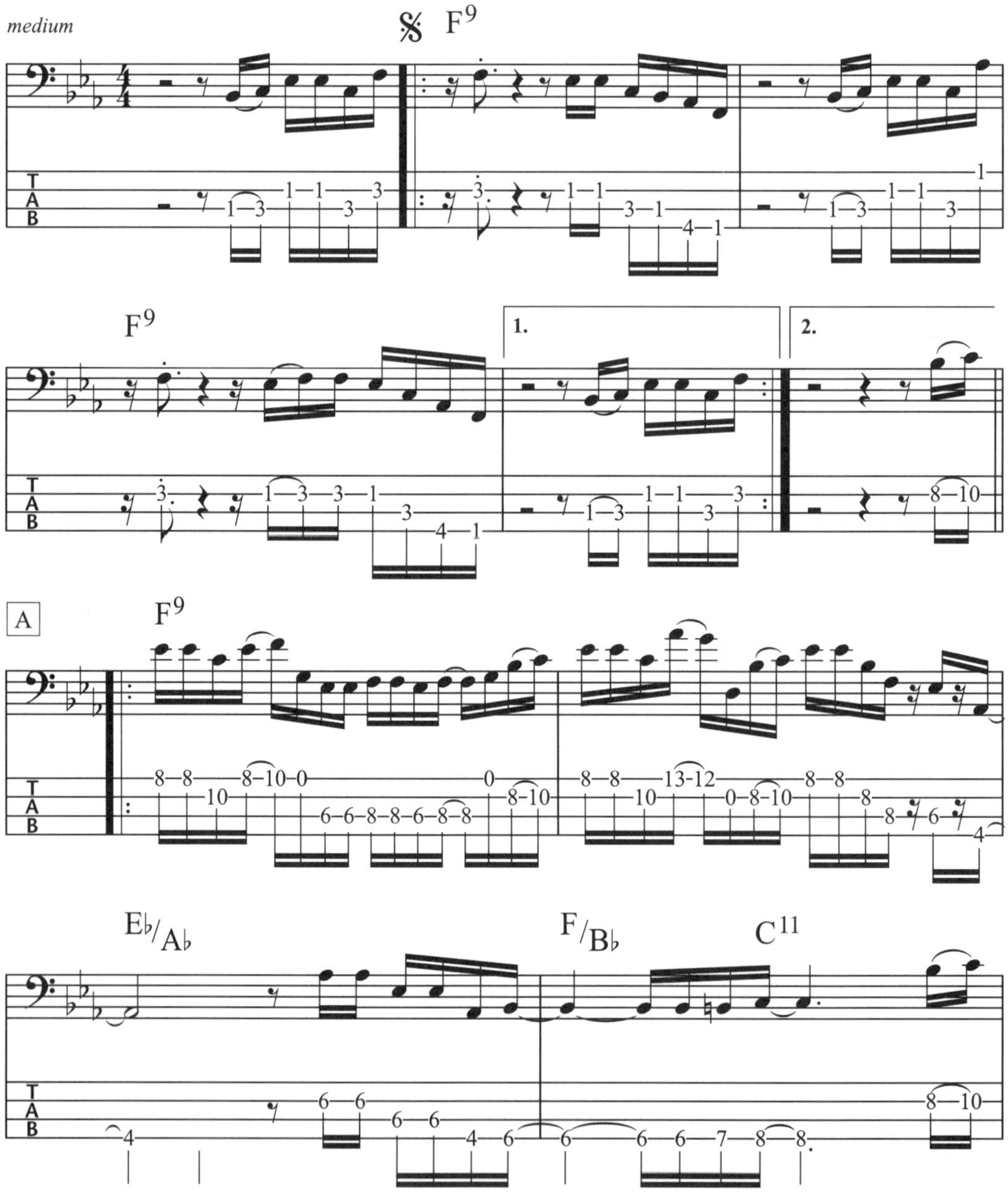
medium
F9
F9
1.
2.
A
F9
E♭/A♭
F/B♭
C11

F9

E♭/A♭ | 1. F/B♭ C11 | 2. F/B♭ C11

C11 | B Dm7 | G

Dm7 | C2 | Dm7

G | C2 | A11

A♭maj9

Fine

Note: Some phrasing may be altered during performance in response to what other instruments are playing and what feels right to improvise at the time.

997

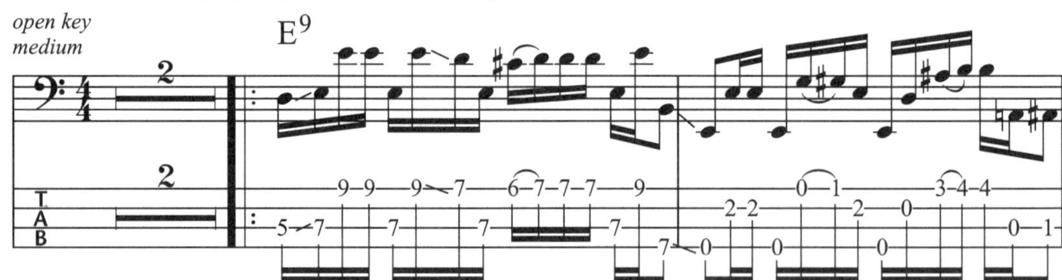

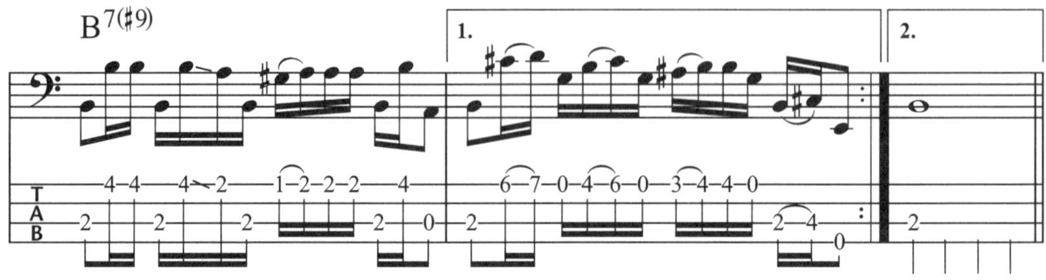

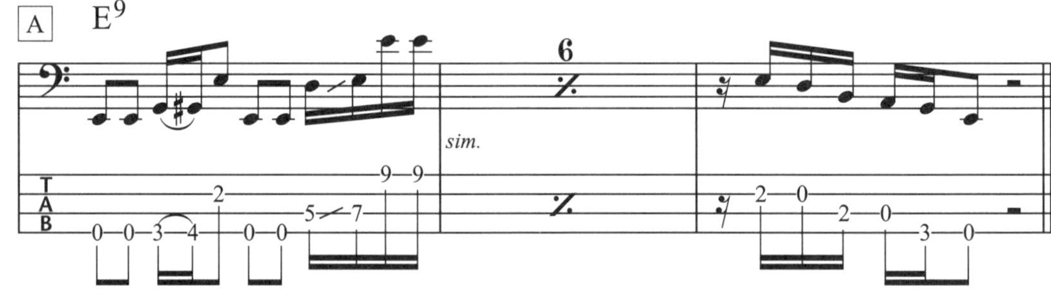

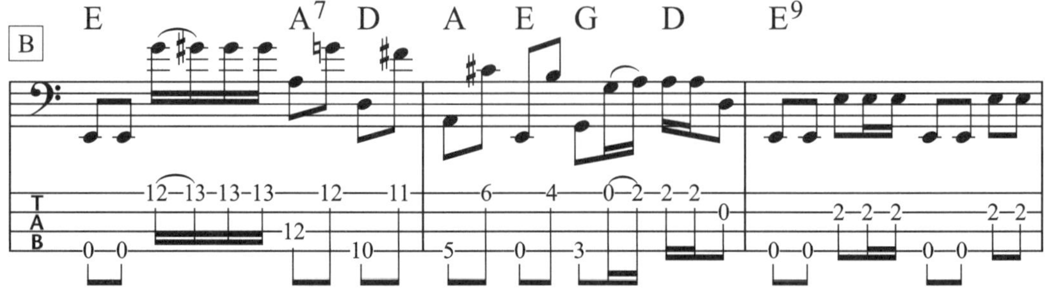

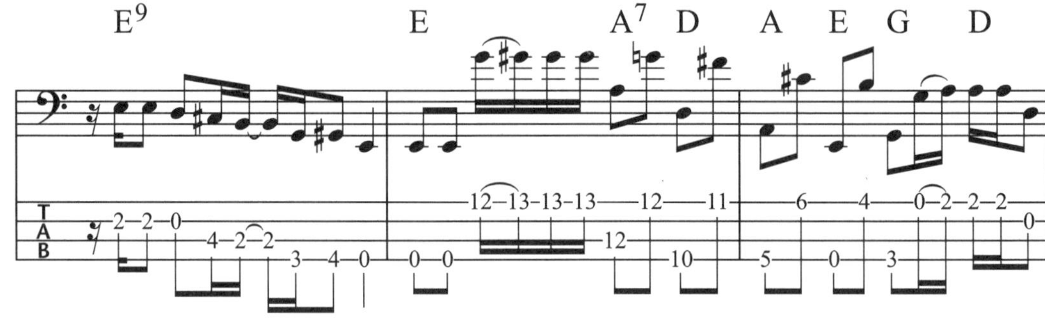

Note: Some phrasing may be altered during performance in response to what other instruments are playing and what feels right to improvise at the time.

998

CD 2 Track 66

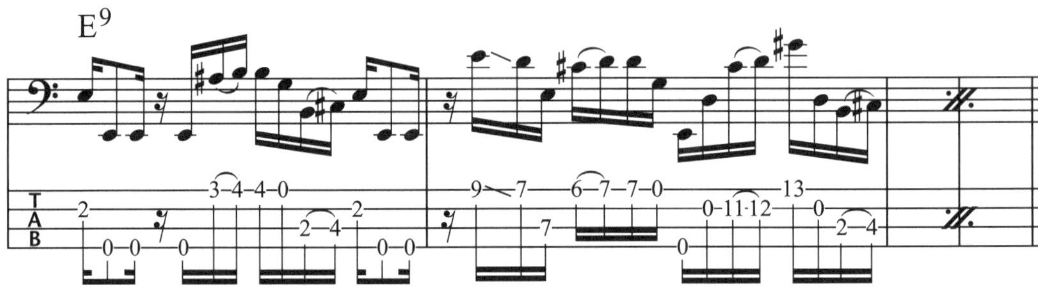

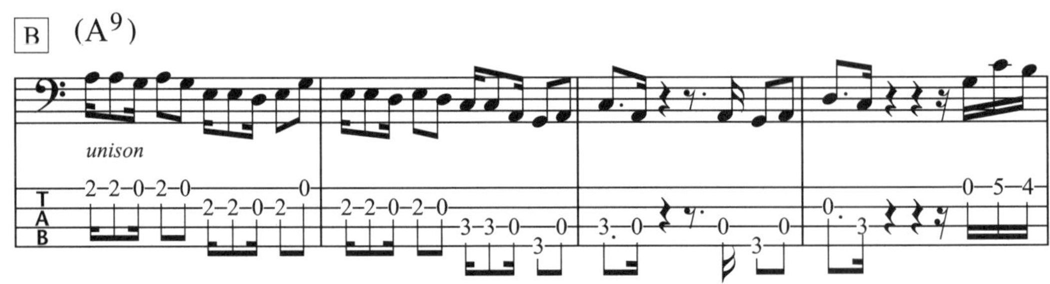

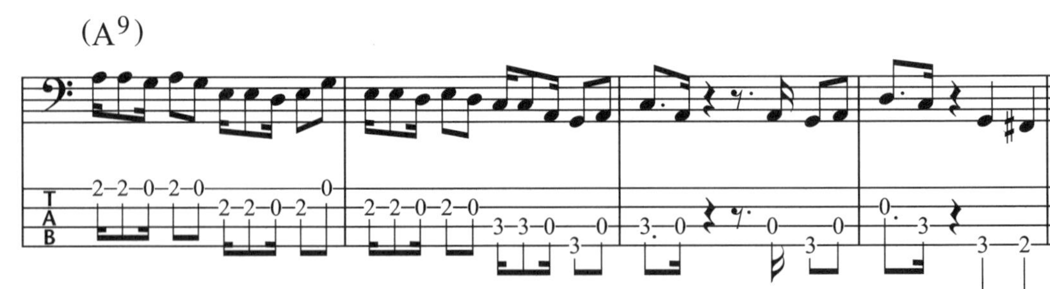

C
E9
T
A
B

D
A9
T
A
B

A9
T
A
B

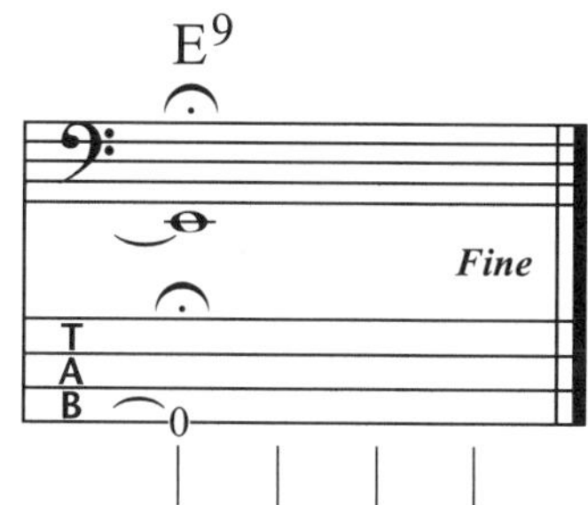
E9
Fine
T
A
B

999

CD 2 Track 67

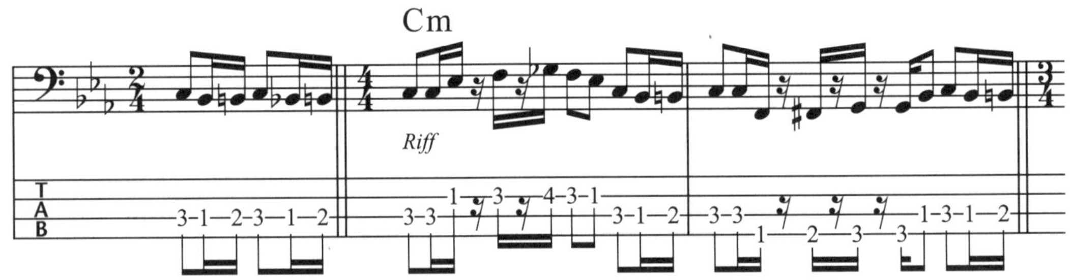

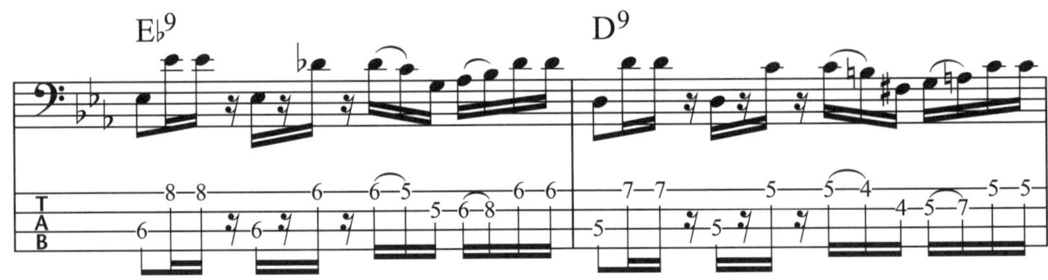

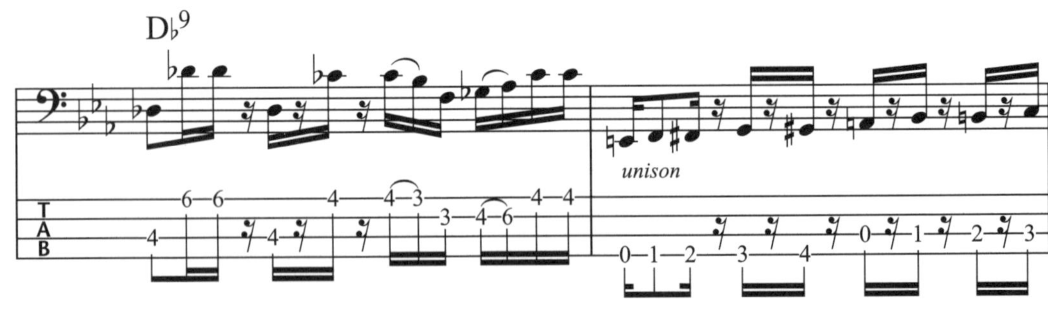

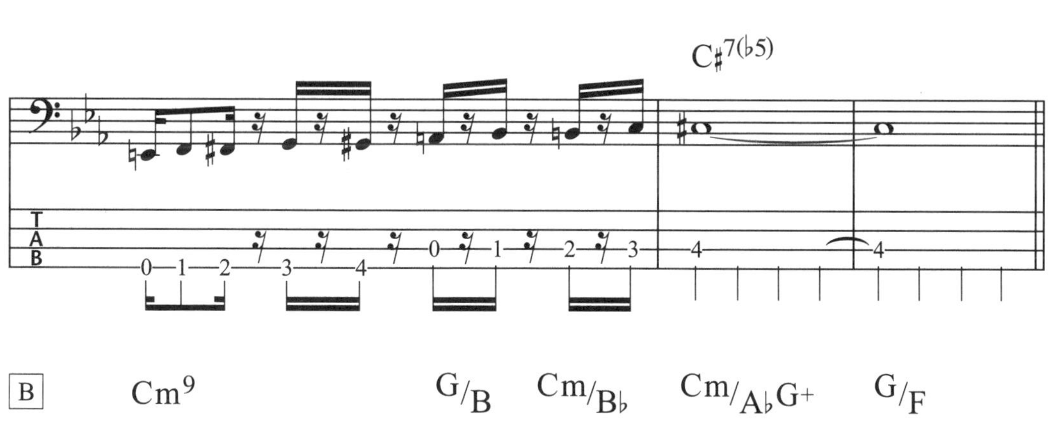
C♯7(♭5)

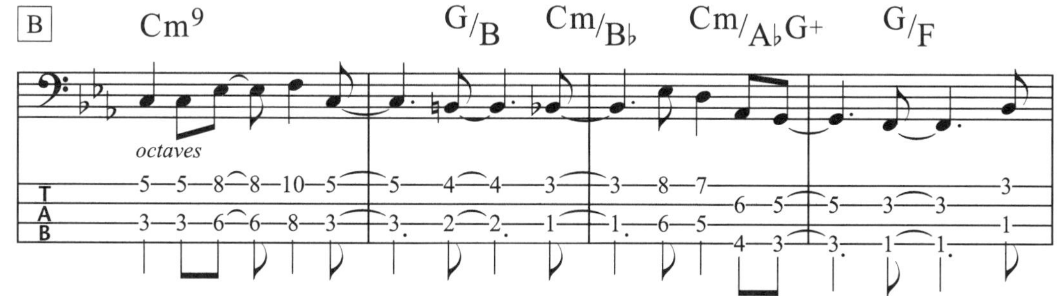
B
Cm9
G/B
Cm/B♭
Cm/A♭
G+
G/F
octaves

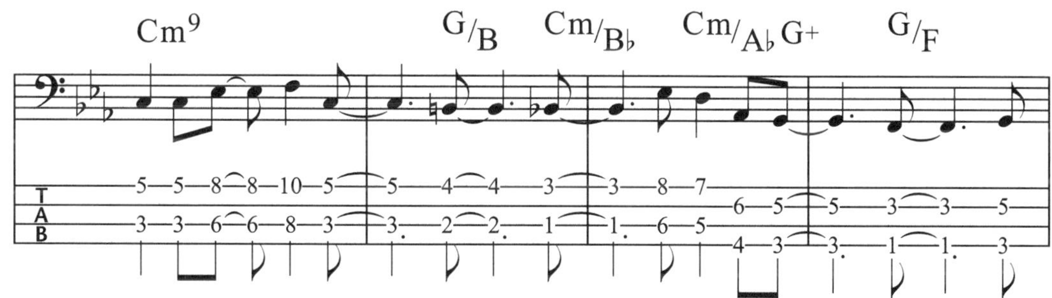
Cm9
G/B
Cm/B♭
Cm/A♭
G+
G/F

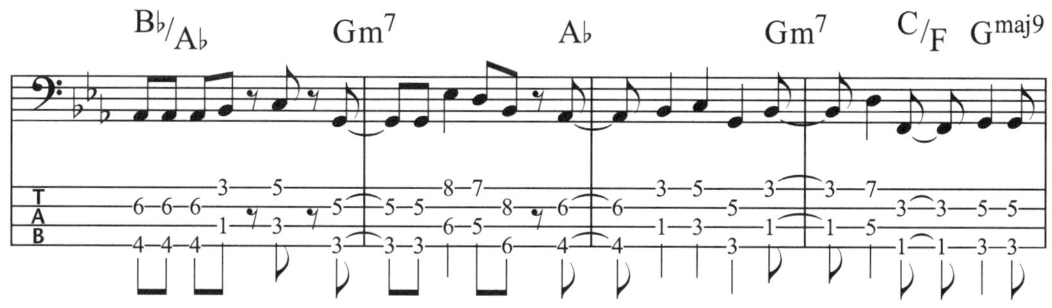
B♭/A♭
Gm7
A♭
Gm7
C/F
Gmaj9

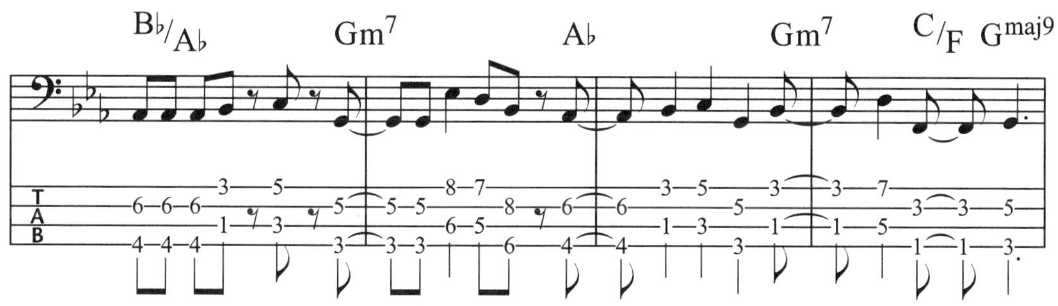
B♭/A♭
Gm7
A♭
Gm7
C/F
Gmaj9

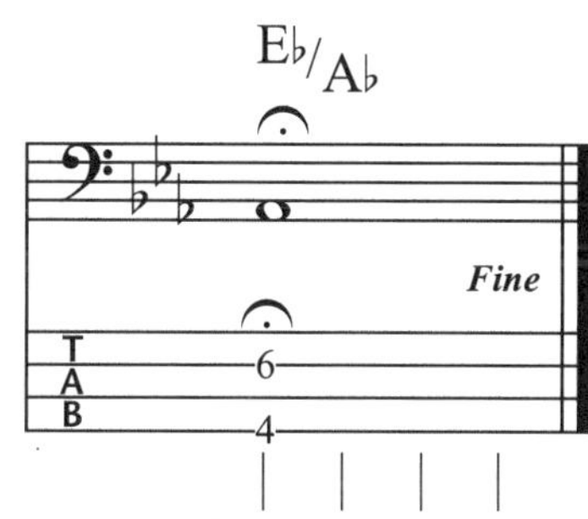
E♭/A♭
Fine

Note: Some phrasing may be altered during performance in response to what other instruments are playing and what feels right to improvise at the time.

1000

CD 2 Track 68

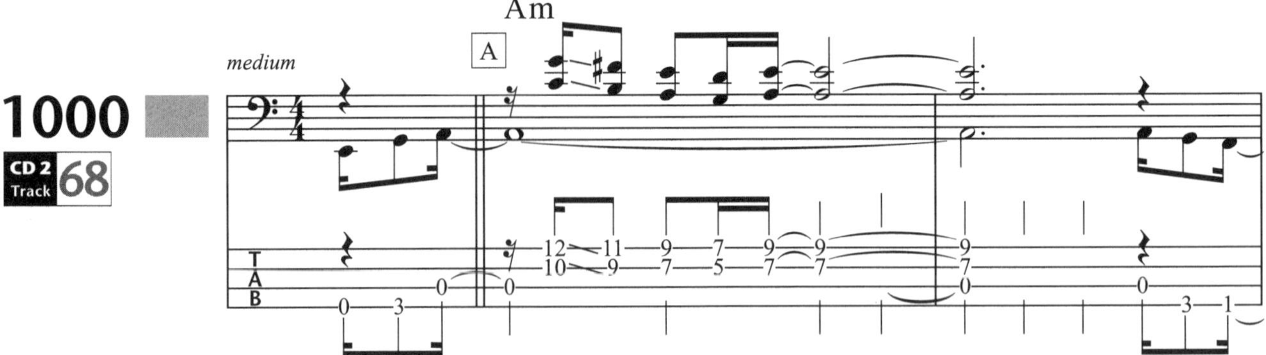

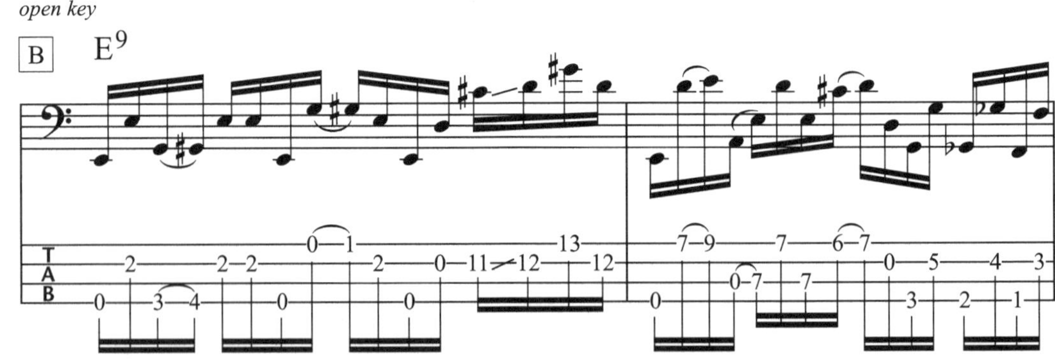

AMA
VERLAG

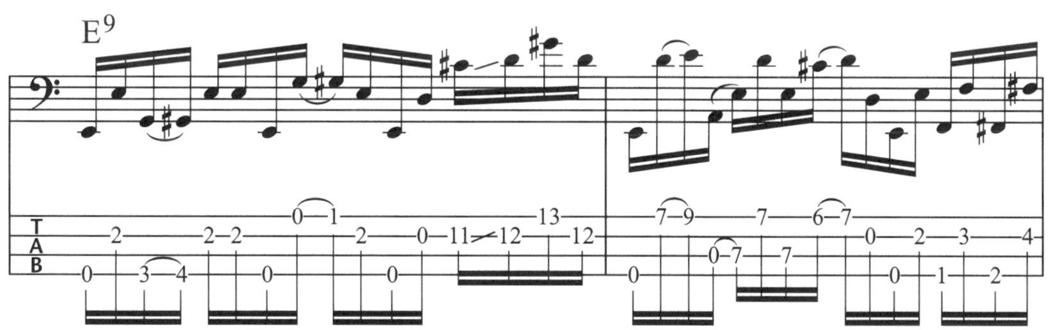
E9

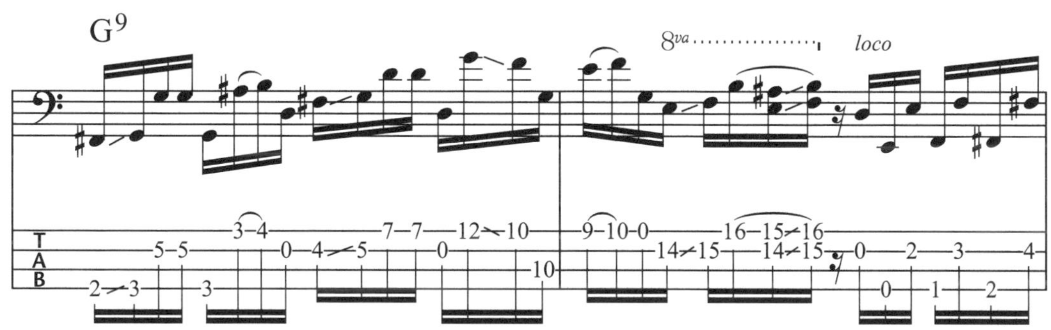
G9
8va
loco

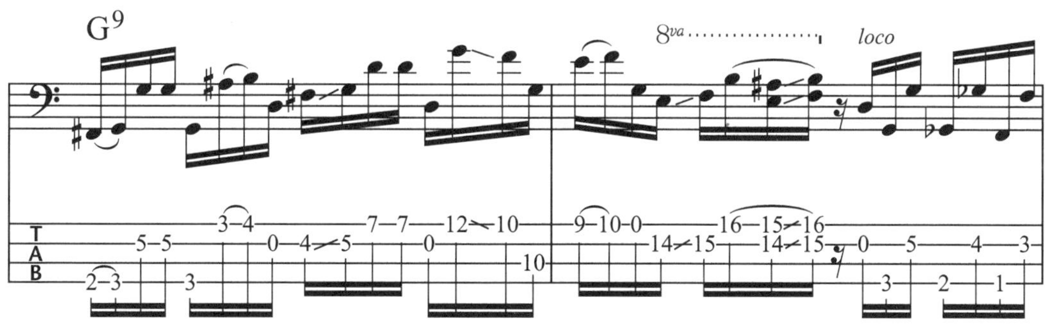
G9
8va
loco

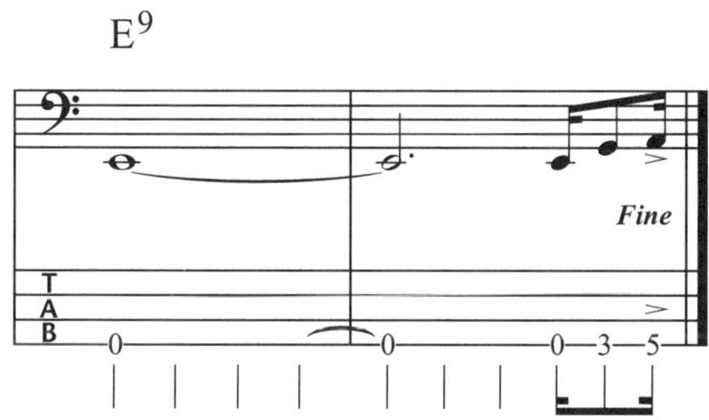
E9
Fine

1001

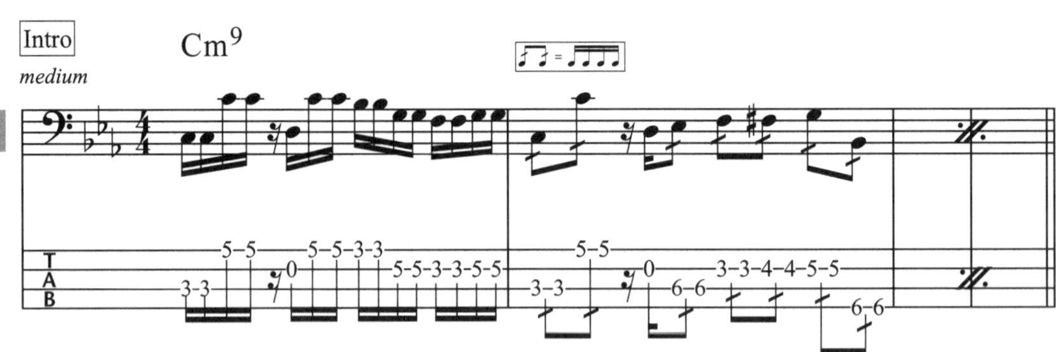

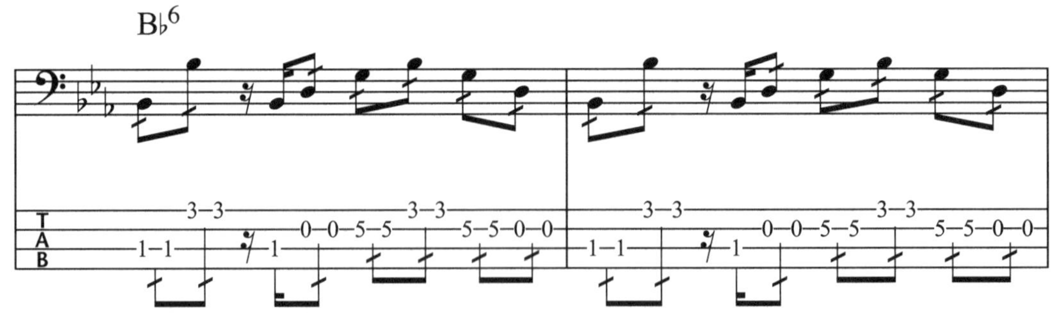

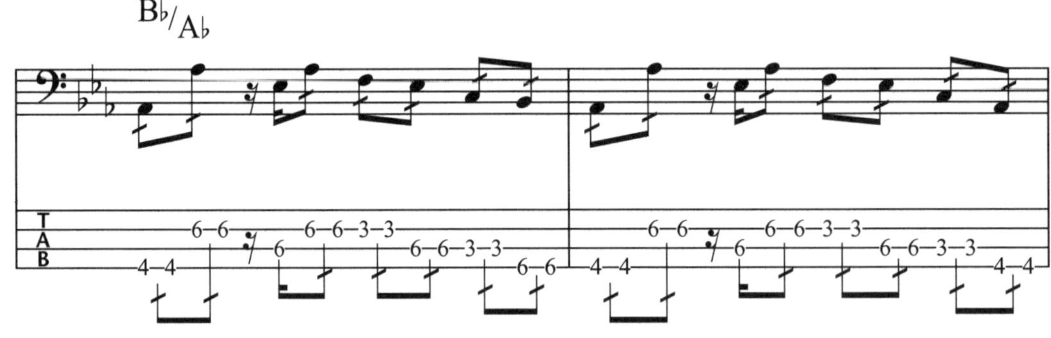

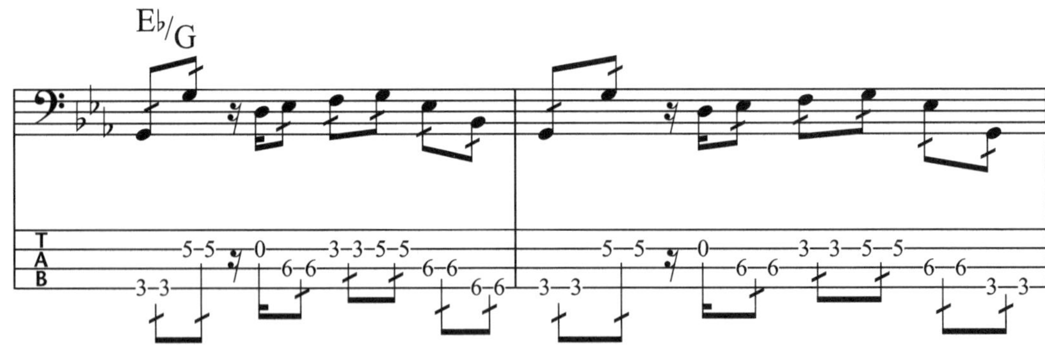

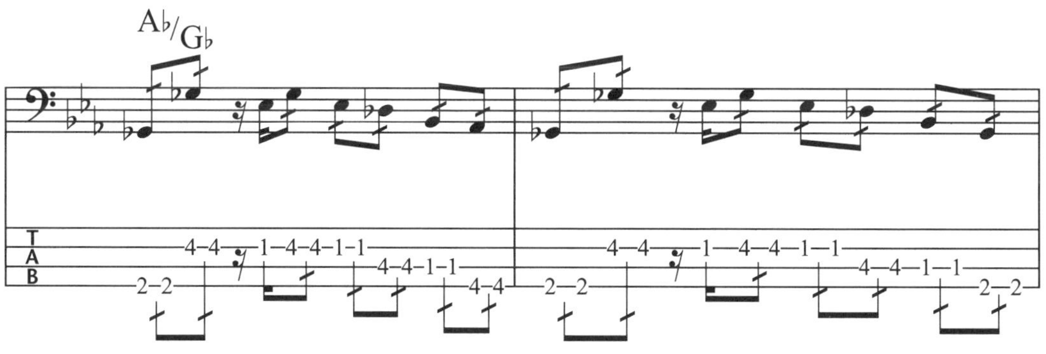
A♭/G♭

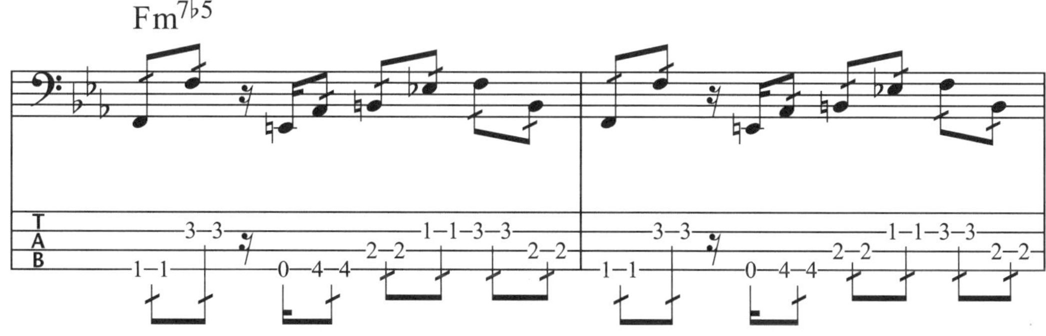
Fm7♭5

Emaj9

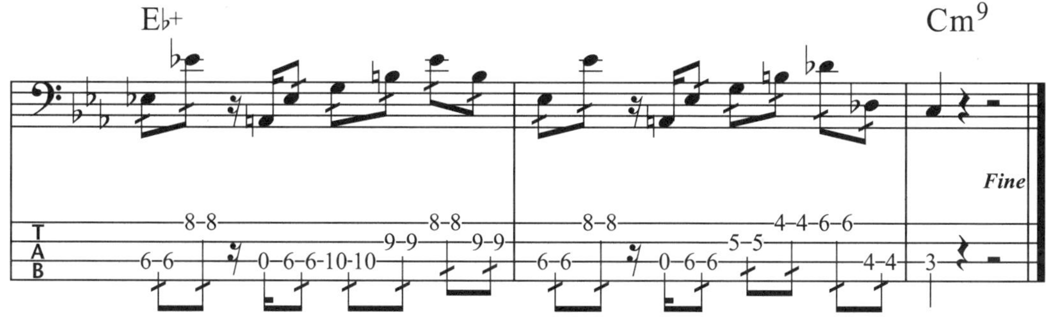
E♭+
Cm9
Fine

Note: Some phrasing may be altered during performance in response to what other instruments are playing and what feels right to improvise at the time.

1002

CD 2 Track 70

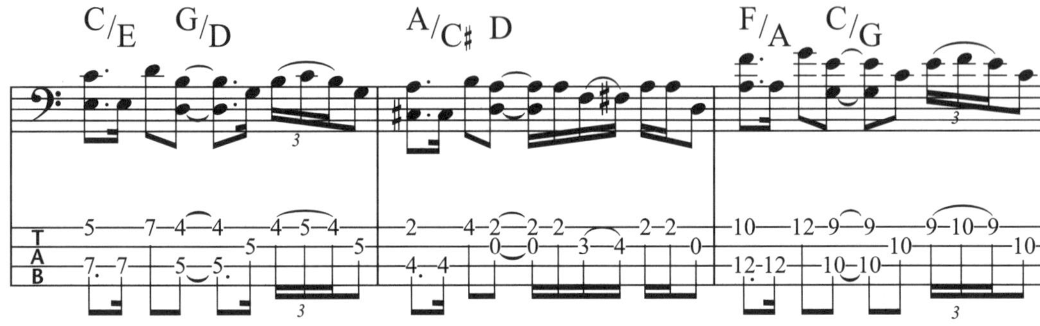

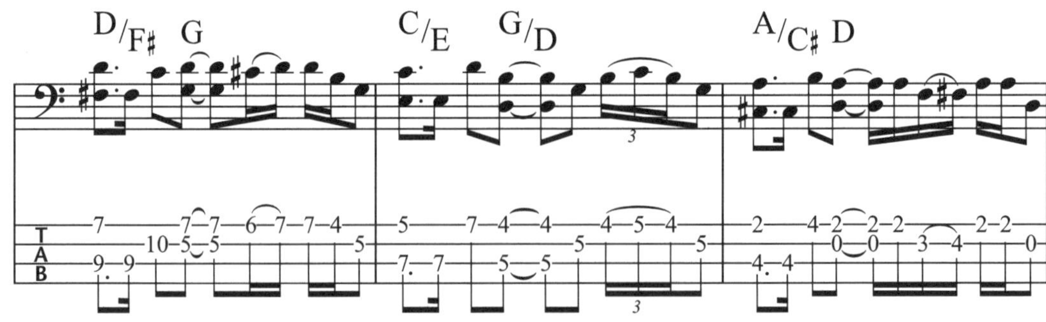

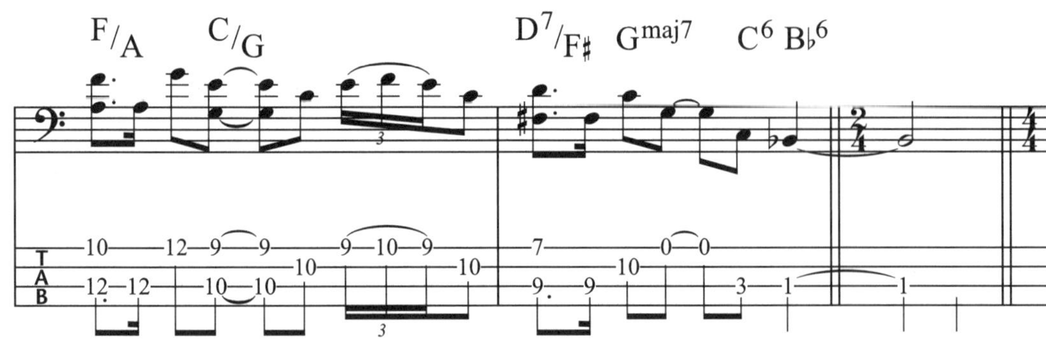

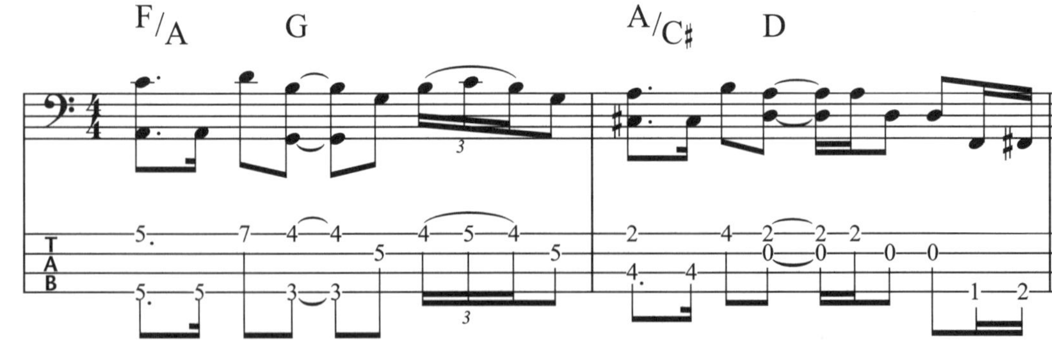

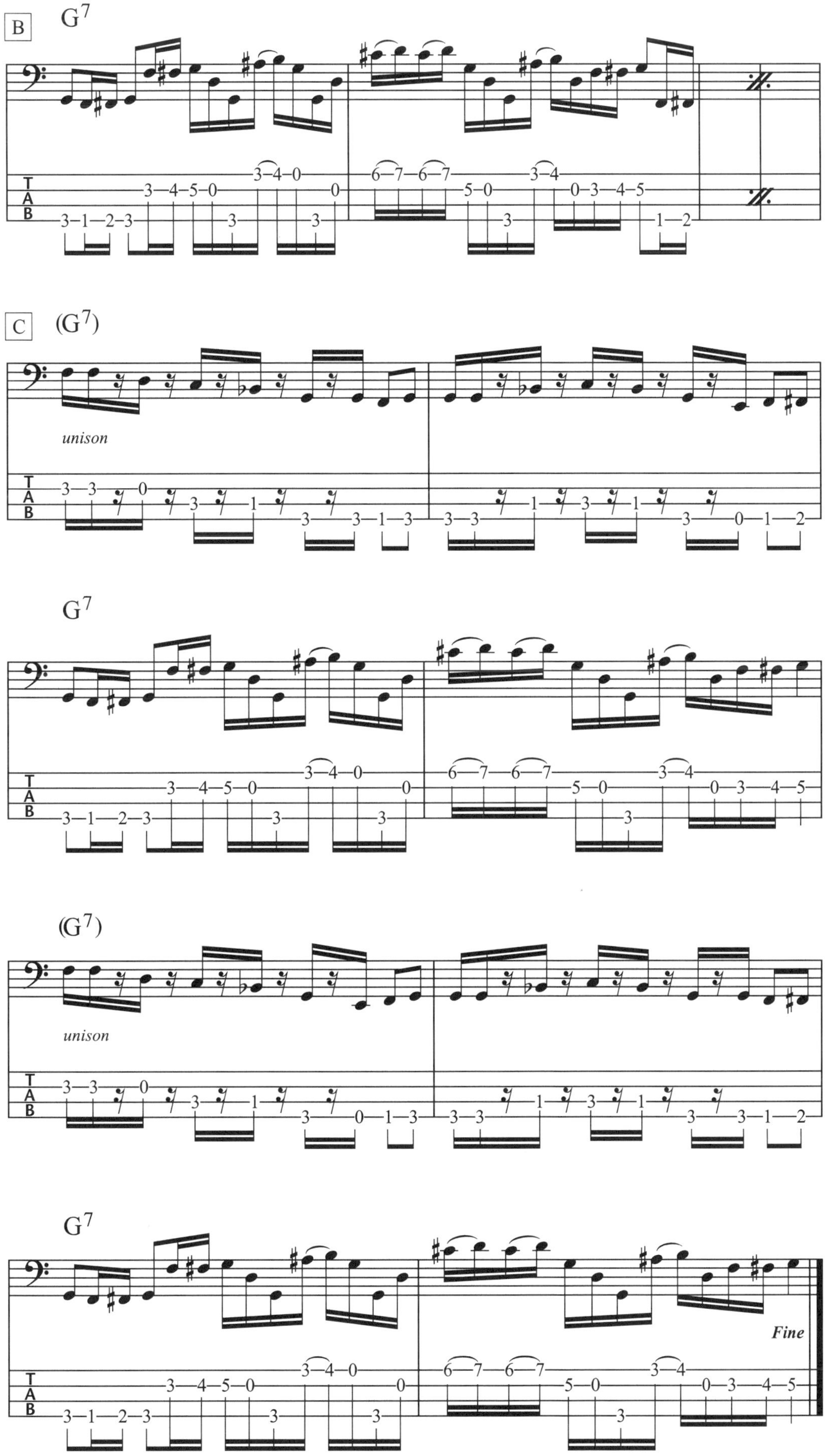

B G7

C (G7)

unison

G7

(G7)

unison

G7

Fine

1003

CD 2 Track 71

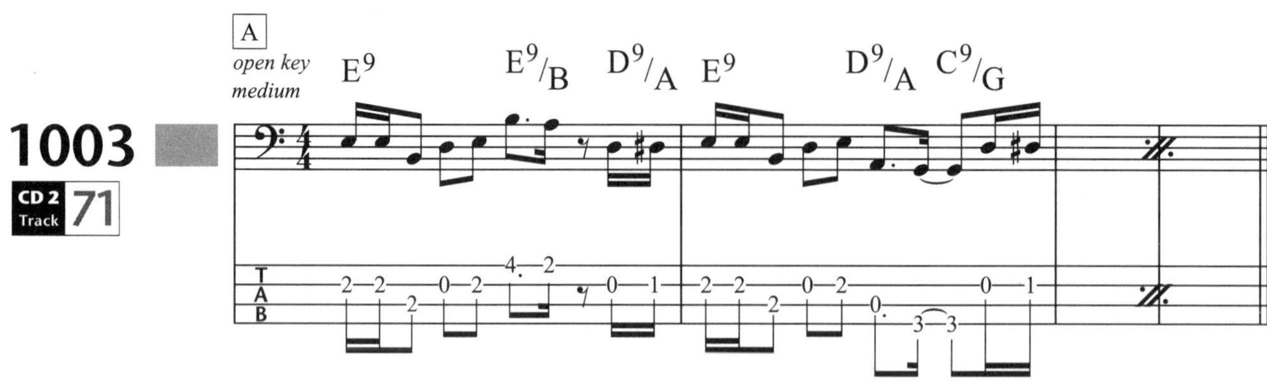

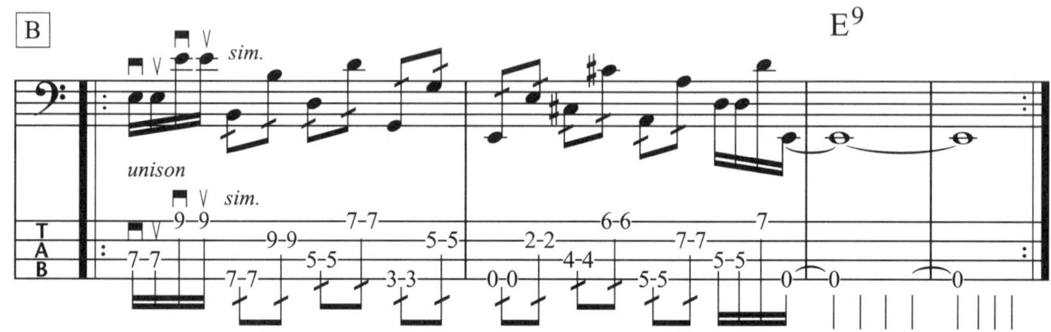

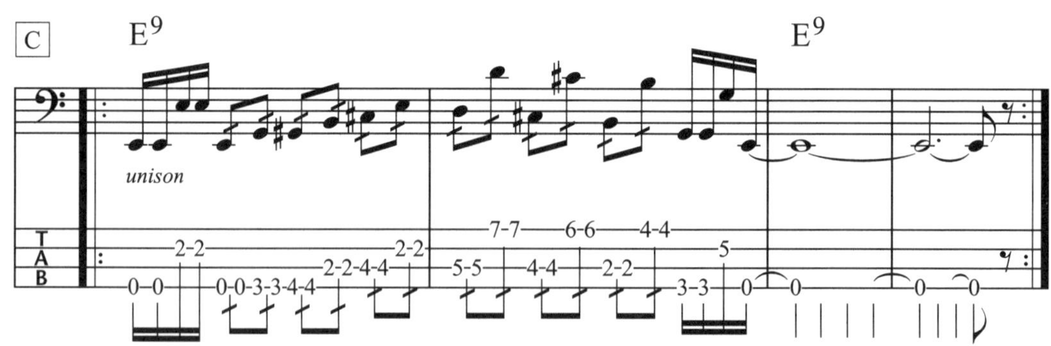

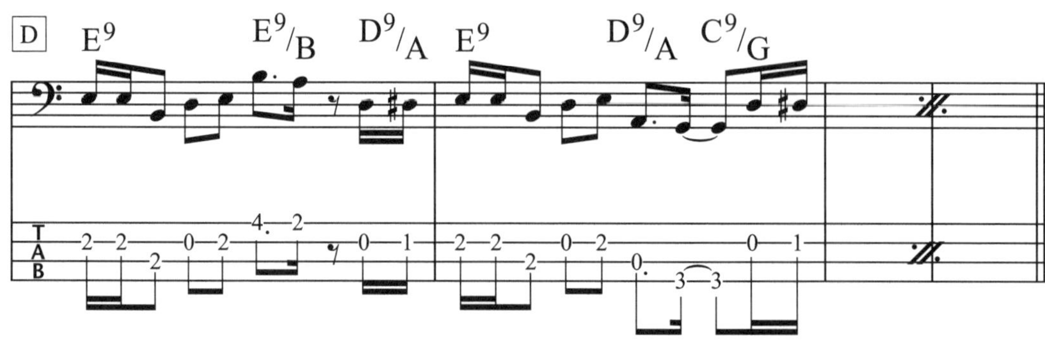

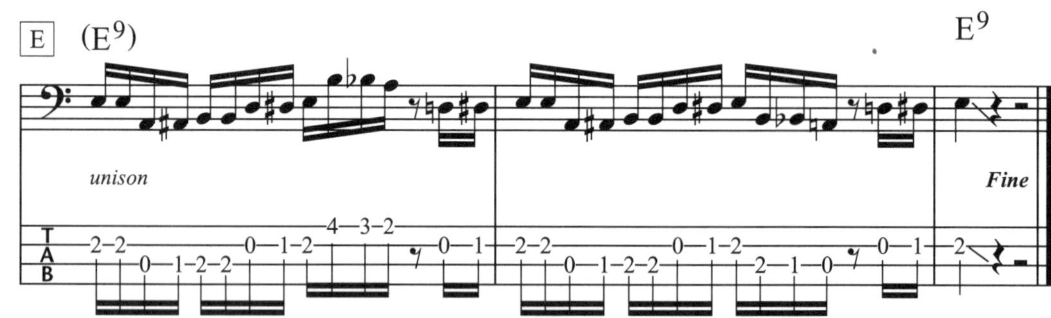

1004

CD 2 Track 72

A

medium/slow

E9

B A7

B7

E9

E9

Fine

1005

CD 2 Track 73

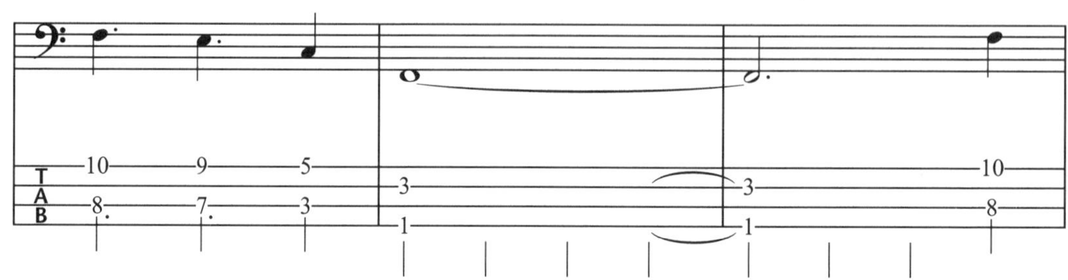

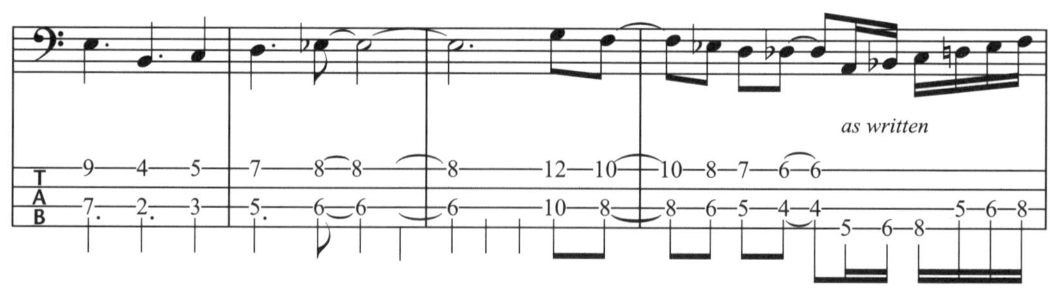

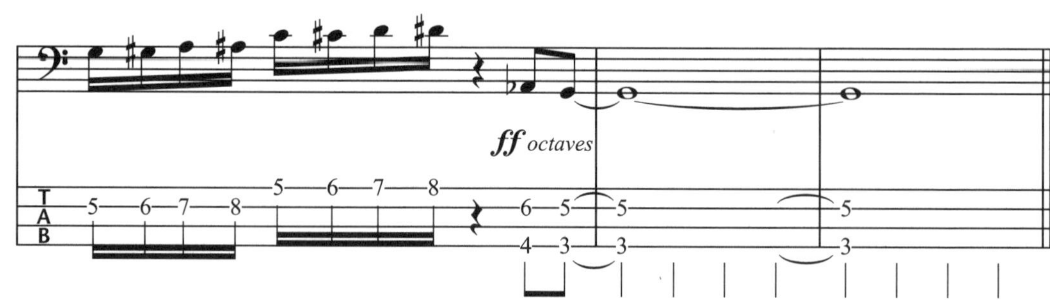

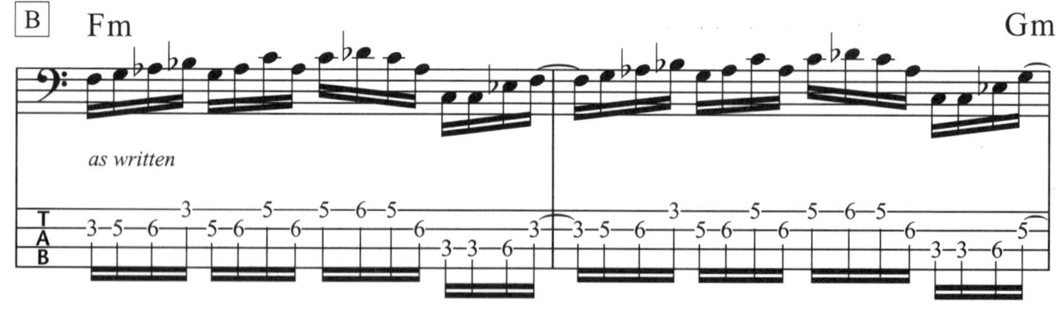

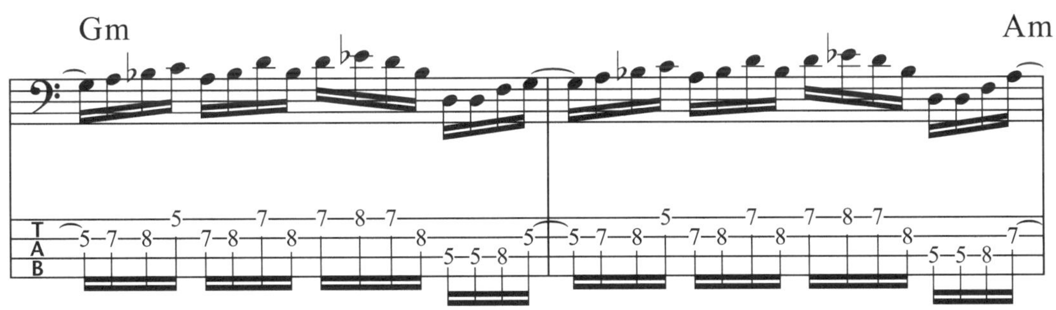
Gm
Am
T
A
B

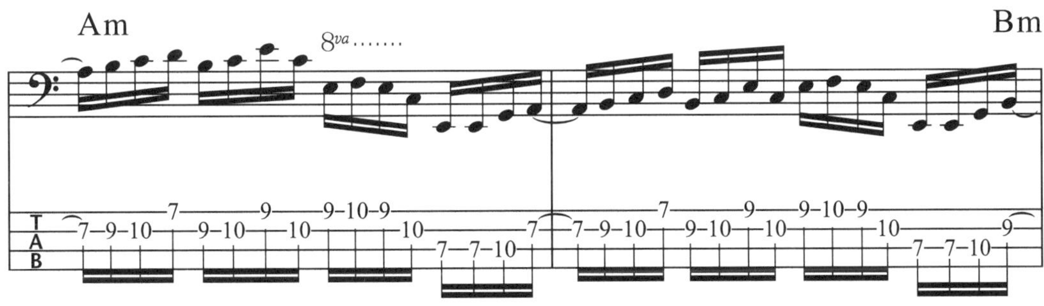
Am
8va
Bm
T
A
B

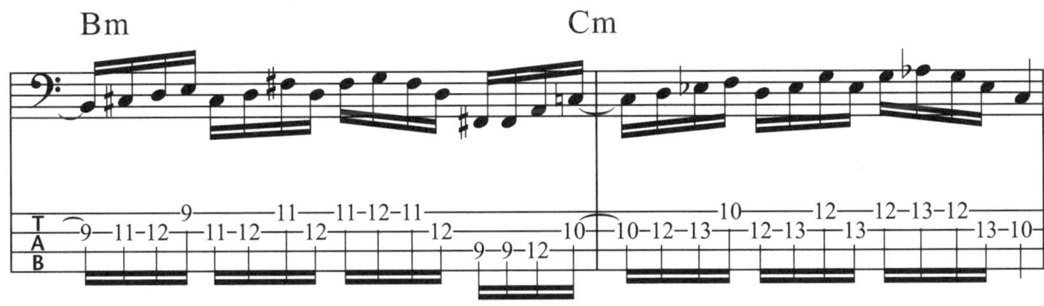
Bm
Cm
T
A
B

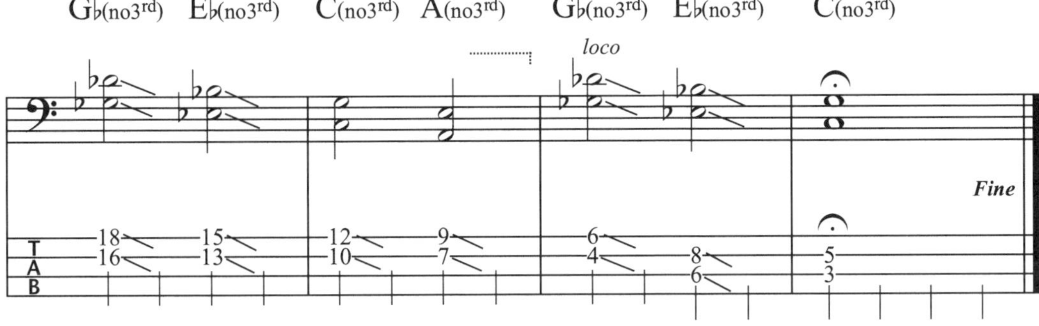
G♭(no3rd) E♭(no3rd) C(no3rd) A(no3rd) G♭(no3rd) E♭(no3rd) C(no3rd)
loco
Fine
T
A
B

Jacky Reznicek:
Rock Bass

152 Pages, Book & CD
The comprehensive method book for the modern electric bassist including notation and tablature. It contains more than 150 exercises and basic grooves for rock, blues, soul, funk, reggae, latin, jazz and other styles.

Order code: 610108E
ISBN: 978-3-932587-98-6
ISMN: M-700185-25-1

Jacky Reznicek:
Die AMA-Bassgitarren-Grifftabelle (chordbook, German)

112 Pages, DIN A5
Chord fingering diagrams for 4 string bass including details describing the correct fingerings and the chord structure.

Order code: 610139
ISBN: 978-3-927190-33-7
ISMN: M-700185-49-7

Frank Haunschild:
The New Harmony Book

149 Pages, Book Only
The standard musical textbook for every musician. Focusses on harmonic structures, scales and modes. Suitable for the classroom or self-study.

Order code: 610165E
ISBN: 978-3-927190-68-3

Dirk Rosenbaum/Harald Heinl:
Rhythmic Reading

188 Pages, Book & CD
For everyone and anyone who wants to make music, whether beginner or advanced and independent of preferred musical style. Suitable as instructional material for the classroom as well as for self-instruction and furthering your musical training.

Order code: 610461
ISBN: 978-3-89922-172-5
ISMN: M-50155-124-8

Peter Fischer:
Rock Guitar Secrets

183 Pages, Book & CD
The ultimate guitarist's reference book with playing techniques, solo and improvisation concepts, exercises and jam tracks.

Order code: 610111E
ISBN: 978-3-927190-62-7
ISMN: M-700136-40-6

Peter Fischer:
Masters Of Rock Guitar

159 Pages, Book & CD
More than 250 licks reflecting the styles and concepts of 40 years of rock guitar.

Order code: 610105E
ISBN: 978-3-927190-60-3
ISMN: M-700185-31-2

Richard Koechli:
Best In The West – Nashville Guitar

276 Pages, Book & CD
Everything about country guitar: rhythm and lead styles, flat-picking, finger-picking, presented in 3 separate progressive sections with comprehensive style analysis of oldtime country, western swing, bluegrass, cajun, rockabilly, country rock etc. Loads of master workshops, traditionals, practice pieces and licks.

Order code: 610228E
ISBN: 978-3-89922-015-5
ISMN: M-700185-47-3

Peter Fischer:
Blues Guitar Rules

167 Pages, Book & CD
Playing techniques, solo and improvisation concepts, exercises, licks and jam tracks for traditional and modern blues guitar.

Order code: 610120E
ISBN: 978-3-927190-64-1